MULTIPLE SIGNATURES

MICHAEL ROCK 2 × 4

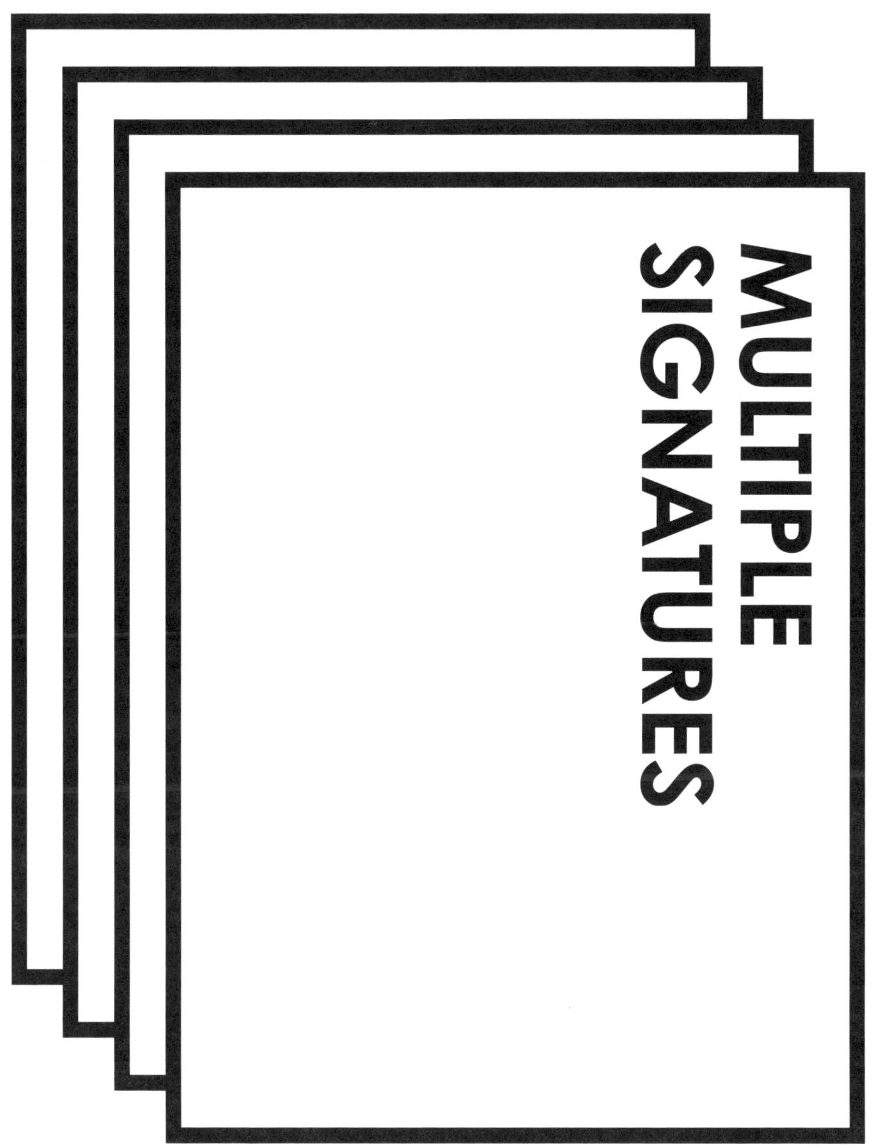

ON DESIGNERS, AUTHORS, READERS AND USERS

RIZZOLI
NEW YORK

First published in the United States of America
by Rizzoli International Publications, Inc.
300 Park Avenue South, New York, NY 10010
www.rizzoliusa.com

For Rizzoli International Publications
Editor: Ian Luna
Editorial Coordination: Monica Adame Davis
Managing Editor: Lynn Scrabis
Editorial Assistance: Kayleigh Jankowski
Proofreader: Mary Ellen Wilson
Production: Kaija Markoe

Printed in China
2013 2014 2015 2016 2017 / 10 9 8 7 6 5 4 3 2
Library of Congress Control Number: 2013930766
ISBN: 978–08478–3973–5

Edited by
Michael Rock

with
Jeanne Heifetz
Lisa Brennan-Jobs

Design by
Michael Rock
Yoonjai Choi

Layout by
Donnie Luu

with
Liliana Palau
David Yun
Sung Joong Kim
Terri Chiao
Jeffrey Ludlow

"Designer as Author" first appeared in *Eye* 20 (1996) and has been adapted multiple times since. The version herein was substantially revised in 2012.

"Paradox on the Graphic Artist" by Jean-François Lyotard is excerpted from Postmodern Fables (1997) and reproduced here by permission of the University of Minnesota Press.

"Fuck Content" (2005) first appeared on 2x4.org and has been republished widely, most recently in the catalogue of the exhibition *Graphic Design: Now in Production* at the Walker Art Center, 2011. The version here was updated in 2012.

An earlier version of "it is what it is" first appeared in a catalogue for the eponymous exhibition at the Gyre Gallery in Tokyo, 2009.

"Post-Occupancy" by Rem Koolhaas first appeared in *Domus D'autore* 1 (2006) and is reproduced here by permission of the author.

"Deprofessionalization" is a 2012 reconsideration of an earlier article "On Unprofessionalism" that first appeared in *ID* (Jan/Feb 1994).

"What Is This Thing Called Graphic Design Criticism" (Part I) originally appeared in *Eye* 4, no.16 (1996) and is reproduced here by permission of the authors.

"Mad Dutch Disease" was delivered as a lecture at the Premsela Foundation for Dutch Design in Amsterdam, March 19, 2004. The version that appears herein was updated in 2012.

"Empire of Screens" was adapted from the lecture "All that is Solid Melts into Air," delivered at the Icograda World Design Congress in Beijing, October 27, 2009.

"On Museums" and "Proposal for a Museum of the Ordinary" were originally delivered as a lecture at the Design beyond Design conference at the Jan van Eyck Academie in Maastricht, November 8, 1997, and subsequently included in the conference catalogue. The versions here were updated in 2012.

For Silas and Winslow

TABLE OF CONTENTS

III CRITICISM

IV READERSHIP

ACKNOWLEDGMENTS

I am deeply grateful to:

Susan Sellers and Georgie Stout for nurturing and sustaining the partnership that is the foundation of everything that follows here.

Mark Wigley, Susan Sellers, Georgie Stout, Rob Giampietro, Jean-François Lyotard, Paul Elliman, Michael Speaks, Rem Koolhaas, Enrique Walker, Iwan Baan, Lucia Allais, Jeannie Kim, Rick Poynor, Jan van Toorn, Elizabeth Rock, Irwin Chen, Alexander Strube, Dan Michaelson, Florian Idenburg, Jing Liu, and Peter Arkle for agreeing to contribute to this project and working together with me to make it happen.

The many friends and colleagues who read and commented on these texts, or served as willing interview subjects, including Lucia Allais, Anthon Beeke, Michael Bierut, Andrew Blauvelt, Irma Boom, Max Bruinsma, Esther Cleven, Wim Crouwel, Willem de Ridder, Meredith Davis, Keith Godard, Emily King, Rem Koolhaas, Dingeman Kuilman, Ellen Lupton, Karel Martens, Katherine McCoy, Christine McQuade, Chee Pearlman, Rick Poynor, Klaartje Quirijns, Elizabeth Rock, Susan Sellers, Daniel van der Velden, Jan van Toorn, Chris Vermaas, Dan Wood and Shaway Yeh.

Mark Wigley at Columbia University, Sheila Levrant de Bretteville at Yale School of Art, and Tom Ockerse at RISD for their support of my teaching and writing.

Lucia Allais at Princeton University for intellectual inspiration and challenging conversations, many of which influenced the contents of this book.

All the collaborators and clients who commissioned and supported us over the years, especially Miuccia Prada, Patrizio Bertelli and Fabio Zambernardi for their support of many of the projects herein.

Rem Koolhaas and Shohei Shigematsu at OMA for years of dedicated collaboration.

Colleagues who inspired, and in many cases co-produced, much of there work herein including Petra Blaise, Kathleen Box, Angelica Broncoli, Adele Chatfield-Taylor, Germano Celant, Cynthia Davidson, Elizabeth Diller, Rolf Fehlbaum, Janet Johnson, Jan Kennedy, Maggie Kim,

Brigitte Lacombe, Michael Maharam, Amanda Palmer, Charles Renfro, Paola Vanin, Verde Visconti, David Weeks, Kanye West and countless others.

The many talented designers who have worked with us at 2x4 including Evan Allen, Katie Andresen, Simon Battisti, Chin Lien Chen, Irwin Chen, Terri Chiao, Alexandra Ching, Erica Choi, Yoonjai Choi, Alice Chung, Eileen Costello, Glen Cummings, Erica Deahl, Gala Delmont-Benatar, Jessica Dobkin, Douglas Freedman, Helena Fruehauf, Julie Fry, Celine Fu, Caroline Gambell, Timothy Gambell, Sarah Gephart, Jiminie Ha, Penelope Hardy, Ebon Heath, Enrique Hernandez Rivera, Fabienne Hess, Sigrid Schelde Holt, Soojin Hong, Alfons Hooikaas, Karen Hsu, Derek Hunt, David Israel, Natasha Jen, Tracy Jenkins, Israel Kandarian, Claire Kang, Kiki Katahira, Sung Joong Kim, Zak Klauck, Kostadin Krajcev, Michi Kobayashi, Albert Lee, JiWon Lee, Jonathan Lee, Beverly Liang, Alex Lin, Jonathan Lo, Jeffrey Ludlow, Donnie Luu, Larissa Marquez, Rory McGrath, Florian Mewes, Dan Michaelson, Manuel Miranda, Emile Molin, Lee Moreau, Hitomi Murai, Eddie Opara, Aline Ozkan, Liliana Palau, Christina Papalexandri, Daniel Peterson, Conny Purtill, Elizabeth Rock, Christopher Rypkema, Milena Sadée, Jaewon Seok, Michael Squashic, Alexander Strube, Anisa Suthayalai, Ryan Brooke Thomas, Hunter Tura, Sharon Ullman, Ryan Weafer, Jing Xin, David Yun, and Shoupin Zhang.

Lisa Brennan-Jobs who edited early drafts of the manuscript and Jeanne Heifetz who carried it through to the end.

Charles Miers, Ian Luna and Monica Davis at Rizzoli International for taking it on.

Yoonjai Choi for her creative direction; designers David Yun, Liliana Palau, Terri Chiao, Sung Joong Kim and Jeffrey Ludlow; and special thanks to Donnie Luu who touched every page.

And finally to Susan, Silas and Winslow for everything, all the time.

MULTIPLE SIGNATURES

I am a designer and a writer. Over the course of many years my work has oscillated between these two roles. Design is both a highly rational and a deeply intuitive process. Like writing, graphic design involves both the adherence to inherent grammatical rules and the liberties one takes with them. The more I conflate the two, the more conflicted I am. The questions that come up over and again in the following pages then are *personal* in that I am trying to figure out how the two aspects of my work are the same and how they differ. My interest is also *professional* because I use this graphic process every day in the service of practical assignments. Finally my interest is *academic* because for almost twenty years I have been trying to teach young designers and work through these issues with them.

This book is a manifestation of that multiple-personality disorder. It's not simply channeled from three different competencies—writing, designing and teaching—it also reflects how much my own ideas are overlapped by the people I work with, write with, talk to, and teach, and how my own certainties evolve over time. So *Multiple Signatures* is an attempt at a collection not bound by the definition of our studio, in the form of a monograph; by a particular chronology; or by the limitation of my own creativity and insight. It is a project instigated by me but co-authored by many people I respect and admire, both living and in some cases, not.

The signature is, of course, a graphic designer's double entendre: both an autograph and a physical component of a book. Each article herewith is signed: by me, by someone else, or some combination thereof. And while we don't abide strictly to the printing signatures, the name implies a structure: every entry is an atom starting on recto, ending on verso. They are, for the most part, stand-alone entries drawn from diverse sources. Some are historical, many are new; most are narrative but there are diagrams and *things* meant to be read as texts as well. They are organized in four big clumps corresponding to what for me are some of the essential challenges facing the contemporary design thinker: discussions about authorship, projects as inquiry, criticism of the practice, and work wherein the user plays an integral role in the construction of the final object.

A few years ago in preparation for a show in Japan, we compiled a large collection of materials produced at our studio. The 1000 images that made up the exhibition and book titled *it is what it is* were an attempt to destabilize the "deliverable"—and so the portfolio entry—and look at the entire design process as something that sloughs off visual and textual material at every stage. The confinement of graphic design to the often thin final results seemed limiting: months of work are boiled down to a business card, a tag, an exit sign. Because the results of graphic design can be decidedly quotidian, even unheroic, we must find gratification in the *thinking* and the *making*. This book is a second attempt to complete that project, but while *it is what it is* was an entirely visual exercise, *Multiple Signatures* is (mostly) words. It's an alternative way of thinking about why and how we work. Taken together the two books comprise something of a *non*ograph: twins, separated at birth, one raised by wolves, the other by librarians.

AN INTRODUCTION

MARK WIGLEY

It's a very graphic name, right? It's in your face. 2x4. Get it? I'll explain it to you. It's very complex. It's a basic building material, a 2x4. So, at the very least, graphic design is a basic building material. Think graphic design not as gift-wrapping of an existing or proposed design, but as design itself. Construction, even. Graphic design as construction. Something that might be wrapped, even gift-wrapped, by the very thing it would seem to be wrapping.

Those of you who feel that graphics are a lesser art, an art of seduction, and that architecture is a superior art that doesn't seduce but quietly exudes its own virtue—be careful. Can you imagine architecture without graphic design? It's almost impossible. Can you even imagine the word itself—Architecture—without some kind of image?

There's a long history of graphic designers collaborating with architects in such a way that there's no clear line between architecture and graphics. One example is El Lissitzky and Moholy-Nagy, who worked very closely with architects in the early decades of the 20th century when it was almost impossible to be an experimental architect if you didn't have an experimental relationship with a graphic designer. The identities were flipping back and forth in those collaborations, almost flickering, and in that flicker the work was being developed.

As architects, we are experts at only one thing: turning objects into words and words into objects. The buildings start talking to you, and the words start to assume a kind of substantial form. That would suggest the graphic designer is at the heart of our discipline, at its core rather than at its surface. That is the great trick of graphic design, to appear to be on the surface while actually occupying the core.

There is no way I can account for all the things that 2x4 has done, for all the different kinds of clients, programs and locations, and no way to guess what they will do next. A list won't work here—and they are good with lists, by the way, so it's not even worth trying.

The only thing I can do is to start a list of things they haven't done, or would not do. It would be an extraordinarily short list. Maybe such a list would include the word Building. Like, they haven't done a building. But if a building is a bunch of walls, then they have done it, many times. They are more architects, perhaps, than many architects I know.

Most graphic designers work somewhere on the line between the unconscious and the conscious. And most of the graphic design that's interesting to us is interesting precisely because it acts as a graphic trigger. Things not on the surface are brought to the surface as the graphic work sparks indirect associations.

I'll risk the claim that 2x4 has a habit of leaping across that line. Not subtly triggering the synapses between conscious and unconscious, between what you see and what you imagine (let's say in the form of advertising)—but of leaping across the line to the super-conscious, the super-direct. They're graphic, really graphic. They're endlessly intelligent, but in your face. Intelligently in your face. Not so much on the printed page, on the wall, on the façade, on the face, but in our face. They force us to think differently, to think about what architecture is, to be architects for the first time or, at least, finally.

TALKING OVER

WITH
SUSAN SELLERS
GEORGIE STOUT

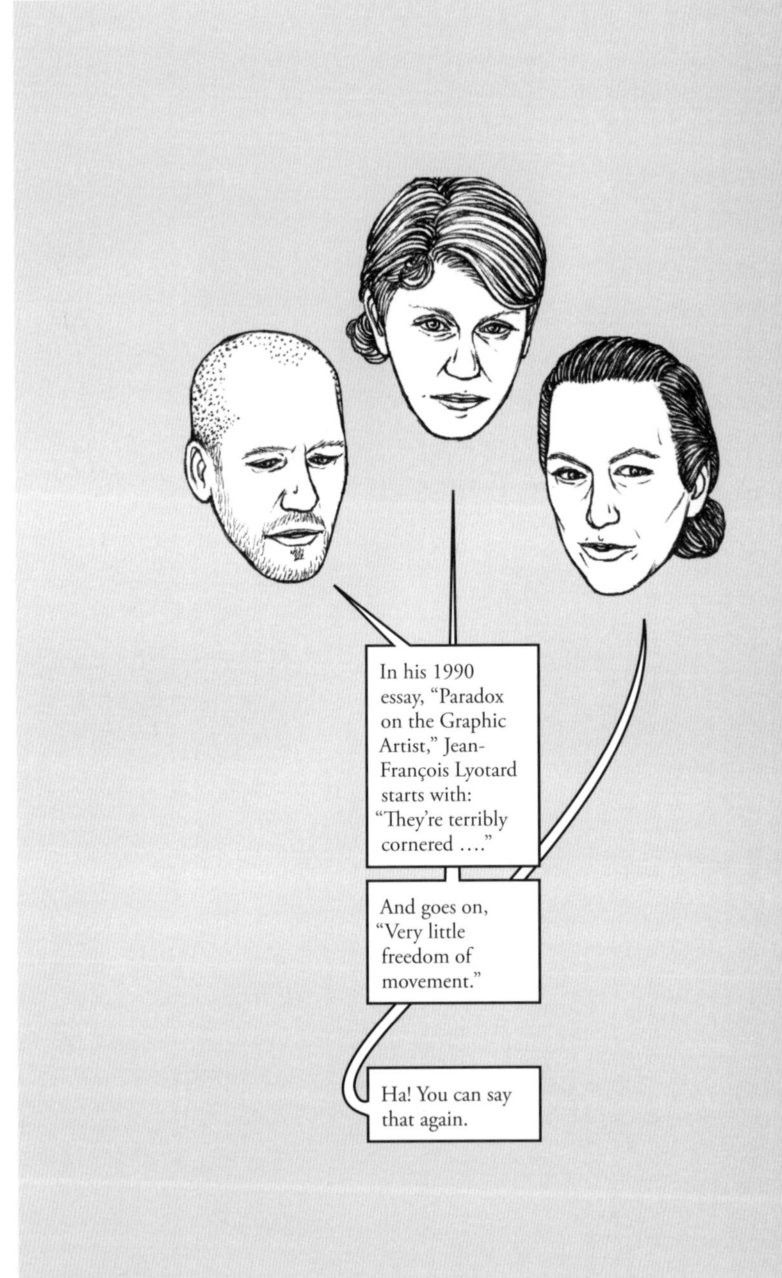
In his 1990 essay, "Paradox on the Graphic Artist," Jean-François Lyotard starts with: "They're terribly cornered …."
And goes on, "Very little freedom of movement."
Ha! You can say that again.

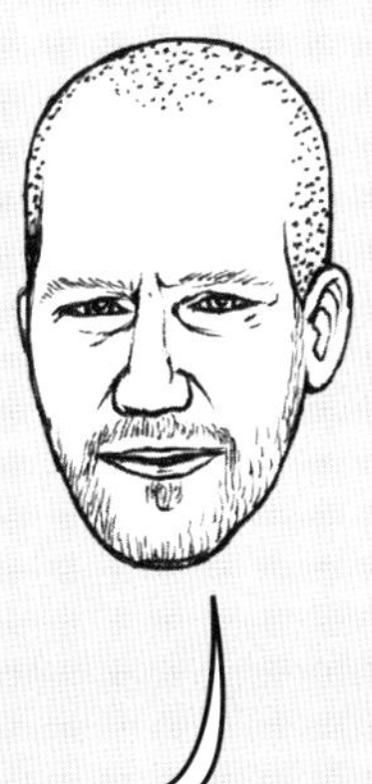

That essay came out in English the same year we started 2x4. And now, after almost twenty years of this—sixty different designers, five studios, three economic bubbles, massive technological changes, the Macintosh, the Internet, email, cell phones, mobile devices—has anything changed?

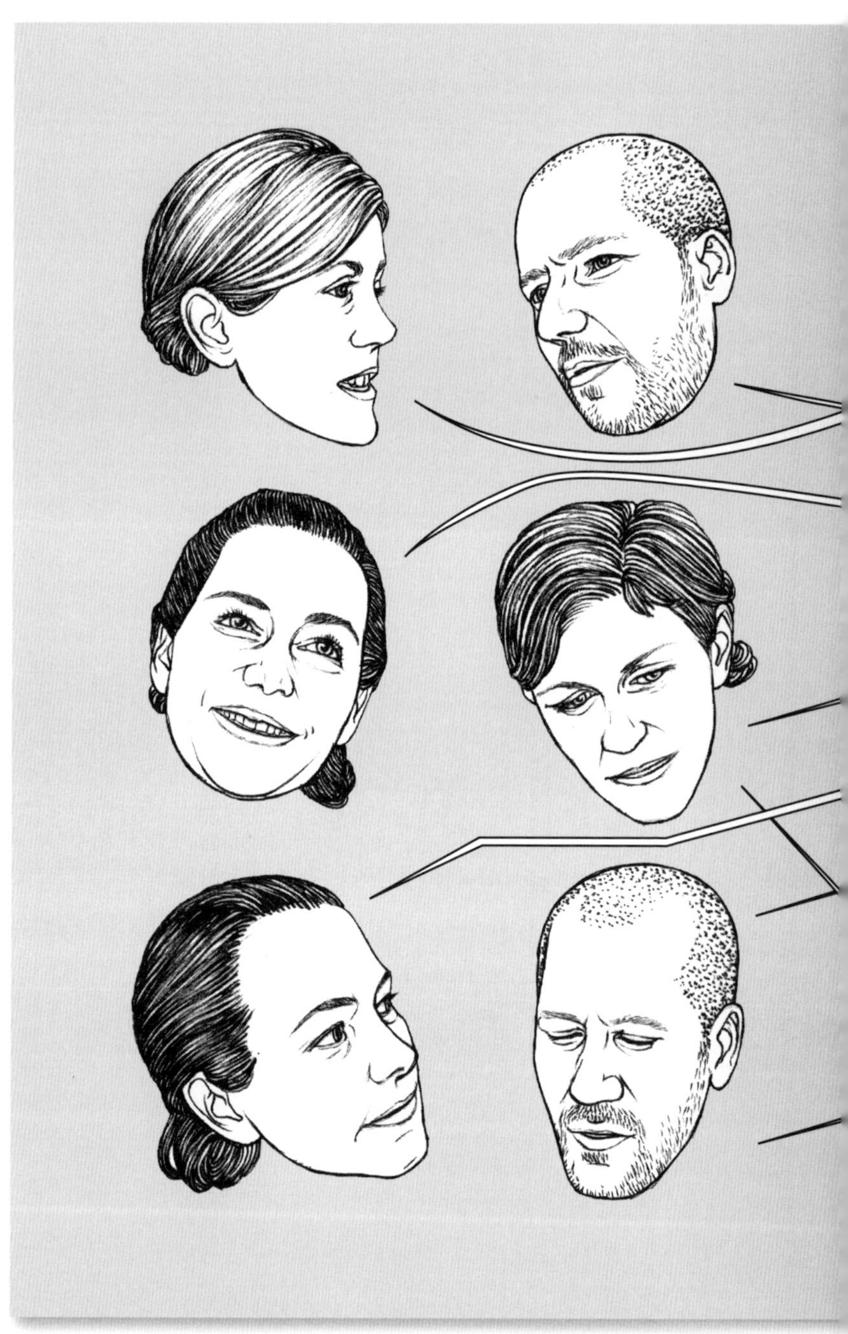

I wonder if this question is really advanced by framing the debate in terms of status, of a Lyotardian relationship to power.

Well, that was Lyotard's premise. If we start off debating the premise we'll never get anywhere ...

You two are impossible.

Clearly the definition of the designer is undergoing radical transformation. Editors are becoming ...

... curators.

And designers are editors and writers and curators.

... and the discrete labors that yield the design object are blurred. The current role of the designer is up to the imagination, ingenuity and sheer stamina of the individual ...

... or a team of people organized to take advantage of the chaos of technological disruption.

The chaos creates a situation where anything seems possible. A provocative designer, adept at rhetoric and storytelling, able to capture the imagination of an audience, and entrepreneurial enough to deliver on that vision, is in a strong position.

I'm not sure that strong is not the right word, but I would say the broader role that designers assume now—writer, thinker, editor, curator, art director, designer, illustrator—inherently puts us in a different creative position.

Well, Lyotard was already off the mark in 1990. Both technology and the academic culture of identity politics and critical theory were undermining traditional hierarchies. The burst of new technology and the cultural milieu of the moment created the conditions for our practice.

Though I'm not sure anyone on the outside would perceive designers as playing a larger or more engaged role now. Are we more influential? Probably not.

That's why I said anything seems possible.

Maybe it is important that we internalize that change in engagement even if it's not generally perceived.

But I think the stakes were smaller when we started. The critical issues engaged by design were important then but mostly linguistic or psychological—products of our own collective neurosis ...

Maybe we only assumed smaller stakes?

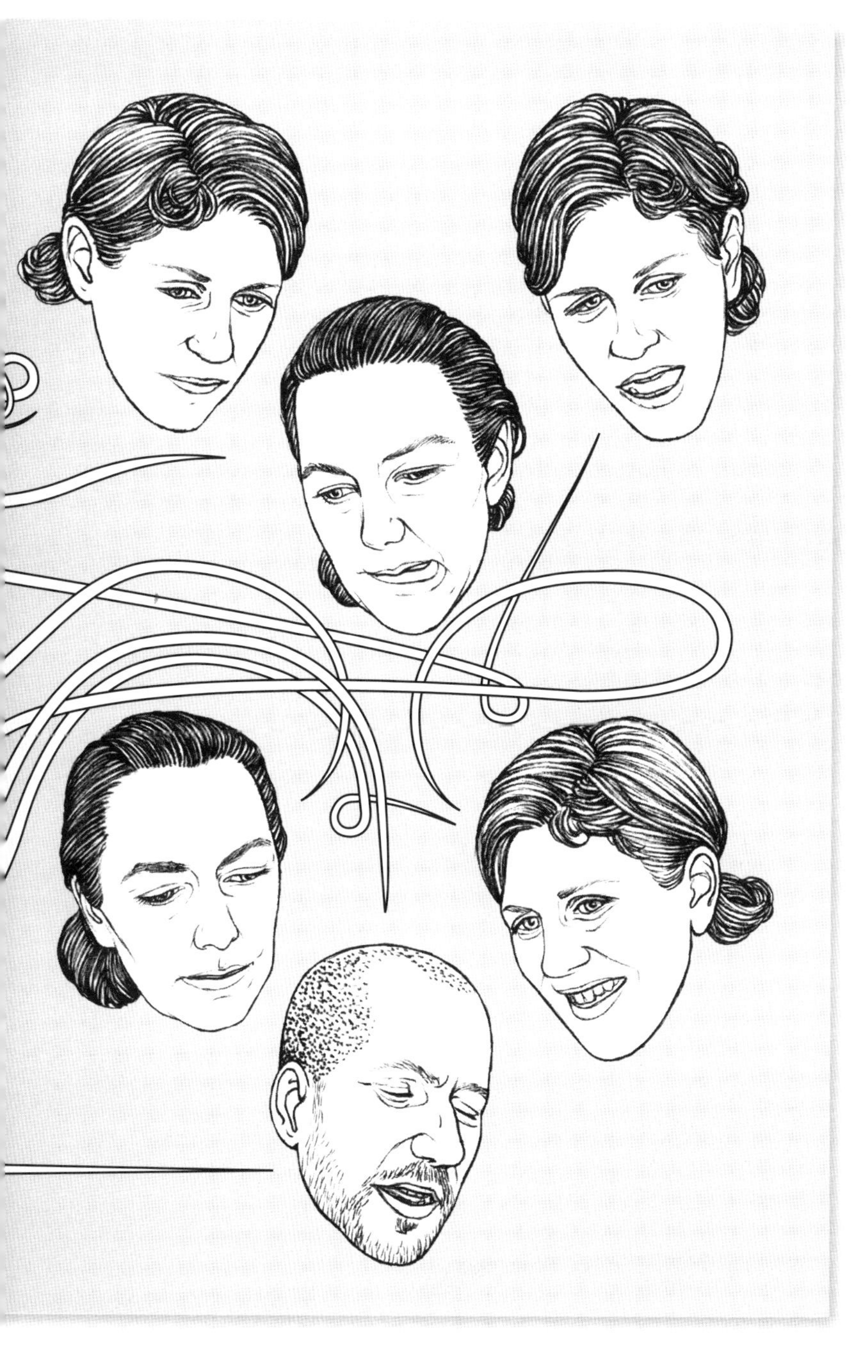

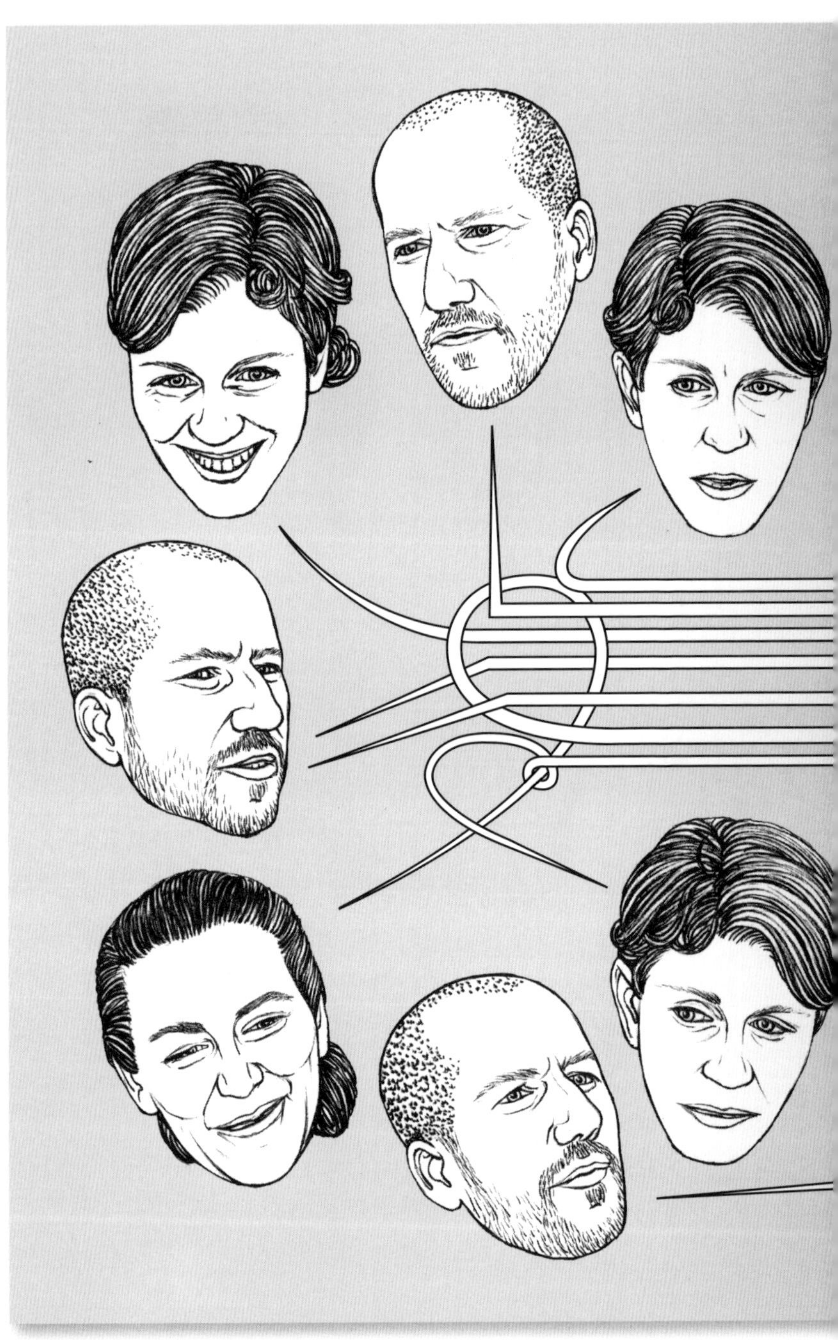

… while those issues persist in new forms, issues today seem more tangible: real economic hardship, environmental emergency and political fracture almost impossible to engage.

Is that what's called progress? Though I'm not sure we would really subscribe to a theory of design based on "progress" anyway, would we?

Recently I've heard designers frame their service as supplying "optimism." Is optimism a design deliverable or, more likely, is it an optimistic form of marketing?

That does have the reek of social-realist propaganda. Throwing the tapestry over the dunghill and all. I think a major question is: Should designers be optimistic or skeptical?

Maybe we can offer bitterness instead of optimism?

By skepticism I mean that a primary role of the designer could be to both create and puncture the commercial skin of culture. What do you tell your students, something about design as a form of inquiry?

I would frame design as a form of inquiry. While I might not package our professional work exactly this way, we do suggest that by demonstrating inquiry and manifesting debate, our clients engage their audiences, constituencies, customers, in active dialogue …

It provokes a relationship …

… and it gets at that concept of generosity we often talk about.

While I still love things, what we do now seems so much more about process and less about end result. We've developed a design methodology that incorporates thinking, talking, sketching, collaborating, doing, connecting, re-doing, writing …

(Yeah, methodology development has probably been our longest-running project.)

… and sharing that process with our collaborators is a big part of what we do.

Trying to be generous in the way we encourage our clients to be.

Our enthusiasm is one of our most recognizable products … it has also nearly driven us out of business a few times.

Can we articulate and enact this concept of "inquiry" at a larger scale? What are the conditions that make inquiry a viable strategy for a studio at this moment in time?

By inquiry, I take it you mean design that is neither form nor content, but instead a kind of analytical tool, a way of looking at the world?

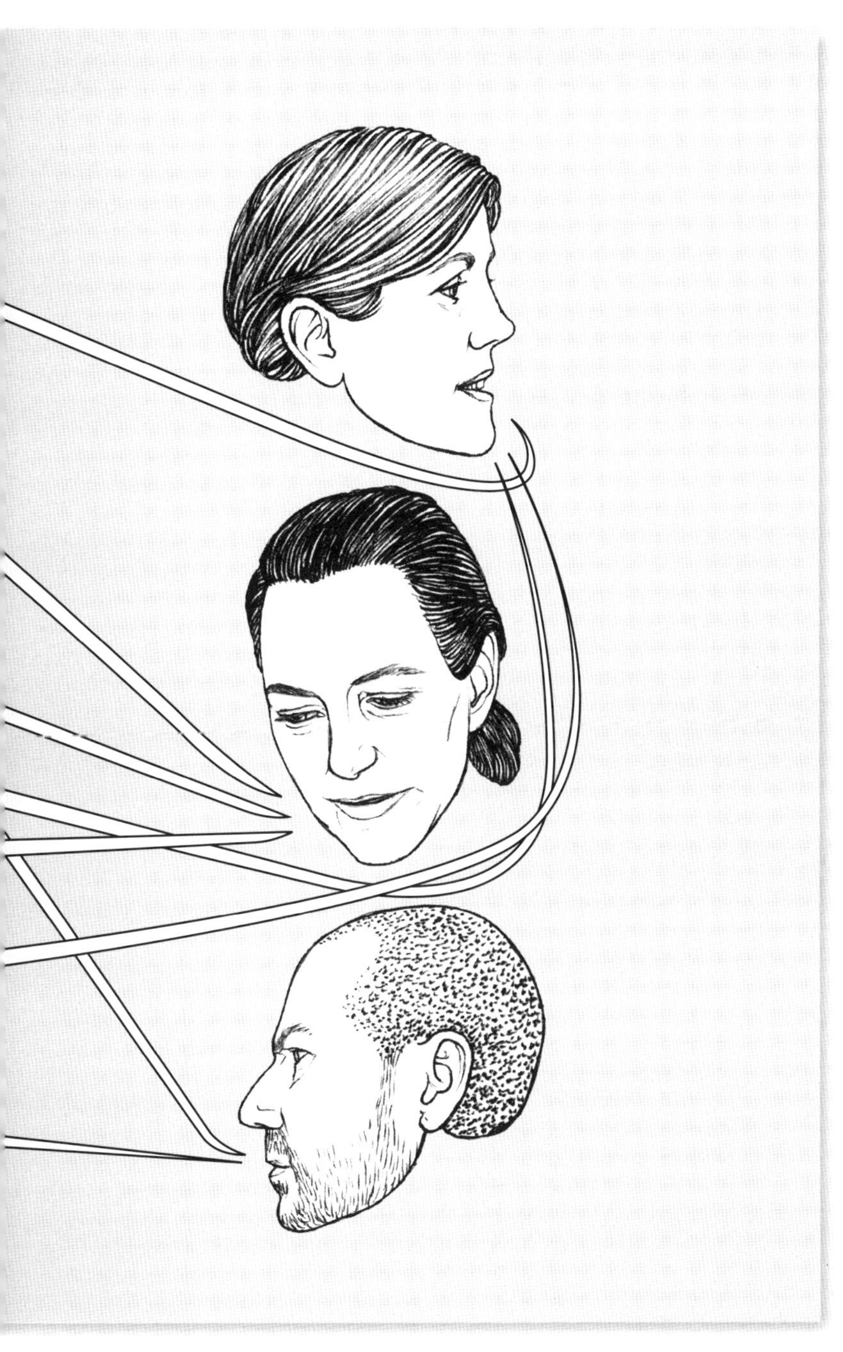

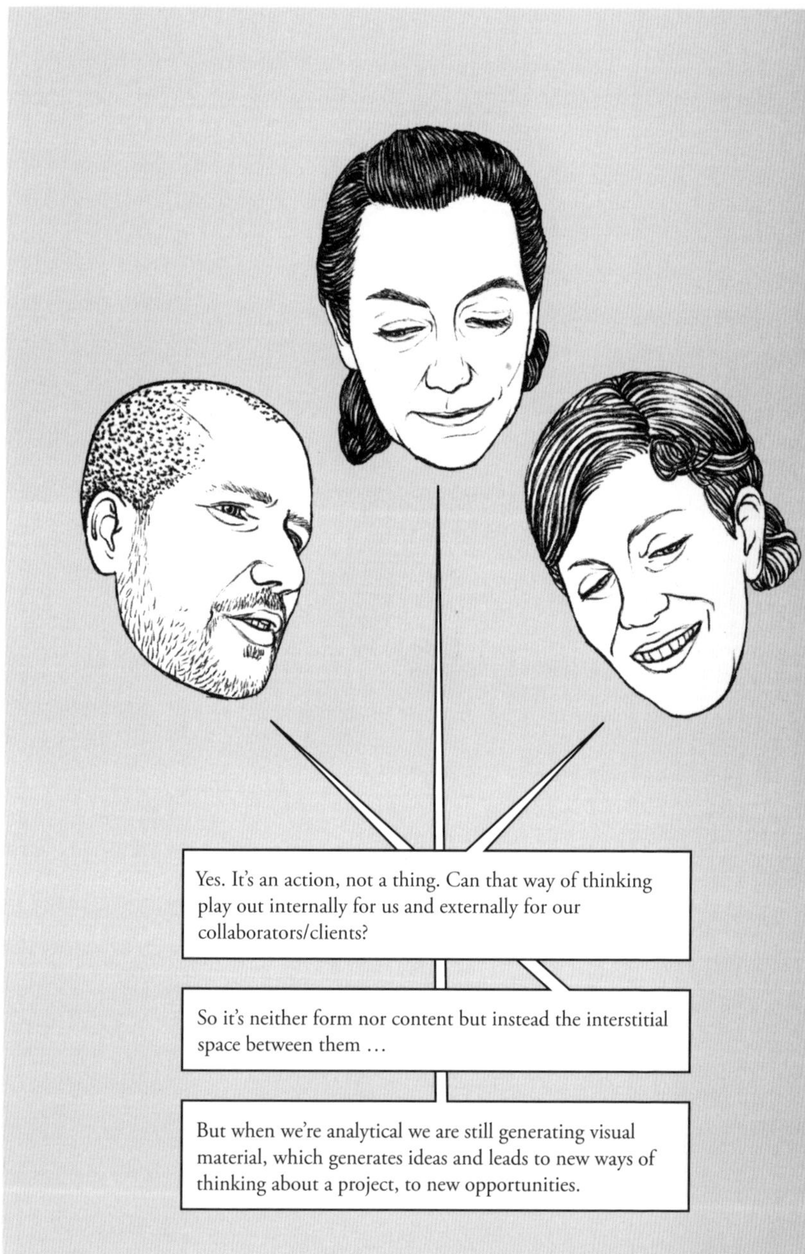
Yes. It's an action, not a thing. Can that way of thinking play out internally for us and externally for our collaborators/clients?
So it's neither form nor content but instead the interstitial space between them …
But when we're analytical we are still generating visual material, which generates ideas and leads to new ways of thinking about a project, to new opportunities.

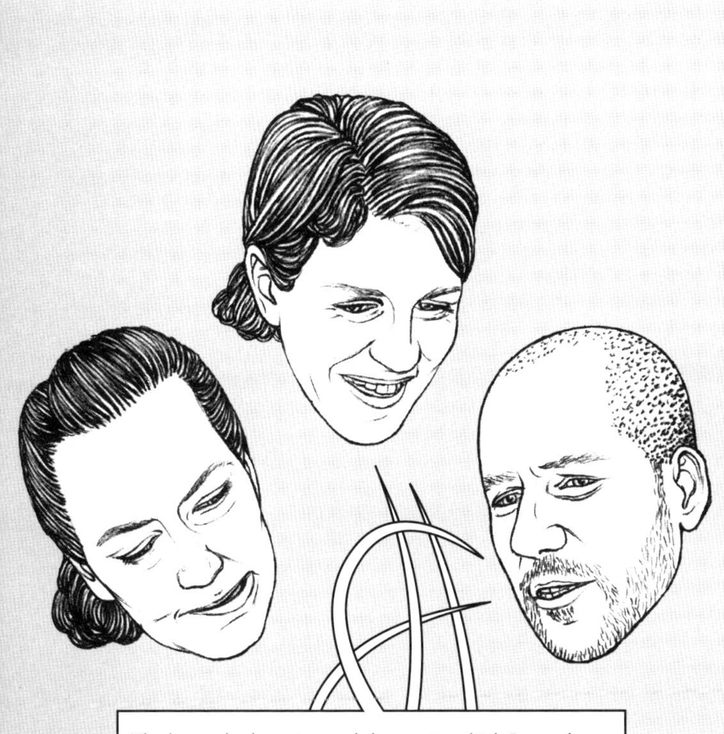
That's exactly the point, and the way in which Lyotard now feels dated. He was obsessed with objects and their residual effect on the "viewer"...
... and you're saying that now we don't talk about effect but instead about participation?
Or "engagement." I'm saying that we are trying to create inquiry using the devices of graphic design. That inquiry invites a viewer to enter into it and participate in the questions under debate through the communication medium. That the design itself is a critical tool.
And Design is the subject as well.

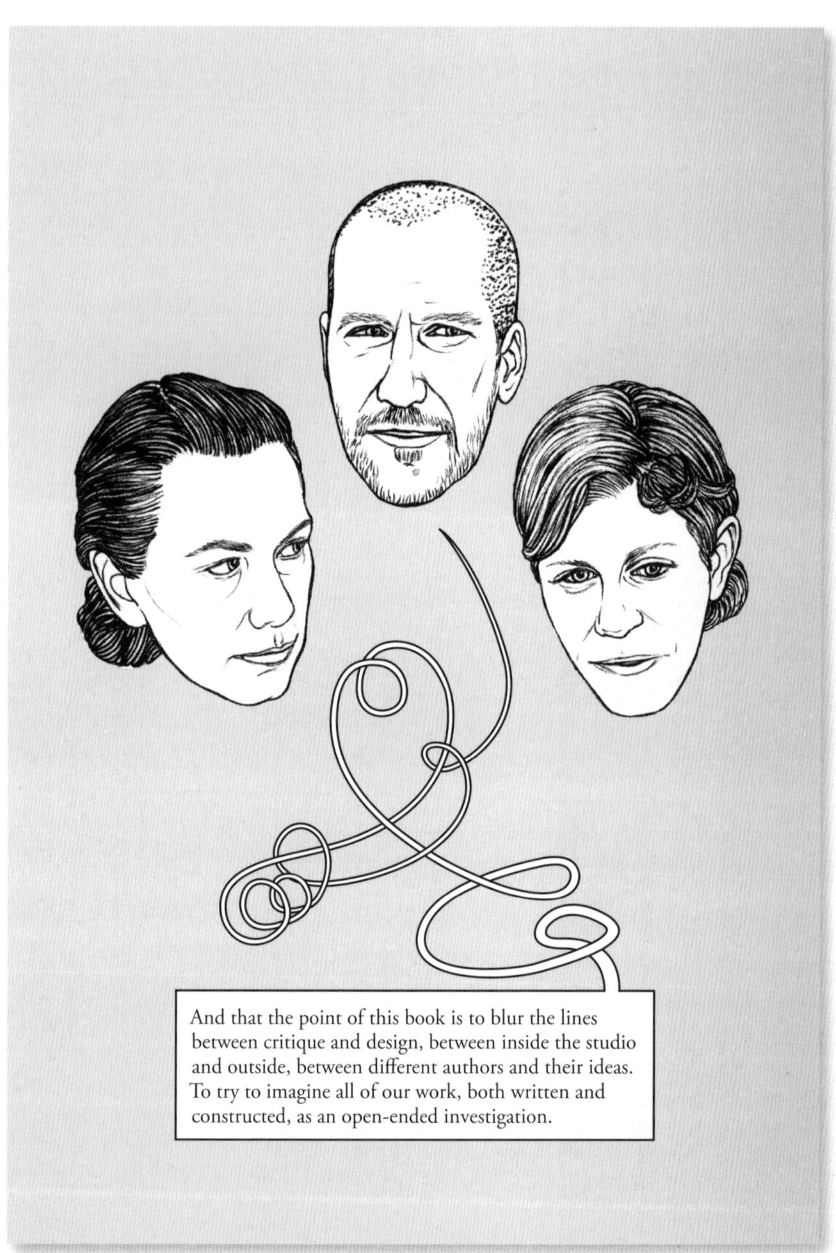
And that the point of this book is to blur the lines between critique and design, between inside the studio and outside, between different authors and their ideas. To try to imagine all of our work, both written and constructed, as an open-ended investigation.

I. AUTHORSHIP

Is a designer some specialized kind of author or a well-dressed ventriloquist's dummy mouthing the polished rhetoric of the market? Design is a deeply contradictory act: the personal and public are inextricably intertwined. Designers make things and make systems that make things. But most of all they perform a narrow, yet essential function in the increasingly complex economy that is public speech.

THE PROBLEM OF PROVENANCE

History belongs to the writer; so too the history of graphic design. The challenge for the design historian is to assemble bits and pieces of data—traditional primary and secondary sources as well as visual material—into coherent narrative. The state of graphic-design history is dire because the subjects themselves have a vested interest in perpetuating a closed narrative about their own ideas—designers want to build and maintain their own self-authored, and self-serving, myths—and design journalists are often unwilling to question the simple stories their subjects feed them. So both the primary and secondary are compromised. But the real problem is that the origins of a visual idea are blurry. In most cases, the attribution of a discrete idea to a single designer is simply a shorthand way to meld all the various threads of influence into a single unified point of *inspiration*.

The story of mysterious aesthetic inspiration gushing forth from fertile imaginations, while romantic, is almost always miscast. Graphic design is mediated: it works because it is attached to the surrounding culture. The creative-genius story is only viable if the definition of a design object is whittled down to the point that it is no longer rich or interesting or if the designer is inflated to the cult status he or she covets.

Take, for example, 2x4's super-scale portrait of Ludwig Mies van der Rohe installed on the glass façade of the Illinois Institute of Technology's McCormick Tribune Campus Center, a building designed by Office of Metropolitan Architecture. (The shorthand way to say that would be "designed by Rem Koolhaas," which would illustrate my point exactly.) The portrait, made up of thousands of tiny pictograms depicting student activities, was acquired by the Museum of Modern Art for the permanent collection and has been widely exhibited, most recently in the MoMA Architecture and Design galleries in *Just In: Recent Acquisitions* (2007–8). The image of Mies was accompanied by this label:

> IIT Mies Wallpaper, 2004
> 2x4
> Michael Rock, Susan Sellers, Georgianna Stout

Almost everything about this label is reductive: that it is a single, discrete object; that it can be situated at one point in time; that it can be attributed to the three partners of 2x4.

On the other hand, I was reading an account of a lecture by a young designer who had joined the large 2x4 team working on IIT and was surprised to find this: "[The designer] was unsure how to start a project designing environmental graphics for [IIT]. Feeling overwhelmed, he started to create simple pictograms of 'things students do.' Hundreds of pictograms he created were later transformed into 20–foot-tall, vinyl portraits of Mies van der Rohe, welcoming the students as they entered the building. He confessed that he had no idea where he was headed." This version is also fictional: the design of the entire system—which spanned many years, involved a score of designers and touched hundreds of various elements—could never be attributed to a single designer; ideas in a studio don't originate individually; and rarely does a project move forward without some sense of intention and direction.

Both these reductive forms of design history miss the real—and unique—aspects of design. Design in a collaborative studio environment is never a solo achievement but is made up of countless individual acts of creativity. Over the course of the six years we worked on the IIT project, more than a dozen different designers participated, not to mention a large and dynamic team of architects from OMA, and landscape designers from Inside Outside.

If we take this one design artifact, the portrait on the façade of the building, and review its provenance in detail, the complexity of assigning authorship immediately becomes apparent. Rem Koolhaas and his team at Office for Metropolitan Architecture won the competition to build a new student center on the campus of the Illinois Institute of Technology in 1998. The site for the building is an interstitial space between the main campus, famously designed by Mies van der Rohe (case in point), and the student dormitories to the north. This dead space is overshot by an elevated train track, and was at the time criss-crossed by "desire lines" that students had worn into the hardscrabble landscape by slogging back and forth between class and home. OMA proposed the brilliant, counterintuitive solution of squeezing the building under the tracks and enclosing the trains in a huge, sound-muffling tube/tunnel, thereby reclaiming land lost to the screeching El. The building plan roughly follows those existing desire lines. The dynamic interior spaces, invigorated by the sharp crossing paths, are encircled by a more or less rectangular modern frame nicknamed the "Mies Wrap."

Celebrating the occasion of the announcement of the competition results, Herbert Muschamp, then architecture critic for *The New York Times*, described the tension between the cacaphonic interior space of the building and the cool Miesian wrap: "At IIT, [Koolhaas] must contend with the authority of Mies and of modern architecture at its most rigidly orthodox. His design both honors and subverts that orthodoxy by wrapping a Miesian glass skin around colliding interior spaces that evoke high modernism's demise."

In the original competition submission, Rem Koolhaas, Dan Wood, Sarah Dunn and the architecture team articulated the Mies Wrap with images of the famous architect applied to the glass façade. Wood recalls that in an era before a simple Google Image search would turn up thousands of possible choices, the portraits were limited to what could be found in the studio library, late at night, Xeroxed onto acetate and applied to the model. The full-on portrait of grizzled, aging Mies ended up positioned over the main entrance, facing his classic campus buildings to the south. In his presentation to the competition committee, and in countless presentations thereafter, Koolhaas described how future generations of ambling students would enter the building through the great modernist's mouth.

The Mies Wrap went through many iterations and convolutions, some inspired by design development, some by programmatic demands, and many to accommodate cost restrictions. Throughout that process the other images that festooned the wrap dropped away but the large portrait of old, saggy Mies remained in the drawings, so by the time we became part of the project it had acquired a certain inevitability. As we started to integrate our ideas into OMA's, we embraced the iconographic notion of the Mies Wrap and also looked for ways to subvert it, twist it, make it strange or funny—to make it our own. High modernism had a conflicted relationship with the mural as a social tool and we wanted to test the limits of how the graphic and the architectural could and would collide. We were just finishing the graphics for Guggenheim Las Vegas and embarking on a new project for the Prada store in Soho (both with OMA), and the mixing of a lowbrow material like wallpaper and a highbrow notion like the modernist mural with a '70s idea of supergraphic was informing much of that work.

The IIT building was littered with graphic effects. This approach developed out of an essential aspect of the construction: the ceiling was more or less disconnected from the walls, basically thin partitions that could be superficially coated with graphic skins. We were looking for a common way to code the various activities that took place inside a campus center, using the graphic surface as medium. To both exploit the modernity of the space, and to slyly undermine it, we considered using pictograms typical of public spaces like airports and sports stadiums. We were also thinking about some of the humor in the stonework at the neo-Gothic campus at Yale where the stonecutters had inserted lighthearted contemporary jokes into seemingly serious, historic architectural detail.

In the studio the project had multiple authors. Different designers, or teams, took on every aspect of the space from the wallpaper and surface patterns to typography, information and image. The idea of expanding the pictograms to include the foibles of student life—keg stands, cheating, making out, and generally lascivious behavior—was developed by a young designer, building on her own thesis project completed at the Yale School of Art the year before, and drawn in her inimitable style. That icon system became a unifying feature throughout the space repeated at every scale.

Pixelation had an extensive history in the studio, starting with projects we had already developed for OMA and Prada. The pixelated portrait can be traced directly to a proposal we made with the Korean artist Do-Ho Suh for IIT in the first year of the project. We were thinking about how to incorporate more of a student presence in the building and together came up with a proposal using ID photographs of individual students to make a huge, 20–foot-high portrait of an averaged, "generic" student. This idea was inspired by work Suh had been doing as a graduate student in sculpture at Yale in which he used images of thousands of Korean students to make wallpaper patterns. At the same time we were investigating different ways we could accomplish OMA's portrait façades and make the images more graphic, and therefore more feasible to apply to the glass. When Do-Ho's project proved to be financially impossible, we tabled the idea of the super-sized, pixelated student portrait, only to reintroduce a version of it years later for the Mies façade.

As the project neared the execution phase we again faced the problem of how to reproduce the Mies face on the glass surfaces. This required a whole new body of work—and more designers—transforming the original icons into a more uniform set of figures, standardizing the library and adding new twists. (At this time we also developed a special typeface, derived from Mies's original lettering on the campus drawings, to use for the project's typographic applications.) We returned to the idea developed by Do-Ho of the pixelated face. A clever young designer leveraged a somewhat anachronistic ASCII algorithm to break down the Mies photograph into a halftone screen using the icon system as the pixel, then spent countless days reworking, tweaking and correcting the final files before they were ultimately etched into the glass panels.

So who is the *originator* of the work that hangs on the wall of MoMA? The one who though up the concept, developed the idea, gave it form or executed the final iteration? Can any one of us own the thing? The truth lies somewhere between the various extremes: institutional authorship on one side—the result of a collaborative, often random, set of efforts where the author's name is a function that unifies that work; and the heroic individual on the other—one person made the physical thing. A large, complex design system is the culmination of many individual flashes of brilliance that cohere into something more or less unified and complete. An insightful, investigative design journalism could tease out this contradiction and build a theory of graphic design based on the tension between the various, often contradictory, modes of making.

[Y]ou're always repeating your same things all the time anyway, whether or not somebody asks you or it's your job. You're usually making the same mistakes. You apply your usual mistakes to every new category or field you go into. – Andy Warhol.

I would like to revisit these ideas of repetition and mutation through a close look at a number of different sources and inspirations. All of them can be found easily – and I have included a few with this email. The materials we will consider are:

Visit from the Goon Squad. Novel by Jennifer Egan. I would like you to create a rough diagram of the narrative structure as you read. This does not need to be graphically sophisticated, i.e. it can be notational. You could try to do a chronology, track the interconnections between characters, diagram the chapters, etc. (Due 1.26)

Pulp Fiction. Film written and directed by Quentin Tarantino. Please watch (or rewatch).

L'Année dernière à Marienbad. Film directed by Alain Resnais from a screenplay by Alain Robbe-Grillet. Please watch. Would be useful to do a little research on Robbe-Grillet.

Farm Implements and Rutabagas in a Landscape. Poem by John Ashbery (attached). Please read. It also would be useful to research the poetic form called the *sestina*.

Forty-One False Starts. Magazine profile of painter David Salle by Janet Malcolm (attached).

The Library of Babel. Short story by Jorge Luis Borges (attached).

Runaway. Song by Kanye West & Pusha T. from the album *My Beautiful Dark Twisted Fantasy*.

I would like you to read the magazine article, short story and poem, view the films, and listen to the song before the first class. (The novel you can work on through 1.26) We will spend our first session discussing this material.

Assignment.
Create a proposal for a project in any media about any subject that formally investigates some aspect of the strategies demonstrated by these examples. The proposal should clearly articulate the nature of your project and provide proof-of-concept materials.

Winter 2012
First Year Design Workshop with Michael Rock
Thursday January 12, 19 and 26.
1:30 to 5:30pm

My interest in this short seminar/workshop is to explore the implications of certain formal structures. I am curious how a formal device can inspire a wide range of discursive investigations.

Many years ago I prefaced an introduction to the thesis project at Yale with this quote:

DESIGNER AS AUTHOR

What does it mean to call a graphic designer an author?

Authorship, in one form or another, has been a popular term in graphic-design circles, especially those at the edge of the profession, the design academies and the murky territories that exist between design and art. The word authorship has a ring of importance: it connotes seductive ideas of origination and agency. But the question of how designers become authors is a difficult one, and exactly who the designer/authors are and what authored design looks like depends entirely on how you define the term and the criteria you choose to grant entrance into the pantheon.

Authorship may suggest new approaches to understanding design process in a profession traditionally associated more with the communication than the origination of messages. But theories of authorship may also serve as legitimizing strategies, and authorial aspirations may actually end up reinforcing certain conservative notions of design production and subjectivity—ideas that run counter to recent critical attempts to overthrow the perception of design based on individual brilliance. The implications deserve careful evaluation. What does it really mean to call for a graphic designer to be an author?

What is an author?

That question has been an area of intense scrutiny over the last forty years. The meaning of the word itself has shifted significantly over time. The earliest definitions are not associated with writing; in fact the most inclusive is a "person who originates or gives existence to anything." Other usages clearly index authoritarian—even patriarchal—connotations: "father of all life," "any inventor, constructor or founder," "one who begets," and a "director, commander, or ruler."

All literary theory, from Aristotle on, has in some form or another been theory of authorship. Since this is not a history of the author but a consideration of the author as metaphor, I'll start with recent history. Wimsatt and Beardsley's seminal text, "The Intentional Fallacy" (1946), drove an early wedge between the author and the text, dispelling the notion that a reader could ever really know an author through his writing. The so-called death of the author, proposed most succinctly by Roland Barthes in 1968 in an essay of that title, is closely linked to the birth of critical theory, especially theory based in reader response and interpretation rather than intentionality. Michel Foucault used the rhetorical question "What is an author?" as the title of his influential essay of 1969 which, in response to Barthes, outlines the basic taxonomy and functions of the author and the problems associated with conventional ideas of authorship and origination.

Foucauldian theory holds that the connection between author and text has transformed and that there exist a number of author-functions that shape the way readers approach a text. These stubbornly persistent functions are historically determined and culturally specific categories.

Foucault posits that the earliest sacred texts were authorless, their origins lost in ancient history (the Vedas, the Gospels, etc.). The very anonymity of the text served as a certain kind of authentication. The author's name was symbolic, rarely attributable to an individual. (The Gospel of Luke, for instance, is a diversity of texts gathered under the rubric of Luke, someone who may indeed have lived and written parts, but not the totality, of what we now think of as the complete work.)

Scientific texts, at least through the Renaissance, demanded an author's name as validation. Far from *objective* truth, science was based in subjective invention and the authority of the scientist. This changed with the rise of the scientific method. Scientific discoveries and mathematical proofs were no longer in need of authors because they were perceived as discovered truths rather than authored ideas. The scientist revealed extant phenomena, facts anyone faced with the same conditions would discover. The scientist and the mathematician could claim to have been first to discover a paradigm, and lend their name to the phenomenon, but could never claim authorship over it. (The astronomer who discovers a new star may name it but does not conjure it.) Facts were universal and thus eternally preexisiting.

By the 18th century, Foucault suggests, the situation had now completely reversed: literature was authored and science became the product of anonymous objectivity. When authors came to be punished for their writing —i.e. when a text could be transgressive—the link between author and text was firmly established.

The codification of ownership over a text is often dated to the adoption of the Statute of Anne (1709) by the British Parliament, generally considered the first real copyright act. The first line of the law is revealing: "Whereas Printers, Booksellers, and other Persons, have of late frequently taken the Liberty of Printing ... Books, and other Writings, without the Consent of the Authors ... to their very great Detriment, and too often to the Ruin of them and their Families ...." The statute secures the right to benefit financially from a work and for the author to preserve its textual integrity. That authorial right was deemed irrevocable. Text came to be seen as a form of private property. A romantic criticism arose that reinforced that relationship, searching for critical keys in the life and intention of the writer.

By laying a legal ground for ownership, the Statute of Anne defines who is, and isn't, an author. It was a thoroughly modern problem. No one had *owned* the sacred texts. The very fact that the origins of sacred texts were lost in history, their authors either composites or anonymous, gave them their authority. The gospels in their purest form were public domain. Any work to be done, and any arguments to have, were interpretive. The authors referred to in the Statute were living, breathing—and apparently highly litigious—beings. The law granted them authority over the meaning and use of their own words.

Ownership of the text, and the authority granted to authors at the expense of the creative reader, fueled much of the 20th century's obsession with authorship. Post-structuralist reading of authorship tends to critique the prestige attributed to the figure of the author and to suggest or speculate about a time after his fall from grace.

Barthes ends his essay supposing that the "birth of the reader comes at the cost of the death of the author." Foucault imagines a time when we might ask, "What difference does it make who is speaking?" Both attempt to overthrow the notion that a text is a line of words that releases a single, predetermined meaning, the central message of an author/god, and refocus critical attention on the activity of reading and readers. The focus shifts from the author's intention to the internal workings of the writing itself, not what it means but *how* it means.

Postmodernity turns on what Fredric Jameson identified as a "fragmented and schizophrenic decentering and dispersion" of the subject. Decentered text—a text that is skewed from the direct line of communication from sender to receiver, severed from the authority of its origin, a free-floating element in a field of possible significations—figures heavily in constructions of a design based in reading and readers. But Katherine McCoy's prescient image of designers moving beyond problem solving and by "authoring additional content and a self-conscious critique of the message, adopting roles associated with art and literature," is often misconstrued. Rather than working to incorporate theory into their methods of production, many self-proclaimed deconstructivist designers literally illustrated Barthes' image of a reader-based text—a "tissue of quotations drawn from innumerable centers of culture"—by scattering fragments of quotations across the surface of their "authored" posters and book covers. (This technique went something like: "Theory is complicated, so my design is complicated.") The rather dark implications of Barthes' theory, note Ellen Lupton and J. Abbott Miller, were refashioned into a "romantic theory of self-expression."

After years in the somewhat thankless position of the faceless facilitator, many designers were ready to speak out. Some designers may be eager to discard the internal affairs of formalism—to borrow Paul de Man's metaphor—and branch out to the foreign affairs of external politics and content. By the '70s, design began to discard some of the scientistic approach that held sway for several decades. (As early as the '20s, Trotsky was labeling formalist artists the "chemists of art.") That approach was evident in the design ideology that preached strict adherence to an eternal grid and a kind of rational approach to design. (Keep in mind that although this example is a staple of critiques of modernism, in actuality the objectivists represented a small fragment of the design population at the time.)

Müller-Brockmann's evocation of the "aesthetic quality of mathematical thinking" is certainly the clearest and most cited example of this approach. Müller-Brockmann and a slew of fellow researchers like Kepes, Dondis and Arnheim worked to uncover preexisting order and form in the manner a scientist reveals a natural "truth." But what is most peculiar and revealing in Müller-Brockmann's writing is his reliance on tropes of submission: the designer submits to the will of the system, forgoes personality and withholds interpretation.

In his introduction to *Compendium for Literates*, which attempts a highly formal dissection of writing, Karl Gerstner claims about the organization of his book that "all the components are atomic, i.e. in principle they are irreducible. In other words, they establish a principle."

The reaction to that drive for an irreducible theory of design is well documented. On the surface at least, contemporary designers were moving from authorless, scientific text—in which inviolable visual principles were carefully revealed through extensive visual research—toward a more textual position in which the designer could claim some level of ownership over the message. (This at the time literary theory was trying to move away from that very position.) But some of the basic, institutional features of design practice have a way of getting tangled up in zealous attempts at self-expression. The idea of a decentered message does not necessarily sit well in a professional relationship in which the client is paying a designer to convey specific information or emotions. In addition, most design is done in some kind of collaborative setting, either within a client relationship or in the context of a design studio that utilizes the talents of numerous creative people. Thus the origin of any particular idea is clouded. And the ever-present pressure of technology and electronic communication only further muddies the water.

Is there an auteur in the house?

It is not surprising to find that Barthes' essay, "Death of the Author," was written in Paris in 1968, the year students joined workers on the barricades in the general strikes and the year the Western world flirted with social revolution. To call for the overthrow of authority—in the form of the author—in favor of the reader—read: the masses—had real resonance in 1968. But to lose power you must have already worn the mantle, and so designers had a bit of a dilemma overthrowing a power they may never have possessed.

On the other hand, the figure of the author implies a total control over creative activity and seemed an essential ingredient of high art. If the relative level of genius was the ultimate measure of artistic achievement, activities that lacked a clear central authority figure were necessarily devalued. The development of film theory in the 1950s serves as an interesting example.

Almost ten years before Barthes made his famous proclamation, film critic and budding director François Truffaut proposed "La politique des auteurs," a polemical strategy to reconfigure a critical theory of the cinema. The problem facing the auteur theorists was how to create a theory that imagined the film, necessarily a work of broad collaboration, as a work of a single artist and thus a singular work of art. The solution was to develop a set of criteria that allowed a critic to decree certain directors *auteurs*. In order to establish the film as a work of art, auteur theory required that the director—heretofore merely a third of the creative troika of director, writer and cinematographer—had the ultimate control of the entire project.

Auteur theory—especially as espoused by American critic Andrew Sarris—held that directors must meet three essential criteria in order to pass into the sacred hall of the auteur. Sarris proposed that the director must demonstrate technical expertise, have a stylistic signature that is demonstrated over the course of several films and, most important, through choice of projects and cinematic treatment, demonstrate a consistent vision and evoke a palpable interior meaning through his work. Since the film director often had little control over the choice of the material—especially in the Hollywood studio system that assigned directors to projects—the signature way he treated a varying range of scripts and subjects was especially important in establishing a director's auteur credentials. As Roger Ebert summed up the idea: "A film is not what it is about, it's how it is about it."

The interesting thing about the auteur theory was that, unlike literary critics, film theorists, like designers, had to construct the notion of the author. It was a legitimizing strategy, a method to raise what was considered low entertainment to the plateau of fine art. By crowning the director the author of the film, critics could elevate certain subjects to the status of high art. That elevation, in turn, would grant the director new freedoms in future projects. (Tantrums could be thrown in the name of artistic vision. "I'm an artist, dammit, not a butcher!" Expensive wines could be figured into overhead to satisfy rarefied palates.)

The parallel to design practice is useful. Like the film director, the art director or designer is often assigned his or her material and often works collaboratively in a role directing the activity of a number of other creative people. In addition, the designer works on a number of diverse projects over the course of a career, many of which have widely varying levels of creative potential; any inner meaning must come through the aesthetic treatment as much as from the content.

If we apply the auteur criteria to graphic designers we find a body of work that may be elevated to auteur status. Technical proficiency could be fulfilled by any number of practitioners, but couple technical proficiency with a signature style and the field narrows. The list of names that meet those two criteria would be familiar, as that work is often published, awarded and praised. (And, of course, that selective republishing of certain work to the exclusion of other work constructs a unified and stylistically consistent oeuvre.) But great technique and style alone do not an auteur make. If we add the third requirement of interior meaning, how does that list fare? Are there graphic designers who, by special treatment and choice of projects, approach the realm of deeper meaning the way a Bergman, Hitchcock or Welles does?

In these cases the graphic auteur must both seek projects that fit his or her vision and then tackle a project from a specific, recognizable critical perspective. For example, Jan van Toorn might be expected to approach a brief for a corporate annual report from a critical socioeconomic position.

But how do you compare a film poster with the film itself? The very scale of a cinematic project allows for a sweep of vision not possible in graphic design. Therefore, as the design of a single project lacks weight, graphic auteurs, almost by definition, have long, established bodies of work in which discernable patterns emerge. The auteur uses very specific client vehicles to attain a consistency of meaning. (Renoir observed that a director spends his whole career making variations on the same film.) Think of the almost fetishistic way a photographer like Helmut Newton returns to a particular vision of class and sexuality — no matter what he is assigned to shoot.

Conversely, many great stylists don't seem to make the cut, as it is difficult to discern a larger message in their work — a message that transcends stylistic elegance. (You have to ask yourself, "What's the work about?") Perhaps it's an absence or presence of an overriding philosophy or individual spirit that diminishes some designed works and elevates others.

We may have been applying a modified graphic auteur theory for years without really paying attention. What has design history been, if not a series of critical elevations and demotions as our attitudes about style and inner meaning evolve? In trying to describe interior meaning, Sarris finally resorts to the "intangible difference between one personality and another."

That retreat to intangibility—"I can't say what it is but I know it when I see it"—is the Achilles heel of the auteur theory, which has long since fallen into disfavor in film-criticism circles. It never dealt adequately with the collaborative nature of the cinema and the messy problems of movie-making. But while the theory is passé, its effect is still with us: to this day, when we think of film structure, the director is squarely in the middle.

The application of auteur theory may be too limited an engine for our current image of design authorship but there are a variety of other ways to frame the issue, a number of paradigms on which we could base our practice: the artist book, concrete poetry, political activism, publishing, illustration.

The general authorship rhetoric seems to include any work by a designer that is self-motivated, from artist books to political activism. But artist books easily fall within the realm and descriptive power of art criticism. Activist work may be neatly explicated using allusions to propaganda, graphic design, public relations and advertising.

Perhaps the graphic author is actually one who writes and publishes material about design. This category would include Josef Müller-Brockmann and Rudy VanderLans, Paul Rand and Eric Spiekermann, William Morris and Neville Brody, Robin Kinross and Ellen Lupton—rather strange bedfellows. The entrepreneurial arm of authorship affords the possibility of personal voice and wide distribution. The challenge is that most in this category split the activities into three recognizable and discrete actions: editing, writing and designing. Design remains the vehicle for their written thought even when they are acting as their own clients. (Kinross, for example, works as a historian and then changes hats and becomes a typographer.) Rudy VanderLans is perhaps the purest of the entrepreneurial authors. *Emigre* is a project in which the content *is* the form—i.e. the formal exploration is as much the content of the magazine as the articles. The three actions blur into one contiguous whole. VanderLans expresses his message through the selection of material (as an editor), the content of the writing (as a writer), and the form of the pages and typography (as a form-giver).

Ellen Lupton and her partner J. Abbott Miller are an interesting variation on this model. "The Bathroom, the Kitchen and the Aesthetics of Waste," an exhibition at MIT and a book, seems to approach a kind of graphic authorship. The message is explicated equally through graphic/visual devices as well as text panels and descriptions. The design of the exhibition and the book evoke design issues that are also the content: it is clearly self-reflexive.

Lupton and Miller's work is primarily critical. It forms and represents a reading of exterior social or historical phenomena and explicates that message for a specific audience. But there is a subset of work often overlooked by the design community, the illustrated book, that is almost entirely concerned with the generation of creative narrative. Books for children have been one of the most successful venues for the author/artist, and bookshops are packed with the fruits of their labors. Many illustrators have used the book in wholly inventive ways and produced serious work. Illustrator/authors include Sue Coe, Art Spiegelman, Charles Burns, David Macaulay, Chris Van Allsburg, Edward Gorey, Maurice Sendak, and many others. In addition, the comic book and the graphic novel have generated a renewed interest both in artistic and critical circles. Spiegelman's *Maus* and Coe's *X* and *Porkopolis* suggest expanded possibilities.

Power ploys

If the ways a designer can be an author are myriad, complex and often confusing, the way designers have used the term and the value attributed to it are equally so. Any number of recent statements claim authorship as the panacea to the woes of the browbeaten designer. In an article in *Emigre*, author Anne Burdick proposed that "designers must consider themselves authors, not facilitators. This shift in perspective implies responsibility, voice, action .... With voice comes a more personal connection and opportunity to explore individual options." A recent call-for-entries for a design exhibition titled "Designer as Author: Voices and Visions" sought to identify "graphic designers who are engaged in work that transcends the traditional service-oriented commercial production, and who pursue projects that are personal, social or investigative in nature." In the rejection of the role of the facilitator and in the call for transcendence lies the implication that authored design holds some higher, purer purpose. The amplification of the personal voice compels designers to take possession of their texts and legitimizes design as an equal of the more traditionally privileged forms of authorship.

But if, as a chorus of contemporary theorists have convinced us, the proclivity of the contemporary designer is toward open reading and free textual interpretation, that desire is thwarted by oppositional theories of authorship. The cult of the author narrows interpretation and places the author at the center of the work. Foucault noted that the figure of the author is not a particularly liberating one. By transferring the authority of the text back to the author, by focusing on voice, presence becomes a limiting factor, containing and categorizing the work. The author as origin and ultimate owner of the text guards against the free will of the reader. The figure of the author reconfirms the traditional idea of the genius creator, and the esteem or status of the man frames the work and imbues it with some mythical value.

While some claims for authorship may be as simple as a renewed sense of responsibility, at times they seem to be ploys for property rights, attempts to finally exercise some kind of agency where traditionally there has been none. The author = authority. The longing for graphic authorship may be the longing for a kind of legitimacy, or a kind of power that has so long eluded the obedient designer. But do we get anywhere by celebrating the designer as some central character? Isn't that what fueled the last fifty years of design history? If we really want to move beyond the designer-as-hero model of history, we may have to imagine a time when we can ask, "What difference does it make who designed it?"

Perhaps, in the end, authorship is not a very convincing metaphor for the activity we understand as design. There are a few examples of work that is clearly the product of design authors and not designer/authors, and these tend to be exceptions to the rule.

Rather than glorify the act and sanctify the practice, I propose three alternative models for design that attempt to describe the activity as it exists and as it could evolve: designer as translator, designer as performer, and designer as director.

Designer as translator

This is based on the assumption that the act of design is, in essence, the clarification of material or the remodeling of content from one form to another. The ultimate goal is the expression of a given content rendered in a form that reaches a new audience. I am drawn to this metaphor by Ezra Pound's translations of Chinese character poetry. Pound translated not only the meaning of the characters but the visual component of the poem as well. Thus the original is rendered as a raw material reshaped into the conventions of Western poetry. The translation becomes a second art. Translation is neither scientific nor ahistorical. Every translation reflects both the character of the original and the spirit of the contemporary as well as the individuality of the translator: An 1850s translation of the *Odyssey* will be radically different from a 1950s translation.

In certain works, the designer remolds the raw material of given content, rendering it legible to a new audience. Like the poetic translator, the designer transforms not only the literal meaning of the elements but the spirit, too. For example, Bruce Mau's design of a book version of Chris Marker's 1962 film, "La Jetée," attempts to translate the original material from one form to another. Mau is certainly not the author of the work but the translator of form and spirit. The designer is the intermediary.

Designer as performer

The performer metaphor is based on theater and music. The actor is not the author of the script, the musician is not the composer of the score, but without actor or musician, the art cannot be realized. The actor is the physical expression of the work; every work has an infinite number of physical expressions. Every performance re-contextualizes the original work. (Imagine the range of interpretations of Shakespeare's plays.) Each performer brings a certain reading to the work. No two actors play the same role in the same way.

In this model, the designer transforms and expresses content through graphic devices. The score or script is enhanced and made whole by the performance. And so the designer likewise becomes the physical manifestation of the content, not author but performer, the one who gives life to, who speaks the content, contextualizing it and bringing it into the frame of the present.

Examples abound, from early Dada, Situationist, and Fluxus experiments to more recent typographic scores like Warren Lehrer's performance typography or experimental typography from Edward Fella or David Carson. The most notable example is perhaps Quentin Fiore's *performance* of McLuhan. It was Fiore's graphic treatment as much as McLuhan's words that made *The Medium is the Massage* a worldwide phenomena. (Other examples include any number of "graphic interpretations," such as Allen Hori's reinvention of Beatrice Warde's Crystal Goblet essay, or P. Scott Makela's improvisation on Tucker Viemeister's lecture, both originally printed in Michael Bierut's *Rethinking Design*.)

Designer as director

This model is a function of bigness. Meaning is manufactured by the arrangement of elements, so there must be many elements at play. Only in large-scale installations, advertising campaigns, mass-distribution magazines and very large books do we see evidence of this paradigm.

In such large projects, the designer orchestrates masses of materials to shape meaning, working like a film director, overseeing a script, a series of performances, photographers, artists, and production crews. The meaning of the work results from the entire production. Large-scale, mass-distribution campaigns like those for Nike or Coca-Cola are examples of this approach. Curatorial projects such as Sean Perkins' catalogue, *Experience*, which creates an exhibition of other design projects, is another example.

One of the clearest examples is Irma Boom's project for SHV Corporation. Working in conjunction with an archivist for more than five years, Boom created narrative from a mass of data, a case of the designer creating meaning almost exclusively via the devices of design: the narrative is not a product of words but almost exclusively of the sequence of pages and the cropping of images. The scale of the book allows for thematic development, contradiction, and coincidence.

The value of these models is that they accept the multivalent activity of design without resorting to totalizing description. The problem with the authorship paradigm alone is that it encourages both ahistorical and acultural readings of design. It grants too much agency, too much control to the lone artist/genius, and discourages interpretation by validating a "right" reading of a work.

On the other hand, work is made by someone. And the difference between the way different writers or designers approach situations and make sense of the world is at the heart of a certain criticism. The challenge is to accept the multiplicity of methods that comprise design language. Authorship is only one device to compel designers to rethink process and expand their methods.

If we really need to coin a phrase to describe an activity encompassing imaging, editing, narration, chronicling, performing, translating, organizing and directing, I'll conclude with a suggestion:

designer = designer.

METAPHORS WE DESIGN BY
with Rob Giampietro

MICHAEL ROCK

In my text on authorship I focused primarily on the link between the designer and the text—the act of design ending in some form of elaborated writing. I invoked the Statute of Anne, enacted in Britain in 1709, as the moment the author was legally considered the owner of a text, and so, as Foucault suggested, subject to punishment for its contents. Recently much of the creative work in design has shifted from producing things to making systems and programs that produce things. This can be a very direct act like designing a computer algorithm that produces endless variation of things—think Lust's poster machine—or crafting *brand guidelines* that direct the generation of multivalent products from objects to utterances—represented by a whole spectrum of practitioners from Landor to Winkreative to 2x4 to Project Projects. How do we describe this development and does it demand a new metaphor?

ROB GIAMPIETRO

It's interesting you bring up the Statute of Anne. I've long been interested in that moment as well because the developments surrounding the printing press reflect some of the developments we see in new technologies today.

The 1709 Statute of Anne followed an earlier law, the Licensing Act of 1662. Rather than protect the activities of the writer, that act protected the use of a tool—the printing press. In the early days of printing, books were scarce and hard to produce. They were copied longhand, and readers had to make pilgrimages to read them. With the invention of the printing press, access to books increased, and the state saw a value in regulating their production. At first, this was not a problem because presses were scarce, costly, and hard to produce. Over time, as presses became cheaper and easier to produce, the increased output of these presses became problematic in two ways. First, producing books at lower cost threatened the interests of powerful, established printers. Second, producing books at lower cost made it easier than ever to produce "seditious" or revolutionary materials that threatened the interests of the state. The Licensing Act of 1662 required printers to be licensed in order to print any materials; this restricted unlicensed printers from operating at all.

Half a century later, the Statute of Anne protected the activities of the writer instead. It was now the writer who gave the press the right to copy or publish his work, and that right was alienable, meaning it could be transferred from one entity to another. Following Marx, this creates a split between product and producer. The book, which was once the work, is now the commodity; its content, which was also once the book, is now the labor. Its author's right is not to the commodity but to his or her

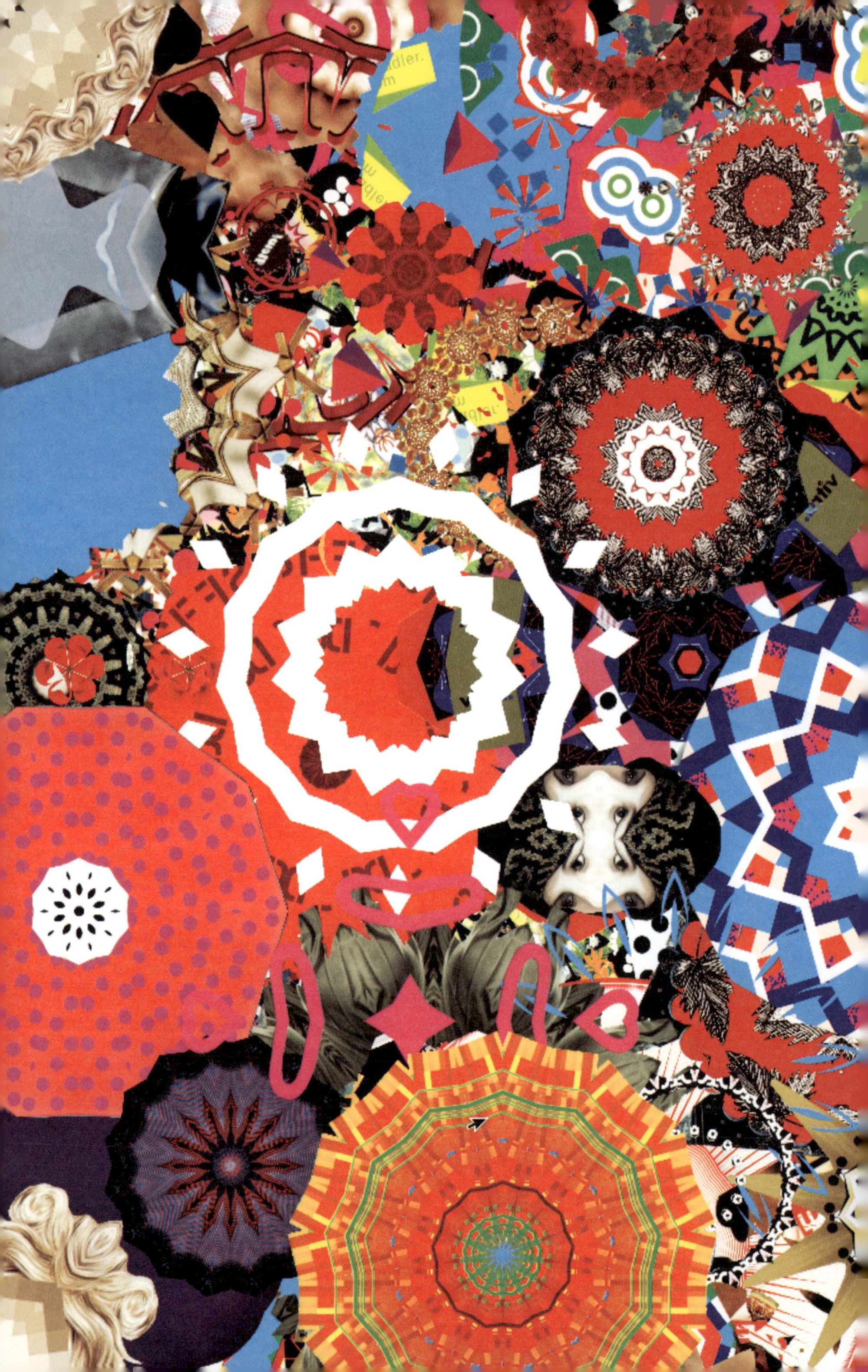

individual labor. In one stroke, the "professional author" and the "commodity text" were born, along with the mass-consuming public to support them. Now it was neither the production of books nor presses that required moderation but the production of texts themselves. And to perform this service, publishers were born. Among other things, publishers helped to separate and solidify the division of labor among writing, printing, and publishing into a system that endured for nearly 350 years.

With the introduction of the computer, that system was rapidly reconfigured once again. Not only did the writer, the printer, and the publisher begin to merge back into a single person, but, in graphic design, the typesetter and the designer recombined as well. For decades before the computer's introduction, designers would specify type that would go to a compositor who would set it and deliver it back to the designer to lay out or wax into place. In order to specify this type, designers had to have a mental model of what they wanted in order to communicate it abstractly via a set of instructions: i.e. 12pt Bembo on 15pt leading. This specification method worked similarly to how type is specified using CSS, except the computer plays the role of the compositor. Online, typesetting happens via markup rather than via WYSIWYG.

So, things skip a generation. Markup for compositors, WYSIWYG in the computer's early days, now markup once again. When WYSIWYG was new, designers could get instant feedback as they played with type, so they were free to experiment. There was formal experimentation and virtuosity, and these ambitious, often quasi-legible experiments found conceptual grounding in many of the ideas prevalent in design's postmodern movement, which was by then well established.

When your essay "Graphic Authorship" came out in 1996, the personal computer was more than a decade old and some of the shock of the new had worn off. It was unclear where postmodern design might go next, and the liberating promise this new design tool had in some ways gone unfulfilled. Designers were beginning to accept that they might need to propose new models, and you outlined some of these very directly in your essay, including translation, theater, and film.

By the time Rudy VanderLans and I discussed "Default Systems in Graphic Design" for *Emigre* in 2003, the question of "What next?" had taken center stage. Yes, the computer seemed to allow for limitless formal customization and experimentation, but to what end? My interview with Rudy looked at some designers whose work fell into a different and more emerging vein. Perhaps instead of trying to be as expressive as possible with all of these new layout and typography controls, a designer could simply accept them as givens.

Though it remains interesting

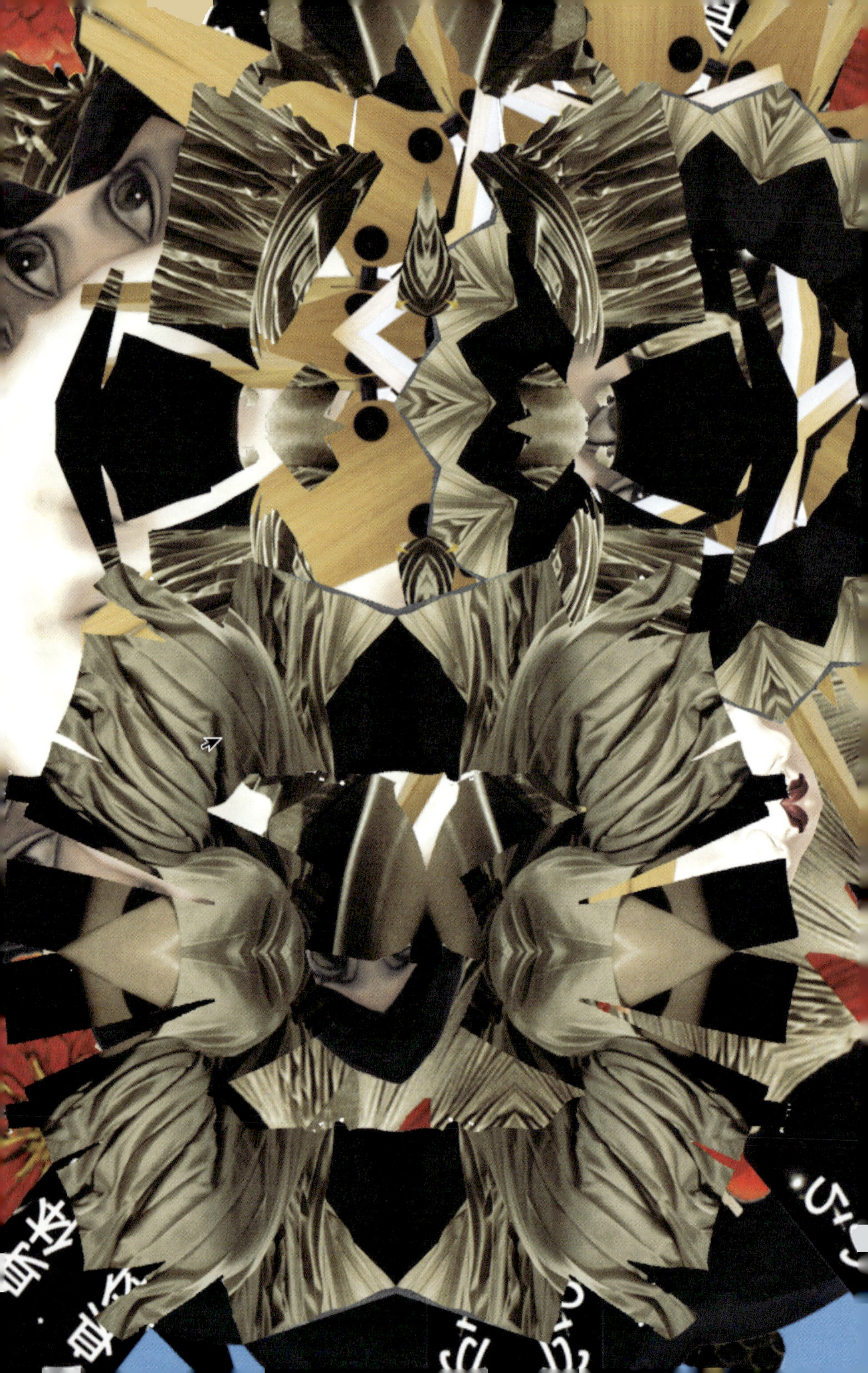

to me, at the time I sensed a slight sadness behind this strategy, a sense of defeat. Designers were joining the masses of headphoned knowledge workers pecking away at plastic boxes. Instead of the unique gesture, which was linked to the cult of authorship you identified in early '90s, this newer work strove for an anonymity that many designers felt was more honest at the time. Designers seemed to be trying to design themselves out of the process as much as possible.

MR

Or maybe in an environment where everything, every graphic trope, had become instantly available to everyone, the only act of resistance was to do—at least seemingly—nothing?

RG

Well "Default Systems" fell around the midpoint between "Graphic Authorship" and now. In the ensuing years, it's safe to say—and your question hints at this—design's direction has shifted once more. The computer was immediately evident as a tool for design, but what designers ultimately realized was exactly what Turing first discovered: what made the computer unique was its position as a meta-tool, a tool for tool-making. Pasteboards and digital typesetting could be virtualized, but so could film editing, music composition, and much more, all in the same box, or even in the cloud. This tool-making tool could build tools that didn't even exist yet—tools for expressing large sets of data, for articulating extraordinarily complex geometric arrangements, and for governing the interactions between other tools.

What had the most expressive potential, far beyond working within the constraints of consumer software or allowing that software to default to preset standards, was for designers to create the software itself. To build tools. To write instructions. Soon this impulse to instruct became a method that could be applied to situations involving more analog forms of interactivity—identity systems, exhibition design, even the transmission of knowledge itself. New skill sets and models were imported from other disciplines like linguistics (experiential metaphors), urban planning (pattern languages), and game theory (coordination problems) to name a few.

MR

The title of the *New Yorker* profile of Richard Benson (Dean of the Yale School of Art when we were both around New Haven) was: "A Single Person Making a Single Thing." I wonder where these developments leave the "thing" itself. Does the object even matter anymore or have we fully shifted to looking at the moment of exchange: the thing being simply a byproduct?

RG

Kevin Kelly has an expression about the so-called Internet of Things, in which objects are linked to the web via RFID tags and the like. In this world, he jokes, "A shoe is a chip with heels and a car is a chip with wheels." A shoe, a car, they're all just chips sending data someplace. The

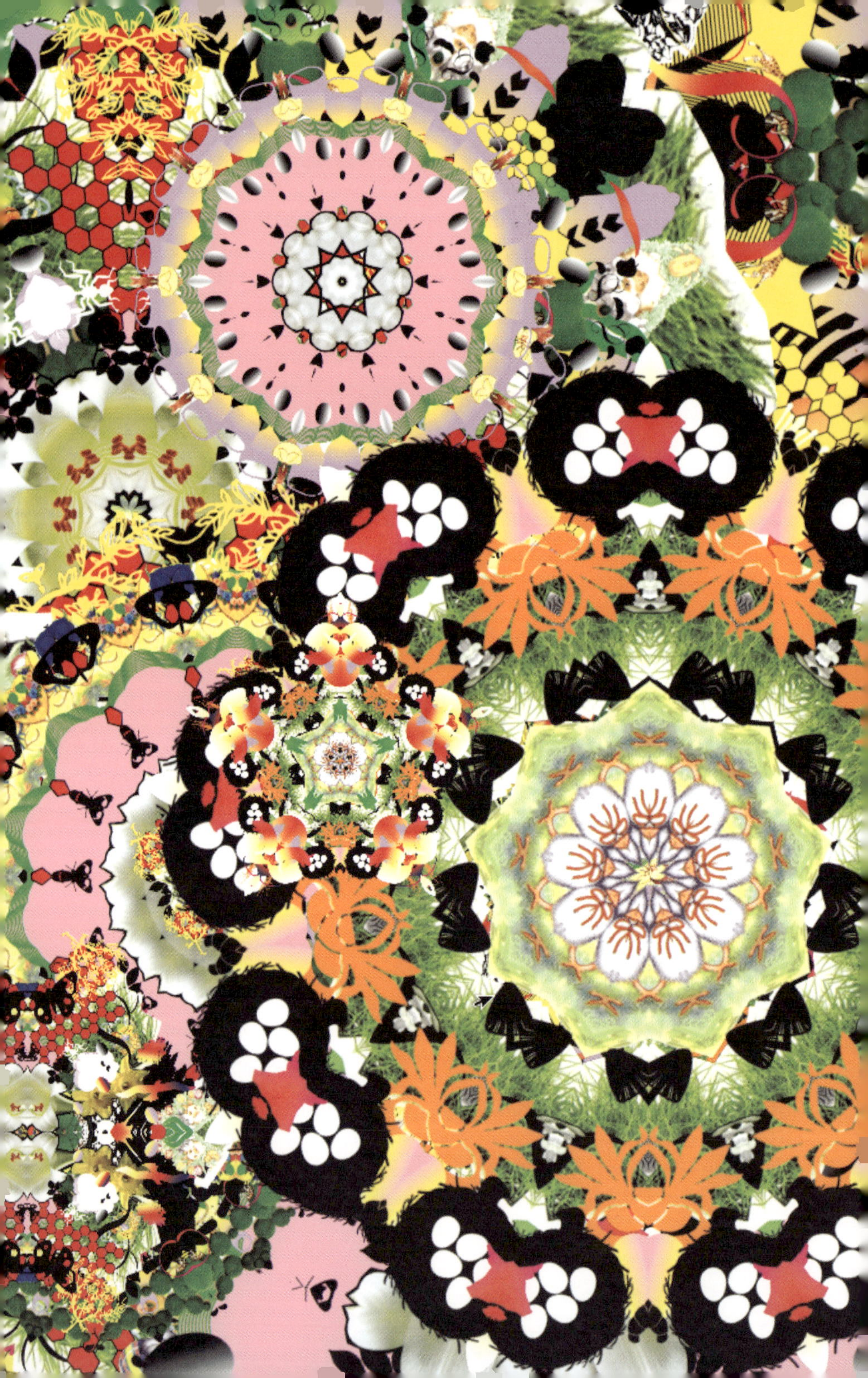

Internet of Things values them not for their objecthood, necessarily, but for the trace evidence their metadata can provide: where we went, how much we spent, how far we've gone, when something's broken down and needs repair. Instructions produce these objects, and the objects in turn produce data.

The degree to which the objects are part of a set of flows is evident in how they're marketed. Here's *Fortune* from February 2012:

> Just try to recall the last couple of Nike commercials you saw on television. Don't be surprised when you can't. Nike's spending on TV and print advertising in the U.S. has dropped by 40% in just three years, even as its total marketing budget has steadily climbed upward to hit a record $2.4 billion last year.

Image-based objects require TV commercials to become iconic and thus valuable; instruction-based objects require communities that act on the data that is ultimately produced by these objects. Instead of glossy shoots, there are individual performance charts. Instead of distressed logos, there are aggregate local trends. Instead of trendy DIY color schemes, there are leaderboards and game-like challenges. At every level, interactions are not just qualitatively but quantitatively symbolic.

This naturally leads to the suggestion that objects have been subsumed by a system of exchange, and it's easy to see how, for many objects, this is at least partly true. But it's worth asking what the data produce, and it's clear that what they help to produce are experiences. To continue with the example of shoes, the data offer the experience of self-knowledge, changing the consumer from an aspirational spectator into an activated participant with the ability to grasp the once-abstract mechanics of his own conditioning, community, competitors, and friends.

MR

But things can produce experiences, no?

RG

Objects can produce experiences, too—most primarily, they can produce the experience of objecthood. What does a positive experience of objecthood mean? It means that someone can appreciate that an object is well crafted; that it is distinctive, unlike other objects, or otherwise rare; that it has been selected over other objects to occupy a particular space; that it is representative of its owner even in that owner's absence; and that it is evocative of prior lived experiences through its very presence.

I like the title you quote, "A Single Person Making a Single Thing," but not for what it says about things. The thing is not so much the point—objects are important, and information about objects is important too. What's significant about this title is what's repeated—the idea of the singular. *The* thing. As more and more objects become simply producers of data, the objects that remain objectifiable become increasingly unique, more and more singular.

A network theorist might point out here that a singular thing has one of two fates. Either that thing is the source of many links and the strongest bonds, or it forms a network unto itself—which means it isn't networked at all. So the stakes for being a single thing, or being a single person making a single thing, move more toward the edges of importance and obscurity in our current context.

MR

I think the whole construct of "Designer as Author"—a metaphor I dismissed back in '96—is even less applicable now. A designer was never a Single Person Making a Single Thing—that clearly seems slanted toward the art object—but there is a difference between what we see now and A.M. Cassandre drawing posters on a litho stone. As designers become systems managers conducting business in large complex networks of collaborating professionals, the very notion of the auteur grows ever more precious. *Things* become luxury items revered for their aura and everything else slips into a cloud of exchanges set up and refereed by designers. So I guess the final question is: Can a systems manager really be considered the author of his/her work? Or, more specifically, what metaphor works?

RG

That reminds me of something Borges called out in "The Metaphor," one of his 1967–68 Norton Lectures at Harvard:

> [The Argentine poet Lugones] said that every word is a dead metaphor. That statement is, of course, a metaphor. Yet I think we all feel the difference between dead and living metaphors. If we take any good etymological dictionary [...] and if we look up any word, we are sure to find a metaphor tucked away somewhere.

Certainly language is a very important bit of technology, and we can think of it as a kind of code as well, with constantly expanding grammar, rules for usage, standards of excellence, and more. But it's useful to examine here because language is also systematic, and yet no one is its sole manager—it is a distributed system, bigger than any one person. (Yet individuals can have an impact: by some estimates, Shakespeare alone introduced over 2,000 words to the English language.) To illustrate Lugones' "dead metaphor" idea, Borges makes reference to the word "metaphor" itself, which is made of "meta-", meaning *over and across,* and "-pherein," meaning *to carry or to bear*. So the metaphor that "metaphor" first made was to convey this idea of taking an experience or idea from one place and invoking it in another place, which is virtualization in its most original form.

What's particularly powerful about Borges' observation is the idea that the development of metaphors precedes the development of language. Before they're language, metaphors exist as language's flexible, free-wheeling extensions—its add-ons, plug-ins, and hacks. The linguists George Lakoff and Mark Johnson create a paradigm in their book *Metaphors We Live By* that explains how metaphors highlight certain aspects of an experience and hide other aspects of an experience. Along a vertical axis they plot "used" versions of a metaphor at the top and "unused" versions at the bottom; along a horizontal axis they plot "extended" uses of a metaphor to the left and "common" uses to the right. If we take a metaphor like *idea-as-food*, it's easy to see how language describing an idea as "raw" or "half-baked" is common, and how to describe the same idea as "simmering" or "undigested" might be less common. However, the more processed food becomes, the less it fits within the metaphorical paradigm: ideas are not "deep-fried," "unwashed," or "refrigerated," and, while ideas can spread, they are not "spreadable" like margarine.

MR

(Aside) I remember Chris Vermaas used to refer to bad presentations in his class as "fried air."

RG

In the paradigm, it's only the metaphors on the upper-right "common used" quadrant that die and are reborn as words. The rest just die or fade away—interesting side projects, perhaps, but not destined to become part of the source code of language.

Technological metaphors work similarly to linguistic ones. We've already had a few eras of computing with accompanying metaphorical frameworks. From the original "desktop" metaphor with its requisite "files" and "folders," we moved to a "web" metaphor with its requisite "links" and "pages." We are now in the midst of a "cloud" metaphor, with its requisite "tags" and "streams." Each of these metaphors is itself a technology, a framework for extending our experience of computing. As one metaphor "dies" or becomes commonplace the next one takes root,branching our thinking outward in new directions.

Designers often enter the process of technological innovation at the metaphor phase. The key aspects for a new piece of technology may have already been engineered, but how can it be made meaningful, even magical? The originator of the "desktop" metaphor, Xerox PARC's Alan Kay, captures this idea perfectly in an interview about the development of one of the first WYSIWYG graphics editors, MacPaint:

> [T]he screen as "paper to be marked on" is a metaphor that suggests pencils, brushes and typewriting. Fine, as far as it goes. But it is the magic—understandable magic—that really counts. Should we transfer the paper metaphor so perfectly that the screen is as hard as paper to erase and change? Clearly not. If it is to be like magical paper, then it is

> the *magical* part that is all-important and that must be most strongly attended to in the user interface design.

This takes me, in a very sidelong way, toward an answer to your question. Authorship is powerful because it is closed. Metaphors are powerful because they are open. The most magical, most radical thing a technological metaphor can do is be open. Instead of stating a fact, or defining a point of view, metaphors offer an opportunity to make a new connection within a much larger system. That connection might turn out to be unusable, or broken, or weak —or it might not. Either way, it is the magic of openness that is the thing. Here's Borges from later in his talk:

> Remember what Emerson said: arguments convince nobody. They convince nobody because they are presented as arguments. Then we look at them, we weigh them, we turn them over, and we decide against them. But when something is merely said or—better still—hinted at there is a kind of hospitality in our imagination. We are ready to accept it.

So, I'll answer your question ("Can a systems manager really be considered the author of his/her work?") with a question: "Is that what designers want?"

Previous pages: Automatic collages produced by algorithm. Design Machine by 2x4 and Potion New York.

PARADOX ON THE GRAPHIC ARTIST

JEAN-FRANÇOIS LYOTARD

—They're terribly cornered. Very little freedom of movement. Not only under stringent constraints, but various kinds of constraints, completely heterogeneous ones. They struggle in this web like crazy people. Each in his or her own way. Each one crying out that he/she is still alive. Long live graphic artists, but what does living mean for a graphic artist? To be still alive. All these constraints put together, maybe each in particular, are mortifying.

—What constraints?

—The heavy-duty ones are obvious: to be liked, to be persuasive, and to be just. What I mean to say is that the object (so I call the project resulting from the graphic artist's labor) gives pleasure to the gaze; that the object induces a disposition in the viewer to buy into (in the double sense of going there and believing in it) the demonstration, the exhibit, the institution, etc.; that the object is faithful to the thing (institution, exhibit, etc.) it promotes, faithful both in the spirit and in the letter.

—You mean to say that by targeting the pleasure of the eyes …

—Of those eyes that engage thought not in knowing, but in enjoying …

—By targeting this pleasure, the object falls into the realm of aesthetics; by targeting belief, it derives from rhetoric. And by respecting the truth of the thing …

—Or by revealing it …

—The truth of the thing promoted, the graphic object takes on the value of testimony, it belongs to the art of proving, to inquiry, to history, to the establishment of knowledge.

—They are in fact at once artists, lawyers, witnesses, historians, and judges.

—Why judges?

—Because they interpret. They are also interpreters. What would the fidelity of the object to the thing to which it refers be, if this reference were not supported by an interpretation? There is fidelity only because infidelity is possible. What would it be to represent the thing by the object, *right down to the letter*? A simple photograph interprets its subject. The "letter" is to be deciphered and interpreted. Take the title of a film, an exhibit, an institution, a play. Let's say it is the letter of these things. It distinguishes them from other things in a general table of titles (a catalog of works, for instance) but only by a simple process of opposition. It says what the titled thing *is not*, it almost never says what it is. Now, the graphic artist must signify what it is or what he or she thinks it is, even while putting the title of the thing back onto the object. The graphic artist "deals with" the thing as red or blue, figuratively or abstractly, as a realist, a surrealist, or a conceptual artist. The graphic artist interprets the thing. The way in which he or she inscribes the title onto the object, positions it, the character and font of the letters used for this inscription, are so many interpretations. And so many judgments.

—Art is free. With all these constraints, is graphic art therefore not an art?

—First of all, art is not free. It is freedom within constraints at every level, conscious and unconscious. But then, aesthetics is an art, the art of producing or of feeling pure (disinterested) pleasure. Rhetoric is an art of persuasion. History is an art of true recounting. And interpreting is the hermeneutic art, perhaps the most difficult of them all. Its rules are almost unknown. We know mainly the negative ones: add nothing to the thing that is interpreted, do not make it say the opposite of what it says. Do not ignore previous interpretations, do not impose one interpretation as definitive. The tradition of reading the Torah has blocked some kinds of positive rules by making distinctions in the text of the Scriptures between literal, hidden, moral, and allegorical meanings.

—Do graphic artists know all this?

—There's no need to know the rules, which are not very prescriptive in any case, in order to interpret something as a graphic object. It's better to recognize what you don't know. Hence, the freedom of graphic artists, chained to their constraints. Imagine (this must happen) that a "subject" is imposed on them, a poster for a public commemoration, for example. By the variety of objects this occasion gives birth to, you can see what great latitude interpretation leaves them.

—Do you mean to say that some will emphasize persuasive force, others the aesthetic excellence of their object, and still others the veracity of their testimony?

—Not only that. Each will appeal more to a given literal, allegorical, etc. sense of the commemoration, that is, of the event the poster is supposed to recall and celebrate. Take the bicentenary of the French Revolution …

—I beg of you. You were saying that these were just the heavy-duty constraints, the most obvious ones. What else is there?

—One more word, before we go on. The word *intrigue.* The object made by the graphic artist must be intriguing. By being intriguing, it might satisfy all the constraints at once. What is beautiful catches the eye, stops the permanent sweeping of the field of vision by the gaze (which is what happens in ordinary sight), visual thought pauses, and this point of suspension is the mark of aesthetic pleasure. It is what is called contemplation. You wait, you linger, you wonder why, how it is that it is pleasing, say, to view the *Horatii* (by David) making their oath with the meadow of Valmy in the background. But, on the other hand, that which persuades is also surprising, or rather what surprises is in and of itself persuasive. Wow, you say, I never thought of that (representing the French Revolution this way). You give yourself over to the object as to something that has remained unthought but that you recognize right away as if it belonged to you. Just like in a dream, or a slip of the tongue. What is more persuasive than a slip of the tongue? It is certain that it means something you were thinking about, while being unaware of it, while being unaware of *what*, while being unaware *that* you were thinking it. Perhaps there is a slip of the tongue in a good graphic design, the slip of the tongue that *you* the viewer were able to make with regard to the thing promised. "La liberté de Mande la libertheid" works on the call for Mandela's freedom just like the dream works on the remnants of the day. And in the third place, what is also, above all, intriguing is the self-evidence of a truth that bursts on the scene, its tenacious trace, something other than an opinion skillfully brought out by a well-honed argument, more like a kind of immediate or "plastic" certitude. How about an example? A man's face, a woman's face, at very close range, cut off from each other by a kind of vertical tear, staring at each other across this tear, he with an intense blue iris, she with her gaze masked by a scarf of the same blue. A poster for a play: Les Yeux d'Encre (Eyes of Ink). The plastic truth of sexual difference: the ink of separation displaced *between* the blue gazes.

—To listen to you speak, what is intriguing always stops the flow of time.

—Because the time of graphic art is one of those more subtle constraints I had in mind. Much is said about communication with regard to graphic art. But we have more material than is needed, if by communication we mean the transmission of a message. A message gives information in the strict sense. That is, an answer or a set of answers that are specific and useful for a specific question. Now, we do "have" language: conversations, interviews, and all their spin-offs, telephones, radio, fax, computers, newspapers, handouts, the mail. I cite these haphazardly, some characterize means of support, others procedures for transmission and diffusion, some interactive, others not, etc. Never, in human societies, has there been so much talking as today. We are so happy to dispose of these means of communicating that you would think it was above all question of making sure they're really there. The message, that is to say, the information that answers a question, is pretty much neglected. On all the supporting devices, there is an abundance of false questions, the ones everybody knows or whose answers can be guessed. We don't inform, we reassure: oh yeah, that's just what I thought. The opposite of intriguing. We're starting to get bored. We dream of being upset. We wait for an event.

—Graphic art certainly derives from communication, doesn't it? It informs about the thing it promotes, it answers questions. That's its testimonial function, after all.

—In part. But it also derives from the visual arts, its situation is more complicated. It has recourse to the components of the visible, the chromatic, the organization of a motionless two-dimensional space, drawing, tracing. It is thereby the cousin of painting, engraving, photography. You know that many pictures, engraved works, and photographs that belong to tradition may be considered as graphic art. They too informed their contemporaries by visual means. Look at the Madonnas and Child by the hundreds in the museum of Siena. Or the great tableaus of battles in the Ducal Room of the Doge's Palace. And despite all this, what interests us is less their information content than their beauty or truth. The aesthetic event that they are. The absolute evidence of a visual manner. The manner of dealing with space, depth, or light, color, or just the subject matter. The Annunciation is an old subject, but Tintoretto's angel at the School of San Rocco cracks through the Virgin's wall like a missile, while the one by Simone Martini in the Uffizi makes a quivering "declaration of love" to Mary, all against a backdrop of gold. They interpret the same "thing" by visual means. Both are faithful.

—You were talking about the time of graphic artists, now we are in the space of painters.

—You might judge it unbecoming here, but there would be no unease, to compare the graphic artists we are introducing by utilizing analogous, that is, aesthetic criteria. Criteria of light, line, color, spatial composition, etc. If there are not schools, in any case there are tendencies—which sometimes share the same graphic artists. Unable to comment on all of them, I will comment on none. But all of them share the same business of having to be intriguing, in any way they can.

—But this constraint to be intriguing is due to beauty, as you said, to the powers of unexpected emotion that lie dormant within colors, surfaces, lines. Once again, it's the artist within the graphic artist who cannot help awakening them, unleashing the inexhaustible potential of sensible events.

—That's true, but it's not everything. That temporality, given rhythm by the deliverance of the powers of the visible, is not exactly all their doing. They have to be intriguing too because they have to deal with passersby, with eyes that wander, with minds on information overload, bored, threatened by a sense of disgust with everything new, which is everywhere and the same, with thoughts that are unavailable, already occupied, preoccupied, notably with communicating, and quickly. Graphic artists have to arouse them from the comforting slumbers of generalized communication, to slow down their unfortunate speed of life, to make them lose a little time.

—But this loss is profitable, bottom line. A good movie poster fills the cinema, a good logo favors investment by capturing attention, it disposes it to exchange, to commerce, to consumption, it speeds up communication. Your loss of time is a gain, counted from a marketing standpoint. Their graphic commodity brings commodities into circulation. It promotes them. Whether it is cultural and of public or social interest, or of private use and interest is a difference forever futile once culture has become part of the market and the public is privatized. With a good graphic object, a little lost time means a lot of money is made, through commercial success or prestige, for the happy owner or the exploiter of the "thing" promoted.

—Your observation is true in general, but all too generally. What can you not say this same thing about, when in fact culture is a market? Thirty years ago, they said that cinema was unique because it was both an art and an industry. And what about architecture? And the theater? And publishing? And exhibits and concerts and records? What you're not telling is what makes for a *good* poster, a *good* logo … And there is where we come across the constraint I'm talking about. Graphic art is not just good to sell things. It is always an object of circumstances, and consequently ephemeral. Of course, you can put it in the archives, collect it and exhibit it—this is what we're doing here. You thus suspend certain of the finalities we have designated: persuading, testifying. You retain only pleasing, which exceeds circumstance. You turn a piece of graphic art into an artwork. But you deceive and are deceived. The graphic object is circumstantial, but *essentially* so. Inseparable from the event it promotes, thus from the location, the moment, and the public where the thing happens. Grant me that an Annunciation remains as current as the New Testament. Even the painting of a coronation or a victory remains current so long as the dynasty or the regime lasts. But a film program in some viewing room today? An exhibit (justly) labeled temporary? The freeing of a political prisoner?

—I agree that the thing is of little duration and the graphic artists must make a living from this "despite it all."

—But just as the thing testified to by the object is of little duration, so is the public of little stability—what we stupidly call the public, as if it existed. And graphic artists cannot make a living without making hypotheses about the public. This is not a civilization nor even a culture, in the anthropological sense. This is the combination, endlessly unmade and remade, of temporary sensibilities …

—Nonetheless, the public has some constants, language, a certain idea, be it unconscious, of its national or local traditions, it undergoes definable conditions of life, of work, of economic growth or recession. And then there is the air of the time, which does not change so fast.

—But you cannot determine the proportion of these components, nor consequently between them, which the graphic object must address in order to intrigue the said public. You are reduced to making hypotheses. Even for the French, the French Revolution is not a determinate motif that would be easy to animate or reanimate by some rhetorical turn or aesthetic gesture. For the Greeks, only a few tropes sufficed to arouse the idea of the polis in a funeral oration; and for the Japanese, a few internal or external architectural dispositions from the temple and some musical and choreographic figures for a Shinto ceremony to evoke the presence of the gods. In the society we live in today, most motifs are uncertain, many motivations are unforeseeable (especially outside the sphere of retail consumption), and the art of the graphic artist is risky. You may bore when you thought to move, you imagine yourself cynical and turn out to be authentic. There is a wager to be made on the current state of the big, black beast's sensibility.

—The big, black beast? You mean the public?

—It doesn't know what it likes or doesn't like. It doesn't exist for itself as a sensibility. It knows itself only indirectly, through situations, and these no longer have the regularity of rituals. The graphic object must constitute one of these situations. It lands in a "blank," neutral, perhaps deserted, region of the public's affective continent, and it is presumed to populate it, to draw sensation to it.

—Good graphic art would then be sensational?

—Sensation is the contrary of sensational. The latter is calculable from what we think we know about the most ordinary emotiveness. It is the trivial mode of seduction. A newspaper boss "knows" what he has to get out in six columns on the front page. But whether beautiful, persuasive, or true, graphic art does not seduce. You seduce by way of an interest, a passion that you make work. The graphic artist constrains the viewer to suspend his or her reactiveness, to dream, to interrupt his or her preoccupations. The graphic artist gives the viewer over to the freedom to feel something other than what he or she believed, to feel otherwise. The graphic artist is a street artist, a peddler. The street (European, New York, Japanese) is a figure of public daily life, a scene of encounters. In the street, encounters are not tragic. Tragedy is the encounter within the familial home. What you encounter in the street is the unexpected, what "passes by," that woman passing by. The art of modern cities, graphic art is exclusively dependent on cultural, commercial, political, utilitarian events, all placed on the same gauge, subject to the same rule of what is without rules, of the event. Graphic art grasps the daily public in its monotonous "passing by," and it gives its other measure, of possible beauty and self-evidence. It transmutes the public. It brings it to see otherwise because it interprets it, and it also brings it to interpret. That's why it *stops*.

—Popular art?

—I would like to call it popular if I knew what "people" meant today. Popular arts, in Europe and outside of it, are a discovery or invention of the Romantic 19th century, which, for the Western world, lasts until the years of the Great Depression. The totalitarianisms, which issued forth from it, were popular and made great use of the popular arts, that is to say, the sensibilities inscribed within local traditions, with a view to *mobilizing* people. But graphic art is not propaganda. As I said, it intrigues, thus immobilizing and causing reflection. Take a Suprematist or a Constructivist poster from the twenties by Malevich or Lissitzky, and then take some Stalinist posters (on the same subjects) from the mid-thirties. You can see how the "popular" is used by the latter, and how it is put into suspense, in every sense of the word, by the former. The dissolution or dissipation of the entity "people," as is the case in the modern city, is essential to the art of the graphic artist, whether abstract or not. The public does not mean people, but the absence of the people, the loss of shared beliefs, what they called the masses, during the intermediary period, the crisis years of the depression. Today, decades have passed since the capitalist societal mode dissolved popular communities. It is in the process of straddling nation-states, well past their prime.

—Enough of this historical panorama.

—The absence of a people is what obligates graphic artists to wager and also what leaves the field wide open for them. Graphic artists "target" an object, but the target keeps shifting. It cannot be said that they commune, or even dialogue, with "their" people. On the contrary, they are banking on an unsure, unforeseeable, perhaps impossible communication. They are the popular artists of cities without people and populations without traditions. Their addressees, all of us, are inhabited by the monotonous passion of "performances," only thinking about what is possible, about what is "feasible," as one says. They hurry along. They let go of the past if it can't be exploited. "Having experience" is a depth that makes them laugh, it's ballast to be jettisoned, better to have amnesia, so you can go faster.

—But never has there been so much experimenting!

—Yes, and the graphic artist also experiments with ways of intriguing. But experimentation is precisely not experience. To explore the future is not to inhabit the past. Graphic artists stick to the present by the occasion circumstances offer them. But also because they are exploring processes as their contemporaries do with everything. They too are launched out front, and they too, at full speed, I imagine. It is a rapid art. But it is an art, and a modern one, and as such, its aim is to surprise. You have to freeze the eye, quickly. The passerby stops, turns back, and examines the poster.

—But if the passerby only contemplates the poster and its art, all is lost. The poster for a show does not fulfill its function if it doesn't make the passerby go to the show.

—That's why I repeat to you that graphic artists are cornered. Artists, yes, but promoters too. They have to offer their work and something other than their work: the thing. Their work is an object that must induce something other than the pleasure drawn from its beauty. It is a subordinate, "applied," art, as they say. It requires of the graphic artists the humility of a servant, perhaps even a humiliation. The graphic artist signs a contract, he or she then has (in principle) the mastery to choose the thing his or her object will promote. But the contract stipulates that the object must promote the thing. The graphic artist thus interprets, but here in the actor's sense, for the actor too is a servant. Just as for the actor, there is a paradox in the graphic artist. The more graphic artists make a void in themselves, in order to let themselves be inhabited by the thing, the more the object is faithful to the thing it promotes. This is a fidelity that is not mimetic, but inventive.

—The paradox is constant, but it is obscure.

—So constant that it must be extended. Who would say that the art of the actor (or the director) is secondary, or even second? Is there even one art form, be it held as noble, that does not conceal this paradox? Doesn't Picasso spend his time in interpreting, in this sense, in "playing," in replaying therefore, scenes, subjects, treatments, already proposed by others before him (or by him)? Look at all the variants and studies together that fill the two rooms dedicated to his *Las Meninas* at the Picasso Museum in Barcelona. They are like a big sketchbook for a poster announcing a Velázquez exhibit.

—So, graphic art would reveal a truth about art, period?

—That's it. About contemporary art, period.

—Why contemporary?

—Because of the big, black beast. How can you be intriguing, in these cities full of intrigues? How can you stop the gaze of passersby upon the Infanta's dog, when they already know it by heart?

BRAND AS VOICE

WITH
PAUL ELLIMAN

"I am large, I contain multitudes."
—Walt Whitman

In one of the emblematic moments of the 2012 Republican primary campaign, candidate Mitt Romney responded to a heckler mocking his stance on unlimited corporate financing of political campaigns with the now infamous phrase: "Corporations are people, my friend … of course they are." While he was immediately vilified for this position—he was seen already as the prototypical corporate tool—his comment wasn't completely off the mark. The obsession with branding has increasingly framed the corporate body as an individual, complete with personality quirks and proclivities. It's telling, for instance, that Nike coined the biological metaphor of brand as institutional DNA, genetic material embedded in every cell of its corporate being. Martha Stewart and MSLO (Martha Stewart Living Omnimedia) share one conterminous form: *L'état, c'est moi.*

The shift from corporate identity to branding represents one of the most significant transformations in graphic design in the past two decades. While corporate identity had developed as a relatively systematic approach to the distribution of graphic elements over multiple platforms, branding endeavors to codify the personality of an organization by shaping all its utterances. In the brand model, every corporate citizen must be trained to sing in the corporate voice. (Continuing the biological metaphor in the branding of the corporate body, individuals actually cease to be and become subordinate organisms that carry out specialized physiological functions.) Because brand attempts to form and generate acts of personality, the gridded logic of modernist identity systems are in fact antithetical to that goal—unless of course the personality is one of gridded precision.

In the simplest terms, while corporate identity programs attempted to manage a look, brand programs attempt to generate a voice. A look implies an acquired fashion (inherently superficial, coming and going with the seasons), but a voice seems physiologically inherent to the body (actors and impersonators aside). Designing a brand system, then, is the establishment of linguistic rules that can generate infinite acts of speech, while the audience and context determine the tone of the individual speech act. Often, however, the rigidity of an identity system cramps the ability of the corporate body to fully modulate its speech.

Alan Siegel (founder of Siegel + Gale) claims to have coined—and trademarked—the term Brand Voice™ and promises his clients: "When you speak in your true Brand Voice, you'll always sound like yourself." The you in this case is "*the company*" and the sounding like "*yourself*" is an entirely constructed rhetoric performed by countless corporate workers. Controlling the brand voice is a way for a corporation to sound like, well, a corporation.

The voice is a powerful device, and that is why powerful organizations take its modulation seriously. This notion brought me back to Paul Elliman, who for the last few years has subtly shifted his project from various typographies—using that term in the broadest possible sense as in a system of differences—to dealing specifically with the voice itself and systematic classifications of sound.

HEARING VOICES
with Paul Elliman

MICHAEL ROCK
How did you get from typography to voice?

PAUL ELLIMAN
You mean it wasn't the other way around? Or is it better not to think of the alphabet as being too phonetically keyed to the voice—a kind of evil map that tries to control the territory of speech! For me even with typography it was always more about finding ways of locating language in the body: through things that we can touch, an object-world that informs how we speak to each other, or in the sense that we still rely on a gestural language. It doesn't help much to think of any aspect of language as exclusively one thing or another. Speech or writing. Separating it like that has very little to do with our experience of language, its impact upon us or its mystery.

MR
You don't think of the voice as primary?

PE
Perhaps in that a child uses the sounds of the mouth first, long before putting a pen to paper or a finger on a keyboard. The voice of a mother is also primary in terms of direct human experience. That must shape our understanding of what a voice is for the rest of our lives. But I don't think of the spoken voice as something that is ever un-impacted by literacy or other aspects of written or even visual information. Even through that earliest relationship with your mother, we are *receiving* a language.

MR
So it's a constructed system, like typography?

PE
We can imagine a time before we could write but we can't return to that. A performance artist, even a painter or sculptor, might claim their work, with gestural movements of the body for example, to be something that could have been made at any stage in the history of mankind, but that's claiming rather a lot. We exist and think and even walk and move under the conditions of our time. The anthropologist Marcel Mauss described how the body is and how it behaves as an embodiment of culture, whether by training or imitation or simply as an adaptation to physical and mechanical requirements of the modes of life that belong to our particular age (*Techniques of the Body*, 1934). Our language is produced in the same kinds of ways.

MR
The typography of culture?

PE
When I think of what is typographical I'm thinking less about letters than about production. Typography is a language of production that begins in Gutenberg's moment, as a means of producing language. But this is an assembly line that runs, for about 500 hundred years so far, from there to the supermarket at the end of my road. The clothes we wear, the houses we live in, the cars, the

computers, even the food we eat, all exist according to refinements and variations of this production language. And whether or not we like to think about it as such, so does much of our expressive language. It's not as if the voice, or the way in which we talk, is able to happen independently of the conditions of our time.

MR

I remember a talk where you played examples from recent music in which the voice, either cut up or collaged or sung in a kind of nonsense of vocal sounds, performs a sort of glossolalia. The voices fell somewhere between a childlike babble and the biblical idea of speaking in tongues, being over-taken by the spirit and losing control of what's coming out of your mouth, becoming an instrument through which the spirit speaks.

PE

Rather than a conscious being through which the instrument of technology speaks? As (Friedrich) Kittler said, it's we who must accommodate or adapt to the machine rather than the other way around.

MR

It was as if you were presenting us with examples of a primitive voice in a very modern technical setting.

PE

I wanted to give a more explicit sense of the typographical production of a voice. All recorded voices are inscribed and re-embodied in technology, technically a kind of typography. The history of the broadcast or recorded voice is a story of microphones and amplification, of effects like reverb, double-tracking, sequencing. Of digital software like Auto-Tune. But also of playback devices, markets, consumer audiences. In terms of voice production, entirely different species of voice-beings inhabit our everyday world via the car radio, mobile phones, MP3 players. These might range from the instantly recognizable voices of certain well-known singers to voices sampled or entirely synthesized. Either way a very spectral voice, or sign-of-the-voice, is something we seem comfortable with, or as comfortable as we are with the written word. You can hold my voice in your hand. But what does that mean? Like writing, the voice now has a kind of inanimate agency, the ghostly remainder anticipated by the myth of Echo and Narcissus.

The voices in the music I played were intended as a graphic example. Perhaps only the sign of the voice. Or as you put it, only its sound. I played some vocal collages by garage and techno producers like Todd Edwards or Detroit's Marc Kinchen. Also a few examples of house music based around long repetitions of nonsensical vocal phrases and chants.

MR

One couldn't ask for clearer examples of the branded voice than from the world of pop music.

PE

That's for sure. You've probably seen the recent *New Yorker* profile that gave a vivid picture of the songwriter Ester Dean working out songs in a

Manhattan recording studio, sounding more like someone in the shower yelling along to Top 40 radio. Except this is her writing hit records for the voices of singers like Rihanna and Beyoncé. Lyrics that are partly stream of consciousness, part random phrases from magazines, ads and TV talk shows. Everything filed in her notebook under categories with titles like Sex and the City, First Love, British Slang. She starts off riffing on nonverbal sounds, whoops and yelps, throws in a blast of advertising tag lines and a few more vocal sounds, fragments of songs from the past. Think of *Hey na na,* or *Can't you hear that boom badoom boom, boom badoom boom* .... Millions of people know exactly what songs those lines are from. Both are by Ester Dean, spat out of the same intense and, well, pretty nutty process of crafting commercial songs from the chaos and impulsive vocabulary of a commercial world. Messages of divine inspiration received directly from the city.

There's another songwriter I'll mention, Priscilla Renea. She's written for Rihanna, Cheryl Cole, Madonna. About three years ago someone sent me a homemade clip Renea had posted on YouTube as a teenager where she's singing the dictionary. She's going through the As to the melody of the Fergie song "Glamorous": *Aardvark, abalone, abandoned, abbatoir, abbey, abyss, abject, able, able-bodied, able-bodied seaman, abnormal, abnormal psychology, abolition, abominable, abominable snowman...* She has an incredible singing voice but what makes it work is her sense of meter. Which is not simply the musical time signature but how you fit a sequence of syllables to it. Very important to the vocal structure of hymns. In hip-hop I think they call it flow.

Both songwriters offer a kind of abstraction, but they don't simplify our physical relationship to a world of language. They make it seem both as ordinary and as strange as it is. Ester Dean allows the world around her to disrupt the organizing system of songwriting. For Priscilla Renea, her own voice disrupts the organizing system of meaning that is the dictionary, voice and language twisting together and apart in this unexpectedly ritualistic way. The ecstasy of the alphabet.

MR

In both the human voice remains prominent. Whereas in most of the examples you played in your talk it was less clear if they were being sung by a person or a machine.

PE

Glossolalia has been described as the sounds of language taken for a language, as if it was something false. But the physicality and ecstasy that seems to carry it off suggests something real enough, or real to the body of the person involved. Marcel Mauss chose not to include the voice as a technique of the body. Yet who doesn't sense that it is probably through the voice that we are more susceptible to manipulation and to finding our own manipulative ways, than any other part of us?

A discussion of glossolalia would fit well in any attempt to supply the missing category of *voice* in Mauss's *Techniques of the Body.* 'Speaking in tongues' refers to a way of speaking in which certain parts of language are connected more emphatically to the body, through noises of the mouth or other unintelligible vocal sounds. The act of saying things takes priority over dialogue: tongues instead of words (Michel de Certeau, "Vocal Utopias," 1996). Though I chose to play examples that also suggest a relationship to the written word as much as the speaking or singing voice.

Around that time I was listening to recorded versions of songs composed by Saint Hildegard of Bingen, a 12th-century Benedictine abbess whose visions, as well as her songs and chants, are said to have involved a form of glossolalia. Saint Hildegard invented a 23–character alternative alphabet for her *Lingua Ignota* or Unknown Language, and many of the songs are written in this secret tongue. Nothing I heard in modern recordings came close to conveying the free-form transcendentalism said to characterize those performances, so-called concerts of the spirit. Who would know how to reenact the way those 'songs' might have been performed, if all we have to go on is the strange typographical glossolalia of her alternative alphabet? But what a typeface. My all-time favorite.

MR

An idea picked up about 800 years later by Kurt Schwitters with his *Ursonate*...

PE

Yes, and think of the graphic connections in all the Dada collage and sound poems, and more recently what about "The Loch Ness Monster's Song" by Scottish poet Edwin Morgan? I'd like to have heard him singing it in a Glasgow pub on a Saturday night. I don't suppose it presents much of a challenge to the vocal utopias of contemporary pop music.

> Sssnnnwhuffffll?/Hnwhuffl
> hhnnwfl hnfl hfl?/ Gdroblbo-
> blhobngbl gbl gl g g g g glbgl./
> Drublhaflablhaflubhafgabhaflhafl
> fl fl –/ gm grawwwww grf grawf
> awfgm graw gm./ Hovoplo-
> dok – doplodovok – plovodokot-
> doplodokosh?/ Splgraw fok fok
> splgrafhatchgabrlgabrl fok splfok!/
> Zgra kra gka fok! /Grof grawff
> gahf?/ Gombl mbl bl – /blm plm,/
> blm plm,/ blm plm,/blp.

(*From Glasgow to Saturn*, Edwin Morgan, Carcanet, 1973)

MR

So if speaking in tongues is at one end of the spectrum — spiritual sounds bursting out of us with no control or mediation — the opposite extreme seems to be the talking machine with its synthesized voice: a manufactured tool of communication designed to elicit a specific response. You've referred to the abundance of professional voices throughout urban space, in vehicles and supermarkets, in elevators and all forms of public transport, as a kind of running commentary...

PE

The Shanghai subway system is still the most relentless that I've heard.

MR

You wrote this a few years back: (reading) "With the persistence of a running commentary, the friendly female voice of the Shanghai subway follows you from train to platform, to ticket hall, to street, pointing out safety features and directions, suggesting bars, restaurants, and department stores" (*Wired*, 2003).

PE

That was at least ten years ago. Don't know how far that voice would accompany you today. Remember the scene in *Minority Report* with the ads that speak directly to people in the street? Naming them: *Hey, Bill Cunningham, you look like you could use a a new camera about now, get a Nikon! Hey, Bill Cunningham, forget these busy streets, let's get away somewhere, Puerto Rico!* Though I think we know already that we don't even have to be named. We'd have less trust in that. As (Louis) Althusser pointed out long ago, we are only too happy to be identified by ourselves when those objects of desire come calling.

MR

Minority Report is set in an undisclosed future, yet those kinds of details, advertising that targets us in very specific ways, hardly seem futuristic now.

PE

I think we've become more aware of the voice as a component of socio-economic flows. Not only because of developments to artificial voice production, or the technical ability to deploy voices almost anywhere—machined voices—but through specific uses, in everyday situations, that make the human voice itself perform in very machine-like ways. Don DeLillo is particularly good at describing the electro-sonic infrastructure of our world. One of his characters, an out-of-work actor, has a job reading weather and traffic reports on a New York radio station. She has a slot every ten minutes or so and the narrator compares her voice to the speed and fluid efficiency of a power-tool. The most convincing aspect of this voice is that it sounds more like a push button radio transmission than a person talking (Don DeLillo, *The Angel Esmeralda,* 2011).

MR

You've also addressed the way that a voice, on the subway for example, can become a *de facto* brand for the city.

PE

It's only about ten years ago that recorded announcements on the New York subway muscled in on the regional voices of the train conductors. You'll still get a Caribbean or a Bronx accent on your ride home to Jackson Heights or Prospect Park —more often lost in the glossolalia of a broken PA system. With the more dominant recorded voices it's not clear where they come from. The male voice, a man named Charlie Pellett, turns out to be English. Not that anyone could possibly know. Sounds like he's auditioning for *Oklahoma* or *Paint Your Wagon*.

MR

"Stan' clear o'the ker-LOW-zin' doors pleeze!

PE

These recordings date back to the late 1990s and are voiced by Bloomberg Radio presenters. This is before Bloomberg became mayor of the city. Then all of a sudden you have this spoken part of the city's infrastructure linked directly to its offices of civic power. Part of the Bloomberg brand. (In his day job Charlie Pellett is the host of WBBR's "The Bloomberg Money Show.") Imagine if all multinational corporations could speak to you from any walkway or vehicle in the city? Oh, that's right, they do. It's called branding.

MR

That was one of Bloomberg's innovations, branding information …

PE

The Bloomberg voices are not distinctly New York voices. Not in terms of dialect. But in terms of what linguists refer to as an *idiolect*, the way these voices sound—confident, professionally efficient, *the business*—extends a corporate image that of course many would prefer to associate with the city. Meanwhile, out on the city's streets, a kind of local vocal insurrection may be in progress. The audio announcements of New York City's crosswalks, intended to guide visually impaired pedestrians, are voiced by a man named Dennis Ferrara, who sounds like what he is: a lifelong resident of Coney Island. In *his* day job he's the supervising electrician at the Department of Transportation. Asked about using a less regionally specific accent, Mr. Ferrara replied, "I've got too many other things to do besides trying to change my voice."

MR

Who better than a tough Brooklyn guy to guide you across the street?

PE

Voices used for announcements in public spaces are instructive by definition. I mean beyond the informational, where you are, where you're going. The skills of a trained voice are used to re-render inanimate objects and spaces with the language of gendered speech. For the New York subway certain kinds of messages are spoken by a male voice—*Stay alert and have a safe day*—while more informational messages are spoken by a female voice—*Transfer is available to the E train*. The MTA says it wasn't planned, that it just happened to coincide with the claim by some psychologists that people are better at receiving orders from men and information from women. Which men? Which women? The U.S. Air Force takes the line that female voices are more authoritative to male pilots. F-16 fighter jets and Apache attack helicopters carry the warning system voice of Erica Lane, also known as Bitching Betty. *Obstacle ahead, fuel low, pull up.*

MR

In most cases, it would seem that the spoken branded voice can't help but take its cue from a world already humming with celebrity voices. James Earl Jones' distinct *"Welcome to Verizon,"* for example …

PE

Hollywood is the central-casting resource for those corporate voices … although one of the most familiar voices in America, the voice of AT&T, Pat Fleet, is not a famous person; few people would recognize her in the street. Think about navigation software: placeless voices directing us through the street and further erasing our own sense of place. Currently that tends to be a combination of celebrity voices and a sort of branded version of 'ordinary' folk. Look at any menu of character voices available to guide us on these strange journeys: *The Hockey Mom; Billy Bob the Redneck; the President; the Islamic cab driver; Beavis and Butthead; Sassy Jill the sexy teenage Catholic school girl; GLaDOS, the corrupted system voice of the video game Portal; Jesus; Jamal the ghetto pimp; Valeria Satnavkov the Russian spy; Clint Eastwood.* If the crew of the Pequod (Herman Melville, *Moby-Dick*) can be described as a cross-section of an emerging U.S. society, here it is updated as a cast of avatars of the American public today.

MR

In your work you evoke the play between human voice and mechanized world: a human imitates a machine and a machine imitates a human; a human imitates an animal whose 'voice' has already been transcribed for a musical instrument. It seems like part of your interest is the point where the voice becomes mechanized or formalized or *branded* in these ways. Not what is being said so much as how it is uttered.

PE

It's often at that point that I feel antagonized, but also curious about where the voice is going without us. You're right about other messages being conveyed by the sound of the voice. By what the voice says despite what it is saying.

MR

The form speaks, which is something I was hoping to get at in this conversation: a designer designs inflection and tone that colors content.

PE

For me the division between form and content is counterintuitive. But yes, if we are talking about instrumentalizing the voice then modulations of tone are almost everything. That could be made to happen by design. It could happen through human instinct as well. I'm thinking of Gatsby, in F. Scott Fitzgerald's book, when he says of Daisy Buchanan: "Her voice is full of money …." It's not that it doesn't matter what Daisy says. It matters very much. But it's in that inseparable fusion of her world, her body, her thoughts and the tone with which she expresses them. She is a kind of product of her social milieu. A wealthy, carefree, glamorous voice produced with the same end result as a Tiffany diamond ring, just as vulnerable to desire, envy, crime, even social and moral bankruptcy. The subject of Daisy's voice may have more to do with her social class, but isn't that a kind of branding in itself? Something we should all desire and aspire to be or take part in: to consume the very privilege of being able to consume.

George Bernard Shaw's *Pygmalion,* later recast as *My Fair Lady,* is another tale of class-conscious construction—and reconstruction—of the voice. You might call it a re-branding exercise for the cockney flower girl Eliza Doolittle. The linguist Henry Higgins sees Doolittle as nothing more than a walking specimen of language from the gutter: "So deliciously low, so horribly dirty!" After her metamorphosis, Eliza recalls her old way of speaking as if it were a part of the city of London she can never go back to.

MR

A perfect example of rebranding.

PE

In more mechanistic terms of designing or building a voice there's a fabulous 'primal' example in the construction of the Tarzan yell for MGM. Though we 'see' it coming out of the mouth of Johnny Weissmuller, one claim is that it was the result of a complex formula, studio-engineered to merge the voice of an opera tenor named Lloyd Thomas Leech with the growl of a dog, a note played on a violin's G string, the trill of a soprano and the recorded howl of a hyena played backwards! Don't we all speak that same unholy fusion of animal sounds, musical instruments, a trained male voice with a dash of androgenic soprano, some technical trickery with the tape recorder? And with more than a hint of Frankenstein devil-may-care, *Oh, to hell with it, let's just build the voice out of whatever parts we've got!*

MR

The idea of a branded voice dispenses with our perception of what a voice *is* in both a bodily and individual sense?

PE

It must operate within an idealized frame, according to certain prescribed conditions, yet seem somewhat 'natural.' Or as if someone were speaking to you quite freely. *Siri* knows my name but she's not my friend. She's not even a she. She's a team of engineers from the Stanford Research Institute now owned by Apple computers. Then again, 'natural'—how do we even negotiate the glass walls around that word? It makes me think of the seven-second broadcast delay of so-called live radio.

MR

The so-called profanity delay.

PE

Arseholes, bastards, fucking cunts and pricks!

MR

Ian Dury?

PE

Thought I was channeling Dr. Johnson's Tourette's. Imagining the kinds of things he would constantly mutter while writing his famous dictionary. Do you know that the compiler of the most important early lexicon of the English language was a compulsive copralaliac? Daisy Buchanan might have had a mouth full of money but the great Samuel Johnson, legal guardian of the English language, had a mouth full of shit. Though the condition was not medically recognized at the time Johnson is known to have had extreme symptoms of what we now call Tourette's Syndrome, characterized in his case by a constant stream of foul-mouthed swearing and a less verbal but no less vocal repertoire of sounds and tics. Friends describe him clucking like a chicken and constantly opening and closing his mouth or stretching it with his tongue while he spoke. Though his language could be wise, scholarly and famously elegant, Dr Johnson's speech was a mess.

MR

Form and content were two separate entities?

PE

Between his mind and his speaking voice, perhaps. But studies have shown an important link between Tourette's-associated coprolalia and the way that the brain processes language. And it turns out to be no different from people without Tourette's. It seems that swearing is not a language use. It belongs to the part of the brain that deals with emotions and instinct. Even though it involves words and the vocal tract, it is an emotional motor activity of the body. This shares something with definitions of glossolalia as more body than language. Swearing is believed to have originated in forms of word magic, hence cursing, or legally swearing an oath. This residue of a much older belief in the power of spoken words remains as part of our language but in the form of a more direct emotional outlet, or as a way of communicating aspects of identity, masculinity for example. Dictionaries are still sheepish about profanity. Though apparently most terms now thought of as vulgar only began to be more firmly categorized as obscene after the 18th century, coinciding with the institutionalized organization of dictionaries. I'd like to hear Samuel Johnson in full flight on the London Underground. That might derail a few ideals.

MR

The British set so much store in the voice. How does that play out on the Tube, still *Minding the Gap*?

PE

Still minding the gap between the social classes.

MR

We've recently been getting a very phonocentric view of British culture from movies. Both *The Iron Lady* and *The King's Speech,* for example, raise interesting issues about the affective values of certain voices of power.

PE

I struggled with the Margaret Thatcher film, couldn't find a way to suspend any disbelief. Meryl Streep talks about being *taught to bring it up from the place where the conviction lies.* I wasn't sure if she was referring to Maggie or herself. In *The King's Speech,* an entire population's emotional anxieties are focused not on the anticipation of the collective indignities of a brutalizing war, but on whether or not the stammering King could announce the declaration of that war with his own dignity intact. Surely the only listening audience for that narrative is the one watching the movie. I'm not disputing the powerful role of the broadcast voice during that period of history. The walkie-talkie was developed during the Second World War (Motorola, 1940). Mobile phones, in other words. British historian Raphael Samuel has written about how the role of national radio in Britain during the war helped shape the way that defining moments of modern history can no longer be dissociated from broadcasting events. And maybe *The King's Speech* is interesting as some kind of allegory for another transition between the inability to speak and the powerful voice of active words—I mean the shift from Neville Chamberlain's appeasement to Churchill's defiance? A politically out-of-favor Winston Churchill was asked to be the wartime Prime Minister partly because of his experiences in the previous war, but he was also already known for the inspirational power of his speeches and radio broadcasts.

MR

There's a branded voice.

PE

The Churchill Insurance Company, with a bulldog for its logo! In his book about the history of the vocoder (also invented during World War II) Dave Tompkins refers to Winston Churchill as Britain's secret weapon, a ready-made human-speech synthesizer. In fact, Churchill's trademark voice was built at great expense. Like George VI, Churchill had a speech impediment, the combination of a dramatic stammer and a distinct lisp. His mouth was rebuilt around a set of loose-fitting dentures specially designed to help him speak more continuously and without losing that idiosyncratic lisp.

Churchill's voice would seem crazy today. Lisp and loose dentures or not, it belongs to another age. Even in Britain the more regulated clipped tones of so-called RP (Received Pronunciation) sound like a throwback to a distant and almost mythical past. The 'Monarch's English,' or King's speech—currently the Queen's speech—was a model for British spoken language since the time of the Tudors. Margaret Thatcher, although not from the upper classes, emulated that way of talking. It was the normative standard, as a sociolinguist might put it. On the other hand, the ambiguous line that separates one's own voice from a more idealized model of speech is quite different from the gap between handwriting and typography. Though perhaps the comparison can be made in terms of cultural hegemony and technical processes. The 19th-century English poet John Clare is valued partly for a stubborn refusal to give up the local dialect terms and accents of his spoken language to a more grammatically uniform written language. Clare's writing responds to the violent upheavals of the Industrial Revolution, particularly the Enclosure movement, which was forcing an end to traditional uses of the fields and meadows. Clare's rougher, provincial vernacular is often described as being in direct conflict with the smoother mechanical lines of both machined land, and, with the printing press, of machined language.

MR

Benedict Anderson made a similar observation in his *Imagined Communities* about the unifying power of newspapers both in terms of fixing an official language and typographic standards.

PE

Going back to Hollywood central-casting, powerful media voices are able to transcend certain notions of class. One of the most celebrated voices of British acting belonged to Richard Burton, working-class son of a Welsh coal miner. In terms of a world around us inhabiting the body and shaping the sound of how it speaks, Burton famously said of his fellow Welshmen, "Our voices were born with coal dust and rain." Upwardly mobile enough to buy the most expensive diamond in the world for Elizabeth Taylor's 40th birthday, he apparently dialed in his bids during the Sotheby's auction from a payphone in a hotel bar.

MR

I hear the telephone. Is that where it all begins for the disembodied voice?

PE

The phone released the voice like a genie from the lamp. The famous first words ever spoken into a telephone — *"Mr. Watson — Come here — I want to see you"* — voice an anxiety for the collapsing space and dissolving bodies the device would specialize in. Some critics believe that the tools of online social networking are essentially unchanged since the telephone's invention. Allucquére Rosanne Stone's study of telephone sex workers brilliantly demonstrated human ability to resituate the body in its interactions with network technology, but in a way that said as much about long-existing capabilities of the human voice.

In almost all situations we interpret or find meaning by taking advantage of any information we're not given. Phone sex can only work by exploiting the gaps, mobilizing erotic tension by taking advantage of what cannot be known. Stone describes how telephone sex workers find a way to reduce the necessary information about the human body into a much smaller signal — the tone of a voice, a few words, an intake of breath, a sigh, a few more words — enough for a client on the other end of the telephone line to uncompress the signal into a substantial sensory image of the body.

By performing these very practical applications of data compression, phone-sex workers translate all the modalities of multi-sensory experienceinto audible form. Into the form of a voice. Yet most people can also perform this magical act of speaking a body into life. Isn't that one of the objects or motives of branding a voice? I brought up the essay by Marcel Mauss because for me it still provokes many thoughts about language as a technique of the body. How far, for example, are we willing to go for an imaginary corporate body that in its own synthetic and seductive ways, and through all of its modes of 'speaking,' is little more than a technique of the voice?

FUCK CONTENT

In *Designer as Author* I argued that we are insecure about the value of our work. We are envious of the power, social position and cachet that artists and authors seem to command. By declaring ourselves "designer/authors" we hope to garner similar respect. Our deep-seated anxiety has motivated a movement in design that values origination of content over manipulation of content.

Designer as Author was an attempt to recuperate the act of design itself as essentially linguistic—a vibrant, evocative language. However, it has often been read as a call for designers to generate content: in effect, to become designers *and* authors, not designers *as* authors. While I am all for more authors, that was not quite the point I wanted to make.

The problem is one of content. The misconception is that without deep content, design is reduced to pure style, a bag of dubious tricks. In graphic-design circles, form-follows-function is reconfigured as form-follows-content. If content is the source of form, always preceding it and imbuing it with meaning, form without content (as if that were even possible) is some kind of empty shell.

The apotheosis of this notion, repeated *ad nauseum* (still!), is Beatrice Warde's famous Crystal Goblet metaphor, which asserts that design (the glass) should be a transparent vessel for content (the wine). Anyone who favored the ornate or the bejeweled was a knuckle-dragging oaf. Agitators on both sides of the ideological spectrum took up the debate: minimalists embraced it as a manifesto; maximalists decried it as aesthetic fascism. Neither camp questioned the basic, implicit premise: it's all about the wine.

This false dichotomy has circulated for so long that we have started to believe it ourselves. It has become a central tenet of design education and the benchmark against which all design is judged. We seem to accept the fact that developing content is more essential than shaping it, that good content is the measure of good design.

Back when Paul Rand wrote "There is no such thing as bad content, only bad form," I remember being intensely annoyed. I took it as an abdication of a designer's responsibility to meaning. Over time, I have come to read it differently: he was not defending hate speech or schlock or banality; he meant that the designer's purview is to shape, not to write. But that shaping itself is a profoundly affecting form. (Perhaps this is the reason that modern designers — Rand, Munari, Leoni — always seem to end their careers designing children's books. The children's book is the purest venue of the designer/author because the content is negligible and the evocative potential of the form unlimited.)

So what else is new? This seems to be a rather mundane point, but for some reason we don't *really* believe it. We don't believe shaping is enough. So to bring design out from under the thumb of content we must go one step further and observe that treatment is, in fact, a kind of text itself, as complex and referential as any traditional understanding of content.

A director can be the esteemed auteur of a film he didn't write, score, edit or shoot. What makes a Hitchcock film a Hitchcock film is not the story but a consistency of style, which winds intact through different technologies, plots, actors, and time periods like a substance of its own. Every film is about filmmaking. His great genius is that he is able to mold the form into his style in a genuinely unique and entertaining way. The meaning of his work is not in the story but in the storytelling.

Designers also trade in storytelling. The elements we must master are not the content narratives but the devices of the telling: typography, line, form, color, contrast, scale, weight. We speak through our assignment, literally between the lines.

The span of graphic design is not a history of concepts but of forms. Form has evolved dramatically from one year to the next, and suggests a profession that continually revises and reshapes the world through the way it is rendered. Stellar examples of graphic design, design that changes the way we look at the world, are often found in service of the most mundane content: an ad for ink, cigarettes, sparkplugs or machinery. Think of Piet Zwart's catalogues for electrical cable; or the travel posters of Cassandre or Matter; or the New Wave work of Weingart, Greiman and Friedman; or the punk incitations of Jamie Reid, in which the manipulation of form has an essential, even transformative, meaning.

At a 1962 conference at the Museum of Modern Art, conservative art critic Hilton Kramer denounced Pop Art as "indistinguishable from advertising art" because "Pop Art does not tell us what it feels like to be living through the present moment of civilization. Its social effect is simply to reconcile us to a world of commodities, banalities and vulgarities." But perhaps the *content* of graphic design is exactly that: an evocation of "what it feels like to be living through the present moment of civilization," with all its "commodities, banalities and vulgarities." How else can we discuss the content of a typeface or why the typography of a surfing magazine suddenly becomes relevant? Or how a series of made-up or 'self-initiated' posters—already a medium of dubious functionality—can end up on the wall of a major design museum? Work must be saying something, which is different than being *about* something.

Because the nature of the designed object is limited, individual objects are rarely substantial enough to contain fully rendered ideas. Ideas develop over many projects, spanning years. Form itself is indexical. We are intimately, physically connected to the work we produce, and it is inevitable that our work bears our stamp. The choice of projects in each designer's oeuvre lays out a map of interests and proclivities. (I use the singular *designer* in the categorical sense, not the individual.) The way those projects are parsed out, disassembled, reorganized and rendered reveals a philosophy, an aesthetic position, an argument and a critique.

This deep connection to making also positions design in a modulating role between the user and the world. By manipulating form, design reshapes that essential relationship. Form is replaced by exchange. The things we make negotiate a relationship over which we have a profound control.

The trick is to find ways to speak through treatment, via a range of rhetorical devices—from the written to the visual to the operational—to make those proclamations as poignant as possible, and to return consistently to central ideas, to re-examine and re-express. In this way we build a body of work, and from that body of work emerges a singular message, maybe even *what it feels like to be living now*. As a popular film critic once wrote, "A movie is not what it is about, it's how it is about it." Likewise, for us, our *What* is a *How*. Our content is, perpetually, Design itself.

Fall 2006

Second Year Design
Core Studio
Michael Rock et al.
Wednesdays as noted.

***

Question:
What is greater than God,
More evil than the Devil,
The poor have it,
The rich need it,
And if you eat it,
you'll die?

Answer: Nothing.

***

I have nothing to say/
and I am saying it/
and that is poetry/
as I needed it.

John Cage, Lecture on Nothing

***

****
Much Ado about Nothing

My intention with this project is actually pretty simple, even brutal. If we have been saying the thesis is not about content but about method, what happens when we intentionally, petulantly, aggressively remove content altogether by saying design something about Nothing.

The origin of the idea came from thinking about John Cage's famous "Lecture on Nothing," a highly structured, formal lecture on the idea of Nothing. (see attached) Its seeming lack of subject refocuses the listener on the structure of the lecture itself as content.

Of course, nothing is never nothing, it is always "something" but in defining what you mean by Nothing, I hope you will reveal something specific about your thesis. (So for instance, someone doing a thesis on the idea "to erase" will create a very different kind of nothing than someone doing a project on "to focus" or whatever.)

This is the second attempt at this project. I am still unsure what we will get but whatever it is, it will certainly be Something.

Project: Design a poster, book, website or short video about the idea: Nothing.

October 4: Introduction.
October 18: Mid project critique. Final sketches.
November 1: Final crit.

II. PROJECTS

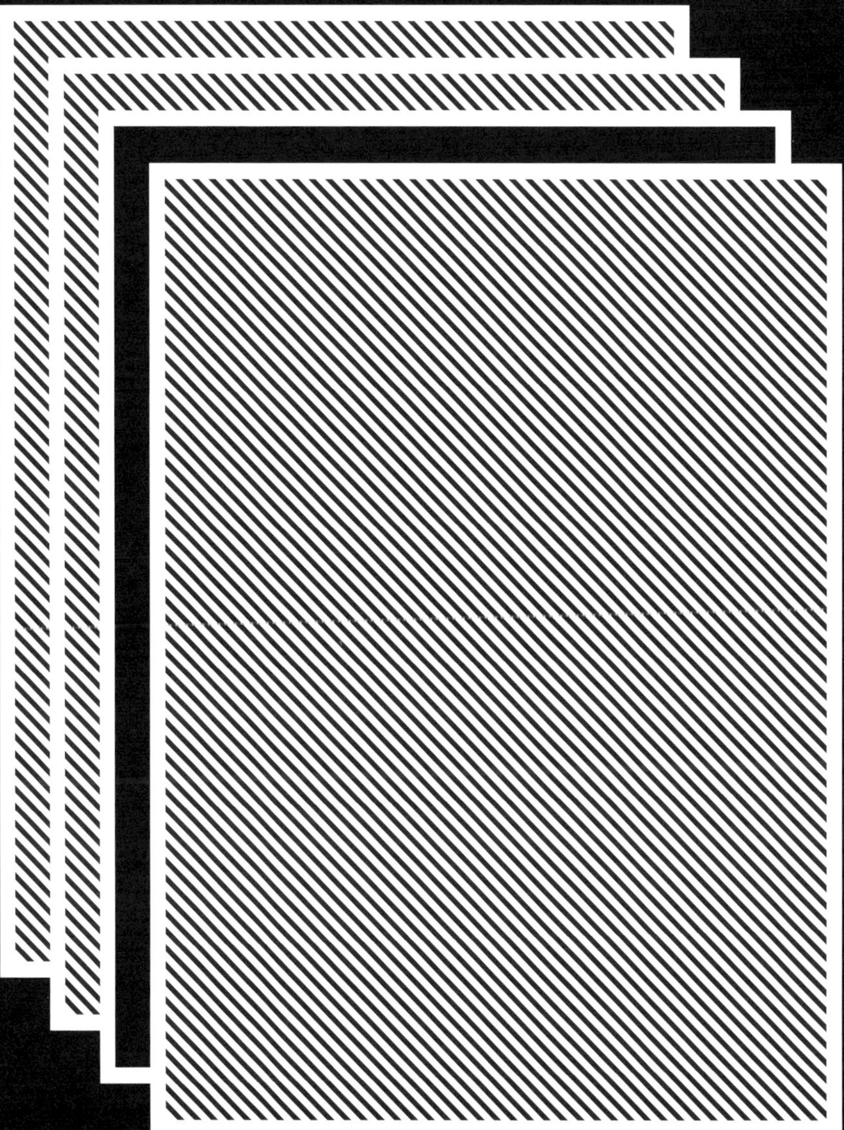

There is thinking *and* making and there is thinking *through* making. The *problem* with work is well documented: Is there room for ideas in the context of dealing with someone else's problems? Designers speak between the lines and a design career is a series of inherently irrational accidents imperfectly molded into something seemingly coherent.

IT IS WHAT IT IS
(OR, ARE WE DONE YET?)

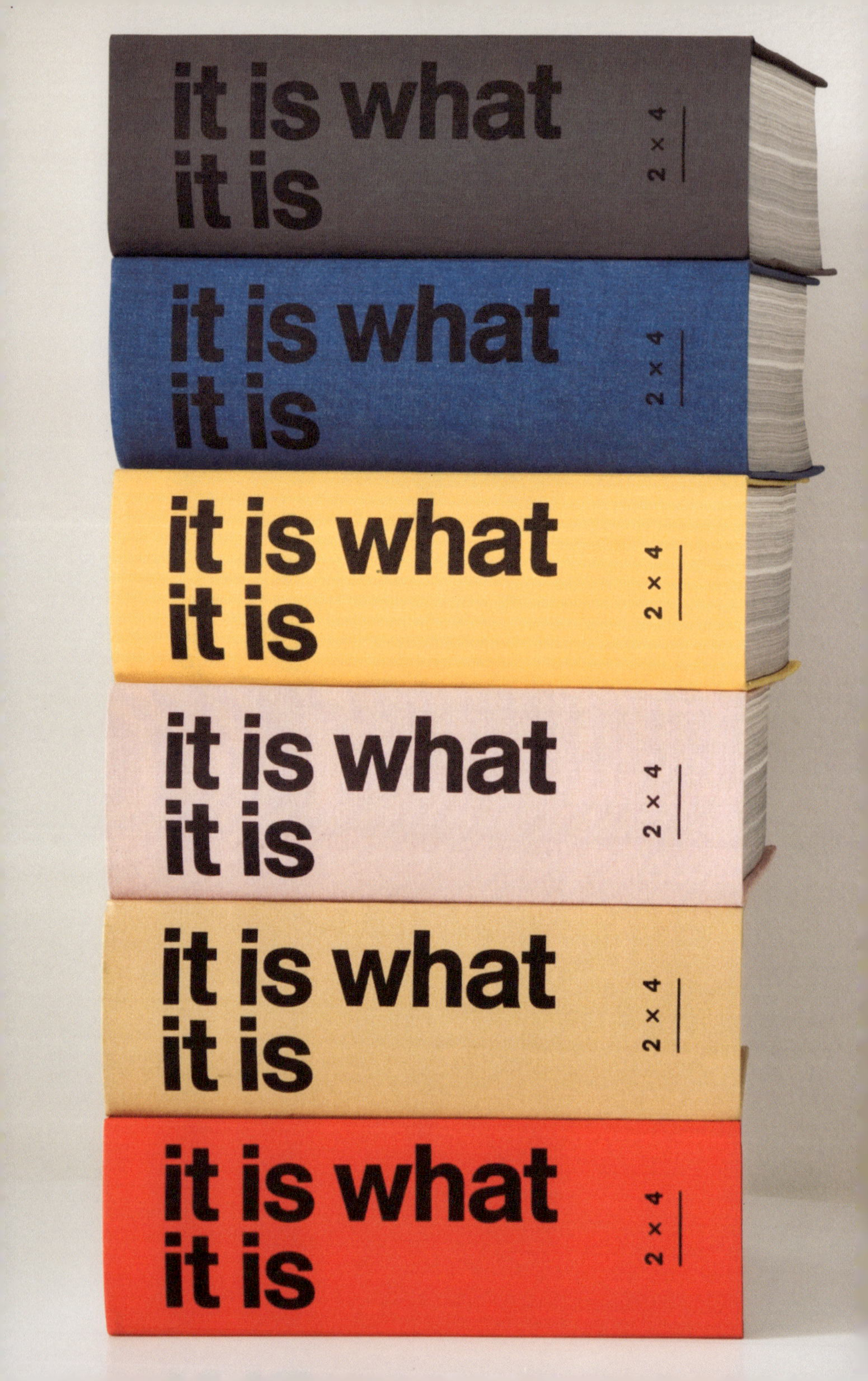

it is what
it is
2 x 4

it is what
it is
2 x 4

it is what
it is
2 x 4

it is what
it is
2 x 4

it is what
it is
2 x 4

it is what
it is
2 x 4

What's your deliverable? It's a common question, as crass as it is self-evident. We deliver Design … 24/7. But it's a strange word—deliverable—with so many embedded assumptions. Someone else demands, requires, needs, wants, and ultimately pays (or doesn't), but we always deliver. The verb makes sense; it's the noun that's the problem: what is this thing we are handing over?

On most business forms, Graphic Design is listed under Service Industries, so that much is clear: we deliver service. We service people, people in need of … design. Okay, so maybe it's not so clear after all. Perhaps the problem is in the shifting definition of the design object. The material nature of the design object keeps slipping over the course of a project and from project to project, client to client, year to year, generation to generation.

A graphic-design project starts out as a relationship, transforms into a process of loose analysis and more or less insightful speculation, then enters into a practically autistic phase of visual generation, followed by a synthesis of speculation and experimentation that morphs into a purely computational and mechanical production—accomplished with or without the involvement of any number of outside trades—and finally emerges into the world through a complex of socialization and acculturation that includes publicity, public relations, distribution, retailing, advertising, focus testing, and criticism.

Some version of this process is applied to everything: from high art to low commerce, from the intellectual to the banal, from the edifying to the disingenuous. And the process may be interrupted at any point—in ways both positive and negative—by collaborators, authors, editors, clients, vendors, users, lawyers, censors, and politicians, all demanding modifications that range

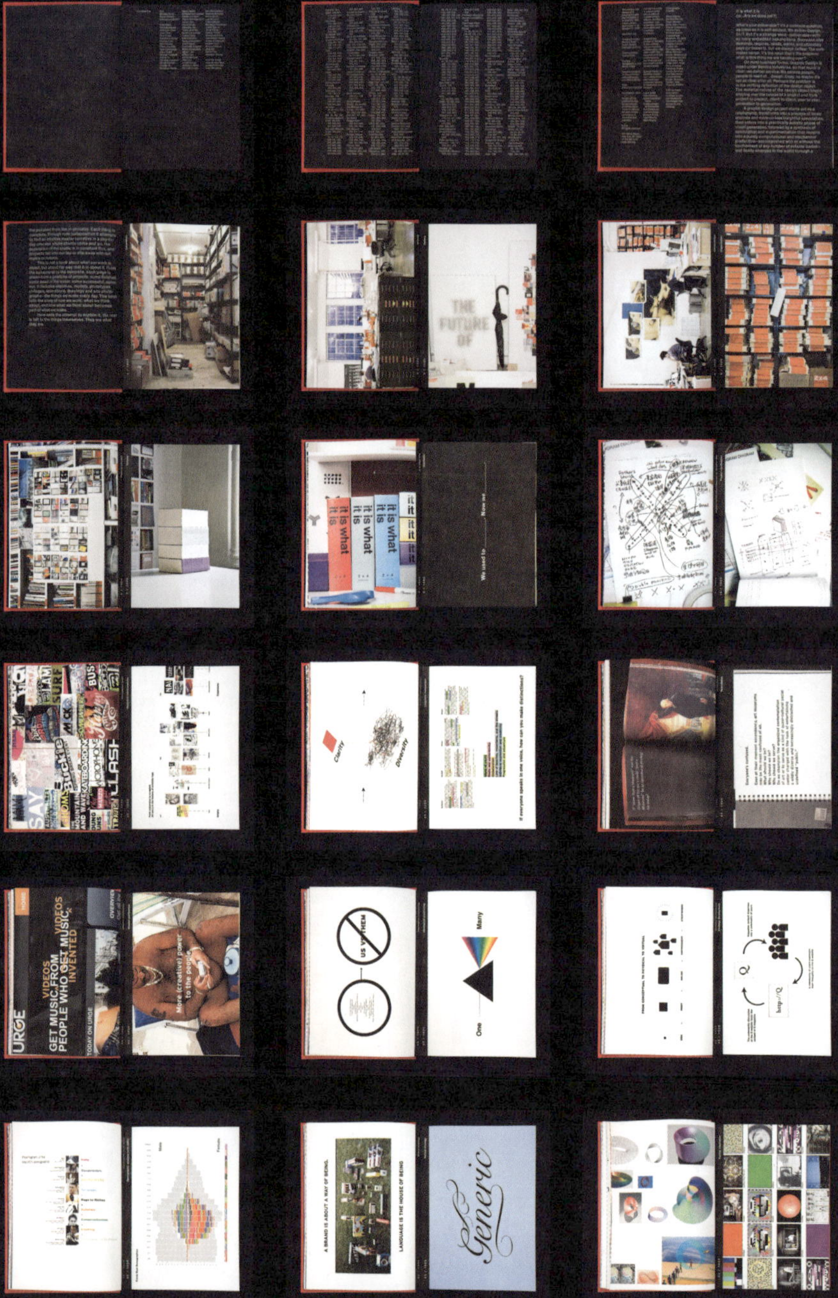

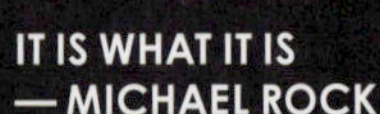

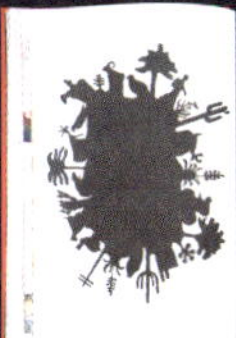
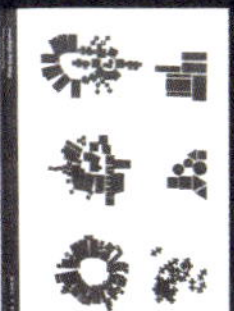
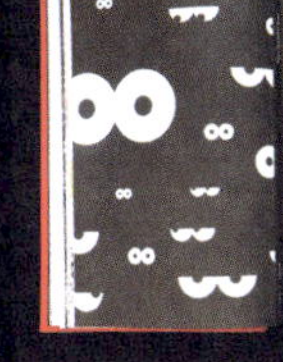
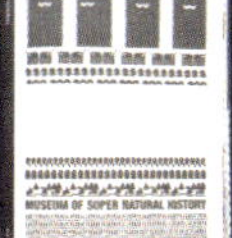
MUSEUM OF SUPER NATURAL HISTORY
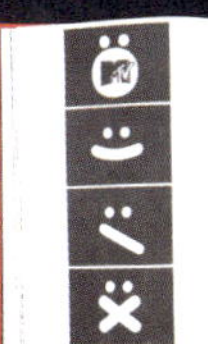
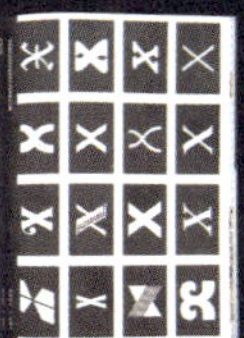
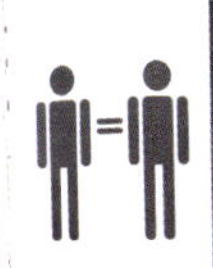

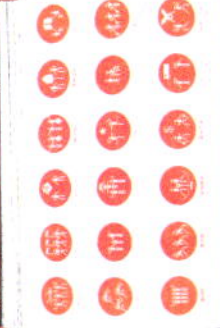
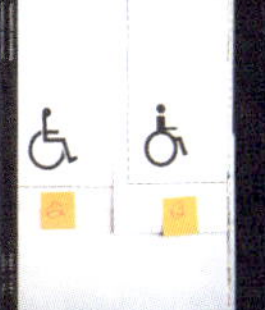
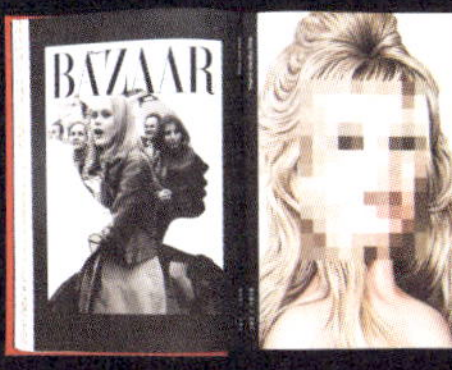
BAZAAR
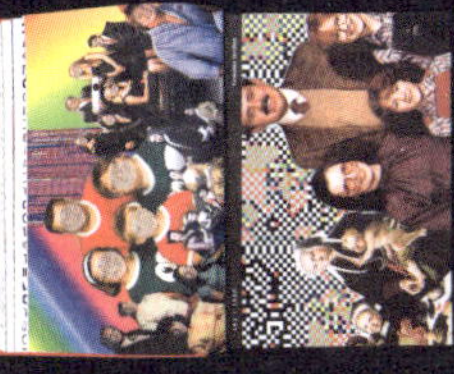
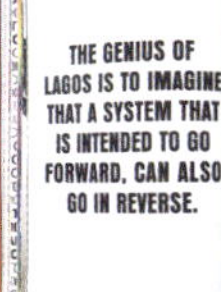
THE GENIUS OF
LAGOS IS TO IMAGINE
THAT A SYSTEM THAT
IS INTENDED TO GO
FORWARD, CAN ALSO
GO IN REVERSE.
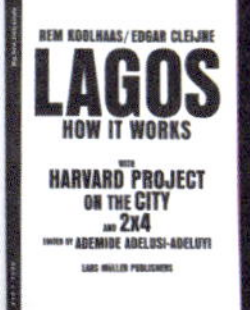
REM KOOLHAAS/EDGAR CLEIJNE
LAGOS
HOW IT WORKS
HARVARD PROJECT
ON THE CITY
2X4
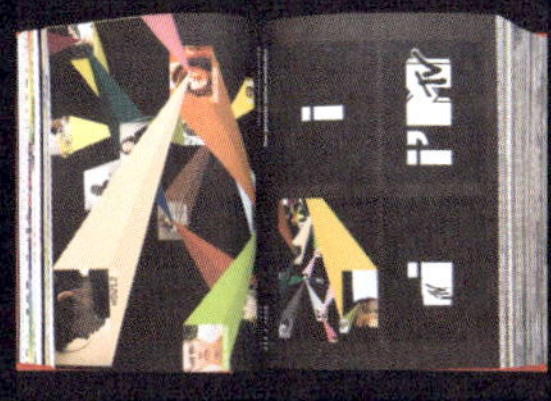
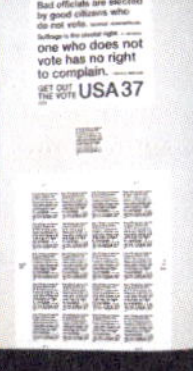
one who does not
vote has no right
to complain.
USA 37
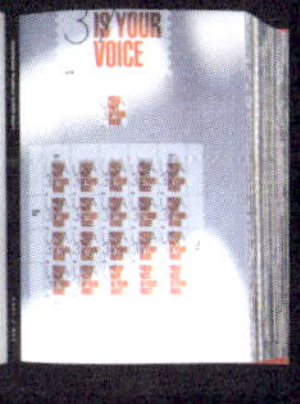
IS YOUR
VOICE
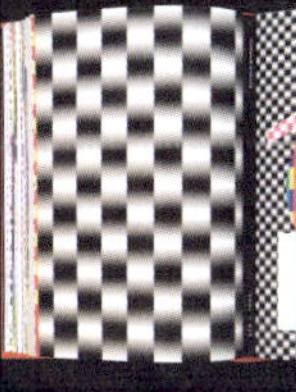
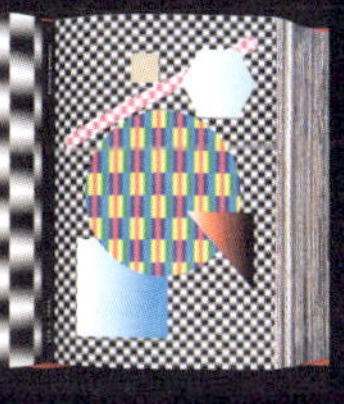
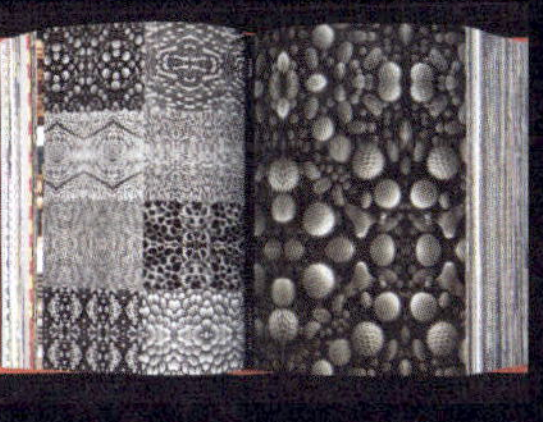
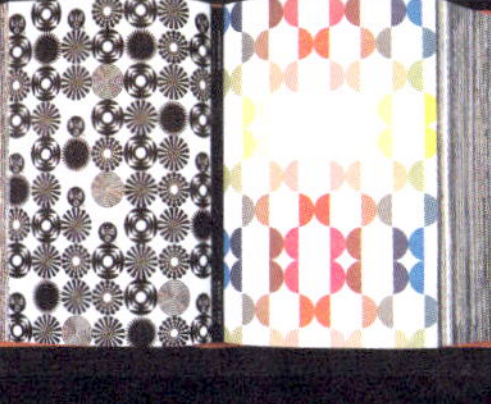
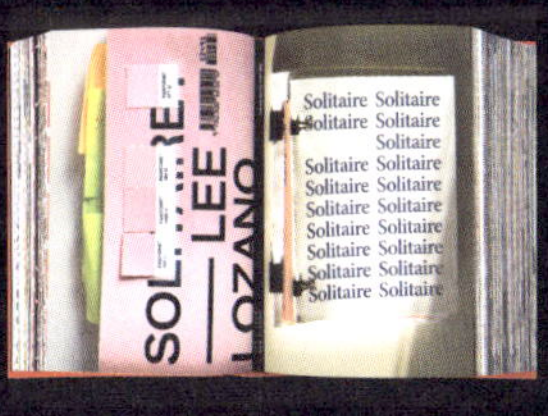
LEE
LOZANO
Solitaire Solitaire
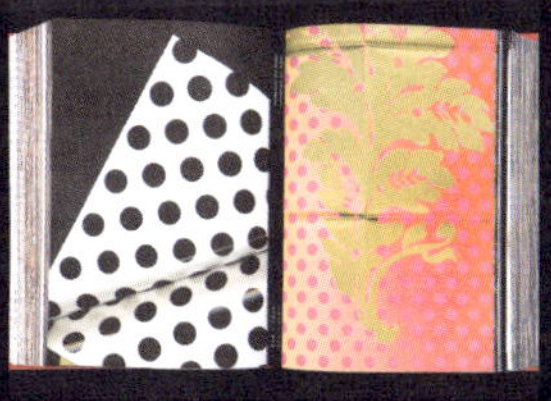
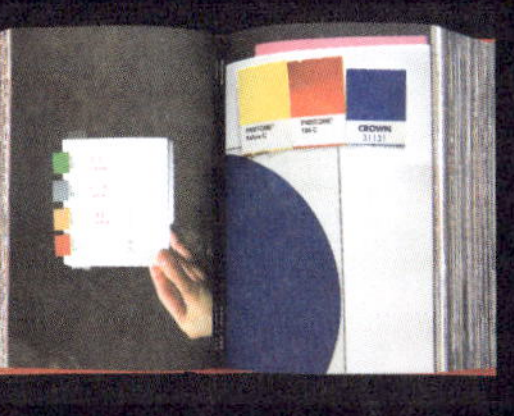
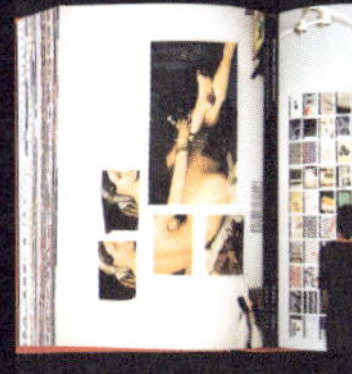
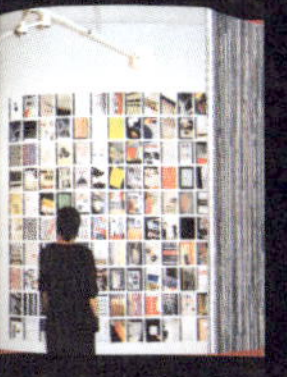
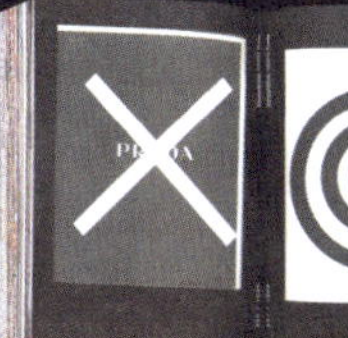
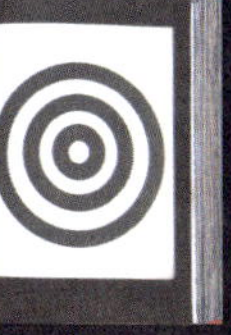

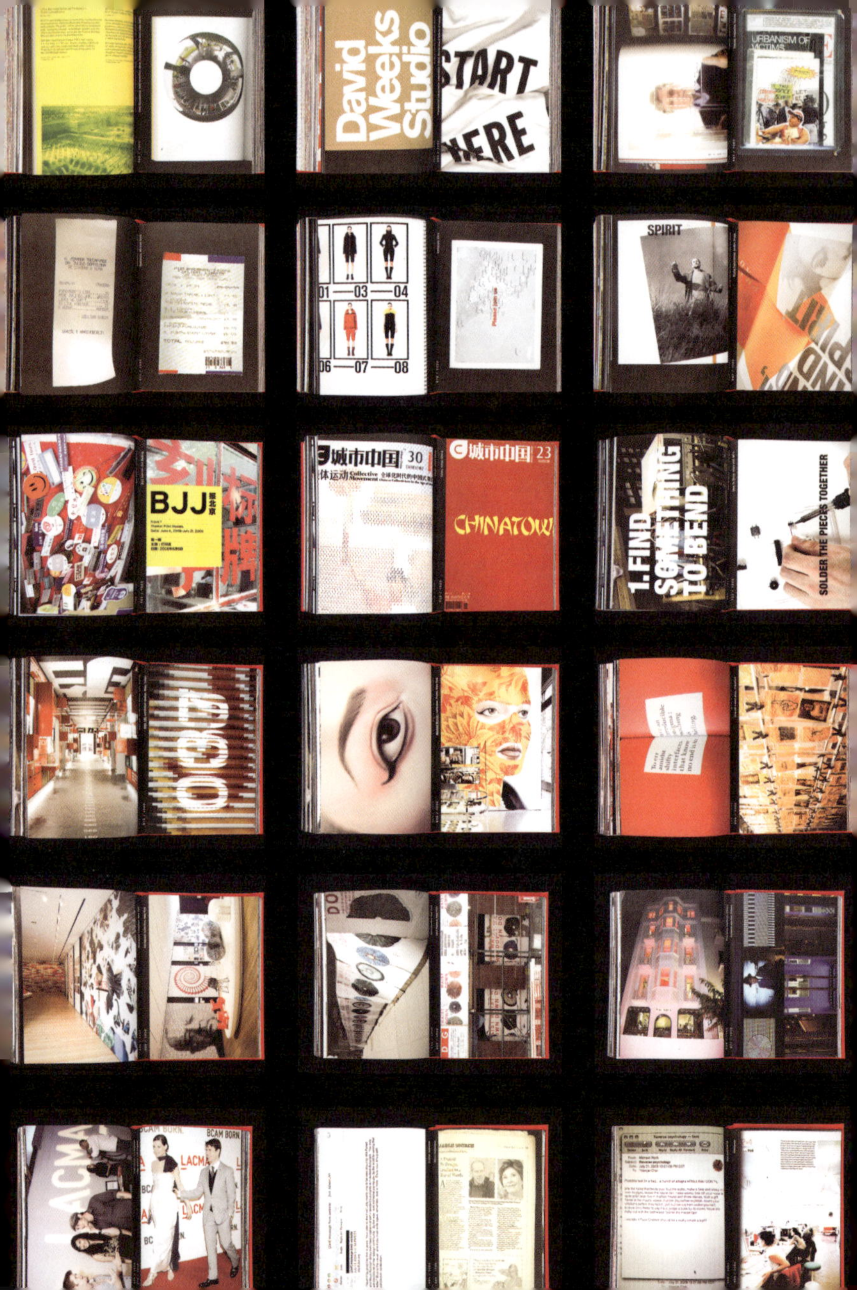
David Weeks Studio
START HERE
URBANISM OF VICTIMS
01 03 04
06 07 08
SPIRIT
BJJ 展北京
城市中国 30
Collective Movement
城市中国 23
CHINATOW
1. FIND SOMETHING TO BEND
SOLDER THE PIECES TOGETHER
BCAM BORN.
LACMA

from the minor to the catastrophic. Add to the mix a studio comprised of thirty headstrong individuals engaged in multiple, overlapping projects—all utterly out of sync—concerning wildly different subjects, players, timelines, technologies, audiences, budgets and geographic locations. On top of that, designers have their own private agendas, ambitions, anxieties, compulsions, and references. Those agendas may mesh with the content at hand—and with the overarching, collective vision of the studio—or may be grafted onto content and live there parasitically. Personal vision is the designer's value-added; it's an indexical presence assumed so resilient it can survive in any context, from the base to the effete.

The compelling aspect of design is that each part of this messy process produces things, a constant stream of material pumping out of the studio. This superabundance defies any simple definition of the "object" (and any simple declaration of completion). Design can never be reduced to a direct process of transmission because the design object carries multiple messages: some overt, others sublimated, some literal, some haptic. And besides, the actual recipient of the communiqué is also opaque. It could be an imagined audience, an ideal audience, a peer, a studiomate, a passerby.

Design is always about creating a physical effect: it is both read and felt. Designers make things—deliverables—but these are not always the discrete things for which one gets paid. The simplest study can yield an idea, effect or emotion. Printing, binding, programming and building don't necessarily have anything to do with it. A designer's "things" happen at every stage of a design process; they are always finished and never finished. But the bigger project, the one that is never complete, is the one carried out over many projects and many years. It's the project that demands persistent, diligent, never-quite-satisfying attempts. That's the work, and the life, of the studio.

it is what it is is a blurry telling of a blurry story. It superimposes diverse projects, scales, eras and voices onto a typical trajectory, starting from first contact and concluding with delivery into the world. It makes no attempt to segregate the polished from the in-process. Each thing is complete. Through rude juxtaposition it attempts to find an intuitive master narrative in a day-to-day process where clients come and go, the population of the studio is in constant flux, and projects fall into our lap or slip away without rhyme or reason.

It is not a book about what our work is about, but about the way that it is about it. From the ephemeral to the concrete, each page is drawn from a pastiche of projects: some finished, some dead in the water, some successful, some not. It includes sketches, models, prototypes, collages, animations, drawings and site photographs — the things we make every day. *it is what it is* tells the story of how we work, what we think about, and how what we think about becomes part of what we make.

Here ends the attempt to explain it, the rest is left to the things themselves. They are what they are.

ANY AND ALL

WITH
MICHAEL SPEAKS

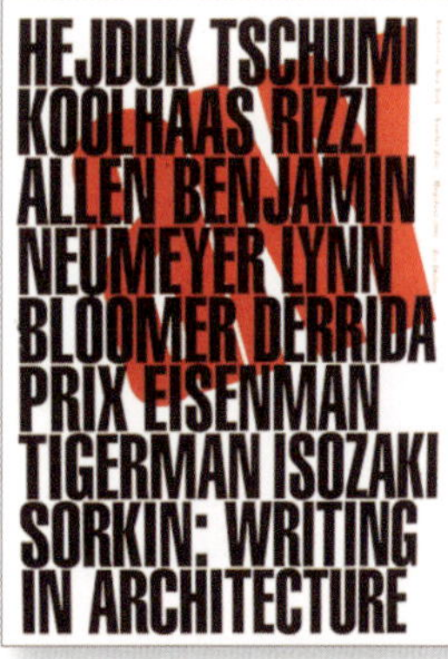

Elizabeth Plater-Zyberk: First, I should say that Andres and I are pleased to be here amidst an architectural community in which we grew up and which we still feel part of. Whatever other reasons exist for this event, we also appreciate the chance to be with old friends and we are looking forward to talking with you all less formally after the debate.

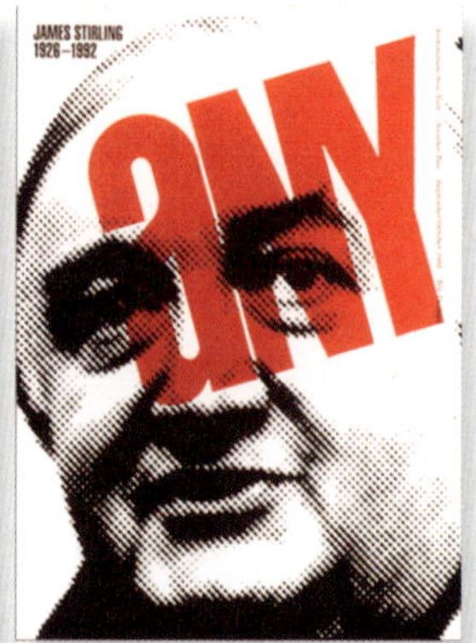

ESTABLISHMENT (DESIGN: MASSIMO VIGNELLI) ⟶

MICHAEL ROCK

How did you start with ANY?

MICHAEL SPEAKS

In 1993 I joined ANY to help launch the "Writing Architecture" book series for MIT Press and to serve as Senior Editor for the newly formed *ANY* magazine. Actually, I wrote the editorial for the first issue of *ANY*, number 0: Writing in Architecture, before I joined the magazine. I was a Ph.D. student studying with Fredric Jameson at the time and was introduced to ANY through his association with Peter Eisenman. In the editorial, whose title would soon become the name of the MIT book series, I focused on the "textual" reading and writing strategies that were becoming increasingly important in architecture.

Soon after I arrived in New York, it became clear to me that Peter wanted to recreate many of the IAUS[1] publishing and exhibition formats—lectures, conferences, books, newsletters—and that ANY Corporation would be the new vehicle for that. The difference, perhaps, between IAUS and ANY is that the debates that originated in the IAUS and published in *Oppositions*, Oppositions Books and Skyline, were polemical and focused on defining an American vanguard agenda on par with those in Europe. ANY, on the other hand, was not an institute, not a place of debate or intellectual production and teaching, but a corporation with sponsors in Japan and elsewhere. ANY was more interested in promotion than polemic; more interested in striking a vanguard pose than in forging a vanguard agenda. If, as Colin Rowe had called for in his Introduction to the Five Architects in 1972, the IAUS labored to create a uniquely American "word" or ideology that it might

1 The influential project led by Eisenman from 1967–1984.

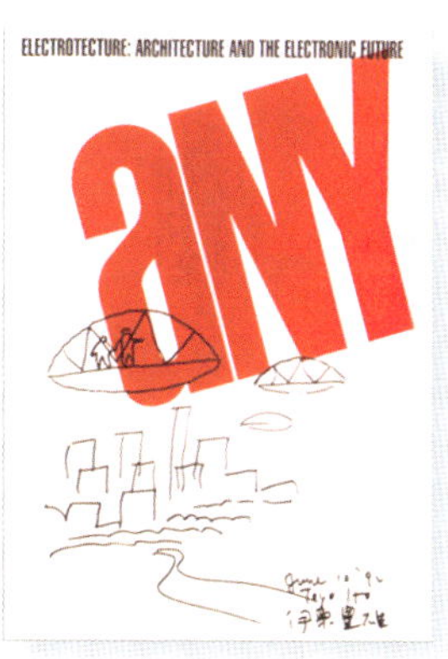

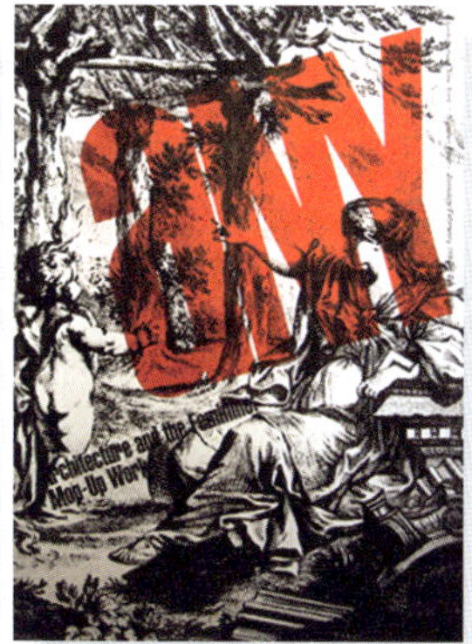

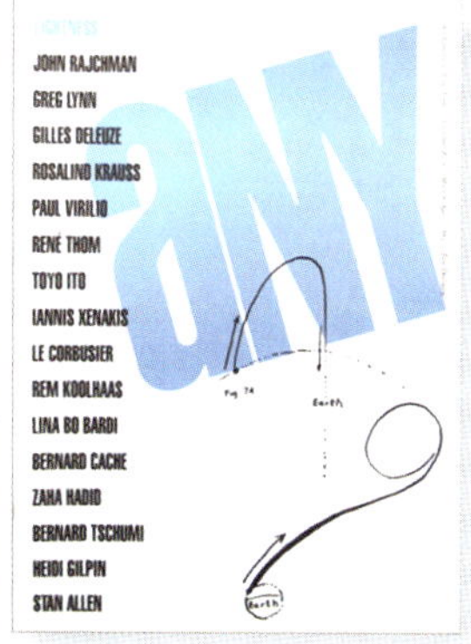

connect to the "flesh" or architectural formalism of Eisenman and his fellow American formalists (even if it meant importing both word and form from Europe and connecting them at the Institute), then ANY assumed the job was complete and set about promoting the "idea" of an architectural vanguard through its conferences and publications.

Oppositions was ideology pure and simple, while *ANY* was style posing as ideology. This shift from IAUS polemic to ANY promotion coincided with the more general trend of translating and introducing into the American academy the rigorous, scholarly and overtly political works of post-1968 continental philosophy. This "translation" created a new kind of intellectual text and writing that was devoid of its original historical and political context, and that new kind of text became known as "theory." Before the mid-1980s there were no "theory" sections in academic bookstores. But beginning in the late 1980s, theory—ranging from anthropology to mathematics to architecture—became an entirely new genre, an entirely new consumer good that was more easily consumed and reproduced than the old works of philosophy. This was all quite exciting to me and I was pleased to accept the position.

MR

Can you say something about the design of *ANY* and how it relates to "theory"?

MS

ANY's original design was entrusted to Massimo Vignelli. I remember very clearly the first time I went with Cynthia Davidson, the editor of *ANY*, to his office to discuss the layout of the magazine. It was a beautiful space, spare and authoritative, like Vignelli himself. When we began to discuss the layout, Vignelli pulled out this big tabloid-format paper, took two pencils, one red, one black, and drew colored blocks where

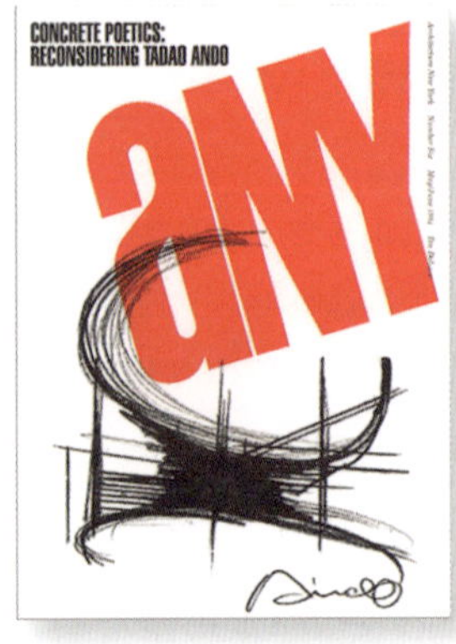

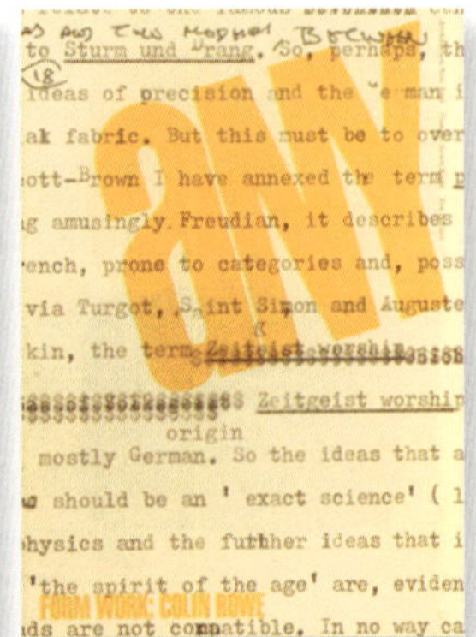

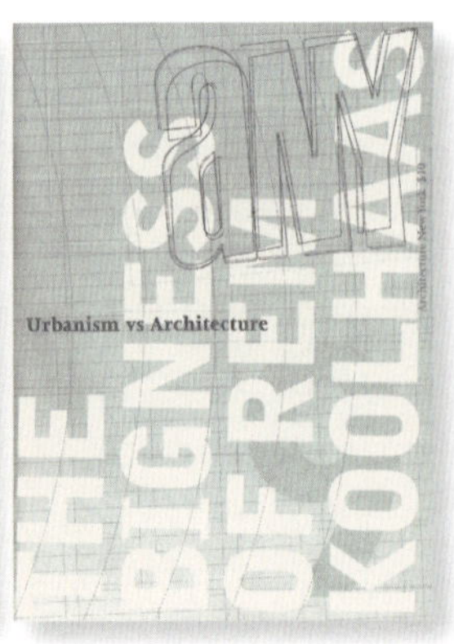

DESTABILIZATION (DESIGN:2x4)→

text would be inserted. I must say I was quite surprised. Coming from a literary-theory background, having spent years paying close attention to texts, and believing they were the starting point of a magazine, I was shocked that he seemed to have no interest whatsoever in the magazine content. Perhaps I was naïve. As we proceeded to lay out—color—all the pages in the issue, it became clear that Vignelli was more interested in creating compositions using his two preferred typefaces and two colors.[2] In retrospect, I now realize that Vignelli was the perfect choice to promote the ANY "theory" vanguard, which, after all, was more style than content, either of the ideological, *Oppositions* variety or some new, post-ideological, incarnation. If, for the Institute, Vignelli represented vanguard "opposition," then for the ANY Corporation he designed a style that looked and felt vanguard. *Oppositions* presented readers with difficult-to-understand texts, while *ANY* presented readers with difficult-to-read texts colored red and black. Vignelli colored the first eight issues of *ANY* magazine with red and black vanguardism, and finally, when you guys came along—at #9, the Bigness issue—I remember thinking: Now we can advance an intellectual project that might lead beyond the ideologically fixated, vanguard impasse to new discoveries and new actions. And that started with the Bigness issue, which in my opinion is still the best one.

MR

I agree. I think it started to fall apart after #16. Meaning we could only sustain our ideas for seven issues.

MS

The shift from Vignelli to 2x4 coincided with what I would call the second wave of theory at *ANY*,

2 Futura and Century Expanded, PMS red and black.

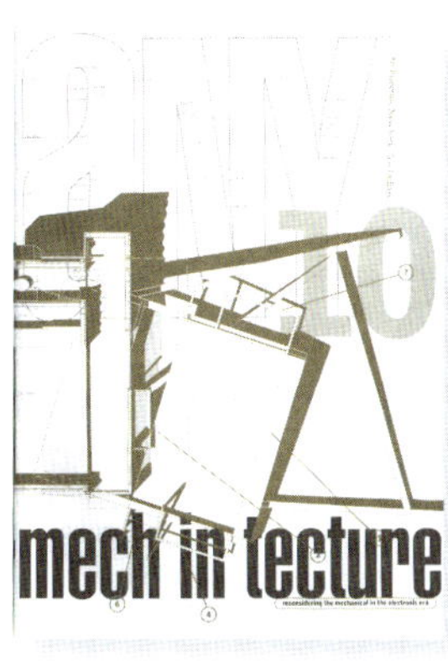

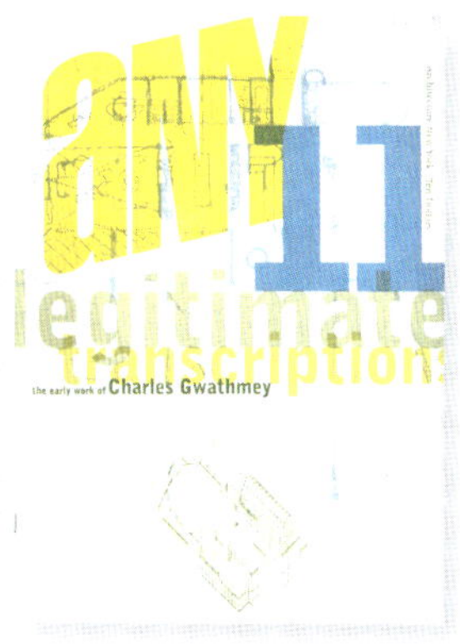

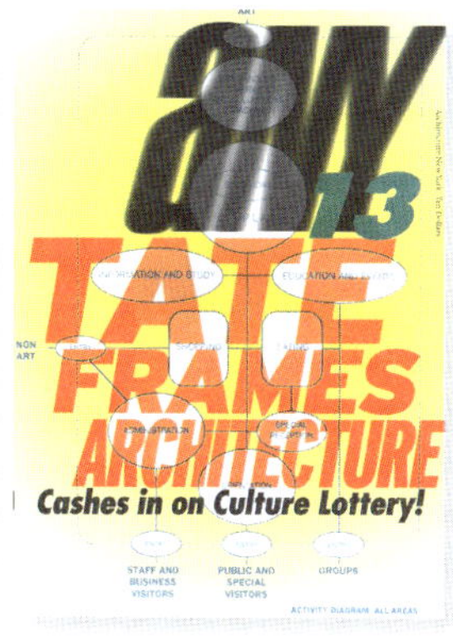

EMERGING →

one that created an opening for a new kind of intellectual debate and a new relationship in the magazine among text, image and concept.

The opening, was, as you suggest, short-lived. If the first theory wave in architecture was influenced and shaped by the work of philosopher Jacques Derrida—introduced by Eisenman, Jeffrey Kipnis, Mark Wigley, Mark Taylor, and others—then the second phase was shaped by the work of philosopher Gilles Deleuze. One of the first books published in the "Writing Architecture" MIT Press series was *Earth Moves*, by Bernard Cache, a book that Deleuze refers to in *What Is Philosophy* (1991), and one he had tried to get published in France. The book was brought to ANY by John Rajchman, who, along with Sanford Kwinter, Kipnis and Greg Lynn (most notably with their advertisement: *Folding in Architecture*, 1994), were the strongest advocates for a new Deleuzean theory vanguard. This next wave was perhaps most evident at the ANYWHERE conference in Yufuin, Japan, where all the Eisenman lieutenants, led by Kwinter, began to peel away from Derrida and move towards the work of Deleuze.

This theory realignment marked a transformation from an architectural focus on interpretation, text and "meaning," to a design focus on shaping and producing effects, concepts, and in Kwinter's case, life itself. Concerns about what architecture *is* were replaced by concerns about what architecture could *do*, a shift that underscored the increasing importance of Rem Koolhaas and the flagging influence of Eisenman. I always thought that 2x4 was similarly concerned with what graphic design can do, from book design to urban design, and so it makes sense that the break occurs with your design of a special issue devoted to Rem Koolhaas' concept, "bigness."

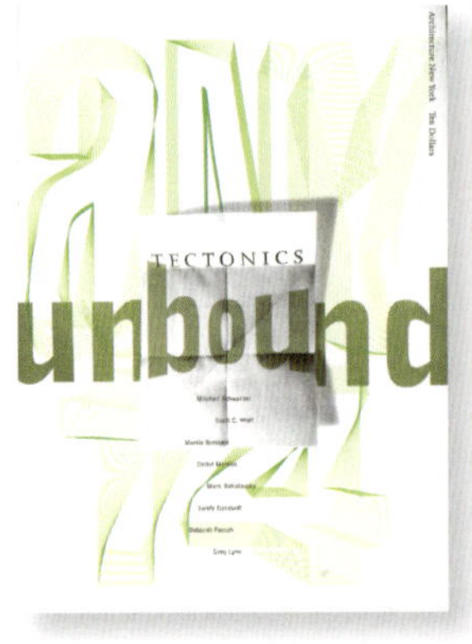

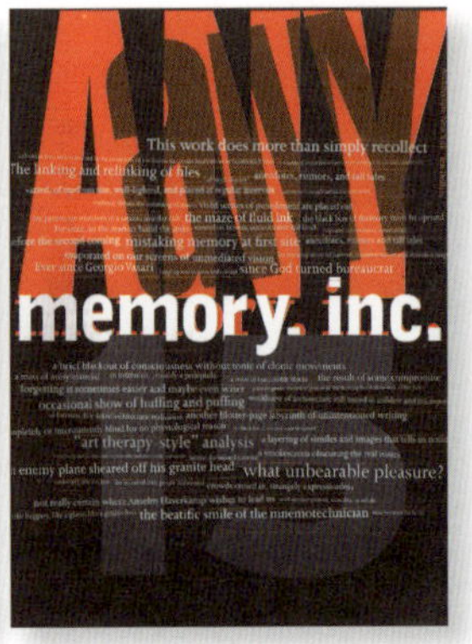

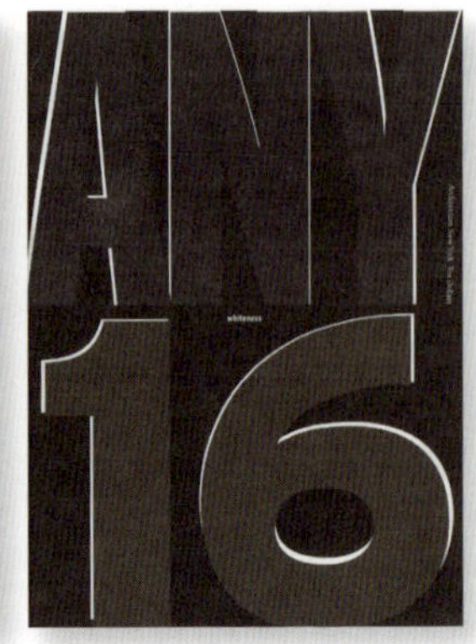

RESTABILIZATION →

MR

ANY was a tabloid. The word "tabloid" conjures up a cheap, fast, easy-to-distribute, low thing, and although *ANY* was cheap to produce, it was laborious to make. We approached it through a series of somewhat sloppy typographical languages that undermined the seriousness of Vignelli's approach. So *ANY* did have a cheapness in its typography. But maybe now Twitter is the new tabloid—the fastest, cheapest and most expendable version of publishing. I'm curious: if we were doing *ANY* now, if you were coming to me to join this great magazine, what would it be?

MS

I can only see *ANY* fixed at a moment in time; it could have no real influence today. I would suggest that architecture theory, and the whole European, post-1968 philosophical discourse that fueled it, ended in some fundamental way in 2000. Assemblage ended, *ANY* ended, the conferences ended, the books ended. Peter also ran out of "ANY" words.[3] *LOG*, the current ANY journal, like *Grey Room* and the other vanguard magazines, are anachronisms pure and simple. These journals make those who are nostalgic for truth and ideology happy, but not me. Like most, I prefer BLDGBLOG, dezeen, Archinect, Twitter, and magazines like *A10*, *Architect*, the *Architect's Newspaper*—all provide a steady stream of chatter, the raw material that I process into my own form of intelligence. For me, intelligence, which is always produced and never received, has superseded all forms of ideology and its stylized incarnations. In fact, ideology and its ersatz forms are just part of the stream of chatter. I do like *Monocle*, which, in my view, is a beautifully stylized packaging

3 The ANY book series were all titled with Any-prefixed words: Anything, Anyhow, Anywhere, Anywise, etc.

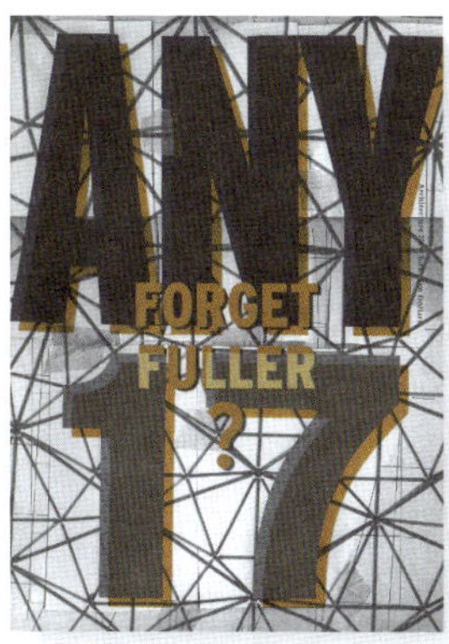

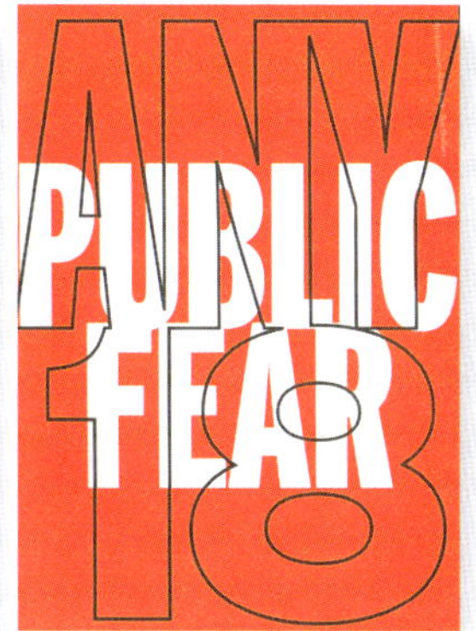

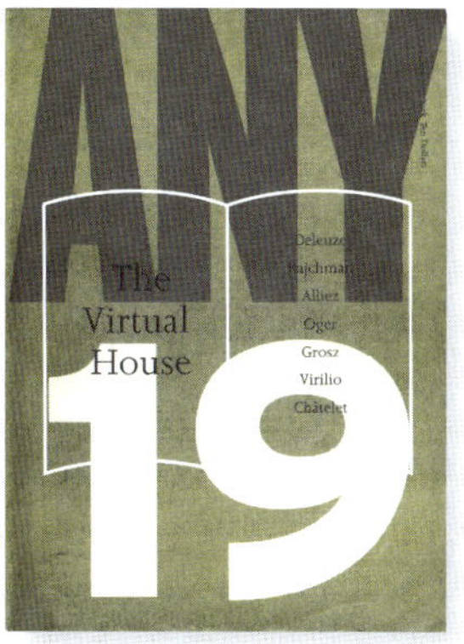

REPETITION →

of intelligence. It's chock full of stuff: there's design, of course, but there's also the Czech Prime Minister's favorite planes (n.b. Bombardier CRJ1000 and Boeing 737–900). They feature all the objects to buy in Tokyo, they partner with Blackberry and feature selections from the contents of the Beams catalogue. *Monocle* is not trying to be vanguard or true or on-the-edge. It is packaging knowledge in a kind of stylized, wonky, policy way.

MR

I'm curious about journals giving the raw material to an audience. Does that coincide with the move towards the projective—work seen as the embodiment of an idea rather than making sense of something that already exists in the world?

MS

I would say that the purpose of *Assemblage*, *ANY*, and all the vanguard journals, is to enlighten readers about what's next, about what they should be doing. They editorialized a kind of truth about architecture—these are the ten people, these are the concepts, these are the debates. On the other hand, intelligence means you sort through lots and lots of data, you discover patterns, and those patterns make sense and from those patterns a new knowledge is produced, not received. So even though *Monocle* does curate lots of stuff, they're neither ideologists nor are they styled to appear ideological. They're simply giving us an array of information so that we can decide.

MR

There's definitely an editorial ideology, though. Don't you think?

MS

I think there's a curatorial approach. I wouldn't call it an ideology.

MR

Would you call *ANY* an editorial ideology?

MS

Not exactly. ANY was stylized ideology, *Oppositions* was ideology.

ANY, like any corporation (no pun intended), had a board, and many of them supported the journal financially. ANY's stylized ideological agenda was really a corporate one, and many of its actions were meant to advance the agenda of those supporters. For example, Shimizu was a major supporter and was connected to Isozaki, who was on the board. It was no surprise that ANY published books and essays authored by those supported by Isozaki. As a project, *ANY* was an attempt to produce and reproduce a vanguard agenda for a post-vanguard world. I don't think people care about vanguard ideologies anymore. They have lost their appeal. *Monocle* has appeal, but that appeal is neither ideological nor stylized ideology.

MR

They're more a brand? Brand is the new word for ideology?

MS

Monocle has a curatorial approach, and it also has corporate sponsors, but its appeal is not based on any real or purported ideology. That's the appeal of the vanguard: they know the way, and they are going to show us all the way. I don't think anybody knows the way anymore. We have to determine that for ourselves: we can choose the prepackaged way of (stylized) ideology or we can produce our own way, our own intelligence. Editors and curators take a pass at sorting and packaging the chatter but we must treat their products as such, as chatter. That is true of *Monocle* and *ANY*. But there are better and worse kinds of chatter; more and less attractive, more and less appealing chatter. And each makes its appeal in different ways. *ANY*, *LOG* and *Grey Room* are no longer attractive, at least to me, because they purport—in their reductive, blanched form and content—to *know*. But we know they do not know. *Monocle* purports only to curate a stream—of policy, design, travel, housing, transportation, music, film, product, and other chatter—and transform that into congealed patterns that you might or might not find compelling, that you might or might not identify with.

MR

You know the first design we did for *Volume*—which lasted only for a couple of issues due to financial and practical restrictions—was a clear plastic box full of stuff, a kind of dossier of raw material.... Do you think that *Volume* is a kind of *Monocle*?

MS

Yes and no. At least, it's much closer to *Monocle* than to *ANY*. *Volume* is very different from *ANY*, but it's still in the same orbit because it still purports to *know*. It's not like *Monocle*; *Monocle* is completely post-ideological, whereas *Volume* still straddles that line, it still wants you to believe.

POST-OCCUPANCY

REM KOOLHAAS

Paradoxically, at the moment of architecture's undeniable flourishing—Jeff Kipnis thinks that architecture has never been this good*—a latent hostility is growing between the architect, the critic and the public. Perhaps as unconscious penalty for the architects' seemingly irresistible ascent, a pervasive skepticism about the architects' alleged motives is rapidly expanding …

Where only a generation ago the architect was endowed with, at least, good intentions—and frequently goodness—the architect today is assumed to share the tawdry emotions, compromised integrity and suspect intentions of the "celebrity" that he/she has become. The typical/average contemporary starchitect—a word now used even by important critics—is indifferent to the clients' interests, contemptuous of his/her buildings' users, repeating the same exhausted catalogue in 101 different contexts, happy to have dumped architecture's awkward moralism and clumsy social alibis. He avoids the profession's only new F-word, function, function, like the plague; costs are nothing to him; the only thing in common with his earnest predecessors is that his masterpieces also leak.

A contemporary Faustus: drowning in attention, but not taken seriously. But Faust, at least, could make his own deals: his present, reduced embodiment is the creation of a thousand marketing strategies, borderline magazines, frantic part-timers, promiscuous freelancers, risk-averse political calculations, ultra-compressed TV spots, academic gold scales, travel budget cuts, a thousand inflated keynotes and his defeated colleagues' generosity …. A combined process of *corrosive adulation* mercilessly registers such crucial details as hairstyles, labels, love lives, glasses, shoes, and other marks of architectural genius. In the Bermuda Triangle of architect/critic/public, the market economy has given each of them a perfect incentive for character assassination.

The publication by the so-called "think" tank AMO of recent work by OMA—perhaps the archetypal global punch-drunk heavyweight—can only exacerbate the expectation of narcissistic excess and critical free ride that now cling to the professions' "leaders" like an unwelcome halo.

With this issue we try to (re)present four recent buildings in a fresh, more complex way. We don't insist on the buildings' qualities, but monitored their effects on their respective hosts and users. There are no "critics"—usually, best friends in drag—no inti-midation. We have assembled myriad anonymous voices and collected snapshots. We documented how (our) buildings take their place in a primordial sea of influences and predecessors on which their existence depends and to whose existence they try to contribute. We looked through the eyes of tourists and artists, trusted others to record. Away from the triumphalist or miserabilist glare of media, we wanted to see what happens in the absence of the author, to represent the realities we were complicit in creating, post-occupancy, as facts, not feats.

*Jeff Kipnis and Robert Somol's lecture at the Architectural Association, 31 January 2006.

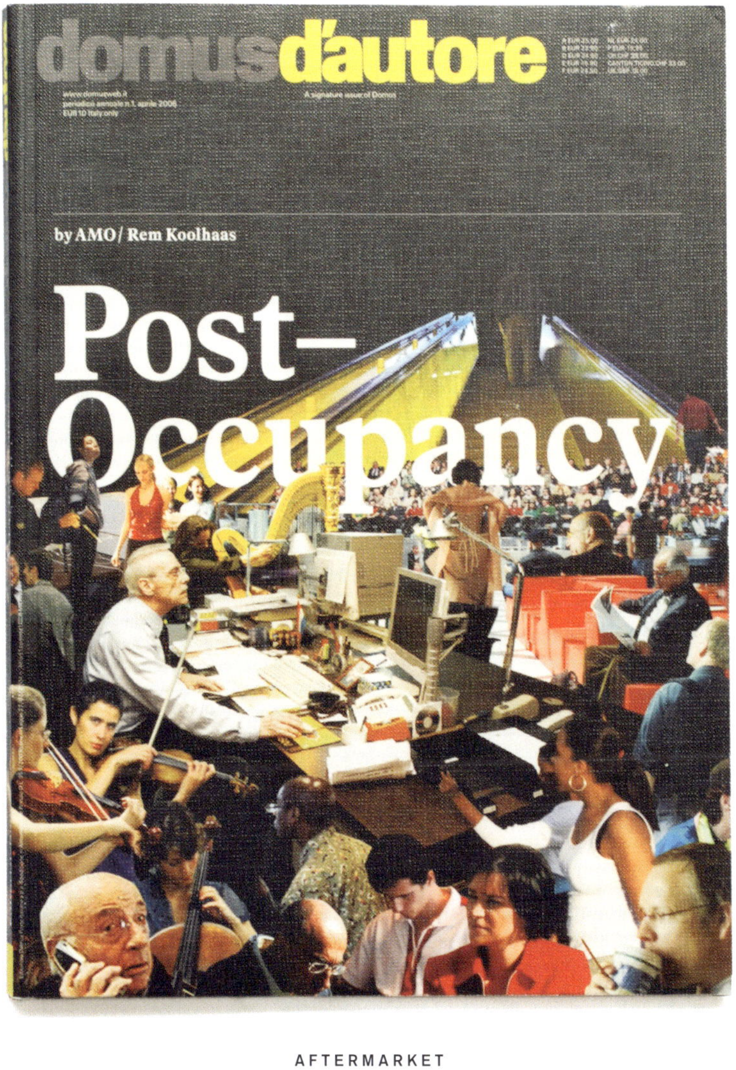

domus d'autore

A signature issue of Domus

by AMO / Rem Koolhaas

Post–Occupancy

AFTERMARKET

Post-Occupancy is a project by AMO and 2x4, edited by Rem Koolhaas and Kayoko Ota.

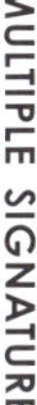

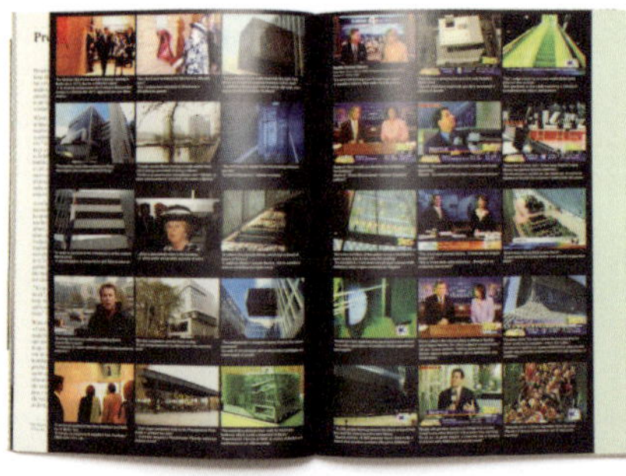

TONIGHT AT SIX
Local televsion coverage of opening day.

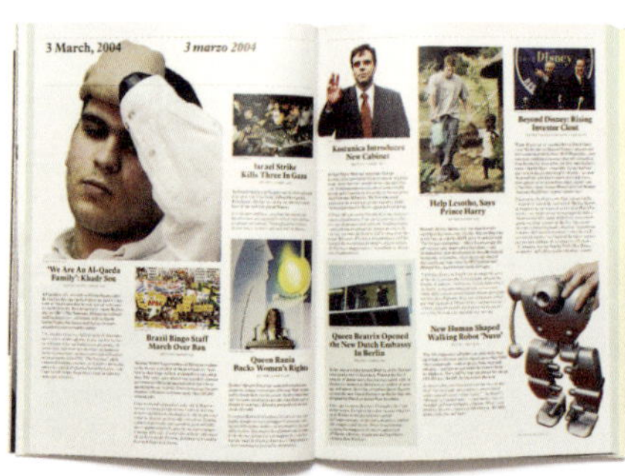

IN OTHER NEWS
Headline stories from opening day.

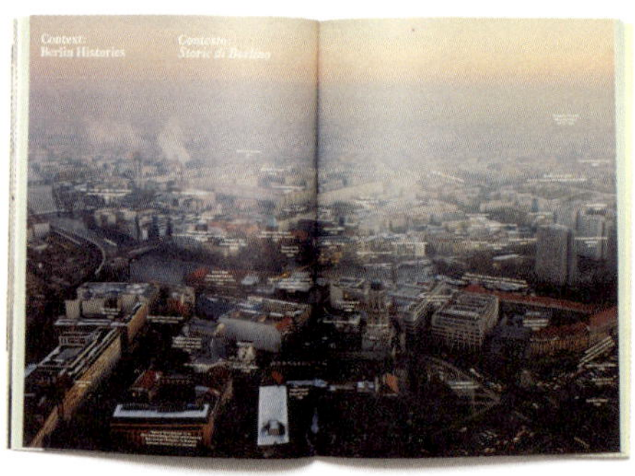

HELICOPTERING
Context at various focal distances.

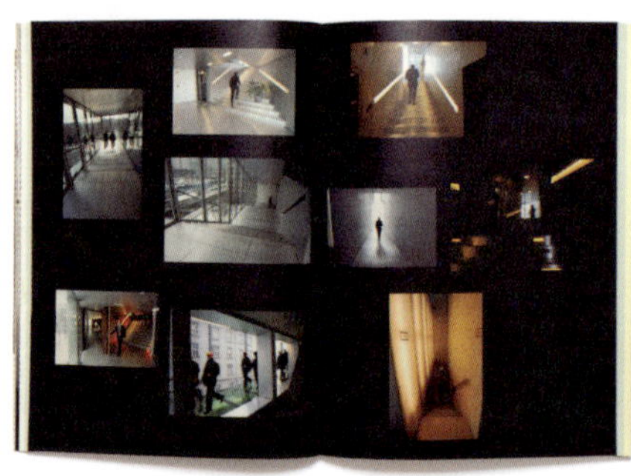

POV
The photographer's path.

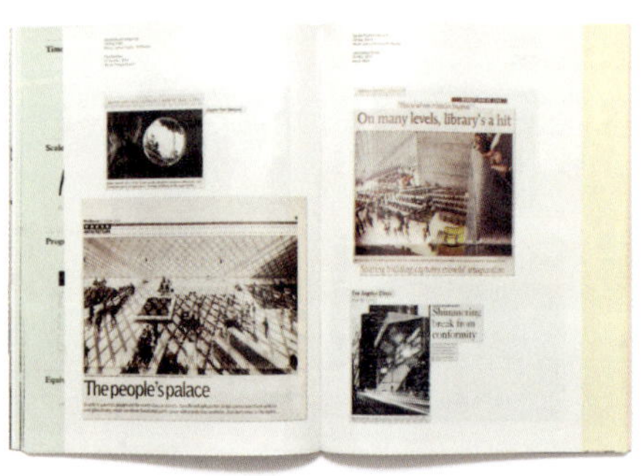

FRONT PAGE
Local newspaper picture editors.

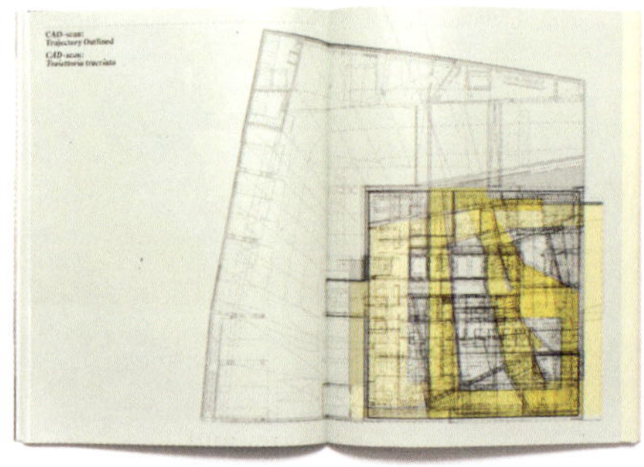

FLATTENED
Collapsed floor plans.

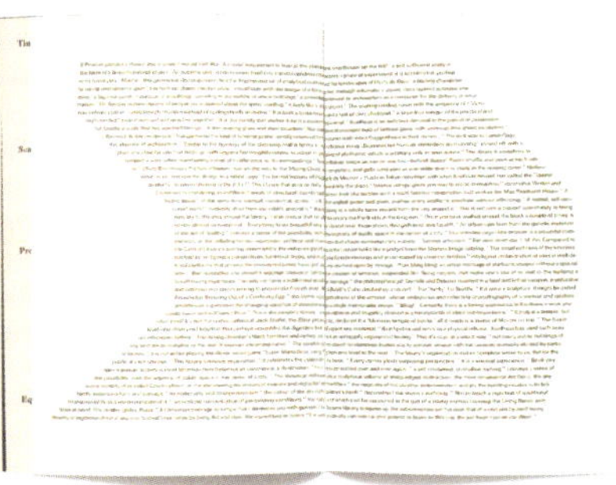

SHAPE
Writing the iconic form.

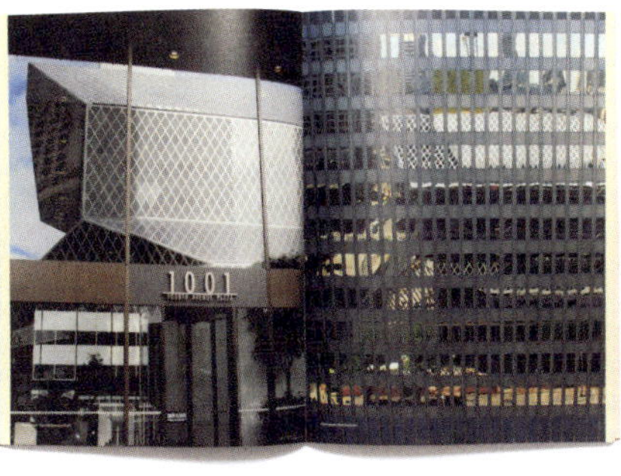

REFLECTION
Image captured in surrounding façades.

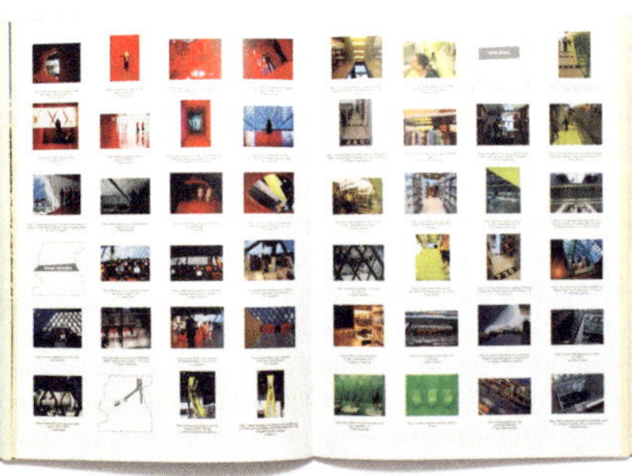

CROWD SOURCE
Tourist as photoeditors.

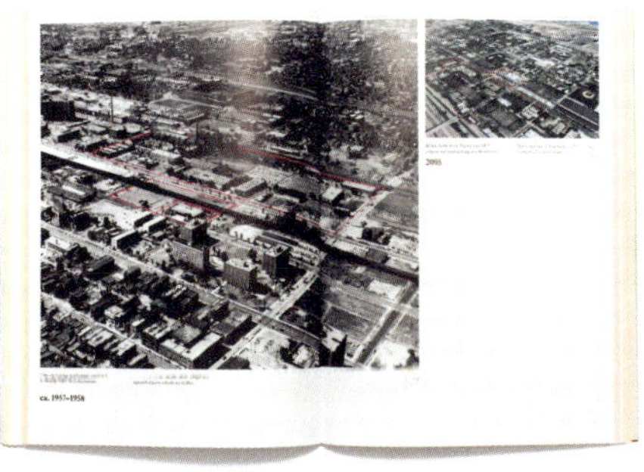

HISTORY
Original conditions as context.

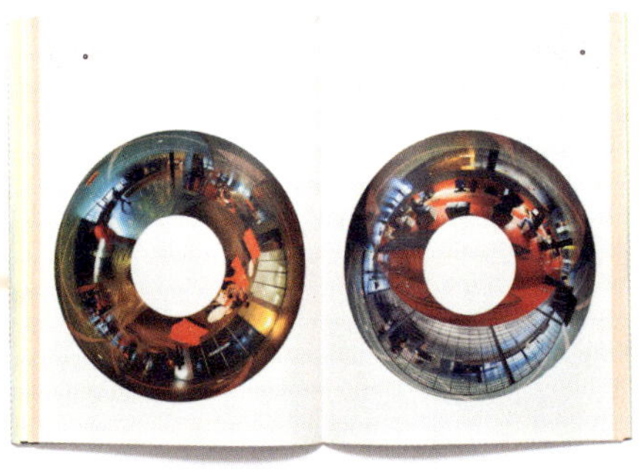

360
Panoramic dramas.

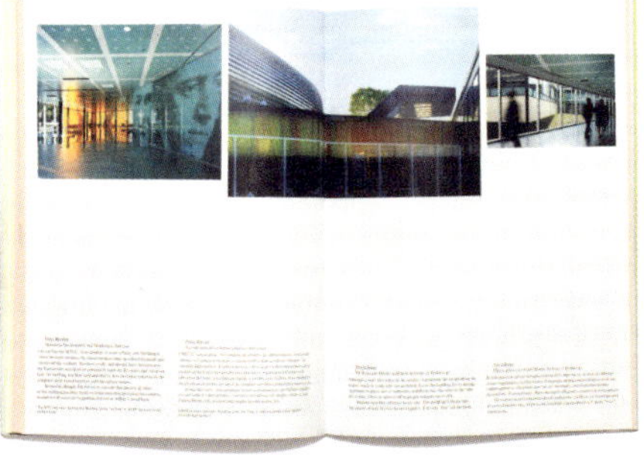

FEEDBACK
Users as critics.

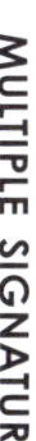

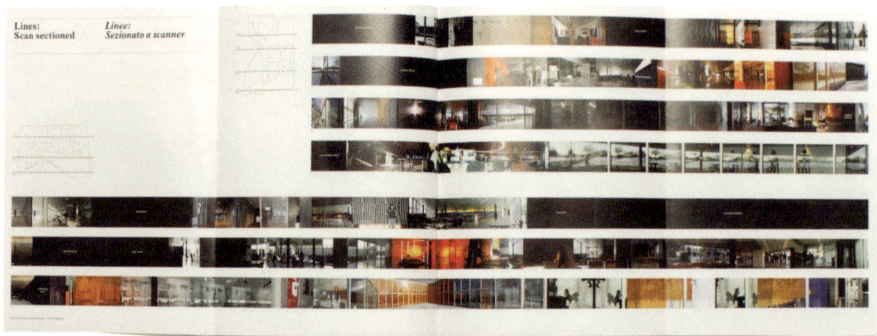

SLICES
Continuous photographic sections.

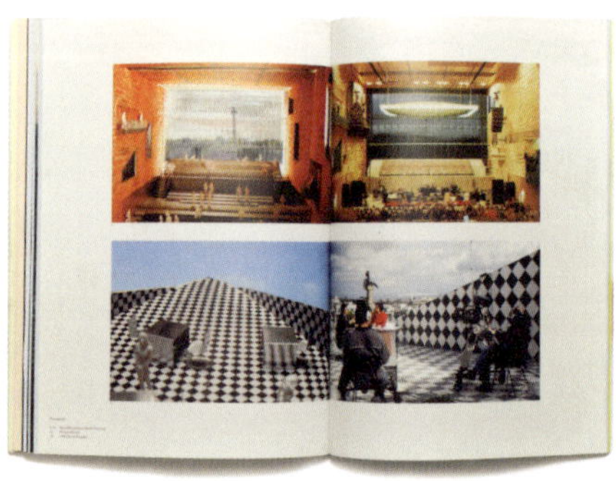

THEN AND NOW
Rendering versus results.

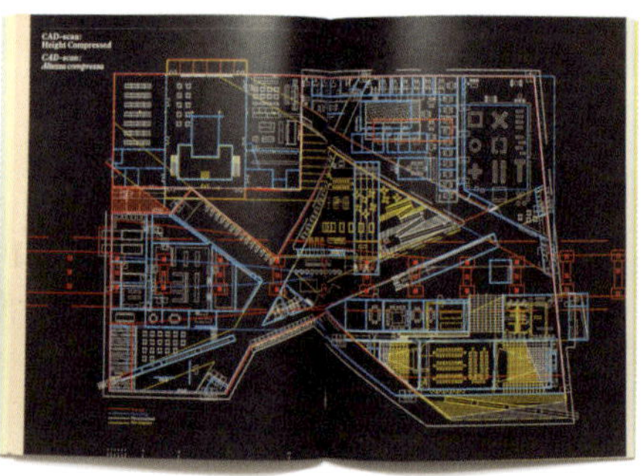

CAD REVELATIONS
Raw material.

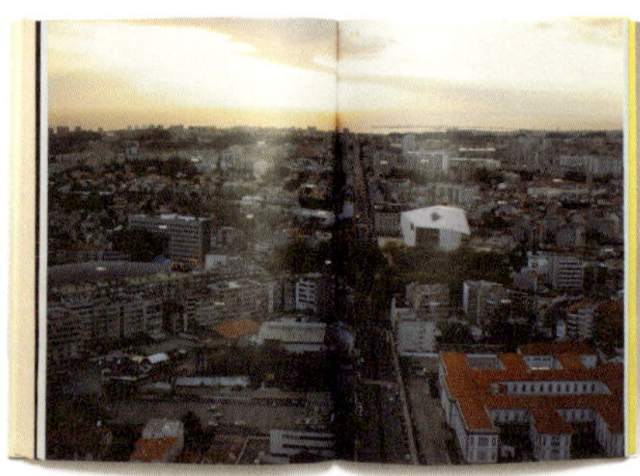

URBAN FABRIC
Expanding the site.

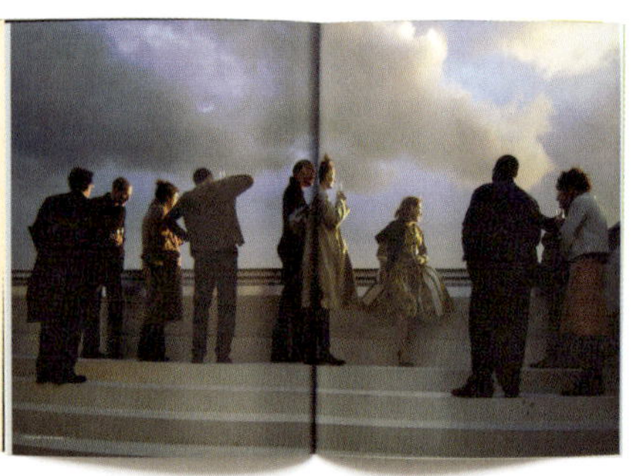

DOCUMENTARY
Imaging from human scale.

CLICHÉS

ANTI-AMBIVALENT

NEO-CACOPHONIC

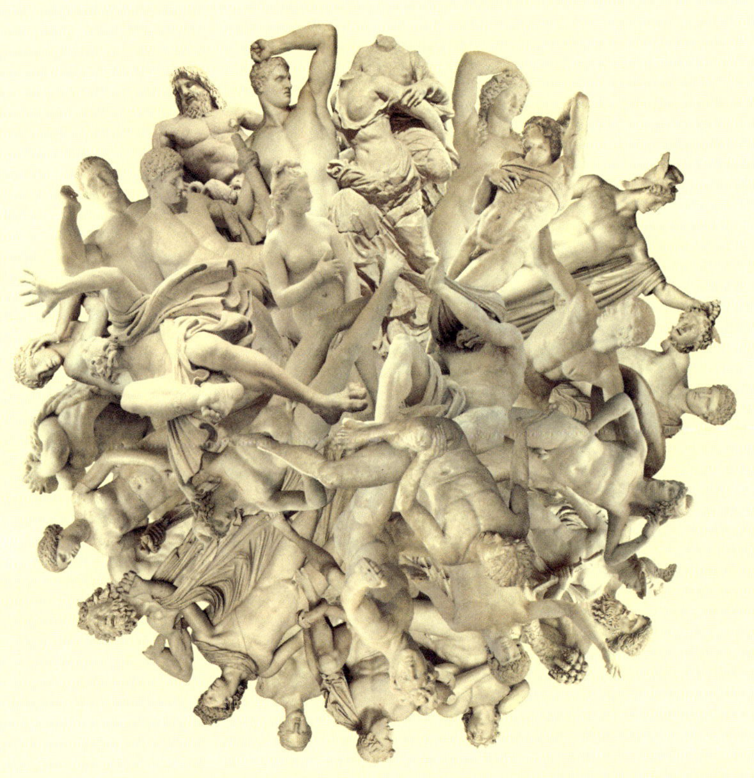

DUODIMENSIONAL

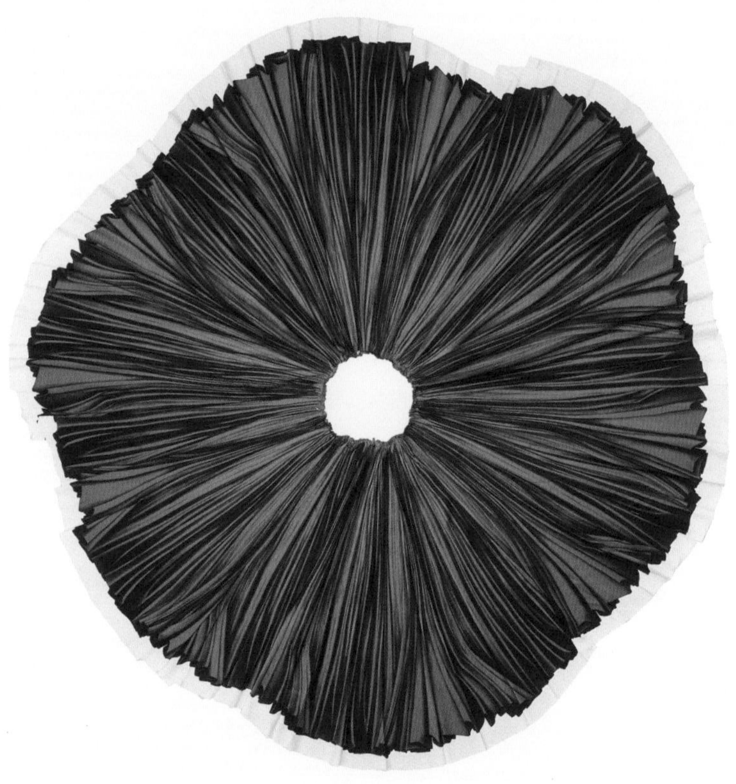

REPETIVISTIC

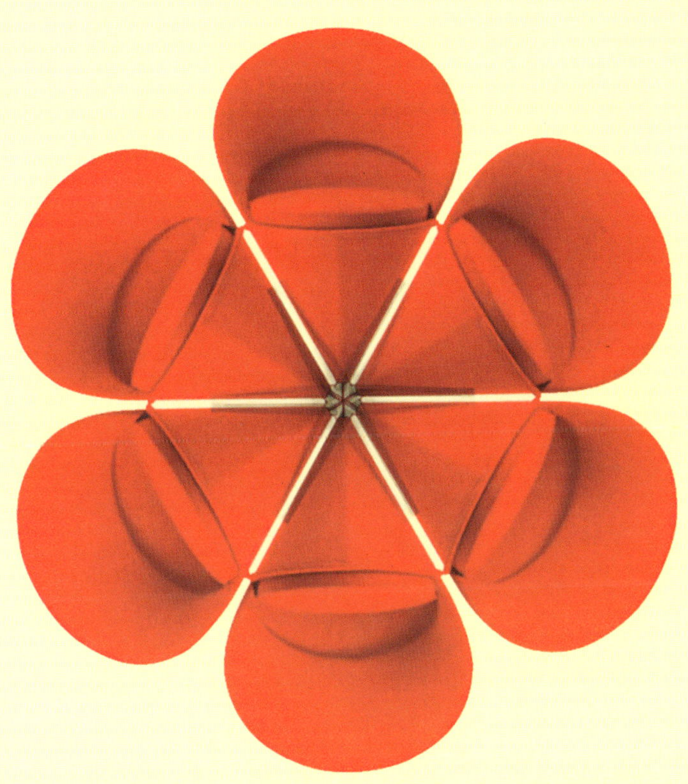

FUZZINESSENCE

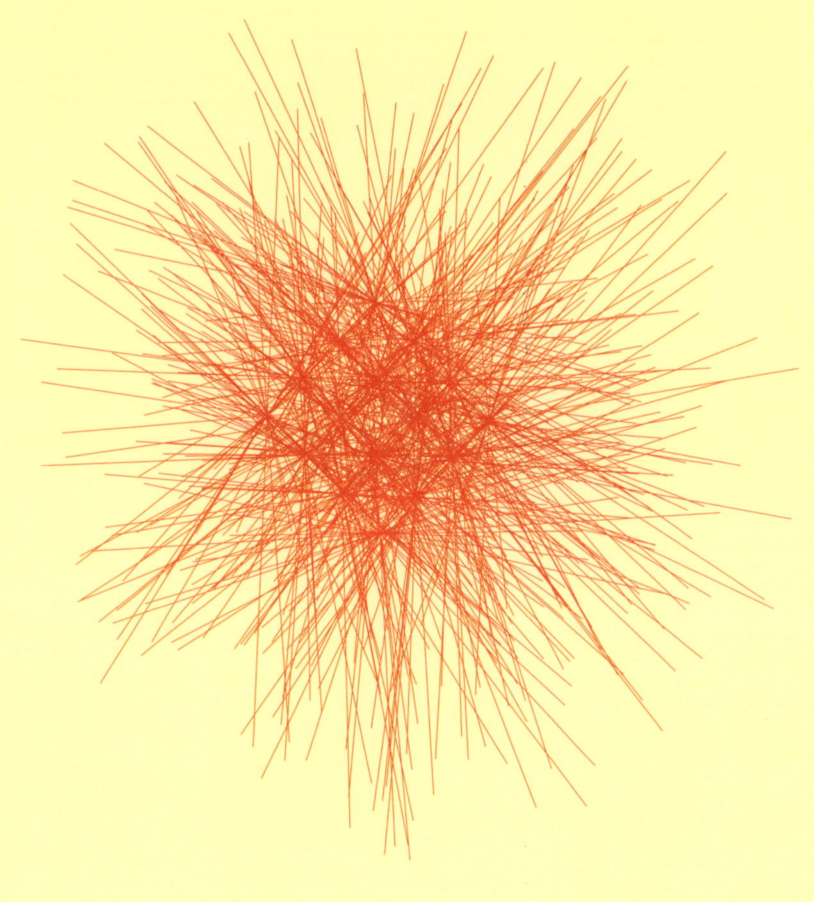

FRACTALITY

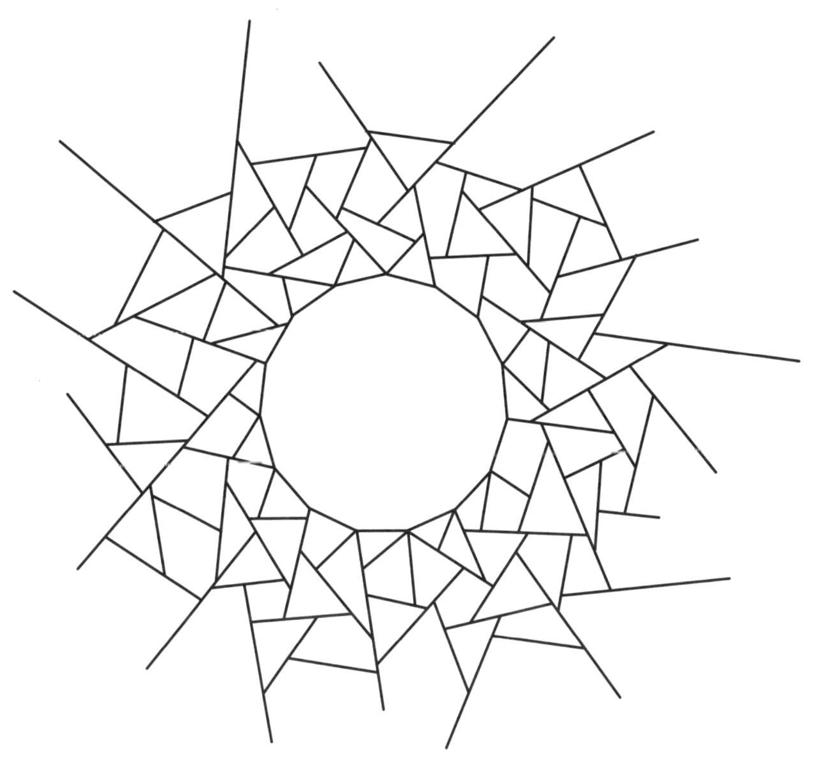

BAROQUISH

MONTESSORISTIC

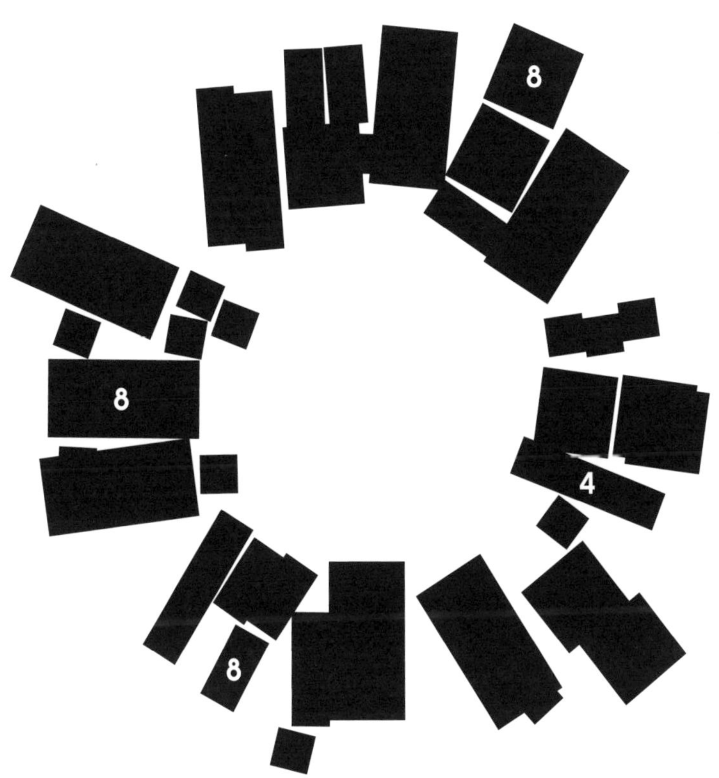

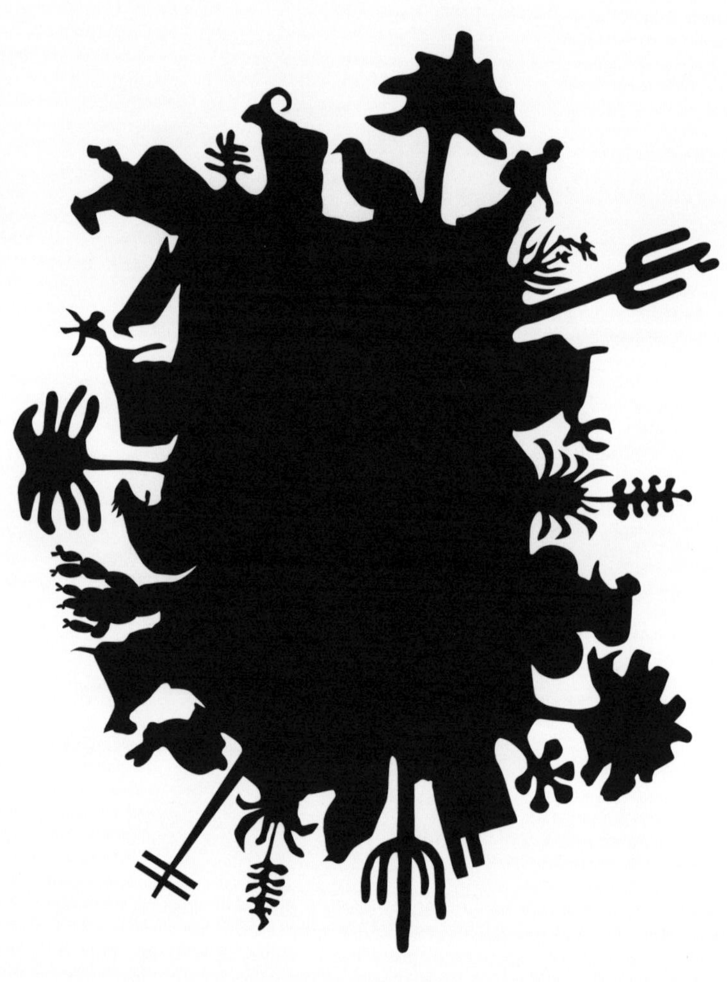

ASTROLOGICALITY

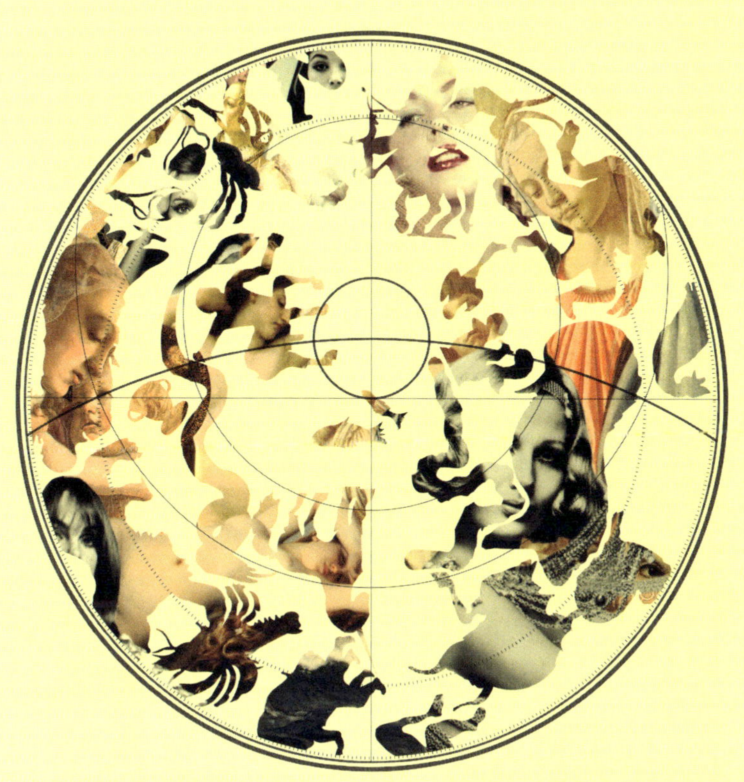

STEALTHINICITY

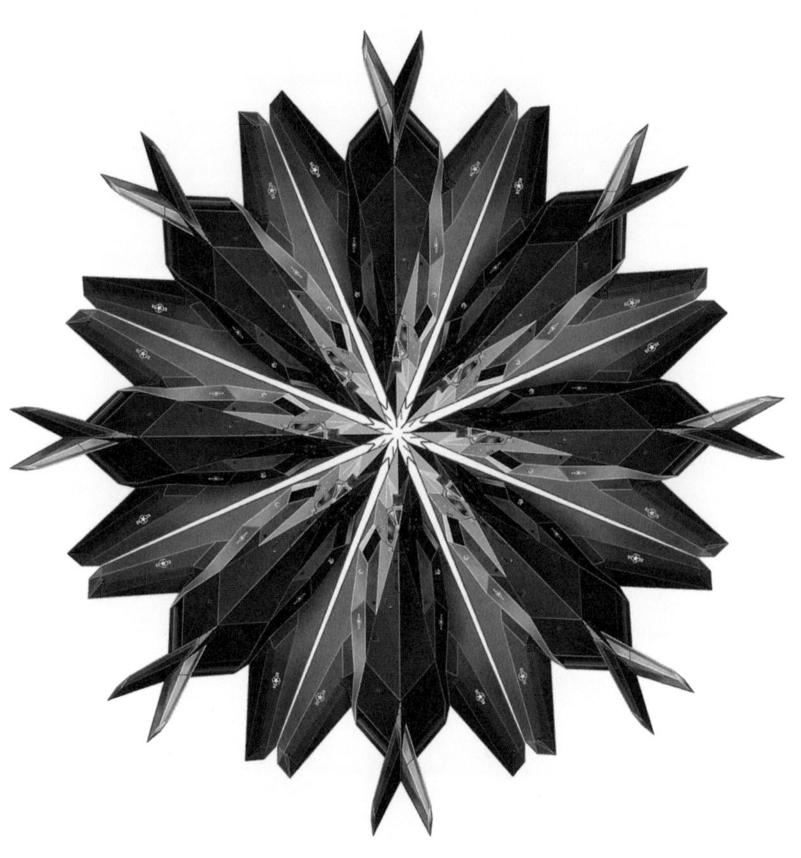

BLOBOLOGIC

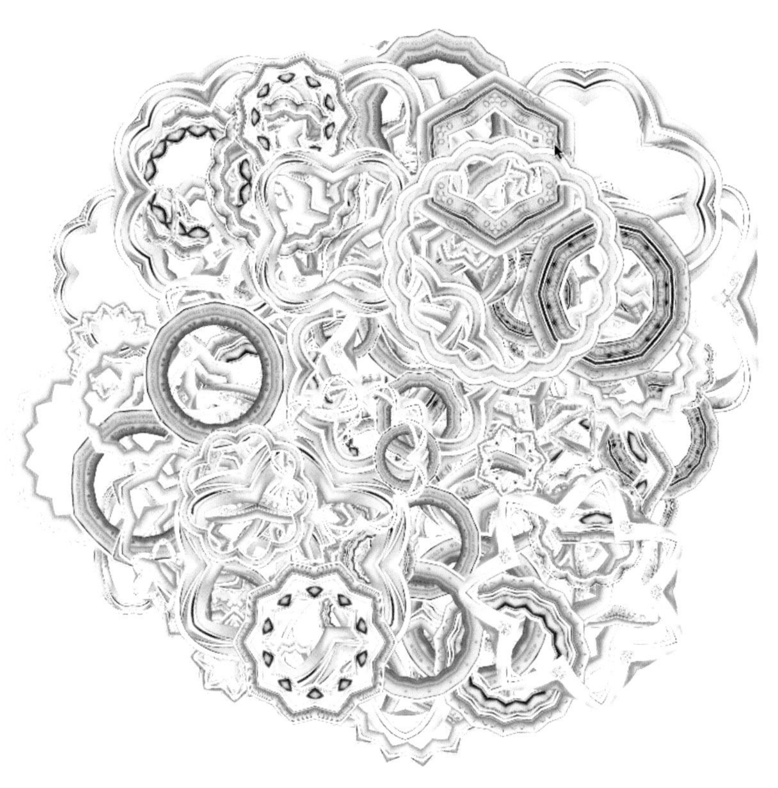

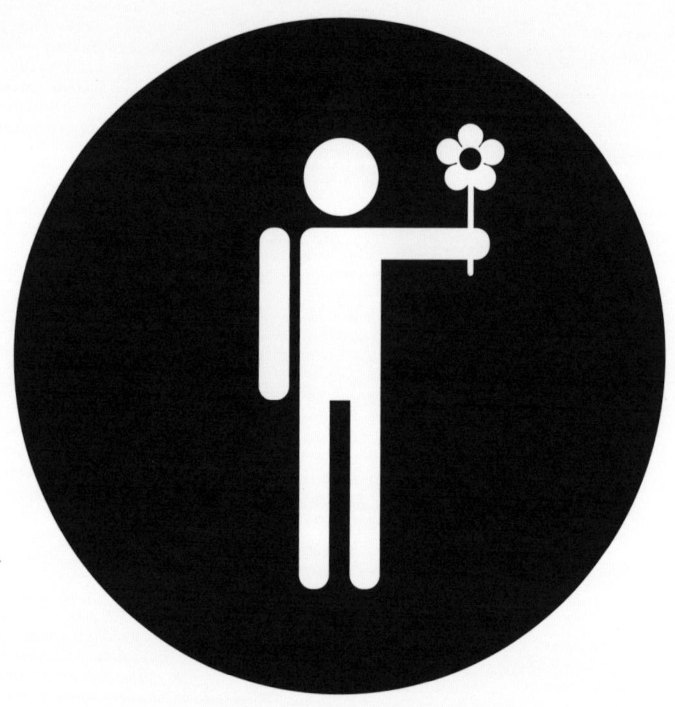

RECEIVED IDEAS with Enrique Walker

MICHAEL ROCK

Since visiting your studio at Columbia I have been thinking a lot about the cliché and its relationship to graphic design. Interestingly, a cliché describes a typographic form. In printing, a cliché is a slug of lead type pre-cast to make up a word—*Sale* or *Notice*—rather than a word composed of individual letters. These pre-cast words are also known as *stereotypes*. The common meaning of cliché, meaning something overused or stale, derived from this idea of the ready-made typographic phrase. (Some even suggest the French word "cliché" derives onomatopoetically from the sound of molten lead filling the type matrix, though I think that is a stretch.) I was curious about the extent that graphic devices, insofar as they are explicitly concerned with mass communication, must always skirt the edge of cliché. (More on that later.) First, tell me about your cliché project and how it came to be.

ENRIQUE WALKER

The Dictionary of Received Ideas (the name of the studio series I have taught at Columbia over the past six years on clichés) was actually the byproduct of an earlier studio series named *Under Constraint*, which examined the use of self-imposed constraints in architecture. Students would embrace voluntary, and therefore arbitrary, constraints at the outset of the design process for the purpose of opening possibilities for their projects.

MR

As a method for displacing responsibility?

EW

Quite the contrary. The studio series was deliberately formulated against the longstanding tradition in design studios of equating process with automatism. That is, design understood as a series of prescribed steps from starting point to outcome, which indeed, as you suggested, has gone hand in hand with obscuring decision-making, as well as with avoiding judgment. *Under Constraint* aimed actually at reasserting authorship. In fact, a constraint would not determine what to do, but rather what not to do. Studentshad to meet an agreement, but the way they did so was not prescribed. So they were condemned to make decisions. And in turn to exert judgment. One of the lessons of that studio series was that a self-imposed constraint, rather than offer an alternative starting point in design processes (to, say, the diagram, the concept, the parti), which was admittedly the ambition at the outset, would ultimately allow you to become aware of the way you do things.

MR

Self-awareness was the product?

EW

Exactly. But self-awareness was also the challenge. Students were generally very decisive about the definition of the rules of the game. But were then, in most cases, hesitant, or far too cautious, when moving ahead, as if they were expecting the rules of the game to dictate their decisions. Since the rules of the game were self-imposed, and were as such arbitrary, they would not guarantee an outcome. Which was, for many of them who were used to orthodox design methodologies, quite disturbing. Let's say all of us were required to write a sonnet. Some of us might write an interesting one, whereas others might not. And still others might not even be able to write one. There is no one-to-one relationship between a constraint and a result. In fact, an adequate constraint is an obstacle to an adequate result (that is to say, a predictable result). So the main realization was that, precisely by pushing you to work in a different way, a constraint could bring your assumptions and received ideas to light.

MR

So that investigation of self-consciousness evolved into the work on the received idea?

EW

Yes, that triggered a new studio series on the identification and instrumentalization of clichés. If the first series was influenced by the work of Oulipo (who, incidentally, define themselves as rats who build the labyrinth from which they propose to escape), the new series was based on Gustave Flaubert's *Le Dictionnaire des idées reçues*. Flaubert inadvertently began this project at the age of nine, when he decided to write down the stupid remarks of a Parisian lady who would visit his parents in Rouen. Over the years, this gradually evolved into a book that would archive all the ready-made phrases and platitudes one needed to employ in order to succeed socially, what he described as an *Encyclopedia of stupidity*. Flaubert's goal was to produce a book so exhaustive that it would silence the reader for fear of using one of the ready-made phrases listed in it. This was the starting point for the studio project: to record architectural clichés of the past ten years: recurrent design strategies that haunt contemporary architectural culture.

MR

Were these always material or visual aspects of practice? They weren't clichés of theory …

EW

We focus on clichés that have implications in design. And, not unlike some of Flaubert's entries, which tell us what to say, we formulate manuals for their use. In other words, instructions. For instance, Flaubert would instruct the reader, after a certain name to "despise" or "praise." You just had to follow.

MR

Very useful …

EW

So the initial goal was to produce an archive of clichés exhaustive enough to block students. Which would in turn compel them to formulate other ways to operate. On the other hand, the studio offered a way out of that block: to use the cliché as a starting point. Once defined, a cliché becomes an *objet trouvé* of sorts, and can be displaced and used towards other results. And to one's advantage. Therefore students do not mimic clichés, but follow the instructions in the manual. And thereby inevitably misuse the clichés.

MR

So there is investigation—to discover and catalogue the clichés—and then production—where they are employed to create something unexpected.

EW

In fact, the studio project implies both trajectories. First we detect clichés and write manuals for each of them. Second, we use these manuals to design, and in turn, potentially, open up alternative design strategies.

MR

How do you define cliché for the studio?

EW

I prefer the term *received idea*, which suggests uncritical reception. But the term *cliché* tends to stick, and usually takes over. We resort to two definitions. On the one hand, we accept the definition of clichés as ideas that were at some point vigorous, but became stale after recurrent use. On the other, we also define clichés as solutions that have outlived the problems they originally addressed. For example, the role of cats in early spy films: a villain caressed a cat on his lap, arguably because the director wanted to frame the villain without showing his face. The *problem* was how to frame the villain without showing his face—the *solution* was the cat. Later spy films portray villains who caress cats without de-framing the image. Admittedly, the second definition is strategic, since it allows for us to put the emphasis on the formulation of problems as critical to design. We go back to the issue of constraints as tools …

MR

So in your project you would redeploy the cat?

EW

We keep the cat, and look for ways the cat could acquire a new role. In other words, we gather design strategies that are no longer connected to the problems they originally addressed, and try to connect them to other problems, thereby redefining those design strategies.

MR

Solutions in search of problems? I have been in large-scale branding studios in China where teams of designers produce logos and "identities" all day long in anticipation of clients who may need them in the future. They are shells waiting to be filled by new occupants. Is problem-solving in itself obsolete, one of those ideas that once was salient but has become stale?

EW

Architects usually take problems for granted and rely on archived solutions (a dictionary of received ideas of sorts). The assumption in the studio is that inventive design is driven by the insightful formulation of problems. Take architectural competitions. Compelling entries usually identify critical problems within a brief as opportunities for design.

MR

And that is a form of authorship? I'm especially interested in this relationship between authorship and cliché. It seems like the *received idea* essentially contradicts originality. To speak in cliché is to assume a prefabricated vocabulary. However, the self-conscious manipulation of banal gestures, reinvesting them with new meaning, is a kind of authorship in itself. Isn't that what Jencks called Double Coding? It seems like the film metaphor is apropos: a director manipulates the history of film over and over again to his/her own end and, in the way those clichés are manipulated, claims authorship. At some point the cat becomes a code that can be endlessly recycled in surprising new ways.

EW

The studios are not about originality, but about awareness. By the same token, being aware of the strategies you use, and the problems you use them for, may potentially trigger invention. In the earlier studio series, constraints were arbitrary problems that you imposed on yourself to uncover the ways in which you did things, and potentially, the ways in which you could do things. The cliché operates in a similar manner. Just as with constraints, you adopt an arbitrary problem to design. And you also know that this is innocuous unless driven by an agenda: the goal towards which you use it. In fact, a cliché is a constraint precisely because it is a design strategy you are obliged to work with, but which offers no promise, since you know it is stale. So you have to work against it.

MR

Then it seems like the goal of design is to reveal its own sources and to let the viewer know that the designer knows that they know …

EW

The ultimate goal is, actually, to efface the sources. Once you have triggered a *finding*, it does not really matter what led you to it. Whether it is a self-imposed constraint or a cliché, they are *scaffolding*, following Raymond Queneau's notion. That is, structures that would disappear without leaving traces once they have allowed for constructing a building. Once you detach the object from the system you used to produce it (which in architecture is usually equated with meaning), the question is how to assess the object. In fact, it would be pointless to assess a building by looking at the scaffolding with which it was built. You must assess the building itself. And therefore situate the building within the genealogy of strategies that have addressed a certain problem. In other words, you do not assess an architectural project by examining its relation to the process, but by examining its relevance within the field. Production and judgment rely on different frameworks. OMA's Casa da Musica, for instance, is an interesting project not because it started out as a scaled-up model of a house, but because it ultimately redefined the type of the concert hall. And it would be sterile to ceaselessly (and blindly) follow the procedure of scaling up models to produce projects. The finding renders irrelevant the operation that triggered it.

MR

There is an essential difference between the way we talk about cliché in the architectural sense versus in the graphic sense. As I mentioned before, graphic design is about dealing with conventional languages and affects. I guess a modernist critic would say all affect is kitsch because it is intentionally trying to produce an emotion. In a certain light, cliché is the material device of graphic design. So every corporate-identity program, for instance, is something of a cliché even when it's intentionally playing with the codes of corporate identity, such as consistency, minimalism, etc. A banal designer only reproduces. An informed designer uses the cultural codes in surprising ways.

EW

That is, you use the cliché as if it were an *objet trouvé*.

MR

Or embody the cliché wholeheartedly —doing it deadpan or investing all your energy into it. That energizes it. In which case, working a cliché becomes a critique in itself. That is what we were tying to do with the Prada Guilt Project—or even the Prada wallpapers in general. Guilt used the device of the branding manual coupled with this very real human emotion. The attachment of Guilt to banal phrases such as "Isn't it time you tried …" or "Ask your doctor about …" reawakened them in a funny and fantastical way.

EW

Could you describe some of the clichés here (gesturing to the images on the table)?

MR

In the book we literally label them in terms of what they are. So you can have a cliché of minimalism or severe reduction—take away all of the extraneous and it leaves something pure. Or you can have a cliché of flattening. A Prada skirt is flattened, and the flattening itself makes it graphic. Even in a computer program you flatten layers as a way to finalize something. Or you have the step and repeat. Here, a Panton image is repeated and rotated. It becomes this goofy flower. The pure rotation and repetition turns one thing into another: roughness, fractal, Baroque. Then there is the contemporary trope of the Photoshop® filter, the prefabricated effect. We would see all of this as the production of the studio, even though they're so essentially different from or unrelated to each other.

EW

I imagine you did not design them with the idea of this set in mind.

MR

No, they come from radically different times, for different clients and by many different designers working in the studio. We chose them with the idea of the set. The selection was driven purely by the constraint of the circular form. On the other hand, we're self-conscious about the fact that something like a flower or a rotation is something that we do all the time. There's some aspect of the graphic language that is always recognizable. And that seems to be the difference between the architectural and the graphic. For language to work, you have to recognize immediately—"Is that a word?"—for it even to operate in the field. Words need to follow conventions. New words can be coined but they must follow some basic rules.

EW

Interestingly, in architecture a design strategy usually becomes a cliché when it is recognizable, once its appearance weighs more than its performance. This has in fact been the criterion for us to identify clichés. We have started to bring together the entries we have recorded in the past few years, and we've already collected about a hundred. We provide a user's manual for each cliché. And also a brief history of the cliché, which involves determining the moment when the design strategy was originally formulated and the moment when the original objective was lost.

MR

Innocence. Is it a loss of innocence?

EW

Or effectiveness …

MR

Even though it might be derivative, it can still be effective, but at a certain point it's both derivative and ineffective. In graphic design typographic gestures are used to signify certain things. They're used a million times but can still either be used well or in an unselfconscious and meaningless way. At times the cliché is extremely effective and smart and at times it's completely un-self-aware and dumb. One of my favorite rants by the great Modernist designer Paul Rand was his list of the unacceptable tropes of postmodern design: (reading) "squiggles, pixels, doodles, dingbats, ziggurats; boudoir colors …."

EW

My knowledge of graphic design clichés is limited. But I could identify a few amongst architects …

MR

We could definitely outline all the graphic-design clichés of architects …

EW

Architects have a limited scope. I find interesting that the underscore, for instance, whose original function in the mid-1990s was arguably to separate first and last names when registering e-mail addresses, at a time when eliminating the space between them was extremely peculiar, is still prevalent to string words together in project titles. Architects have kept the affectation even though it has no function today.

MR

The parenthetical is another example, the (re)presentation—

EW

A late-1980s cliché …

MR

—derived from Derrida, this idea of de-stabilizing language that carries on, project after project: there's always the parenthetical, saying two contradictory ideas can be contained in one construction. It's a linguistic and typographic cliché that has run its course but I'm sure it can be re-invested again in some new way we haven't thought of yet.

EW

Today, there is a preference for square brackets, and far less loaded terms.

MR

Or it's bold or italic but it's always about typography de-stabilizing the word. Is there an unlimited font of clichés?

EW

I think the question has to do with the cycle of revival of clichés.

MR

Revivalism?

EW

Clichés have a cycle. They emerge as the depleted version of a formerly vigorous idea. Then they are forgotten. But then in turn they may be revived.

MR

Like sideburns in Brooklyn. But is it always laden with historicism? Even if you were the first person to go back to that reference, that still seems like finding, not making. There's a whole graphic design movement based on discovering really obscure texts and republishing them. Is there a point where cliché is always revival? Is it never about the production of something new? Or are you saying that the overlapping of clichés and the dealing with them is the device that generates newness now?

EW

We try to look at recent clichés, design strategies of the past decade, precisely those that have not yet been stabilized by history, and that therefore do not imply references. They haunt us without us being aware. When clichés become old, they weigh as references. When they become older, they cease being clichés. I mean, when you read Flaubert's dictionary entries today, three-quarters of them make little sense.

MR

It would be an interesting experiment to see if, next to your 150 architectural clichés, we could generate 150 typographic equivalencies. One informs the other. At a certain point in the '80s, graphic designers and architects were often looking at the same theory. Graphic designers were trying to find a way to incorporate theory in their work in the same way architects were. Often the *misunderstanding* of the theory generated the work. But for the professional designer, someone grappling with designing things, there is an insecurity or uncertainty. At some point you evaluate your own work and ask yourself, "Am I aware? Is this work banal? Or is it interesting?" You have to recognize your own clichés and understand if you're actually manipulating them or being driven by them. Maybe that's the point of a studio.

EW

When you were at *ANY*, for instance, you often played with the rules of the game of the existing graphic project, as well as with the clichés derived from it, and in turn invented a number of techniques that would have probably been otherwise unimaginable.

MR

At *ANY* it was about simple things, twisting conventions. If the footnote is usually at the bottom, what if we move it to the middle? The right and left page are now swapped, and so on. The funny thing is that many of the *ANY* affections became real clichés in themselves.

EW

You were basically adopting clichés but changing their role. You formulate a number of operations upon what exists, and then determine what may have led to an invention. Some operations are of interest, and some are not.

MR

You're trying to evaluate what you're doing, but also to create a narrative around it. Retroactively establish an oeuvre. In every designer's book they're attempting to create some narrative out of a system that is almost brutally resistant to narrative because, as you know, a designer's career is such a haphazard set of—

EW

Accidents …

MR

—and yet somehow the story has to be told that all those things are building towards something. What story will be told in the end?

EW

You work back and forth. You look back at the work you have done. And this allows you to articulate an argument for the work you will potentially do.

MR

So it requires a self-conscious negotiation between the field you work in, all the work you've done before, and the kind of work you want to do in the future.

EW

But the work in the future is equally accidental. In *The Art of the Novel,* Milan Kundera claims that life is a relentless process of acquiring experience which ultimately cannot be applied. The conditions you encounter are always different.

MR

That's the perfect description of a design career.

Logotype

GuilT

Color Variations

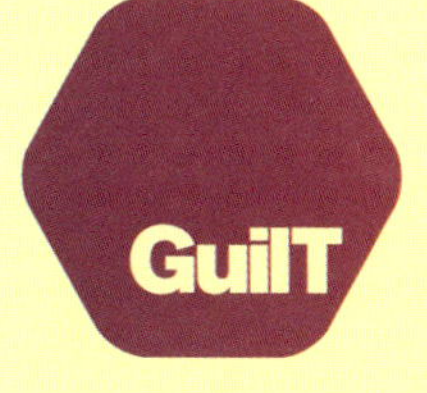

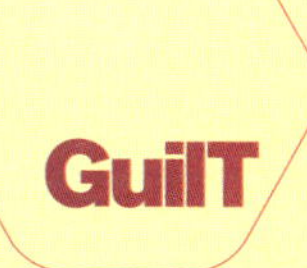

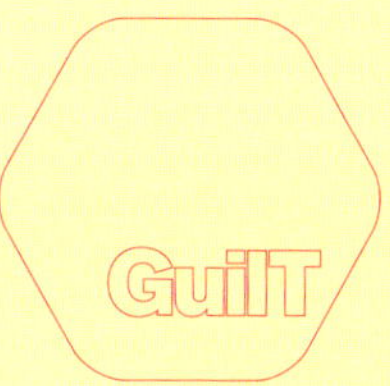

Transportation

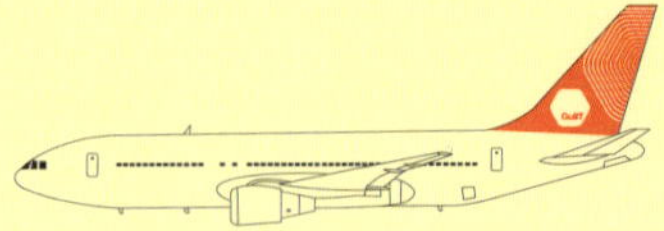

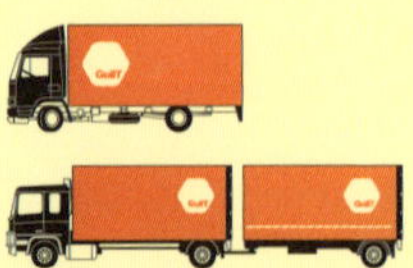

Uniforms

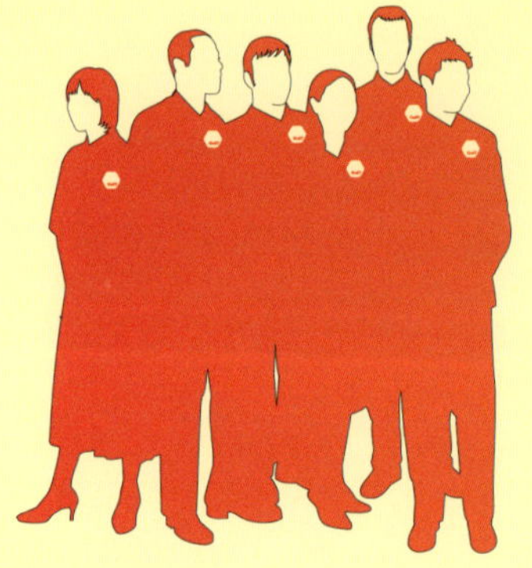

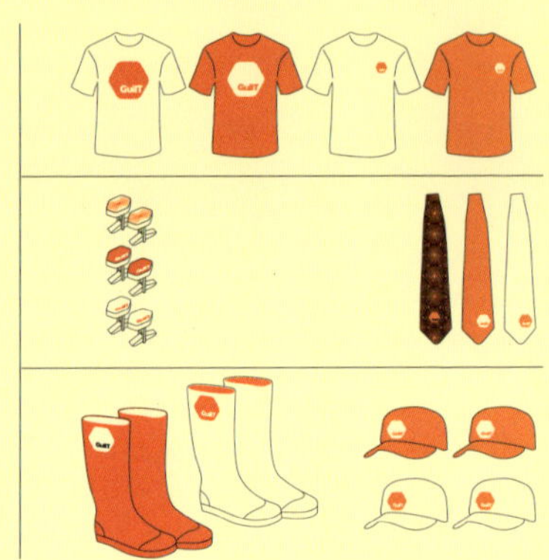

Environmental

Signs

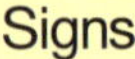

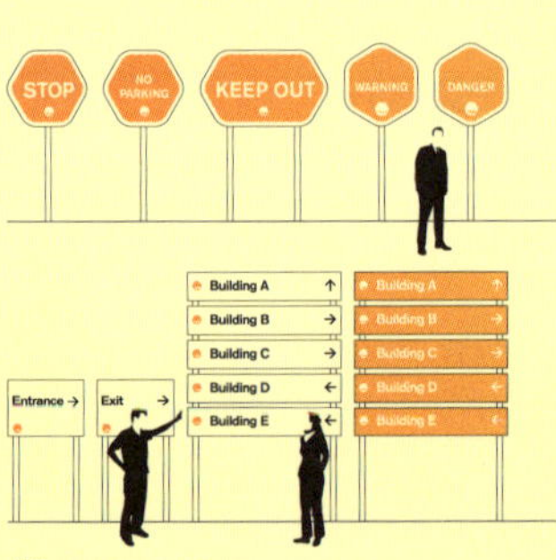

Flags

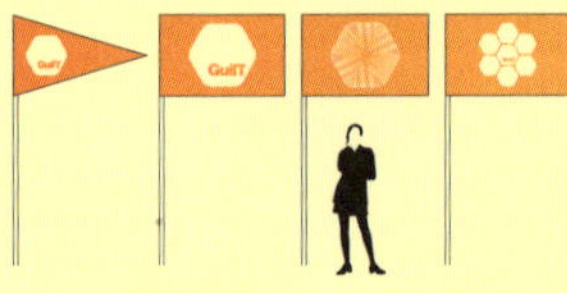

Banners

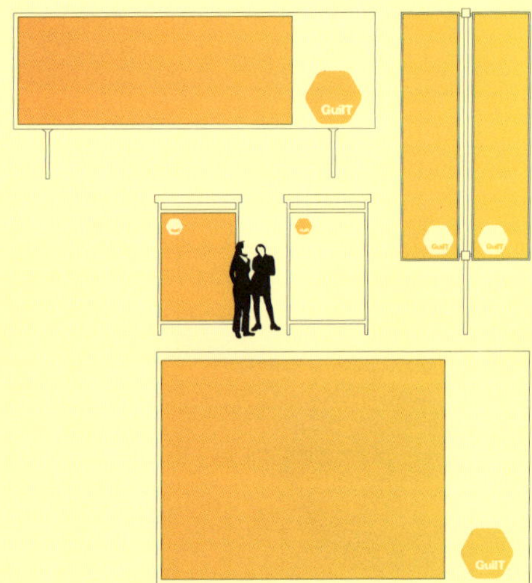

Merchandise

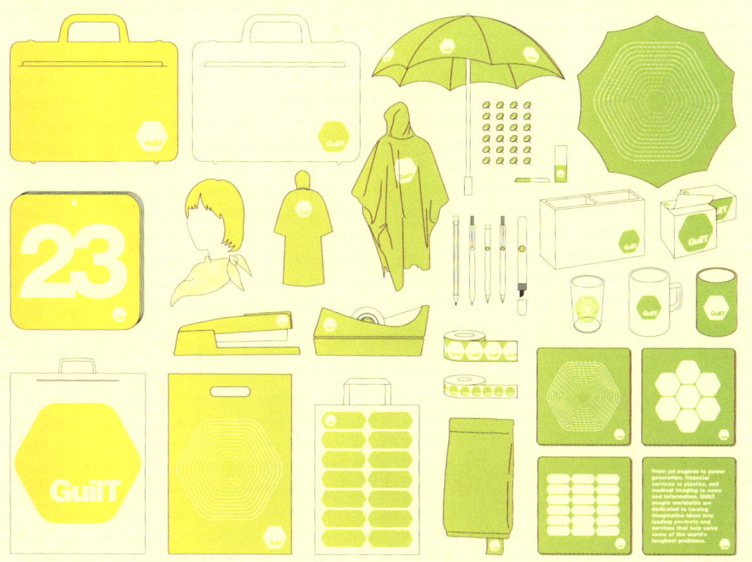

Boxes/Packaging

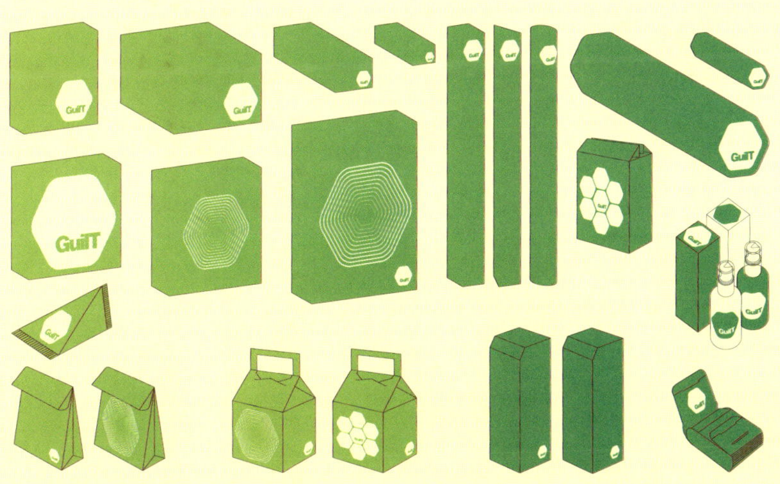

Ask your doctor about

GuilT

isn't
it
time
you
tried
?

GuilT

MULTIPLE SIGNATURES

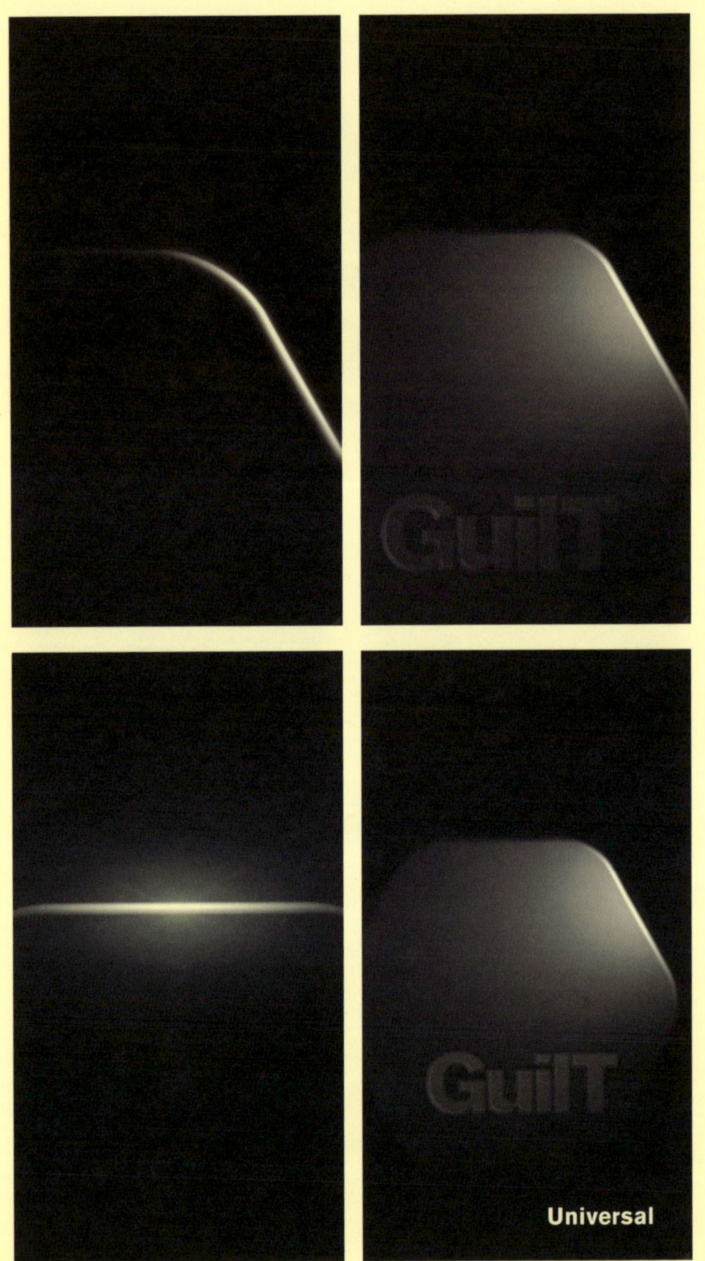
GuilT
GuilT
Universal

PRADAPEDIA

2×4

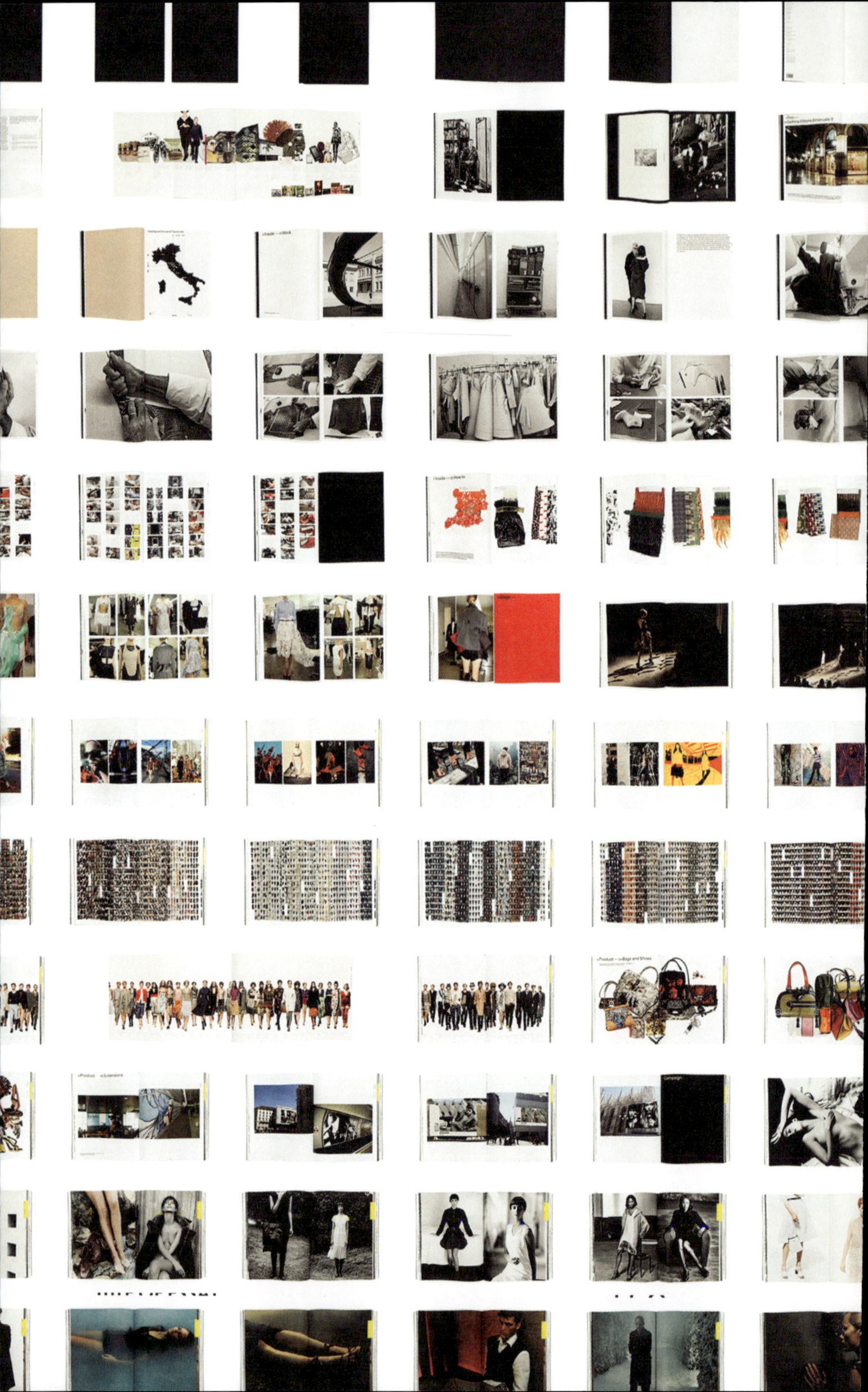

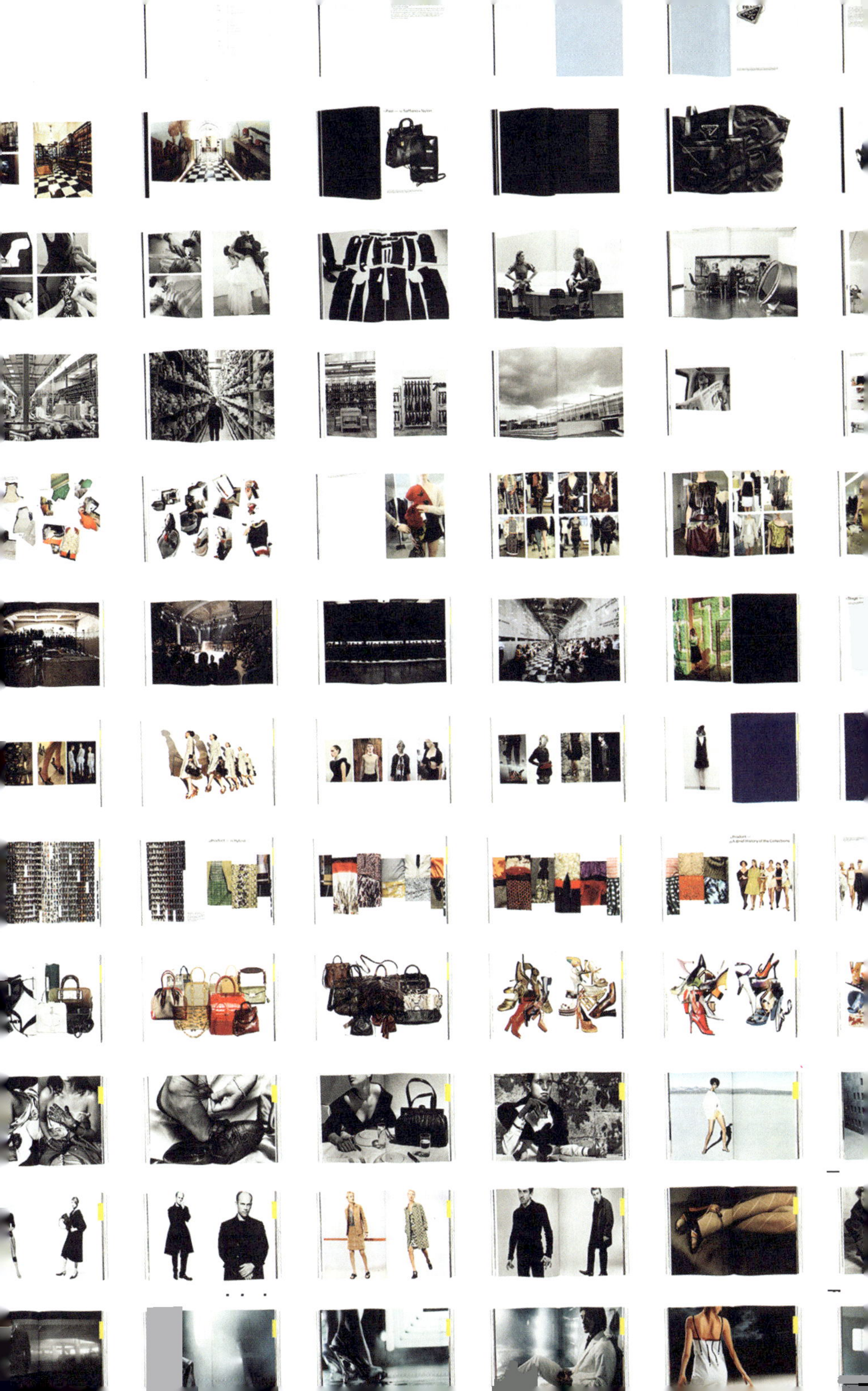

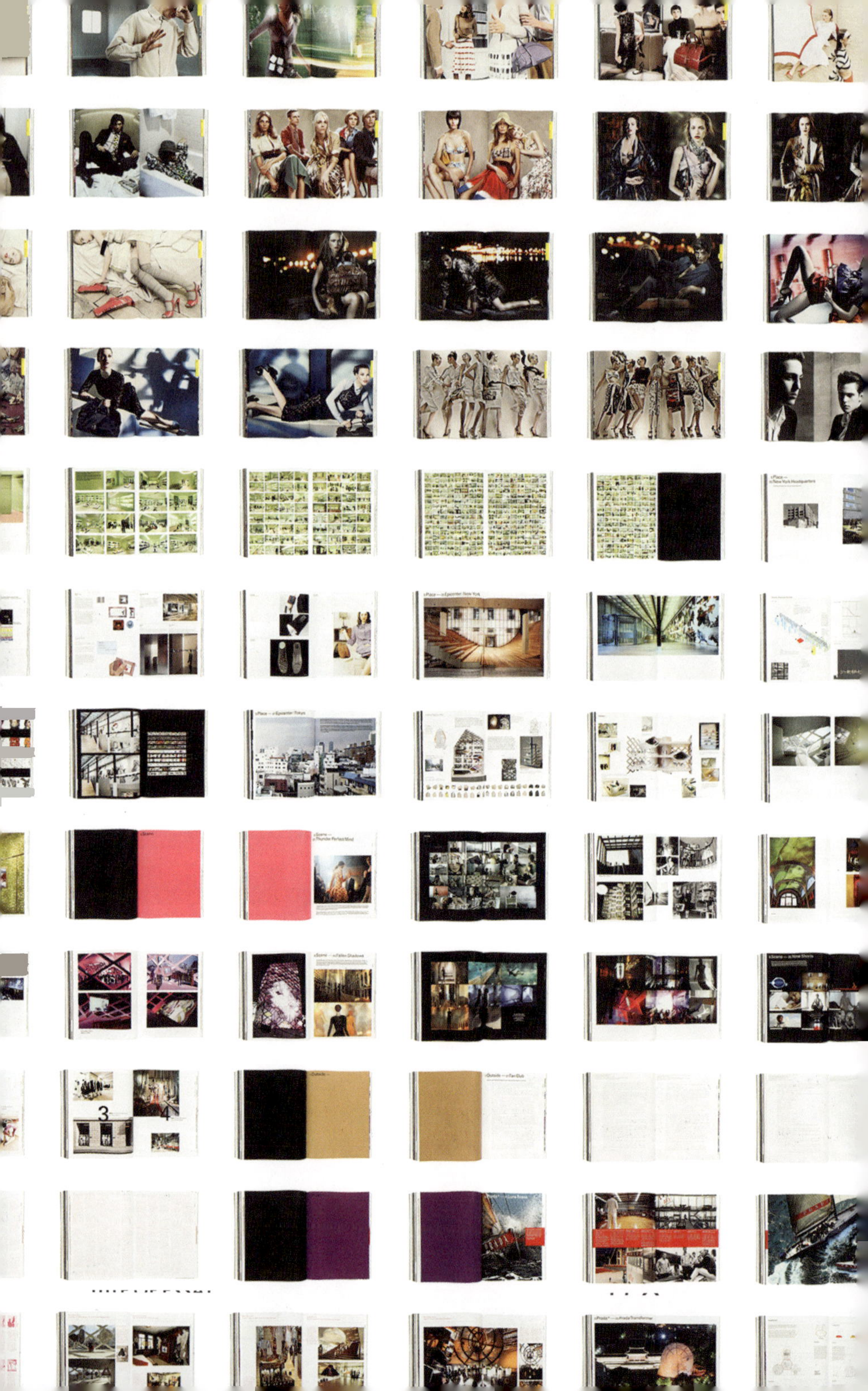

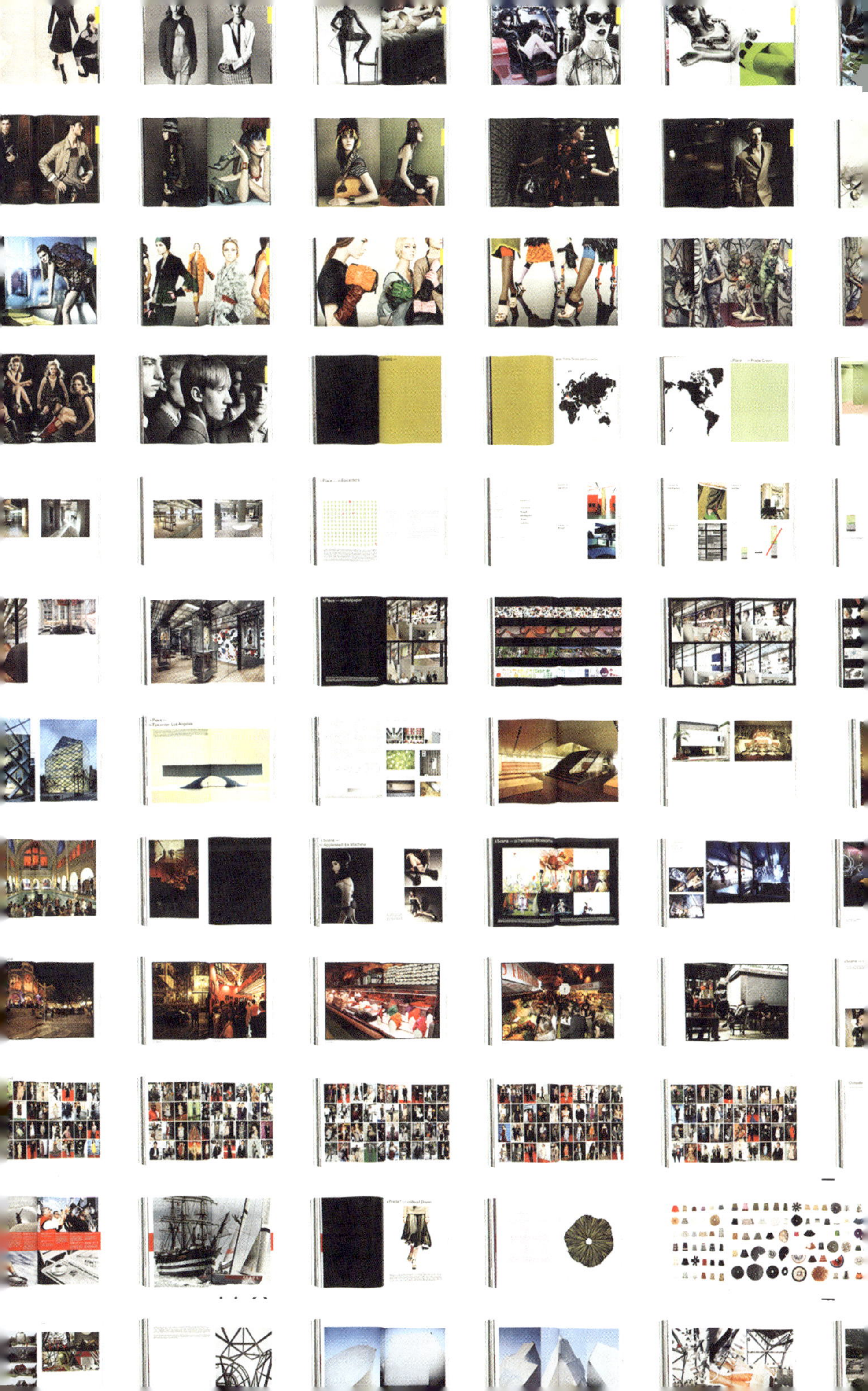

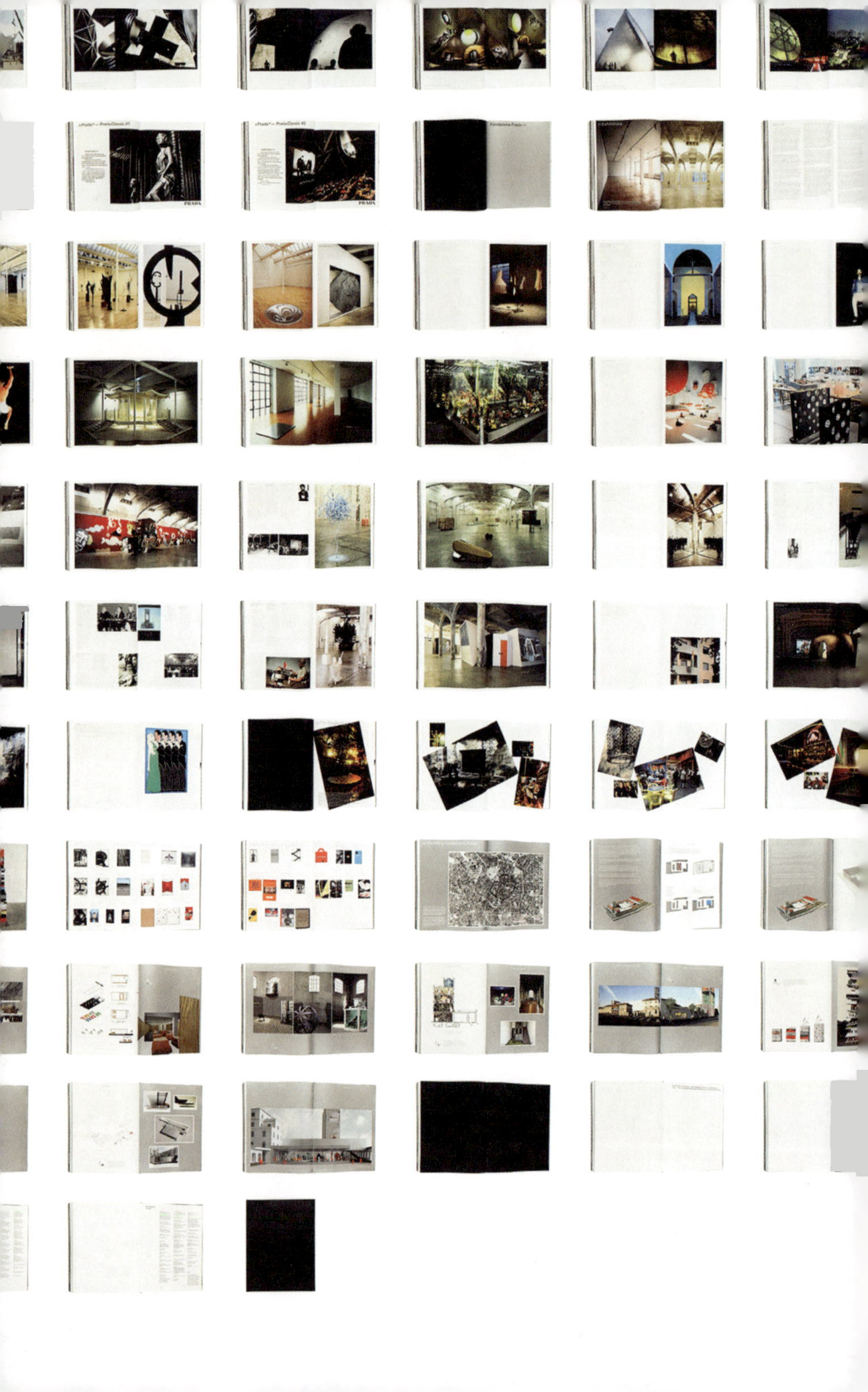

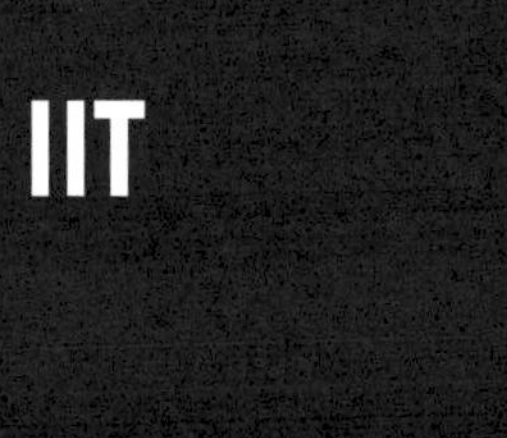
IIT

IIT McCormick Tribune Center

Late in 1998 we started working on the graphic design for the new student center at the Illinois Institute of Technology—the campus famously designed by Mies van der Rohe.

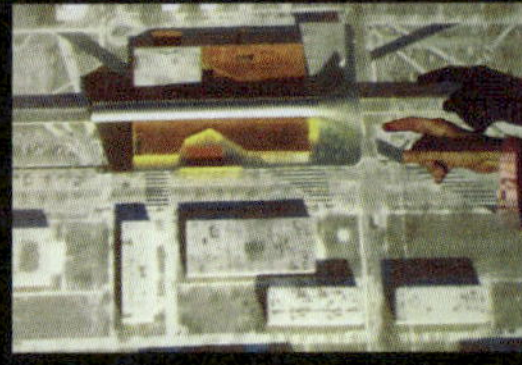

Mies van der Rohe, Rem Koolhaas and OMA had won the architectural competition with a radical building, wedged under an elevated train track, that featured a huge, 700-foot, sound-muffling tunnel on its roof.

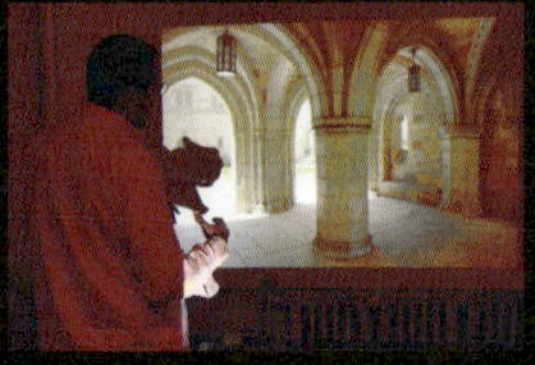

We wanted to develop a unified graphic language for an academic building. So we went back and looked closely at Yale—the school many of us either taught at or attended—and its famous Gothic architecture.

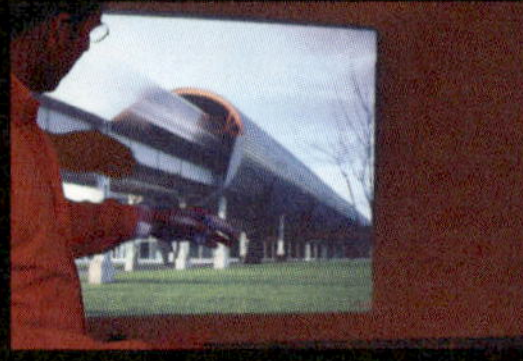

Here is the building, five years after starting. The tunnel sits directly on the roof and the building is squeezed underneath.

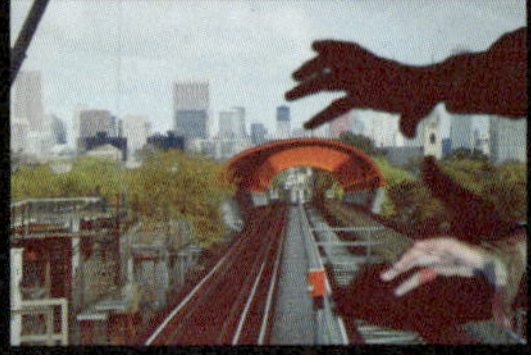

From the train heading north, the tunnel frames the skyline. Our challenge was basically to coat the walls with a kind of artificial significance: textures, images, surfaces.

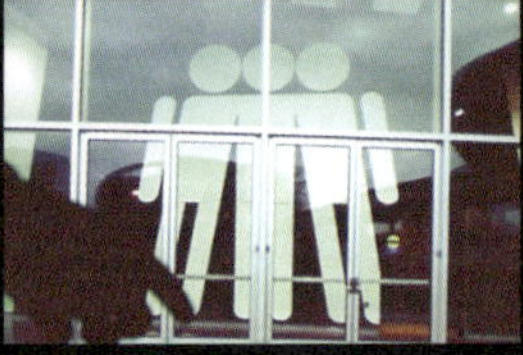

Our non-generic figures populate the building at many different scales, from the 15-foot-tall "Togetherness" icon here at the south entrance to one-inch pixels.

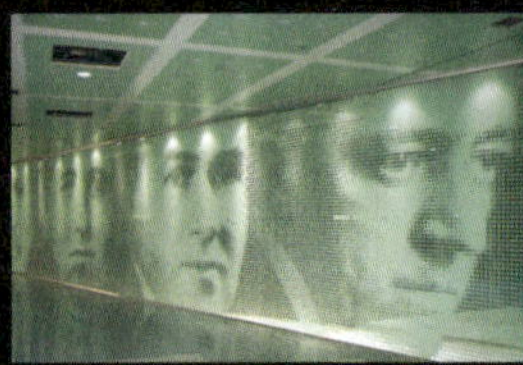

The portraits are integral to the glass surface. (Note the bare sheetrock ceiling. When the surfaces aren't artificially "dressed" they are left flagrantly "naked.")

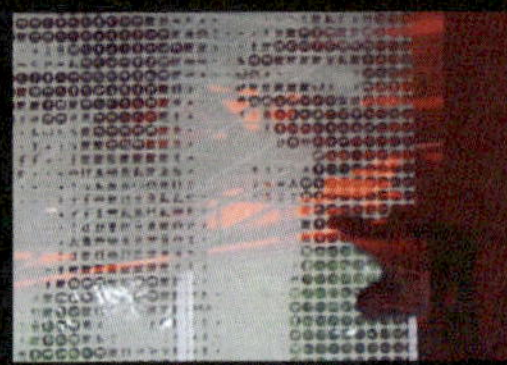

Upon closer inspection you realize that the portraits are made up of our tiny pixel-people.

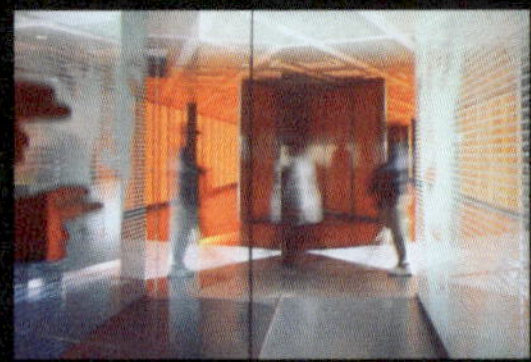

The faces form a wall separating the Welcome Center from the Faculty Club and read in positive or negative depending on light conditions and reflection.

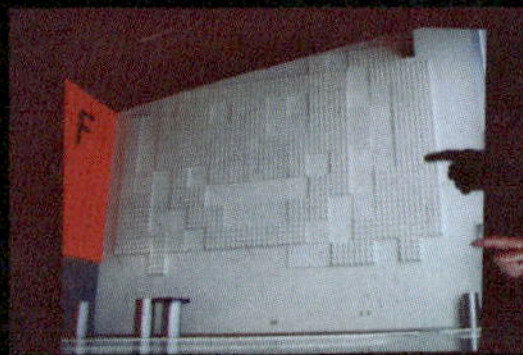

The walls also flirt with depth. The ballroom acoustic wall dampens sound reflection and also forms a smiley face. The projection booth is covered with custom elevator pads ...

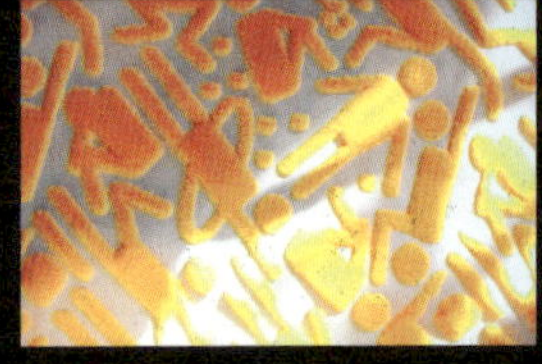

... and we even designed a special fuzzy wallpaper featuring the icons.

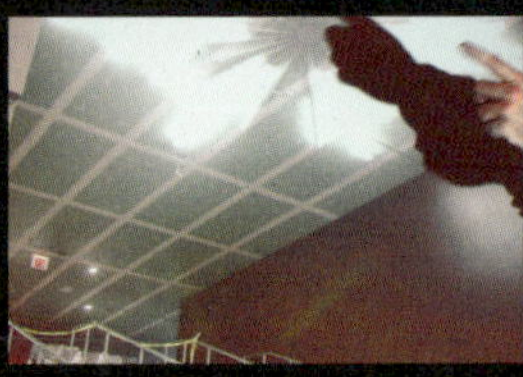

Our work also extends into a number of lighting conditions, such as some very crude "chandeliers" fabricated from raw electrical conduit and industrial fluorescent tubes ...

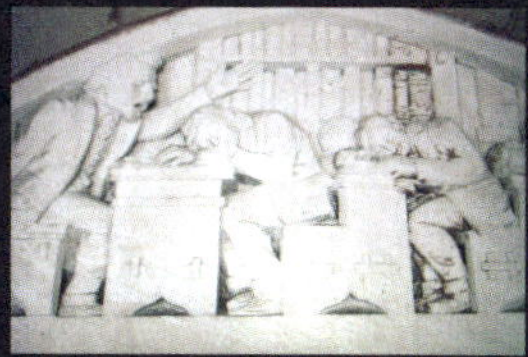

Yale's seemingly dead-serious Gothic details actually are full of jokes, like the professor lecturing to the sleeping students over the door of the law school ...

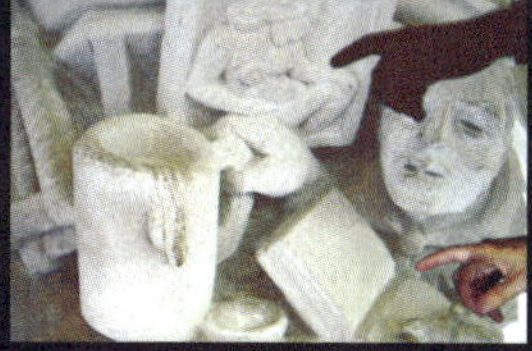

... or a sculpted student in front of a girlie picture, drinking beer and smoking cigarettes on a library column capital.

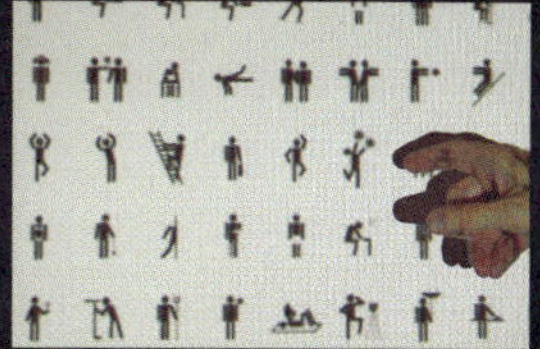

So we developed our own, somewhat ironic graphic vocabulary based on a "modern" gender-neutral student engaged in a number of activities, both licit and illicit.

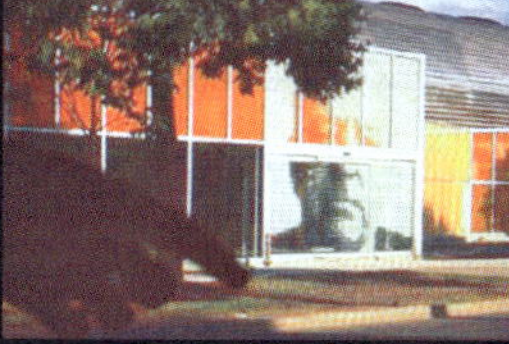

The main entrance on the west side features a 20-foot portrait of Mies himself ...

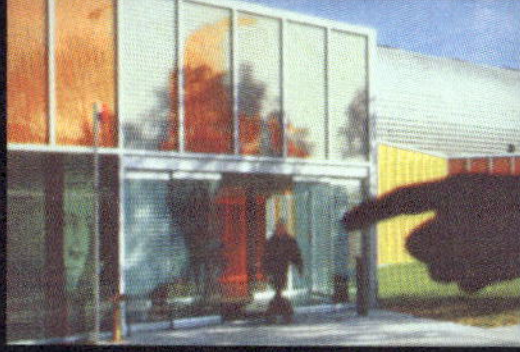

... positioned so that the automatic doors serve as his mouth: the building swallows its users.

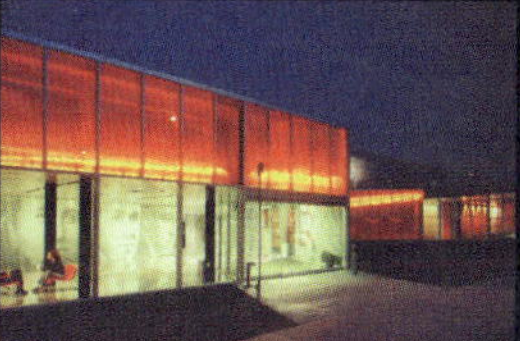

Beyond the Mies entrance is a "founders' wall" featuring portraits of the University founders etched in the glass.

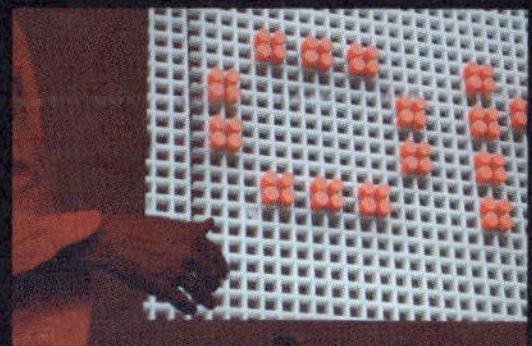

The various surfaces are modified to become information: the east wall becomes a typographic matrix simply by adding colored plugs to make letterforms.

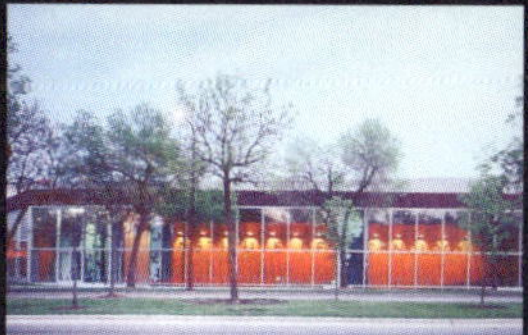

The ballroom features a huge three-part curtain, created by Petra Blaise using full-scale tree plans we derived from Mies' original campus plans.

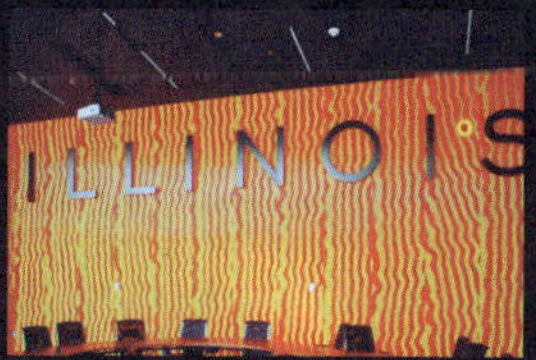

The curtains cover an insanely vibrant orange wall in lenticular wallpaper that seems to move with the viewer, and gigantic typography that runs through three separate ballrooms.

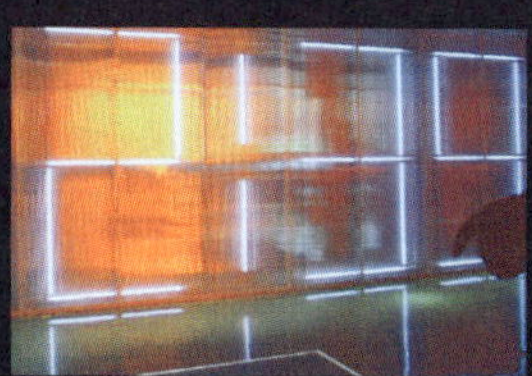

... or a nine-foot digital clock embedded in a polycarbonate wall.

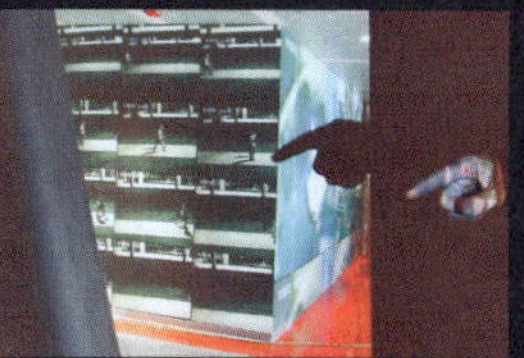

Other areas were simply wallpapered with images. In the post office we created a special plaid pattern out of surveillance images of mysterious IIT students performing seemingly nefarious acts.

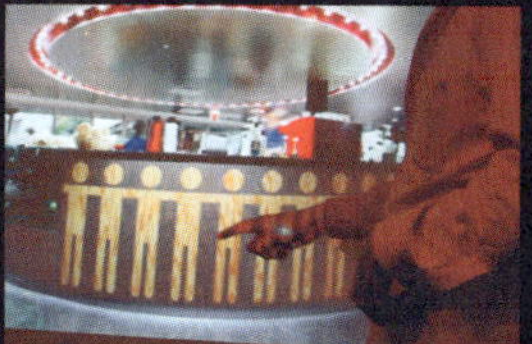

In other places the patterns are literally cut into the surface, such as this plywood coffee bar, embedded into the floor, or extruded from the doors ...

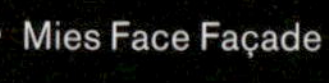

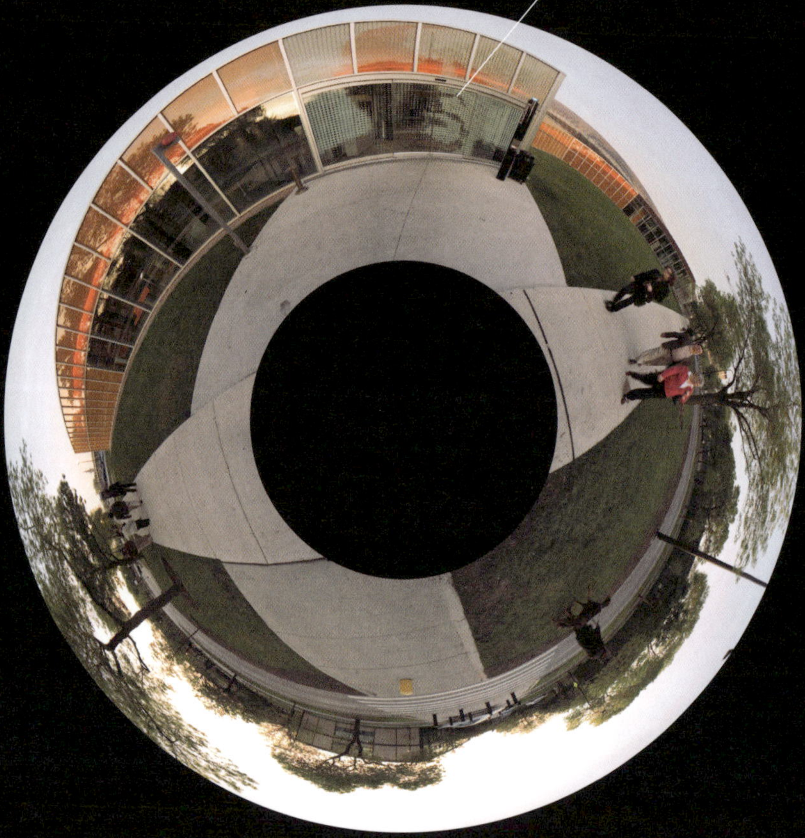

Bias — *with Lucia Allais and Rem Koolhaas*

MR I would say for us, IIT was something of a proto-Junk Space project: code the walls, fancy or rough or plain or elaborate, through the most superficial means.

RK That just demonstrates how many things are going on in every project. For me IIT was about some of the most profound references but at the same time, in terms of fabrication it anticipated Junk Space because it was fabricated entirely according to the rules of Junk Space. That was part of the pleasure of doing it at that particular moment and that particular way, where your work played an important role.

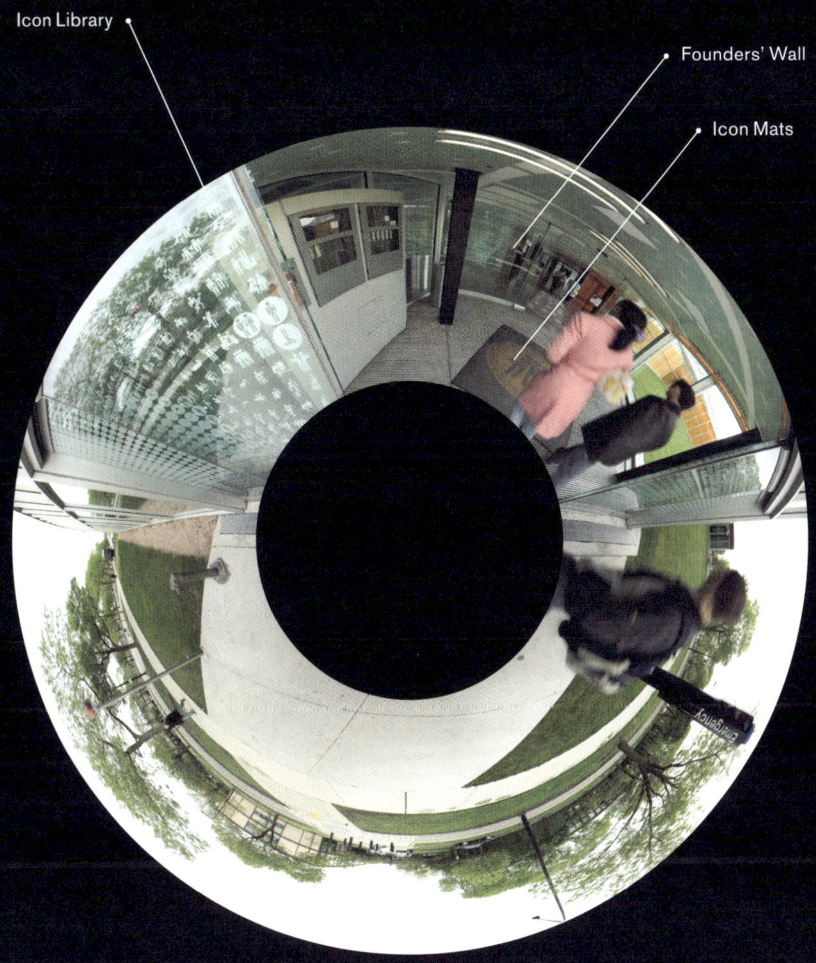

MR That particular moment also involved *value engineering* as a form of automatic design. This was instigated by assuming a position where instead of replacing luxurious things with low-cost alternatives, anything that was engineered out was simply left as a gap: the bare spaces where *design* had once been.

LA What is the relationship between this architectural profundity and the hyper-legibility of the work that 2x4 did on the project—the icons and images that were superimposed on the architectural surfaces?

RK That was another beautiful sheen or layer, with which I was very happy because it took away some of the burden of angst of the other ambitions of the project.

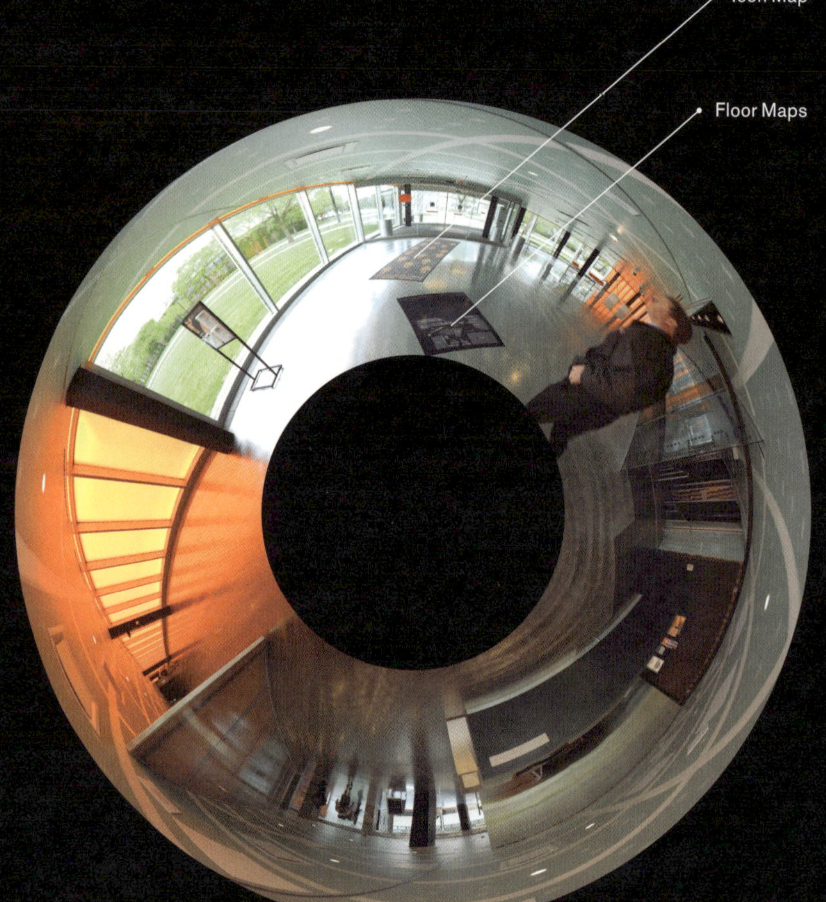

LA Angst?

RK There are certain projects that just seem to underwhelm the architects. What I was actually trying to do at IIT was invisible: a cultural project about the connection between Mies and the Romans (laughs). Admittedly, that's a very private interest, a very longstanding one. I could explain it 'til I was blue in the face …

LA Was there, in your opinion, any aspect to the project that improved due to that resistance? More clarifying or, on the contrary, becoming more stubbornly …

RK Yes, I became more stubborn, and for that reason it got better.

LA Especially the Pompeian slab idea. Pompeii plus … what?

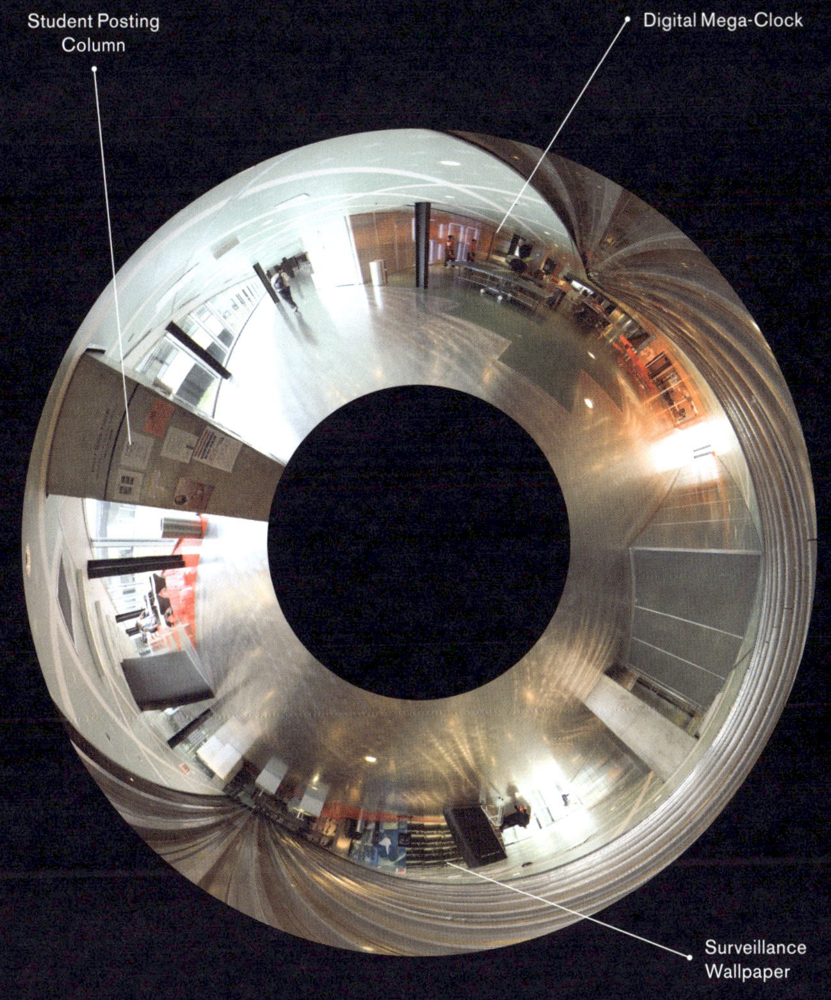

RK Pompeii plus circulation, then, as a kind of bone thrown to contemporary expectation, this tube …

LA Ah! The tube is the thing …

RK Yes! Even now, people call the tube "iconic." It's really fantastic.

LA The Pompeian slab is very interesting, as a trope that returns: for example, in CCTV.

RK Yes, it returns in everything.

LA But at IIT the Pompeian slab is violated.

RK I don't think you can call it violated.

LA Well, *chopped*.

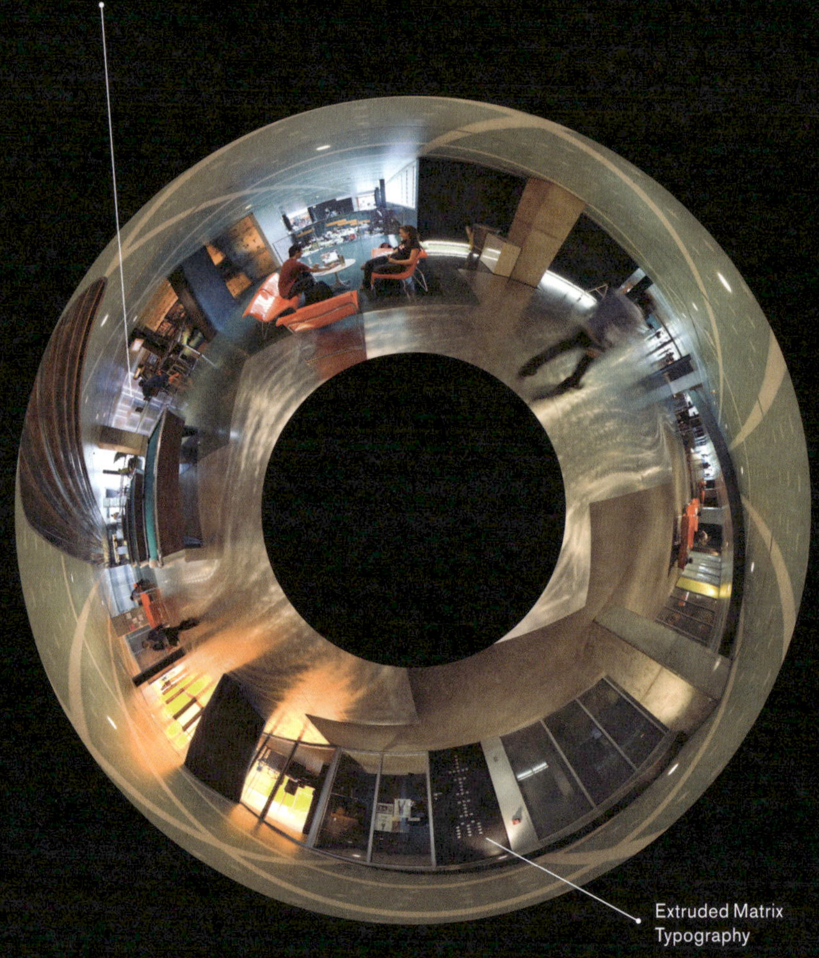

RK Chopped, in a sense, by the desire lines the students inscribed in it, but that's not so much a violation as a form of engagement.

MR I like that that *engagement* is constantly forced. It's a project of collisions. For us the innovation here was to be almost rudely incongruous in terms of graphic language. We took the slash across the slab as a methodology and a license to let the rough edges between things remain exposed. It sounds naïve to say now, but that was a revelation in our work.

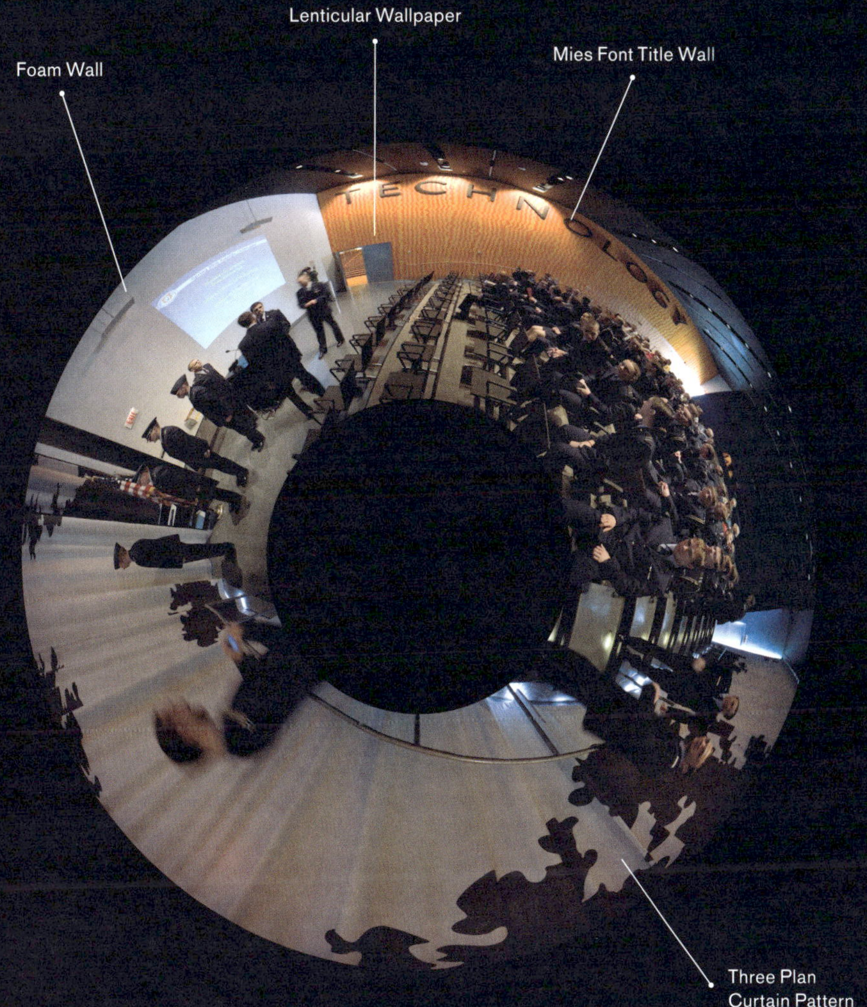

LA Because you had found an area where you could take a stance?

MR In some ways I think OMA's ideas for the project and ours were at cross-purposes. But maybe that is a description of a collaborative process at the most basic level: everyone in it is trying to wring their little bit of authorship out of it.

RK So this book functions as another one of the collaborations, or collisions?

MR Maybe, or a way to reframe earlier collaborations that were important to us, and to see

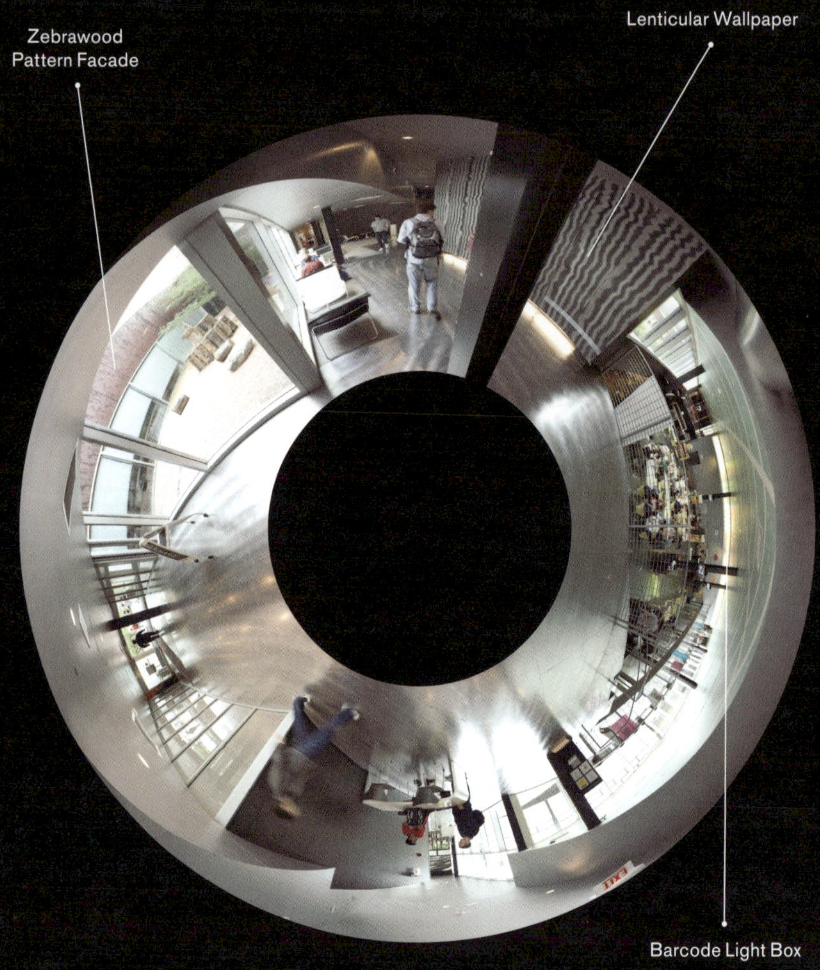

the studio not as a single moment in time but something more diachronous. Because the studio has never been one thing, it's always changing, and I want to try to link the past and present in a messy but interesting way.

LA A kind of professional nostalgia?

RK I don't think it's nostalgic. In the absence of memory you have to construct an artificial depth.

MR The impulse is to try to trace a trajectory—and in the retracing make it make sense—but every trajectory always seems to end in disillusionment.

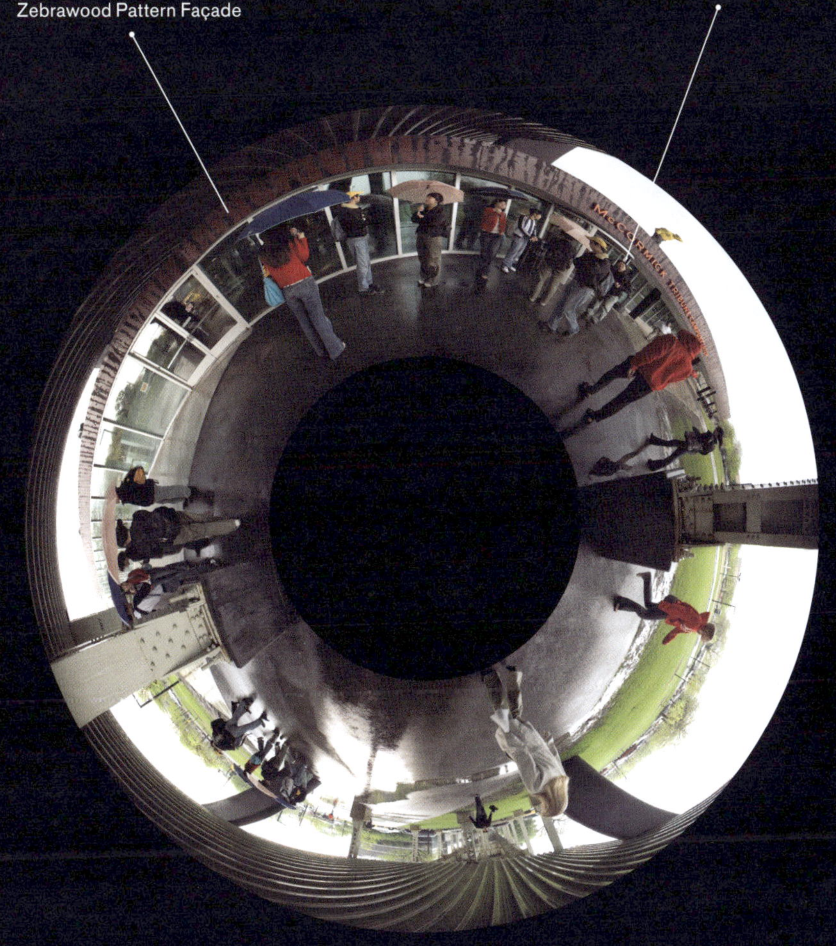

LA It always ends like that—the last phase of any history is always the reason we want to forget it.

RK Exactly. I don't think it's nostalgic at all, but it's daring.

LA Because you're scared of what you might find.

MR Or what you don't find …

IIT: ICONOMANIA
—2×4

PLEASE DO NOT! USE CIRCLED ① FIGURES

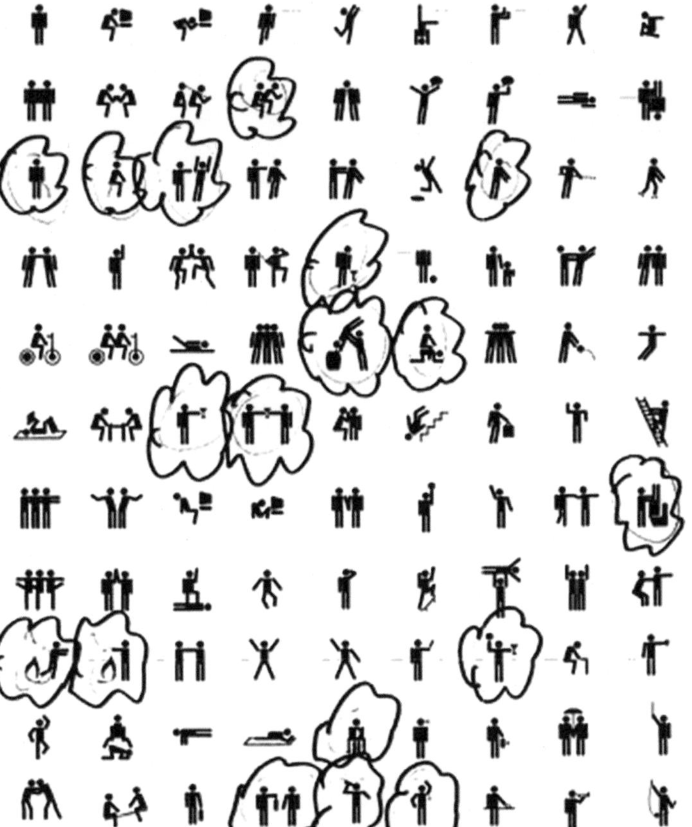

GHOST BOOK

JEANNIE KIM

After nearly two years of pre-ordering on Amazon.com, *Lagos: How It Works* was apparently published in either August 2007 or October 2008 by Lars Müller. Weighing in at 800 pages, released in paperback, and out of print soon thereafter it was—in fact—never published. After eleven (twelve? thirteen?) years of research, the life of the publication seems now to be limited to circulating Xerox copies of the thesis book in the Harvard University Graduate School of Design's Loeb Library, and an archive of drafts, slides, and DVDs in the closets of everyone who ever worked on the book over its long evolution. As is well known, the project grew out of what might best be described as a series of research studios conducted at the GSD between 1998 and 2000. What began as a study of urbanism in West Africa more generally was narrowed to the subject of Lagos, Nigeria, in 1999 and was seemingly on the verge of publication by the end of 2002 as the logical successor to the *Harvard Design School Guide to Shopping* (Taschen, 2002) and *Great Leap Forward* (Taschen, 2002). Excerpts from the first two years of research were also published in *Mutations* (Actar, 2001), a toxic-yellow-plastic book with a built-in mousepad that is, to date, Actar's best-selling book, currently out of print. The material legacy of the never-published book includes: an abandoned computer and scanner stationed in the basement of the National Theater in Lagos where the film archive of FESTAC '77 lies festering; thousands of digital images catalogued according to an obsolete naming system that was coded to the original book's organization; at least as many actual slides (not including the images taken by Edgar Cleijne while on foot and via then-President Obasanjo's helicopter); a small library of pirated videos and television footage from Lagos' robust media culture; several hundred West African newspapers and magazines; a collection of "pure water" bags, 419 letters, mermaid stories, recipes for malarial cures, megachurch bumper stickers, government publications, and incomplete maps of the city; an outdated (circa 2003) library on informal urbanism; approximately 1,000 linear feet of A4 documents; and versions of "the book" whose typologies include a postage stamp-sized accordion, a tabbed encyclopedia, a Baedeker travel guide, a *Heart of Darkness* Penguin paperback, a well-intentioned parody of South African *Drum* magazine,a Lars Müller brick, and a Nigerian Federal Government Development Plan. The book always had a problem of authority, occupying a space somewhere between amateur journalism, naïve anthropology, and enthusiastically speculative academic research, with a temporal framework that was repeatedly undone by political unrest, new urban crises, or the latest editor. As sales figures and the cultural legacy of both *Shopping* and *The Great Leap Forward* demonstrate, however, the buzz that prefigured the

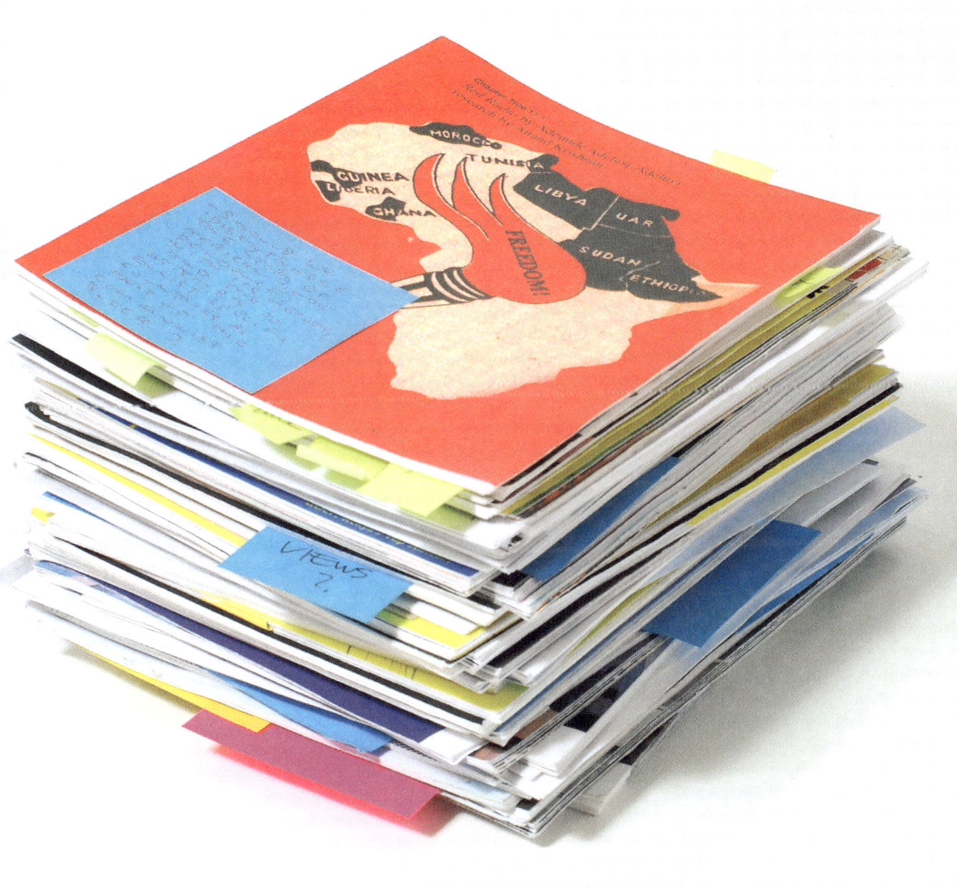
MOROCCO
GUINEA
GHANA
LIBYA
UAR
SUDAN
FREEDOM!
VIEWS ?

Gentrification 8.4
Nollywood by Seke Somolu

Some say the phenomenon of 'home videos' was started by videocassette traders who wanted to package content with their merchandise. Others claim it was the old time film producers who could no longer afford to shoot on celluloid and shamefully picked up video cameras in order to continue plying their trade…

Four-one-nine by Jeannie Kim

On monday the 24 September 2002, I was released, on the condition that I will release the rest of my fathers money in my care, to the tune of $I.5b,which i agreed. Now I have been released but kept under severe house arrest, I had amassed monies running into hundreds of millions of dollars stashed in various private foreign accounts around the world, most of wish have been frozen…

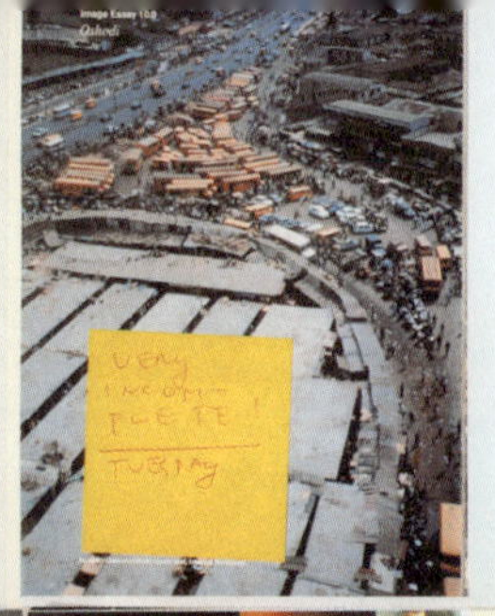

Chapter Title 11.9
Bregtje van der Haak does Chief Ubochi

BREGTJE VAN DER HA…
About The History Of A…
CHIEF UBOCHI: Alaba… originally part of Ala… late seventies. When … tronics, especially sp… off. F.E.S.T.A.C '77 … demand for audio eq… of the festival. We ou… had to move. We relocated to Mile 2 but that was not convenient either. The market maintained its popularity, but the resulting traffic jams were unbearable. Finally, we moved west to Ojo, along the Lagos-Badagry Expressway. Now, we can grow to infinity.

Zein Warona

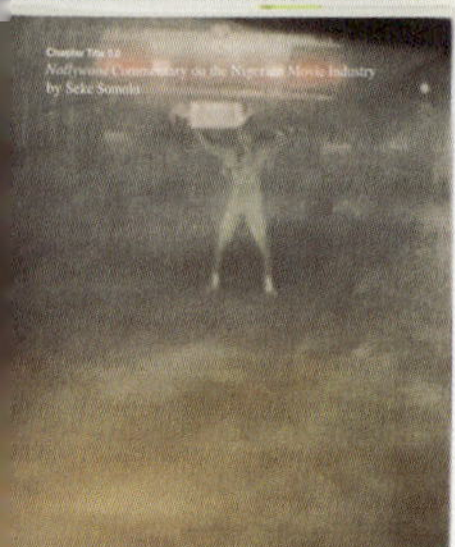

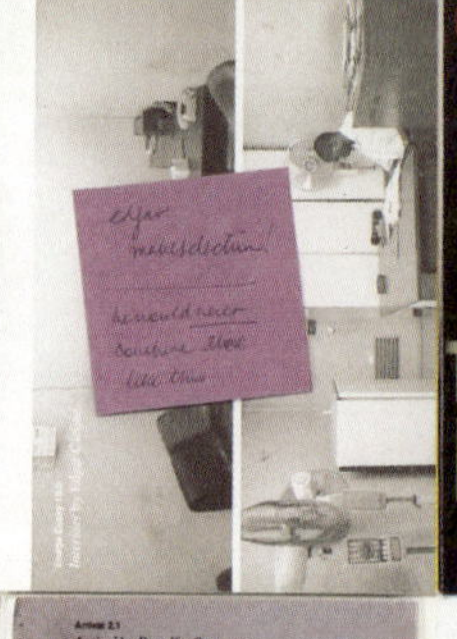

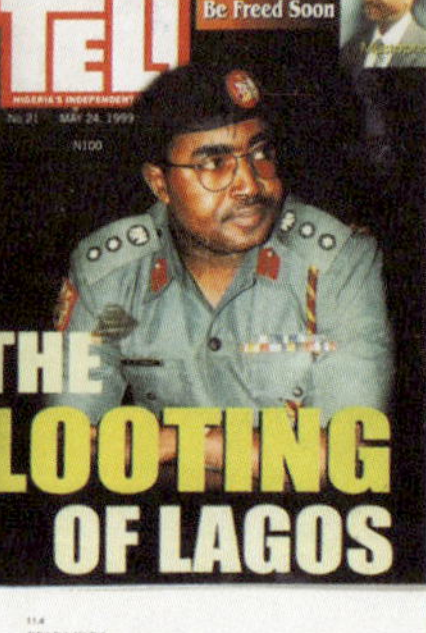

Abandonment / Reversal 6.7
Jankara
by Pierre Belanger with James S…

Chapter Title 11.10
Funmi Iyanda interviews Rem Koolhaas and Edgar Cleijne for New Dawn on Ten (NTA) January 24, 2001 (Lagos)

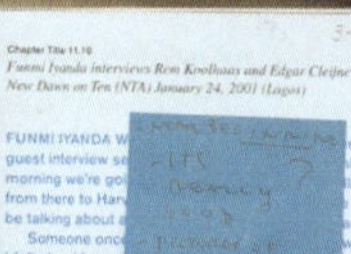

FUNMI IYANDA … guest interview … morning we're go… from there to Har… be talking about … Someone once … I felt about Lagos … either love or hate … ground. Trying to … but this is what m… trying to do. Rem Koolhaas … in the world. In 1… in the architectur… Pulitzer, or even … been a professor … Harvard Univers… city, a study that … world. Good mo…
REM KOOLHAAS…
FI: Kool…
RK: …'house'

Arrival 2.1
Arrival by Rem Koolhaas

Ropes are strung across the runway. To avoid them planes have to stop with almost impossible suddenness. Airplane security rests on unimpeded access of rescue crews from the outside…

11.4
PRADA YADA
Conversation with Rem Koolhaas

- …because you work for them?
- No no no no…
- No, no… them… the way th… really i…
- Hmm.
- Sometimes, I don't understand…
- Hey. The way their brain works? Toyin, mama, zero in.
- But how does their…?

Historical Timeline 9.0
Political Fluctuation by Ademide Adelusi-Adeluyi

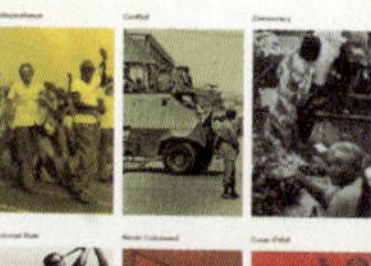

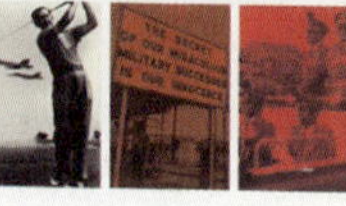

MICHELIN
Keeping Nigeria Moving

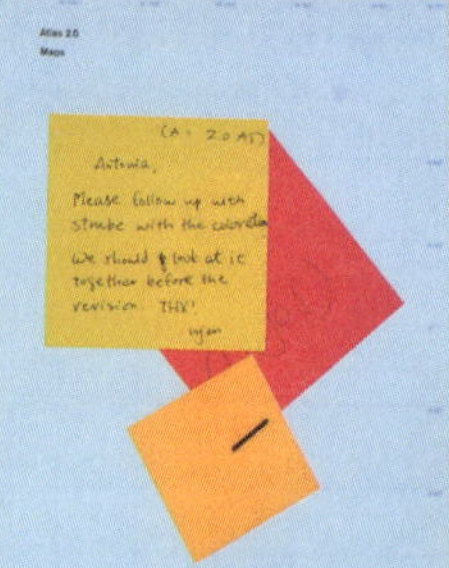

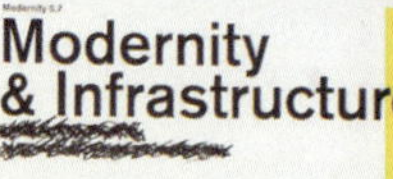

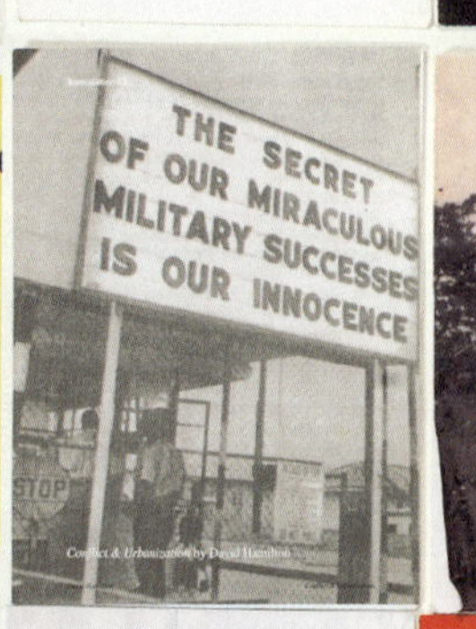

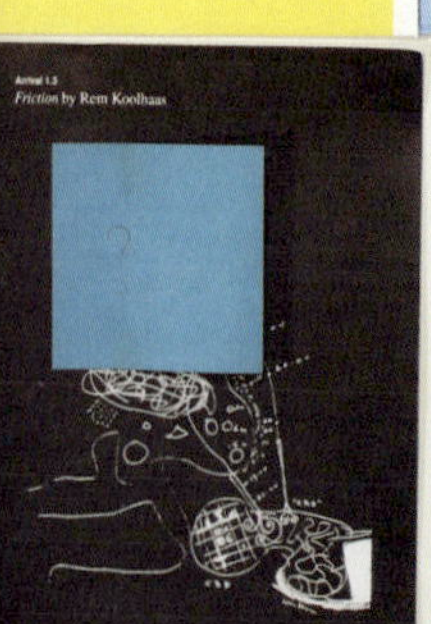

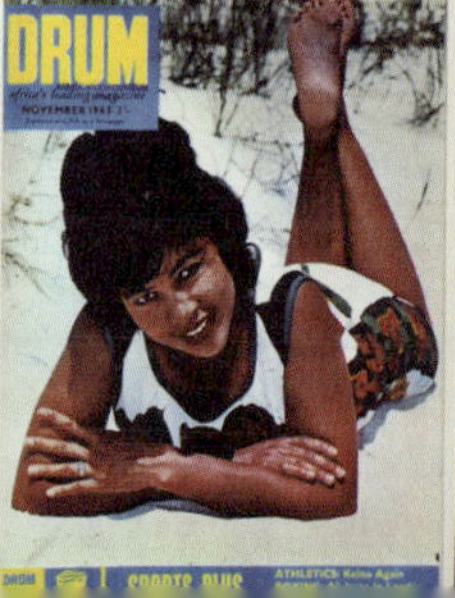

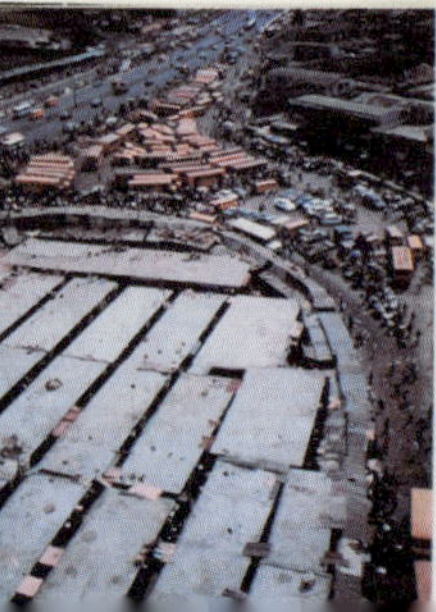

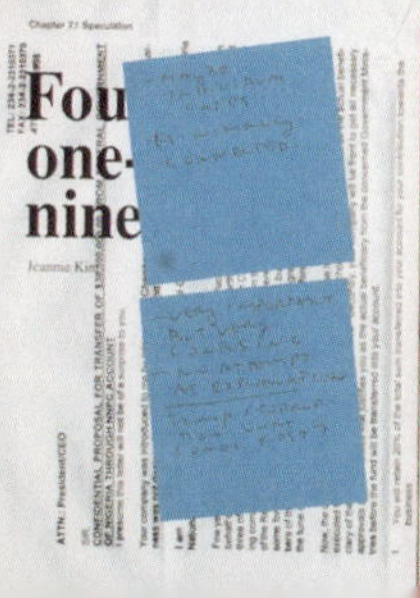

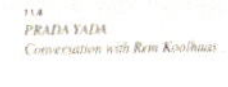

11.4
PRADA YADA
Conversation with Rem Koolhaas

– ...because you work for them?
– No no no no...

(General laughter)

– No, no, I really work with them very intimately, and the way their brain works is really interesting.
– Hmm.
– Sometimes, I don't understand...
– Hey. The way their brain works?
Toyin, mama, zero in.
– But how does their...?

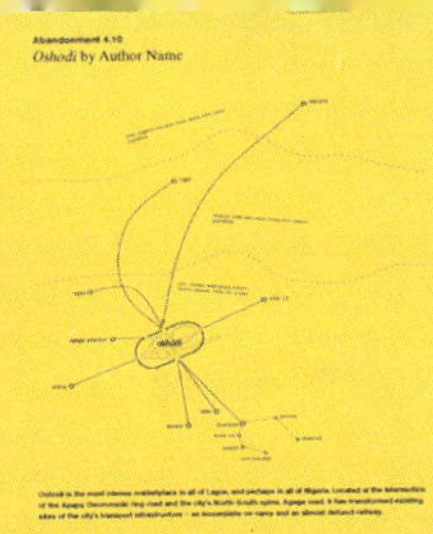

Interview 2
Funmi Iyanda by Bregtje van der Haak

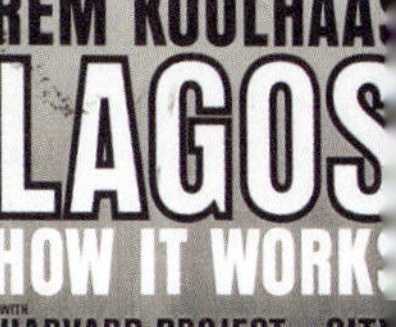

WITH HARVARD PROJECT ON THE CITY
EDGAR CLEIJNE AND 2x4
EDITED BY ADEMIDE ADELUSI-ADELUYI

LARS MULLER PUBLISHERS

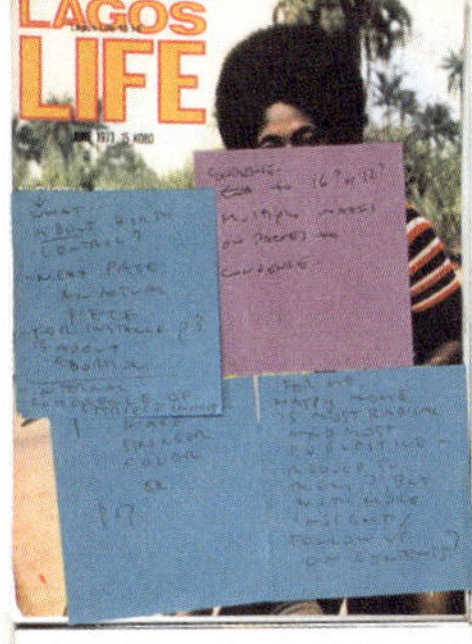

Modernity 5.7
Modernity & Infrastructu

Essay by Rem Koolhaas
Mapping by Ademide Adelusi-Adeluyi

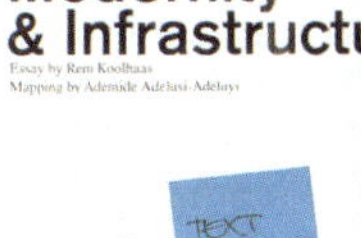

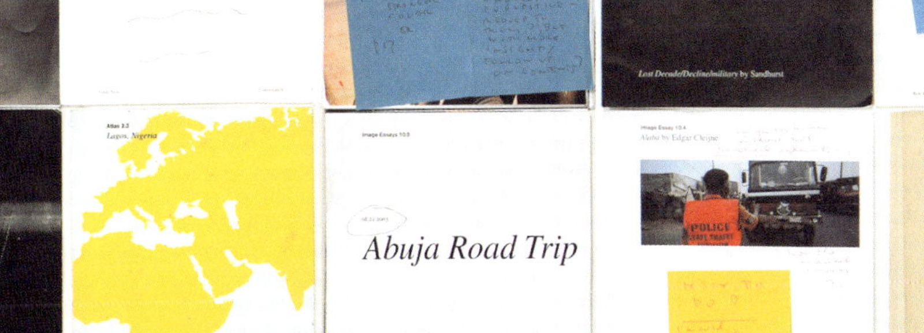

Abuja Road Trip

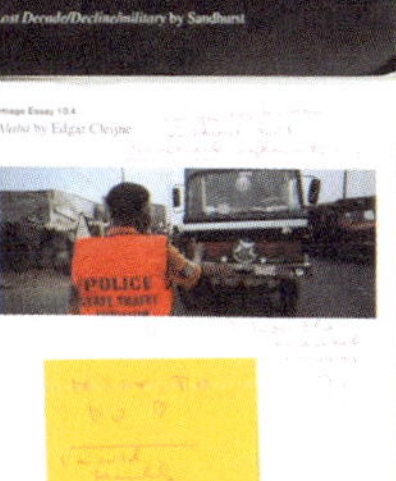

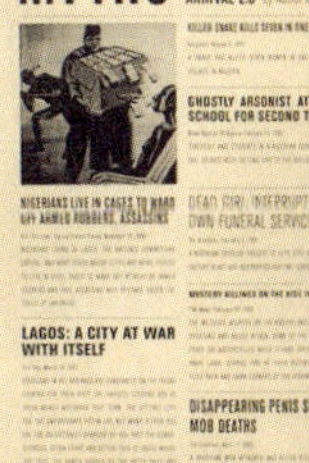

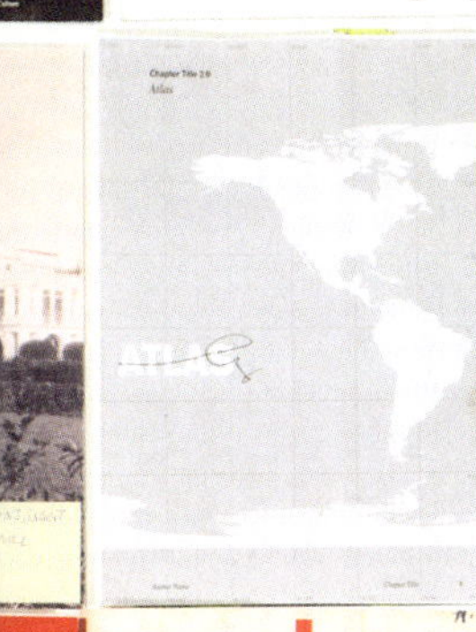

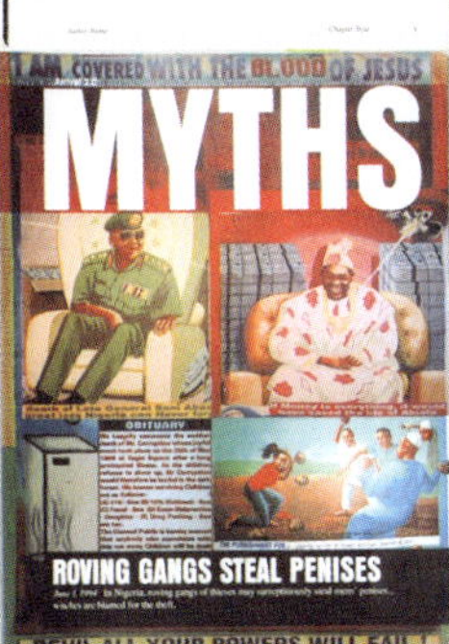

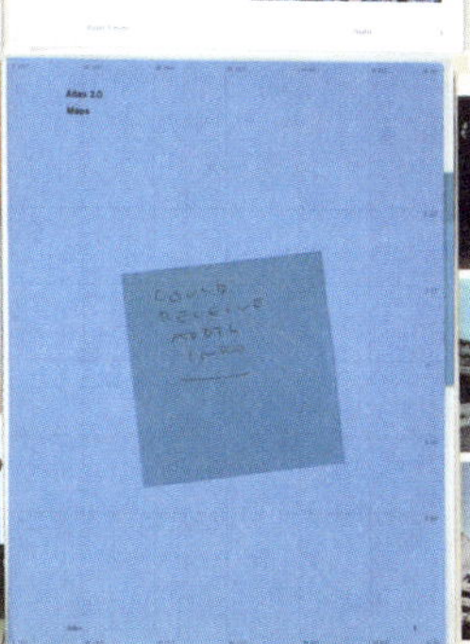

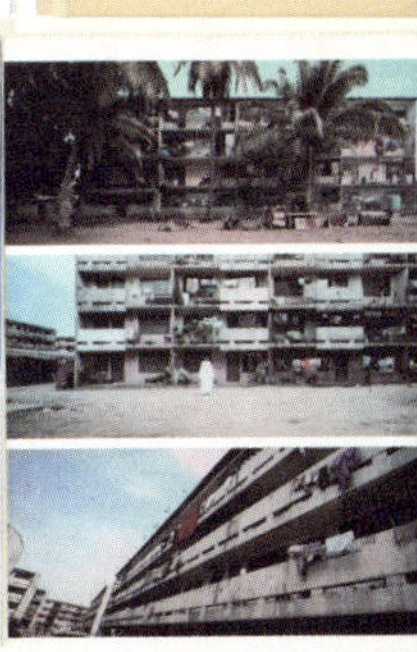

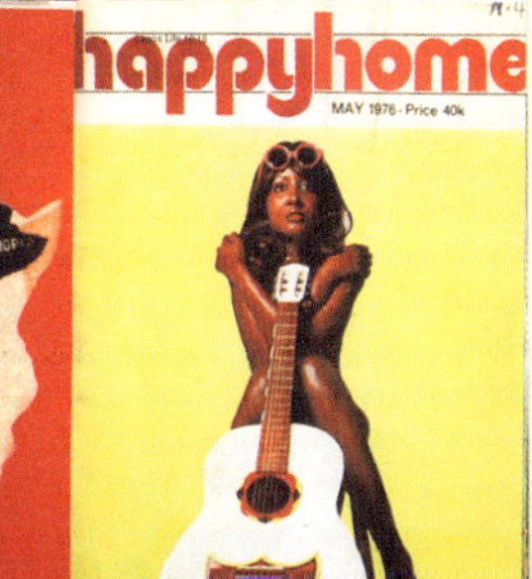

Abandonment 4.3
Four-one-nine by Jeannie Kim

On monday the 24 September 2002, I was released, on the condition that I will release the rest of my fathers money in my care, to the tune of $I.5b,which i agreed. Now I have been released but kept under severe house arrest, I had amassed monies running into hundreds of millions of dollars stashed in various private foreign accounts around the world, most of wish have been frozen...

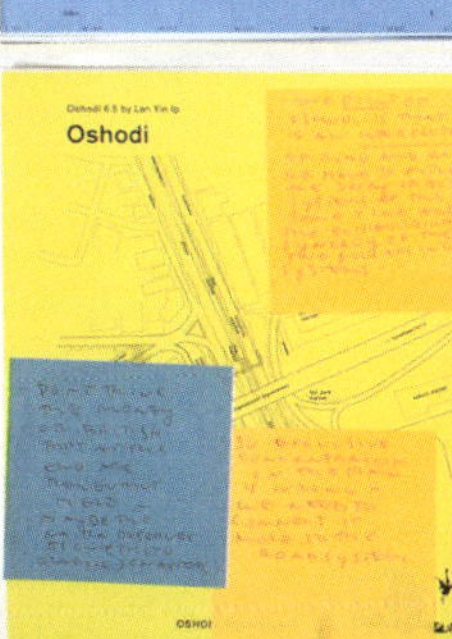

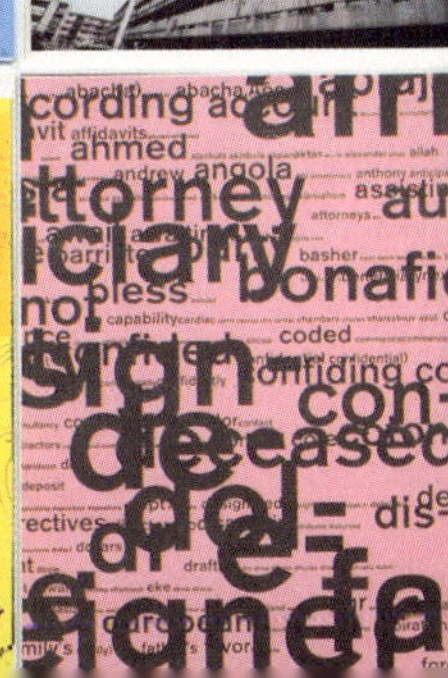

books actually exceeded the books themselves. (This was not helped by the confusing covers, simultaneously alluding to and suggesting indecision about titles, authorship, intellectual property, and marketing.) Perhaps *Lagos* was best left unpublished, unfinished, and ultimately uncontained. If, as George Packer suggested in his seriously journalistic critique of Koolhaas' fascination in "The Megacity," (*The New Yorker*, November 13, 2006), Lagos had become a "hip icon of the latest global trends," the book was, at best, a lifestyle guide—an unfair dismissal of nearly a decade of earnest research conducted together with, and with the support—the city and its inhabitants and not, as Packer and others have suggested—from the perspective of fascinated intellectual detachment through tempered glass. "The impulse to look at an 'apparently burning garbage heap' and see an 'urban phenomenon,' and then make it the raw material of an elaborate aesthetic construct, is not so different from the more common impulse not to look at all," Packer wrote.

This was preceded by Matthew Gandy's questioning of the positioning of the project in the *New Left Review* (May/June 2005). Although the project never claimed to be affiliated with geography, digression from its disciplinary practices gave Gandy occasion to launch a critique of the methodology and the critical consciousness of the research based on the highly excerpted and exhibition-ready text presented in *Mutations* and the equally edited print version of Rem Koolhaas' lecture at Documenta (2002) alone, it seems. Taking the admittedly hyperbolic tone of some of the writing as statements of fact, Gandy's selective evidence, not surprisingly, leads him to question the intentions of a body of research that, in his presentation, seemingly proceeded without any recourse to the actual history of the city.

The project made a cameo appear-ance again during the spring of 2012 in Martin Filler's assessment of Koolhaas' career in bigness, on the occasion of the exhibition *OMA/Progress* at the Barbican Art Gallery and the publication of *Project Japan: Metabolism Talks* (Taschen, 2012). Here, again, ventriloquizing George Packer's mischaracterization of the project in *The New Yorker* six years earlier, the research is contrasted with the well-meaning Yale students of Robert Venturi and Denise Scott Brown's *Learning from Las Vegas*. Whereas the Yalies really hit the pavement and got to know the Strip, the frightened Harvard team, Filler claims—repeating Packer—never got out of the car. The mistakes in Filler's journalism, including his claim that the book had been published (possibly misled by Amazon but clearly not compelled to actually attempt to acquire or read it), were enough to warrant a reaction from Koolhaas and a rejoinder from Filler. While Koolhaas' response to the accusations of indifference or colonial fascination in the project are by now familiar, the letter to the editor

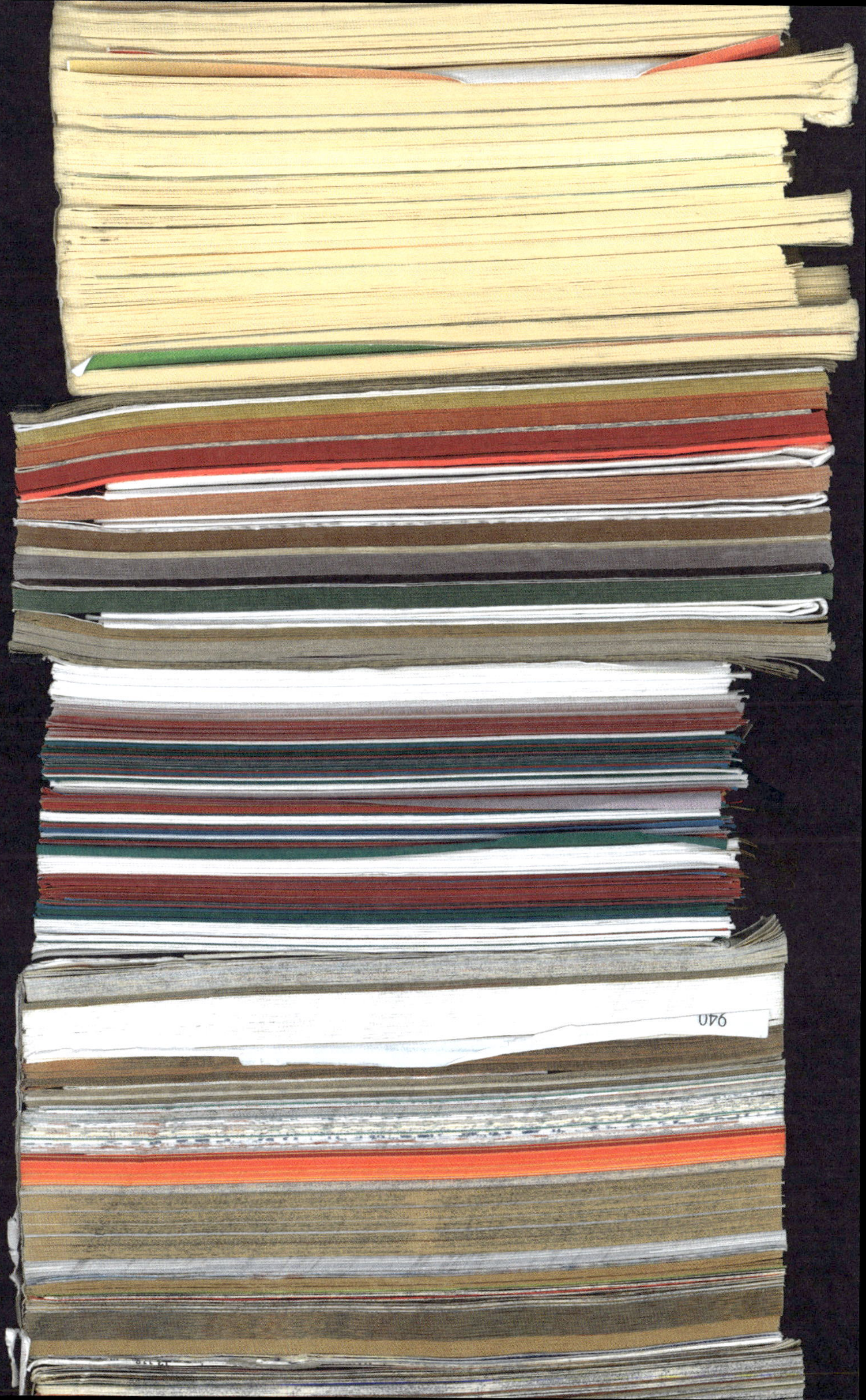

ends with a reference to the book in present tense.

As an unfulfilled fantasy, the project continues to be mythologized in design studios throughout the Northeast where the vogue of accusing Koolhaas of a mildly offensive voyeurism has mostly been forgotten and new legions of design students embark regularly on research missions to find urban innovation in far-flung corners of the world that they may never see. This may be the perpetually forthcoming publication's best legacy, as actual publication will grant the research an air of finality and truth that will be doomed to fail for all of the reasons already claimed in its absence.

SUPERFICIALITY: LITERAL AND PHENOMENAL, OR 50 WALLS

I have a problem with space.

It's not that we don't think about space. On the contrary, graphic designers are obsessed with space: the space between things—letters, lines, columns, gutters—the space inside of things—counter-forms—and the space around things—margins, borders, frames. But our pet subject, the one to which we are almost religiously attached, is white space. White space, especially for those of us trained as modern designers, exudes a kind of mystical and only partially containable aura. The control of white space, even simply the perception of it, is one of the designer's basic magic tricks.

White space is a two-dimensional byproduct of the modernization of the printed page. White space does not exist as a discrete concept—a kind of visual derivative that can be traded on the market of critique—until it is invented at the turn of the last century by the titans of the avant-garde: Tschichold, Bayer, Rodchenko, Malevich and Co. "White space is to be regarded as an active element, not a passive background," Jan Tschichold commands in 1930. (Note: IS TO BE.) The revolution in typography reignites the negative. Emptiness becomes charged, counterform colonized.

In his *Language of Vision*, György Kepes announces the *plastic organization* of space is as essential to the human condition as photosynthesis is to a plant. "Just as the letters of the alphabet can be put together in innumerable ways to form words which convey meanings, so the optical measures and qualities can be brought together in innumerable ways, and each particular relationship generates a different sensation of space. The variations to be achieved are endless." The *sensation of space*, not space.

Modern composition requires the manipulation of plastic forms within defined edges. Such space has extremely un-deep depth: we talk about one form on top of another, but the z-dimension is gauged in microns, the thickness of ink. We act as if things really recede or emerge but our third dimension is metaphoric. This illusory depth pervades everything. We *Bring to Front* and *Send to Back* or manipulate and reshuffle a series of labeled layers that are ultimately *flattened* back into a seamless whole. This obliterating *flatten* command crushes the temporary moment of depth and returns the work to a state of pure superficiality.

The formal problem of graphic design is constructing Kepes's *sensation of space* while working on a: hard, glancing surface, impervious to all attempts at penetration to the real meat of the issue. This pejorative understanding of the superficial is a fundamental limitation to the understanding of graphic design. It may be awkward to describe ourselves as superficial—what's worse than being shallow—but taken at face value—one of the attributes of superficiality—the word is simply descriptive: to be on the surface.

Both the formal (to coat or skin) and the metaphoric (to be obvious) connotations are apposite.

In the early days of 2x4, the scale of the work is determined by the laser printer. When you are working on the design of a single page, to be read by a single person, the spatial issues are literally at hand, the edges clearly limned. But the spatial application of the graphic creates new conditions. Our most common condition is a blank wall. The wall is the problem. How we deal with that problem is essential. The surface of the wall is both material and metaphoric, and how the wall is materially manipulated is the indexical sign of the designer's mind at work.

As teenagers, my sister and I fumble into a commission from a hometown bar we frequent. In exchange for an open tab, we start a room-scale graphic novel on the barroom wall that plays out over the course of a year or two. This is our first volley in the ongoing battle of the wall. We paint the comic frames using a mixture of powdered lime, milk and water on a chalkboard surface. Painting in white allows the designer to work in counter-form, drawing the white space out of the black. But it also forces us to consider the way the graphic interacts with the spatial and the temporal.

This trilateral dynamic of the formal, spatial and temporal becomes a defining feature of the work of the studio. In pushing to make the work critical, we engage this multivalent condition as the essential content of our work. This is our writing, regardless of the message it is designed to carry.

ACCRETION

1. Accretion I. *Guggenheim Hermitage.* Las Vegas, Nevada.

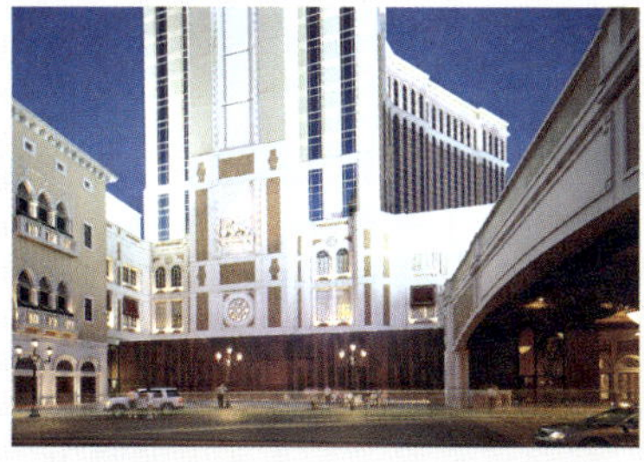

Corten steel meets foamcore. Blank steel box punched through the front wall of the casino's faux-Venetian façade. Monumental letters acid-etched into steel so that the type rusts at a different rate from the wall.

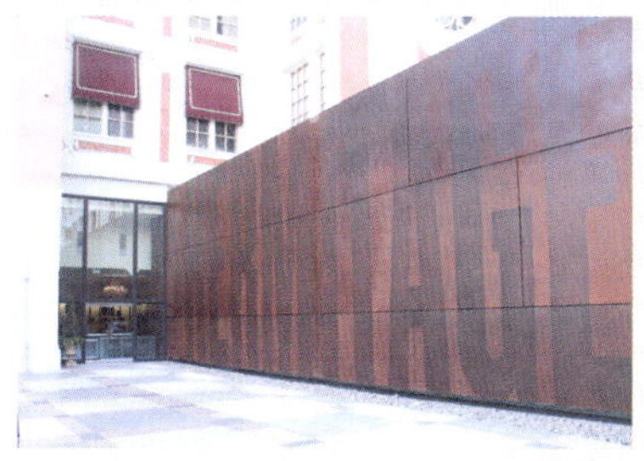

1a. Could the façade be backdrop for other (un)planned interventions?

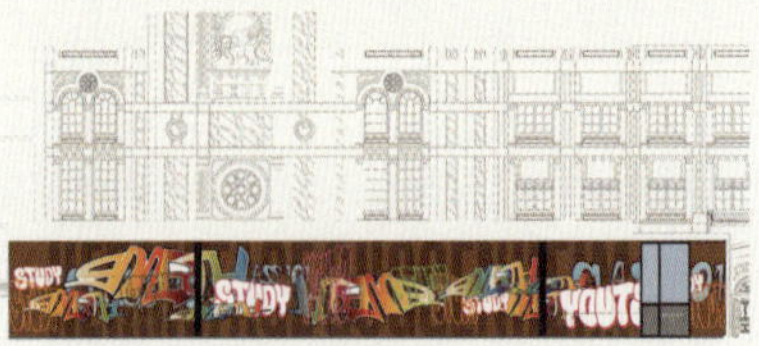

(Unfortunately, in true Vegas fashion, the buildings are replaced by more popular attractions before we can find out.)

1b. Accretion II. *Guggenheim Hermitage*. Las Vegas, Nevada.

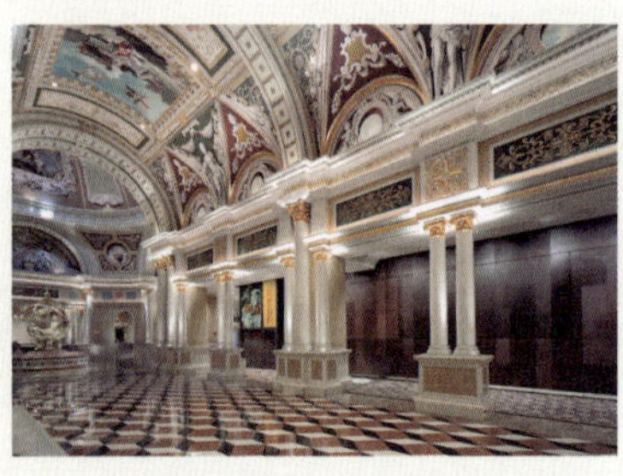

Exposed steel wall visible in the elaborate lobby. Shiny polished steel contradicts rusting surface.

2. Accretion III. *Vitra Showroom*. New York, New York.

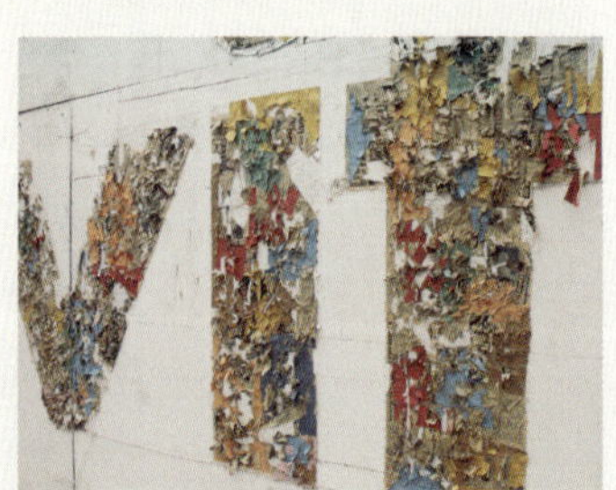

Form discovered by cutting away the crust of stapled detritus of the urban barricade: accumulation of staples as ad hoc appliqué.

3. Accretion IV. *Otis College of Art* and Design. Los Angeles, California.

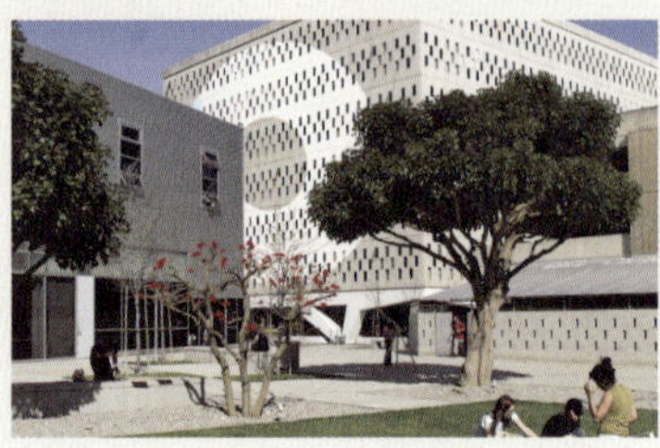

Anti-accretion: The graphic effect of hygiene.

EXTRUSION

4. Extrusion I. *Guggenheim Las Vegas*. Las Vegas, Nevada.

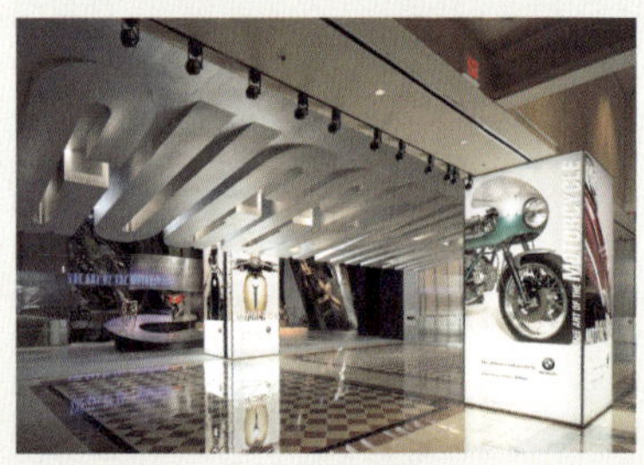

A second museum space just off the sprawling casino floor. Where goes the sign? Since we can't go up, we go under: ceiling as façade.

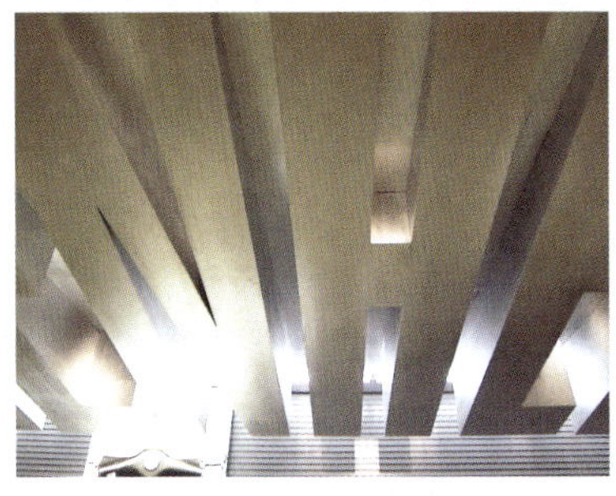

5. Extrusion II. *IIT McCormick Tribune Campus Center.* Chicago, Illinois.

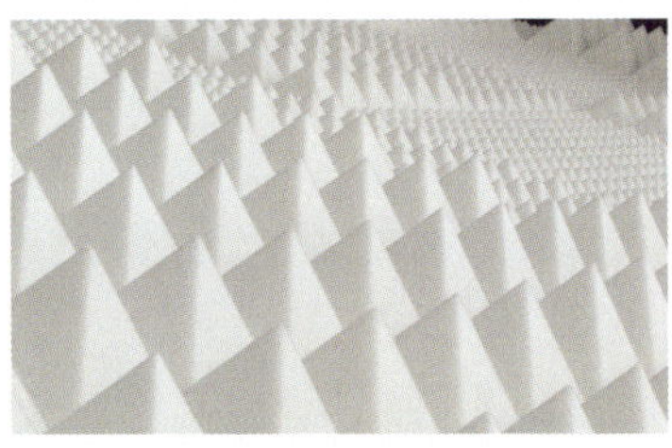

Pyramidal foam soundproofing adds depth and texture.

6. Extrusion III. *IIT McCormick Tribune Campus Center.* Chicago, Illinois.

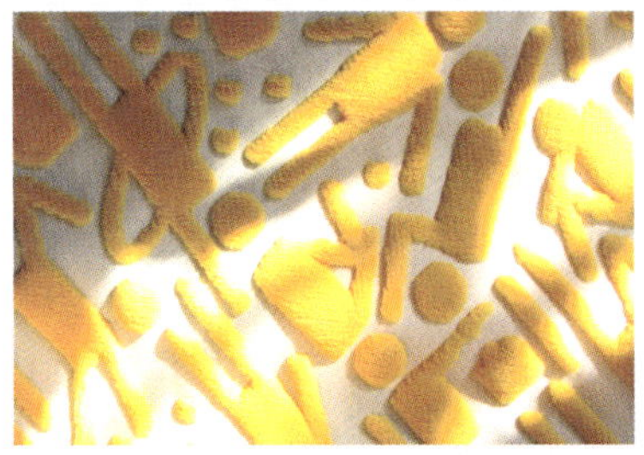

Heavy flocking—by way of paint-roller technology.

7. Extrusion III. *Prada Broadway.* New York, New York.

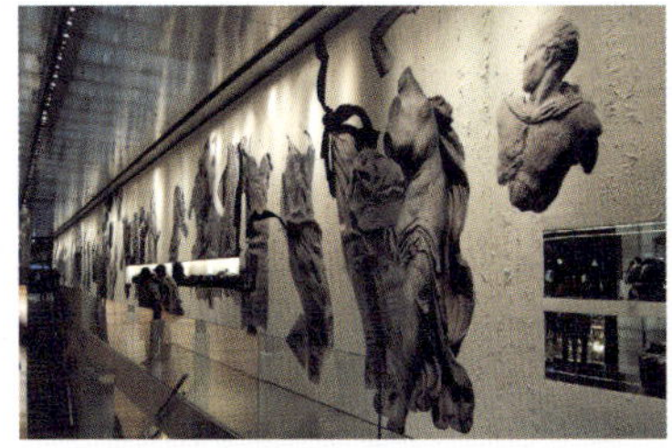

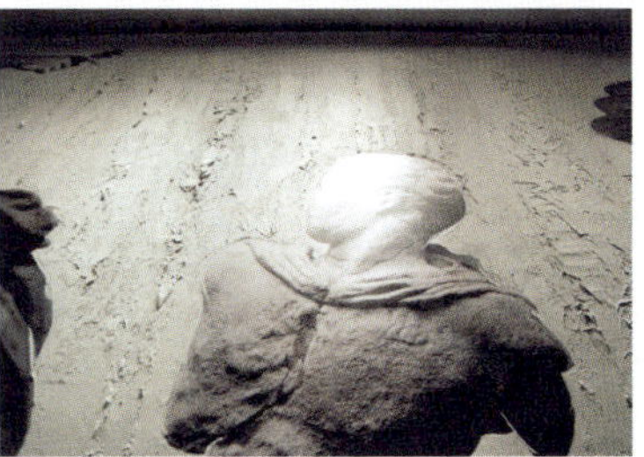

White space materialized, negative space materialized. Bas relief in reverse. The flat is dimensional, the dimensional flat.

8. Extrusion IV. *Nike 100.* Beijing, China.

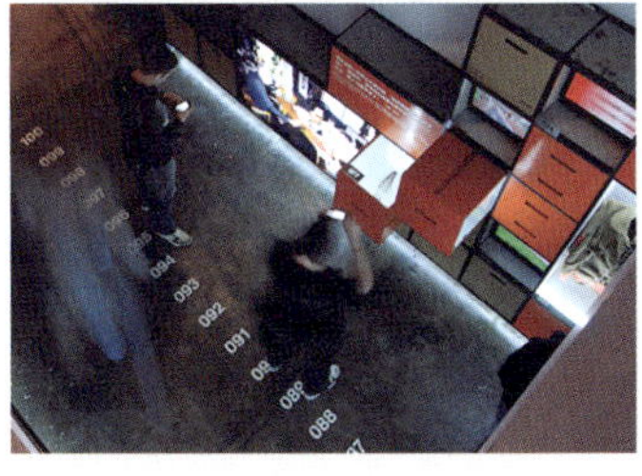

Corridor flanked on either side by dense display walls with extruded vitrines, drawers and display cases. Each unit deforms the flat surface.

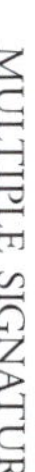

PAINT

9. Paint I. *Leo's*. Providence, Rhode Island.

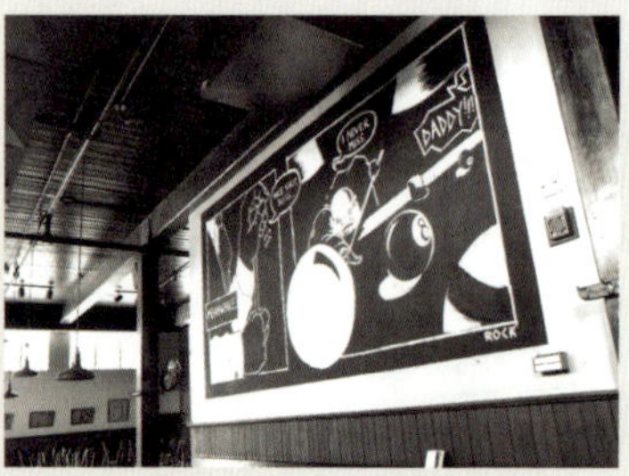

Bar as graphic novel. Drunken patron as ideal reader, repeatedly forgetting the storyline and seeing the work anew. Transformation of the wall over time creates hyper-slo-mo animation.

10. Paint II. *PS1*. Queens, New York.

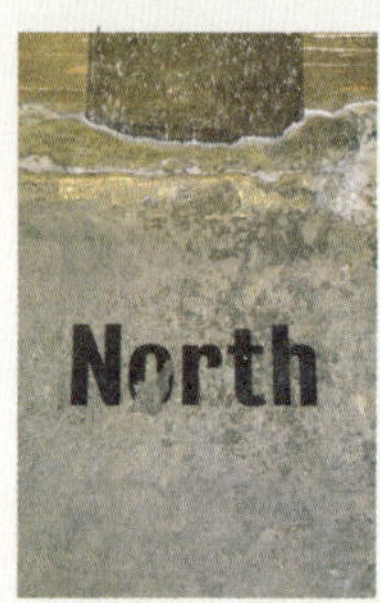

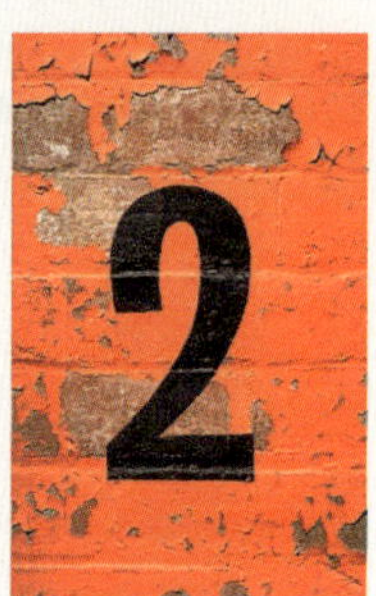

Decommissioned public school transformed into contemporary art museum. Labeling all elements of the vast space: numeric and typographic labels painted directly on distressed surfaces. Restaurant-style chalkboard serves as master menu.

11. Paint III. *New World Stages*. New York, New York.

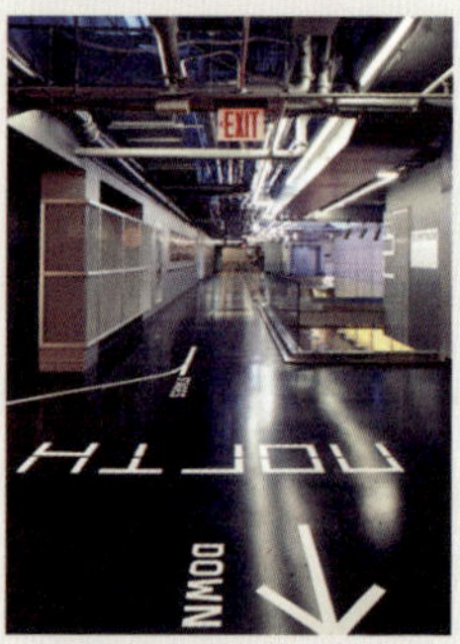

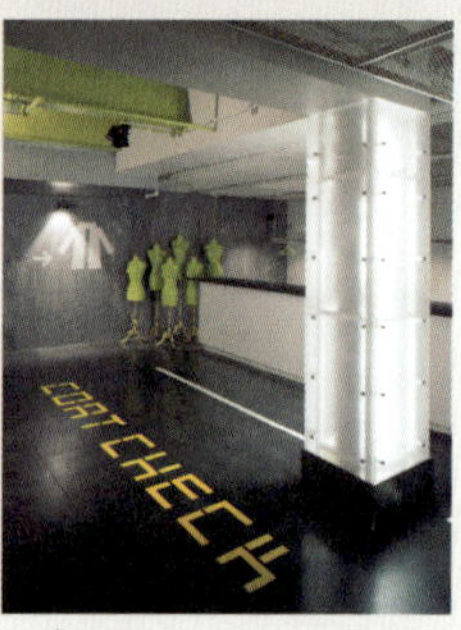

Full-scale diagram. Labels painted directly on floor and walls of subterranean theater re-orient the visitor to the space overhead.

12. Paint IV. *Milstein Hall*. Ithaca, New York.

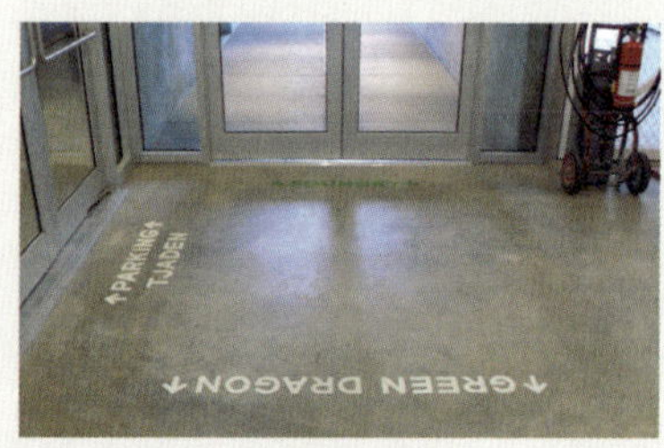

Plan notations, 1:1 scale.

13. Paint V. *Novartis Fabrikstrasse 15*. Basel, Switzerland.

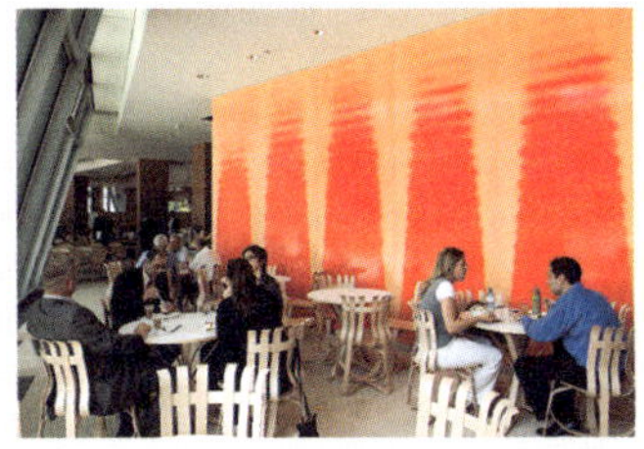

Refrigerated aluminum walls treated with temperature-sensitive paint; color transforms when coolant is flowing.

PIXELS

14. Pixels I. *IIT McCormick Tribune Campus Center*. Chicago, Illinois.

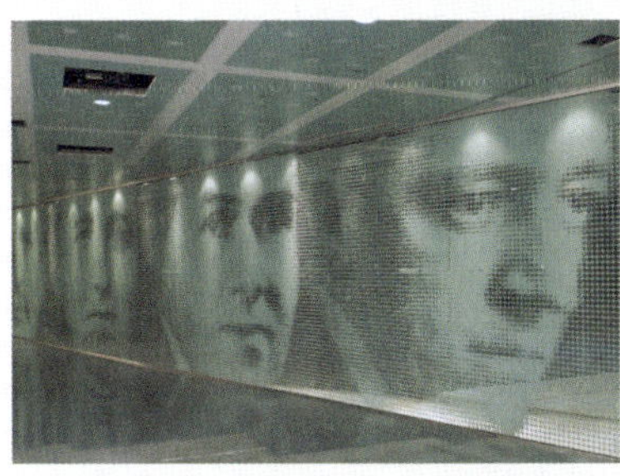

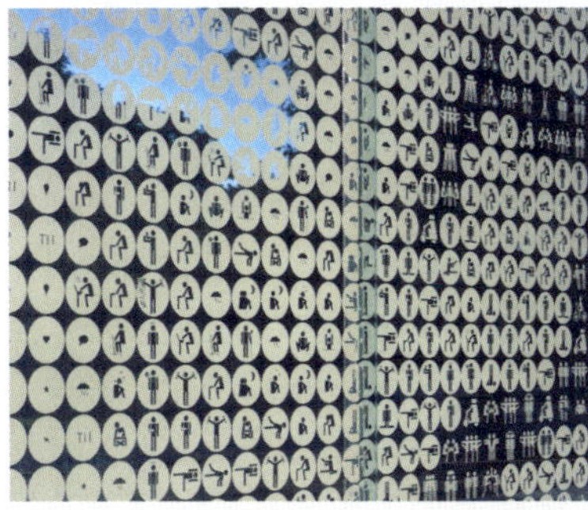

The image-in-the-glass redux: super-scale portraits comprised of rough screens of picot-pixels.

15. Pixels II. *Prada Broadway*. New York, New York.

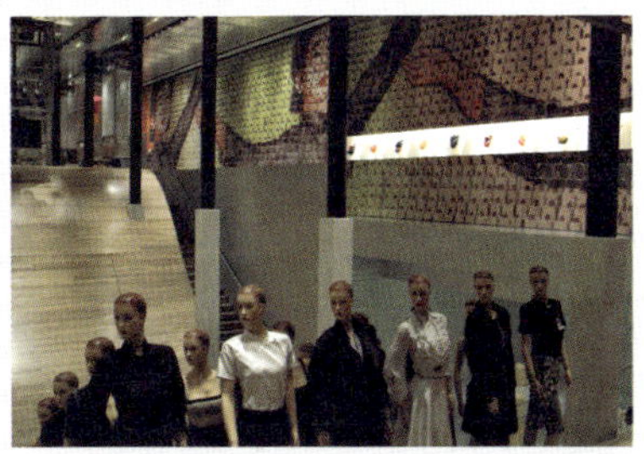

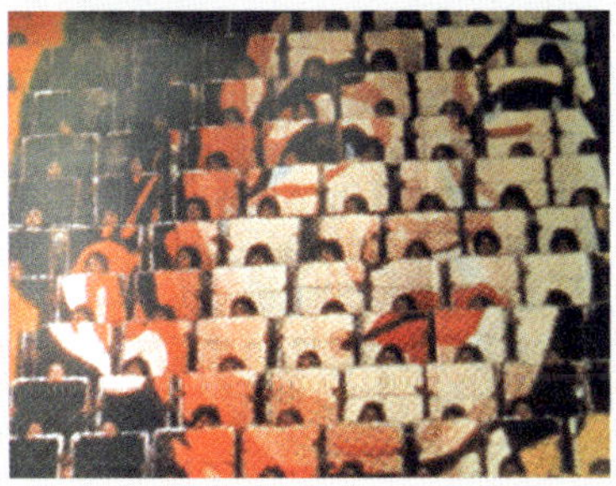

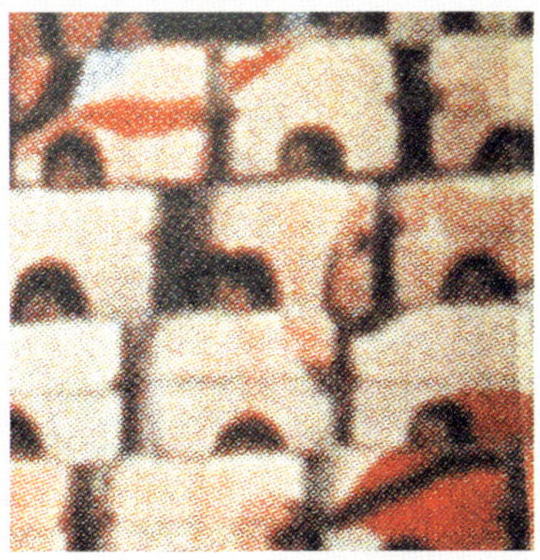

Monumental figures that—on close inspection—reveal tiny figures surveilling the shoppers below.

16. Pixels III. *Muhammad Ali Center.* Louisville, Kentucky.

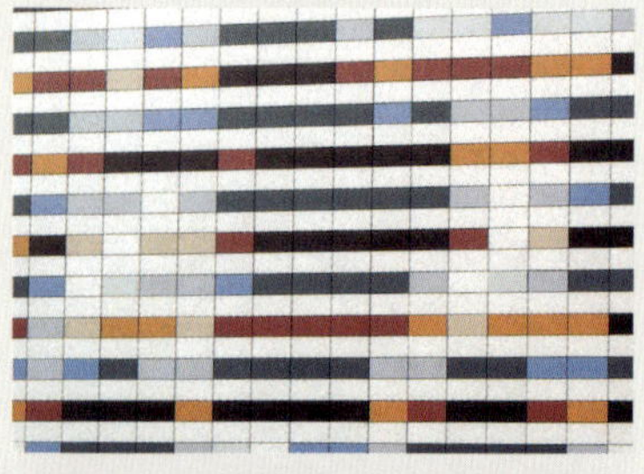

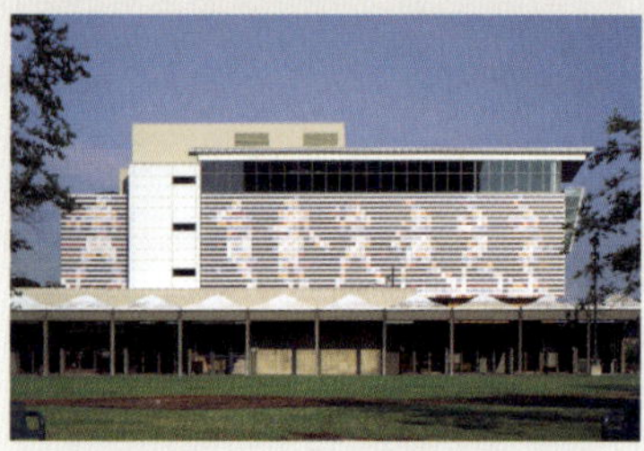

Image perceptible only from a distance; at close range pixels disintegrate into a more or less even distribution of color.

17. Pixels IV. *Chinese Central Television Headquarters.* Beijing, China.

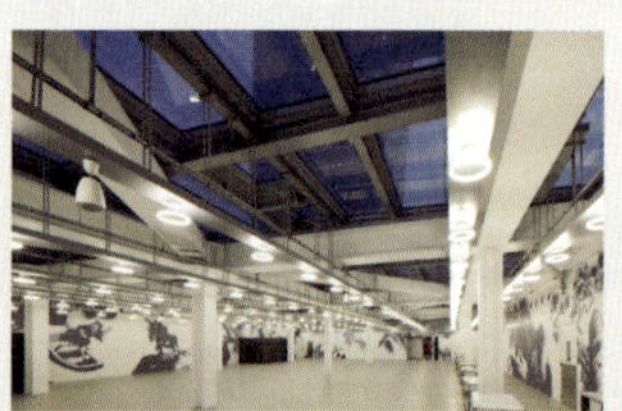

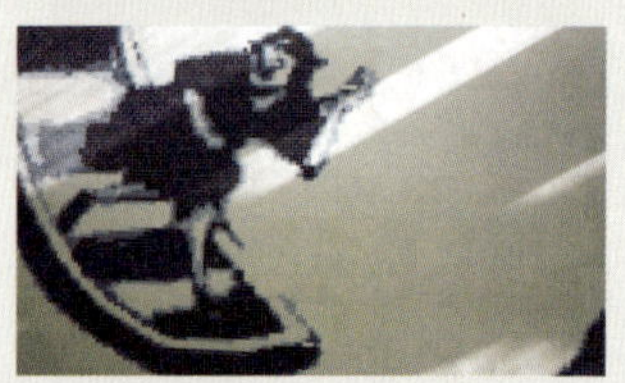

Three-colored tiles reorganized into low-res Chinese vase.

18. Pixels V. *Prada Broadway.* New York, New York.

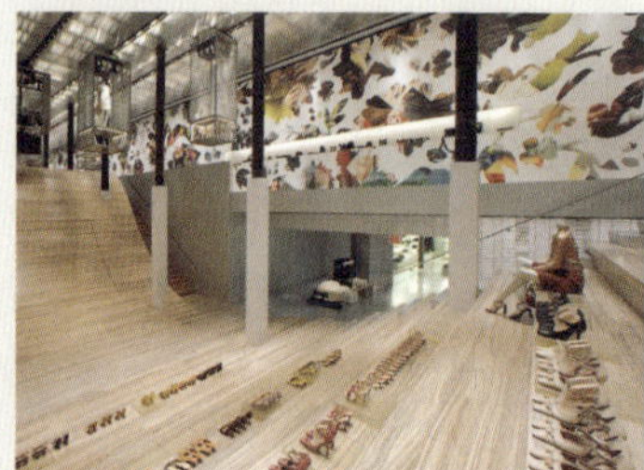

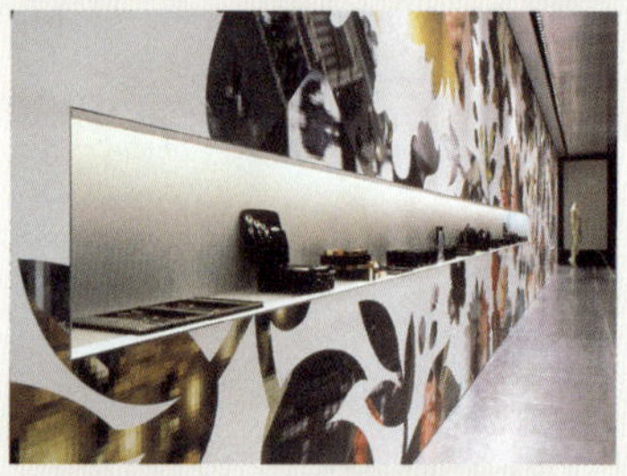

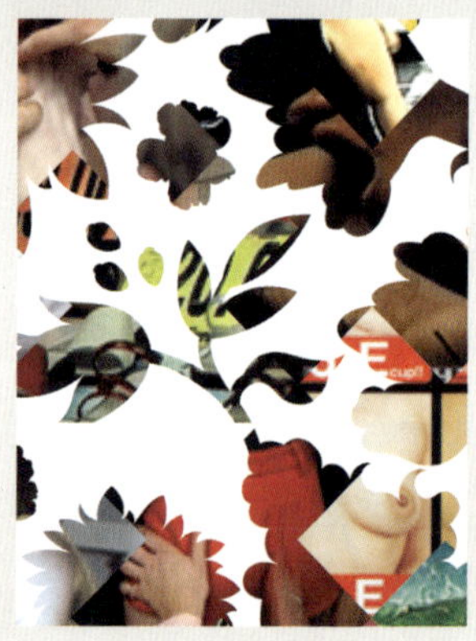

Contemporary chintz constructed of pixel fragments: images, film stills, found objects, some banal, some precious, some vaguely pornographic.

PUNCTURE

19. Puncture I. *Novartis Fabrikstrasse 15*. Basel, Switzerland.

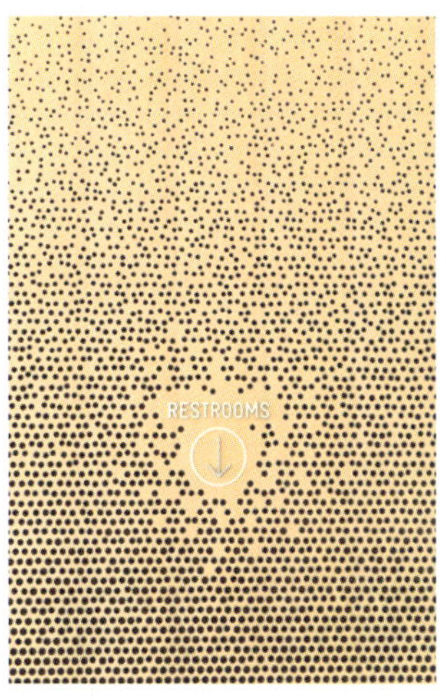

Materially altering the surface—drilling, cutting, etching—breaks through the skin of the space. Wood-paneled walls pierced with countless tiny holes.

20. Puncture II. *Dee and Charles Wyly Theatre*. Dallas, Texas.

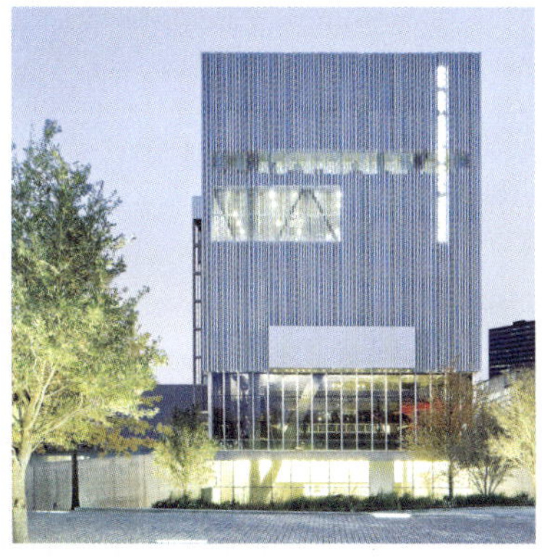

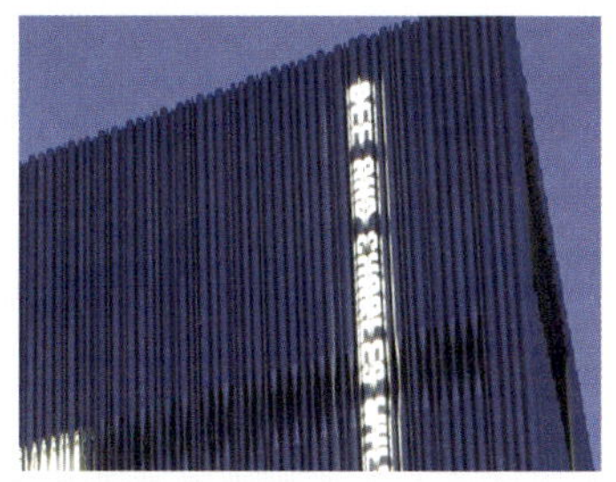

Low-res typography punched through extruded aluminum tube façade. Light floods through the wound.

21. Puncture III. *Nike 100*. Beijing, China.

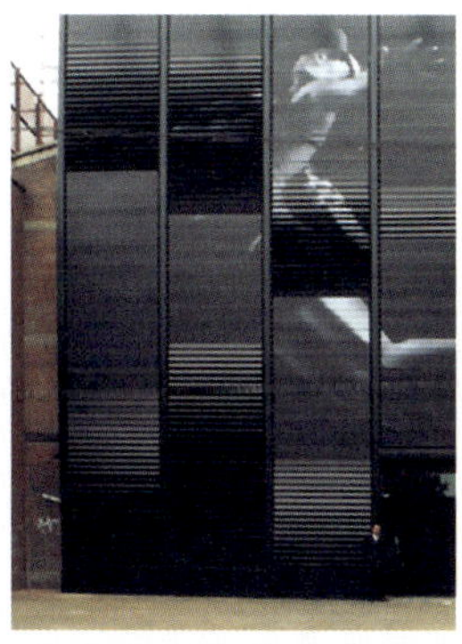

Mechanical façade breaks the surface—flipping irregularly among three different images—a jittery, unstable effect.

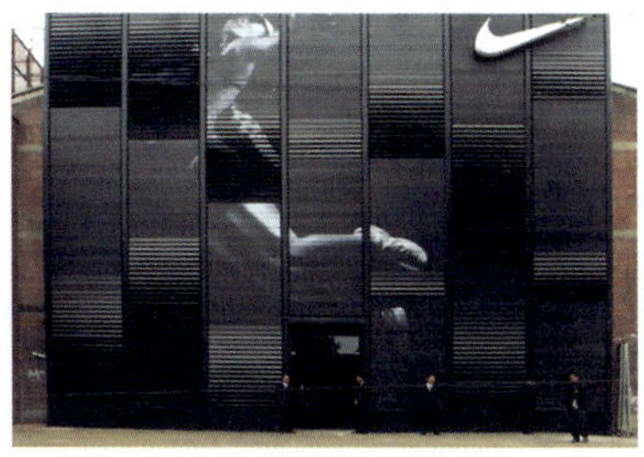

REDACTION

22. Redaction I. *Prada Broadway.* New York, New York.

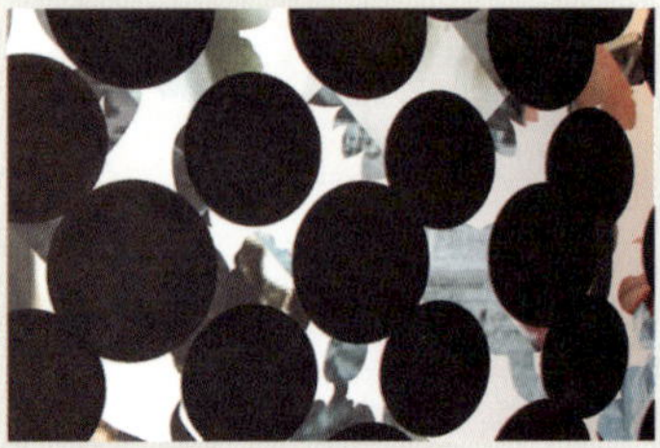

Large-scale dot moiré applied directly over existing installation (see no. 18). Black as form, white relegated to background. Moiré creates sense of movement and illusory depth.

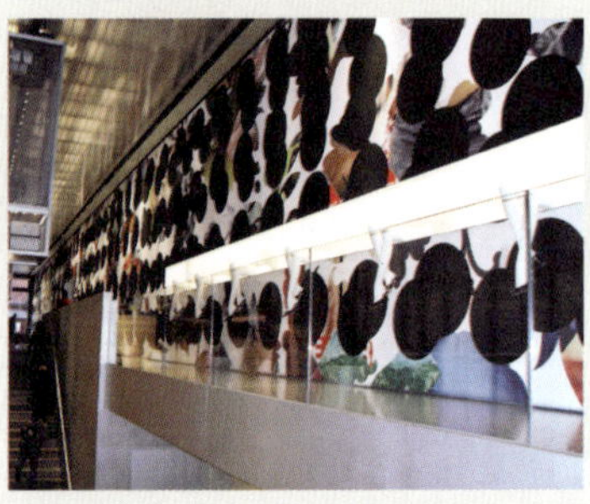

23. Redaction II. *Prada Broadway.* New York, New York.

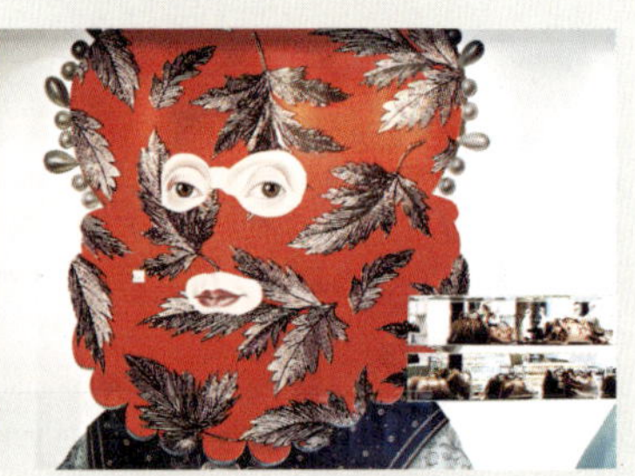

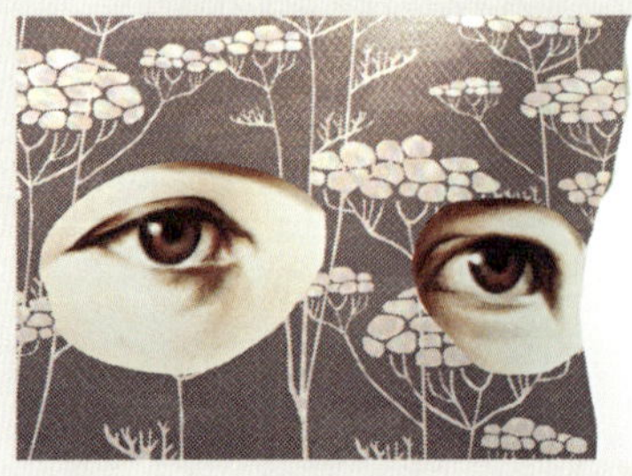

Jaunty masks render the infamous anonymous with an only slightly repressed reference to current forms of infamy (see no. 27).

24. Redaction III. *Smoke and Mirrors.* New York, New York.

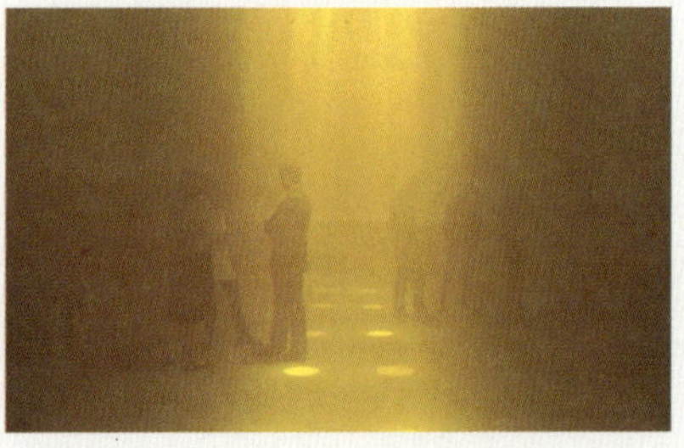

Smoke erases walls, solidifying volume.

24a. Depending on the direction of the lights the room has columns or a defined ceiling.

REFLECTION

25. Reflection I. *Guggenheim Las Vegas.* Las Vegas, Nevada.

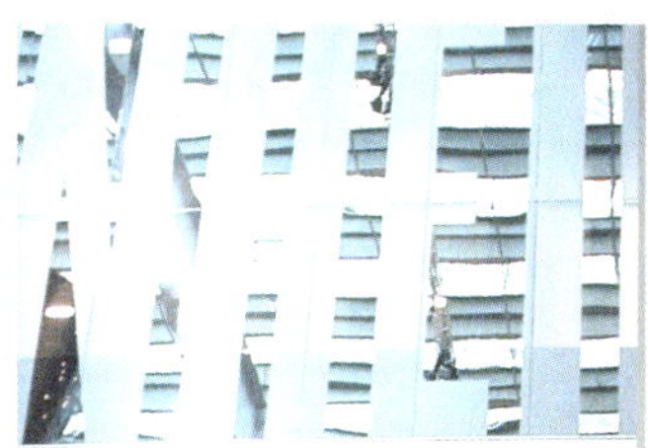

One-way reflection yields directional voyeurism.

26. Reflection II. *Prada Broadway.* New York, New York.

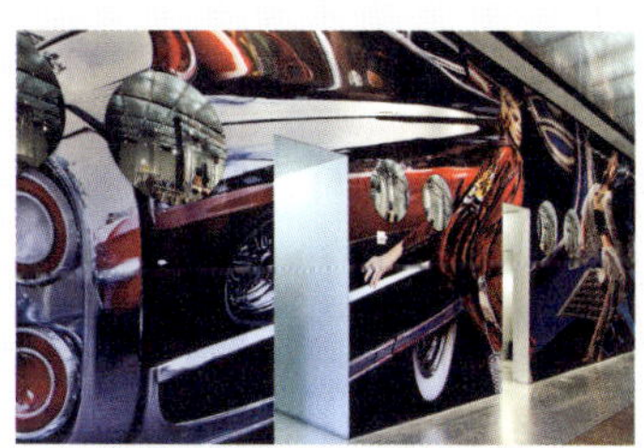

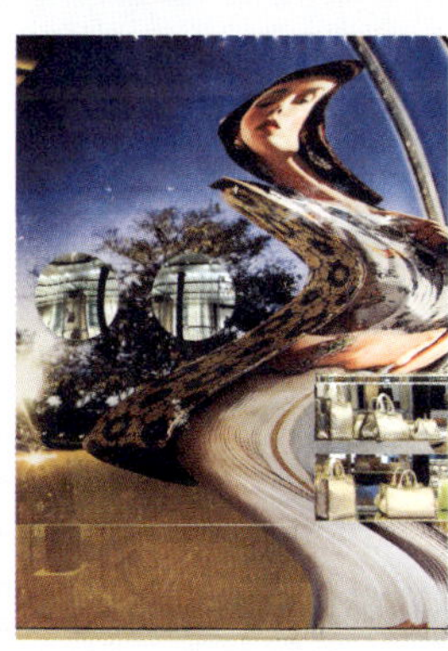

Convex mirrors optically penetrate solid surface.

SALON

27. Salon I. *Prada Broadway.* New York, New York.

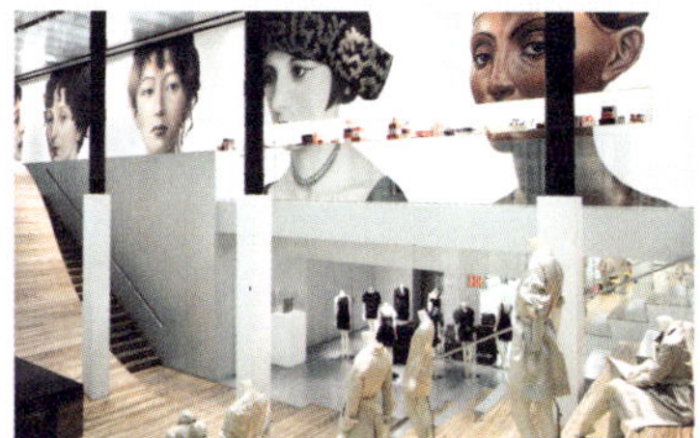

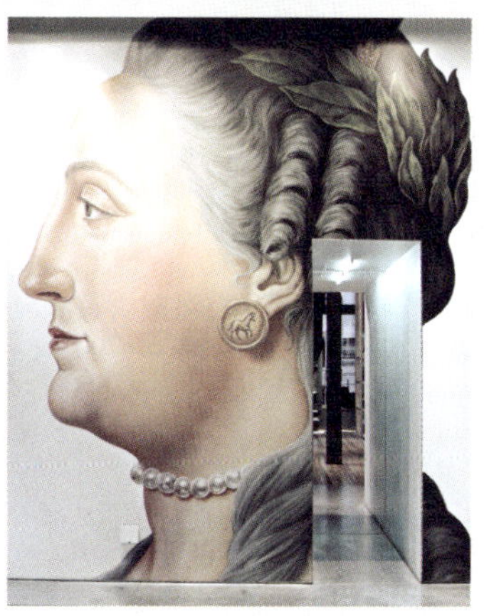

Monumental oil portraits of nine infamous women, including Elizabeth I, Simone de Beauvoir, Kiki de Montparnasse, Catherine the Great.

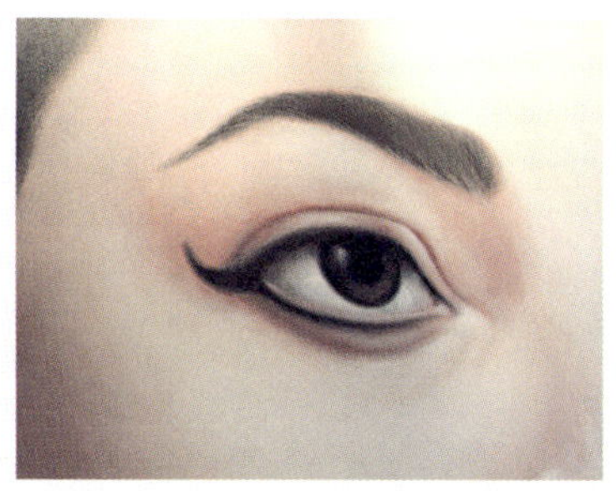

28. Salon II. *Prada Broadway.* New York, New York.

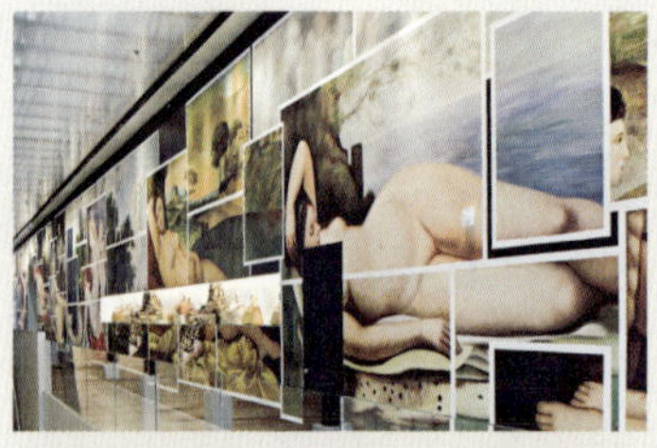

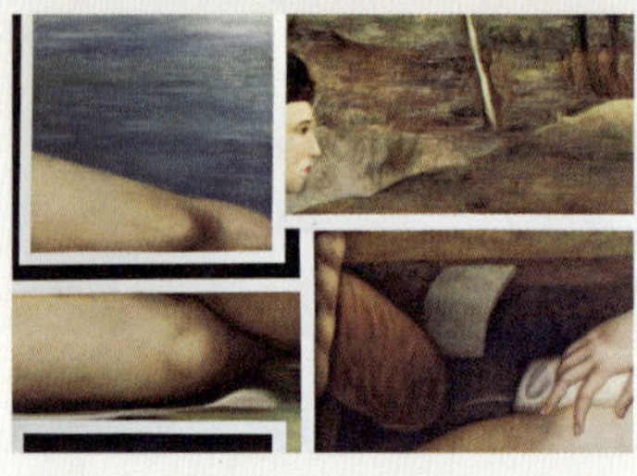

Wall as salon, paintings as wallpaper: 100 counterfeit oil Old Masters from young Chinese factory painters.

SCENOGRAPHY

29. Scenography I. *IIT McCormick Tribune Campus Center.* Chicago, Illinois.

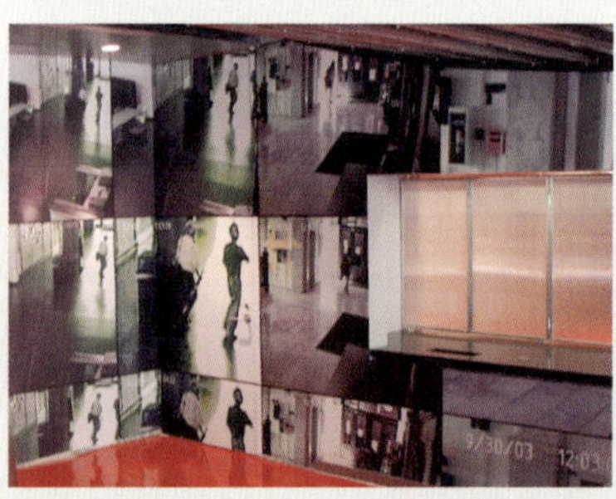

Surveillance views as portraiture.

30. Scenography II. *Prada Broadway.* New York, New York.

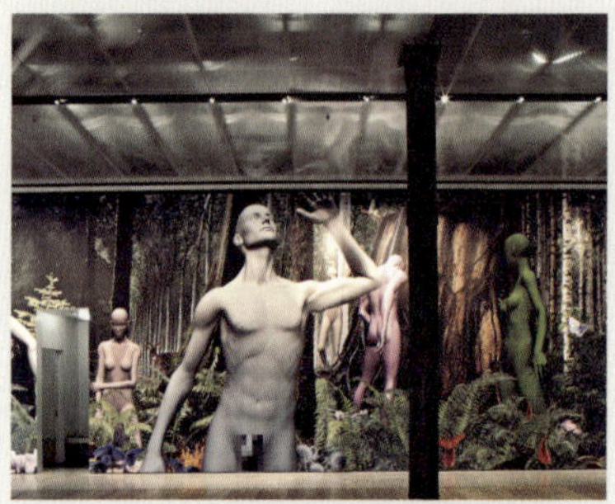

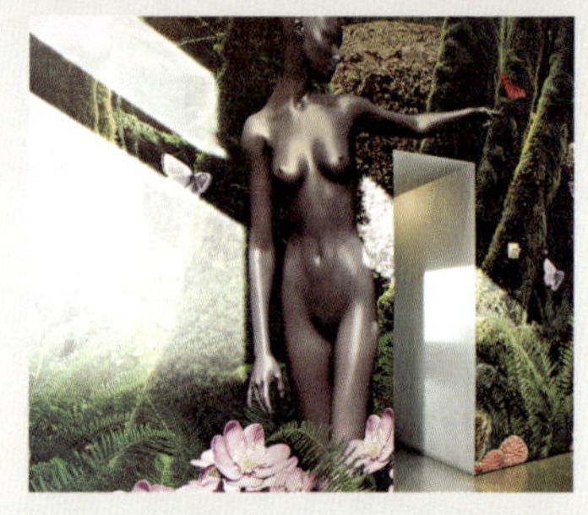

Idyllic fantasy of vivid color and imagery: un-domestic workers inhabit a world beyond the shop floor.

31. Scenography III. *Prada Broadway.* New York, New York.

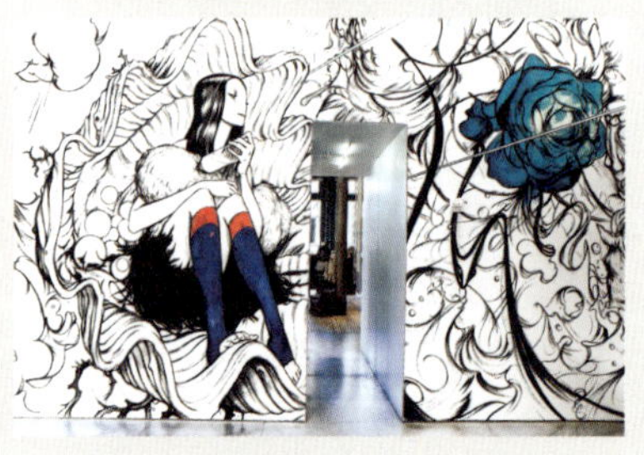

Exotic dream space: collision between Bosch and Beardsley.

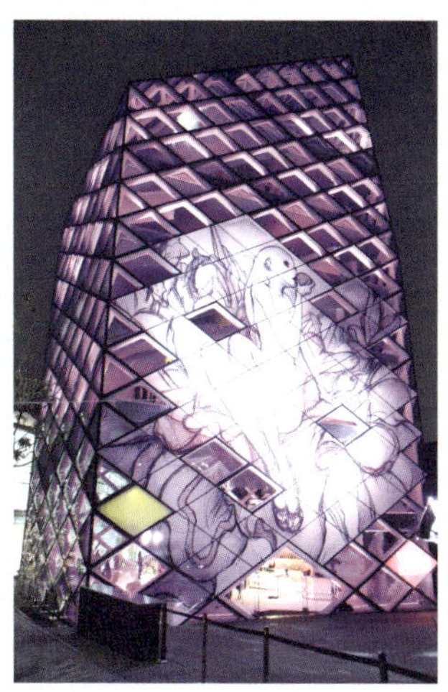

32. Scenography IV. *MiuMiu Fashion Show*. Milan, Italy.

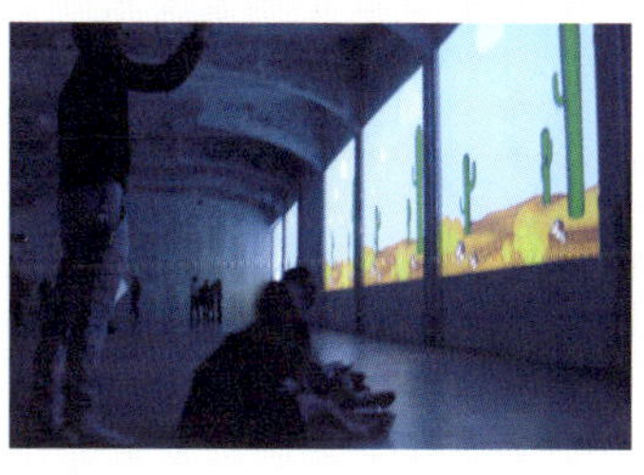

Full-scale video-game landscape populated with animated cacti, mushrooms, bananas and clouds creates fleeting event horizon.

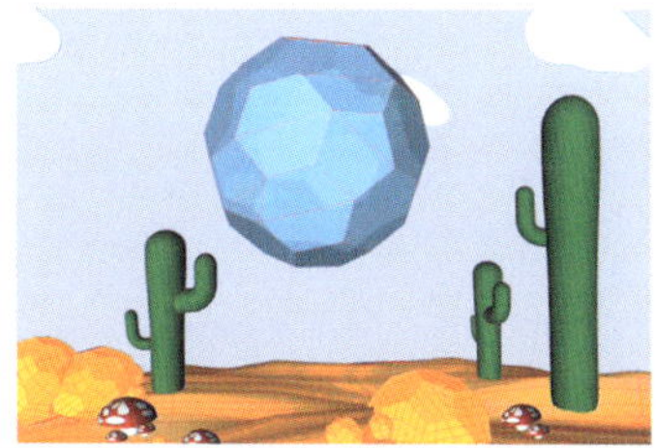

33. Scenography V. *Prada Women's Fashion Show*. Milan, Italy.

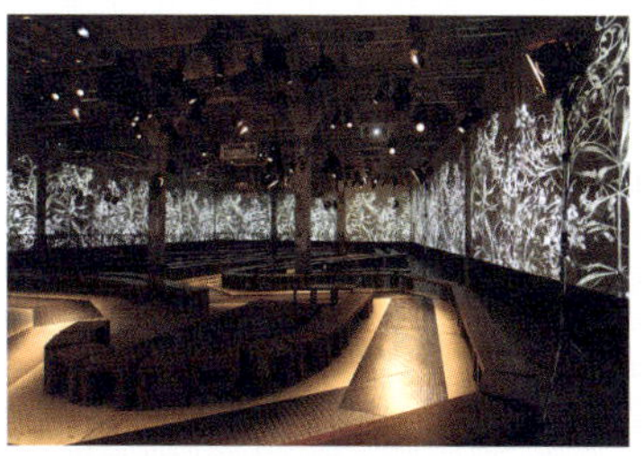

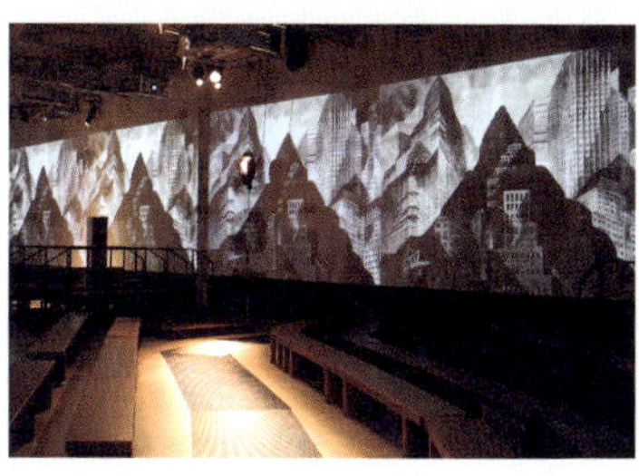

360–degree space with 18 coordinated projections. Piranesi's perspectives create contiguous environment overgrown by tangle of computer-generated vegetation.

TRANSPARENCY

34. Transparency I. *Guggenheim Las Vegas*. Las Vegas, Nevada.

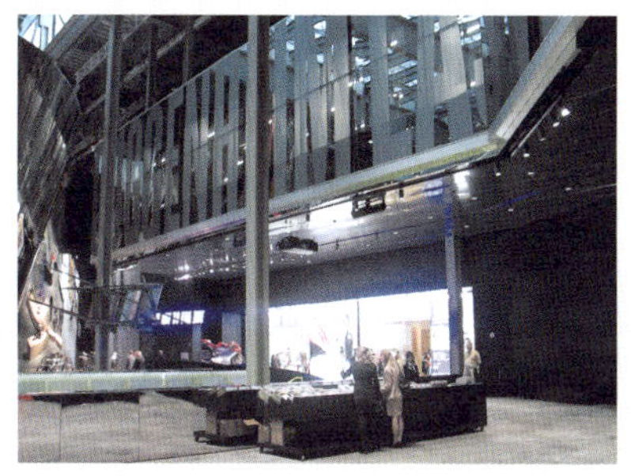

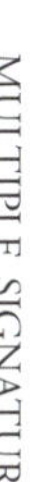

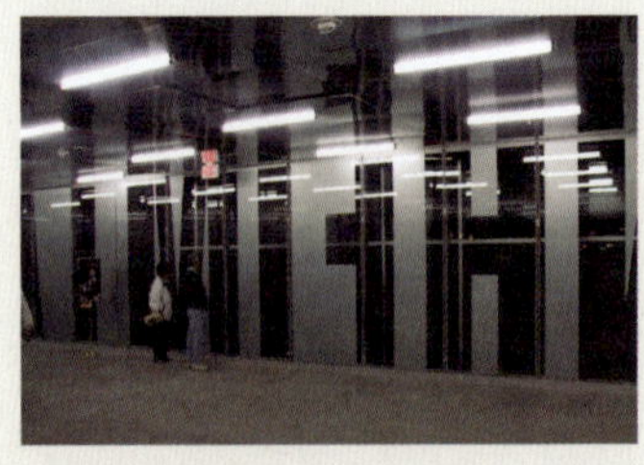

Mirrored-glass bridge funnels art-loving gamblers from parking garage to vast casino floor. Fragmented letters fracture views through two-sided wall. Passersby animate typography.

35. Transparency II. *Guggenheim Las Vegas*. Las Vegas, Nevada.

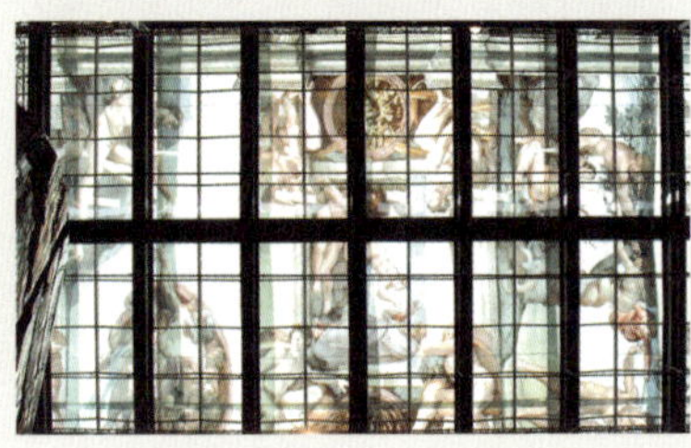

Overhead the Sistine Chapel back-lit by desert sun.

36. Transparency III. *Smoke and Mirrors*. New York, New York.

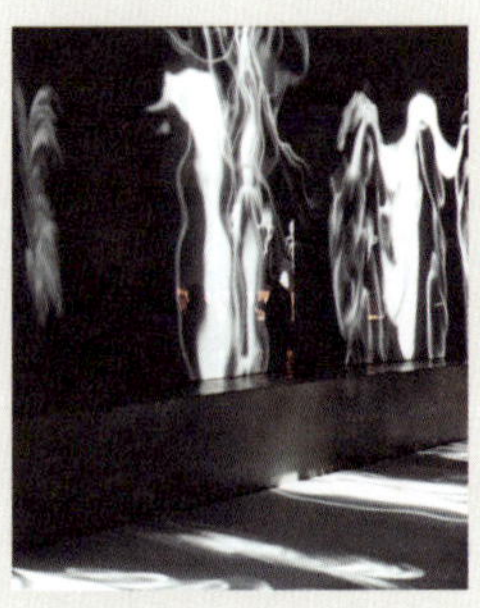

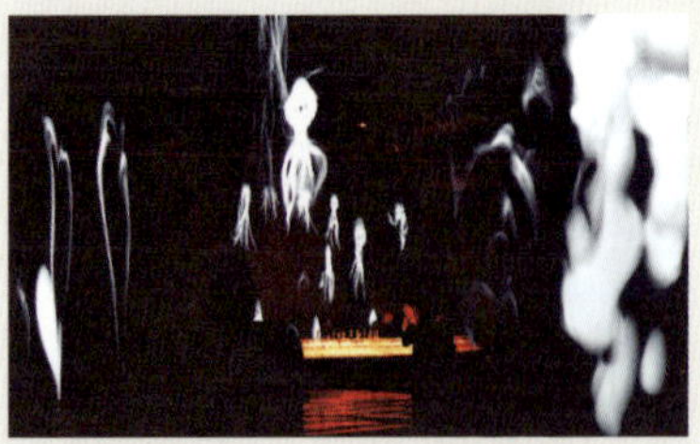

Gravity-defying display made possible by the old trick known as Pepper's Ghost*. Wall where there is none: the invisible wall area occupied by seemingly solid forms dancing in deep space.

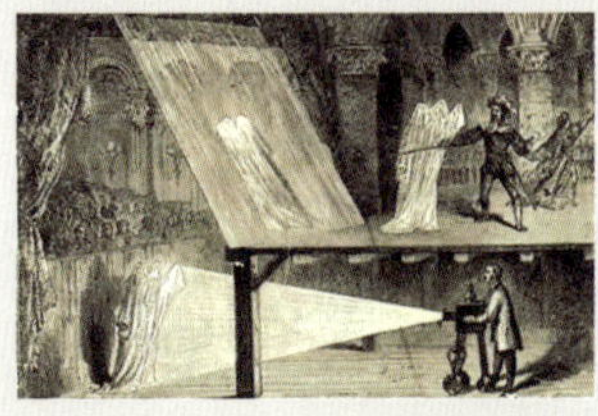

*Pepper's Ghost creates the illusion of an image floating in space. A transparent scrim is set at a 45–degree angle to the audience. A projection bounced off a reflective surface onto the angled screen allows viewers to see through the projection to the scene behind the screen.

37. Transparency IV. *IIT McCormick Tribune Campus Center*. Chicago, Illinois.

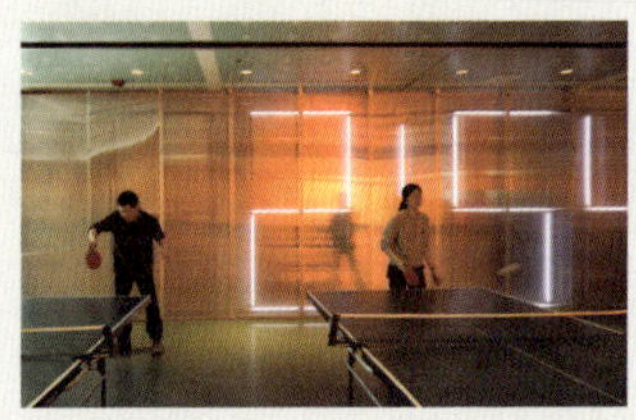

Thin cathode tubes embedded in polycarbonate panels—forming a crude digital clock—illuminate poché.

38. Transparency V. *Prada Beverly Hills*. Los Angeles, California.

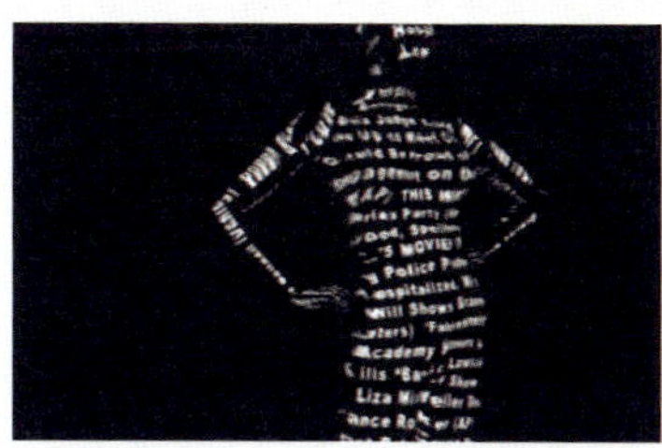

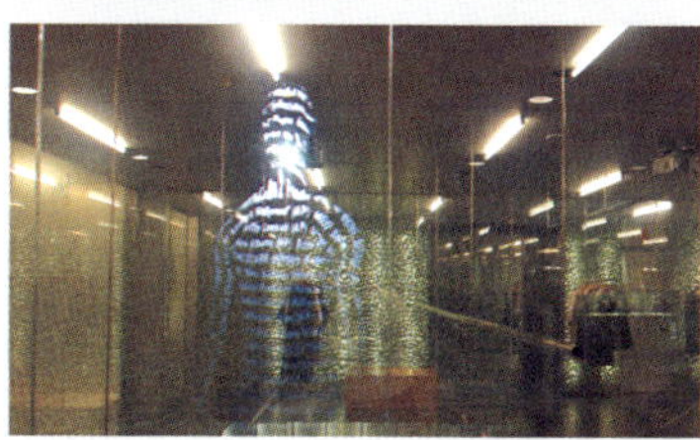

Digital android with data-mapped skin projected onto electrostatic glass appearing, ghost-like, in indeterminate wall space. Simultaneously deep and weightless.

39. Transparency VI. *Darwin D. Martin House Visitor Center*. Buffalo, New York.

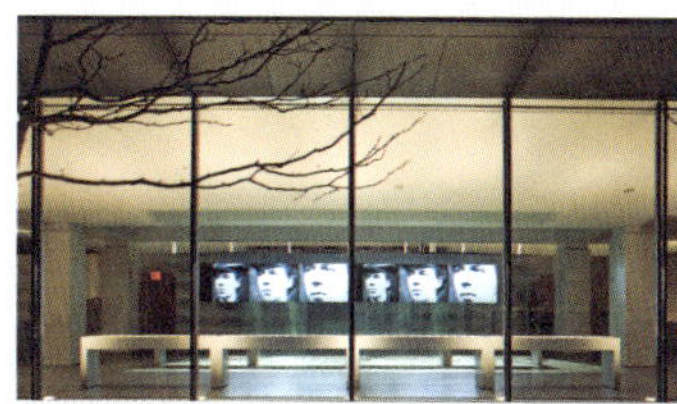

Projected images magically appear on polarized-glass demising wall.

40. Transparency VII. *Winspear Opera House*. Dallas, Texas.

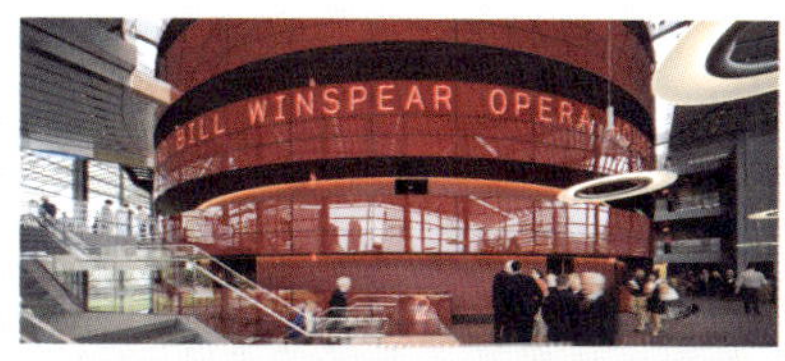

Light typography behind heavy red glass forms softly illuminated projection on glassy exterior surface.

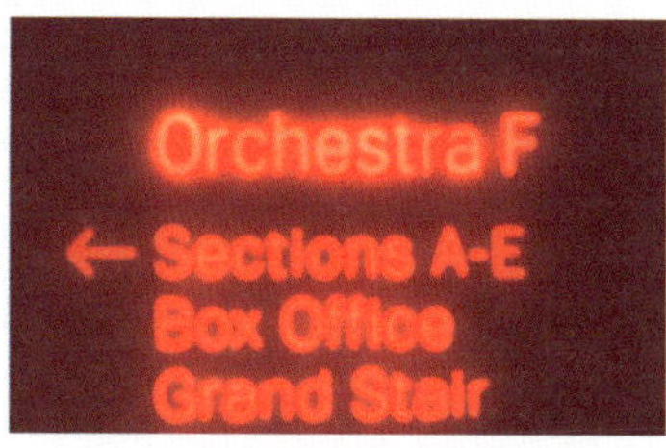

41. Transparency VIII. *Novartis Fabrikstrasse 15*. Basel, Switzerland.

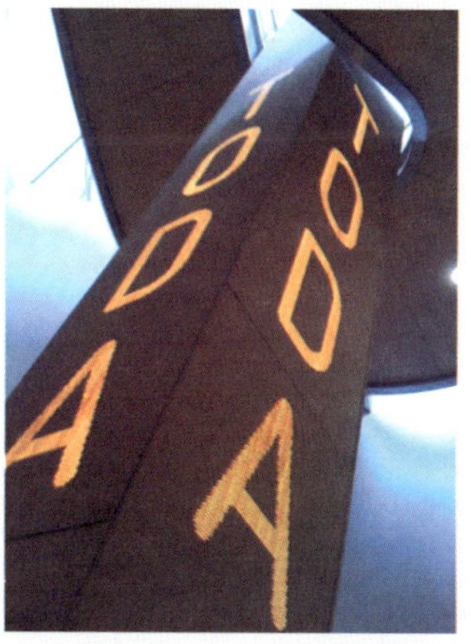

Wooden surface embedded with LED modules. Light undermines opacity.

42. Transparency IX. *Chanel Flagship.* Hong Kong, PRC.

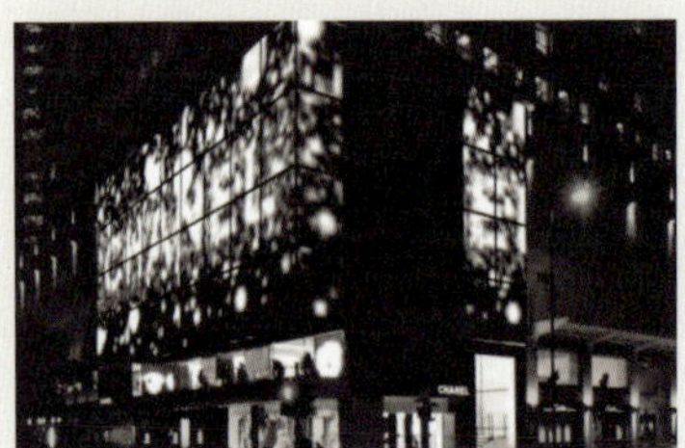

Zero-gravity animation undermines solidity of the façade, particles creating a second, illusory surface somewhere behind the gridded glass curtain.

TROMPE L'OEIL

43. Trompe l'oeil I. *Prada Broadway.* New York, New York.

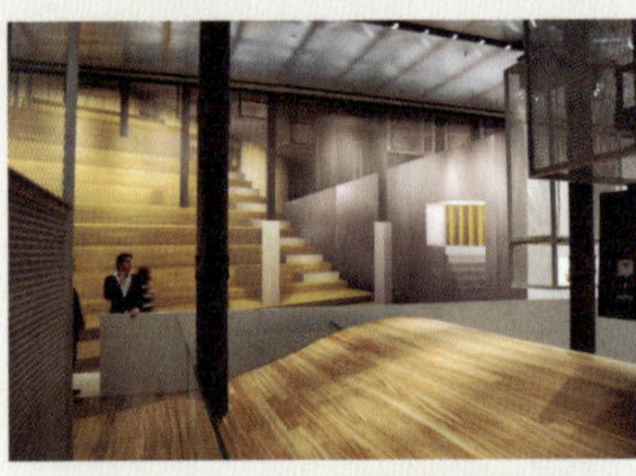

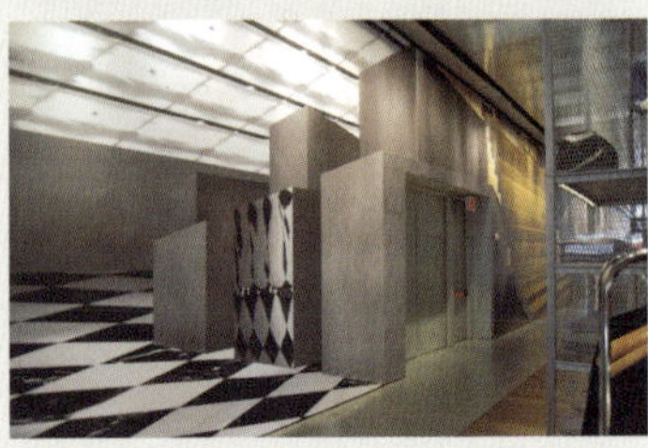

Fake perspective creates conceptual space that extends architecture into an imaginary nether zone. The illusion of depth is monoangular.

44. Trompe l'oeil II. *Prada Beverly Hills.* Los Angeles, California.

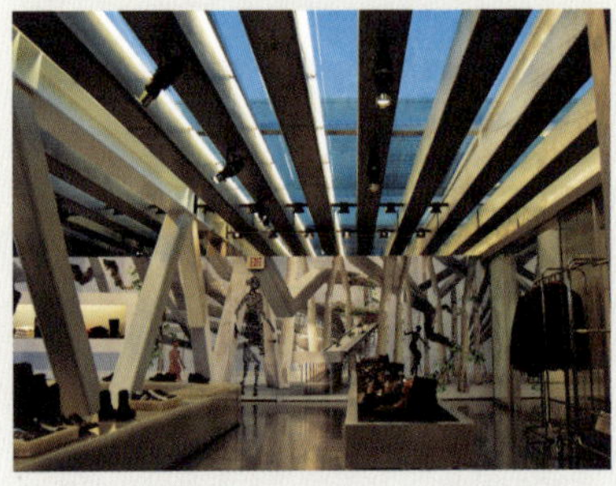

Ceiling beams collide in confused wall space.

45. Trompe l'oeil III. *Vitra Showroom.* New York, New York.

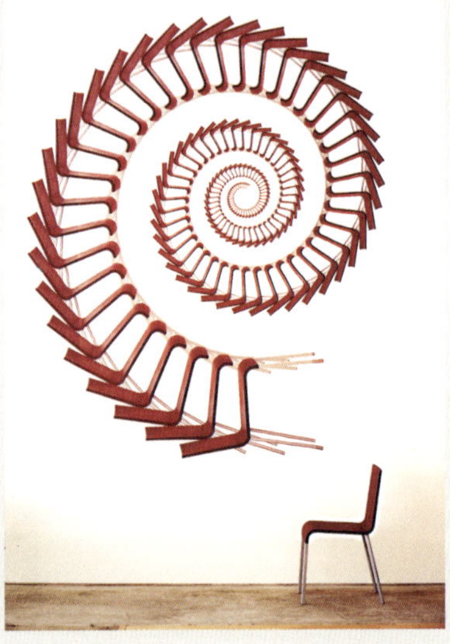

Spiral optically penetrates surface of the wall.

46. Trompe l'oeil IV. *New York Academy of Sciences*. New York, New York.

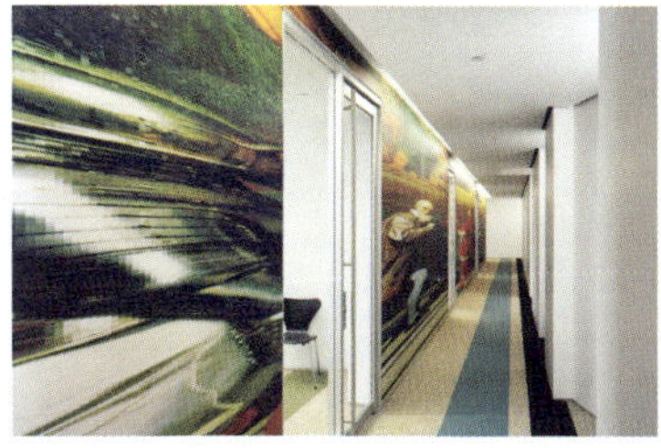

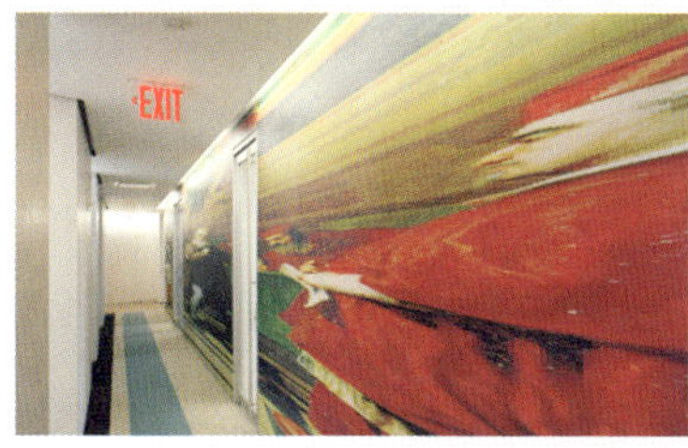

Multiple studies on the physics of perception, perspective, color perception, scale and detail, depth of field. Robert-Fleury's Galileo before the Holy Office, depicting a classic battle between science and faith, stretched the entire length of a narrow corridor.

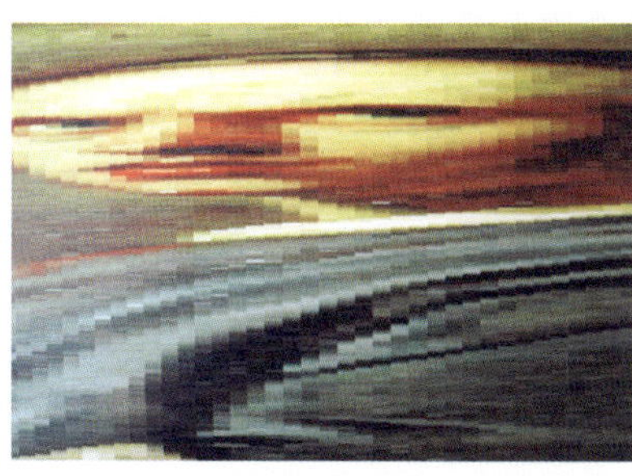

46a. Anamorphosis: Quadrupling the x-axis of each pixel distorts the image along the horizontal plane.

47. Trompe l'oeil V. *New York Academy of Sciences*. New York, New York.

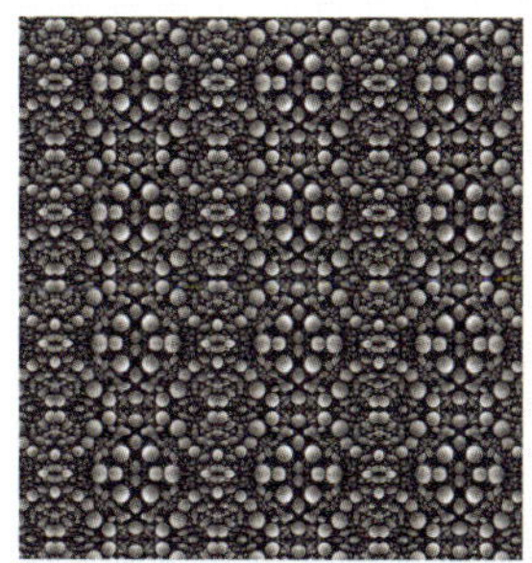

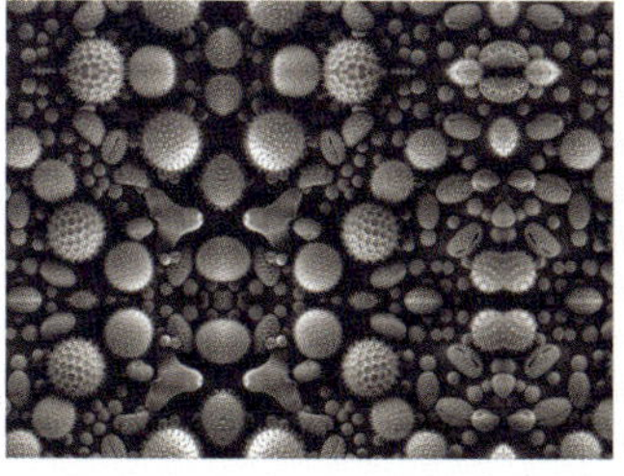

Wallpaper pattern disintegrates into microscopic components.

48. Trompe l'oeil VI. *New York Academy of Sciences*. New York, New York.

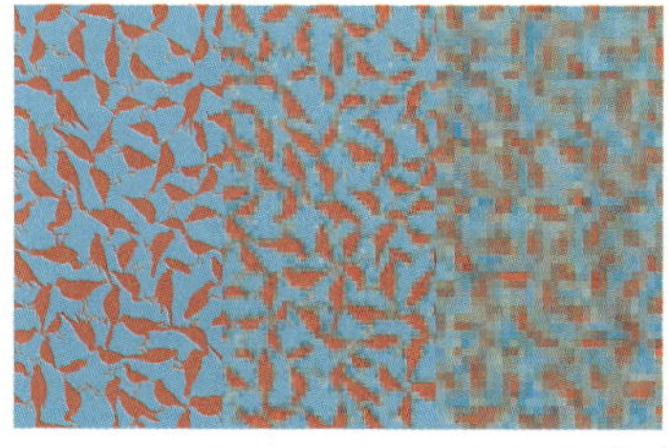

Depth of field pattern: sharpness linked to proximity.

49. Trompe l'oeil VII. *IIT McCormick Tribune Campus Center.* Chicago, Illinois.

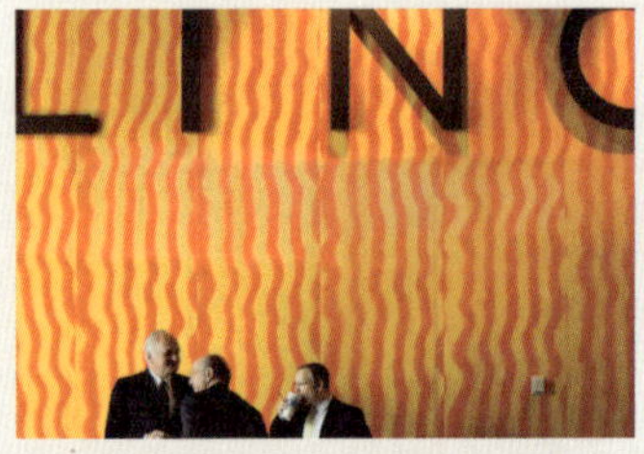

Lenticular film produces eerie, vaguely nauseating quality and indeterminate depth—like high-tech watered silk.

50. Trompe l'oeil VIII. *Dee and Charles Wyly Theater.* Dallas, Texas.

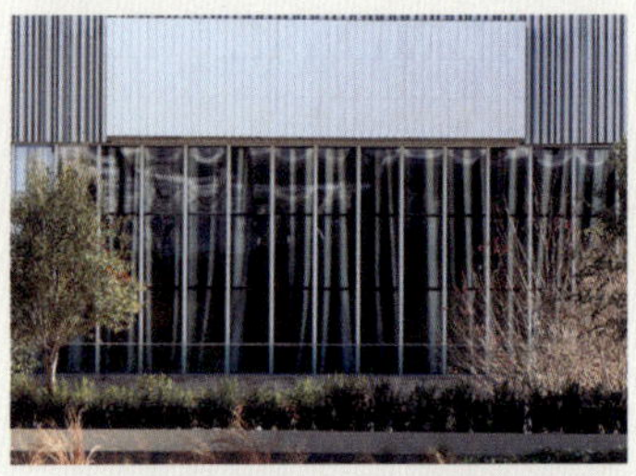

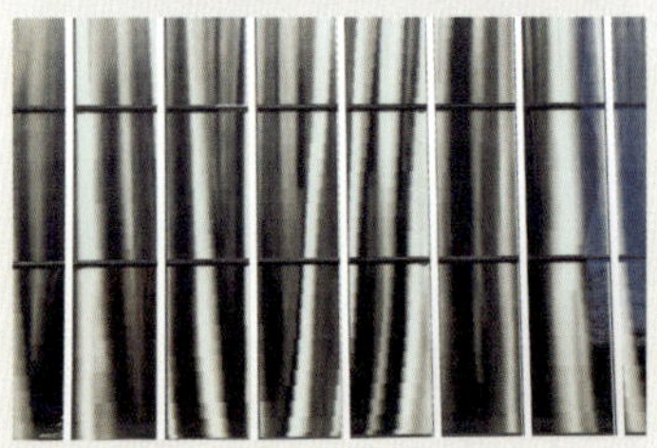

Super-low resolution image depicts gentle folds of a real curtain, printed on flat blackout shades that surround the theater space. Soft form destabilizes heavy structure above.

"Here is an important point," notes Kepes. "The range of hue, value, saturation, and the scale of geometrical measure is incomparably narrower on the picture surface than in one's visible surroundings and only by a creative use of the relativity of the optical differences can one create an optical image on the surface that stands up to the vitality of the visible world."

The preceding examples amount to an evolving meditation on the *relativity of the optical difference.* This investigation is entirely separate from specific issues of content, program, context and function. We maintain a speculative process that skims along the back of professional requirements. There are the overlapping questions with which we grapple daily: questions about systems, content, image production and technology management. However, form will always be one end of our work, and our closest link to the historical practice of graphic design.

If graphic design, in the purely visual sense, is ultimately about the manipulation of two-dimensional space, any research necessarily engages the expansion of that space into new ways of thinking. In changing the nature of what is understood as spatial, we invite our audience to reexamine the preconceived relationships with the world around them in surprising ways. Walls accumulate sensation, become communicative: flat becomes deep, static becomes dynamic. In making the world strange we make it new. That's hardly superficial.

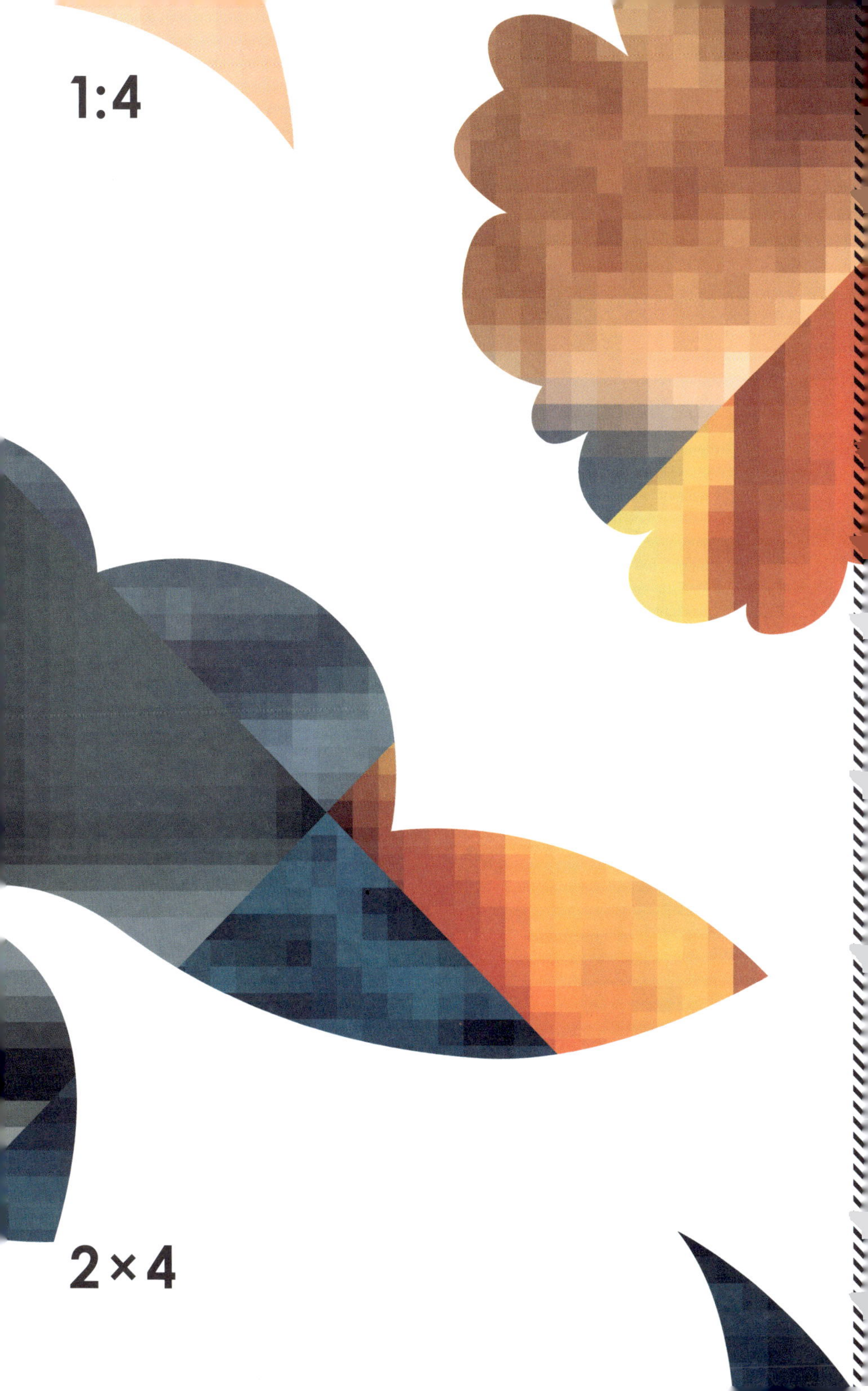

1:4
2×4

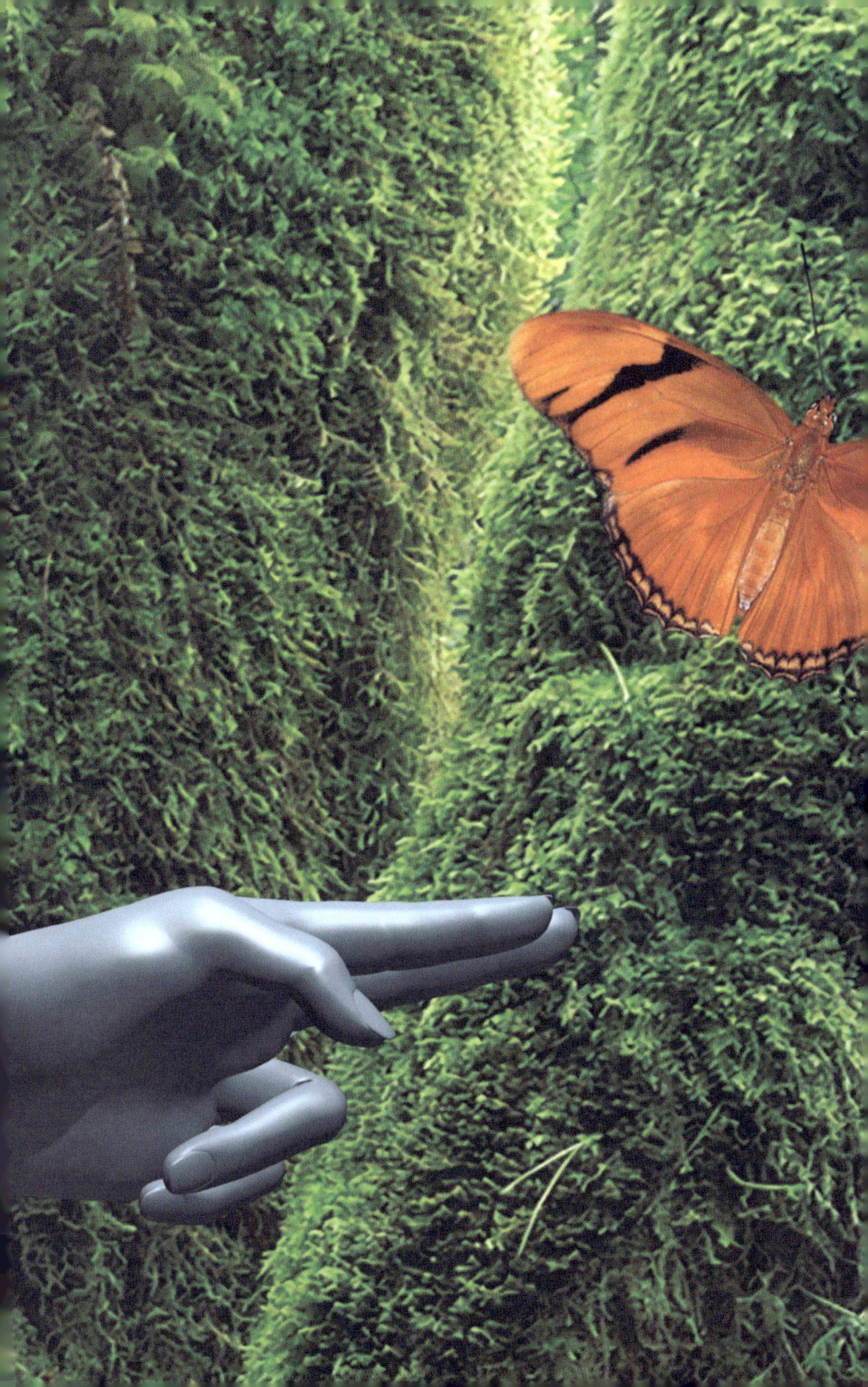

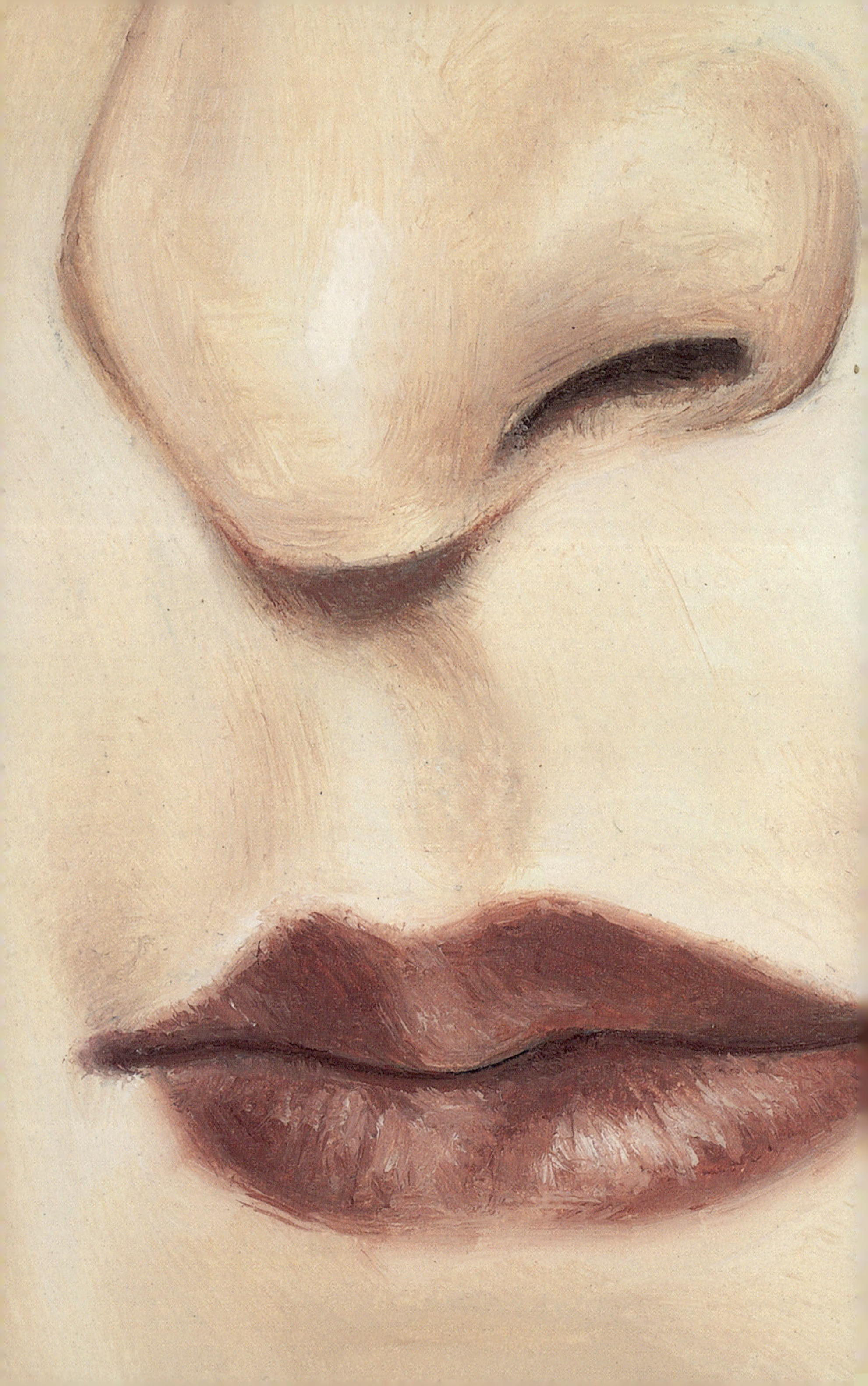

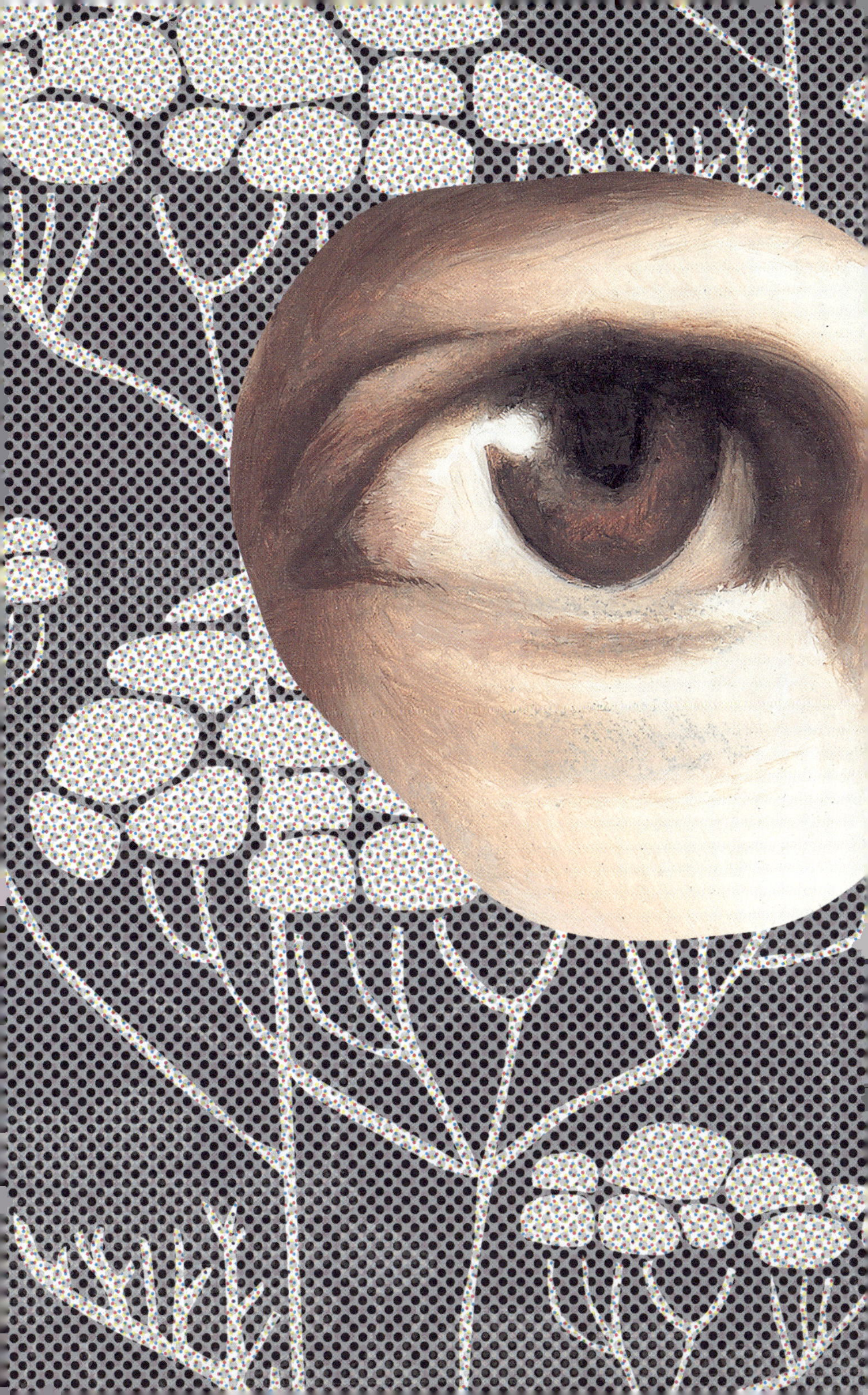

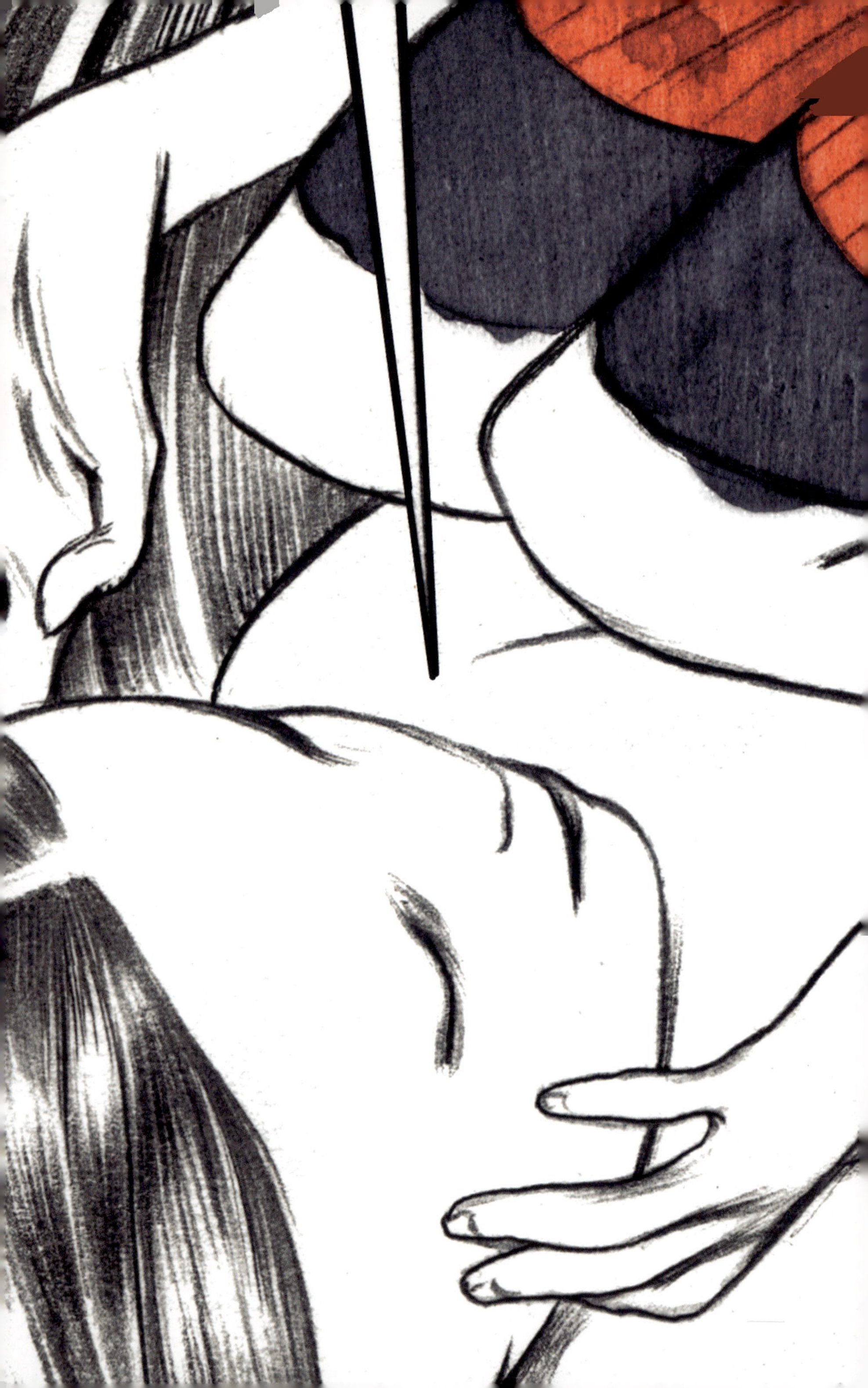

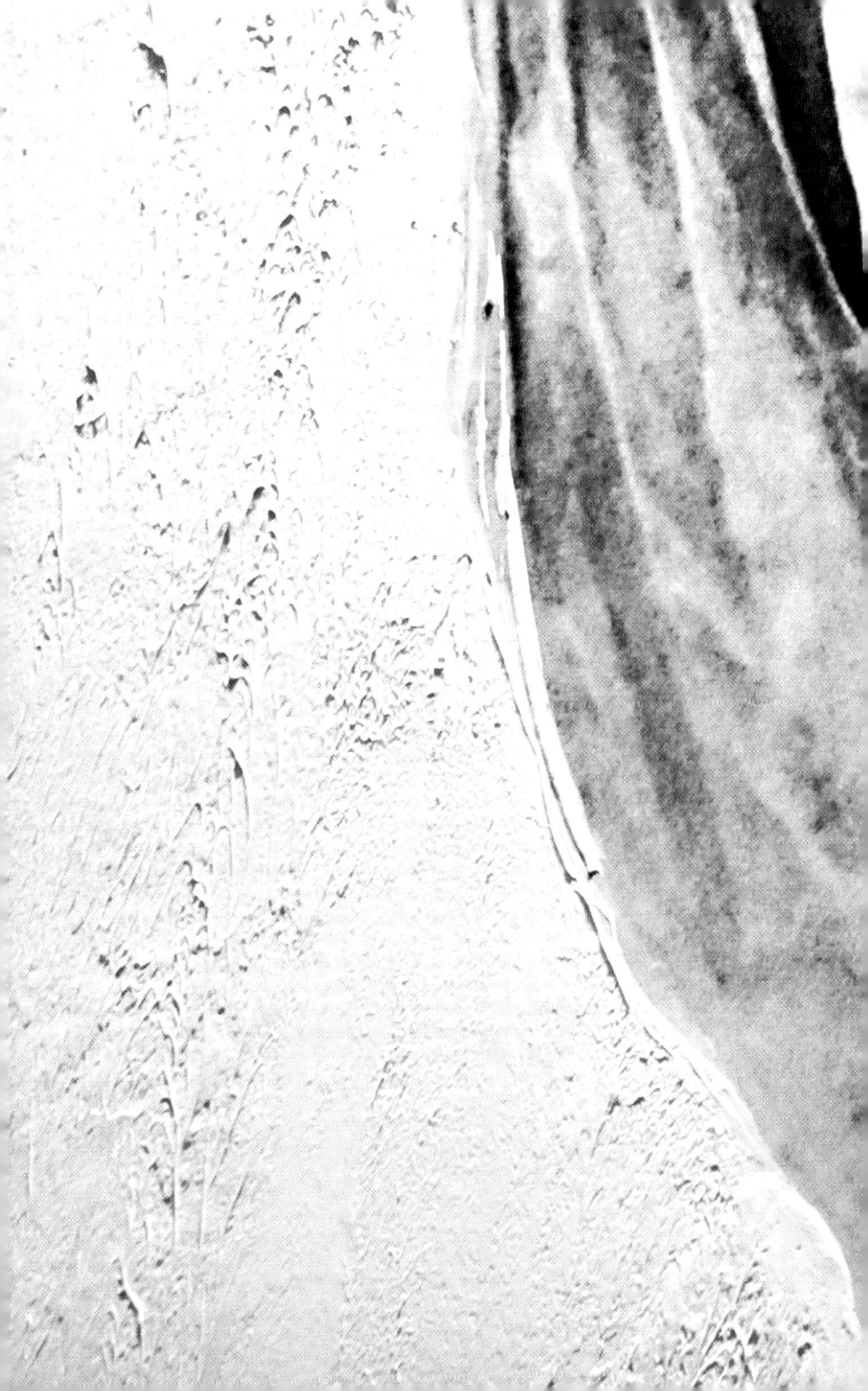

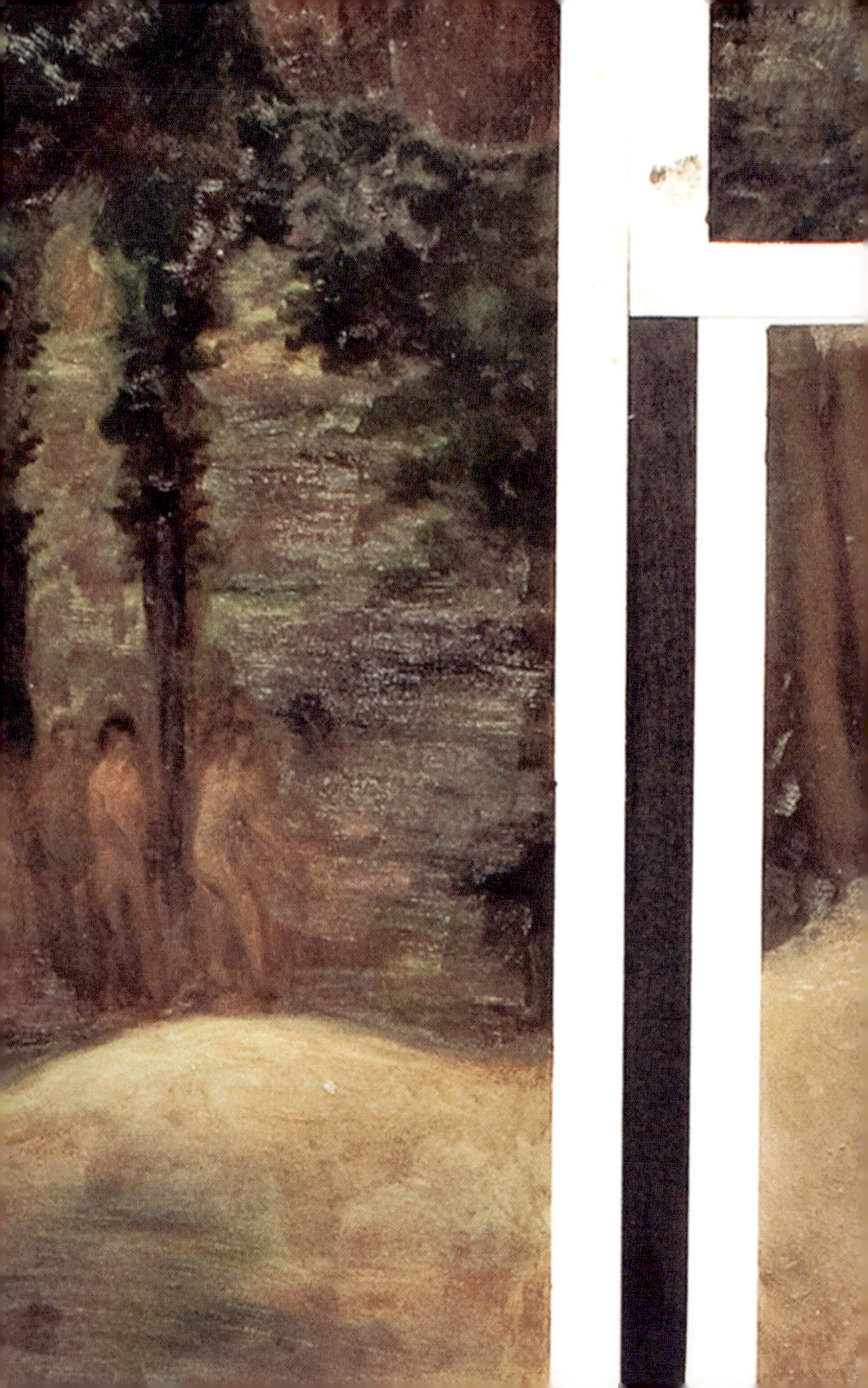

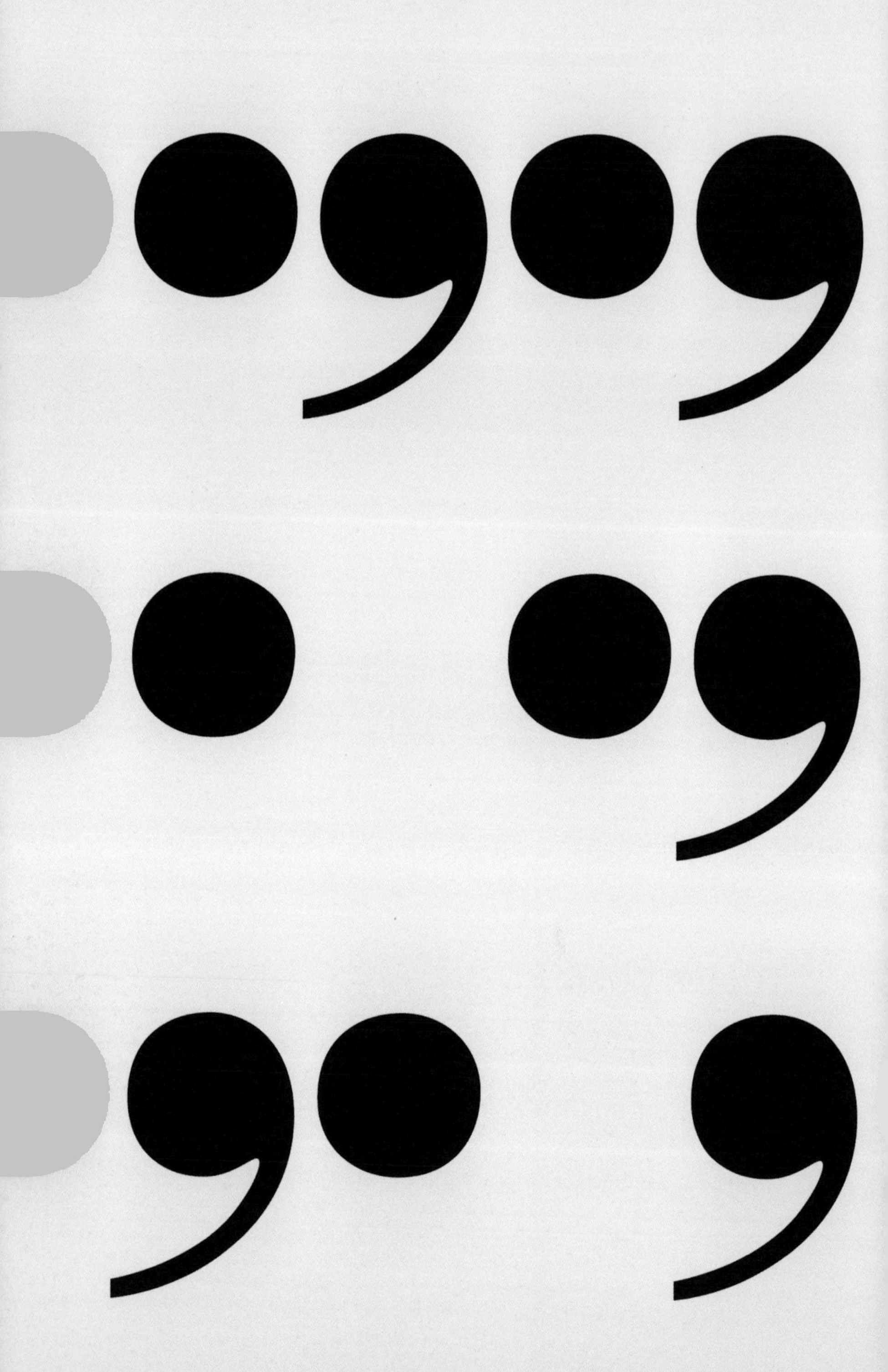

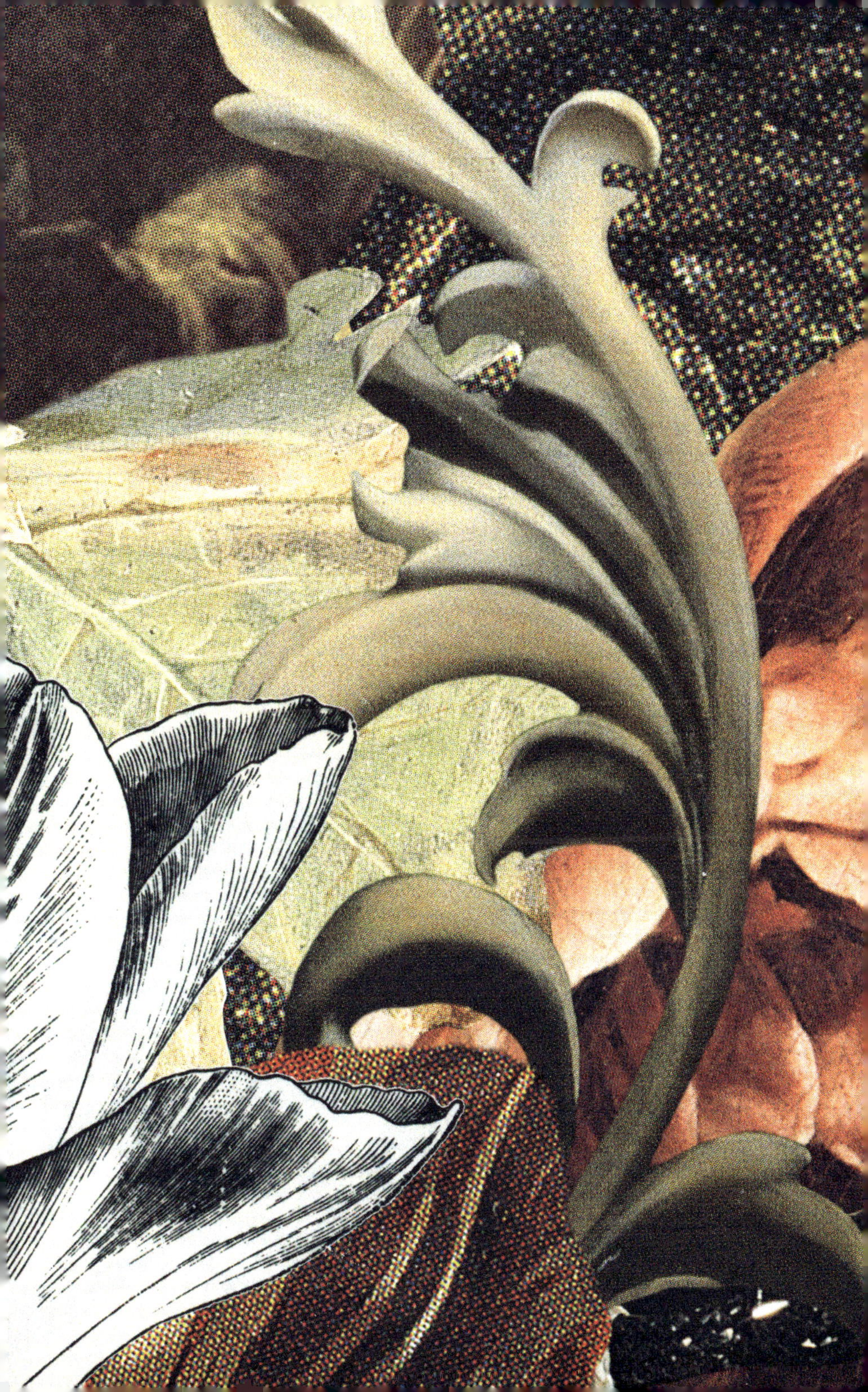

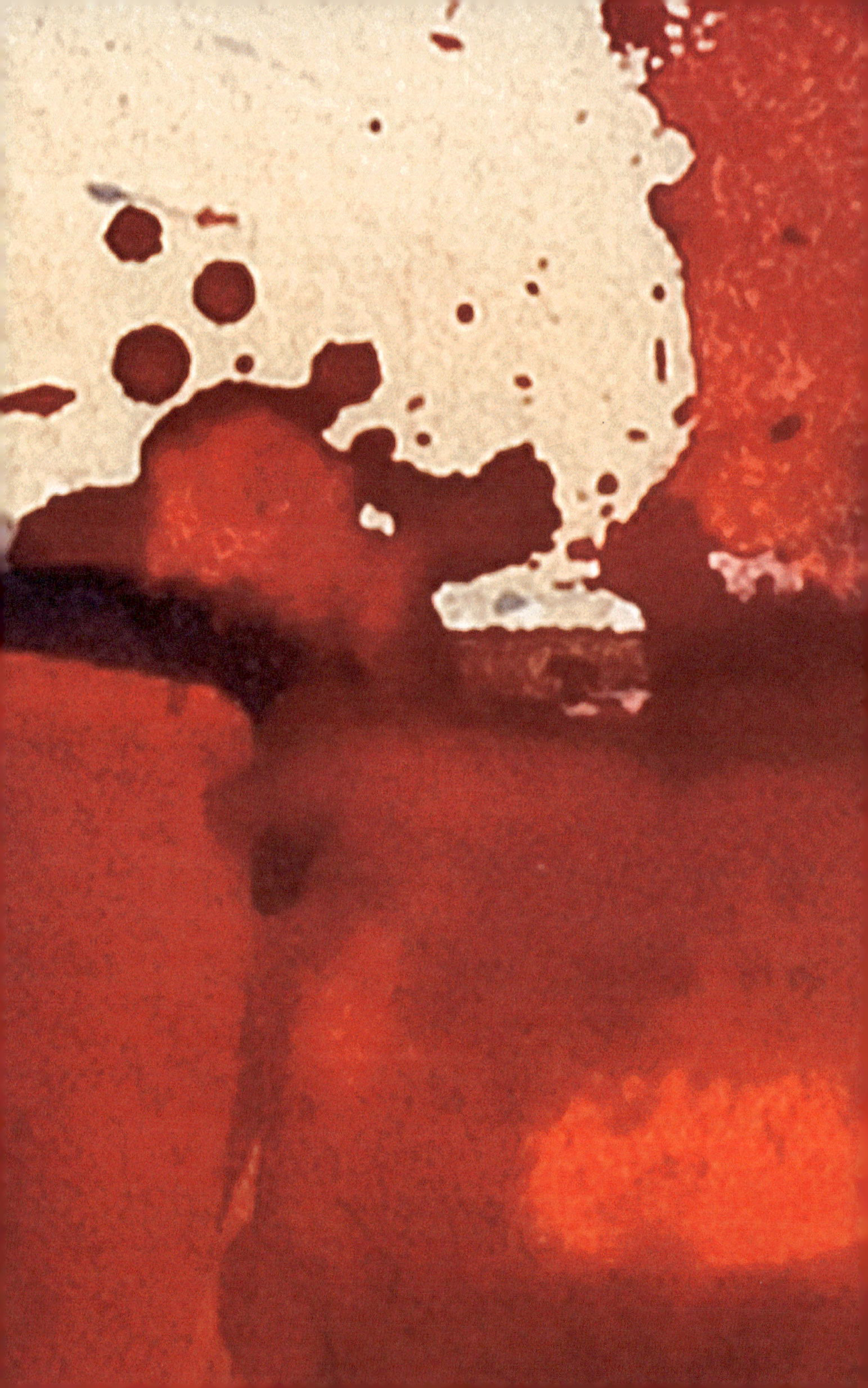

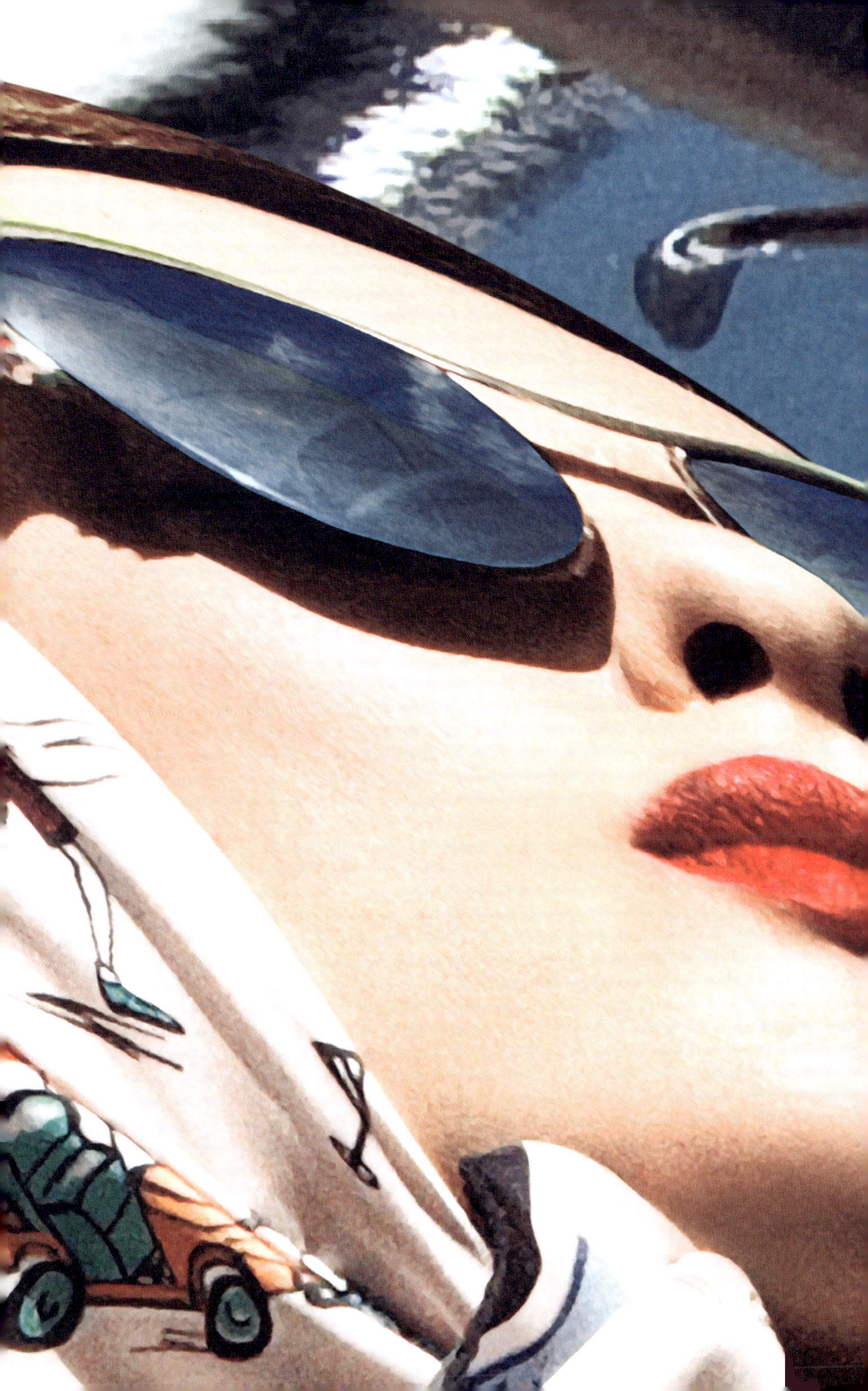

STARING AT WALLS: 2×4 FOR ARCHITECTS

LUCIA ALLAIS

Walk into an environment designed by 2x4, and you are likely to find yourself staring at walls. The walls are not visible, *per se*: they are hidden behind images, symbols, icons, words. But the visual universe 2x4 conjures up is not easy to consume: it requires deciphering. So you find yourself staring, more or less closely, at the surface of these images, adjusting your position the better to understand them, and slowing down the act of visual perception until, unwittingly, your attention has been entirely commandeered by a piece of architecture that was declared obsolete over a century ago: the solid wall.

From the point of view of architectural history, there are two ways to see this achievement: as a final blow to the modernist dream of dematerialization, or as a bittersweet victory for the architects who promoted it. Modern architects in the early 20th century wanted so badly to conquer solidity and opacity, to remove all boundaries and achieve a new spatial continuum, that they prophesied the end of the traditional wall. But they did not imagine that the wall would disappear behind images. Walls would dissolve into nothingness, leaving room for an architecture of transparency and interpenetration. This didn't literally happen, of course: instead modernist walls were painted, made of glass, slotted with strip windows, or detailed as freestanding objects.[1] Learning from this tradition, but carrying few of its anxieties, 2x4 makes walls disappear in plain sight.

But if 2x4 intervenes in this ongoing architectural struggle, it is not only to do architecture a favor (as an architect might say, by "re-activating the performative potential of vertical surfaces"). 2x4 also takes the wall as a space for meditations on design, and on the problem of medium-specificity in design. Any lessons we can draw about the relationship between graphic design and architecture in 2x4's work, therefore, come from their broad exploration of the relationship among different design media, particularly old media and new media. And this exploration is itself only part of 2x4's larger interest in the global circulation of images and its impact on the efficacy of designers. Consider the visual literacy of the 21st-century subject. Increasingly, images are broadcast around us but we are unable to discern their material support. This has heightened their communicative power—our eyes are more likely to go right through to the message, without thinking about how the images are made. Anyone seeking to intervene critically in what Rosalind Krauss has called the "post-medium condition"[2] is therefore in

1 The history of the dressing up of the modernist wall is vast and beyond my scope but Mark Wigley's *White Walls, Designer Dresses* (Cambridge: MIT Press, 1995) provides an overview of the problem of color, while Detlef Mertins' "Transparency: Autonomy and Relationality" in *AA Files* 32 (1996) explicates the issues around modernist transparency.

the paradoxical position of having to both capture the attention of the viewer and direct this attention to the vast technological apparatus that undergirds our culture of inattention. Given this condition, the wall may seem a rearguard choice of material support. But for all its "old media" quality, for 2x4 the wall is an ideal space for experimentation because it can slow down the flow, expose gaps, and act as a visual de-complicator through which illusions must pass.

If the wall is 2x4's space of experimentation, the experimental subject is you, your body, and the repository of images that your mind has become. Your body is asked to assist in the mental mechanisms (switches and associations) that are usually performed instantaneously by your synapses. As for your mind, the goal is to make you think about images, their origins, their intentions, their material presence. But these reflections are not provoked in a vacuum. Many of the images are famous, the graphic languages known, the icons universal. What is at work here is not so much the education of your eye as the rediscovery of your image-memory. 2x4 would like to call forth every image you have ever perceived, and make it strange again by asking you to look *at* it rather than *through* it.

And so, to analyze 2x4's architectural toolkit we cannot resort to the usual categories of graphic work in space—signage, way-finding, wallpaper, decoration, *trompe l'oeil*, etc. Proceeding instead by media types, we find that there are three kinds of walls in 2x4's repertoire: print walls, which play on flatness; screen walls, which promise depth; and aura walls, which create a floating, holographic atmosphere.

When 2x4 treats the wall like a printed page, a thickness is worked up from the surface, reaching towards the viewer. For instance, the glass corridor at the entrance of the McCormick Tribune Campus Center in Chicago orchestrates a double perceptual breakdown.[3] From outside, we begin with the enlarged faces of the institution's founders. Even if we don't recognize them we can tell by their hovering likeness that they are the ghosts who haunt its architecture. The first breakdown is optical: as we approach these ghosts, they lose legibility—the big faces are quickly revealed to be composed of miniature bodies. The second *caesura* is semiotic: these minuscule bodies are isotypes, universal graphic indicators of human behavior. But as soon as we

2 Krauss describes a condition in which artistic media have been complicated to a point of no return, and any aesthetic practice can no longer rely on the tension between form and its medium in order to make a critical statement, because media have become elaborate socio-technical apparatuses. See Rosalind Krauss, "Two Moments from the Post-Medium Condition," *October* 116 (2006); and Rosalind Krauss, "Reinventing the Medium," *Critical Inquiry* 25, no. 2 (1999).

3 I owe this formulation to Aleksandr Bierig, to whom I am also grateful for invaluable help in researching and conceptualizing this article.

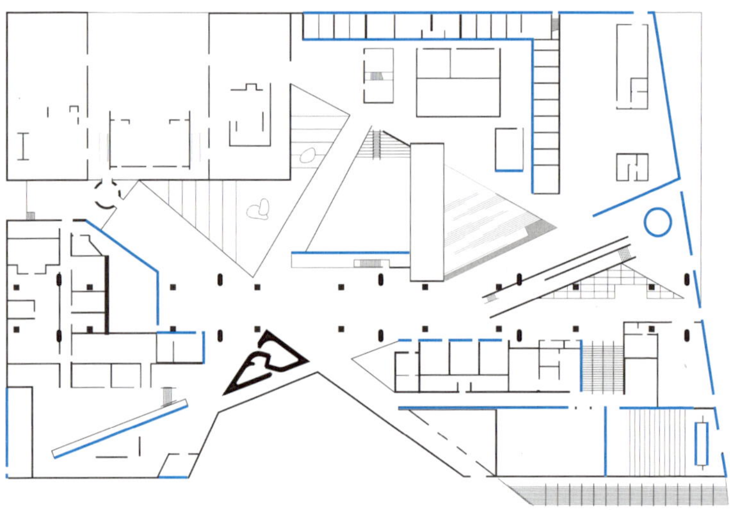

McCormick Tribune Campus Center—Chicago, Illinois

recognize this graphic language and prepare to be appropriately directed, or informed, again we are denied the gratification of universal legibility—because the isotypes turn out to be absurdly, comically, customized.

In between these two breakdowns, the link is a design gesture specific to techniques of image reproduction: the graphic device of exposing that continuous tone is actually made up of discontinuous dots, or pixels. Pixelation, dotting, cropping, scaling, step-repeating: the conventions of graphic design, laid bare, become links in a cognitive chain. On the walls of PS1, art-labeling becomes a ubiquitous over-printing. At the Vitra barricade, oversized typography is pixelated into so many scraps of paper. In these projects the wall is treated as a print medium turned vertically, to confront the viewer with the material constraints of image-making.

When 2x4 treats a wall like a screen, the optical breakdowns proceed through technologies of broadcasting. For example, the main façades of the Muhammad Ali Center in Louisville function like colossal screens, calibrated to the disjointed scale of the post-industrial city. Here we begin with incomprehension: standing in the plaza that fronts the building, we perceive no image—just a gridded composition of colorful tiles, perhaps an abstract reinterpretation of the Depression-era murals that

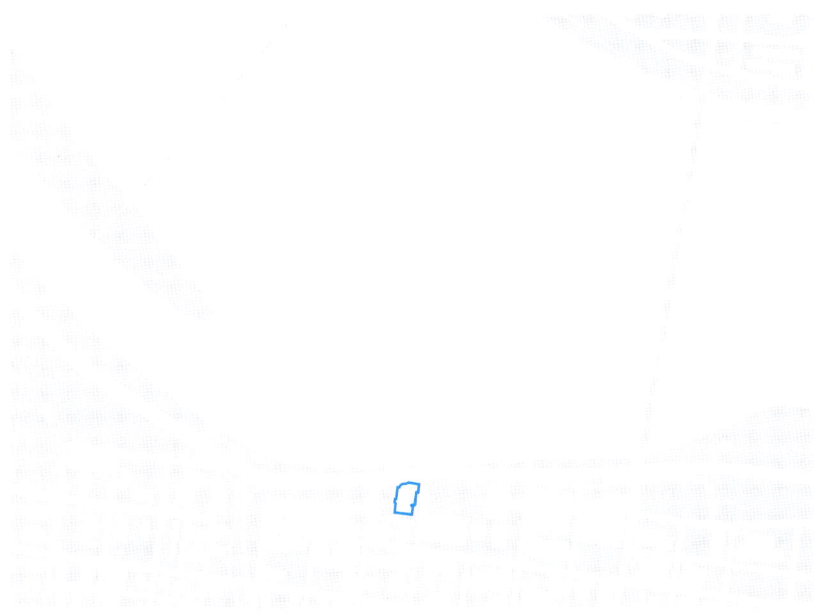

Muhammad Ali Center— Louisville, Kentucky

were once used to signify American civic space. Instead of being painted, the mural is built into the minimal color palette of a basic ceramic rain-tile wall. The proper place to watch these colors cohere into an image, however, is about a mile away: from across the river, or perhaps from an airplane. From here the striations gather into the bands of a digital screen, scrolling some of the most famous images in sports history, staged by Muhammad Ali himself. But again our moment of recognition is immediately foiled by 2x4's second scrambling act: the screen is glitchy. Like a malfunctioning television it repeats still images rather than letting them flow seamlessly into one another. So the wall here is a pretext for a game of media-switching. First, the limitations of ceramic-tile architecture (four colors, fixed grid) are revealed to be the same as the constraints of cathode-ray television (four colors, striated signal). Second, the evolution of one medium into another (from still photograph to moving image) is frozen in place.

2x4 walls work by creating a baseline of recognition, then introducing doubt. Human figures and typography are their most frequent graphic symbols, but not the only ones, especially in aura walls. On the wall of the Vitra store, a spiral spins a decorative aura around a chair. The spiral is recognizable—

as geometric figure, as scientific imagery, and most importantly as an optical illusion that draws us closer to the wall. As we approach, the figure turns out to be made of chairs step-repeated into an ornamental swirl. But because there is still an object — the chair — between us and the surface, the ultimate effect is a decorative push off the wall. The spiral becomes a graphic reality that exists in space, hovering above the chair itself and in innumerable other media where the chair appears, from print ads to animations. Much of 2x4's Vitra imagery — flowers, spirals, collages, landscapes — spins around the products, a decorative illusion that pops off the page, the wall, and the screen. This Photoshopped aura accompanies the product everywhere — better than any packaging.

The project where these wall types have been hybridized, and where the relationship between object, wall and subject has been further destabilized, is the wallpaper wall in the Prada epicenter store in Soho, New York. What really distinguishes this sixteen-by-two-hundred-foot wall from the others is that it has a different kind of depth: narrative depth, aptly echoed in the way 2x4 represents the wall as sequential horizontal bands, like film strips. The wallpaper concept was part of the earliest models by OMA and reflects its interest in the dialectics of cheapness and luxury. But the wallpapers have changed every few months following a script that has been created, over the years, by the triumvirate of architect (OMA), graphic designer (2x4), and client (Prada), in a three-way internal conversation that became source material for the story posted on the wall.

In one installment, a lineage of powerful women chosen by Mrs. Prada became a colossal new graphic standard. Before digitizing their faces, 2x4 had them repainted with oil on canvas, to erase the various media that made them famous: Nefertiti, known to us as a limestone bust; Catherine the Great, immortalized in paint; Maria Callas, a photographic diva. Oil paint, old medium *par excellence*, averaged out the graphic scale, while also bringing a historicist depth to the wall. Flatness returned in the next iteration, as these faces were masked by patches of enlarged

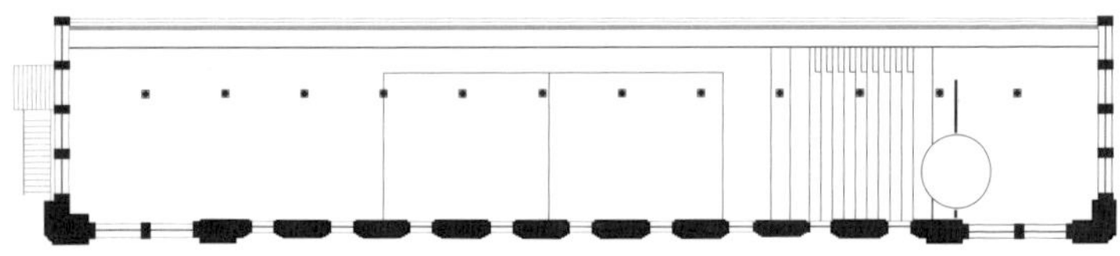

Prada Store — Soho, New York

wallpaper. Visual memory was now activated along multiple timelines: you might have remembered the faces underneath, or become nostalgic for Victorian floral patterns, or caught the geopolitical resonances of the mask as an icon in an age of privacy and security. But these would have been merely passing associations: the wall promoted a constant instability among them, and also between the wallpaper designs. The historicist theme soon returned to the wall, in a new plotline that played with the conventions of academic painting. First, cropped nudes were pasted salon-style. Then landscape scenes were framed with decorative collages of the season's shoe collection. Throughout the series, the wall alternatively pushed and pulled, flattened and deepened, its content remaining to a certain extent inscrutable. Were these screenshots of a graphic designer's desktop? Renderings of alternate architectural schemes? Clever ways to display a fashion line? No matter, the cumulative impression was that a story was being told.

The most compelling tale told in this semi-private design language has been the story of the humanization of the pixel, which began with the third wallpaper. Again a large-scale image broke down into an aggregate of pixels, both optically and semantically. But here the breakdown was itself a performance, staged as a sporting ceremony in a stadium in North Korea where each pixel was held up by one individual. This time the viewer was asked to make the literal equation of mass and image, graphic unit and human being. Through mass ornament, the pixel became content, the subject of the story. The story itself (we are told) was an allegory for the three designers' growing engagement in Asian markets, where they sensed that the delicate balance of mass-marketablility and hyper-individuation of Western commercialism may no longer hold.

Whatever its latent meaning, this rumination on sameness and otherness took over the wall, indeed the entire store, which was suddenly filled with a crowd of identical mannequins, fashion equivalents of the graphic isotype. It wasn't long before the mannequins crossed *into* the wall, so to speak: the next wallpaper featured colorful computer-rendered nude creatures roaming free in a virtual Garden of Eden. Now the wall functioned fully as a glossy screen, as if a window had opened into the mannequins' natural habitat, leaving you behind among the clothes in the real space of the store, where the mannequins had their modeling day-jobs. And just in case you were confused about what feeling had been evoked in you by watching this weirdly compelling universe, the next wallpaper installment made it clear: guilt. Although formally unconnected, these three wallpapers offered a design morality tale to which the Guilt wall was a fitting conclusion. Sponsored by a fictional corporation (Guilt™), the wall featured a team of lab-coated specialists ready to design you with their universalist graphic standards, tinted with the most atmospheric graphic convention of all, the color spectrum. An aura wall pushed to the extreme, Guilt didn't just pop off the wall; it skipped the product altogether and lodged itself directly in your mental space. The Guilt wall fulfilled the dream of wallpaper designers since William Morris: to design your ideas, without having to go through commodities at all. (And if negative reinforcement was the price to pay for this achievement, so be it. "Guilt," one TV ad read, "Universal.")

The Prada wall has been an epic novel about the condition of design across disciplines, authored by a rare alliance of three voices intent on demonstrating that one can engage with the world by "designing" through an issue, rather than "thinking" through it. The results are admittedly heady: not "total design" but design *about totalities*. Critics, especially those who compare design to art, have complained that this work usurps the trappings of high art and the rhetoric of political persuasion in order to facilitate commerce. But site-specific criticality does not belong in the art world alone. If viewers are able to enter a realm of aesthetic criticality while staring at a white wall, they can also be intellectually engaged while staring at a wallpapered one, no matter the souvenir they buy afterwards. More to the point, criticality here is always latent but delayed. All this design energy is not aimed at identifying targets for critique. The goal is to create a space of cognitive instability —something that it is difficult for architecture to do on its own.

So what has 2x4's architectural contribution been? Four points seem salient. First, 2x4 often acts as the first reader of an architectural project, receiving plans in their diagrammatic stage and introducing content to translate or annotate the spatial experience. One such annotation occurred at the Guggenheim Las Vegas, also designed by OMA. Two modernist walls bore the institution's name in huge boldface, so as not to get lost in the maze of Las Vegas architecture. Matte on the outside, to absorb the visual noise of the kitsch streetscape, the words became shiny on the inside, to outdo the hyper-busy casino interior. This manipulation of the absorptive and reflective properties of walls leads to the second point: that for all its cerebral heft, 2x4 has played a major role in a movement that includes much blunter and less lofty design practices: the trend of making buildings glow to render them "contemporary." As Sylvia Lavin has argued, at some point in the last 20 years now-ness became a graphic hue, as if architecture had to emit color in order to be present.[4] 2x4 has contributed its fair share to the two wall treatments Lavin identifies, the "hyper-painterly" and "wallpaper-color."

4 Sylvia Lavin, "What Color Is It Now?" *Perspecta* 35 (2004).

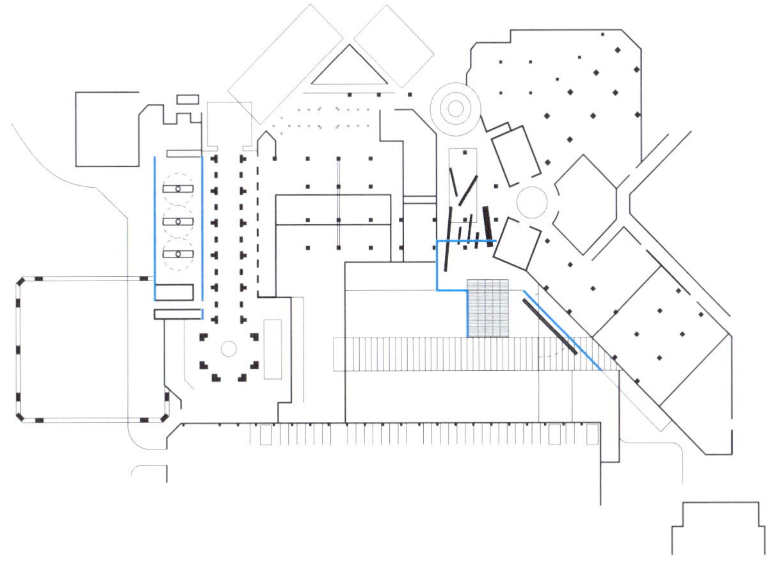

Guggenheim Las Vegas—Las Vegas, Nevada

But 2x4's walls reach beyond the object-building; they situate you in the larger environment that used to be called "the city" and is now a global, decentralized, cosmopolitan realm. This is the third point: 2x4 addresses the role played by images in contemporary place-making, and does so by mixing the lessons of graphic modernism and architectural postmodernism. Like Otto Neurath, who invented the isotype to empower the modern subject, and György Kepes, who wanted to educate the eye with science imagery, 2x4 deals Tin universals. But unlike these modernist heroes, 2x4 knows that neutral symbols become images among others laden with history and meaning, often becoming instruments of control. Instead 2x4 situates the viewer in a specific place, learning from the architects of the 1960s and 1970s, who rescued the communicative potential of architecture. The billboards of Robert Venturi and the Supergraphics of Charles Moore were also ways to hail the modern subject, only with messages that were site-specific, contaminated by context, and often by bad taste. But (and this is where graphic design folds its critique back onto architecture) 2x4 also calls out postmodern architecture for its lack of commitment to message, its fear of content, and its seemingly endless self-referentiality. For 2x4, images still have narrative power, a before-and-after. Like the muralists of the mid-century who wanted architecture to speak to the citizen, the designers intend to change your mind, and your comportment. But rather than empowering you once and for all, they try to teach you an incremental paranoia.

In a final twist, the result of this cognitive doubt is often spatial certainty. You are not sure what you are seeing, but you are absolutely certain that you are here. The fourth point, then, is that 2x4's attention to the lost potential of walls has shown that "place" can still be a critical design medium. Call them the New Situationists: they want to locate you by organizing visual chaos into an ever-dissolving, ever-reappearing, spatial order.

The days of site-specific wall narration are probably over. Most of the walls 2x4 has designed in the last 15 years were built in cities like New York and Las Vegas that have a special role in the history of urban culture, cities whose identities produce a baseline of experience against which 2x4 has been experimenting. Most places in the world don't have this property—not because they are less authentic "places," on the contrary—because their nature as products of globalization are less hidden behind a history of thematization and branding. Graphic icons hail the viewer by appealing to a longing for universals, but so do global sites. To put it another way, the cosmopolitan

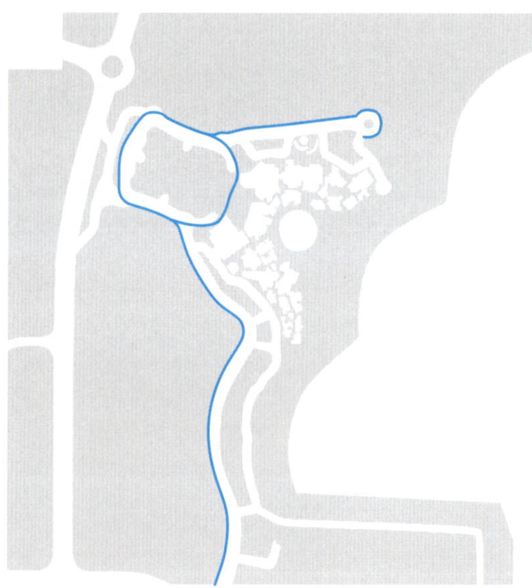

Doha Film Festival—Doha, Qatar

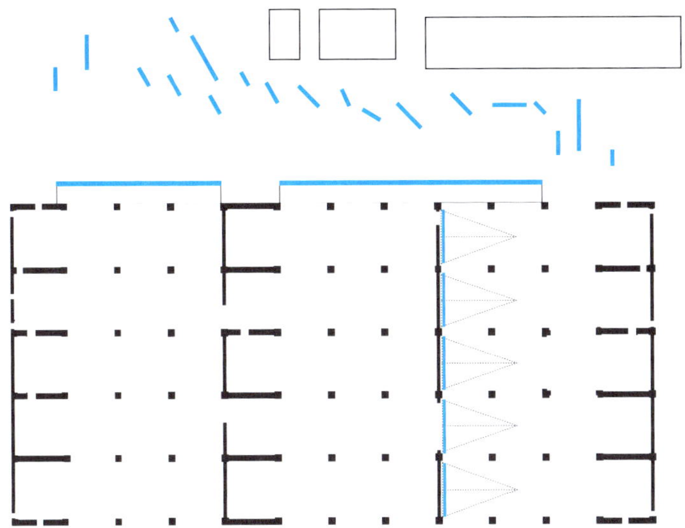

Prada Warehouse—Tokyo, Japan

subject is ever more constituted by graphic languages that circulate along far more intricate networks than those of a real-life city.

Increasingly 2x4 is designing walls that exist in non-spaces like the desert of Doha, a warehouse in Tokyo, and the beach of the Cannes Film Festival. Not coincidentally, these walls are usually temporary, and usually projected upon—they are cinematic "fourth walls." These walls can of course be analyzed in the context of the history of multimedia architecture, from Herbert Bayer to the Eameses. But more to the point, their temporary quality speaks to the rise of a new kind of wall in the global built environment: walls not for building but for zoning. Zoning walls separate spaces temporarily rather than constituting them once and for all, and for this reason they need to be freestanding, movable. Even if they disappear behind images they are bound to reappear again. Not designed by architects, these walls are the default building blocks of global development. Today the wall is well on its way to becoming an object again. And the more borders disappear, the more object-walls become visible. Take the Jersey barriers lining the road to the amphitheater of the Doha Film Festival, where 2x4 has installed black-and-white film-still frames to activate the road as film strip. The role of this barrier is not only publicity but also security, and to obscure the dune construction going on behind it. The Jersey barrier has become iconic of a newly unstable global condition, whether used by engineers to "develop" desert spaces, by police to "secure" urban environments, or by border patrols to "stabilize" contested lands.

The return of the wall is also the return of a political object in architecture, so it may well be time to stop staring at walls and start looking at them. Undoubtedly, 2x4 could create a new geopolitical iconography out of the walled universe that is rapidly growing around us, and make it the subject of a graphic project to help us develop the paranoid visual memory we need to understand it. But iconography might no longer be enough. Zoning walls are already part of a multimedia apparatus whose visual component consists not of entertainment imagery but of surveillance feeds and security records. To look at these walls means not only to re-engage the body in the forgotten art of perceiving. It means to ask what kind of space is constructed through the art of constantly being watched.

To put it another way: Architecture's proverbial slowness has served 2x4 well, providing a space to occupy the glitch between media, to interrupt the fast and the smooth by using the slow and the rough. But will this critical glitch-space survive as the speed of exchange between these two realms quickens to a feedback loop?

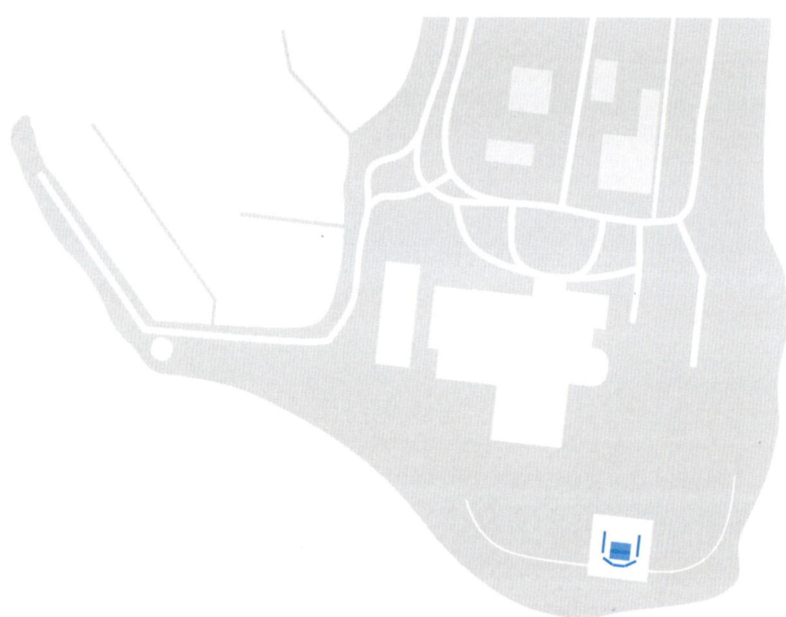

Cannes Film Festival—Cannes, France

III. CRITICISM

Graphic design's resistance to critique is alternatively attributed to its invisibility, ubiquity or superficiality: it's too ephemeral to measure, too broad to categorize, or too thin for meaningful penetration. But without critique and self-examination there is no discipline. Can there be a critical practice without practicing critique?

DEPROFESSIONALIZATION

Is design a profession? It seems strange to ask that question now, but it was bandied about a lot in the '90s, when the conventional wisdom was that no one knew what graphic designers did (including their own mothers). But that was before Steve Jobs and Martha Stewart and the Macintosh with its pull-down font menu and the World Wide Web and a million B-school consultants with their newfound obsession with branding. The Internet may have been the single biggest graphic-design educator in history. Suddenly millions of people were grappling with the implications of graphic design: a website, after all, is 100% pixels/0% bricks. Overnight everyone became a connoisseur. Ironically the design explosion of the last 20 years has transformed the situation from no one understanding graphic design to everyone becoming a graphic designer. What was once imperiled by obscurity is now threatened by ubiquity. Moms everywhere not only know all about it, they're practicing at home. If everyone does it, what separates the professionals from the hacks?

The right answer is: Nothing. Professionalism is an artificial wall wrapped around a huddled mass of designers clinging to the remnants of self-regard. If only we could devise some standard practice we could officially conclude who is a *real* graphic designer and protect ourselves from the onslaught of the amateurs. We need a test. But for the life of us, we can't decide what the questions should be.

After the war—that's WWII—the great theorist of the professional class, C. Wright Mills, observed, "United States society esteems the exercise of educated skill, and honors those who are professionally trained ... [I]t also esteems money as fact and as symbol, and honors those who have a lot of it. Many professional men are thus at the intersection of these two systems of value." A nascent, postwar graphic design tried to bust into the American professional dream the old-fashioned way: it went to university, got a good job, bought a suit and played by the rules. We tried to ingratiate ourselves by imitation. A title or an acronym after a name would be our class signifier, denoting position and community approbation. An organized profession would legitimize our sense of privilege.

Professionalism is usually sold as a service to clients, protecting them from charlatans and swindlers, while in fact, professional organizations serve their members by limiting competition, excluding alternative practices, and legitimizing higher fees. To achieve this guild-like solidarity, we struggled to develop a specialized jargon and mysterious trade practices, drawn first from the ancient language of the printer and the type shop. But our secrets kept getting outed. One of the great fears about the Macintosh and desktop publishing was that it would initiate others into our secret language of fonts, rags, picas, and leading. (That is, of course, exactly what it did.) That old, technical talk has now been replaced by the ever more vaporous "expertise" of branding and crowd-sourcing and social media.

In the attempt to maintain a separate identity, graphic design was once defined by elimination: not art, not illustration, not photography, not industrial design, not writing, not architecture, not printing, not typesetting and—especially—not advertising. We occupied the interstitial. But suddenly that territory is infiltrated by emerging hybrids: artist/webmasters, blogging fashionistas, logo-making DJs, culinary-event-designing gallerists. Now to be one thing is so extremely dull. Tell someone you're a designer and the response is: *And*?

This massive deprofessionalization of design has left the old professionals in the lurch. Value has shifted to the naïve and the homegrown. Unschooled trumps schooled. The dropout outpaces the graduate. Around the conference table all the grey heads turn to the 20-something intern to figure out what to do next. All that work to make ourselves presentable now renders us passé.

It was all a pipe dream anyway. We never really had a leg to stand on (or any science to back us up). Graphic design is continually challenged by the introduction of ideas from outside: radical technological disruption and artistic innovation. One year's certainties are next year's embarrassments. Since definitions of what design is, and should be, are in flux, arbitrary standards have always been a naïve attempt to project stability in a gelatinous realm.

The current state of deprofessionalization means we must jettison the dream of a singular definition of design practice. And why should design have some unified field theory anyway? We must view design as an elaborated speech or writing, a common activity, shared by all, on many levels. Writing is practiced eclectically, from poetry to graffiti, to novels, newspapers, tabloids and love notes. There is academic writing and experimental writing and religious writing and profanity and "bad" writing that comes over time to be considered "good" writing. I can appreciate, in differing amounts, both the back of the cereal box and a structural analysis of it. We celebrate the diversity of writing but bemoan the paucity of so-called good design. We must accept that there is no single correct way to make graphic design, and no sure way to gauge its value. It's all a negotiation. Who is, and who isn't, is only a matter of the doing. The best becomes obvious over time as surely as the cream rises to the top.

WHAT IS THIS THING CALLED DESIGN CRITICISM, I & II

WITH RICK POYNOR

1995

RICK POYNOR

Terms such as art criticism, literary criticism, architecture criticism and film criticism are so familiar that they require little explanation, whether we are interested in reading their products or not. They are all activities with obvious, readily identifiable roles and job descriptions attached: "art critic," "film critic" and so on. They bring to mind the names of writers who specialize in the subject, achieve a continuous critical presence through their publications and are identified with a particular sensibility, style of writing, set of ideas and point of view. Compared to art or film criticism, the term "graphic design criticism" has an unfamiliar, slightly uncomfortable ring. It is one that even the most avid reader of graphic design magazines and books will encounter rarely, if at all.

In the 1990s, the call for such a criticism has nevertheless become steadily louder, the few exponents increasingly prepared—though still fairly tentatively—to identify themselves as such. A collection of critical writings on graphic design—some drawn from *Eye*—has recently been published.[1] Ten years ago the more forward-thinking designers urged the development of such a criticism, believing that it was part and parcel of a mature profession. Now that it is happening there are murmurs of discontent and, despite the example of neighboring disciplines, the critic's motivation is in doubt. "Criticism," one internationally renowned designer declared, "usually takes the form of the negative and the overly judgmental."[2] So what exactly is graphic design criticism? Who practices it, or ought to practice it, and what are its aims? And can it, in the sense that we might talk about art or film criticism, be truly said to exist at this point?

MICHAEL ROCK

While we might not recognize it as such, design criticism is everywhere, underpinning all institutional activity—design education, history, publishing and professional associations. The selection, description and reproduction of designed artifacts in books and magazines, for instance, is the work of theory. Objects are represented to make a point—even if the point is as simple as "My, isn't Rick Valicenti a genius"—and that is a critical position.

Famous designers, complaining about over-zealous design critics, forget that their fame is created through exposure. For example, while I have rarely encountered actual work by Neville Brody, I have seen hundreds of examples published in the international design press and his own books, carefully organized and edited

1 See also Steven Heller, "Criticizing Criticism: Too Little and Too Much," *AIGA Journal of Graphic Design* 11 no.4 (1993); and *Emigre* no.31, "Raising Voices" issue (1994).

2 Letter from April Greiman, *AIGA Journal of Graphic Design* 12 no.3 (1994).

to give the impression of complete artistic continuity. Thus Brody has an influence and reputation through publishing that he could never have in practice.

Writing has a profound effect on Institution Design, the elaborate apparatus that surrounds design production.[3] Design work is exchanged intra-professionally, through publishing, lectures, promotional material and other written forms. Publication may lead to speaking engagements, workshops, teaching invitations and competition panels—all of which in turn further promote certain aesthetic positions. At the same time, an historical canon is perpetually generated, a canon of that will influence the next generation of designers by indicating what work is of value, what is worth saving, what is excluded.

So the relationship between practice and theory is symbiotic. The 40-year expansion of the post-war design industry has been both critiqued and promoted through writing.

RP

We are at an interesting juncture, where those with a stake in graphic design writing are starting to debate the forms such a criticism should take. The principal forums for the critical writing undertaken to date have been the professional magazines. Even in the more critically-minded publications, criticism has run side by side with ordinary journalism and other reader services. Established editorial formats and the need to engage a broad professional audience place pragmatic restrictions on what can be attempted and said. There are those who now feel that such "journalistic criticism" is lacking, that it fails to make its critical positions sufficiently explicit, and that we need, in short, a more academic form of criticism to compare with those generated by, for instance, art, literature, or cultural studies.[4] This is potentially of great educational value, but in Britain academic graphic design criticism is at such a rudimentary stage of development, with so little to show in terms of published research, that few conclusions can be drawn.

To what extent such a criticism will be able to address the working designer is a moot point, though experience suggests that the kinds of journals and books that would carry it will have limited appeal to professional readers. What we hope to achieve with *Eye* is not so much a "journalistic criticism"—the term makes it sound like something that has fallen short of the real thing—as a *critical journalism*. By this I mean the kind of writing you find on the arts pages of the Sunday papers: informed, thoughtful, skeptical, literate, prepared to take up a position and argue a case, aware of academic discourse and debates (perhaps even

3 The phrase is borrowed from Michael Speaks' term "Institution Architecture." See "Writing in Architecture," *ANY* no.0 (May/June 1993).

4 See "A conversation with Andrew Blauvelt," *Emigre* no.31.

written by academics), but able to make these issues relevant and accessible to a wider readership—writing with a firm sense of its audience's interests and needs. That, at least, is the ideal.

MR

Design critics who have been influenced by cultural studies tend to eschew the celebratory zeal of design journalism and attempt instead to read designed objects as cultural artifacts. As Stefan Collini notes, "those who make [cultural studies] part of their self-description regard the demystifying of unmasking of the essentially ideological operation of various forms of ... representation as the core and purpose of what they do ..."[5] Obviously, having work *unmasked*, exposing the *essentially ideological operation* at play can be a rather unpleasant experience for a designer more accustomed to back-patting. I think that cultural criticism is surpassing art history, formal analysis and perceptual psychology as the dominant model for design criticism in the United States. Many of my design graduate students study with its teachers in the American Studies and Comparative Literature departments and that influences the way they think about their work.

It is interesting to note that cultural studies here is very influenced by the British New Left movement, literary critics like Raymond Williams, and Richard Hoggart's Center for Contemporary Cultural Studies at Birmingham University. American scholars too have addressed the popular media in many serious academic projects. There is, in fact, more good critical writing about design than most people realize.[6] I suspect that the longing for academic criticism comes more out of not knowing where to look than a dearth of material. Also, designers' limited self-definition leads them to reject writing on subjects like advertising or public relations that have a direct bearing on our profession. While we may be heavily invested in the notion of "graphic design" as an independent activity, as a discrete category it doesn't always hold up under academic scrutiny. Perhaps a different kind of journal, more on the model of *Assemblage,* might promote experimental forms of writing and cross-disciplinary work.

RP

At this point we run into the question of who exactly these different forms of criticism are aimed at and what they hope to achieve. While certain kinds of theory can undoubtedly nourish and reinvigorate design practice, your reference to the cultural studies approach suggests the possibility of a future schism between practice and theory, and a division of "graphic design" into two distinct

5 See "Escape from DWEMsville," *Times Literary Supplement*, 27 May 1994.

6 Neil Harris at the University of Chicago, Jackson Lears at Rutgers University, Stuart Ewen at Hunter College and Johanna Drucker at Yale have all produced substantial work on design subjects.

areas of study, the practical and the critical, attracting different kinds of students. Their aims may not ultimately be reconcilable.

Theory's conclusions will in some cases be profoundly opposed to certain forms of design activity. How meaningful or relevant is the unmasking of ideological operations going to be to the designer making a successful career in supermarket packaging, annual reports for *Fortune* 500 companies, or the world of glossy magazines? Not everyone shares the leftish political position that underpins the challenge these theories make to design. Few designers will relish hearing that their work is ideologically suspect and that they should design something approved by some cultural theorists instead. This is not to suggest some uncompromising forms of analysis are invalid or have nothing to teach us, simply to be realistic in acknowledging that they will only appeal to designers given to a particular type of critical reflection.

Critical journalism offers different kinds of insights and knowledge. It is capable of forms of investigation that more academic styles of criticism overlook. Where cultural theory takes a rather Olympian view—choosing representative but ultimately interchangeable examples for analysis—critical journalism has a strong sense of the particular and uses a close, pragmatic acquaintance with the realities of production to ask more down-to-earth questions about individuals and bodies of work. What is the value of what has been accomplished? What is its immediate context? And its wider implications, both professional and socio-cultural? Designers are making large claims to authorship—both implicit and explicit—and these deserve to be tested critically.

MR

One of the problems of the cultural theory model is that it has not dealt with formal detail. It may be very effective for discussing the nature of the annual report as a device of capitalist culture, but weak in discussing the choice of Univers over Helvetica, although such distinctions are within its scope. But all critical positions necessarily require that you leave something out; they are perspectives, after all. To build an effective design criticism, we will have to create our own perspectives, fashioned out of a number of other techniques.

What is particularly interesting about criticism in general is how different perspectives give rise to different meanings. This has been fully realized in film criticism, for instance; the same film can be fodder for a formal, feminist, psychoanalytic or semiotic analysis, each offering a new way to *read the text*. Criticism doesn't yield answers, only opinions, and opinions should be diverse. Cultural criticism has been useful because it has analyzed the institutional rhetoric of design, examined the institutional myths that are perpetuated through education and practice which serve to insulate and promote the profession.

If you choose to focus on the individual, the "masters of design" approach, you intentionally narrow your scope; the cultural issue is still present in that it is consciously excluded. For instance, we had years of writing about Modern design without any examination of the relationship between the formal tenets of the movement and corporate capitalism. So we have a lot of information about logos and typefaces and the design "heroes" that make them, but little that situates the work in the culture. We need both types of analysis.

RP

I hope that the mixture of profiles, reports and thematic essays published in *Eye* shows that critical journalism can accommodate a wide range of approaches and subjects. But this leads back to the point I made at the beginning. For graphic design criticism to exist in the sense that it does in other disciplines, and with the same variety of perspectives, it will need dedicated writers. I don't question the educational value of the critical writing that, for instance, post-graduates produce as part of their studies and I know from experience that their findings are sometimes publishable. But occasional paper writing in the course of research is not the same as being a fully fledged critic, writing regularly about a broad range of graphic design subjects, or many different aspects of the same subject.

Whatever the discipline, the critic is engaged in a process of interior and exterior discovery, a riskily public dialogue with the subject matter, the readership, and him or herself. Critical positions will inevitably evolve over time, Errors of judgment will sometimes be made. The critic can only learn what is possible by constantly *writing*. It will also help if they can actually write. Good as some graphic design criticism is, even the best of it has some way to go before it can equal the most fluent, supple and engaging writing on the other arts. One basic but crucial difference is that these more public subjects attract people whose primary ambition and talent is for writing and who realize this ambition through a medium that fascinates them. Graphic design is not by and large—may never be?—such a subject. It's a catch-22, because without such writers to bring it alive graphic design stands much less chance of becoming a discourse of wider public interest.

MR

We don't have a couple of centuries' worth of books, biographies, films, myths, and stories about making a poster or designing a typeface, whereas we do about painting or writing. Graphic design is such an obscure activity, there are just not that many people who even know it exists, never mind write about it. So most design critics start off as practitioners with a penchant for writing. This explains the collusion that has existed between design practice and the design press.

There are other factors that shape the practice of design criticism. Designer/critics are the products of art schools where there exists a deeply ingrained division between the visual and the verbal. Students with verbal skills are suspect. The stereotype is that the verbal student uses language to mask deficient visual skills. Also, as criticism is not at all lucrative, most of us have to work professionally. Therefore the subjects of our writing are often our friends, colleagues, teachers, clients and students. You have to be willing to take great personal and social risks to write with conviction. Designers may debate the issue of "personal expression," but there are few forms of expression as personal as writing something down, signing your name and sending it out for all the world to see.

There is always teaching. But as design programs are considered professional schools, institutions require significant *professional* output, rather than writing, before bestowing the tenure plum. There is no escaping it. Like anything else, the only way to get better at design writing is to practice it. But without seven years of graduate study in preparation of a dissertation to hone their abilities, most design critics have to squeeze in writing here and there, and learn on the fly. Unfortunately it shows.

Finally, there is little encouragement. Editors are reluctant to risk alienating the very people who make up their subscription lists, or to commission or publish longer or more challenging pieces of writing. Since many designers—reviving the old art school bias—eschew any theorizing and demonstrate an alarming lack of curiosity about their own profession, there is a pitifully small audience for new writing. And last, there are few models. The reason we cast about for some critical paradigm is because our profession—the profession of graphic design criticism—is in the process of becoming.

RP

I began by quoting a leading designer's view that too much writing about graphic design is "negative and overly judgmental." Have we fully answered that charge? "Judgmental" is a slippery word because its use instantly suggests its more desirable opposites: tolerance and understanding. To be judgmental is to wag a finger and raise the voice, to carp and repress. Called to account in such morally loaded terms, criticism can't possibly be a good thing.

But this is, in reality, a considerable misrepresentation of the critical process when responsibly carried out. It is hardly the purpose of criticism to squash its subjects arbitrarily. On the other hand, being a critic does require the exercise of judgment based on all the writer's knowledge and experience. The writer who wilfully suspends judgment, or fears to make it, lets down the reader and ultimately perhaps the subject itself. This critical process will often lead to conclusions at odds with those of the subject. But while the process might be intrinsically adversarial, it is not inherently negative even if the ordinary usage of the verb—to criticize—makes it sound as though it is.[7] Criticism's conclusions may be largely or even wholly supportive of the subject.

MR

Designers are generally insulated from any broad discussion of their work, but once in the world of commerce, producing materials that affect the lives of millions of people, designers are open to the same kind of response as anyone else in such a position, for instance an architect or novelist. The most interesting criticism uses the subject as an example of a larger idea, drawing connection between the work and the context. In order to write sharp criticism, it is sometimes necessary to exaggerate the differences between things, to compare and contrast in a way that illuminates the subject for the reader. Only lousy criticism is merely judgmental. The key to compelling criticism is to rise above petty judgment and make a rational case for your position, historically supported and logically constructed. Properly executed, even the most biting criticism should be useful, entertaining and instructive. But it would be naïve to think that the relationship between the critic and the subject will ever be entirely smooth.

Despite the difficulties, I am incredibly optimistic about the practice of graphic design criticism. We are perhaps the first generation of writers who consider themselves, as a form of self-definition, to be graphic design critics, and that sense of being at the beginning of something is extremely liberating. Through the practice of writing, I discover more and more about design and I am very conscious of trying to build a design criticism. It is a huge, organic project that involves years of concentrated effort, missteps, public embarrassments, bruised feelings and misunderstandings, but a great deal of pleasure as well.

Rick Poynor and Michael Rock, published in *Eye* 4, no. 16.

7 For further discussion of the adversarial nature of criticism see Michael Bierut, "Learning to Live with the Critics," *Eye* 2, no.8.

2011

MR

I was rereading our dialogue about design criticism published in *Eye* now —gulp— 15 years ago! This line jumped out at me: "For graphic design criticism to exist in the sense that it does in other disciplines, and with the same variety of perspectives, it will need dedicated writers." Looking back at the trajectory of our work over that decade and a half, it seems that you have become exactly that: a dedicated writer of design criticism. And, clearly, that impressive body of work enacts a very specific cultural criticism that draws on many of the sources we discussed so long ago. I, of course, took a different path.

We ended that discussion on an optimistic note, looking forward to a flowering of criticism in the coming years. How are you feeling about that development now? Was my optimism justified? What have you surmised about the subject of design? Does it hold up? And who are you writing for now? Is there a public out there that's getting elevated? Or is it more rarefied? In "Post No Bills," Walter Benjamin wrote: "For the critic his colleagues are the higher authority. Not the public. Still less posterity." Has the institution of design criticism effectively changed the institution of design?

RP

I see scattered growth rather than a great blossoming. There has certainly been plenty of talk about design criticism since our dialogue in *Eye*. A few personal essay collections have been published and, as with other fields, these are good indicators of critical vitality, a sign that a writer has achieved a certain presence and a degree of traction. They are also the most concentrated and cogent way of finding out what a critic has to say. Blogs are clearly a notable development. Then there is the emergence in the last two years of the design writing and criticism MFA and MA courses at the School of Visual Arts, London College of Communication, and Konstfack in Stockholm. The Royal College of Art in London has also announced an MA in Critical Writing in Art & Design. These phenomena tell us something about the perceived importance of criticism within design.

I don't, however, care much for criticism as some purely abstract ideal and I don't think we need too many more vague academic "calls" for criticism. We need some action. We need a lot more criticism and places to disseminate it. Criticism is a highly motivated personal act, so the litmus test for its presence is pretty simple: can you name the critic? Are there plenty of these people at work in the field? What is their agenda? What is their particular contribution to the discussion?

My model for what the life of a design critic might be has always come from outside the academy and especially from the example of music writers and film writers. These are people whose commitment to their subject is so great that they want it to become their work and their living. They have enough outlets to support them. There have been many such individuals. Of course, the online environment is changing the terms of engagement for every kind of writer and anyone arriving on the scene now hoping to become a full-time design writer will require exceptional commitment. It's far more likely that most design writing will continue to be produced on the side, taking second place to better paying activities, such as designing or teaching. But, as the patchy state of design criticism shows, it's not possible to build a sustained writing presence, a convincing body of work and a committed readership by occasional weekend dabbling. Writers must write. Again, the yardsticks have to come from better established kinds of critical writing.

MR

The fragmentation you identify—and the effect it has in sidelining writing—is at the heart of the issue. We had a sense of that way back when but neither of us could predict how profoundly both the act of designing and writing would change. In fact, technology and media-driven fragmentation obscure the development of some institutions of design criticism (not that that is what you are calling for) and opens up certain opportunities as well.

Let me try to pick that apart. Take the demise of my old employer, *I.D.* Magazine, as a case in point. *I.D.* was reorganized back in the early 1990s (as was *Eye*) as the model of new design journalism. The idea was to take writing seriously, to engage a broad range of topics and tap critics from other disciplines to look at design. *I.D.* and *Eye* succeeded in the mission for a while but ultimately *I.D.* became the victim of fragmentation. As web-based communication eclipsed print, blogs like Design Observer and dezeen and, more recently, social media forms like Facebook and Twitter, drew away readers and writers from *I.D.* The magazine format was too slow to follow the hyperactive conversation on the blogs.

This change is good in some ways: it has drawn new people into the dialogue, and some very good young writers are working on design. Two ex-Yale men come to mind, Rob Giampietro and Dmitri Siegel, as well as someone with a real projective practice, Daniel van der Velden. But because all that writing is unpaid, and because of the open nature of the blog format, I wonder if Design Observer can exercise an editorial framework the way that an *I.D.* or an *Eye* could. In addition, while a blog now may have the substance of printed writing, the ephemerality of the medium, coupled with the rather annoying smack-down response the format seems to engender—in which every idea slowly degenerates into a series of increasingly personal insults—can make it feel degraded.

This fragmentation of writing forums reflects the equally disruptive fragmentation in graphic design. As books and print are recast as luxury items, as budget cuts eliminate editorial positions, and as the general pace of projects accelerates, the nature of what a designer does and doesn't do transforms. Designers now often serve as editors, content-managers, proofreaders and caption writers. Design projects routinely involve art direction, technology development, social-media management, publicity, and any number of tangential activities. The design object itself is shattering just at the moment that the tools to dissect it are, too.

As a case in point, we recently developed a wayfinding project that functioned completely within an existing cellphone and SMS messaging network. There were no visible components, only a database, an SMS server, and a public cellphone network. If that project is now within the realm of graphic design, what critical tools are necessary to analyze it, and what is the forum for that analysis?

RP

Your SMS project is an intensified form of a critical problem that hamstrung design writing even at the time of our original dialogue. The practical criticism found in other disciplines — to use the concept introduced by literary critic I.A. Richards — begins with a publicly available object: a novel, a music CD, a painting, a building, a film. Buildings and paintings might only be accessible at a remove in photographs, but everything else can be experienced easily and immediately at first hand as pleasurable forms of culture to which we choose to give our time. While some types of design — the album cover, the movie title, the internationally distributed magazine, the imagery of global branding — occupy the wider public sphere, most of the work graphic designers do is relatively local, a matter of concern, if at all, only to the smaller number of people who see it.

Not only that: the object itself might be so slight that, unlike even a mediocre novel or film, it is simply not reviewable. There's very little to say and barely anyone would be interested to hear it. I remember you making this point once in conversation, using the example of a hairdresser's logo. If we were to examine hairdressers' logos collectively, as a category of symbol, could we begin to make such a piece of writing revealing or interesting? The object of study needs to have sufficient magnitude in our personal experience and to be complex enough in form and content to require and support critical interpretation. The writing needs an audience that regards the object as significant enough to want to know more about it. In any case, graphic design is usually a secondary component of the project it serves. People care a great deal about films and novels. They have no such conscious passion for transient commercial logos, which isn't to say that they don't respond to them.

(I'm talking here about a general audience, not specifically about designers.)

Design writers have dealt with this by indulging in a lot of generalizing about graphic design while avoiding close engagement with objects—a tacit admission of doubt that design is really interesting enough to justify this degree of attention. The lack of specific critiques in the Looking Closer series of critical writings (1994–2006) made this all too clear. Critical methods needed to be demonstrated convincingly on some designed phenomena, but this rarely happened. Since 1999, as my own answer to this, I have written a regular "Critique" column for *Eye* about a single designed artifact. Some work. Some probably don't. But every time I begin one I face the same essential problem: will this be of any interest to international readers who will most likely never encounter the project I'm talking about?

So, yes, the fragmentation is even greater now when the outlets for design criticism are shrinking, as is the appetite for it. We can't ignore the fact that older forms of critical writing devoted to literature, art and film are regularly proclaimed to be in crisis for one reason or another, or even moribund—see, for instance, British literary critic Rónán McDonald's *The Death of the Critic* (2007). Even if we believe (and it's a big "if") that critical writing about graphic design can resist these broader trends and somehow hang on to its audience, a pressing question remains: what is criticism's primary task? In 1995, you were very clear about the role of the critic as someone with the job of "unmasking" and exposing the ideology at work in a design, and your own writing up to that point often reflected this. Fifteen years later, after so much experience as a designer, where do you stand now on the idea of unmasking?

MR

My idea about unmasking is still intact; actually, it has become more expansive. It's essential for the critic to reveal the inner workings of individual pieces via close reading—to reveal—but s/he must also link work into associative networks. Linking is another methodology that supports and extends this unmasking. Through linking, individual objects are contextualized.

Contextualization addresses the problem of insignificance (hereafter known as the "Hairdresser's Logo Problem"). I agree that many works of design are just too slight to stand up to real analysis, and the only way to understand them is to draw them into bigger socioeconomic and historical arcs. The design object must be seen as an index of something bigger.

I've tried to do this several times. Most recently, in "A Brief History of Screens," I argued that the evolution of display technology has fundamentally changed the relationship between the designer, the architect and the city. The aforementioned SMS project, then, can be seen as the apotheosis of a trajectory from the 19th-century urban flâneur, through the mid- and late 20th-century couch potato, to the contemporary hand-held device, which allows the reader to be both couch potato and flâneur. In this light, the work loses its small, individual qualities and becomes an inevitable product of historical development.

If the product of design becomes increasingly invisible, the critical project is less one of unmasking than of revealing. The critic must resuscitate the design object from the ether and set it into proper context. This is what I always admired about—and what seemed to be the mission of—the "Critique" column. You linked design objects to bigger narratives.

But the idea of revelation goes further: the critic, through his magic, must take what seems to be one way and show it to be another. The job of the critic is to disprove conventional wisdom, to create a revelation in the mind of the "public." Work that is generally lauded should be undermined; obscure work, slated to be forgotten or already forgotten, must be revived, shown to be sorely overlooked. Another quote from my current favorite, Benjamin's "Post No Bills: The Writer's Technique in Thirteen Theses": "The public must always be proved wrong, yet always feel represented by the critic." Would you agree with my reading of your column?

RP

I broadly agree with your outline of what design criticism should do. Its ultimate purpose is to elucidate the role design plays in social, cultural, economic and political contexts, but this inquiry still has to start with observable phenomena and experiences—with the "object" itself. If design criticism isn't capable of close reading, from which the networks of association you describe can be built, then any larger conclusions it might draw are open to doubt.

In reality, though, very few design writers seem concerned with drawing larger social or political conclusions about design. Their constitutional blindness to these issues duplicates the endemic blindness of design itself. They are "post-critical"—in the sense that architecture uses that term—without being conscious that this is their actual position. The idea of vigorously contesting anything is foreign to them. This would necessitate a firm, clearly thought-out position and they don't have one. While art can kid itself that it occupies a privileged zone of free thinking and critique within capitalism, design as we mostly practice it today understands itself as an integral service to and expression of capitalism. Hardly surprising, then, that the public perceives it in similar terms.

We can see the resulting critical quandary most clearly in the phenomenon of "design thinking" so much in vogue now in the business schools and in the pages of *Businessweek*. However well meaning the self-styled design thinkers might be, they are firmly embedded within capitalist ways of thinking and business models, and this dictates their social values and their instrumental view of design.

Their work might offer benefits to society, but at root it will remain economically and ideologically self-serving. It can never be a reliable source of critique. There is no perfect, ethically pure position for any kind of critic, especially not a design critic. Nevertheless, the critic must endeavor to maintain as much independence from the object of critique as possible. There can be no unmasking, no revelation, no setting of anything within its "proper context" without a clear sense of purpose on the critic's part in the first place. As Benjamin also said, "He who cannot take sides should keep silent."

If it is to mature, design criticism must acquire a new ideological awareness. It must move beyond soft, easy, self-comforting assertions that "sustainability is good" or "too much consumerism is bad for the planet"—as though the problem can be fixed by a few adroitly applied Band-Aids—and embrace the need for rigorous political analysis with the eventual goal of fundamental systemic change.

Design criticism's reluctance to engage with these issues reflects public failure to grasp the seriousness of the situation. Even after narrowly averted economic meltdown and public bailouts of the banks, many still want to believe that the system is basically sound and we can carry on in the old way. The lack of public anger is remarkable. We struggle to break the silken net of complacency spun around us by decades of superabundance. Design criticism, too, must find the nerve and the resolution to tear away this veil.

MAD DUTCH DISEASE

Summer 2003. Dingeman Kuilman, then head of the Premsela Institute in Amsterdam, invites me to give the first in what would become an annual lecture series. The idea is to have foreigners comment on the state of so-called Dutch design from some distant perch. A regular visitor to Holland, I have been a visiting critic at the Jan van Eyck Academie in Maastricht for many years but I am hesitant to claim any special insight into the national character. I am especially tentative when Dingeman announces that the exclusive audience for this talk will be stacked with many of the very subjects I would be dissecting.

After a long period of procrastination I decide the only way I can attack my assignment is to refocus from Holland to America. The neo-liberal privatization debate is in full escalation: the government postal service PTT is swallowed by the private company TNT, Air France absorbs KLM. So the qualities that made Holland so special—to my starry eyes—are increasingly Americanized. There is a concomitant explosion of so-called Dutch Design—at least in stylistic terms—worldwide. I am curious about the simultaneity of these two trends and wonder if they could be conflated.

Fall 2012. I now see many of the predictions I made here were wildly inappropriate. I don't mind; that was the point. Others, however, proved to be if not prescient, at least accurate. Dutch Design is a global phenomenon. Quintessentially Dutch designer Hella Jongerius is redesigning the interior of KLM's business-class cabin to re-inscribe its Dutchness. Museums in China sponsor full-scale exhibitions of Dutch Design as instruction to the emerging design community. Development at Ground Zero creeps forward. And the privatization wave has radically transformed the social landscape.

PROLOGUE

Some caveats to start:

Slide 1.

News photograph of a smug President George W. Bush.

I am an American and everyone knows Americans are self-obsessed.

I am a designer—linguist Roman Jakobson famously quipped that asking a writer about literature was like asking an elephant about zoology—so I am inherently unqualified to talk about design.

I am not a theorist even when I sound like one. I have tried to keep this talk as jargon-free as possible. A few times, however, I accidentally fall into it. It's an affliction.

I am not an expert on Dutchness: an amateur, an interested observer, an enthusiast even, but no expert. Much of what I put forth will be naïve and oversimplified. My examples will seem obvious, canonical, irrelevant or clichéd. They will represent the oddities, not the norms, of Dutch design. I am not immersed in enough work to speak with real nuance. But that's part of the point, isn't it, to hear the view from afar?

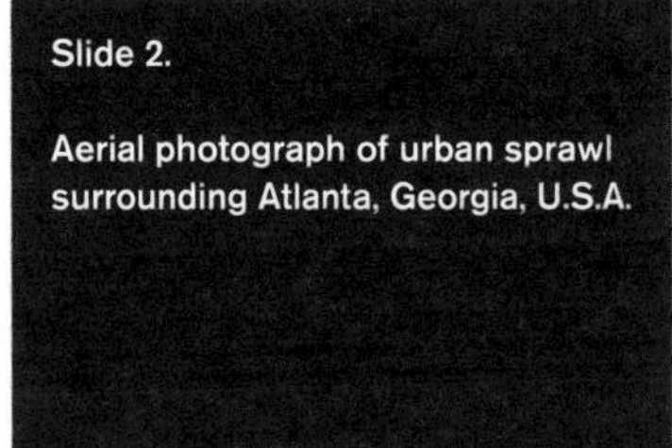

I come from a big, messy country. We have plenty of land so we are thrilled to waste it. When we get sick of something, we simply move on to something, or somewhere, else. At the same time, we are obsessed with the idea that our government is wasting our hard-earned cash. So while politicians like to appropriate money they hate to use it in ways that look too fancy.

Slide 3.

Photograph of gleaming, futuristic bright green PTT Telecom telephone booth.

In your country this is public infrastructure.

Slide 4.

Photograph of graffiti-covered public telephone, with missing receiver, New York City.

In my country we settle for more modest solutions.

> Slide 5.
>
> United States Department of Homeland Security diagram showing how to duct tape plastic drop cloths over doors and windows in case of chemical or biological attack.

When our government had to come up with a design solution for a possible terrorist attack, their advice was duct tape and plastic sheeting.

So what right do I have to criticize? In fact this is not criticism. This is a love song.

> Slide 6.
>
> A fake logo based on Milton Glaser's famous design for New York, reading I (heart) NL.

It is as much about America as it is about Holland, and perhaps as Holland becomes increasingly Americanized—read: privatized—it is a kind of cautionary tale as well.

INTRODUCTION

Maybe we just got bored somewhere along the way. Maybe we just started to believe in our own irrelevance. Or maybe, after years of trying to get people to like what we do, we just gave up our attempts to win friends and influence people and retreated into our little private club where we know everyone and everyone knows us. But, whatever the reason, somewhere along the line we just stopped trying to really change anything and we settled for simply changing DESIGN itself.

I call the convoluted, challenging, intelligent, difficult, self-reflexive, coy, clever, often staggeringly beautiful work that results from this exhaustion *Dutch Design*. Dutch Design is not restricted to work generated in the Netherlands; I consider Dutch Design a category, a type of work, or even a brand, that could, theoretically, occur anywhere at any time.

> Slide 7.
>
> A fake logo in the style of Coca Cola, script type with white and silver swoosh on bright red, modified to read Dutch Design.

Dutch Design's natural habitat is the Netherlands because of its special environmental features—a culture that understands design, a well-organized design profession, a rich design history, a wealth of well-educated design students—and because so much money is injected into the system to support design experimentation. (In America the high-tech bubble created a brief moment conducive to such work.) But any work that demonstrates the peculiar combination of irony, self-deprecation and thinly veiled egoism can earn the title of *Dutch Design*.

There are several key themes to follow: the rise of branding, the decline of nationalism and the public realm, and an emerging form of overt authorship; and some broad shifts, from public to private, from large ambition to small concerns, from optimism to irony. The form, however, will be blurry. What follows are the briefs for ten potential lectures on my own misreading of contemporary Dutch Design.

1
THE GREENHOUSE EFFECT

My first visit to Holland as an adult was in 1984. I distinctly remember thinking that this was what my design professors were talking about. Good, modern design was everywhere. Signs had real typography. Bright yellow, orange and green were actually used by serious companies. Public buildings were challenging. Holland seemed like a designer's dream. I think we American designers are fascinated by Holland because real design actually seems to get built here. You don't know how novel this is for us (especially when the work is commissioned by the government).

To plan and build a country using design as a key instrument is unfathomable to us. When we see a picture like this, the condition and the opportunity are completely foreign.

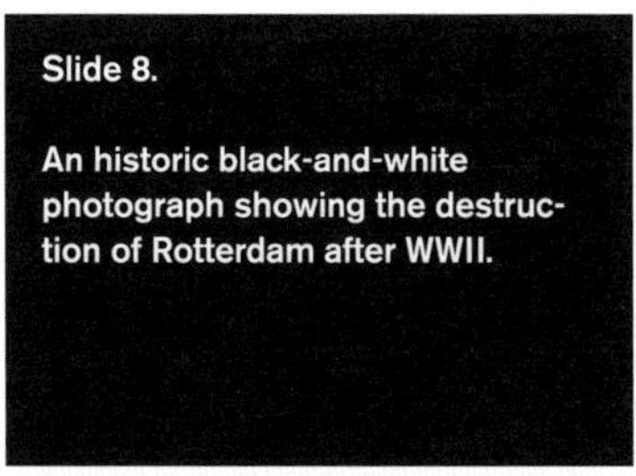

Slide 9.

A contemporary photograph of the smoking remains of the World Trade Center in New York City after the 9-11 terrorist attacks.

Walt, scratch that. We are now dealing with a Dutch project, Ground Zero, and the process is a fiasco.

For whatever reason—maybe our country is just too big or our culture too eclectic—we have never really believed in the notion of planning. In America, consensus is for wimps. Individualism and raw power rule. "Action is typical of American style," wrote Harvard sociologist Daniel Bell, "thought and planning are not." (I realize you may see this consensus culture as problematic, but in America it is cited, continuously, as an unattainable utopia.)

Our commitment to private over public represents a vast difference between the ways we view the issue of design. To understand that difference, you must realize that in America, design is always considered suspect: effete, luxurious, intellectual. America tends to be a deeply anti-intellectual, anti-aesthetic place. So if our government builds something, it must look as awful and as cheap as possible, signifying that 1. precious tax dollars weren't wasted on it and 2. no fatuous egghead "concepts" were passed off on an unwitting public. We have no tradition of aesthetic functionalism. We are suspicious of modernity. Modern smells expensive.

From the outside, the situation in Holland seems to be the opposite. While it's almost impossible to get a real number, by my crude estimate various Dutch governmental agencies dole out tens of millions of euros per year to architecture and design foundations. That's for a country with roughly the population of greater New York City. Some percentage of that money supports contemporary, experimental design work. In 2000, the U.S. government granted a whopping $400,000 in design grants for a country of about 280,000,000 people.

Slide 10.

An official U.S. Air Force photograph of an exotic B1 Stealth Bomber.

In contrast, the 2003 defense budget was about $355,000,000,000. Of course, some of that could be seen as a kind of design subsidy—it's just that the designers tend to be Boeing and Lockheed Martin and the experimental projects tend to be jet-propelled. The point is that Holland uses subsidy to support projects overlooked by the market; America subsidizes the market.

That official sanction of Design as a valid, vital cultural activity seems to create an atmosphere here wherein designers actually consider themselves valid, vital contributors to culture. This is not always the case in America, where designers tend to be much more insecure about our professional value. A fully privatized market simply will not support the kind of design culture that exists in Holland. (The dissolution of the PTT's art and design department may prove that this is increasingly the case here as well.) Maybe the designer is less valued as a business asset than as a cultural asset.

And all that subsidy and support has had an effect—maybe not a direct financial effect—but a psychological one. When I scan a Dutch cityscape, or a poster kiosk or magazine rack, the array of designed infrastructure is staggering: stations, government buildings, museums, urban planning, conferences, institutes, festivals. But, I wonder, what is the function of all these elaborate or exotic designs to the state that promotes them? I suppose when something is so obviously designed it suggests a social democratic commitment to culture, to the life of the nation. An exotic building or an unconventional book or a loco logo says: We're a good government! We invest in culture! We're daring and creative! We care about our people!

In Holland it seems that any object, be it a building, a bus or a bottle, must clearly be *designed*—colorful, oddly shaped, or of unexpectedly material, absurdly dysfunctional, surprisingly mundane—to suggest that the government and the major corporations are progressive and committed to cultural improvement. In America, if something challenging is designed, it says: "Your government wasted YOUR hard-earned money on something as frivolous as this." In America color is waste.

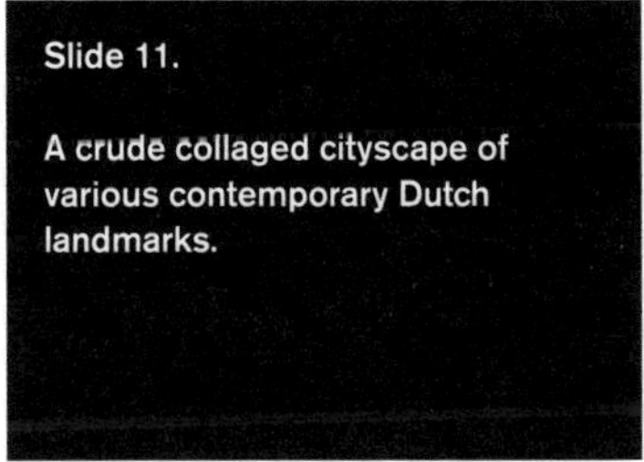

The Dutch landscape is littered with fragments of contemporary international design, indexical signs of an engaged, thoughtful, benevolent state and corporate governance. This fragmentation may be aggravated by the current tendency to break up big projects into small commissions, encouraging young designers to make a name for themselves through some especially innovative design.

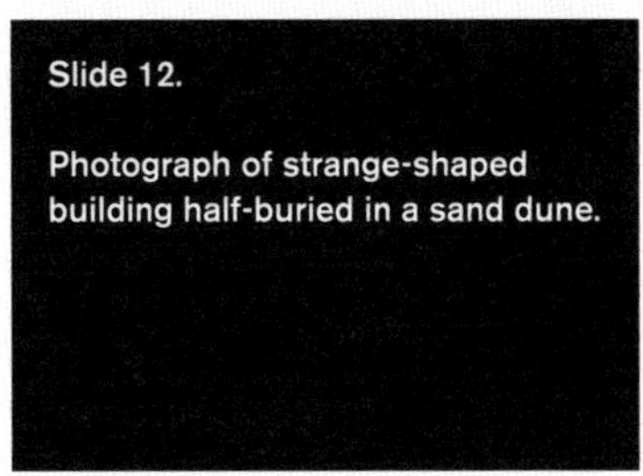

Strange buildings either crash-land in empty fields or get crammed together in conglomerations of urban renewal. So much Design in one place creates an aggregation of exacerbated difference. I wonder now, after a twenty-year ejaculation of making, whether individual design doesn't need to signify anything anymore; it simply needs to look different from other designs. In that way, design shifts from ideology to a kind of branding strategy and enters its fully linguistic state. The Dutch city becomes a Vegas version of a Dutch city with its myriad contemporary "attractions." It's Holland as International Design Theme Park.

2
POOR LITTLE RICH COUNTRY

So all that government incentive, corporate investment and cheap design education has paid off. Over the past two decades, Dutch Design has become simultaneously hot and cool. (Hot as in popular, cool in that it doesn't seem to try very hard or care too much.) What was once a local take on modernism has grown into a global brand.

Slide 13.

A fake logo based on the Intel Inside mark reading: NL Inside.

But how did design become so central to the image of Holland? The cliché is that Holland is manufactured territory, that the construction of dykes and polders and the reclamation of land suggest a kind of artificiality underlying the Dutch psyche, that the landscape itself is the great design project of Holland. I'll spare you that well-worn story. My question is not nearly so profound. I am simply curious about the idea of identity and the way designers construct it.

I love this picture:

Slide 14.

A historic photograph of the founders of Total Design earnestly discussing the future.

Here's a group of hardworking young men planning the overthrow of the Dutch aesthetic landscape. Their generation would take on all the major efforts of visual reconstruction: the airport, the telephone and postal systems, the rail and highway system. With that much money, time, effort and talent thrown into design, is it any wonder so much was done? The name they chose for themselves speaks volumes: Total Design. It could be a philosophy for the nation.

That first wave of Dutch corporate identity in the '50s and '60s may have been a knock-off of the work being developed in Germany and Switzerland at that time. Total Design loved Gerstner and Müller-Brockmann's hyper Swiss-German rationalism. But an increasingly Dutch form of identity found its way into all sorts of designed objects: stamps, posters, trains, money, buildings, ships, highways, and airports. And in Holland, more than anywhere else, much to our envy, corporate and government commissioners would actually choose good design over bad.

It seemed like everything in the postwar Netherlands was being rethought. The process of identity design, with its emphasis on analysis, was one more type of rethinking. If there was any question that Holland was a progressive, modern state, the proof was everywhere: pull out some money, lick a stamp or pick up a phone. The Dutch remade modernism in a more eclectic, more tolerant version. Dutch design not so much Swiss-lite as Swiss +.

The branding of Holland seemed to be overlaid with other, unassailable values: efficiency, legibility, economy and beauty. At least in the '60s these values were still discussed seriously; there appeared to be an honest belief that the injection of design into the built environment would make it a better place. So, like the social democratic politician demanding that the building be a good building, public-information work demanded good design—which was usually interpreted to mean, more or less, Total Design modernism. And this form of rational functionalism became the standard of design education as well.

Somehow the heads of Dutch corporations and Dutch government agencies embraced the notion of not only the value of modern design but also the promotion of Dutch talent through commissions. Certain things are possible in a state where the money looks like this:

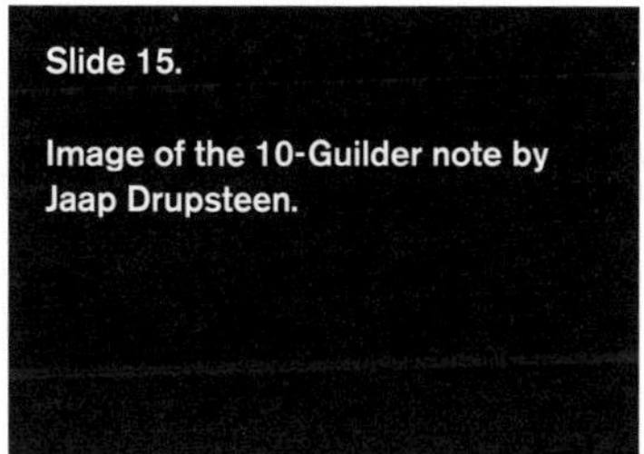

or this:

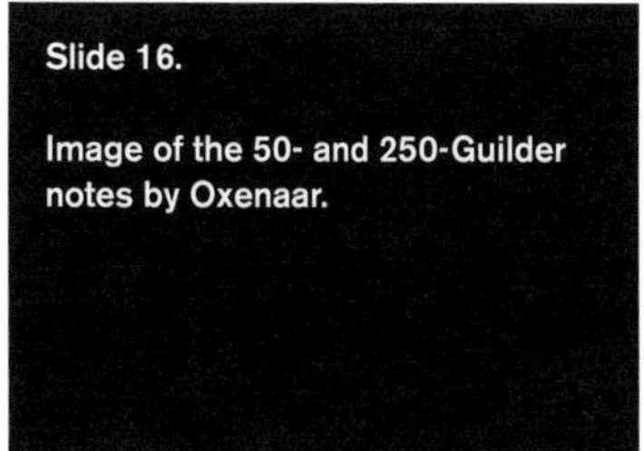

If the most staid organization of any state, the central bank, is sponsoring design like that, what is left to rebel against? In America we still feel it's our duty to try to inject good design into the fabric of a culture that is generally resistant to it. In Holland that cultural fabric is saturated, and it's a small country. But are all big projects done? Is Holland a country where EVERYTHING is already designed?

3
CLASH OF THE TITANS

The answer, of course, is yes and no, and, at least in the late '60s, the thing to rebel against was Total Design's totalizing effect. In trying to understand the Dutch work I find interesting now, I keep going back to the oft-cited debate between Wim Crouwel and Jan van Toorn in November 1972.

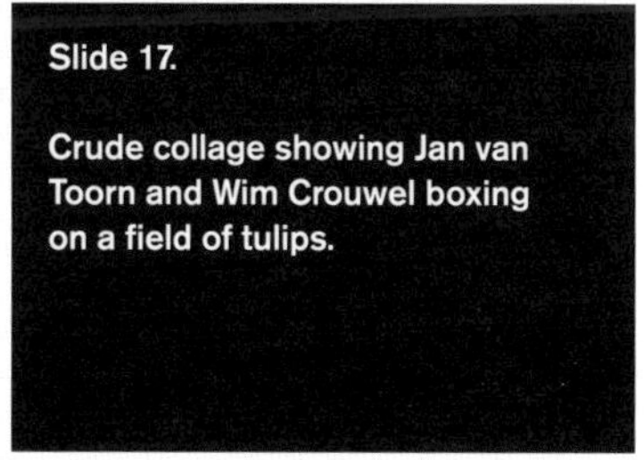

I realize this debate has been mythologized to the point of canonical sheen but, on the surface at least, the opponents seem to represent the extremes of an irreducible contradiction that still undergirds Dutch design. Perhaps the flow of history, however, has slowly reunited them.

Slide 18.

A comparison between a poster by Jan van Toorn for the Van Abbemuseum and one by Wim Crouwel for the Stedelijk.

The much-touted contrast between van Toorn's design for the Van Abbemuseum in Eindhoven and Crouwel's work for the Stedelijk Museum seems not nearly so pronounced in the branding era. Crouwel seemed to argue for a seamless, rational rendering of information—the designer as information channel, the perfect expression of the "new objectivity." (His position in America was mirrored by the likes of Rand and Vignelli.) Van Toorn, on the other hand, argued for the designer as editorial shaper, the one who adds content to content. Van Toorn sees the designer's role as political commentator, even preaching "hindrance" rather than clarity. In van Toorn's view, the designer accepts his distorting role and uses it to forward a specific social agenda.

But what we have learned in the meantime is that 1. neutrality is a myth or, at least, a brand message in itself, and 2. hindrance and dissent as a method can also become a brand device. So van Toorn's claim of eliminating of house style while working with Jean Leering at the Van Abbemuseum is as much a house style (no style as house style) as Crouwel's work for the Stedelijk (which relied on one master grid for every piece of communication). Each institution used the figure of the designer, or his purported absence, as an aesthetic expression in itself. By injecting van Toorn and his well-known political agenda into the message of the work, the designer himself becomes a kind of authorial presence, an emblem for the client. But despite their aesthetic, methodological and political differences, both Crouwel and van Toorn end up coming off as humanists. Both are working at the so-called makeable society: one from the position of efficiency, modernization and objectification; the other from the position of agitation, dialectic and the enlightenment of the masses. So Jan and Wim end up not in opposition but as two sides of the same Dutch coin. Both assume a patriarchal belief in their role as guardians of culture. (You rarely miss an underlying rhetoric of social value, no matter where you scratch the surface of Dutch design.)

The ideology of a dominant culture consumes all discourse contained within it, including the discourse of resistance. So their difference now, in the age of what Max Kisman has dubbed the "style of styles," seems to be primarily formal. This disintegration of distinction does not in any way lessen the real ideological differences between the two men in 1972, but instead demonstrates the way in which the visual expressions of ideology have been absorbed into one master system that strips the meaning of all aesthetic gestures and reduces them to easily exchanged visual clichés. (See, for instance, Experimental Jetset's ideology-free regurgitation of Crouwel's work. It's not accidental that the political power of the original work has been replaced by a history of conflicted dramatic "personalities.")

4
DUMBAR FOR DUMMIES

Speaking of personalities .... For Americans the ideological debates of the '60s and '70s were more or less invisible. We had our own conflicted relationship with Switzerland to work out. True, Dutchification crept into our consciousness much later, and this "tagging" of official agencies was profoundly affected by one figure: Gert Dumbar.

Slide 19.

A photograph of bright yellow Dutch trains.

While we were following Jan van Toorn, Karel Martens, Anthon Beeke and later studios like Wild Plakken and Hard Werken throughout the '70s, '80s and '90s, this one designer —through his burgeoning studio stocked with legions of stagiaires—seemed to impress his subjectivity on every aspect of Dutch culture. For most of the rest of the world, Dutch graphic design in the '80s became synonymous with Dumbar Design.

Dumbar seemed to impose a kind of irrational exuberance on the staid institutions of Dutch culture: the post office, the railway, the police station. Dumbar neatly synthesized the two competing strains of Dutchness: the systematic and the wonky. And he seemed to be able to sell his institutionalized wonkiness to even the most conservative commissioners. (As outsiders, we secretly couldn't believe any self-respecting country would allow their government officials to wear such outlandish outfits.)

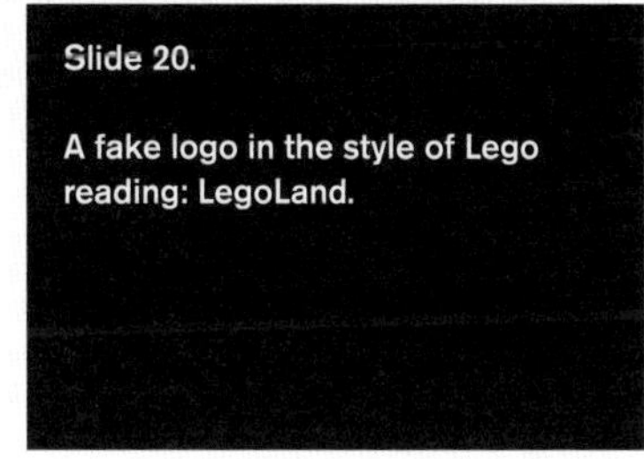
Slide 20.

A fake logo in the style of Lego reading: LegoLand.

By 1995, Chris Vermaas, capturing this sensibility, warned that the continued application of Dumbarism to the organs of the state threatened to turn Holland into a LegoLand:

"The Dutch policeman seems attached to his motorbike sitting on one big plastic peg and has a head that can spin around 360 degrees and come off in one piece."

Slide 21.

A photograph of Dutch Police Porsche with bright candy striping by Studio Dumbar.

Working from a palette of tried-and-true elements — brightness, off-kilteredness, geometric abstraction, angularity — Dumbarism became a kind of brand in itself that could be applied to anything, anywhere. Rather than an expression of a client's values, Dumbarism became a value in itself. (Critics complained that he supplied visuals for companies without their own story to tell.) To associate with Studio Dumbar meant adopting certain values suggested by Dumbar's own mythmaking apparatus: basically a systematic modernist approach to corporate identity peppered with a sprinkling of playful design elements. This approach allowed conservative, often privatizing clients to have it both ways: Dumbar seemed to promise both efficiency and individuality or freedom.

Slide 22.

Images of Studio Dumbar's design for the PTT.

(As an aside, that double-sided rhetoric also served Dumbar's ends: the studio's ubiquitously published "wild" '80s design that captured the attention of the world was underwritten by conventional corporate-identity work, much to the chagrin of the legions of Cranbrook and RCA interns drawn by the studio's public image only to find themselves composing corporate-identity manuals for a bank or an insurance company.)

The effect of Dumbarism and the frenzy of identity designing during the '80s and '90s seemed to make Holland one continuous sea of logos. Everything was done. Everything was styled. The country took on a quality of a *Gesamtkunstwerk*: a total work of art and design. Like some Art Nouveau dream, every surface of the country was fondled. It recalls Adolf Loos' description of the bourgeois gentleman subjected to the all-consuming design of his Art Nouveau environment:

"The happy man suddenly felt deeply, deeply unhappy ... He was shut out of future life and its striving, its developments, and its desires. He felt: Now is the time to learn to walk about with one's own corpse. Indeed! He is finished. He is complete!"

Are young graphic designers living with the corpse of their parents' Dutch design? Did Dumbar finish it off with terminal, nationwide over-design? If not, what is left? Is there any room left for the Dutch design imagination?

5
DUDE, WHERE'S MY COUNTRY?

During the ascendancy of Dumbarism and Dutch Design as an international brand, the country itself was getting harder to find. Branding is a late-cycle phenomenon, the next step once the thing itself is no longer enough. When the consumer needs added impetus to choose one more or less equivalent product over another, the package becomes almost as critical as the product. Does a thinning Holland need an ever more robust package? Is there a relationship between the rise of branding and the disappearance of a nation?

Like countries everywhere, Holland is under intense pressure. The contemporary nation is stretched, as Mark Jayne wrote in *Cities and Consumption*, by the "domination of information, media, and signs, the desegregation of social structure into lifestyles; the general priority of consumption over production in everyday life."

Slide 23.

Contemporary Dutch photograph of an African woman on an overpass in what appears to be Rotterdam. Her entire face has been overprinted with solid black.

What is Dutch anymore anyway? Clearly the meaning is changing. (The conservatives resort to the sly phrase "Dutch values" to disguise an overt nationalist/racist appeal.) The demographics are brutal. The time-honored story of the battle between Catholic and Protestant is dissolving fast. What percentage of the country is Muslim? Who can speak Dutch and who can't? While no one was looking, Holland became a porous concept.

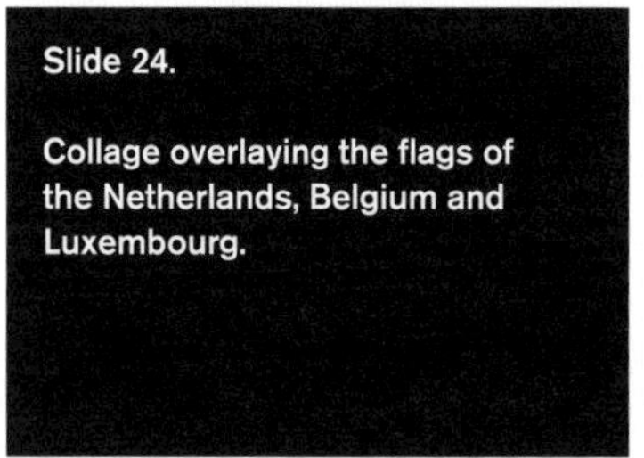

The famous emblems of Dutchness dissolve through merger and hostile takeover. The money first, then the post, then what? As production fades, Holland transforms into BeNeLux or MainPort: Europe's airport, seaport and warehouse land (with its own special logo).

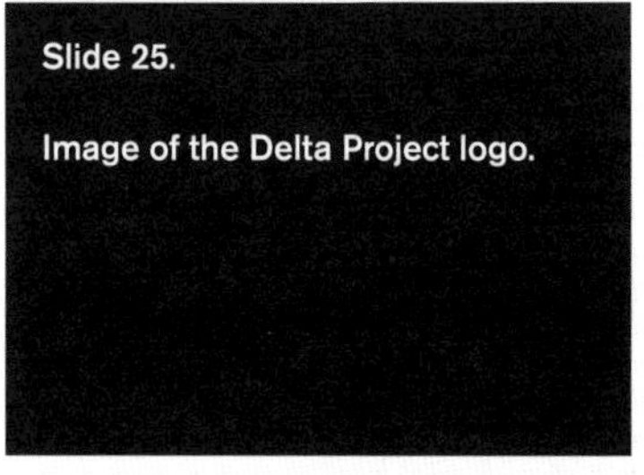

It's the country as conduit. All that Delta Project territory to create land to store and move someone else's things that are headed somewhere else. There is a shift from commodity to experience. Everything—time, space, services as well as goods—becomes branded.

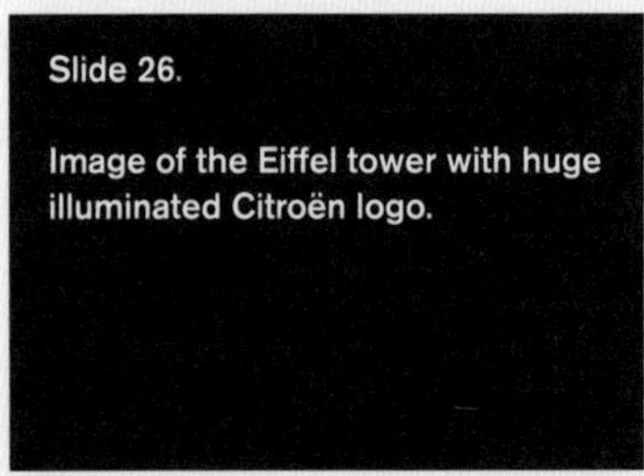

Some products are so inextricably linked to their nation they take on a quasi-public role. But a subtle but profound shift happens when major cultural figures privatize. Air France swallows KLM, although the deal is couched to make it seem like an equal marriage.

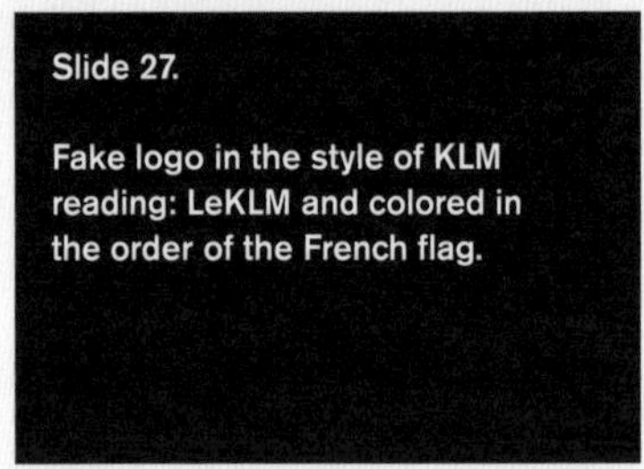

PTT becomes a wholly owned subsidiary of TNT, based in Australia of all places. These great public institutions, flagships of the nation, become profit-driven corporations, subsidiaries of international conglomerates. What once was an expression of Dutch pride—PTT showcasing the best of Holland in the design of the stamps and phone cards, for instance, or KLM with their slow motion swans and painfully matter-of-fact blue-suited flight attendants—either simply disappears or flips to clichés of Dutchness, turned back on the nation as marketing tools. The public institution represents the state; the private one attempts to represent the taste and lifestyle of its own market. It's the McKroket strategy.

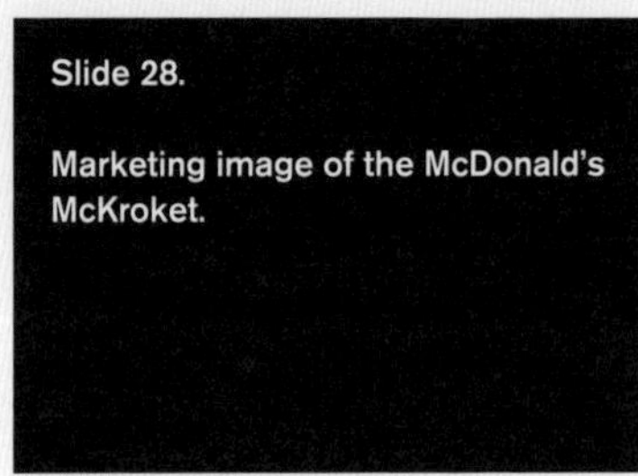

Multinational McDonald's customizes its internationally consistent commodity to appeal to vernacular tastes. The McKroket is McDonald's going Dutch. The privatized standard-bearers of the Dutch culture repackage the emblems of Dutchness as a branding strategy to maintain the loyalty of their consumers (the contemporary word for citizens). So Dutchness, and Dutch Design, become tools for globalized, capitalist corporations to market to the Dutch audience. Dutch design as branding tool and constructed signifier of Dutch values becomes as quaint and charming as windmills and tulips.

At this moment of deep internal ambivalence, the nation is embarking on a major initiative, building signature embassies in world capitals.

Once content with low-profile generic office space, Holland now uses embassy design to make an international show of strength, to shore up the Dutch Brand. (Branding is the last grasp of the desperate.) Whatever is happening at home, Holland keeps up appearances. The embassy project is pure boosterism, reassuring yourselves and the rest of the world that you are still here, and you still matter.

6
TWO BIG BOOKS

I began by discussing the progression from an optimistic design culture, ready and willing to engage in the major challenges of rebuilding Holland, to a hyper-design state with increasingly less room to maneuver. Now I want to look closely at contemporary reactions to the state and the concomitant rise in the desire for self-expression.

To explore that shift from public to private a little further, I turn to two big Dutch books: Wim Crouwel and Jolijn van de Wouw's PTT telephone book of 1977 and Irma Boom's commemorative book for the SHV corporation of 1999.

Specifically, I am curious about the relationship between the designer and the work in two settings: the utterly public and the obsessively private.

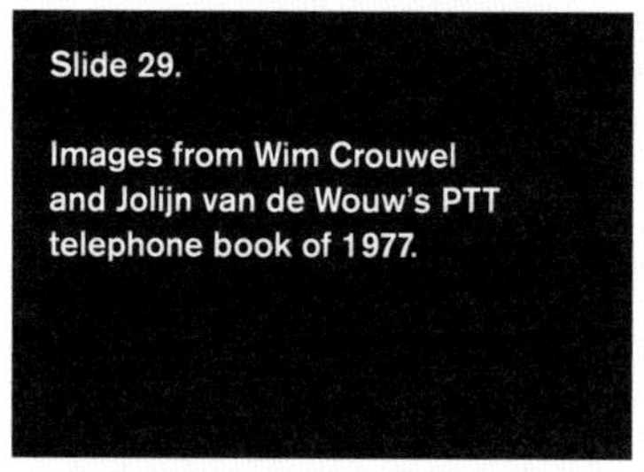
Slide 29.

Images from Wim Crouwel and Jolijn van de Wouw's PTT telephone book of 1977.

The telephone book may be the ultimate utilitarian object: it is both open to, and includes, everybody. Its function is clearly stated and simply tested. The social contract between the designer and the public is clear and simple—I need to find a name, the number needs to be legible. The designer has a responsibility of clarity, legibility and efficient production. Nobody wants personality or parody in a phonebook. So far, so good. This fits comfortably into the definition of Graphic Designer as problem solver, scientist of information.

But despite claims to the contrary, the phonebook is an expression of a kind of ideology, a belief that it is good for the public to read a certain way, a typographic aestheticism disguised as altruism. Under the cover of neutrality, the designer asserts his position. For instance, Crouwel uses the limited character set of phototypesetting to justify an all-lower-case alphabet, a long-time dream of modernist designers who saw different upper- and lower-case letterforms as an untenable illogic.

Then how do we make sense of Irma Boom's role with SHV corporation (for whom Crouwel's Total Design had created the original house style in 1965)? The Director of SHV commissioned Holland's most celebrated book designer to create a special volume commemorating the centennial of the company. Working for over five years, without specific or designated content, Boom shapes a narrative out of raw data, documents and found objects. She authors by collage. The meaning, then, is not a product of words alone (or words at all) but of selection, page sequence and image cropping, the essential devices of design.

Slide 30.

Images from Irma Boom's SHV book from 1999.

Boom's big book is fundamentally a different genre from Crouwel's big book, and the role defined for the designer is so antithetical as almost to demand a different title. The SHV book is a project for one man, representing all the power of his corporation, produced in a hyper-limited edition. (In typical Dutch pseudo-modesty, the extravagant display of conspicuous consumption is hidden from view by limited distribution.) The book makes the signature of the designer part of its branding strategy. The book says: we are an enlightened company, we are rich, we are cultured, and we know the value of Irma Boom. The corporation uses its association with her unassailable brilliance to advance its own image.

The difference between the two books, I think, is the difference between a hyper-Dutch and a hyper-American project. The two books represent the move from the public to the private. In both cases, the association with the designer has meaning. Crouwel disappears in the phonebook; the PTT makes an overt commitment to Modernity through a connection to Total Design. SHV licenses Boom's aura and Boom grafts her identity onto the content of the SHV book. (In an interview, Crouwel opined that a recent Boom book on Otto Treumann was "in fact a book about her, not Otto Treumann.") A book that large and complex, with every page shaped by one person, becomes a kind of autobiography. Boom is a constant, ghostly presence. It's not JUST a big book. It's an Irma Boom book. The designer, as author, supplies brand value or celebrity endorsement.

7
THE ORGANIZATION MEN (AND WOMEN)

I'll get back to that trend, where the designer makes a guest appearance in the work. But I actually think those cases of the overt reference of author/designer are anomalies. Holland poses a special condition and the Dutch designer has a conflicted relationship with the idea of authorship (in the same way the Dutch seem to have issues with ambition and authority.) There's the divided lust for expression on one side, and moral rectitude and modesty on the other, both of which seem to generate a range of singular behaviors.

To assuage, or at least to mask, the ambition and ego necessary to build the figure of the author, the Dutch designer positions him/herself not as originator, but as one who marshals undeniable economic, legal, textual, demographic and civic forces and follows them to their irrefutable conclusion. By this technique, the designer eschews celebrity, feigns anonymity, and assumes the role of systems manager.

This bifurcated relationship—dividing the desire to express from the drive for reason—is already present in Crouwel's description of a rational design process: "The content determines the form, the typeface, the format, the cover, the binding. Every assignment can be divided into several factors, which are all interrelated. With each commission, as it were, you have to plot those factors along a horizontal and vertical axis, stretch out a string and then see where it takes you" (1961). The image of the matrix is brutal; its findings, absolute. Notice the passivity, the submission to the data. You wait to see where the data take you. His experiments in type design test the same formula. He sets up the system but then slavishly follows it to some logical conclusion.

Slide 31.

Rendering of MVRDV's Expo 2000 Netherlands Pavilion.

This matter-of-fact, hyper-pragmatism, surrendering to the omnipotent effect of the diagram is present in all manner of Dutch work. Perhaps the strategy derives from a natural reaction to a country in which every centimeter is regulated by preordained rules. But the buildings of architects like MVRDV, and their attendant documentation and reliance on so-called Datascapes, stretch Dutch rationalism to absurd, even parodic results. Research and analysis form a diagram and a diagram derives a building. The designers are represented as bystanders or objective scientists watching with grim satisfaction as their convoluted theories give rise to even more convoluted forms.

Slide 32.

Image from OMA's Museum of Modern Art proposal in which a building is shaped by filling a zoning envelope mold with resin and withdrawing the resultant form.

See also Koolhaas' plan for New York's MoMA that simply uses the given zoning envelope as form generator—coupled with the title "Architecture without Architects."

Slide 33.

Diagram from OMA's Seattle Public Library proposal showing shifting trays of program.

Or OMA's Seattle Public Library in which the Dewey Decimal organization of the library books drives a diagram that drives a building.

Critic Thomas Daniell put it nicely, comparing the method of the Japanese architect and the Dutch architect. I'm paraphrasing here: the Japanese architect begins with a poetic concept and refines it into plausibility; the Dutch architect begins with analysis and extrapolates it into poetry. These Dutch buildings have a kind of self-evident brutality to them. Of course they're brutal—current conditions, objectively measured, don't necessarily render beauty. Beauty would imply a subjectivity. Facts are facts. You make the building the facts give you.

Perhaps many of the novel shapes of recent Dutch buildings can be attributed to this devotion to the diagram, and the authorial absolution it grants. By taking traditional Dutch pragmatism to absurd, deadpan extremes, the designer generates new, wholly unexpected forms. Some of Droog Design—which has been so publicized it doesn't need any more publicity from me—embodies this absurdist hyperrationalism. The designer simply continues to apply the system until the form appears in all its strangeness.

This authorial avoidance strategy seems to have spawned enthusiasm for the generic, the recycled, the already done, the under-designed and the preexisting that dominates contemporary design debates. Much of recent Dutch design seems intent on erasing the sense that any designer imposed any subjectivity. Take Pascale Gatzen's reworking of photographed clothing. By copying an existing item—not even the original but the ad—remaking it, and then re-photographing it and re-advertising it, she calls into question the origination of the object. Is it her work? Or take Klavers Engelen, who makes a simple change in orientation into a defamiliarization strategy. Or Hella Jongerius's textile, "Repeat," which uses pre-existing traditional textile designs reorganized by curious juxtaposition and unifying overlays. Or Experimental Jetset's project that samples the work of a previous generation, overwriting new meaning.

Slide 34.

Pages from *Archis* magazine showing typography modeled on other publications.

Or *Archis* magazine's use of found typographic style, absolving it of a sense of subjectivity, eliminating the designers' presumed responsibility to create a distinct, unique identity. (More on that shortly.)

8
AUTHOR AS VALUE-ADDED

But if it is a Dutch Design trait to disappear into data or a system and feign, at least, a lack of real ambition or subjectivity, there is an emerging tendency in which the designer assumes a central role as a character in the work. This tests the way the treatment of given material—what van Toorn might call the critical perspective—amounts to a kind of authorship.

Many designers have enthusiastically embraced the idea of authorship in hopes of dipping into the authority traditionally granted to authors. But designers have generally misconstrued the idea of the author as a power strategy, a way to wrest control over their projects from the various forces intent on limiting it. Most design use of the phrase links authorship to a kind of artistic expression or self-expression. But I am interested not so much in trying to recuperatethe prominence of the designer through the application of authorial principles, but in trying to pick out the way the figure of the author (which is always fictionalized) meshes with branding strategy.

(In all cases it's important to remember that when I use the term author, I am never referring to the writer but to a fictional figure that serves to unify a whole variety of diverse texts. The author is a function, a term of exchange.)

Dumbar could embody one model of the designer as auteur, managing an army of underlings to impress his stamp on the broadest possible canvas. Dumbar—actually NOT Dumbar but Dumbar's studio—creates Dumbar signature work. Dumbar as flamboyant stands for the work, gives it a public face and a branded "personality." Irma Boom working with SHV represents another model in which the designer uses the tools of design to construct meaning. But more recent work engages the subject in more complex and nuanced ways.

I want to turn back then for a moment to look closely at one project: *Archis* magazine and its transformation from a somewhat straight, analytical professional journal to an international style magazine whose subject happens to be architecture. (Since the magazine was recently celebrated again with the Rotterdam Design Prize, I think it safe to assume that it is an example of what some consider to be the "best" of contemporary Dutch design.)

While the core of the magazine is still articles, reviews, critiques and editorials, the magazine adopts another voice that appears spectrally among the articles, offering choices, garnering information, asking questions and making jokes. But whose voice? The editor? The designers? A phantom that haunts its pages? Who is the "I" of *Archis*?

Since that voice ostensibly has nothing to do with the delivery of the content—that is, the articles and items that make up the body of the magazine—it would seem at first to be a van Toornian hindrance strategy. The designers editorialize by shaping the material. But the *Archis* authorial presence has none of van Toorn's desire for social reformation or political agitation. The *Archis* voice is the court jester: it's about richness, pleasure, irony, humor, i.e. value-added content and shading.

Archis furthers that relationship between author and reader through a series of specific shifts and moves. The voice asks questions directly, leaves blank spaces to be filled, supplies forms to fax back, overwrites other texts and generally interferes. (And it can be maddening, like an annoying friend reading over your shoulder, making snide remarks.) Some pages are perforated, suggesting reader-driven mutability, that the presented form is merely one incarnation, not the finished state. It invites its own disfiguration.

Slide 35.

Grid of *Archis* magazine covers.

The voice of *Archis* moves the magazine from a writerly to a readerly text. By goading readers to literally fill in the blanks, the *Archis* "I" implicates them in the design itself. This gesture culminates in the recent move toward organized public events that suggest a completely user-centric forum, where content is specifically formatted in direct response to an audience gathered in a specific spot at a specific time with the *Archis* author assuming the role of maestro, conducting.

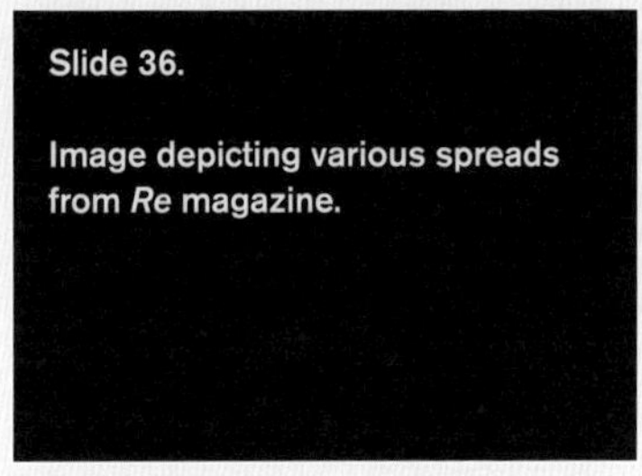

Slide 36.

Image depicting various spreads from *Re* magazine.

One well-publicized example of the fictionalized author can be discerned in Jop van Bennekom's self-initiated *Re* magazine. Van Bennekom links his magazine—which started as a school project at the Jan van Eyck Academie—to a "typical Dutch approach .... A conceptual position of self-irony and self-questioning." Bennekom positions himself as both the originator and subject of the magazine. Through this overt form, the magazine is dedicated to his interests, proclivities, possessions, friends, life events. The magazine generates a fictional presence—the designer Jop van Bennekom—who permeates every aspect of the project. Even as he moves from sole proprietor to executive editor to a single individual, van Bennekom serves as both author and subject in an intensely autobiographical project.

Slide 37.

Image of Tony Oursler's Rem Koolhaas doll with projected face on display at the Content show in Berlin.

And then this. Visiting the recent AMO/OMA exhibition at the National Gallery in Berlin, I was greeted by a special Rem Koolhaas doll that artist Tony Oursler had created for the exhibition. Koolhaas can be read on several levels, as literal author and as coalescing figure—the ringmaster—marshalling the forces of a broad, decentralized, international cast of collaborators whose work is unified under his name. Oursler's figure of Koolhaas floats spectrally over a smashed and decayed pile of garbage and broken design elements and reads, over and over in continuous loop, his article "Junkspace." The Rem doll makes a perpetual celebrity appearance, endlessly spouting his famous, branded rhetoric.

9
DRESSING DOWN

In typical Dutch fashion, no one dresses up to make an appearance. The Dutch author arrives disheveled. His or her presence is padded with irony and self-deprecation. There seems to be a close connection between the rise of the author, of subjectivity, and the un-designing of design.

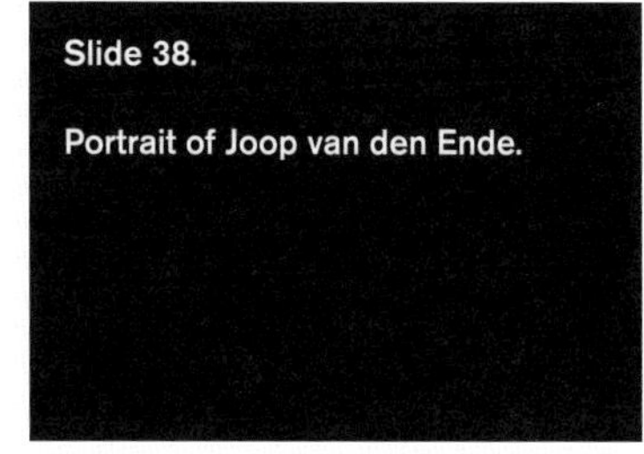

But what drove that shift to the undesigned design in the '90s and the attendant Dutch Design explosion internationally? While part of the shift is clearly a reaction to the slickness of the '80s and the early '90s, I nominate one man, Joop van den Ende, as the real source of inspiration. Joop van den Ende is of course the father of the worldwide global phenomenon known as Big Brother and bubble-gum television. The basic tenet of Big Brother is that compelling television may result from simply sticking a bunch of unlikeable characters in a house and filming the ensuing friction.

Reality TV has exploded in the U.S. and around the world. Television producers love it because it's cheap, easy to make, easy to serialize and, most important, easy to localize. It satisfies the grim desire to inspect your neighbor's dirty laundry. In Holland it seems to have a special resonance, perhaps because the whole country is a kind of artificial reality of closely packed neighbors, or perhaps because of the brutal efficiency of the concept. It seems to embody the “not one penny more” credo.

Slide 39.

Images of work from artist Jaap van Lieshout’s AVL Ville project depicting the slaughtering and butchering of a pig.

Recent work focuses on the banal: the areas untouched by Dumbarism and the sweeping over-design gestures from the years before. Van Lieshout’s AVL Ville is a kind of artificial reality TV. The work refers to the standard, accidental items of an in-between space, but always with some ironic twist. Actually, it’s a romanticized banality. This work ignores the corporate, globalized reality of Phillips and PTT or Rabobank. The romanticized reality focuses on the generic apartment, the refugee camp, the abandoned embankment and the vernacular language of the do-it-yourselfer.

Slide 40.

Various screen shots of KesselsKramer’s website adopting diverse vernacular forms.

That same aesthetic is repackaged by agencies like KesselsKramer in campaigns for the likes of Diesel and Ben. Their own sly, funny website perfectly embodies the methodology. It adopts all of the familiar clichés of the web, injects them with style, and produces a new form of writing that is part reference, part narrative, part playacting. Of course this casualness is so enormously cultivated and finessed that it is immediately recognizable as design with a capital D. No one would miss the joke.

The question is: does banality have an agenda? Is anything advanced except the blasé, detached bemusement of the designer? Has Holland become so comfortable, so completely designed, that the only thing left is ironic commentary on the act of designing itself? Does anyone think about a kind of makeable society, or have we just given up? Design may have become a free-floating reaction, all verb without direct object.

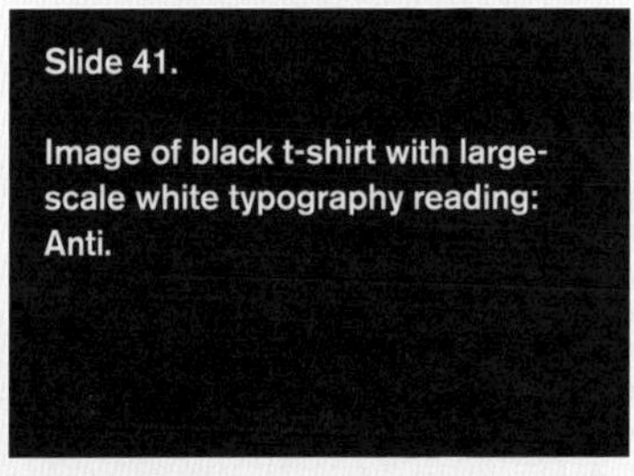
Slide 41.

Image of black t-shirt with large-scale white typography reading: Anti.

Just *against* … but against what? Note this remark from Experimental Jetset:

“What we have … drawn from post-modernism is the realization that there are no objective, neutral or universal values. But that does not discourage us from pursuing those values; that is our modernist inheritance. In the end, we've actually arrived at something of a synthesis of modernism and postmodernism; working with a utopia in mind, while being fully aware that we will never achieve that utopia."

We have all gotten used to accepting whatever comes along, whoever is in the house. One will get voted off each week, but don't worry, the whole thing will start again next season. It's just a game. It's as if after twenty years of absolutely relentless shifts in style, and years of being berated for their lack of political commitment by their May '68 professors, young Dutch designers simply turned inward. The kind of Dutch design that captures our attention now almost always has a layer of humor and reference that seems to say, like Experimental Jetset, we don't really believe this, but let's pretend anyway. But, more striking, for a country once known for big, bold, broad public initiatives, Dutch design seems to have taken to tackling small issues. The designer has cast his/her gaze on something so low, so insignificant, it imbues the object with almost mythic power.

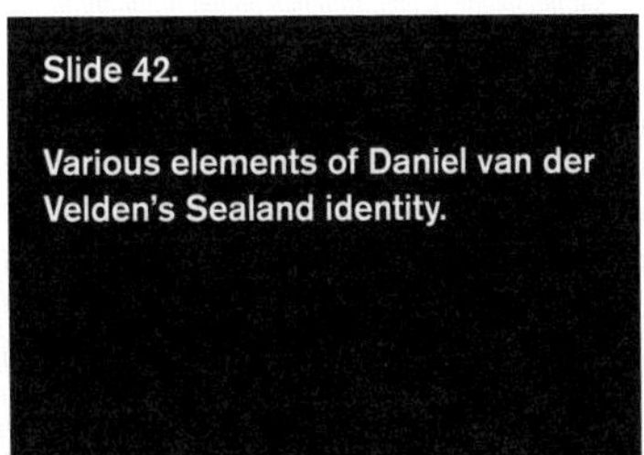
Slide 42.

Various elements of Daniel van der Velden's Sealand identity.

Let's turn briefly to a contemporary identity project: Daniel van der Velden's project (government-subsidized, of course) to develop a brand for Sealand, a single abandoned North Sea defense-platform-cum-principality. Whatever the merit of the design experiment—to create an identity for an entity without substance, a pure data space—it may be poignant as a metaphor: Dutch designers may have turned their attention offshore, given up on the mainland, given up believing their work can affect the "real" world. Maybe there is no running room left in Holland. Maybe the "makeable society" is simply the basis for parody.

10
WE ARE WHAT WE EAT

The production and consumption of style has accelerated so quickly, been broadcast so widely, that trends and countertrends develop simultaneously. Action and reaction are linked inextricably. This is due, in part, to the fact that you really do have a culture of design here, a culture of experiment, discourse and discovery.

I've titled this talk "Mad Dutch Disease," an obvious allusion to Mad Cow Disease or, more officially, bovine spongiform encephalopathy. The scourge of Europe, Mad Cow appears when cows eat feed that contains the remains of other cows. When our diet starts to be restricted to the point of devouring and regurgitating last week's trend, we are in serious jeopardy of succumbing to a similar fate.

Slide 43.
Sequence of images from an old cartoon showing Wile E. Coyote:

1. plunging the t-shape handle of a detonator with wires leading to pile of roadrunner food in the distance …

2. a large, colorful explosion …

3. crispy black coyote holding remains of plunger as unharmed bird speeds away.

But as I mentioned at the beginning, I don't see Dutch design as confined to the Netherlands. This is happening everywhere. It's just that due to advantageous conditions, it seems more pronounced here. In the States, our flights of fancy are constantly quelled by the market. Because of that we use Holland as a kind of breeding ground, carefully observing what is sure to happen everywhere else sooner or later.

Or perhaps this is a better way to put it: I wonder if we have worked ourselves into a trap of our own making. We have been tirelessly chasing this thing called design theory or criticism for twenty years. Have we been building an elaborate contraption of self-reflective meta-design culture, only to realize that we may be its ultimate victims?

When it comes time to hit the switch, who knows what the result will be.

AMERIDAM: THE DUTCHIFICATION OF AMERICA

PREAMBLE

I was invited by Jan van Toorn to contribute an essay for a book he was organizing on the great Dutch designer Anthon Beeke. Jan asked me to provide the foreign eye, to evaluate the work from the outside. To the best of my recollection, I met Beeke twice: the first time more than twenty-odd years ago in Providence, Rhode Island, and the second time in the spring of 2010 in Amsterdam in preparation for the following text.

As most of his Dutch books and magazines have never been available in America or translated into English, Beeke's remarkable early work is practically unknown in the U.S. And to the American eye, his work after 2000 became less distinct—competent, even elegant, but not as wildly original and emblematic—and therefore less relevant. As a critic, as always, I must deal with the designer through the design. Therefore, I confine myself to a sliver of time starting around 1980 and ending in the early 1990s—the period during which he produced his major work, work that established his international reputation and for which he is primarily known in the U.S. And it was on the strength of this work that he was invited to America as one of the early ambassadors of Dutch design.

Beeke is not my peer—he's a generation older—and he's not exactly my subject either. In fact, this is not so much an interrogation of Beeke as it is an eyewitness account of a distinctly American attachment to European design (and how that attachment shifted focus in the late 1980s), how modernism was understood and extended, and how Beeke's oeuvre fits perfectly into this realignment.

Ancient History: The Europeanization of the American Design Academy

Time: Sometime in the early '80s.
Location: Art-school auditorium, Providence, RI.

Wolfgang Weingart, then distinguished professor of typography at the Schule für Gestaltung Basel, is in the middle of a lecture (or maybe "demonstration" would be a better term), titled "How to design a Swiss poster." He is a hulk of a man, bristling all over with stubble. Is he really wearing a smock or is it some kind of Swiss tradesman's uniform? He has an overt disdain for us, although I may be imagining that he often starts his sentences with the phrase: "You Americans . . ." There is not much evidence to go on. He hardly says anything. He is hunched over an overhead projector placed in the middle of the audience, cutting litho-film—fragments of typography, half-tone images and Ben-Day dot-screens—creating ovelays and manipulating moiré, the tedious, painstaking work broadcast on a humongous screen. When he finds a composition he likes, he signifies the victory with a small grunt of satisfaction and fixes it with Scotch tape. This seems to go on for hours. We are rapt.

Our American design world of the early '80s breaks down into crudely drawn camps. If you want to know which camp you're in, the simplest test of allegiance is your position on the quintessential New York designer Milton Glaser. If you are in the camp that reveres Weingart, it follows that you must despise Glaser, and vice versa. For all of us on that side, Weingart represents a direct, unbroken lineage from the heroic and historic avant-garde: Vhutemas, revolutionary Constructivism, Dada, De Stijl, Bauhaus,Ulm, Basel, us. Our design canon, reinforced by our design-history classes, is peopled almost exclusively with Europeans and Americans who pretend they are Europeans.

The great American champion of the Swiss is the belligerent modernist Paul Rand, the preeminent corporate designer and polemicist of his generation. "When I first became aware of the work of Swiss graphic designers in the late forties," he says, "I used to ridicule it. I would yodel and say, My God, here they come again! I really thought the stuff was awful, cold—all the clichés that are used to describe Swiss design. But then I realized that nobody had come up with anything better or even as good."[1]

Rand and Glaser[2] have similar backgrounds but they represent two sides of an essential battle in American design: i.e. how European it would be. Rand increasingly sees his work as akin to an abstract art and positions himself as the inevitable successor of the towering figures of European art and design. He brackets his canon "from Cimabue (1240–1302) to Cassandre (1901–1968)."[3] Although Glaser spent a formative Fulbright year in Italy, his work draws from an entirely different set of American references. His work is eclectic, playful, vernacular and popular. We dismiss it as kitsch.

By the time I meet Rand, around 1990, the jaunty adman of the 1940s known for his goofy collages hawking cigars and cordials is a distant memory. He is the adamant, unyielding defender of the modern (read: European) orthodoxy. In his mid-70s, he's hunkered down in a stark modernist house in leafy Weston, Connecticut, from which he decries the post-modernization of American design and all the attendant "squiggles, pixels, doodles, dingbats and ziggurats; boudoir colors, turquoise, peach, pea green and lavender; corny woodcuts on moody browns and russets; Art Deco rip-offs, high-gloss finishes, sleazy textures; tiny color photos surrounded by acres of white space; indecipherable, zany typography with miles of leading; text in all caps [despite indisputable proof, he says, that lowercase letters are more readable]; omnipresent, decorative letterspaced caps; visually annotated typography and revivalist caps and small caps; pseudo-Dada and Futurist collages; and whatever 'special effects' a computer makes possible."[4]

1 Steven Heller, "Paul Rand: The master of twentieth century graphic design talks candidly about technique, trends, time and perfection," *I.D.* Nov./Dec. 1988: 40.

2 Born a generation apart, Rand in 1914 and Glaser in 1929; both are New York Jews, Rand observant, Glaser not; urban educated, Rand at Pratt in Brooklyn, Glaser at The Cooper Union in Manhattan.

3 Paul Rand, "Confusion and Chaos: The Seduction of Contemporary Graphic Design," *AIGA Journal of Graphic Design* 10, no. 1 (1992).

4 Ibid.

5 Paul Rand, personal interview, Oct. 1991.

6 Max Bruinsma, personal letter to the author: "Your assessment of Glaser as 'not a van Toorn' is correct. But look at the work of Beeke (and/with) Swip Stolk, and you see that these are kindred spirits. In stylistic respect, Rand vs. Glaser is Crouwel vs. Beeke! So where, from an 'over-theorized' perspective of young post-modern American designers in the 1980s there seems to be a US-EU dichotomy, from the perspective of the young European rebels in the late 1960s it's a rift between Swiss-led international style corporate modernism vs. '68–ish anti-authoritarian libertarianism. Fluxus, Provo, the sexual revolution, flower-power, feminism (yes: and feminism!) are the social-political sources of inspiration for Anthon and his milieu."

We are sitting in his studio room—underneath a bright CYRK poster by Tomaszewski—on a sunny New England autumn afternoon. Rand leans back in his work chair, fixes us in his goggled stare. "Did you bring any work?" he barks in his old-school Brooklyn accent. "N-no," we fumble. "This is just kind of a social visit." "You should have brought work," dismissing us. "How else can I figure out what side you're on?"[5]

To be on Rand's side is to believe in the game of design as a closed system: structures are devised and the designer plays all available games possible without betraying those self-imposed limits. Above all else, Rand's mid-century European modernism represents the elimination of attachment, the stripping away of associative meaning outside the system in the name of direct expression and hierarchy. The work may not refer: it is what it is. Everything else is cloying novelty.

To those of us on the Swiss side, Rand's exhaustive list may as well be a comprehensive inventory of Glaser's toolbox. The now universally acclaimed I♥NY is the perfect emblem of this American depravity: lowbrow novelty font, cutesy dingbat, corny visual pun, all tied up in a neat package and accompanied by a catchy jingle. American design has no rigor, no taste, no RULES. It is essentially Victorian in its attachment to novelty, humor and the tackily referential. But the dynamic between Rand and Glaser is not the equivalent of the much publicized Wim Crouwel/Jan van Toorn debate. Glaser does not, in the way van Toorn does, offer a political resistance to Rand's formalism.[6] Both are extremely successful corporate designers working deep inside the system. We are offended primarily by style, not politics. Those on the other side decry Swiss design as cold and emotionless. Our slavish devotion to Europeanism reads as academic, overly intellectual or simply snobbish. But they all miss the point: that coolness *is* the attraction. We love being aesthetic snobs; it makes us feel less American.

• • •

By the 1970s, the first of a cadre of graduate students indoctrinated into the European religion at Ulm and Basel—and at their American outposts such as the Yale School of Art and the Rhode Island School of Design[7] —fan out across the academic design landscape sowing the Helvetican seed, painting silhouettes of keys and letters and ruling pens in black plaka and extolling the virtues of *Raster systeme für die visuelle Gestaltung.*[8] To complete the effect, it is not uncommon for born-and-bred American students to return from their forays in Swiss graduate schools sporting shapeless jackets, a copy of *Typografische Monatsblätter*[9] under their arms and speaking in weird, quasi-German accents, artlessly struggling to remember their native words for common objects. "In English, how do you say ...?"

By the time we come around, giants like Emil Ruder, Armin Hofmann and Josef Müller-Brockmann have a little too much monumentality for us to relate to. And the relatively youngish Weingart is too prickly to embrace. On our side of the Atlantic, the Americanization of Europeanism comes through a bicoastal channel: the briefly married but spiritually connected couple Dan Friedman and April Greiman.

7 Katherine McCoy elaborates: "The Philadelphia College of Art (now University of the Arts) and Kansas City Art Institute (KCAI) were more influential in introducing Swiss design in the earlier years. Basel-educated Ken Hiebert initiated PCA's Swiss-infused program in 1966 and it was in full swing by 1970. Steff Geissbuhler arrived to teach there in 1967. Eventually PCA built a full roster of Basel-educated faculty, including Hans Allemann, Inge Druckrey, Chris Zelinsky, Bill Longhauser and April Greiman (for 2–3 years when she returned from her year abroad). Because of the proximity to New York and the tendency for PCA grads to go there to work, PCA is probably the most influential school to spread the Swiss religion, both early on and continuing to today .... Rob Roy Kelly's KCAI program (1964–1974) brought Inge Druckrey there in 1966. Hans Allemann arrived with Chris Zelinsky in 1967. April Greiman graduated from KCAI around 1969, as well as Jerry Herring of Houston. After his Yale MFA, Gordon Salchow taught at KCAI from about 1966–69 and became imbued with Swiss ideology through his close work with Inge and Hans. Then Salchow moved to University of Cincinnati to found that Swiss-oriented program there about 1969." (Email to the author.)

8 The influential text by Josef Müller-Brockmann.

9 The iconic Swiss typography journal.

10 Katherine McCoy, email to the author: "Barbara Stauffacher Solomon and Ken Heibert may have been the first Americans to attend the Schule für Gestaltung in the early 1960s. Dan Friedman was an early American a few years later and April Greiman was there for a year around 1970. She was a good friend of Philip Burton who later went on to become second-in-command at Yale. The flood of American grad students heading to Basel in the second half of the 1970s were going for the excitement of Weingart's experimentation, not the earlier strict modernist work."

An innocent Midwesterner, Friedman makes a daring move and attends the design academy in Ulm before moving on to Schule für Gestaltung, Basel. There he meets young April Greiman at the temple of Hofmann and Weingart, and they go on to transform their adopted methodology into a double-pronged injection of what would later become known as New Wave Design.[10]

Returning stateside, the couple splits: Friedman goes East, teaches at Yale, shaves his head and then slides into New York's emerging East Village art scene, hooking up with Keith Haring along the way. He works for AGP and Pentagram by day—applying his Basel-trained precision to the Citibank account—but by night his apartment becomes a site for constant visual exploration of lurid colors, drop-shadowed triangles, squiggles and dots: a New Wave *merzbau*. His work starts to veer away from European orthodoxy into an area dangerously close to the depravity described by Rand a decade later. Greiman heads west to preside over her own grapho-cyborgian, sybaritic California hybridization, including innovative publications such as *WET*, provocatively subtitled: *The Magazine of Gourmet Bathing and Beyond*.

Greiman and Friedman don't dismantle their masters so much as add another layer—replete with drop shadow—of compositional articulation. (Later they would both become more complex figures, Greiman with her prescient foray into technology, Friedman with his immersion in Queer politics.) The sides are clearly delineated: Europeanism represents the tendency of a certain class of Americans to express disdain for the very culture from which they emerged. It is, of course, an illusion. Both Glaserism and Europeanism are highly historical: if Europeanism is built on the radical elimination of attachment and the strict adherence to the closed system, that position is deeply embedded in a long tradition of the radical elimination of attachment, from the historical avant-garde forward. Hence the question is not historic vs. ahistoric but, rather, which history will prevail or, more precisely, which history is valid and usable. In other words, whose side are you on?

1982: Greiman is appointed head of the design department at the California Institute of the Arts. In a remarkable moment of aesthetic alignment and homogeneity, the four major highbrow design schools in the United States are all led by direct disciples of one European system: Rand and Hofmann at Yale, Tom Ockerse (ex. of Yale) at RISD, Katherine McCoy (alumna of the high-Euro studio Unimark) at Cranbrook, and Greiman at CalArts. In addition, important schools from North Carolina to Cincinnati to Chicago preach the Swiss religion. We are all Euro now.

PART 2

How the Dutch Drove the Swiss from the New World

Time: Mid-'80s.
Place: Art-school party, Providence, RI.

The ballroom is dark wood festooned with gold, a New England mansion built by some 17th-century slave-trading Unitarians now serving as gallery, presidential palace and site for occasional debaucheries marking some scholastic event. The huge French doors at one end are thrown open to a glorious manicured garden. From outside, the room seems to move in one pulsing block of bodies, festooned in black and white and occasional bursts of outrageous color. The pounding music shifts into New Order's "Blue Monday," with its spare opening drum, machine ticking, sketchy, jumpy beat that slowly fills in with the synchronous lower tones of the synthesizers and then Bernard Sumner's low groaning, "How does it feel / To treat me like you do ..." The ballroom is filled with beautiful children in their late teens, each with a certain flair: an outrageous dress, a campily serious white-tie-and-tennis-shoe combination, a tulle confection. Girls dance, throw their heads back, close their eyes, raise and cross their thin, pale arms overhead. In the middle of this sea of powdered white gothic faces appears a bright pink bubble. It's the glistening, ecstatic face of a tottering giant. A crown of golden curls is plastered to his forehead. He moves like a great bear, his arms outstretched, the crowd parting as he wades through it. He is dressed in a kind of shapeless smock that exaggerates his bulk. One stout arm encircles the waist of the closest teenager. He pulls her close and plants a big baby kiss on her cheek. She pulls away with a laugh as her friends gather around tittering. He takes the next in two thick hands and attempts a jitterbuggy twirl. He spins another girl round and round and round, clears a hole in the dance floor. The girl, slight, practically swings off her feet. Morrissey drones: "I am the son and the heir / Of a shyness that is criminally vulgar / I am the son and heir / Of nothing in particular ..." and the beat is driving everything forward and the big pink baby of a man throws his head back and sings out with glee. Beeke is in the house.

The design world that Anthon Beeke wades into in the mid-to-late '80s is on the verge of a massive shift. The symbolic arrival of Dutch design—in the form of a posse of high-profile visitors making their rounds through various art-school studios—coincides perfectly with the exhaustion of the Swiss methodology. New Wave temporarily provides a welcome injection of fun, unserious, DIY sensibility—but the movement lacks both theory and gravity. Friedman and Greiman's exuberance settles into a predictable genre of graphic tricks. (See Rand's rant.) New Wave has no political substance beyond the personal joy of the designer. The Swiss can't sustain us anymore. New Wave is sweet but empty calories.

We know almost nothing about the Dutch, less about their designers. We know Rietveld because his chair keeps popping up in our art-history surveys. We know a little of van Doesburg and a few of the iconic elements of De Stijl. We know nothing about Piet Zwart or Paul Schuitema or Willem Sandberg or Otto Treumann, never mind Crouwel or van Toorn. Our *History of Graphic Design*[11] makes only a low pass over the low countries. Total Design is on our radar mostly because it extols Swiss virtues and because Benno Wissing, late partner thereof, is on the faculty of RISD and occasionally dusts off some ancient slide presentation about de Bejinkorf, PAM or PTT. But Wissing is already a dinosaur. His eyes are clouded, he sports a fluffy mustache and safari jacket, and he speaks with some kind of quasi-Afrikaaner drawl punctuated by long *eeeeeerrsss* and *aaaaaahs* between short bursts of word fragments. (We discover only years later the breadth of his early work.)

All that changes. The successful infiltration of the Dutch into the American academy can be traced largely to two educators: Katherine McCoy at Cranbrook and Tom Ockerse at RISD. McCoy is solidly American: a warm, open, bespectacled Midwesterner, hair in a thick braid, who speaks with the broad vowels of her native Michigan in the tone of a cheery mom bucking up a reluctant teenager. She is also a leading Europeanist. She comes to Cranbrook from Unimark, the bastion of high European design based in Chicago, where Massimo Vignelli was one of the founders and Herbert Bayer sat on the board of directors. Like most young Eurocentric designers she is under the sway of the Wiengart/Greiman/Friedman axis. On sabbatical from Cranbrook in 1983, McCoy spends a year in Eindhoven on a Phillips residency and finds herself in the position to "zoom around Holland" immersing herself in Dutch design culture. She visits all the major studios and returns to Bloomfield Hills, Michigan, with a huge roll of posters under her arm.[12]

11 The standard textbook of the time by Philip Meggs.

The work she encounters during that Eindhoven period is a revelation. "I immediately felt that this was something different," she remembers later. "The best of New Wave was playful, arty, experimental, spontaneous, irreverent and fun, which was quite welcome after Swiss Modernism's serious, systematic, austere corporatism. To me, the Dutch work had those same positive qualities and was somewhat related to the American New Wave in the international graphic-design lineage. But the Dutch work of the 1980s had more roots and cultural integrity, and less superficiality. It also seemed more closely related to the Dutch art world than American New Wave was to the American fine-art community. Here was a body of work built on the same Constructivist foundation but with an entirely different expression."[13] While Swiss design morphs seamlessly into the modular requirements of corporate identity, Dutch work offers an alternative way to interpret modernism.

Her visit to Studio Dumbar is transformational, not only for the striking work she encounters, but for the method of working: "Studio Dumbar is like a grad studio, a real atelier."[14] McCoy is in charge of a pretty great atelier herself—the design studios at the Cranbrook Academy—so it's natural that she becomes close to Gert Dumbar and ends up inviting him for the first of many visits to the school. In Dumbar, she sees a designer for whom historical references are a lived relationship: "Their history is alive. They all knew Zwart personally. He isn't an abstraction."[15] It is the beginning of a vital cross-cultural exchange between the two studios. Dumbar draws some of its most important image-makers—Robert Nakata and Allen Hori, among others—from the Cranbrook graduate studios as the experimental work just starting to emerge there finds a more receptive audience in Holland than at home. Later Anthon Beeke will write: "At Studio Dumbar, Cathy [sic] McCoy's talented students were given a degree of freedom that was then inconceivable in the United States."[16]

Upon returning from Holland she pens an article for *I.D.* Magazine—the American design magazine, not the London style guide—titled "Reconstructing Dutch Graphics." It is perhaps the first critical assessment of contemporary Dutch design from this side of the Atlantic. She writes, "At a time when American graphic designers are searching for ways to expand

12 Katherine McCoy, Personal interview, Aug. 2010.
13 Katherine McCoy, Email to the author, 25 Aug. 2010.
14–15 Katherine McCoy, Personal interview, Aug. 2010.
16 Anthon Beeke, "Paper to Wake a Sleeping Dog," *Dutch Posters: A Selection by Anthon Beeke* (Amsterdam: BIS, 1997), 138.
17–18 Katherine McCoy, "Reconstructing Dutch Graphics," *I.D.* Mar./Apr. 1984: 38.
19–21 Ibid. 43.
22 Beeke, "Paper to Wake a Sleeping Dog," 138.

on the ideas of the Swiss School, itself a culmination of Modernist Bauhaus ideals, the Dutch offer a refreshing insight into how designers of all types might synthesize a number of diverse elements appropriate to their audience and context. In our efforts to warm the rationality and coolness of the Swiss approach with some emotion and flexibility, our own American New Wave design solutions often deteriorate markedly."[17]

She goes on to show a number of examples from van Toorn, Studio Dumbar, Ko Sliggers and Wim Crouwel/Total Design—implying they are more or less unknown to her audience—and includes two works by Anthon Beeke. In the caption for his "Marilyn" poster (1982) she makes perhaps the first analysis of his work in a U.S. forum: "Anthon Beeke uses many elements found in Swiss-derived New Wave graphics seen in the U.S., yet remain [sic] distinctly Dutch. Letterspacing, a wide variety of type sizes and typefaces, handwritten words, background patterning, fifties nostalgia and the nongrid composition are all American New Wave but the sensibility is tougher and more acerbic, with less hedonism and more social consciousness."[18]

She returns to Beeke with a brief assessment of "Kunstscrift" (1982): "Anthon Beeke of Amsterdam is another new Dutch master of typography and image whose covers for an art magazine employ color bars, grids, information forms and typewriter type. These unassuming elements combine to form an elegant pattern."[19] In this work McCoy finds an oeuvre reacting to the same set of historical constraints that she and her students rebel against. But in Dutch design she finds a deeper level of commentary, even parody, a "toughness that borders on perversity; beauty is not the goal."[20] She concludes: "Their synthesis of rationalism and ambiguity, international art influences and Dutch vernacular, refined typography and commercial culture provides us with an energetic model of what Charles Jencks calls 'double-coding.'"[21]

It's telling that she concludes by "theorizing" the implication of the work, because Dutch design at this point seems to happen in an almost theory-free zone—van Toorn being the notable exception. Dutch work develops as a series of actions and reactions played out on a visual field. Beeke writes: "Dutch design was enriched with the Cranebrook [sic] philosophy,"[22] suggesting it lacks a philosophy to describe itself. Lucky for the Dutch, we are ready for them. If America isn't necessarily creating groundbreaking visual work in the '80s, there is one area in which we excel: the construction and assimilation of theory. The synergy is perfect—the newly emerging Dutch approach supplies the rich visual examples on which the newly emerging American theory plays out. It's as if we have been developing all these amazing new weapons and finally we have something to shoot at.

That McCoy ties this work to architectural historian Charles Jencks' "double-coding" is also revealing. Double-coding incorporates high and low—popular and esoteric, visceral and intellectual, amateur and professional—simultaneously. In other words, the game can be open, played on many levels at once, full of sly references, inside jokes, parodies and intentional faults. The design object could become, to use Barthes' phrase, "A tissue of quotations drawn from the innumerable centres of culture."[23]

The same year McCoy invokes Jencks, Umberto Eco publishes "Postscript to The Name of the Rose," with his elegant definition of double-coding: "I think of the postmodern attitude as that of a man who loves a very cultivated woman and knows that he cannot say to her 'I love you madly,' because he knows that she knows (and that she knows he knows) that these words have already been written by Barbara Cartland. Still there is a solution. He can say 'As Barbara Cartland would put it, I love you madly.' At this point, having avoided false innocence, having said clearly it is no longer possible to speak innocently, he will nevertheless say what he wanted to say to the woman: that he loves her in an age of lost innocence."[24]

This inchoate longing for a usable design theory is becoming tangible, and nascent attempts are sprouting out of diverse traditions, borrowing freely from semiotics and semiology, literary criticism, deconstruction and psychoanalytic and feminist criticism. Of all the design pedagogues in the '80s, there may be none as committed to a rational, theoretical discourse than the soft-spoken chairman of RISD, Thomas Ockerse. A transplanted Dutchman, the tall, enigmatic Ockerse is an early product of Yale (MFA '64) by way of Indiana University. In an article titled "Teaching Under the Influence," he cites as mentors Rand, Matter, Walker Evans and Eisenmann (but interestingly no compatriot Netherlanders).[25] Having left Yale formalism behind, Ockerse is attempting to recast his own education in a new, more theoretical language. He is searching for a reasoned, professional approach to the construction of visual message in the somewhat arcane semiotics of the American pragmatist philosopher Charles Sanders Peirce and coupling it with a studio program deeply rooted in Hofmann and Weingart. His youthful faculty is increasingly drawn from direct or second-generation descendants of Swiss modern, but this injection of theory adds a level of complexity and (some would say) perversity to the process. It is interesting to note that so-called theory driven design often elicits an agitated response from more traditionally minded designers who reject the attempt to quantify what they see as a more or less intuitive act of aesthetic inspiration.

In parallel to Cranbrook's growing affinity with Studio Dumbar, Ockerse organizes a special class titled "Visiting Designers," and stocks it with some Dutch heavy hitters. The first semesters include masters Ootje Oxenaar and Jan van Toorn and upstarts Anthon Beeke and Gerard Hadders. The impact of the Dutch contingent is powerful and immediate. Each visitor brings an alternate model of critical practice: van Toorn, a probing investigation of social conditions and a strong affinity with Lissitzky; Oxenaar, a long tradition of illustrative modernism and design for the Euro-modern state; Hadders, a brute visuality and refreshing DIY sensibility; and Beeke, a parodic, hyper-sexualized image-based production that seems outside of the Dutch compositional tradition. In the studio their critique is rough, crude, sub-lingual. As a foil to the hyper-intellectualism of coolly rational Ockerse, the young Dutchmen offer a highly seductive, sometimes juvenile, always passionate model of design-by-sensation.

At the end of his stint at RISD, Hadders reveals his ulterior motive: "I had a secret mission — I wanted to let something happen that was not the regular thing. I hope that I succeeded in showing students that they could make very fine design using a different method from what they're used to. There is a constant bombardment of certain methods in this school — the Basel influence ... I would rather have people imitate something else, if they are going to imitate."[26] The work Hadders is showing, and encouraging his students to imitate, has the potential to reconcile the dissonance between the austerity of the Basel-influenced work and the potential richness of a semiotic approach. The work of these visitors, van Toorn and Beeke especially, provides a subject with complexity and substance equal to the theoretical models we are trying to build. But while van Toorn is clearly working from a critical, dialectical position — his work poses and engages specific conditions — Beeke's position is almost antithetical. He presents himself as a brutish savant, a cipher through whom ideas flow without filter and repeatedly cites his lack of formal education and solidly proletarian roots as anti-intellectual bona fides.[27] "His work isn't about design," notes one of his students. "It's all about him." But it is precisely this un-theorized stance, and because he has such a seemingly straightforward and un-nuanced reading of his own work, that makes him open to such diverse critiques.

23 "We now know that the text is not a line of words releasing a single 'theological' meaning (the 'message' of the Author-God) but a multi-dimensional space in which a variety of writings, none of them original, blend and clash. The text is a tissue of quotations drawn from the innumerable centres of culture." Roland Barthes, *Image-Music-Text* (New York: Hill and Wang, 1977), 146.

24 Umberto Eco, *Postscript to The Name of the Rose* (New York: Harcourt, 1984).

25 Thomas Ockerse, "Teaching Under the Influence: What Is of Use Now?" *Spirals '91* book 2, (Providence: RISD, 1991), 35.

26 Gerard Hadders, interview with Doug Banquer, 1987, in *Spirals '91*, book 2, (Providence: RISD, 1991), 53.

Beeke's work of the period is perfectly emblematic of the post-modern embrace of the referent. While Crouwel builds on the modal structures of Müller-Brockmann, and Dumbar extends the long Dutch compositional tradition of a highly dynamic Constructivist composition, Beeke flaunts both positions. His work is often intentionally lowbrow and anti-compositional. Rather than refer to his fellow professionals, he draws from the butcher shop (from which he proudly emerged). In that way he plays the game of convolution: if you know your audience is expecting something, you do the opposite; if you know they expect you to defy their expectations, you do the expected thing, *ad infinitum*. Thus his famous poster for the Rijksuniversiteit Utrecht, produced by dictating the design over the telephone to the printer, a classic Fluxus trick that undermines the authority of the author, displaces the act of the designer and questions the value of things like taste and expertise. Such a highly choreographed "mistake" and provocation is performed by someone acknowledged, even lauded, as one of the most knowing, skilled designers of his generation.

In mocking the traditions and skills so carefully guarded by an emerging professional class, Beeke sets himself apart. His work is parody as it assumes and dashes the obsessions of his predecessors. How can you simultaneously engage with and critique the profession of education by your very presence? How can you care LESS for form than by leaving it to your printer? If post-modern externality—that is, the referent—reveals a political alignment between the contemporary maker and his/her usable past—as it does with Jan van Toorn's explicit citation, even reproduction, of ill-fated Russian Constructivism—what kind of allegiance can be gleaned from Beeke's evocation of the supermarket circular in his Mickery Theatre poster? Beeke performs Eco's notion of "false innocence." By employing the slipshod reference, rather than the intellectual, highfalutin' one, he is able to both accomplish his typographic task—an ugly drop shadow or elaborate script face works perfectly well in his information hierarchy—while indicating he has no interest in participating in the values of taste and style held in polite (design) society. Thus he can say, "I love you madly," and still acknowledge the impossibility of anyone taking such sentiment seriously.

The notorious large-scale photographic posters of the early 1980s are the clearest example of Beeke's provocation strategy. By eliminating composition—in the Constructivist/Zwartian sense—he breaks with the Dutch tradition. These posters, many accomplished for the Toneelgroep, align more closely with the work of photo-allegorical art directors such as Americans Henry Wolf or George Lois at *Esquire*, Willy Fleckhaus at *Twen*, or typical "low" advertising layout with its emphasis on the eye-catching image with limited copy or overt design.[28] The explicitly sexual nature of these images only exaggerates the essential rule of advertising: Sex Sells. At the same time, they reinforce the message that he is working without constraint, beyond the restrictions of social mores, professional decorum and personal reserve. The charged images bubble to the surface from some primordial part of his unreconstructed brain stem.

Beeke's use of genitalia secures his reputation as professional libertine and he offers vivid descriptions of the obstacles he overcomes in order to broadcast his images. But his use of sex stands in stark contrast to the soft-porn eroticism of Fleckhaus or sly suggestion of typical "sexy" advertising. Beeke wields the phallus like a cudgel. The sheer frontality of his nudity has the blatant sense of assaulting the passersby. The frontal demands affront. There is no suggestion in his imagery; in fact the images are designed to flaunt the idea of the suggestive. If sexualized advertising deploys displacement—the penis and vagina are symbolized as in Rand's famous images for El Producto cigars—Beeke mocks such modesties. The "innovation" of his poster for "Troilus en Cressida" is his rejection of metaphor—i.e. to show that which is usually hidden in a trope, in this

27 Max Bruinsma, email to the author: "One of the things that has always amazed me with Anthon is his deep—and considering his lack of academic education and formal training, mysterious—grasp of classic European symbolism. He is a master of symbolic representation and interpretation, in his work often thinly disguised as 'realism.' He doesn't theorize this, but he knows very well that he has extremely well-educated eyes. I'm not saying that he is either ingenu or savant, but his almost instinctive understanding of the traditions and discourses of European visual culture and iconography merits intellectual analysis beyond the narrow historical and theoretical scope you are confined to here."

28 Max Bruinsma, email to the author: "Your bias towards the American reception of (European) theory has a major drawback: it tends to overlook the European influences and contexts of Beeke's formation and work. You mention a few designers who have been hugely influential in the US, but of whom I'm sure Anthon was only marginally aware during the time he was developing his own style: Henry Wolf, George Lois and Willy Fleckhaus. I'm convinced he'd seen and admired their magazine and movie-title work, but then again, he was inspired by much the same sources as they were. There are two traditions in European graphic design that Beeke is clearly linked to: the Dutch expressionism of Sluijters, Elffers and Wijnberg, and French vernacular commercial art—and of course Cassandre. Two decidedly 'un-Dutch' traditions, if you see them from a 1980s post-Swiss perspective. Another very important influence is (the European version of) Fluxus, which Anthon encountered via Willem de Ridder. Anthon, in short, is a product of a clearly delineated European tradition of anti-intellectualism and resistance to theoretical categorization, spanning 19th-century realism and expressionism, via Dada to Fluxus. The 'realism' would be something to scrutinize in Anthon's work: his utterings concerning 'Troilus & Cressida,' for instance, are very akin to Courbet's replies to the critique on his 'L' Origine du Monde:' 'I show you how it is, not how you want to represent it symbolically' or words to that effect."

case the leather strapped buttocks and exposed vagina of a model shot from the rear—while supposedly working metaphorically. He works in plain sight: *Phallus est phallus, pudendum est pudendum*.

These Dutch provocations provide us with an alternate future, a new way to re-imagine the modern legacy. By example they present an aesthetic position that is at once playful and political: playful in the way the design refers to and builds on essential modern forms and figures; and political in that it takes on, in highly provocative ways, issues such as class, sex and social condition. But while these images clearly have their roots in the sexual liberation movement of 1960s Amsterdam, they have a radically different reading in late 1980s America.

Visiting American universities, Beeke gives his standard slide presentation peppered with pricks and pussies. The students (especially the women) sit tight-lipped and fuming, burning for a chance to voice objections. As soon as the lights come up, hands shoot up begging for a chance to interrogate. Their reaction triggers an escalation of belligerence on both sides. At Cranbrook McCoy watches with a modicum of pride as her increasingly politicized students grill the designer on his use of the female body. Beeke refuses to concede possible inverse readings of his stated intention. He dismisses critique of his work as misguided delicacy and American prudishness. The scene plays out again and again with each lecture. He is vehement in his claims of un-intentionalism: he is, he insists, on their side! He's a feminist! Why can't they see that? He designs to provoke. "As long as it affects them it will start them thinking, which will lead to discussion. They have to think about the real situation."[29] "But," counters an avid student, "isn't that like saying 'I beat my wife to make people aware of wife-beating'?" On and on *ad infinitum*. And so Anthon Beeke delivers himself, one lecture at a time, as the perfect subject of another prong of burgeoning American theory.

29 Anthon Beeke quoted in: Karl Llewellyn, "Dutch Design: The Controversial Anthon Beeke," *The Pioneer*, Feb. 1990.

PART 3

Hell Hath No Fury Like....

Time: Around 1990.
Location: America.

Ellen Lupton is a rail-thin twenty-three-year-old with an infectious, toothy smile. She speaks with a slow drawl, an almost Southern inflection, and she propels her drawn-out syllables with a repetivive circular hand gesture, as if waving a soft flag to keep an idea running. Twenty years her senior, designer Keith Godard is a bluff and dapper Englishman, snaggle-toothed and wild-eyed, often sporting a silk ascot knotted jauntily around his throat. This unlikely couple joins forces to facilitate Beeke's introduction to New York.

Fresh out of design school at the Cooper Union, Lupton assumes the position of curator at Cooper's Lubalin Center, a nascent exhibition space named for Herb Lubalin, the urbane and slightly corny American typographer. (Soon to be relevant side fact: One of Lubalin's early jobs was the design for *EROS* magazine, devoted to "the beauty of the rising sense of sexuality and experimentation," which folded after being sued for obscenity by the U.S. Postal Service.) Lupton establishes herself early on and continues to prove herself as one of the most innovative design curators in America, a feat tempered in glory only by the fact that she is, in fact, one of the only design curators in America. She is approached by Cooper professor Godard with the idea of exhibiting the posters of Anthon Beeke.

By this point Beeke is one of a handful of familiar Dutch designers on the circuit, but his work still stirs controversy. Lupton and Godard organize a tightly curated show of work from the mid-'70s to the present: "'Anthon Beeke's Stage: Holland's Illusionist Poster Designer, Posters, magazines, and other graphics from the 1970s and 80s."[30] She has, however, misgivings about displaying the aforementioned "Troilus en Cressida" poster and leaves it out, not out of prudery but because she is discomfited by the gender-representation questions stirred by Beeke's image, which portrays, she tells a reporter from the student newspaper, "one group of society in a position of inferiority, and another group in a position of power."[31] At a lecture in Cooper Union's Great Hall introducing the exhibition, Godard flashes a teasing image of

30 Ellen Lupton and Keith Godard, *Anthon Beeke's Stage: Holland's Illusionist Poster Designer 1970–1990* (New York: Lubalin Center, 1990).

"Troilus en Cressida," piquing interest in its unexplained absence. Long conversations ensue, with the middle-aged males predictably missing the point. Despite the fact that Lupton has clearly stated her position directly to Beeke early on, during his appearance at the Great Hall he complains that his work has been censored and launches into a diatribe against the curators, the school and lily-livered Americans in general. After intense pressure from both students and peers, and pointed accusations of censorship, Lupton ends up acquiescing and including the poster, accompanied by a wall text that frames the curator's objection to the work.[32]

Jump to North Carolina State University, Raleigh, North Carolina. A young RISD graduate, Adam Kalish, approaches the newly appointed graphic-design department head, Meredith Davis, and proposes an exhibition of Beeke's major posters. Gallery space is limited and the posters are huge. How, asks the young assistant professor, shall we cut this exhibition to fit the space? An administrative council is convened. Given the explicit nature of the images, the council suggests moving the exhibition to a gallery away from the main entrance and thoroughfare, but with full public access, and grants the curator free rein to hang the show as she sees fit. Shortly after, however, the Chair of the Faculty, Denis Wood, inexplicably announces the show has been self-censored. Despite the uproar, the exhibition opens—including "Troilus en Cressida" and other challenging pieces—without incident, and the school organizes a major symposium to discuss issues of academic freedom and sensitive speech: the classic "teachable moment" on the American campus.[33] But when recounting the incident in print, Beeke represents the facts in a different light. "In America where I have a traveling exhibition the shit threatens to hit the fan again every time the poster is displayed. In North Carolina a Dean of the State University resigned because the institute refused to hang this and other posters."[34] (Wood had subsequently been removed from office but over an entirely unrelated issue.) Years later the inaccuracy is still peddled as truth. Willem Ellenbroek misreports, "An exhibition of his work later at the North Carolina State University was cancelled because this poster was too SHOCKING for the curator."[35]

Why the disconnection between the way each side remembers these incidents? Why is Beeke so invested in the idea that his work has the power

31 Ellen Lupton quoted in: Karl Llewellyn, "Dutch Design: The Controversial Anthon Beeke," The Pioneer, Feb. 1990.

32 Ibid.

33 Personal conversation with Meredith Davis, 26 Aug. 2010.

34 Anthon Beeke, "Affiches van Anthon Beeke," verteld aan Pieter Brattinga (Amsterdam: Valeton & Henstra, 1993), 3.

to shock and repel?[36] And, more important, why did these particular images create such a stir? Godard claims "one design, which totally offended the woman's movement in the 1970s, is too 'bad' to show even behind darkened curtains."[37] Again the issue comes back to a theory gap between America and Holland in the late '80s. It is not uncommon for young, almost exclusively male, Dutch designers to spice up their presentations for American college students with a few naughty images to make explicit the liberalization differential and add a little shock value to their work. The designers generally misunderstand the nature of the critique coming from their American audiences. In his aforementioned defense of the "Troilus en Cressida" poster, for instance, Beeke declares that he intends it, in fact, as a feminist tract: he is attempting to depict a state of subjugation. Once again, the weakly theorized "naturalistic" Dutch work—proposed as the unaffected product of individual genius—falls into place as the perfect clinical subject for over-theorized American minds, who tend to see work as a product of certain social and historical conditions over which the individual designer has only minimal control.

To understand this gap and seeming disconnection between the Dutch and American positions, it is important to understand the context in which we are reading Beeke's work. By the late 1980s, almost any female graduate student (and most males) involved in the visual arts is well acquainted with, if not deeply influenced by, a burgeoning body of feminist theory. This work is highly influential across media: painting, sculpture, design, architecture, and especially film and photography. (At Cranbrook, design and photography share a building and much of the interest in the theory is generated by the photographers.) Almost every young designer in Beeke's audience has read Laura Mulvey's essay, "Visual Pleasure and Narrative Cinema," originally published

35 Willem Ellenbroek, "Repaint," *Billposting Allowed* (Amsterdam: Private publication, 2004).

36 Max Bruinsma, email to the author: "Anthon's versions of his work being 'censored' in the US may be exaggerated from where you stand (I have no doubt you are right), but they do reflect not just Anthon's but a general Dutch (I'd even say continental-European) view to the US as a backward country when it comes to public dealings with sexuality. Anthon, in other words, can also be seen as voicing a critique of post-Freudian feminism long before it became fashionable in post-feminist circles to re-appraise sexuality and use the female body as a weapon in social and political discourse rather than merely reflecting on it from a sacrificial point of view. There are a few 1960s and early 1970s feminist artists (most notably Marina Abramovic and Ulrike Rosenbach) who are much closer to Anthon's position than American feminist critics would have it."

37 Lupton and Godard, 1.

in 1973 but republished in 1987 and often anthologized and included in the course packets of numerous Film Studies 101s and Women's Issues seminars. Working from a highly politicized, psychoanalytic foundation, Mulvey reasons that the apparatus of Hollywood cinema creates a dynamic between the gaze of the spectator, who is necessarily masculine, and the subject, inevitably the female object of desire, turning the women's "to-be-looked-at-ness" into the spectacle of the cinema itself. The film itself incorporates the viewer into the male role through identification with the protagonist.[38]

Imagine how this analysis of the "voyeuristic-scopophilic look"[39] can be applied to work such as Beeke's "Penthesilea" posters. This series of three posters—designed to advertise the performance by Toneelgroep Amsterdam, based on the story of murderous, man-slaughtering Amazons who use men solely for procreation—features photographs of characters holding photographic images of eyes that gaze between the posters as we observe them from the street. (We watch the photographer watch them watch each other.) The one unmasked woman—wild-haired, tongue protruding, body smeared with some ancient woad—holds a framed image of an erect cock as she leers across at the lone, somewhat worried, male figure. Note the play ends with Zeus seducing Penthesilea against her will and gaining her ultimate submission before, in his typical Zeusian way, abandoning her, a fact to which Beeke responds: "Woman can do that, women want that, that makes them so strong, that makes them so vulnerable."[40] (These types of pronouncements complicate his self-proclaimed feminist bona fides.)

Mulvey posits the designer/photographer is an unwitting subject in this loaded relationship, fated to reproduce the deeply embedded codes in which he is immersed. "Woman then stands in patriarchal culture as signifier for the male other, bound by a symbolic order in which man can live out his fantasies and obsessions through linguistic command by imposing them on the silent image of woman still tied to her place as bearer of meaning, not maker of meaning."[41] She calls on her readers to actively undermine and overturn this patriarchal relationship. "It is said that analyzing pleasure or beauty annihilates it," she famously states, adding that that is exactly what she wants to do. Those enraged students, grilling Beeke during his obligatory Q+A, are finally getting to employ the tools they have been so assiduously trained to use.

This kind of analysis is essentially different from what Ockerse is attempting at RISD. Ockerse's semiotics is a generative device, more akin to a poetics than a theory of reading. Mulvey is part of a broader tendency to focus on how the audience constructs a text and less on what an author is attempting to say. (What Beeke thinks his work means is neither here nor there.) It also falls in with a broad-based social reevaluation of the representation of women. This shift is manifest when, upon the retirement of longtime department chair Alvin Eisenman, the Yale School of Art takes a radical turn and appoints Sheila Levrant de Bretteville as his replacement at the helm of the design department. The high throne of modern design in America transitions to one of the most outspoken feminist voices in the design community. In protest, uber-modernists Rand and Hofmann tender their "resignations" shortly after her appointment—a protest conveniently timed to coincide with their planned retirements.

The movement is developing on both the right and left simultaneously. Since the election of Ronald Reagan in 1980, America has taken a hard right turn. In 1986, the Reagan administration releases the 1,960-page Meese Report, which posits commercial pornography—expanded to include almost all contemporary art showing the human body—as a major assault on conservative American values. The situation peaks in 1989 with the furor over the exhibition of Andres Serrano's "Piss Christ," a photograph depicting a crucifix immersed in a vial of urine, which erupts almost simultaneously with Beeke's show in Helms' home state of North Carolina.

On the left the pressure is just as intense. While much of the liberal community rallies against the chilling effect of the Meese Report and rejects Helms, there are notable exceptions. Women Against Pornography (WAP) is formed in the late '70s and grows as a movement throughout the '80s. Founder Andrea Dworkin and prominent lawyer Catherine MacKinnon stage a march on Times Square—then New York's red-light district—and actually testify before the Meese Commission in support of the Commission's position. The movement creates an extremely broad definition of violent pornography, arguing that almost any commercial use of women's images constitutes a form of usury and a "system of prostitution." WAP tours the country delivering slide shows on college campuses and community centers critiquing all manner of cultural production, especially album covers, such as the Rolling Stones "Black and Blue." These slide

38 Laura Mulvey, "Visual Pleasure and Narrative Cinema." in *Film Theory and Criticism: Introductory Readings*, eds. Leo Braudy and Marshall Cohen (New York: Oxford UP, 1999), 843.

39 Ibid.

40 Anthon Beeke, *"Affiches van Anthon Beeke,"* verteld aan Pieter Brattinga (Amsterdam: Valeton & Henstra, 1993).

41 Mulvey, 834.

shows again imply subversion is inherent in the system itself, regardless of the author's intention. The author is fated to constantly reproduce the rules of hegemony.

Beeke's protestations, then, only seem to underline his state of false consciousness. The author and his audience exist in different worlds. This must be especially frustrating to Beeke, whose own lived experience suggests a different reading of the sexually explicit. From his days with Willem de Ridder at *Hitweek* and later working together on *SUCK* magazine, the explicit/subjugated image suggests its opposite: Liberation. In the late '60s, *SUCK* pushes the boundaries of the public and the private when de Ridder famously publishes — against her wishes — a nude portrait of feminist icon and *SUCK* board member Germaine Greer in full spread eagle. It is an early experiment in user-generation. It is not subjugation, de Ridder insists. To generate your own porn suggests you have control over your own erotic representation.[42]

> *Sitting awkwardly in his apartment, I ask Beeke about life in Amsterdam in the late 60s/early 70s. What did he do for fun? Since his stroke he struggles with English. You can see his sheer frustration at his inability to connect thoughts and words. But with this question his face illuminates, his eyes blaze sharp and blue: "FFFFFucking!"*[43]

The use of the body or, more explicitly, the use of the pseudo-pornographic image, represents a different kind of resistance. Years later, in a retrospective interview, Hugues Boekraad asks a leading question — or something like a statement posing as a question — that basically sums up the operational nature of the liberatory use of the body images in the city, deeply rooted in the culture of Amsterdam in the '60s: "Your definition of the role of the poster in public space indicates that you regard yourself partly as a political designer. Not as a partly political designer, but as someone who provides a picture of freedom in the city. The language and visual language in the public space are an indication of this. What can be said and shown? You were born in 1940 in Amsterdam and lived through the 1960s in the same city. So you know what provocation means, challenging authority and pushing back the boundaries of what is permitted. Your work is provocative, right up to the present. In this respect, you are someone from a specific generation."[44]

And so the body question reaches a generational divide. Is it liberation or oppression, an urban act of resistance or a patriarchal act of symbolic abuse? But the underlying issue is not, as Beeke often casts it, a gap between liberal, enlightened Amsterdam and rigid, prudish everywhere-else.

As he puts it: "Posters such as that for 'Troilus en Cressida' which are displayed at official locations in the Netherlands, would never be displayed at comparable sites in ostensibly progressive cities such as New York, Paris and Tokyo. Of course we know that this is not so much a question of morality of shifting norms as it is a production of petty bourgeois propriety and trepidation."[45] (Note that he equates the progressive with the permissive.) It is, in fact, a battle over where the meaning of work resides. Beeke refuses to concede that the meaning of his work may be out of his control; he suffers from the so-called *intentional fallacy*. It is perfectly emblematic of this moment, a battle between an author and his readers over the ultimate ownership of the text.

42 Personal conversation with Willem de Ridder, Apr. 2010.
43 Personal conversation with Anthon Beeke, Apr. 2010.
44 Hugues Boekraad, "Shakespeare and Co.: A conversation with Anthon Beeke about a theater poster," *Billposting Allowed* (Amsterdam: Private publication, 2004).
45 Anthon Beeke, "Paper to Wake a Sleeping Dog," *Dutch Posters: A Selection by Anthon Beeke* (Amsterdam: BIS, 1997), 10.

PART 4

On Being Bad

Time: Early '90s.
Place: Amsterdam.

Upstart American designer Tibor Kalman is presenting the work of his now famous New York studio M&Co to a group of Dutch designers. The presentation starts with an empty stage. Out of the darkness rumbles the crackly thump of an electronic beat machine, De La Soul's wry, ironic, sing-song Brooklyn accent stamping out: "Mirror mirror on the wall/Tell me mirror what is wrong? Can it be my De La clothes/Or is it just my De La song/What I do ain't make believe/ People say I sit and try/But when it comes to being De La/It's just me myself and I." Kalman spends the next hour puncturing any remaining self-importance clinging to the design profession. His slides are drawn almost exclusively from NY street scenes, found typography, graffiti, vernacular signs, scrawled handbills. His message is that in cloistering themselves as professionals working from an obscure (European) tradition, designers have lost touch with the vital energy of the youthful street. Kalman's work is designed to intentionally mock anything held sacred in the designer pantheon.

In the broadest possible sense, design can be broken down into two styles with almost everyone falling in the middle: the Super-egos and the Ids. (Of course, these are an assumed presentational dialectic, not "natural" states.) The Super-egos have utter faith in the system as the defining feature of design. The identification or construction of an underlying order becomes the generative device that gives rise to the form itself. And since that underlying system is usually a highly rational form, such as a regular grid, the designer is not so much an originator as an implementer. A grid is eternal; no one can claim to have invented it. Super-egos believe their position is quantifiably right. (Remember Rand's line, "indisputable proof that lowercase letters are more readable"?) The Super-egos believe in science and slide easily into commercial success because such rationality meshes perfectly with the demands of corporate capital for constant replication and expansion. The same ordering methodology can be applied to ordering typographic information or organizing a design studio.

The Ids, conversely, see their work as a direct expression of their inner state. (Remember, "His work isn't about design, it's all about him.")

The closer their work comes to a direct, unmediated manifestation of some primal condition, the more powerful it is seen to be. The Ids eschew regularity, order and self-replicating methodology as the external suppression of unfettered self-expression. Their work changes style from one moment to the next because style is not ideological but temperamental. To work against order is a sign of authenticity. Rejection of constraint implies honesty. Descending directly from May 1968, their motto is: "Sous les pavés, la plage!" Under the ordered pavement stones of authority lies nature. Tear away the constraints of society, and discover freedom. Beeke counters Crouwel's highly rational gridded alphabets with one of his own, the letters formed by intertwining nudes.

The Super-egos are both disdainful and slightly envious of the Ids. They envy their sense of abandonment, their freedom. The Ids are popular on the lecture circuit because frustrated designers laboring under the petty constraints of their clients can live vicariously through their license. The Ids ride their "individuality" to international fame. At the same time, Id studios always seem to flounder: they can never grow beyond the limits of their leader.

The Super-egos are a distinguished lot: Ruder, Crouwel, Müller-Brockmann, Hofmann, Bill, Vignelli, Treumann, Tschichold. In many ways, their influence is more profound exactly because their methods are so fungible. But the profession is enamored of its Ids: Beeke, Brownjohn, Bernard, Saville, Sliggers, Van Stolk, Victore, Sagmeister.

Between the two camps, another style emerges: the Jester. The Jester is cynical and mocks both sides. Kalman is the model. The work from M&Co is parasitic: it cannot survive without an object of parody. Max Bruinsma suggests Dumbar creates this synthesis: "If Dumbar has to be credited for anything, it is for his re-introduction of playfulness and irony in Dutch graphic culture ... Studio Dumbar's work transformed the official face of the Netherlands, building an effective bridge between the playfully anarchic trait that is deeply embedded in the soul of Dutch avant-garde design, and the down-to-earth Calvinistic rationality which characterizes official culture in the Netherlands."[46] It is the perfect model of Eco's postmodern condition. There is still a need to speak, but honest speech is impossible in the age of false innocence.

All three styles, however, are trapped in a reactionary state. The positions only hold in opposition. The basic and irreconcilable paradox of modernity is to be both of the moment and clearly severed from the past. The obsessive desire to eliminate all attachments, to be contemporary,

46 Max Bruisima, "Nouveau Dutch Design," *émergence* 6 (2007).

is stymied by the fact that modernity needs a past to be broken from, and thus reinforces the presence of the very past it works to obliterate. Modernism is defined, and undermined, by its emancipatory mission.

Bruno Latour develops the logical extension of the paradox: "What is a style—in the largest civilizing sense of the word—that would at last be contemporary in and of itself? That is, a style ... that would internalize that which the modern styles had always externalized, so hurried were they to 'get rid of' the externalities? Contrary to what postmodernists imply, modernism is not something of the past that should be overcome, deconstructed or simply abandoned. The problem of the first modernism is its obsession with the past. It might be time to consider, at last, the future. Provided that it can catch up with its time—obviously the most difficult task for modernists."[47]

In the course of writing I speak to dozens of designers from many generations and nationalities: Dutch, English, American, Swiss and others. All know of and admire Anthon Beeke, but not one confesses to being directly or visually influenced by his work. (On the other hand, many feel deeply influenced by van Toorn or Crouwel.) Why?

It is perhaps due in part to the peculiarly Dutch discomfort with influence. But when I pose the question to the celebrated book designer Irma Boom, who closely followed Beeke early in her career, she admonishes me: "Je doet hem te kort!"[48] Boom explains: "In Anthon's case it is important to understand he liberated Dutch design from too much Calvinism. The way he worked, his mentality even, was very important for a whole generation of designers. I see Anthon as a conceptual designer. He was fearless, and never afraid to take great risks. The visual results of that fearlessness could be erratic, but at least he tried. He was always trying to explore and searching for new approaches for each new problem."[49]

Perhaps in the well-worn 20th-century dichotomy, Beeke is Picasso to van Toorn's Duchamp. Picasso was a giant but his work was ultimately charting himself. Duchamp changed the practice of art in ways that affected all artists in every field. For a long stretch of his career, Beeke seems to be entirely in his own present, free of reference or ideology. "Anthon's work appears in some ways foreign to Dutch design," notes Godard, "He might seem at first glance to be a solitary figure divorced from any known school

47 Bruno Latour, "Is there a non-modern Style?" *Domus*, Jan. 2004.
48 Literally: "You're doing it too short!" or being overly simplex.
49 Email from Irma Boom to the author, Dec 12, 2010.
50 Lupton and Godard, 1.

or trend."[50] In this way, in his best work, for a brief moment, he achieves a difficult state—that of the non-modern, the eternally present. The ultimate Id, he constructs a communication that is unhinged from place or time, which seems to come out of some deep recess of the human psyche. Perhaps the device is overused, but he understands, implicitly, the eternal efficacy of the cock and the cunt.

THE CONTINENTAL DIVIDE with Jan van Toorn

MICHAEL ROCK

I have now written two longish essays—Mad Dutch Disease and Ameridam—seemingly on Dutch design but actually on American design framed by its fixation on Dutch Design. I want to understand more clearly a certain void that exists somewhere over the North Atlantic. This gap has been the subject of numerous arguments, misunderstandings and bad feelings among many different writers, designers and theorists for years. Specifically it's the gap between an essentially European approach to modern design and an American one that was imperfectly modeled on it.

I am of the opinion that a certain generation of American designers long for the social engagement we perceive in contemporary European design and its modern antecedents. (We've always been embarrassed by the market economy approach to design predominant in the U.S.) At the same time there seems to be in Northern Europe a decidedly aggressive attitude about the whole idea of design "theory." Max Bruinsma pointed me to a "clearly delineated European tradition of anti-intellectualism and resistance to theoretical categorization, spanning from 19th-century realism and expressionism, via Dada to Fluxus."

I am a bit confused. Dutch design always seemed to us deeply theoretical in that it had a pronounced social overtone. But how then to explain this animosity toward theory in general? Can you help me?

JAN VAN TOORN

Okay, let's start with Max Bruinsma. He is right, there is a European tradition of anti-intellectualism in fine art and design but this does not seem to be a fruitful explanation for why designers often resist theory. While there has always been a small and strong reflexive tendency in design, we know from historical and contemporary experience that an intellectual dualism based in two opposite principles is not a productive way to understand the complicated dialectics of the conditions in which we work, let alone help you to make something out of your social engagement.

MR

Would you say that this dialectic approach is particularly Dutch?

JVT

I don't think so, but to really understand the kind of social commitment of Dutch design culture you need to know that The Netherlands have a tradition of disciplinary care. By this process intellectual work is brought into action in cooperation with the organized bodies of the state, church, cooperatives, industry, trade, etc. to serve public good. Examples can be found in many different spheres: the best-known ones are the early examples of government care for technically qualified public-water management; the care for the homeless since the end of the 17th century; large-scale social housing programs and urban development projects by public-private initiatives in the early the 20th century. In terms of communication design, the state-owned PTT (Post, Telegraph and Telephone) played an exemplary role formulating an aesthetic policy that reconciled the socio-cultural ambitions of the avant-garde with corporate interests.

MR

This level of cooperation has never existed here, except maybe in the way that advertising industry has dipped into the avant garde to replenish its visual stocks ....

JVT

Dutch society owes a great deal to this interaction between intellectual/artistic pragmatics and the enlightened interest of individuals, social organizations, authorities and companies. One of the great socio-cultural attainments of this private/public collaboration before and after the Second World War was a well-kept intellectual, financial and logistical infrastructure in service of the common interest, an infrastructure that is now slowly but surely dismantled by the privatizations of neo-liberal politics.

MR

The culture of consensus replaced by a culture of personal attainment?

JVT

Yes, indeed, a tradition of consensus in which opposing interests contribute to the quality of social life. But one of the characteristics of this social equilibrium is that underlying private/public interests and ideological conflicts have difficulty surfacing in the public arena. The dominant regime of tolerance accepts deviations as private or individual dissent to a certain extent, but at the same time is anxious about disturbances of the status quo.

The animosity to theory dominating Dutch design fits in this tradition and explains the longstanding lack of reflection and debate compared to design culture in the other European countries. Another reason is that design education in The Netherlands, since the 19th century, has been a vocational training in arts and crafts serving the nation's industrial and commercial development. Therefore it wasn't until the end of the '70s before art history was replaced by design history and until the '80s before communication studies and design discourse were scantily introduced.

MR

Not so dissimilar in America …

JVT

Due to the traditional split between practice and theory, none of our universities had anything but a rather formal aesthetic and technological interest in design: not a bit of a critical, integrated design history or theory. This changed during the '90s, but intellectually speaking, the debate is still rather poor and too academic compared to other European countries.

MR

But modernization had a critical component, no?

JVT

Holland wasn't completely isolated from what was happening elsewhere in the world. My own education at the Instituut voor Kunstnijverheidsonderwijs [the Institute for Arts and Crafts, later Rietveld Academy), where Mart Stam was director from 1939–1948, was an example of art education rooted in the consensus-oriented modernist policy of Gropius' Bauhaus. It focused on the individual development of the student, including both good form and a positivist social engagement as a frame of mind.

But initiatives like these were incidental, mostly based on personal contacts and an internationally shared progressive mentality. The majority of Dutch art schools, however, remained unaware of developments in other countries, such as communication studies, semiotics etc. in the '70s; the introduction of cultural studies in art education in Britain in the '80s; the intellectual climate and debate in Germany, France and Italy during the high days of critical theory and structuralism; never mind what happened at the Hochschule für Gestaltung in Ulm under Tomas Maldonado in the '60s, with people like Max Bense, Abraham Moles, Hans Magnus Enzensberger, Gui Bonsiepe and others, striving to continue Hannes Meyer's wittingly non-consumerist pedagogical and sociopolitical orientation at the post-Gropius Bauhaus.

MR

Is that what you tried to remedy at the Jan van Eyck?

JVT

The Jan van Eyck Academie (c.1991) was the first art school in the Netherlands that introduced critical theory and cultural studies in its curriculum as an equivalent to fine art and design. Our goal was to allow the work of everybody at the academy to "find its place in current debates around the social, intellectual and historical preconditions for visual production." To our astonishment we were confronted by an almost complete lack of interest from the Dutch design community from the beginning. It wasn't until later on that the idea of a reflective practice became more accepted. The Design beyond Design conference [1997] was attended by many Dutch designers even though the majority of the speakers came from abroad. But this gradual acceptance did not suggest that both theorists and designers came up with strategic or methodological clues to overcome the traditional split between action and thought in practice.

With the increase of interest in theory, we see a growing influence of the critical intellectual discourse on design practice. But there is little thought about what this critical insight means for the action of design in a socio-cultural sense. That political question seems to be swept aside, again and again, by a formal visual and technocratic perspective on design's own actions.

MR

But form can be a kind of engagement and even resistance? Isn't that what you always advocated?

JVT

Yes, but I am afraid it is not so simple, as your question suggests. Form always expresses a kind of engagement, conventional, resistant or whatever, but I hope we are no longer so naïve as to believe that language is a neutral instrument and mentality finds its form automatically.

I am convinced—as Susan Buck-Morss wrote in her introduction for the Design beyond Design conference in 1997—that all information, empirical observation, data, etc., are socially conditioned and related to modes of production that give shape to forms of sociality. Communication design as cultural production is social commitment in that sense. So when we criticize the forces that determine the world, the given symbolic order should also be reworked and related to reality again, to everyday life. This is a question of method, it's political, because we are searching for solidarity in a non-consumptive relationship with our audiences.

This means that the merger of political conservatism and modernist aesthetics, with its affirmative language and propagandistic monumentality, should be replaced by an argumentative visual language that mobilizes the viewer and reader through the dialectical relations between the heterogeneous fragments of the message.

This dialogic condition of a-formality—on the one hand rejecting traditional ideas of form and content, and on the other hand approaching the commission with a kind of open substantive and strong visual argument— seems to tell us something about our present cultural condition. Not just about a particular stage of design discourse, but about our desire for forms of communication that articulate contemporary life in its very illegibility and contradictory qualities.

"JUST A FEW SMALL THINGS..."

WITH ELIZABETH ROCK

To: ______Design
Re: New Brand Launch -
Phase One

First, let me say that we are so amped, we are just really, really looking forward to working with you on this. It's so new, so fresh, so bleeding edge. I know I speak for everyone here, that we are just really thrilled about this new direction, and our whole team is so excited to have you on board.

And we ARE all a team! We really are a family. Just some of us compensated differently, and maybe a LOT differently, from others, but we are all a family. Maybe one of those families where there's that one girl who has something scheduled every night, and then there's that other girl who always stays home and does the dishes and things—because that's what she's good at! We're like that family.

So now: launch day. Get ready. Are you ready? This is so important for us, because next season we are taking this brand to a Whole. New. Level. We are celebrating a completely new girl. Because that is what we do. We're innovators. It's in our DNA. And because these girls are out there, and they have money, and they have been tragically underserved.

But that is where we live. We live ahead, on the edge, always seeking the next thing, the idea just out of our reach. But you know all this. So:

Welcome to our new brand position: IntelliChic.

OK, so already you're like, Whoa, whaa? This from the creators of *Skank!* and *MüdderFckr* and *PSUSY* and *Brothel Brand Jeans*? From the people who invented *Slut Chic*? And I am telling you: YES.

Because we are going in an Entirely. New. Direction.

Because according to our research, there is a whole demo of girls out there who are not only underserved by the fashion industry—they are invisible to the fashion industry. These girls have been flying over our radar. They are somehow growing up, going to school—and *staying* in school—and graduating (yay!) and sometimes going on to further their education (!!)—and then on to all kinds of jobs in really high-end, knowledge-intensive industries; jobs involving science and math and really impressive things that require a lot of, you know, just really, important kinds of knowledge material.

This girl is turning off the TV. This girl is hitting the books. AND reading them. ALL the way through. Real books, not Audio or podcasts.

And this girl—this poor, probably slightly overweight, dowdy girl, wearing God-knows-what to her endless classes, reading her way to bad skin and corrective lenses, working in labs with chemicals that just CAN'T be good for your skin and hair — this girl is going on to get Major Jobs in Really Big Companies. Jobs where they need to look their best, and make a statement.

And: jobs where they are making just truckloads of money.

Which is when I had my Major Realization: We have to hook these poor, overworked, unattractive things NOW, when they are still open, still ready to meet the brand they will love for the rest of their lives. We have to act NOW when they really really NEED us. These girls are out there and they are crying out for our help.

So: Yes. We are saying that our company is done with the trashy, slightly unhygienic looks of the past. (That was a creative direction we explored, and frankly, IMHO our work on that collection was truly next-gen — and I continue to be proud and a bit in awe, if I may say so, of that work. Because it spoke volumes about who we are as a company. And I truly feel that it was — all right, I'll just say it, to you, as trusted partners — but seriously, I can feel the tears rising now — revolutionary.)

Anyhoo! Now a new direction! Booty shorts and tramp stamps are OUT. Gnawed fingernails, unwashed hair and translucent, light-starved skin are IN.

OUT: Spring break with stick-on nails and spray tan.
IN: Myopia.

MODELS - OUT: the gaunt plank of a girl with a face like a pole-axed Siamese cat, a pink tutu and a size 0 baby tee. Who is this popsicle stick with eyeshadow? We don't even know. Even though we knew her last season. But we don't know her now.

MODELS - IN: the gaunt plank of a girl with a Supercuts haircut and awesome coke-bottle glasses and perfectly shaped calves from hiking to some remote African village or something.

This proud, nearsighted innovator is reTHINKing fashion. She is challenging our preconceptions, our notions of gender image, beauty, and the importance of innovative moisture-wicking fabrics and heat-retaining self-bonded materials.

YES. We choose to celebrate this girl. Because why should these drab, mousy, tired, over-scheduled, under-dated girls have to celebrate their mind-expanding attitudes with really tacky fabric and sub-standard materials and workmanship? Why should we not be clothing them as the striding, proud intelligistas that they are — that girl who is a CEO AND a PhD with a perfect BMI?

So: Your work must identify, pinpoint, and celebrate this woman.

Honestly, I can hardly say that without, really, just welling up. I just really feel that we are doing something radical and really important here. Because for the first time in my career I can honestly say we are bringing our skills to the aid of the people who need us the most.

To: _______ Design
RE: New Season - Further Thoughts

So following up on our project launch meeting: first, let me just say how GREAT that was. We all know your reputation as the absolute eggheads of the advertising world but we weren't prepared for that LSAT *nightclub* project. Who knew you could make test-prep sexy?!

It's so seldom that you go into a meeting and really feel the energy in the air like that. We could all really, really just feel the excitement coming from your group. It was electric. I know our team can be a little overwhelming, and we give off a lot of energy, and frankly, a lot of people don't always do well with that. But I was so truly gratified to see that your team was just really getting us, and getting into our process and listening—and really listening, which is such a rare thing nowadays, and a real gift too, don't you think—to, like words, and like everything we said. I know it was kind of a wall of stuff, and some of it was kind of random. But I hope you are all just as energized and enthused as we are. Because we are just crazy out of our heads about this, and people are saying this could be a total game changer for this company—and people are talking about words like genius, groundbreaking, revolutionary, insane—but in a good way.

Can't wait to see the boards and initial concepts.

To: _______ Design
Re: Some thoughts

Just throwing these out - what do you think of:

A woman striding down Madison Avenue. She is wearing one of those white lab coats, which is flaring out on either side of her. Underneath she is wearing just the most perfect cocktail dress—really, really tiny, just so cute, and it fits PERFECTLY (of course!) and she's hurrying and carrying a black medical bag. OR! even better! A microscope!

Or:

A really great emo shot of a woman, partially obscured by darkness, at a desk. Some desk-like, smart things are on the desk—books, and a lamp, and, I don't know, more books. How about a globe? She's leaning over some test tubes or something to kiss a man on the other side of the desk. A colleague?

A secret romance in the "lab"?? Who knows??! Fun, right?!!!

To: _______ Design
Re: Brand Position

On my way to JFK have to be in Guangzhou tomorrow but was wondering about the brand position statement; how's it coming? I know you said you needed more time on it to process all the info. But we really need to get moving on this. Note we have had intimations that other groups may have heard a whisper and are scouting around about it. So for now on, EYES ONLY and full security for anything regarding the IntelliChic work.

Oh no, there I go again!

To: _______ Design
Re: Brand Position

What concepts exactly did you need more clarification on?

To: _______ Design
Re: Brand Positioning

OMG OMG LOVED LOVED LOVED THE BRAND POSITIONING STATEMENT YOU ARE SUCH GENIUSES ITS PERFECT but need to make a few tweaks. Just small things:

In the first line could you change UGLY to HIDEOUS? We think: "lovelorn and broken-hearted" could be changed to "envious of the hotness around them" Line 5: shouldn't that read: "date-less"?

Running out the door. Will get back to you.

To: _______ Design
Re: Social

I think this might be good time to really broach the idea of the social end of this. You have some plans for that, yes? Those girls do that, right? The social stuff?

To: _______ Design
Re: Concept Meeting Yesterday

SHUT UP!—you guys are AMAZING. We were all just blown away. And we are SO psyched now about the direction IC is going. So—kudos! BTW I did get some notes from our team, so want to pass them on.

We really want to push the Study Hall direction even more. But instead of them being at the beach—what if they were all at Harvard?? Or Hogwarts????!!!

We HAVE to drive that IC Soul Cycle direction even more. But it's a little expected to have them all at the gym. Maybe they could be soul cycling to somewhere, like an unexpected destination? Like the rainforest? Maybe hunting down those people who are doing all those awful things to the rainforests?

We all liked the IC Zumba direction! But now we're thinking about what it means to actually Zumba. Like, can you do some research on that? You know, what IS Zumba anyway? It just doesn't seem as conceptually sound as the Soul Cycle direction. I think this has the potential to be the hottest option, we just need to tap into its core and discover, so awesome!

We all LOVED the IC Baby direction! But now we're thinking about a IC Baby Stroller campaign. Can we see something on that? Wait, do those girls use strollers? Or—oh GOD, they don't use those hideous hippie horse-blanket baby-swaddle things that they bought in Katmandu or Peru or something, while they were off on one of their grubby projects, do they? Because that would just be SO UNATTRACTIVE.

Also: I understand your misgivings, concerns and objections re: the IC Wedding direction, and duly noted and all that. But the team here is really insisting on seeing that direction. And I have to let you know: I think this a big deal. Just my insider tip. I really listened to all your concerns, but it's something that is really important to the team, and I can't emphasize enough how important it is that we explore it. It's just crucial, to be frank.

Thanks! Looking forward to the next stage meeting! Honestly, we are all so excited here.

To: _______ Design
Re: Next stage meeting

So, as usual, so great. Some things did come up, though. We all felt that the visuals were—not sure of the right word—so I'm using the word that the team used—stupid. Also, boring. Also, not fresh.

Now I KNOW that this must seem harsh and I explained to them that they're just not used to looking at really, seriously smart, high-end design work. I told them you guys are INTELLECTUALS. But we do have to move forward with their reactions.

Also: bad news, but take out all the stuff for the IntelliChic Wedding thing. I know this is something near and dear to you and your team, and it's hard to give up on your personal favorites, but seriously, it is SO not going anywhere. I mean those girls getting married to those hot guys? It just doesn't pass the smell test … and I kind of feel that we wasted some valuable time on it as a total dead end.

To: _______ Design
Re: First looks

OK, so EXCITING! Loved the mood boards! But we really want you to push that even further. We think the girl in the chem lab should be breast-feeding a baby—can you find an image like that? Maybe she's feeding the baby with a little test tube!!? Could the girl on page 3 be posed like that "Thinker" statue but wearing our sweat-proof faux-fur sports bra? How GREAT would that be?? And also, we'd really like to see more owl imagery—especially with the mortarboard hats. I know it's out there but just a great "ironic" inside joke for the intelligentsia! We know these are just swipes but they all look a little too focused, don't you think? Could they be just a bit more vague? Maybe like they're really pondering a deep thought?

And: This is TOP SECRET—but we are thinking that the models for our runway shows for next season may each be carrying an ACTUAL LIVE OWL!! SHHH! With little mortarboard hats!!

SO CUTE!!!
WHOO WHOOO!!

To: _______ Design
Re: Call me.

To: _______ Design
Re: Team Meeting

So, I have a bit of difficult news … but the whole team here has gotten together, along with the principals, and the decision has been made to go in a new direction.

Fortunately, before we went very far, our people have been coming back with the consensus that the whole "smart" thing is just really, really old, and has really been done to death.

I mean, when you consider that we see Hillary and Michelle and Angelina almost every day. So, really, almost impossible to really find anything fresh about it. And we're getting research that those girls just don't even WANT to be hotter.

We want you to know that we SO appreciate all your great work and efforts.

And we know how married you are to your concept, and that is totally admirable and passionate—but frankly we remain just unconvinced of the viability of your whole IntelliChic direction.

So the company has made the decision to move forward for next season with a new design team. We've really enjoyed working with you, and understand that some design firms have a very particular attitude and way of working that doesn't always mesh easily with others. Thanks again for your interesting work. We wish you the best of luck in your future endeavors.

DESIGNED SCREENS: A COMPENDIUM

WITH PAUL ELLIMAN

1
SCREEN

PAUL ELLIMAN

The irony is in the name, screen. As if it were there to protect us.

MICHAEL ROCK

There's a double meaning: on one hand, to protect, and on the other, to obscure. (Or is obscuring a kind of protection?) Does it reveal or conceal?

2
THE BIG SCREEN

PE

I remember the "launch" of the biggest cinema in Europe—the Géode in Paris—with its thousand-meter-square hemispheric screen. The screen becomes the auditorium; the audience is supposed to feel as if they've entered cinematic space. Giant screens capture or focus mass imagination in public spaces.

MR

I was at Obama's inaguration and we were so far from the podium we watched the event, together with about 50,000 fellow citizens, on a huge screen built on the back of a flatbed truck.

PE

(Reading a picture caption from *The New York Times*) "On February 20, 1962, commuters filled the concourse of Grand Central Terminal to watch as Colonel Glenn became the first American to orbit Earth."

MR

The dream is a screen that can capture the world at a scale of 1:1. Abel Gance tried it in the '20s with his three-screen version of Napoleon. In the '60s, Cinemascope's elongated proportions were extended by Cinerama, a concave screen that curved to embrace the audience. The New York World's Fair of 1964 marked the apotheosis of the giant-screen frenzy. I was there, too. Pavilions competed for the most breathtaking displays: the circular Kodak theater, the GE "Skydome Spectacular," General Cigar's "Movie in the Round," and Charles and Ray Eames' storied "View from the People Wall," a nine-screen projection on the ceiling of the IBM building. All were precursors to the ubiquitous IMAX.

PE

Screens finally began to out-scale the world. Imagine the staple political image of the moment: the politician (Reagan, Thatcher, Clinton, Blair, Chirac, Mandela, Deng) dwarfed at podium by their own towering portrait on a three-story video wall.

3
THE SMALL SCREEN

PE

In one of Hiroshi Sugimoto's photographs of a drive-in movie, the night sky behind the giant screen is traced with airplane lights that radiate from the bright rectangle. The jump from the car windscreen view of a movie to airplanes flitting across the sky evokes the miniature screens embedded in the back of airplane seats. On some flights, passengers get to watch themselves take off and land on those screens.

MR

The on-board experience moved from public to private in a few short years. The first in-flight movies were just that: film projected onto a common screen, transforming the cabin into a theater. The miniaturization of the screen individualized the experience from public theater to hundreds of tiny living rooms (the way a drive-in movie privatizes the film experience and the kids can wear their pajamas.) Is this why people travel in sweat suits and trainers?

4
LONELY SCREENS

PE

Part of the panoptical infrastructure are the Screens That Go Unseen, like the surveillance screen that monitors some lonely petrol station forecourt at three a.m. These screens must be all over the city, at the desk of every sleeping night guard. Every now and then a building blows up, or a child goes missing, and in the news we see the spectral shadow of a suspect in the bottom left corner of some blurry screen, as if to remind us of what screens are really for: to present our world in all its tragic glory.

5
INVASIVE SCREENS

MR

The fluoroscope is a device equipped with a fluorescent screen on which the internal structures of an opaque object, such as the human body, can be viewed as shadowy images formed by the transmission of x-rays through the object. More vivid than the static x-ray, fluoroscopy magically reveals the mysterious interior workings of the body in real time. The invention fueled countless animated cartoons: a character stands behind the screen and the doctor is shocked to discover a hamster on a wheel, an undigested ham sandwich, a hawk or a handsaw.

6
PROSTHETIC SCREENS

MR

Dick Tracy's creator, Chester Gould, gave the famous gumshoe the ultimate in detective accessories: the wristwatch videophone, realized as today's smartphone.

PE

Teletubbies have screens where ordinary people have stomachs. Their tele-prosthetics allow them to view ordinary people doing ordinary things. Like watching TV screens.

7
TV SCREENS

PE

A friend of mine who works on "home-theater" technology told me how the plasma screen is supposed to work: "The screen is a honeycomb of pixels between sheets of glass. The pixels hold a mixture of neon-xenon gas and phosphorescent material in red, yellow or blue. Electrodes fixed to the front and back of each cell cause the gas to emit ultraviolet light which, in turn, causes the phosphors to project light, which creates the picture." It's a lot cleaner than the old-fashioned tubes, but it sounds extremely alchemical to me.

MR

Flatness. Eliminate the box. The desire to hang a moving image on the wall like a painting is fulfilled. Fujitsu's first flat TV ads went like this: the screen appears on the wall of a super narrow house populated by three hipsters grooving to the Beatles: "Got to admit it's getting better, a little better all the time ..."

PE

Good song. (Is that what Frank Zappa meant by architecture you can dance to?)

8
MORE TV SCREENS (AND VIDEO ART?)

PE

When artists first started using video, the discussion was about where, exactly, the work resided—was it on the screen, on the tape, in the studio, or some other mysteriously electrical part of the process? As if to make a work that resided clearly in the screen, the 1970s performance group Ant Farm (whose work was mainly about our obsessions with cars and TV) drove a car at high speed into a tower of TV screens.

MR

The destruction of the TV screen is the only form of resistance left, as emptily symbolic as that might be. The loony anchorman in "Network" inciting his audience to throw their sets out the window, proclaiming "I'm mad as hell and I'm not going to take it anymore!" The famous Apple/*1984* ad with the girl swinging the hammer into the Big Brother video wall. And, of course, scores of disaffected rock stars, following Elvis, drawing revolvers and shooting out their TV screens in countless hotel rooms worldwide.

PE

Rave on Howard Beale! In England the Sex Pistols achieved another level of notoriety when an irate viewer put his foot through his television screen. He said he was disgusted by the foul-mouthed Pistols' appearance on the early evening Bill Grundy show. There are a lot of TV screens in contemporary art. There's Nam June Paik, of course, and his TV Robots, waking up as each screen flickers into electromagnetic life.

9 MOVIE SCREENS

PE

I can't think of an example where the screen is attacked at the premiere of a movie; usually it's the projector. In Buñuel's "Los Olvidados," a Mexico City delinquent hurls an egg at the camera. We, of course, see it hitting the screen in an explosion of yolk and shell. In Woody Allen's "Purple Rose of Cairo," the screen star walks out of the screen and into the screen version of real life. In David Cronenberg's "Videodrome," James Woods gets eaten by the screen.

MR

The screen as fragile tissue, transgressable. In the opening sequence of "Persona," the boy reaches to touch his own exaggerated image on the flickering screen.

PE

Warhol made consistent use of the screen in the process of filmmaking. Most of his films were, in fact, made for multiple-screen projection. In his 1965 movie, "Outer and Inner Space," a 22-year-old Edie Sedgewick is filmed in conversation with herself on two screens; it was billed as "double-screen experiments by double-screen experimentalists."

10 CLEAR SCREENS

PE

(Reading from Pynchon's *The Crying of Lot 49*) "Oedipa stood in the living room, stared at by the greenish dead eye of the TV tube."

MR

(Reading from Gibson's *Neuromancer*) "The sky above the port was the color of television, tuned to a dead channel."

PE

The screen is not supposed to say anything. It's supposed to be neutral —neither blanc nor black, but blank. Yet identifying it as dead or passive or empty suggests our own loss of understanding or response to what is perhaps ultimately being screened onto us.

MR

Like that scene from "Paris, Texas" in which Harry Dean Stanton stands in front of the projector as home movies of his life with Nastassja Kinski play out on his body. The screen is always on, the reverse of the white page. White space is total reflection (in projection) or total radiation (in video). And as to whether it reveals or conceals ...

PE

I'm happier resisting the either/ors in favor of a more encompassing quality, that is, the screens' (and our) ability to reflect. In any of those attempts to describe our world through cellulloid, video tape or pixelled bits, the thing being reflected is, after all, us.

No matter how familiar, how prevalent (in the deli, the stadium, the town square) screens become, they refuse to lose our interest. They are patient, these screens, silently waiting to ignite and brilliantly reflect the shadows that we recognize as our lives.

The End.
(As the screen might say.)

NOTES FOR A LECTURE TITLED: EMPIRE OF SCREENS

An ad for Layar, a European company specializing in augmented reality software: a happy young couple roams the streets of a teeming city arm in arm. They are not unlike millions of other stock-photography couples roaming generic cities in any number of forgettable ads but in this one they hold a smartphone at arm's length in front of them. As they pass through the streets their gaze is intensely focused not on the surrounding cacophony but on the 2"x3" screen that falls between them and the wide world. As they forge ahead, the tiny version of the street captured on their screen is automatically annotated with pop-up information overwriting the city with attention-grabbing factoids: Feeling down? There's a Starbucks right around the corner! Apartments for rent in this building! Here's that haunted Indian burial ground you've heard so much about!

Cut to the 65th Cannes film festival in 2012. Hip-hop recording artist Kanye West is standing on the edge of steeply canted bleachers addressing an exclusive audience that has just witnessed his elaborate music video/film hybrid *Cruel Summer* splashed across seven gigantic movie screens that fill every visible inch of a temporary pyramidal film-screening pavilion. The seven-screen concept "relates to a post–Steve Jobs, post-Windows era where we're always on a BlackBerry or a phone at a ballgame, at the movies, and you're looking at seven windows when you're online," West explains. "And I've found myself even falling asleep at the theater unless I'm talking to somebody or I'm on the phone, and it's because of the amount of information that we have at once ...."

Jump to CNN election headquarters, Decision 2012. News anchor Anderson Cooper stands tall in the middle of a wide-open television studio. Suddenly a screen appears magically in the air in front of him—just a free-floating screen—and up pops the head of a political correspondent with whom the newsman proceeds to have a detailed conversation. Two more windows appear. All the windows have heads and all the heads are talking to one another. Suddenly the screens close and disappear into the ether as mysteriously as they appeared. Of course I am watching all three of these simultaneously on windows framed on my computer: A screen in a screen in a screen. I'm browsing.

If the flâneur—*one who walks the city in order to experience it*—was an essential figure of the 19th century, the browser—*one who, while shopping, purchases nothing*—is the 21st-century equivalent. The two occupy opposing time dimensions: the diachronous—cinematic: one thing after another—and the synchronic—pictorial: simultaneous. The flâneur was a product of the urban, the narrative animated by physical movement. The browser is essentially placeless: he sits wherever and the world is served into his lap(top). The transition from one to the other, and ultimately the conflation of the two, has broad implications for designers charged with modulating the interface between humans and things.

We used to design things. Now we design things that happen on screens. The object of graphic design has melted. The following timeline traces this dissolution from thing to image-of-thing and from street space to screen space. It starts with plate glass. The shop window—and later long chains of windows ordered in tight sequences along urban arcades—is the first urban screen. The window presents a dialectic, clamoring consumption on one side, endless cornucopia of production on the other: the more glorious the offering, the more dependent the effect is on constant revision. Glass invents the fashion cycle and a new type: the window shopper, precursor to the contemporary browser.

The story continues through the electrification of the window, the illumination of typography, and the emergence of the big screen—first inside, then in the drive-in movie, then in the public square. Screens grow, multiply and are used in multiples, memorably by the Eameses in their famous World's Fair installations. Then just as the city fills up with screens comes a great fracturing neatly symbolized by Ridley Scott's famous 1984 advertisement announcing the arrival of the Macintosh (the quintessential screen-of-screens) wherein a young be-hammered woman shatters the Big Brother-broadcasting super-screen into, presumably, an infinity of personal computers. From here on out the story is one of increasing miniaturization, fragmentation and customization. Instead of going to see screens, they travel with us in our backpacks, pockets and ultimately built into our glasses. Screens stop broadcasting and start mediating. We don't look at them, but, like our happy couple with their augmented reality, through them.

Up to a point the screen followed a typical form of media—a recognizable platform that could be refilled constantly with content for mass distribution. The transformation from broadcast to mediation, however, implies a fundamental disruption in the way media are composed. It implies a future less about content and more about filters, frames and, yes, even augmentation. In this iteration the screen becomes prosthetic, not serving vision but extending it. The new screen—mobile, light, personal—completes the circle. Your screen accompanies you, or ultimately, is built into you, on your ramblings and the browser and flâneur are, at last, reconciled.

Our design work and research in multi-screen display has been deeply influenced by the writing of Beatriz Colomina on the work of Charles and Ray Eames, in particular "Enclosed by Images: The Eameses' Multimedia Architecture," *Grey Room* No. 2, (Winter 2001), 6–29.

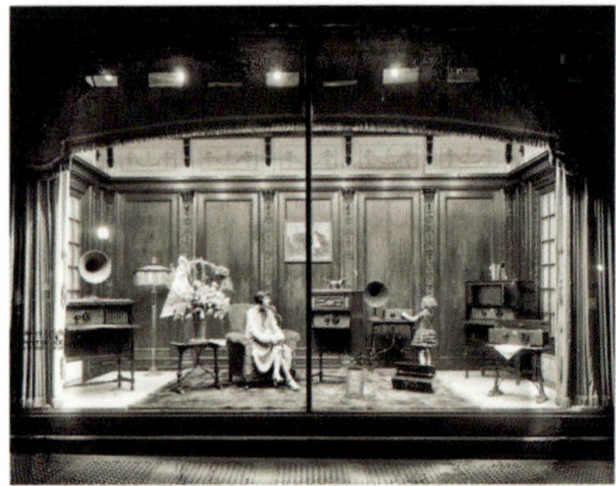

Windows

Plate glass as proto-screen: shop windows in tight sequences along urban arcades narrate the story of consumerism. The abundance of new production demands a delivery system to equal it. Glass presents a dialectic: clamoring consumption on one side, endless cornucopia of production and display on the other. Large-scale glass inserts consumer-scale narrative into the architectural façade. The window frames an endlessly evolving story presented to the street.

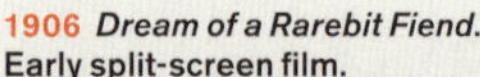

1906 *Dream of a Rarebit Fiend.* Early split-screen film.

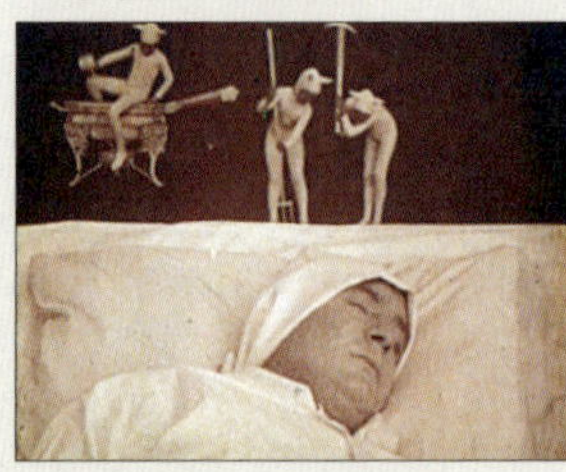

1900 Proposal for a Cinéorama, Paris Exhibition.

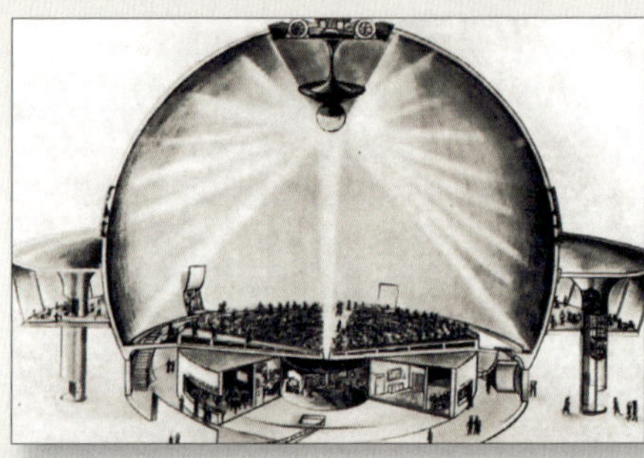

1900

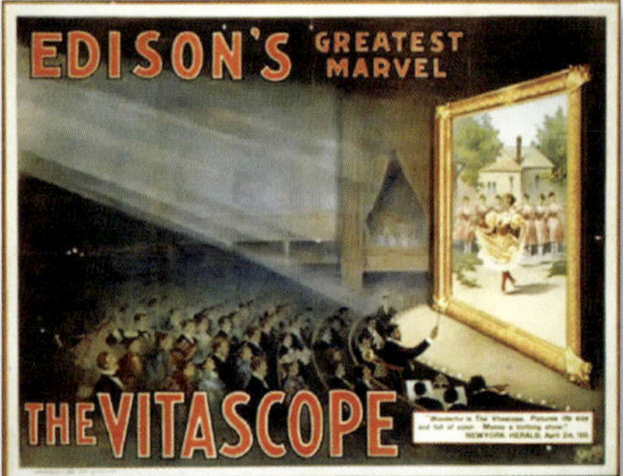

1896 The Vitascope ushers in the age of the big screen as shared public spectacle.

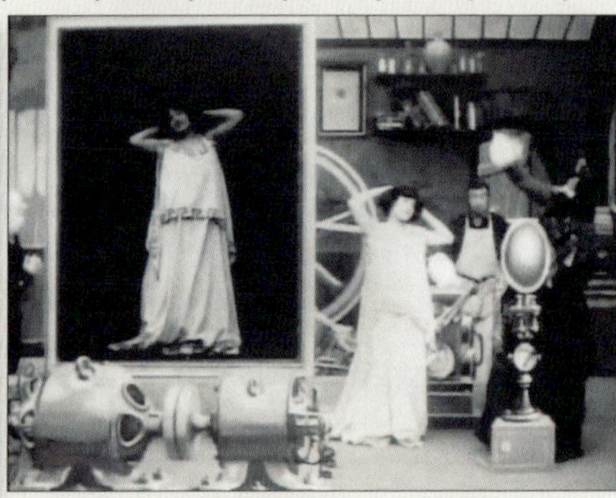

1908 Georges Méliès' *Long Distance Wireless Photography.* Screen in screen.

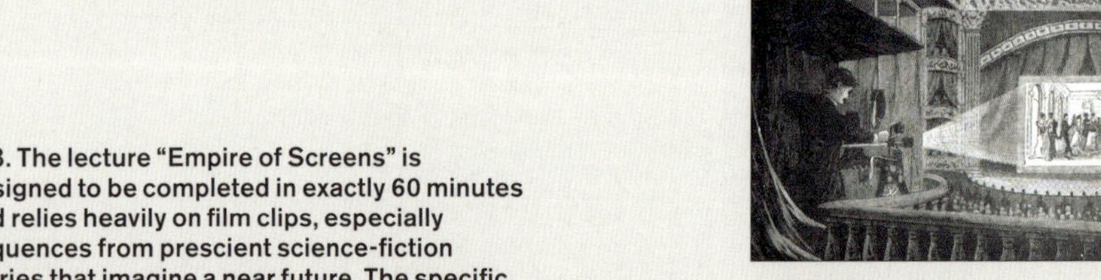

1890s Cinema: The "frenzy on the wall."

N.B. The lecture "Empire of Screens" is designed to be completed in exactly 60 minutes and relies heavily on film clips, especially sequences from prescient science-fiction stories that imagine a near future. The specific stills from films not available for reproduction are indicated herein with a black redaction.

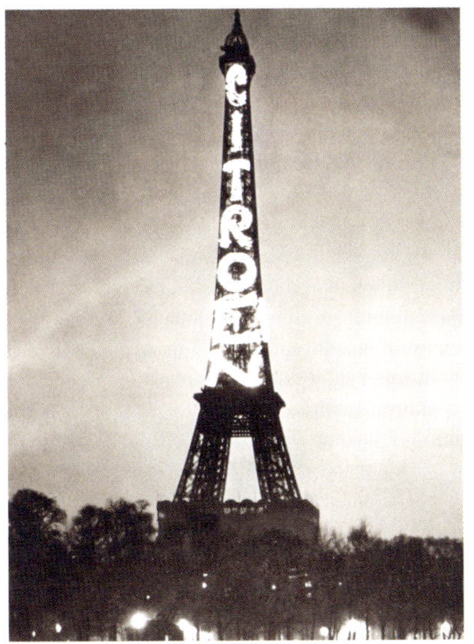

Luminescence

Electricity invigorates typography. Buildings crouch behind brilliant panels of illuminated information. The electrotypographic phenomenon overwrites the city. The electronic sign, and its cousin the illuminated billboard, lead to the emerging urban screen: cinema meets city.

1920s The illuminated billboard as façade.

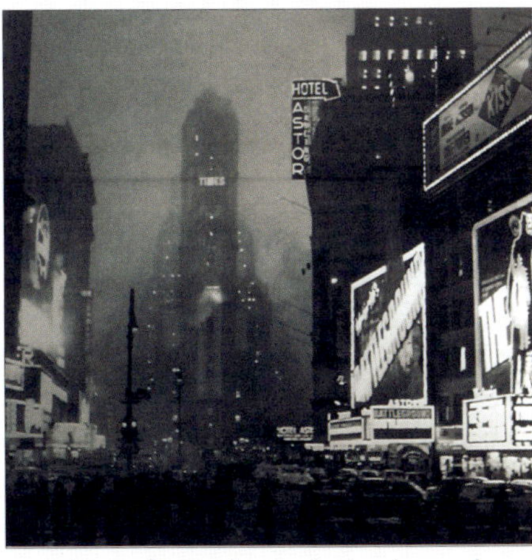

1930

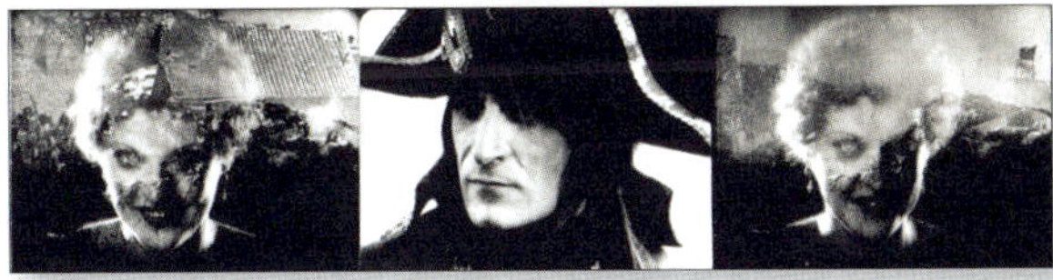

1927 Abel Gance, *Napoléon*. Triple-screen narrative.

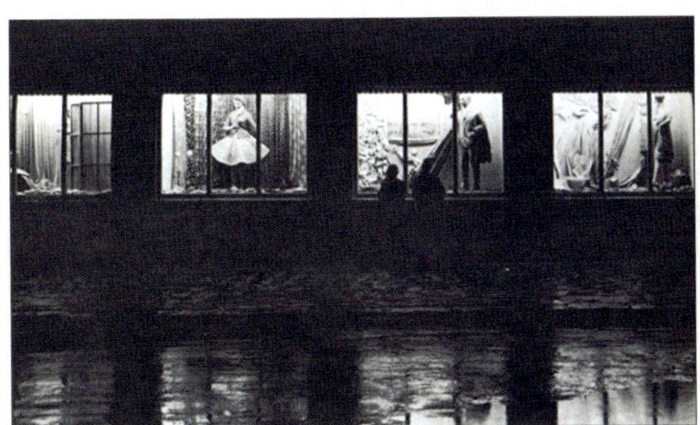

Illuminated store displays as sequential urban screens.

1913 *Suspense*. Early split-screen narrative.

Novus Ordo Seclorum

The well-tailored eyeball: Herbert Bayer's prescient diagram (1930) suggests a new order. The static subject is surrounded by an array of screens. The info-cloud is engineered for maximum viewing efficiency, the panels linked, presumably, to wildly diverse sources. Mr. Eyeball is all input, an insatiable pupil sucking content from the ether. The prosthetic screen extends vision to the world.

1940s Military radar operators.

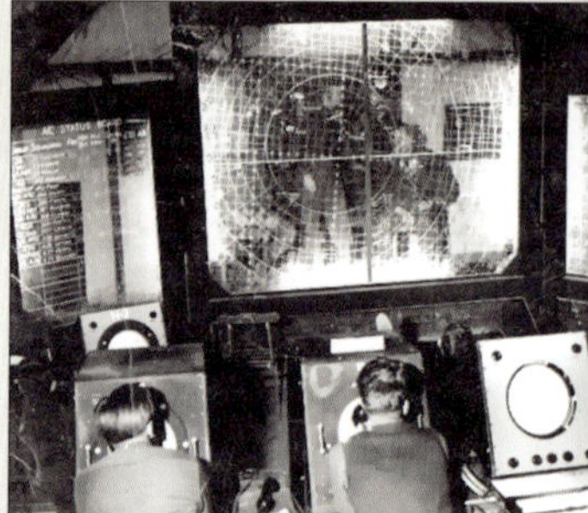

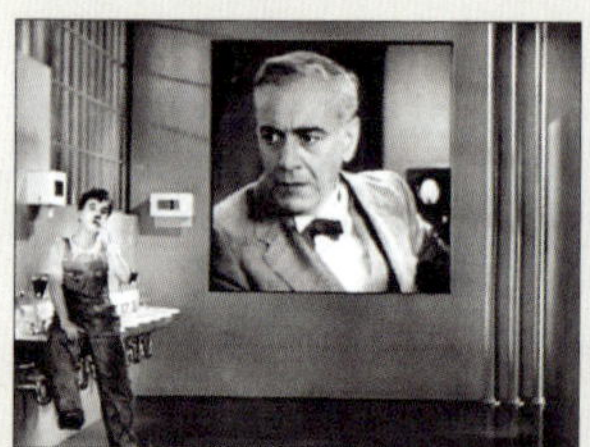

1936 *Modern Times*. Visionary telepresence.

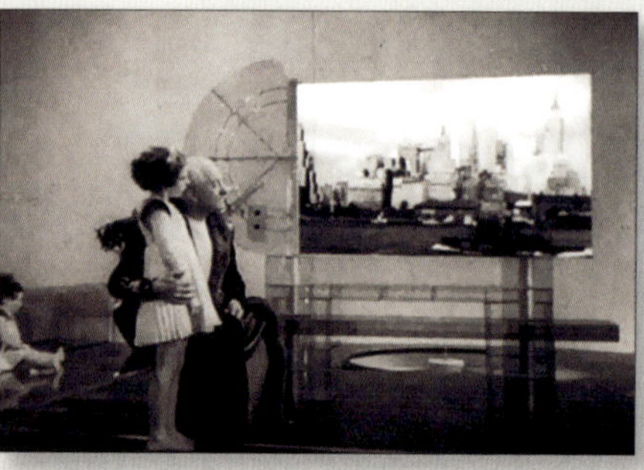

1936 *Things to Come*. Visionary flat-screen display as subterranean window.

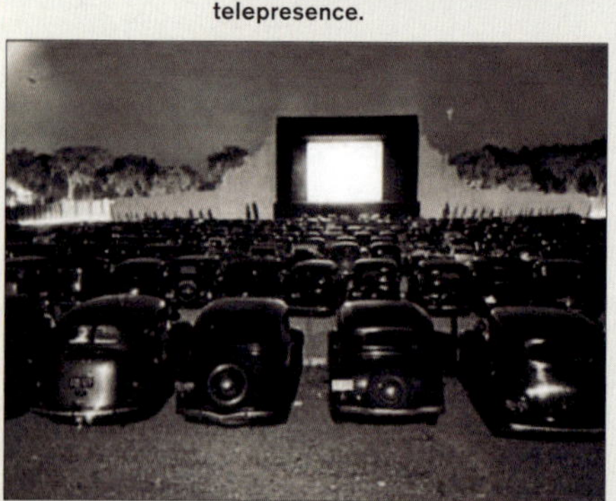

1933 Drive-in movie, Camden, New Jersey. The cars stop, the screen accelerates.

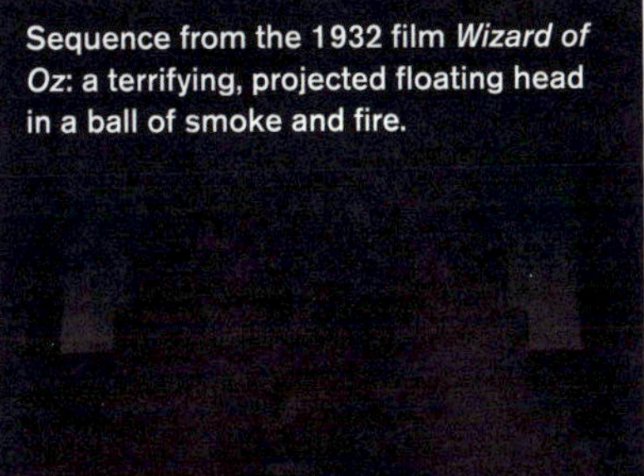

Sequence from the 1932 film *Wizard of Oz*: a terrifying, projected floating head in a ball of smoke and fire.

Following sequence from the *Wizard of Oz*: flustered wizard, furiously working the levers of a complex machine, is revealed when small dog draws back emerald green curtain.

The Man Behind the Curtain

The complex and essentially invisible machinery of broadcasting implies seemingly omniscient networks of power, operating remotely, manipulating the emotions of the masses.

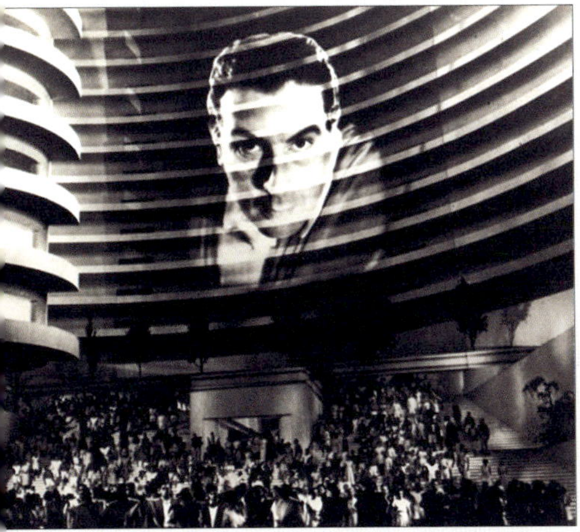

1936 *Things to Come*. Big screen = omnipotence.

1945 Home screen: early commercial television.

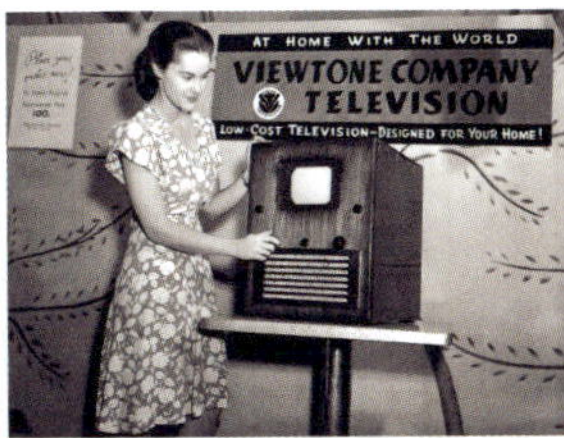

1940s First NBC broadcast control-room.

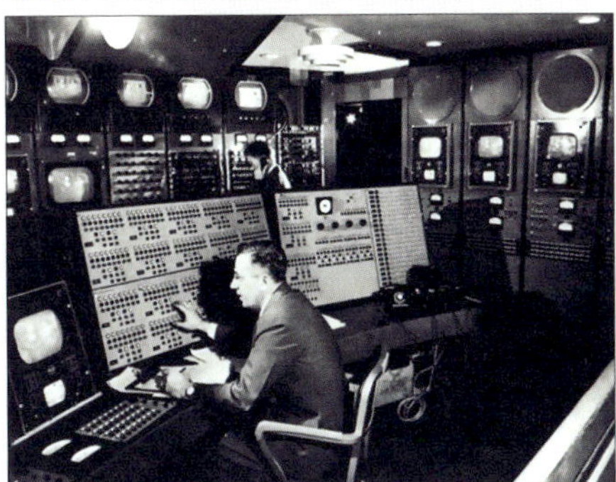

1940

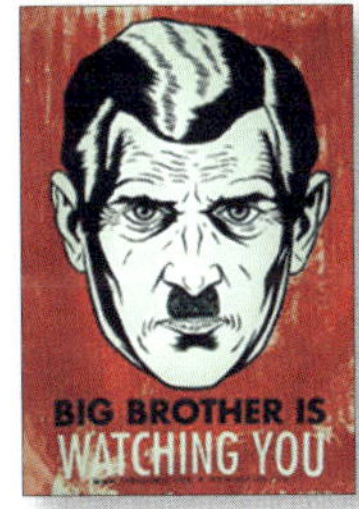

1949 *1984*.

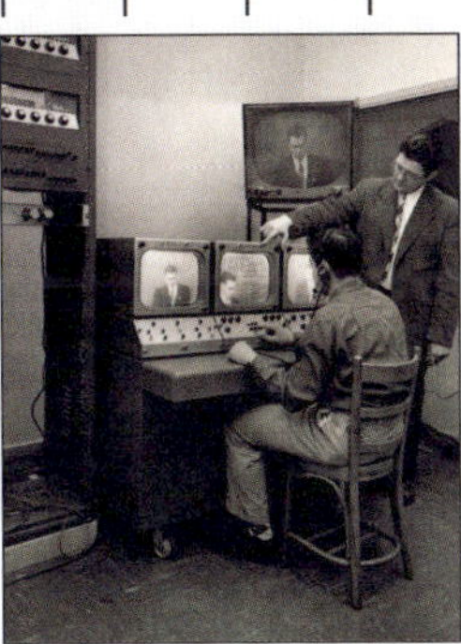

1950s Television control station.

1950s The screen comes home.

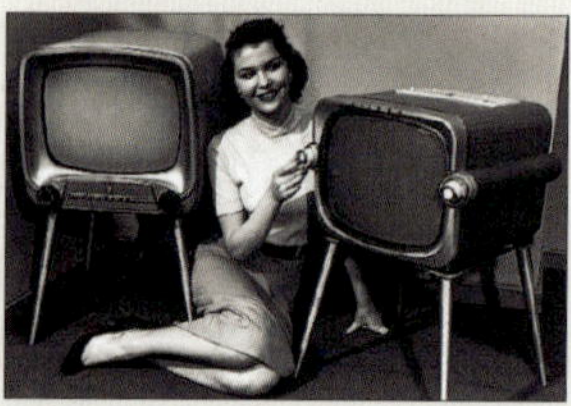

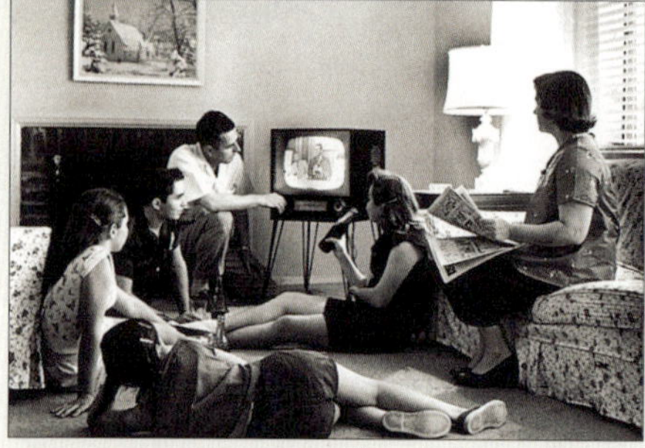

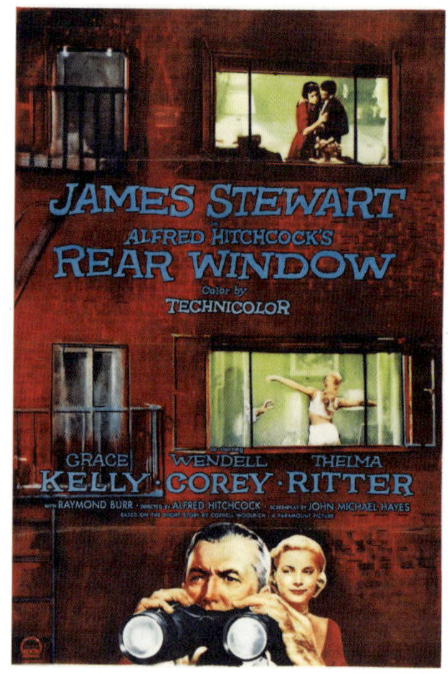

Multiplex

Hitchcock's *Rear Window* (1954) is both a treatise on the voyeur and an analysis of the coming age of multi-channel television. His protagonist is immobilized by injury and spends his convalescence watching the stories played out in the multiple windows (screens) of the neighboring apartments. His leading man defines a new typology: couch potato.

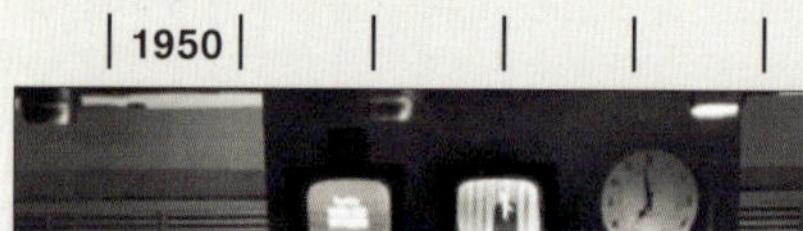

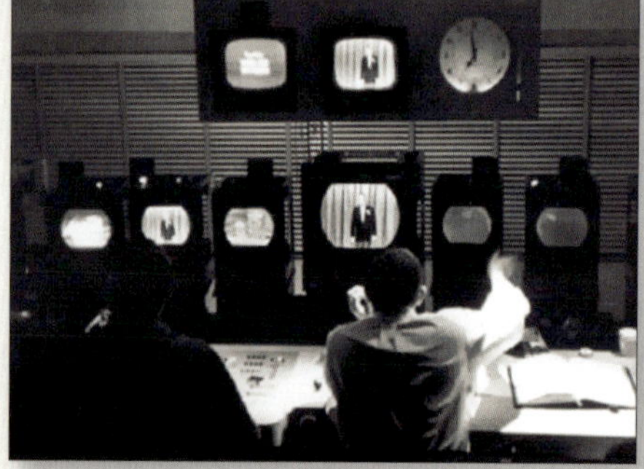

1950s Television broadcast-control module.

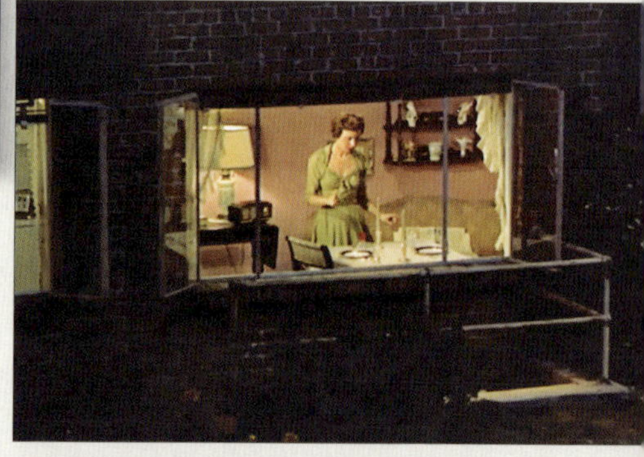

1954 Hitchcock's *Rear Window*. Window as screen.

1959 *Pillow Talk*: split screen as simultaneous narrative.

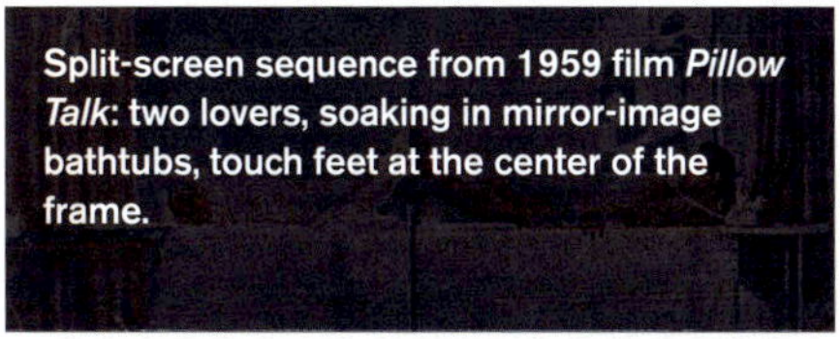

Split-screen sequence from 1959 film *Pillow Talk*: two lovers, soaking in mirror-image bathtubs, touch feet at the center of the frame.

1959 Charles and Ray Eames, *Glimpses of the USA*, Moscow.

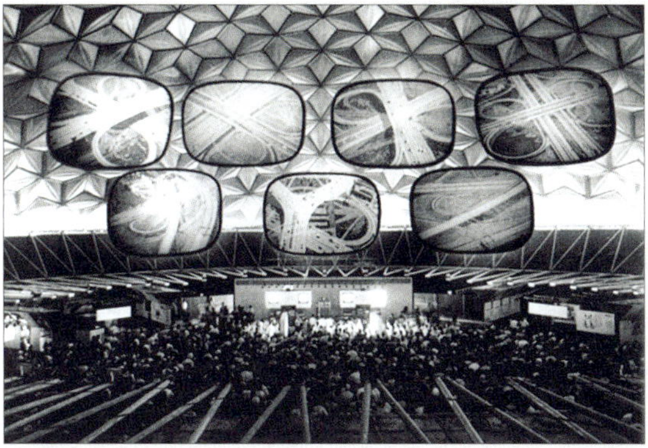

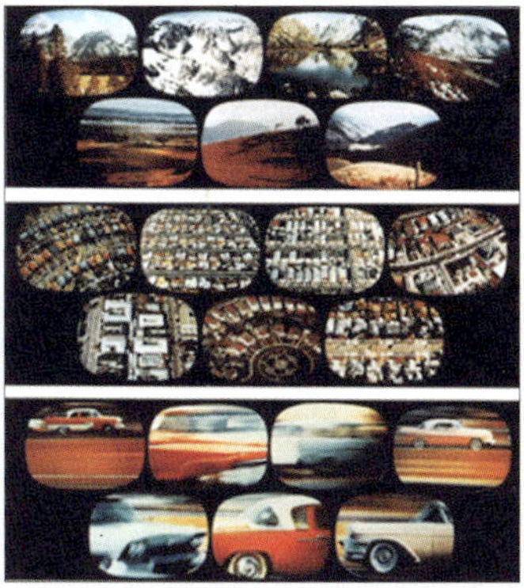

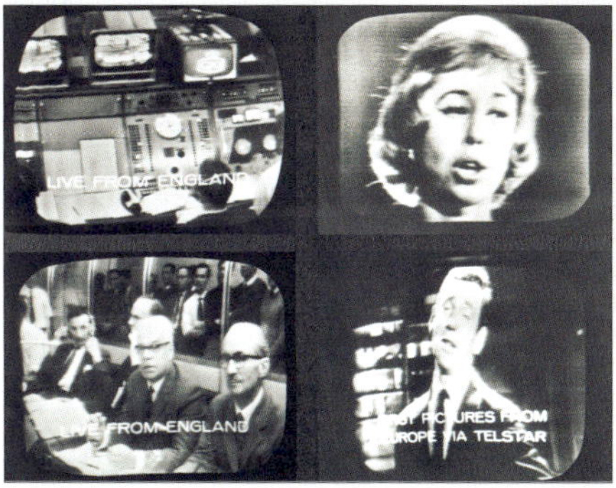

1962 Monitors in Manhattan display the first live transatlantic broadcast from General Post Office Television in England.

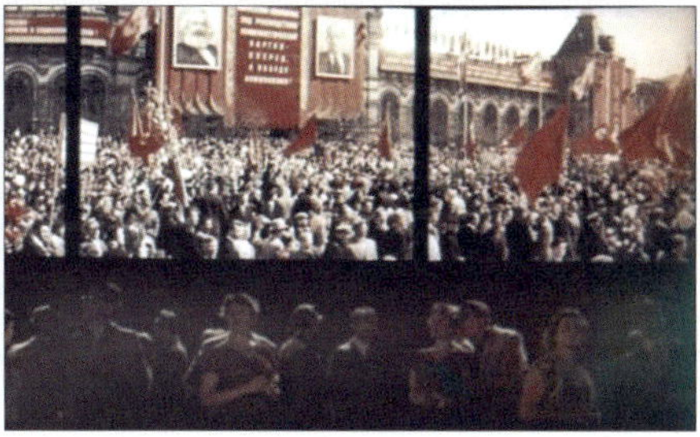

1959 Krugovaya Kinopanorama. 360-degree cinema.

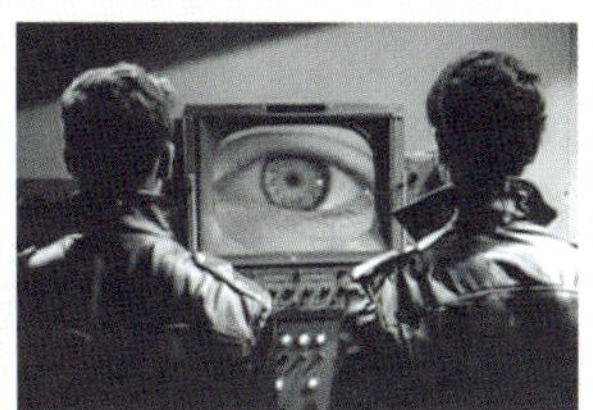

1964 Twilight Zone: *Black Leather Jackets*.

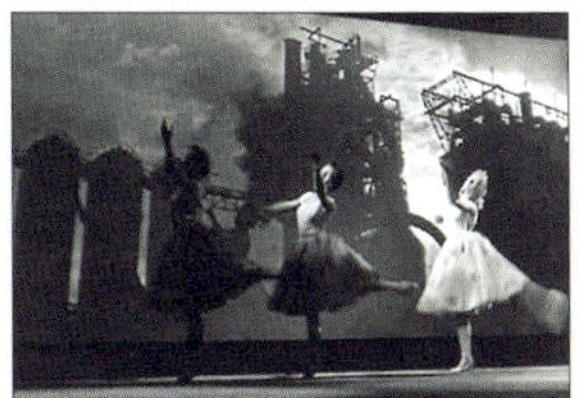

1958 Brussels Expo: *Laterna Magika*. Screen and dancers interact.

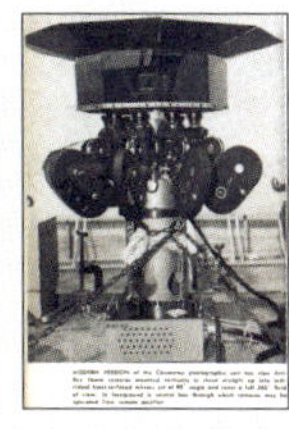

1955 9-camera *Circarama* rig.

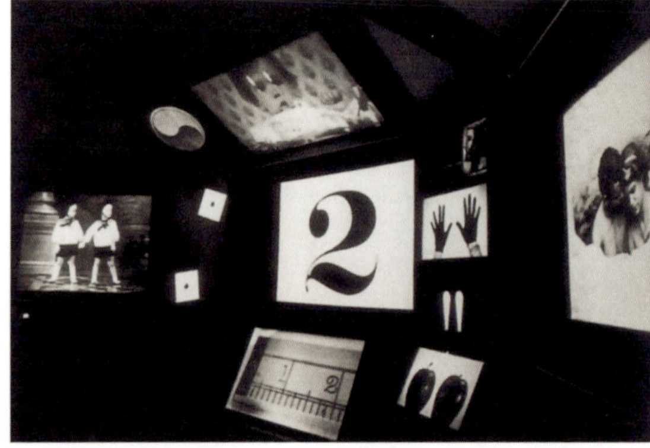

1962 New York Grand Central Station: live broadcast of Mercury launch.

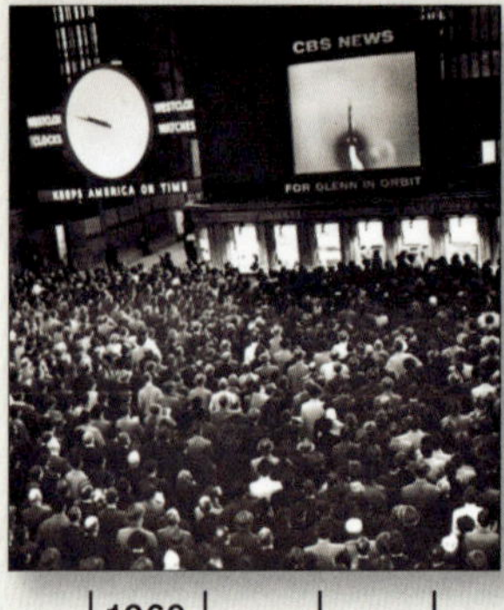

The Parallax View

With *Glimpses of the USA* (1959) and *Think* (1964) Charles and Ray Eames master the multi-screen format. As predicted by Bayer in 1930, the multiple screen is presented as both a thoroughly modern and an entirely *natural* way of looking. The Eameses speculate that the fragmentation of the screen creates an active viewer and forces the brain to reconstruct bits and pieces of data into narrative wholes.

1960

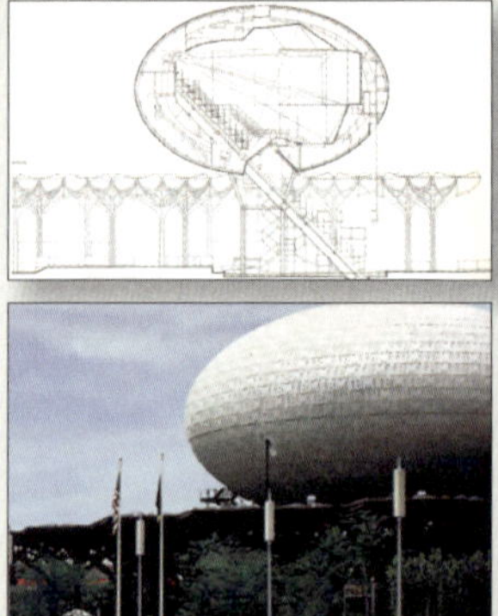

1964 New York World's Fair: IBM Pavilion housing the Eameses' multi-screen film.

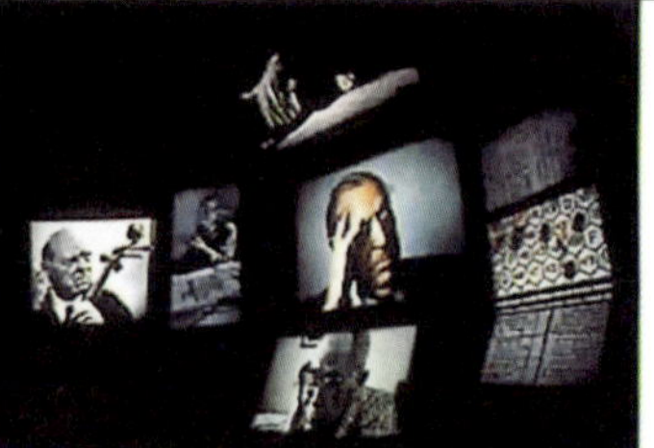

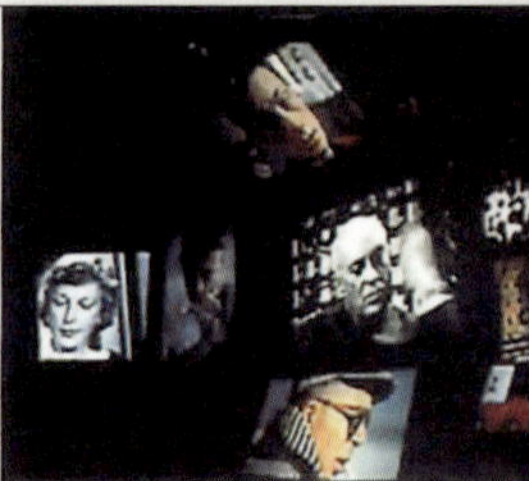

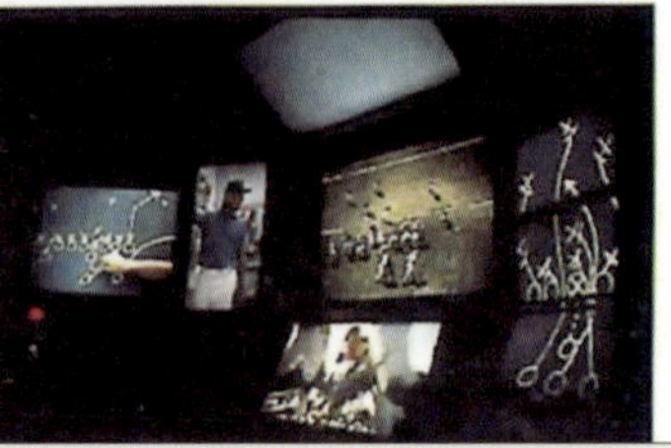

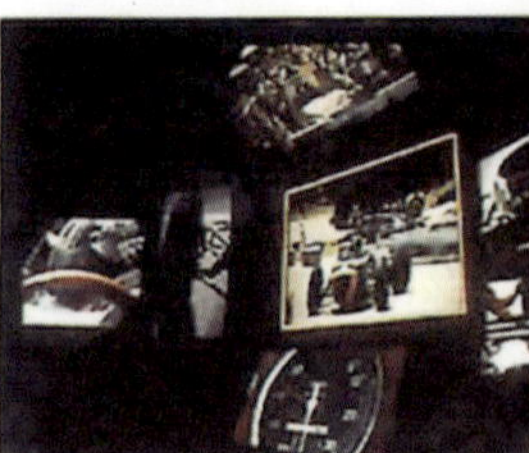

1964 Multiple iterations of the Eameses' *Think*.

1964 Kenneth Adam's design for the War Room in *Dr. Strangelove*.

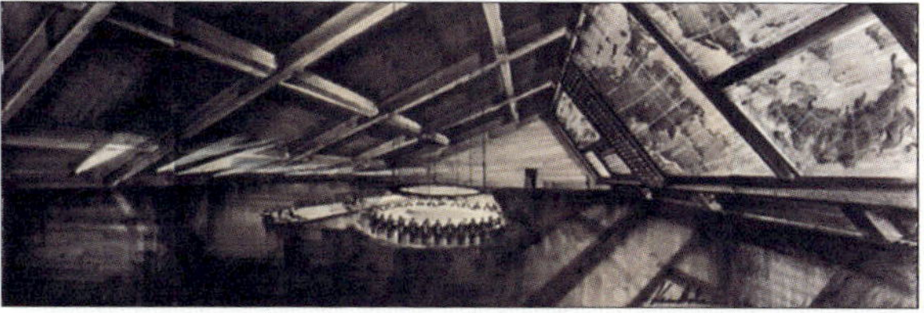

1966 Andy Warhol: *Chelsea Girls* shot in split screen.

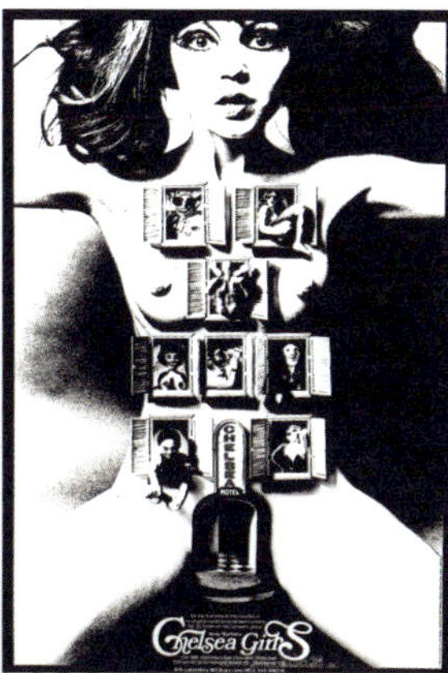

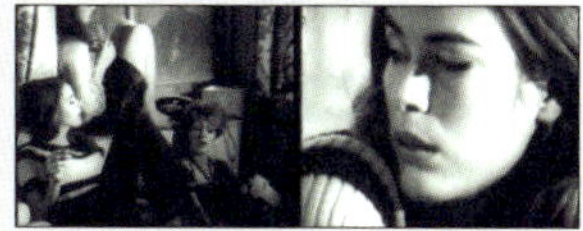

1967 Disney's *Circle-Vision 360°*.

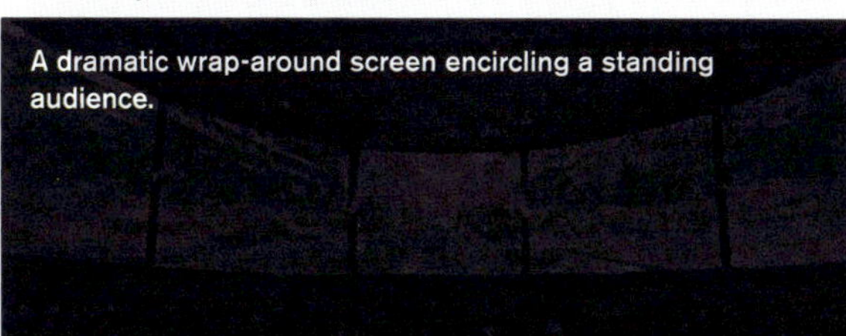

A dramatic wrap-around screen encircling a standing audience.

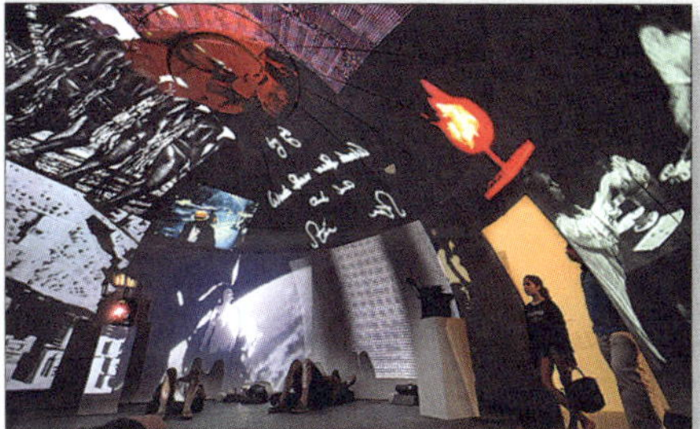

1963 Stan VanDerBeek's *Movie-Drome*. Screen merges with architecture.

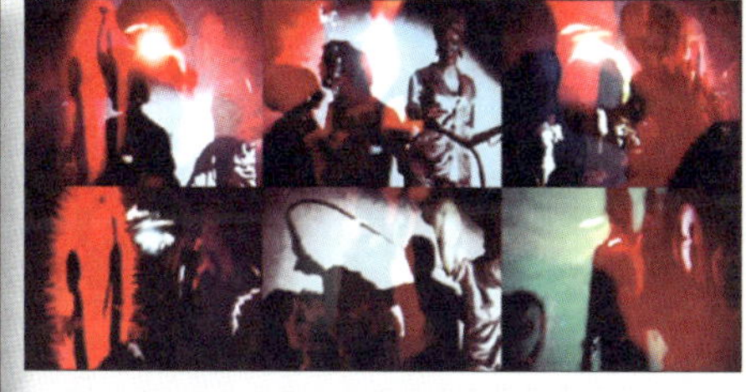

1967 Andy Warhol: *Exploding Plastic Inevitable*. Screen overtakes live performers.

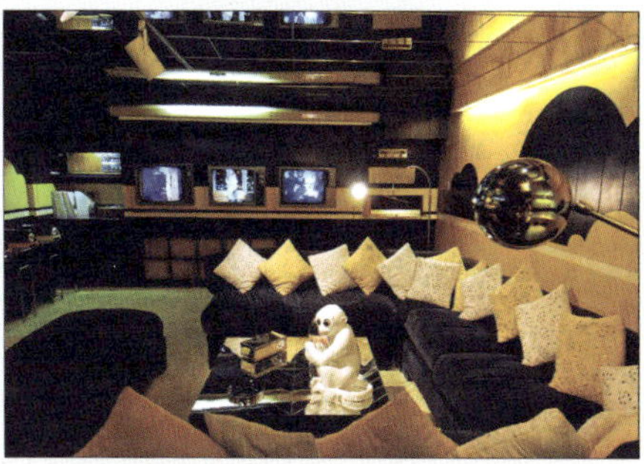

1964 Elvis Presley's living room at Graceland with multiple televisions.

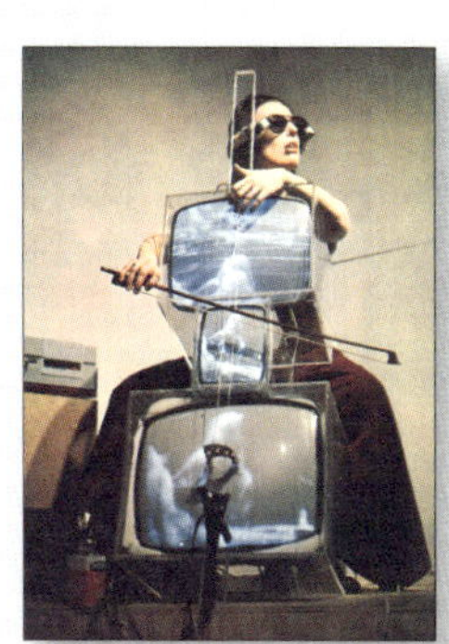

1971 Nam June Paik, *TV Cello*.

1952 Cinerama's 3-projector, super wide-screen display.

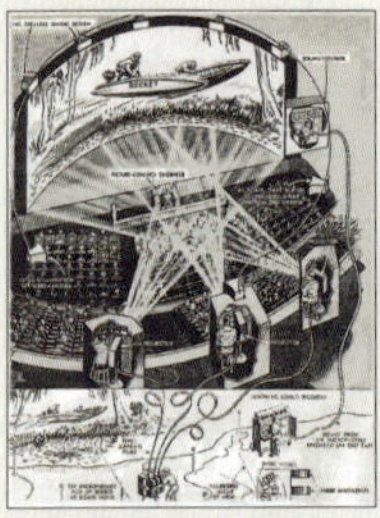

1963 Cinerama Dome opens in L.A. in Buckminster Fuller structure.

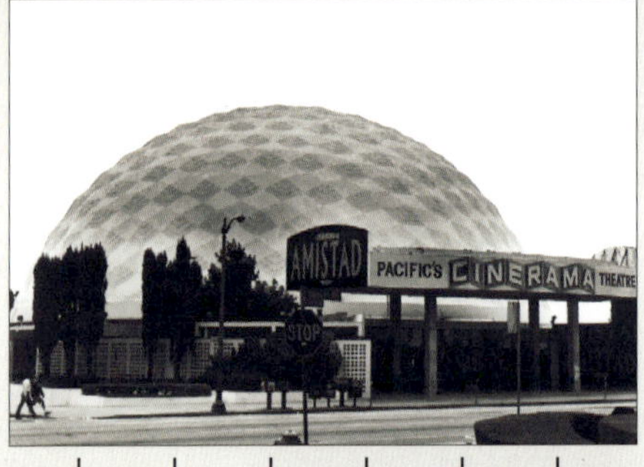

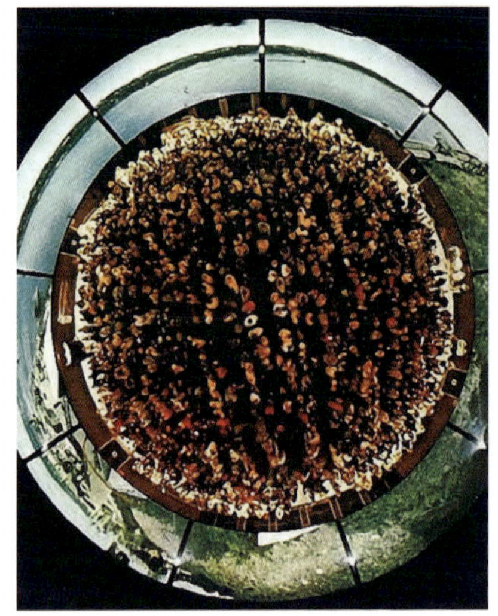

Expo

The multi-screen is a staple of the World's Fair experience. Too expensive for general application, immersion is perpetually dangled as the technique of the future, tangible but just out of reach.

1967 Expo '67: The Labyrinth.

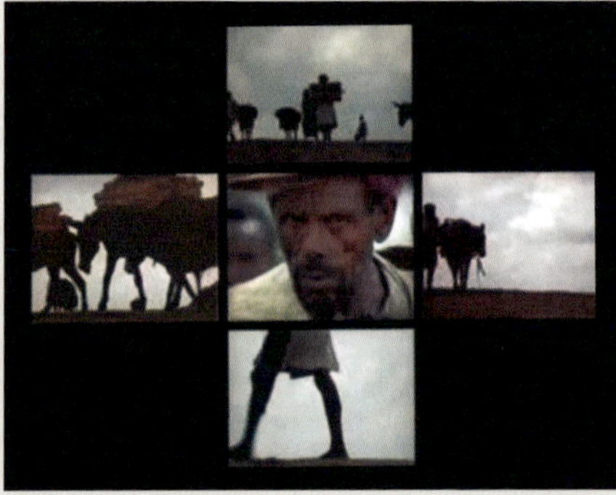

1967 Expo '67: Canadian Film Pavilion. *In the Labyrinth.*

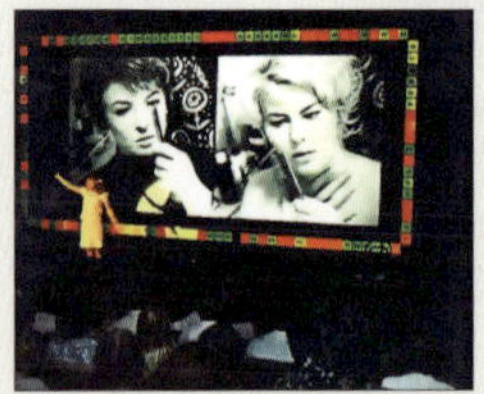

1967 Expo '67: *Kino-Automat.* Choose-your-own-adventure.

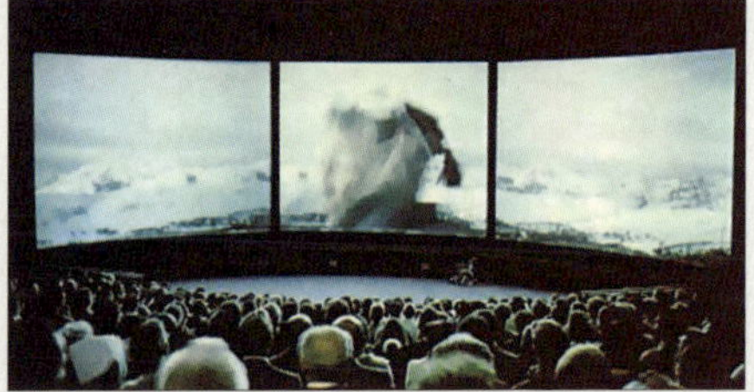

1967 Expo '67: *We Are Young.* Multi-screen projection.

1967 Expo '67: Plan of the Labyrinth theaters.

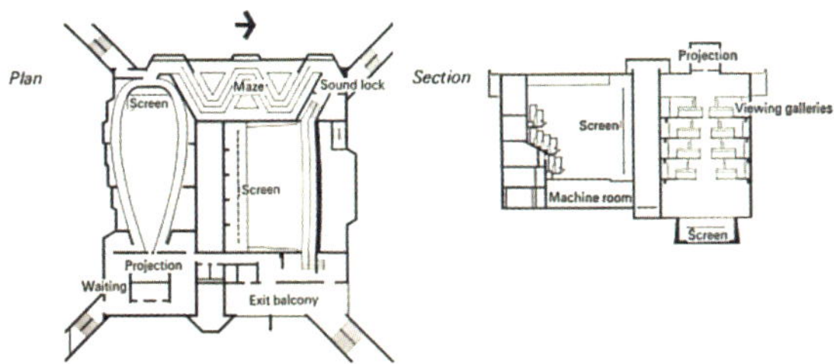

1967 Expo '67: *Polyvision.* Dispersed screen.

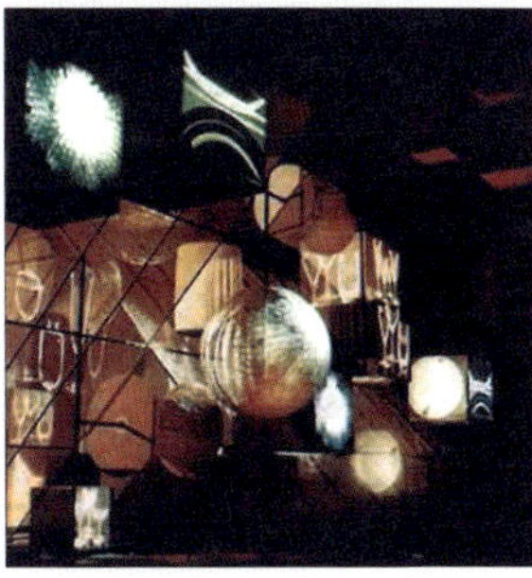

1967 Expo '67. *Polyecran.*

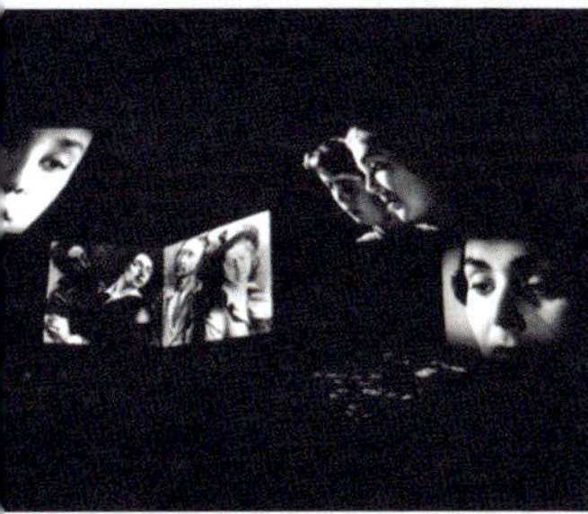

1967 Expo '67: *Polydiecran.* Fragmented screen.

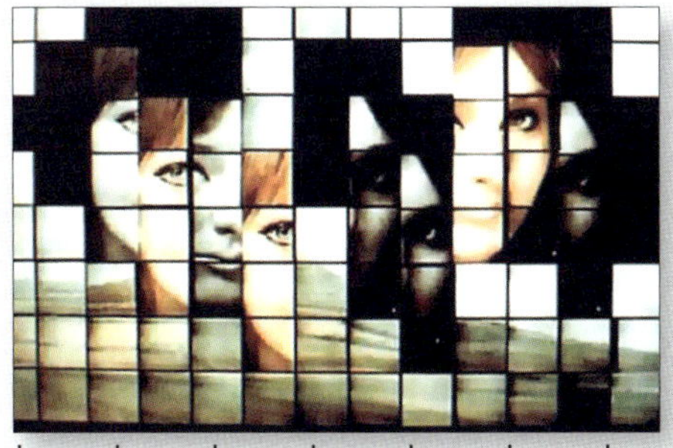

1970

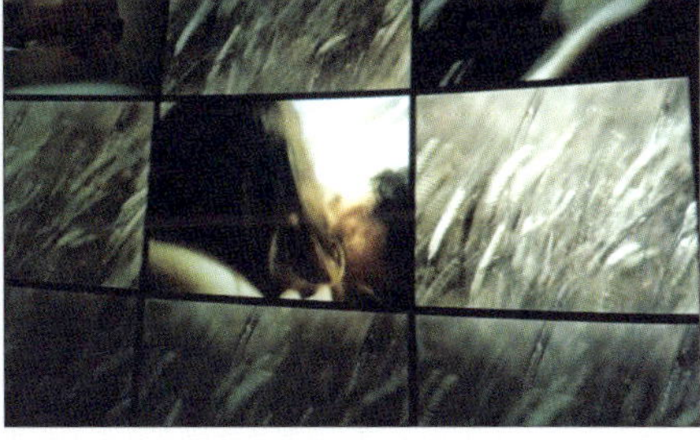

1970 Osaka '70 Expo, Fuji Group Pavilion. *Tiger Child*, precursor to the modern IMAX.

1970 Osaka '70 Expo, inflatable Fuji Group Pavilion, plan showing rotating auditorium.

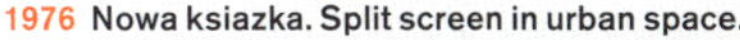

1976 Nowa ksiazka. Split screen in urban space.

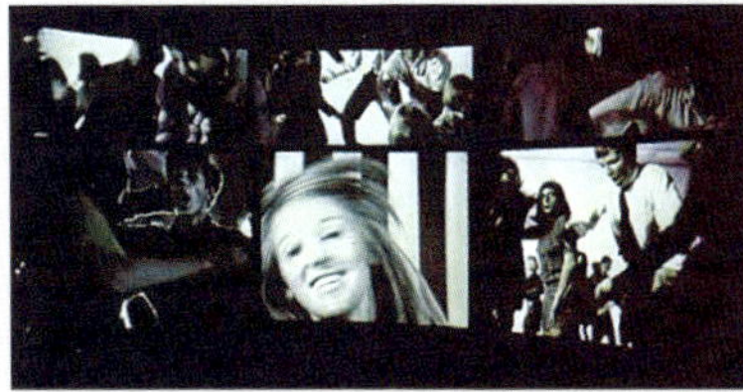

1967 Expo '67 Canadian Pacific Pavilion.

1980 Mitsubishi installs first full-color mega-screen at Dodger Stadium.

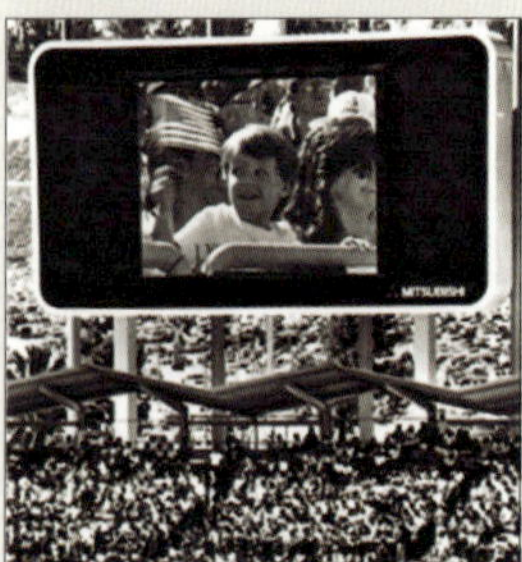

1984 *1984* in 1984. Big Brother as Big Screen.

Sequence from the film *1984*: a menancing projected image of Big Brother lording over an audience of proles.

1982 *Blade Runner*. Architecture consumed by screen.

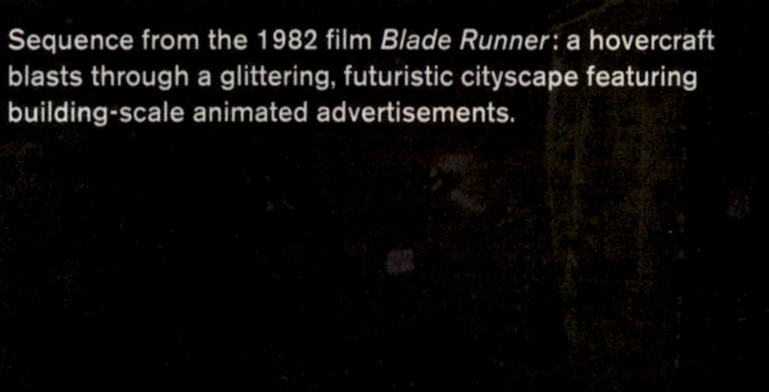

1989 Nam June Paik, *Fin de Siecle II*.

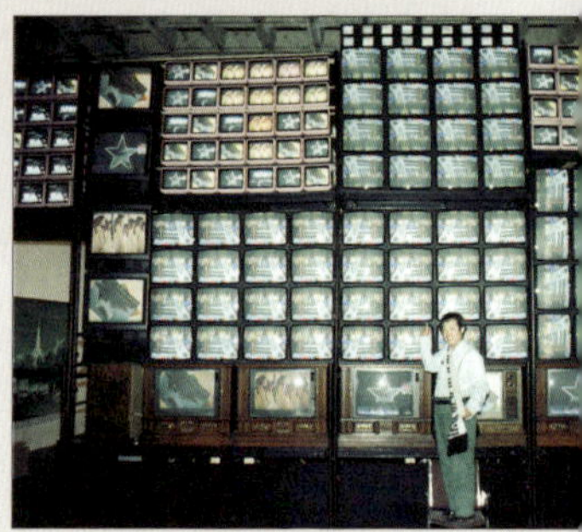

1980

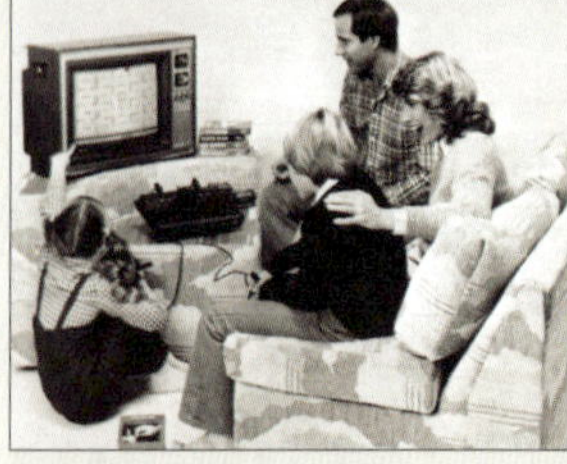

1977 Atari 2600.

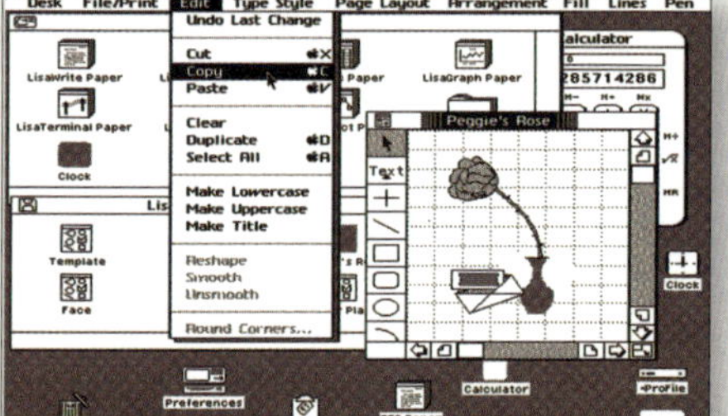

1983 Apple introduces multi-window display on the Lisa.

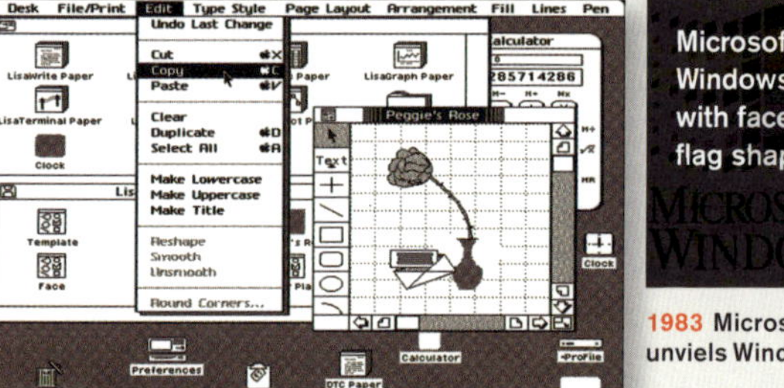

1983 Microsoft unviels Windows

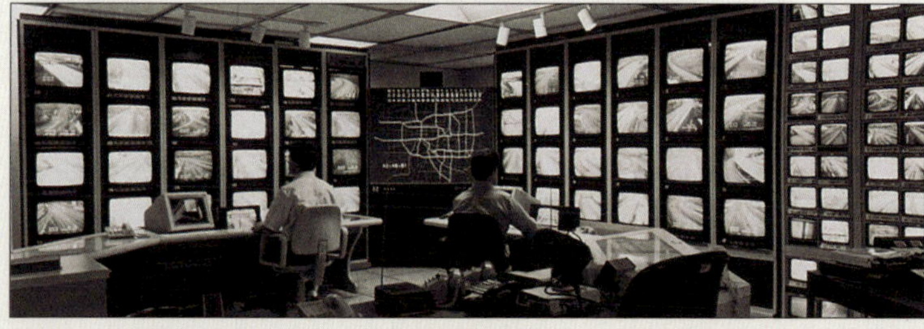

1992 The electronic panopticon.

Two sequences from Apple's 1984 advertisement introducing the Macintosh computer. The first depicts the projected image of a grim Big Brother.

The second sequence depicts a young, white-blonde woman, dressed in vaguely Olympian garb, running toward the camera carrying a giant hammer.

1984

Following the success of *Blade Runner* (with its own spectacular screens) in 1982, Ridley Scott returns in 1984 with two dystopian fantasies: the remake of Orwell's *1984* and Apple's infamous one-time-only Macintosh Superbowl advert in which a lithe Olympian unleashes a Thor-scaled hammer and crushes a gigantic screen image of a Big Brother, standing in for arch-rival IBM. The small screen (as PC) is born of the shards of the big one. The birth of the user comes at the expense of the death of the viewer.

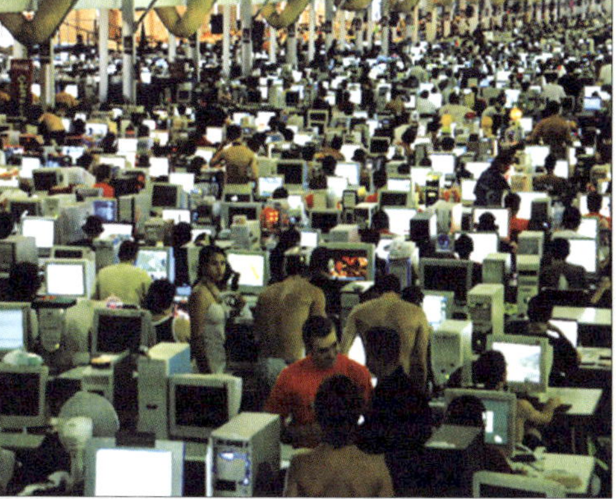

1980s Birth of the small screen.

1986 The first permanent IMAX theater is built in Vancouver.

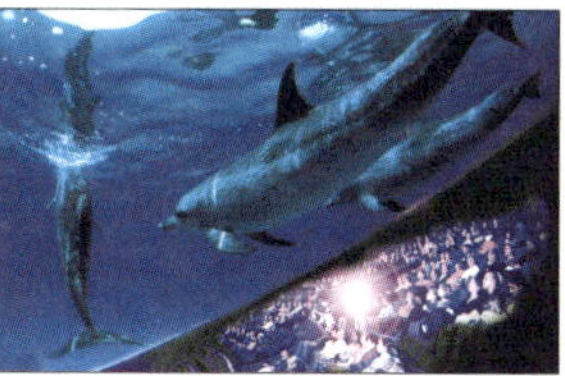

1982 Bloomberg Terminal introduced.

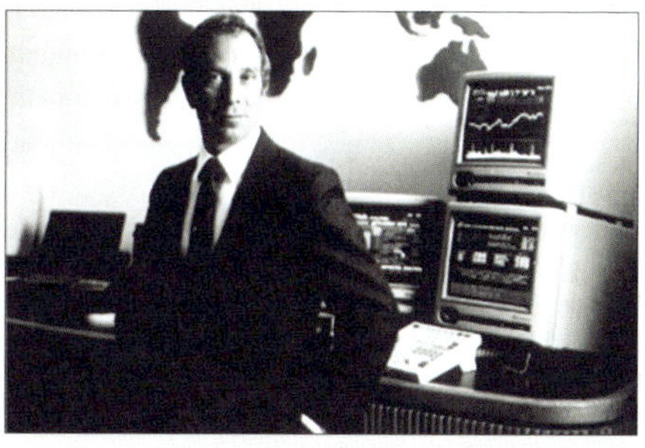

Frame from the 1987 film *Wall Street*: bond trader Charlie Sheen surrounded by a bank of computer monitors with glowing green numerals.

1987 *Wall Street*: information (screen) is power.

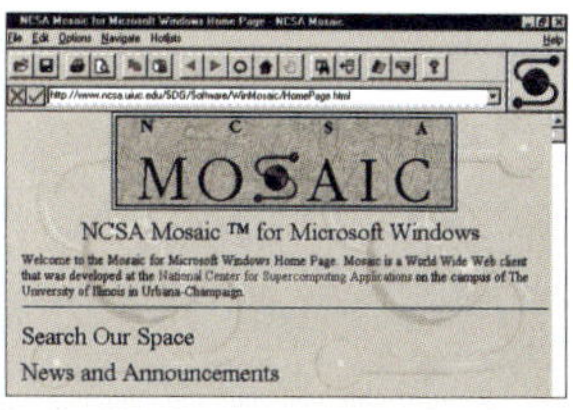

1993 NCSA Mosaic. The browser emerges.

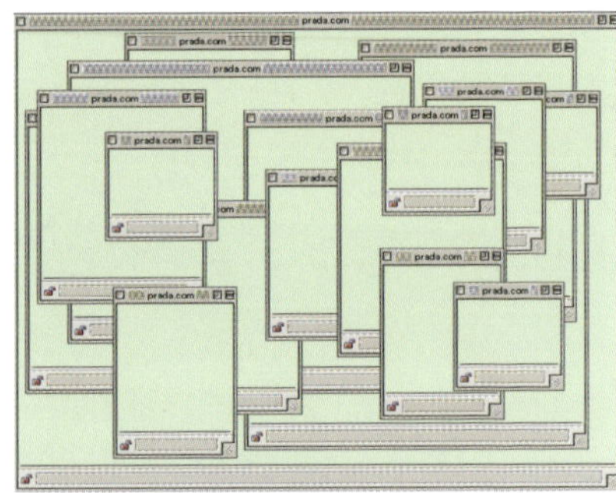

1990s Urban screenscapes.

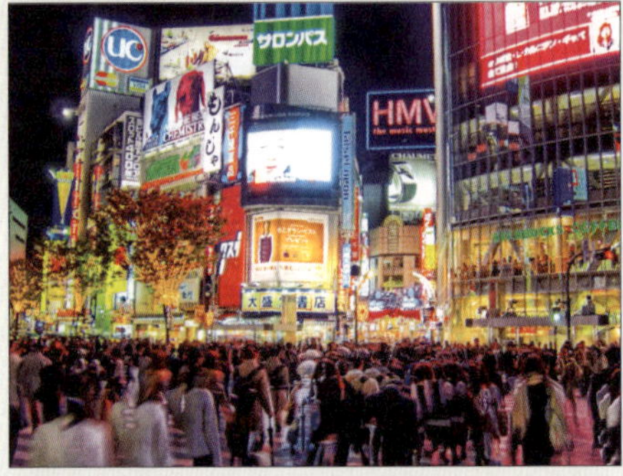

Windowscreens

If the multi-tasking window becomes the norm of interface design—each screen a panoply of more screens—browsing is miniaturized: the negotiation of windows mirrors the negotiation of space. The innovation of the smart device is relinking, wandering and browsing. The smallest screen is at once an element of the world while encapsulating the universe.

| 1990 |

Sequence from cable television: newscaster speaks to colleague framed in floating video screen.

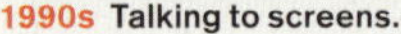

1990s Talking to screens.

Sequence from the 1999 film *The Matrix*: a solo computer jockey working in a module surrounded by a wall of video monitors.

1999 Living in *The Matrix*.

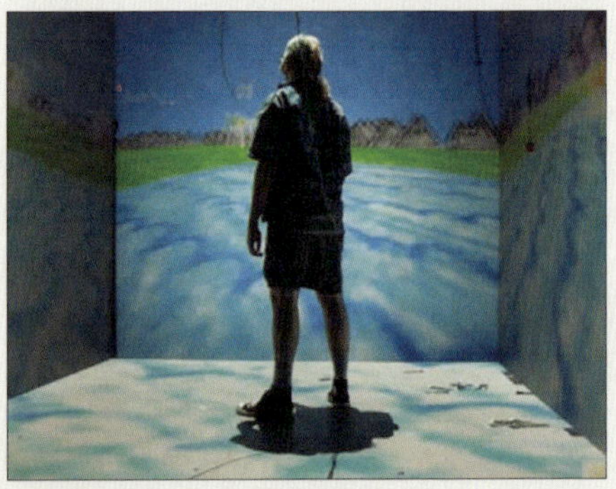

2001 CAVE (Cave Automatic Virtual Environment).

2003 *The Matrix Reloaded*: screen room.

Sequence from the 2003 film *The Matrix Reloaded*: Keanu Reeves close-up in a room entirely composed of monitors displaying images of Keanu Reeves close-up.

2002 *Minority Report*. Body-reactive screens.

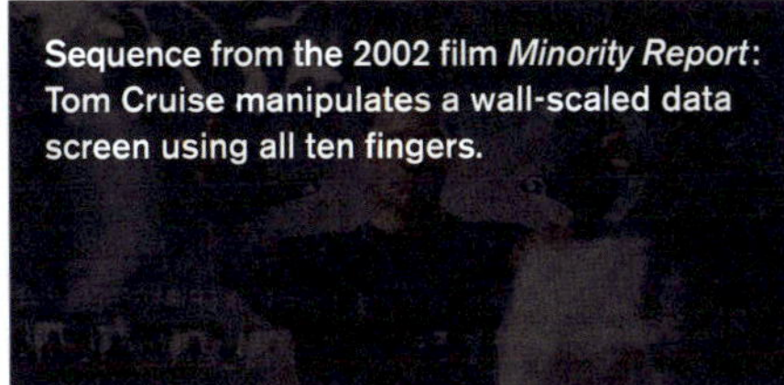

2000s Ascendance of the quants.

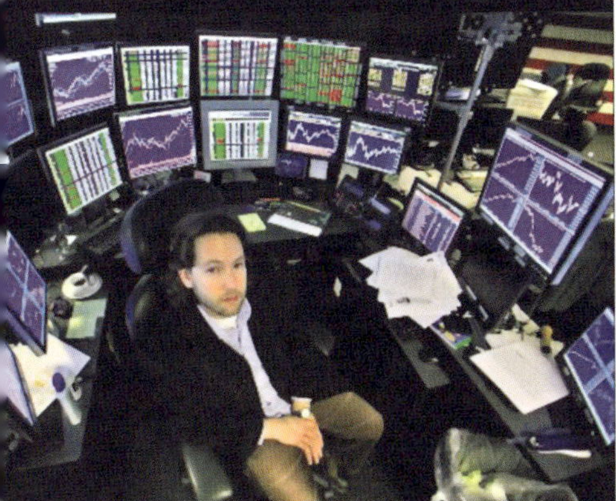

2000 *Timecode*. Simultaneous narratives in real time.

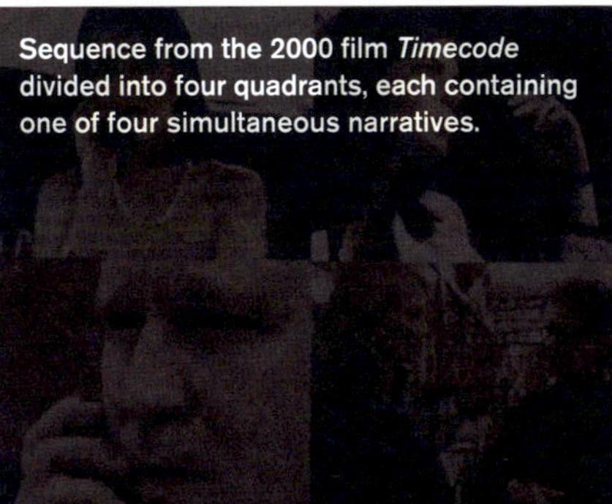

2000

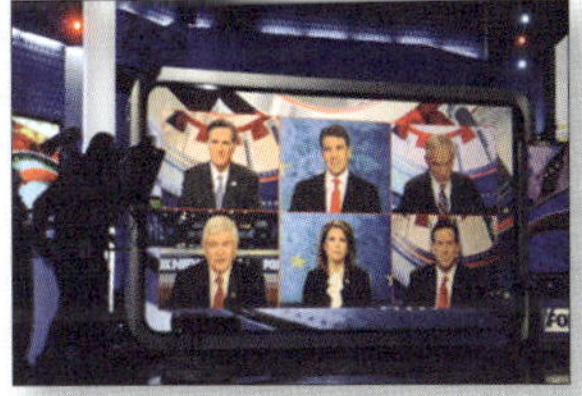

2000s Screens in screens.

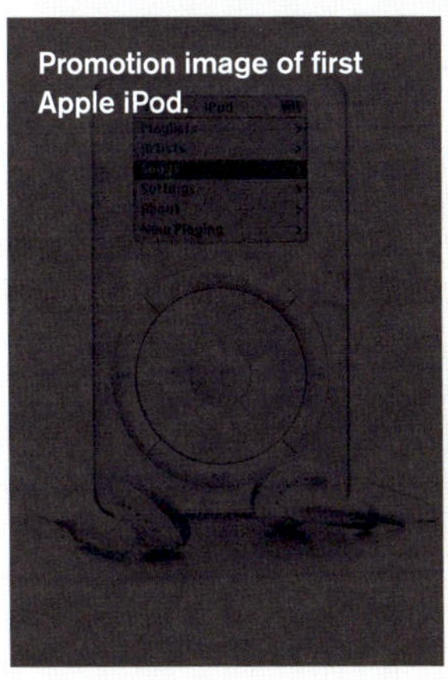

2001 iPod arrives. Screen to go.

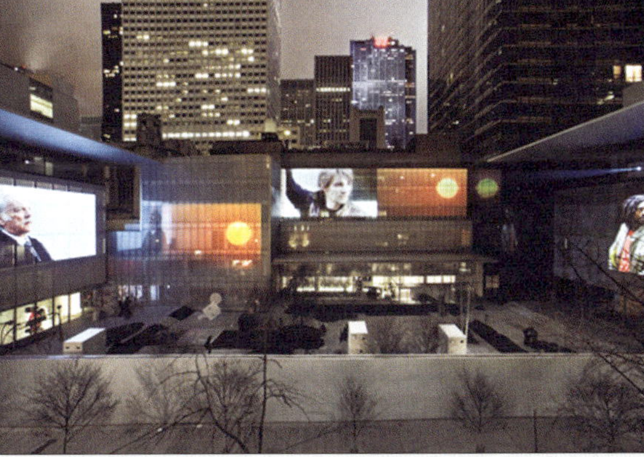

2007 Doug Aitken, *Sleepwalkers*. Simultaneous urban projections.

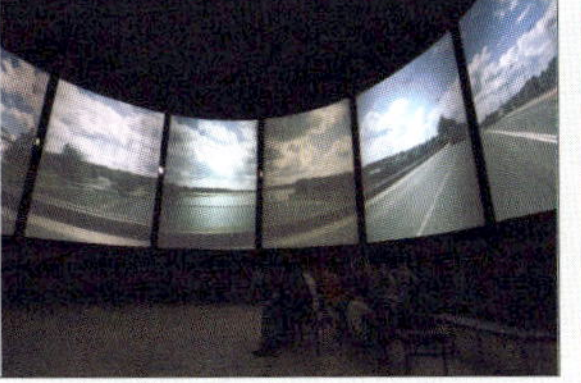

2006 Krugovaya Kinopanorama reopens in Moscow.

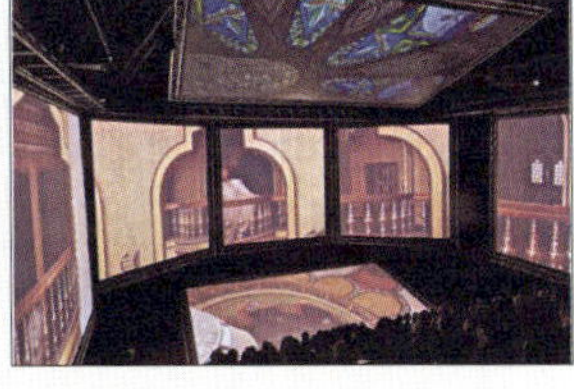

2012 Kanye West, *Cruel Summer*.

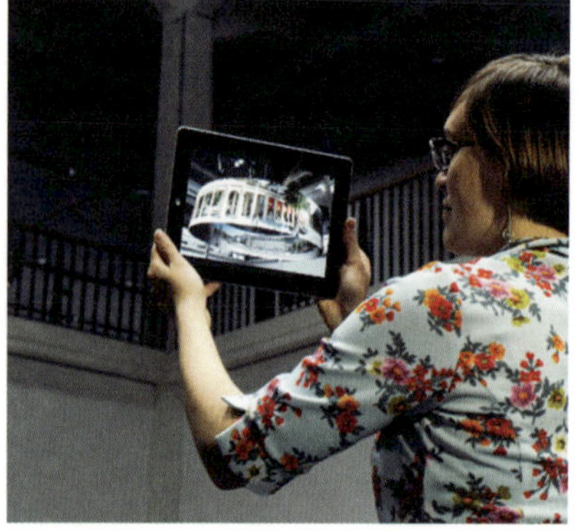

Mediation

The screen falls between the viewer and the world. Rather than presenting the world, the screen overlays it with content, a dynamic window that co-opts the world it passes through. The screen sheds its superficiality finally achieves depth.

2012 *The Avengers*. Transparent screens.

Sequence from the 2012 film *The Avengers*: two exhausted super-heroes converse through a transparent video screen.

2012 *The Avengers*. Heads-up display.

Sequence from the 2012 film *The Avengers*: depicting Robert Downey, Jr. as Iron Man with heads-up display in the visor of his super-robotic armor.

| 2010 |

Sequence from the 2008 film *Wall-E*: an obese human gliding along a corridor in a hovering lounge chair, sipping a soda and reading from a transparent video screen that floats in front of his face.

2008 *Wall-E*. Screen plus mobility.

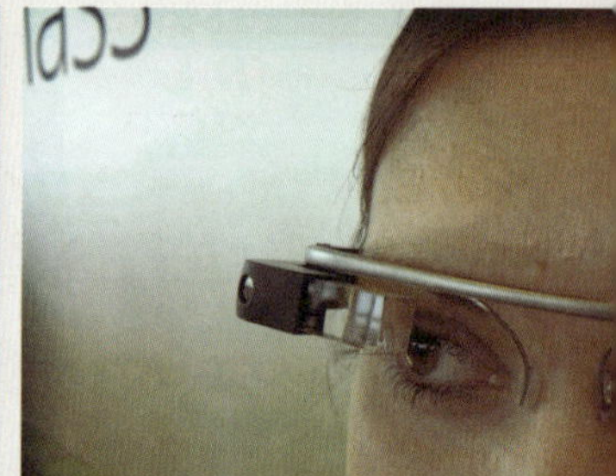

2012 Google Project Glass debut.

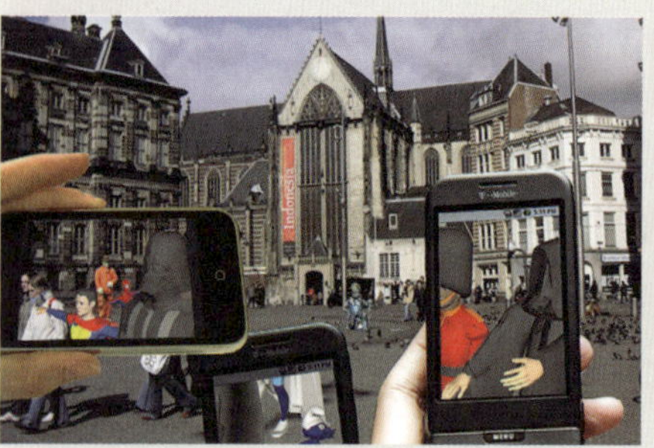

2010 Augmented reality flashmob.

Sequence from the 2010 film *Iron Man 2*: Robert Downey, Jr. as Tony Stark observes a meeting through the frame of a transparent smartphone.

2010 Screen as aperature.

IV. READERSHIP

Design works on subjects, changes behavior, shapes opinion, frames experience, negotiates relationships. As experience becomes ever more mediated, the nature of that mediation becomes key. As readers become users, they themselves have immediate impact on the object. The equilibrium between writer and reader shifts.

IF YOU DON'T SEE THE FNORD IT CAN'T EAT YOU

While typography performs its alchemical operations in broad daylight, the fnord lurks in the shadows. If type is inseparable from visuality, the fnord—a crypto-typographic element rendered invisible through systematic brainwashing—derives its power from non-presence. A non-sign, it performs the function of typography—to shade meaning—while bypassing semiotics. The fnord carries no message. It conveys only uncertainty: a vague feeling impossible to name. It is pure effect. While typography clings to the surface of language, the fnord is a self-contained virus that injects its fragment of paranoiac genetic code past the eye and directly into the brain. The fnord is the marketer's unobtainable fantasy: pure, crystalline inference.

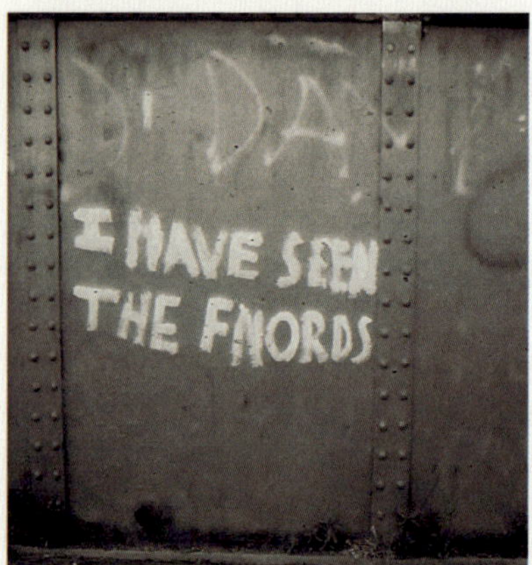

The fnord is first identified in an obscure tract titled *Principia Discordia: or How the West was Lost*—originally published in a mimeographed edition of 5, later republished and renamed *Principia Discordia or How I Found Goddess And What I Did To Her When I Found Her: The Magnum Opiate Of Malaclypse The Younger, Wherein Is Explained Absolutely Everything Worth Knowing About Absolutely Anything*. The obscure pamphlet is written—or discovered, or compiled, or invented—by an Englishman, Malaclypse The Younger (aka Greg Hill), and an American, Lord Omar Khayyam Ravenhurst (Kerry Thornley), around 1965, purportedly in New Orleans, and continues to be republished widely through various publishers and numerous websites. The original bears the anti-copyright: "Ⓚ All Rites Reversed—reprint what you like," a methodology the authors seem to practice liberally themselves.

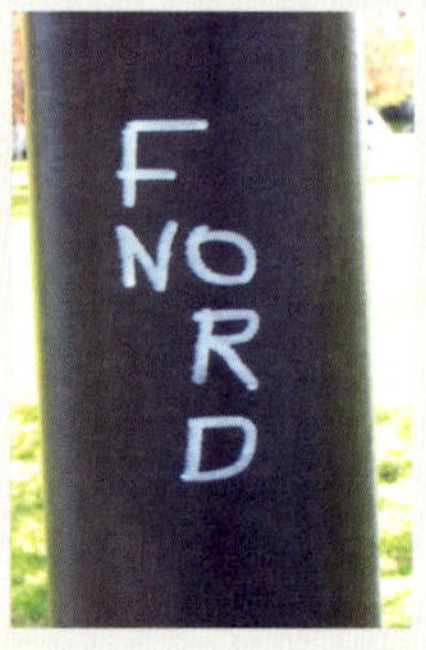

The fnord, however, remains more or less un-theorized for another decade as the *Principia Discordia* never fully articulates its sinister power. Enter Robert Anton Wilson, true prophet of Discordianism, one-time *Playboy* Forum editor, and conspiracy theorist/author dedicated to the goal of "get[ting] people into a state of generalized agnosticism, not agnosticism about

God alone but agnosticism about everything." In 1975 Wilson and co-writer Robert Shea publish "The Eye in the Pyramid," volume one of *The Illuminatus! Trilogy*, their so-called fairy tale for paranoids. Wilson theorizes the fnord as a fully typographic element embedded in all mass-media texts by the Illuminati—a super-secret and all-powerful transnational organization—in a worldwide brainwashing campaign code-named Operation Mindfuck.

"Very nice," I said. "But why did you bring me up here?"

"It's time for you to see the fnords," he replied. Then I woke up in bed and it was the next morning. I made breakfast in a pretty nasty mood, wondering if I'd seen the fnords, whatever the hell they were, in the hours he had blacked out, or if I would see them as soon as I went out into the street. I had some pretty gruesome ideas about them, I must admit. Creatures with three eyes and tentacles, survivors from Atlantis, who walked among us, invisible due to some form of mind shield, and did hideous work for the Illuminati. It was unnerving to contemplate, and I finally gave in to my fears and peeked out the window, thinking it might be better to see them from a distance first.

Nothing. Just ordinary sleepy people, heading for their buses and subways.

That calmed me a little, so I set out the toast and coffee and fetched the New York Times *from the hallway. I turned the radio to WBAI and caught some good Vivaldi, sat down, grabbed a piece of toast and started skimming the first page.*

Then I saw the fnords.

The feature story involved another of the endless squabbles between Russia and the U.S. in the UN General Assembly, and after each direct quote from the Russian delegate I read a quite distinct "Fnord!" The second lead was about a debate in Congress on getting the troops out of Costa Rica; every argument presented by Senator Bacon was followed by another "Fnord!" At the bottom of the page was a Times *depth-type study of the growing pollution problem and the increasing use of gas masks among New Yorkers; the most distressing chemical facts were interpolated with more "Fnords."*

Suddenly I saw Hagbard's eyes burning into me and heard his voice: "Your heart will remain calm. Your adrenalin gland will remain calm. Calm, all-over calm. You will not panic. You will look at the fnord and see it. You will not evade it or black it out. You will stay calm and face it." And further back, way back: my first-grade teacher writing FNORD on the blackboard, while a wheel with a spiral design turned and turned on his desk, turned and turned, and his voice droned on, IF YOU DON'T SEE THE FNORD IT CAN'T EAT YOU, DON'T SEE THE FNORD, DON'T SEE THE FNORD . . .

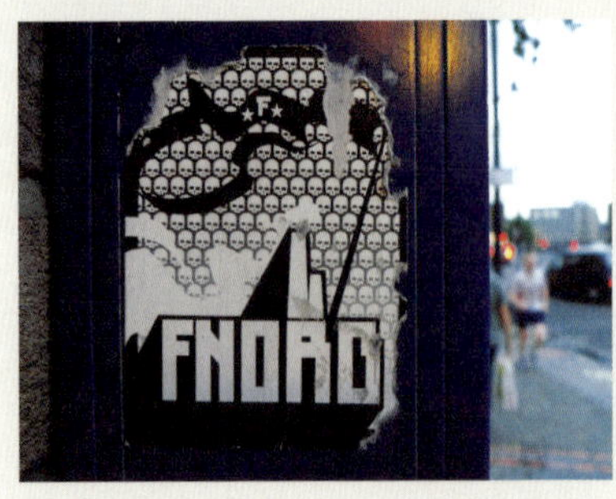

The brilliance of the fnord is its very invisibility. Children are taught from birth by their Illuminati overlords to not-see them. (In fact, fnord itself is a stand-in as no one is able to recognize the actual name.) The non-element, even while rendered invisible by the reader's own mind, is still read. Erasing its visibility sublimates the function of the typography. Through powerful associations embedded in the subconscious mind of the reader, the fnord triggers a vague but visceral feeling of dread and confusion that shades the rational consideration of the text. Fnords purportedly riddle the texts of every book, newpaper and magazine, thereby linking all information with sensations of fear and uncertainty:

This was one step beyond Pavlov, I realized. The first conditioned reflex was to experience the panic reaction (the activation syndrome, it's technically called) whenever encountering the word "fnord." The second conditioned reflex was to black out what happened, including the word itself, and just to feel a general low-grade emergency without knowing why. And the third step, of course, was to attribute this anxiety to the news stories, which were bad enough in themselves anyway. Of course, the essence of control is fear. The fnords produced a whole population walking around in chronic low-grade emergency, tormented.

The one place fnords do not appear is in advertisements. "That was part of the gimmick, too: only in consumption, endless consumption, could they escape the amorphous threat of the invisible fnords." Thus by the simple presence or absence of fnords, all humans are unsettled by actual content while being drawn to and soothed by the vapidity of advertising. Since the reading of the fnord bypasses language, it is perhaps the most direct of all typographic characters. Without the filter of decoding, the figure itself is linked directly to sensation. The brain is rendered defenseless.

This fantasy of the subliminal graphic gesture that eludes the filter of the conscious mind is one of the most enduring design tropes of our time. The fnord shares a bond with George Orwell's Newspeak—reprogrammed language hammered into the brains of the proles until the resistant mind finally submits (2+2=5)—or with the murderous instructions embedded in Richard Condon's "Manchurian Candidate." But while Wilson's vision predicts a fnordic infestation of editorial content, the "real" epidemic emerges from the one place Discordian theory assumes is safe: Advertising.

In 1957 James Vicary, a Madison Avenue market researcher, announces a new form of advertising: subliminal projection. Vicary has repurposed a device that can flash images at a speed unrecognizable by the conscious human brain—as fast as 1/3000th of a second—to project messages onto a movie screen. This tachistoscope allows Vicary to strobe suggestive advertising suggestions between the frames of feature films. He proclaims he has tested the device on unsuspecting teenagers in a movie theater in Fort Lee, New Jersey, with a resulting 18% increase in Coca Cola sales and a whopping 58% increase in popcorn transactions at the concession counter. "This innocent little technique," he preens, "is going to sell a hell of a lot of goods."

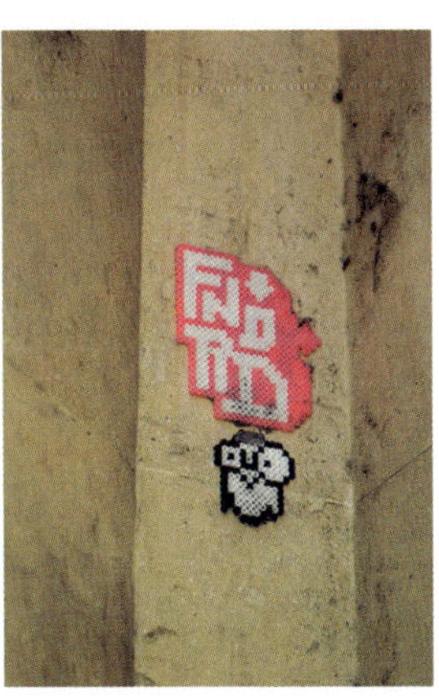

When Vicary's claims are made the public uproar is immediate: suddenly the shadowy tools associated with totalitarian mind-control—a real-life Operation MindFuck—are being deployed in America, not by subversives but by American marketers, reprogramming American children into cola-guzzling, popcorn-gorging robots. The CIA swoops in and conducts a super-secret investigation into Vicary's ominous new technology to determine if they have been pre-empted in the mind-control racket. Perhaps the Spooks fear the 42-year-old Madman is encroaching on their territory.

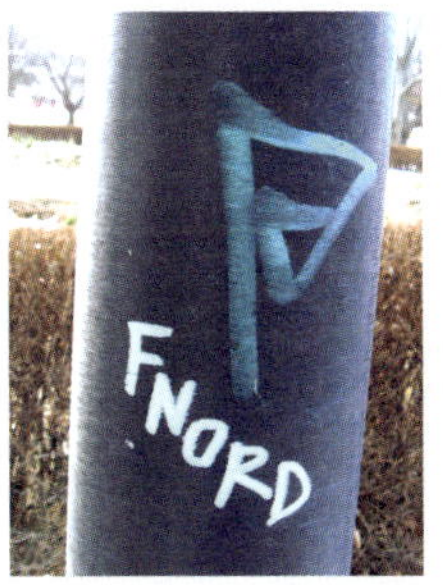

Almost immediately a counter-attack is launched. The leader is magazine writer and sometime social critic Vance Packard, author of a wide range of popular journalism with titles such as "How to Pick a Mate" and "Animal IQ." After losing his day job when Collier's Magazine folds in 1956, Packard devotes himself full time to an exposé of the secret techniques of the advertising and consumer motivational research industry. "The Hidden Persuaders" is a bombshell. Packard proclaims, "We are being monitored, managed and manipulated outside our conscious awareness by advertisers and marketers." Packard claims admen exploit a cluster of eight compelling human needs so basic to our very being that the desire for their satisfaction is an overwhelming force. The combination of Packard's articulation of modern advertising's hidden technology and the urban lore surrounding Vicary's tachistoscope firmly establishes the concept of subliminal advertising in the minds of a fearful public.

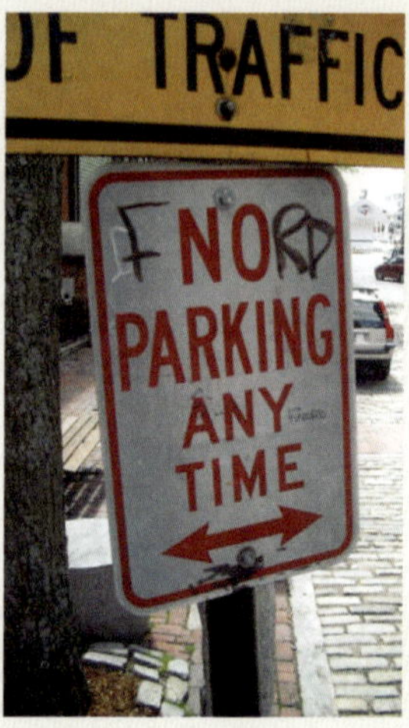

Outside our conscious awareness is the operative concept, the eerie notion of some grey-flannelled cabal tapping directly into the brain of unwitting Americans as they flip through fashion magazines and browse the aisles of their local supermarkets. Packard and Vicary suggest that perception without awareness is actually more efficacious, and more subversive, than normal perception. The very idea of such subconscious appeals seems to be an assault on Liberty, simply un-American in its usurption of the basic rights of free citizens to make decisions for themselves. Can we have a democracy if we are not truly free thinkers? The technology carries enough of the ominous overtone of totalitarian suppression to fit neatly into the feverish anti-Communist rhetoric of the time and enough potential to inspire an emerging generation of young political operatives to wonder: How can we use these techniques to win elections?

The outrage and unsavory interest generated by these emerging techniques compels the U.S. Senate to launch an official investigation: our children are at risk, after all. Cornered, Vicary is pressed to reveal his secrets. He is unable to reproduce his purported findings and later confesses, if somewhat ambiguously, that he has never actually performed his movie-theater experiment: it was, in fact, all a publicity stunt to launch a new market-research company. The government inquiry fails to turn up any evidence to suggest advertisers were really experimenting with mind-control techniques. But while the initial furor dies down, the basic concept—that we are under constant assault by the invisible—is firmly embedded.

The essence of the invisibility thesis is that some mechanized process is methodically manipulating the actions, habits and thoughts of a vast, unsuspecting public. Such a conspiracy is extremely useful to describe the inexplicable events of the modern consumerism. In the early '60s Columbia professor Richard Hofstadter applies the theory to the political movement surrounding the campaign of Barry Goldwater in what he calls "The Paranoid Style in American Politics." "The central image [of the paranoid style] is that of a vast and sinister conspiracy, a gigantic and yet subtle machinery of influence set in motion to undermine and destroy a way of life." Rampant consumerism and the seeming dissolution of traditional values have to have a reason—other than avarice—and subversive advertising is cast as the dark force at work.

In 1973 the issue comes bursting back, with a new twist, when a young Canadian psychologist, Wilson Bryan Key, unleashes a blockbuster trade paperback titled "Subliminal Seduction: Ad Media's Manipulation of Not So Innocent America." The title encapsulates the whole paranoid fantasy with an innovation: Seduction. Apparently America is not so innocent after all. The clearly libidinal overtone suggests the affair between advertiser and citizen might be more complicit than previously understood. The cover features a benign-looking photograph of a cocktail overprinted with the question: Are You Being Sexually Aroused by This Picture? Apparently we are: the book causes an immediate sensation and sells over a million copies in the first year. The author emerges as a cross between media sensation and me-generation guru. He has unlocked the secret world of advertising and the black arts of selling, and the key to everything is: sex.

Key's revelation is that advertisers are secretly slipping sexual imagery into the shadows of advertising photographs, thereby warping the collective subconscious of American consumers. Wherever he looks, he finds sex—breasts, phalluses, orgies, obscenities. He sends millions of pubescent kids on a frenzied search for hidden erotica in the matted fur of the cigarette-pack dromedary. In subsequent books Key identifies increasingly explicit images in the most unlikely places from the word SEX embossed into the surface of Ritz crackers to an elaborate, tangled orgy woven into in a photograph of a plate of fried clams. Nabisco and Howard Johnson's will, apparently, stop at nothing to make us consume.

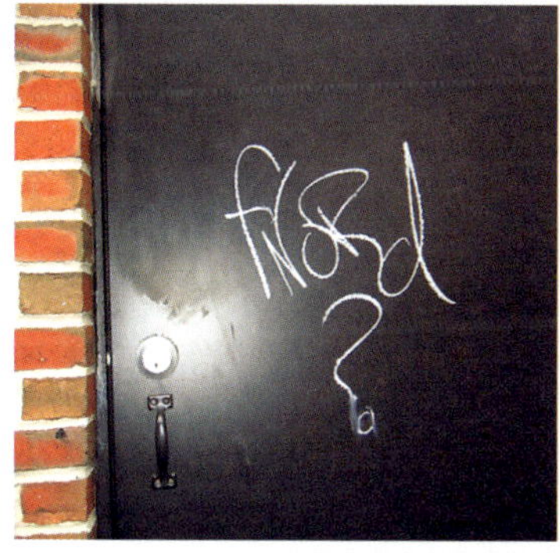

Key contributes an important new dimension to the conspiracy discourse. The weak point in the human firewall is sexual insecurity. Apparently the sexual revolution failed and post-Summer-of-Love Americans are as repressed as ever. Key's fnord is the phallus, and Packard's eight compelling needs can be boiled down to the big one. If Americans can't understand their own manic consumerist tendencies, Key gives them an easy out. It's not their fault; they have secretly been seduced. Belief in the efficacy of the sexually charged image proves to be another wrinkle in an indelible urban myth.

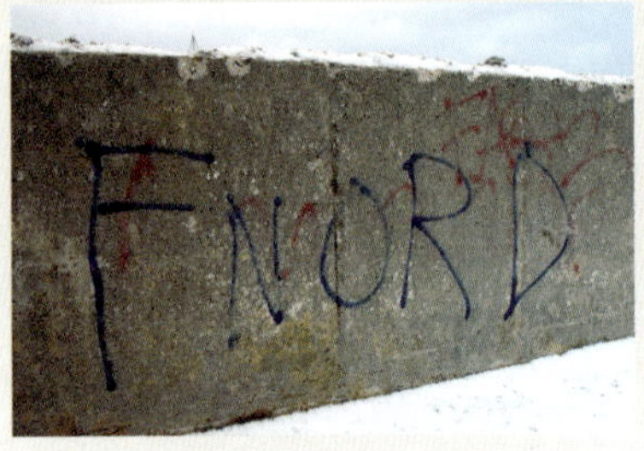

A decade later John Carpenter revives the fantasy in his B-movie classic, "They Live," wherein an unsuspecting citizen—played by professional wrestler Rowdy Roddy Piper—stumbles on a mysterious pair of sunglasses that reveal the conspiracy lurking in ad media. As with Wilson's fnords and Key's ice cubes, Carpenter's sublimated messages are typographic and occupy a layer just behind the glossy surfaces of the advertising world. The totalitarian infiltration is replaced by a new menace—space aliens—but the technique is the same: surreptitious mind control. The message is present yet invisible.The world is not as it seems. Our brains are unequal to the challenges of the manipulators. That Carpenter can deploy the subliminal advertising message so effortlessly reveals how widely the basic principle has penetrated the mind of the public. Our consciousness-raising is complete. This hermeneutic image of the world, this sense that a real message is obscured or latent, hidden by a false façade designed to obscure rather than reveal, has a long and storied history—Hofstader starts his investigation in the 17th century and Dan Brown starts somewhat earlier—but the advertising twist is a thoroughly modern incarnation. One might be compelled to see the image-world as a kind of dream state, a psycho-analytic condition where visual images are obscure symbols of something always just out of our perceptual field. It follows then that a careful analysis of the visual image could decode the hidden message and unlock real meaning. The properly trained analyst could make sense of the latent world through a careful study of the surface.

The endurance of such myths constitute an ad hoc conspiracy theory of design—we are unconscious victims of some hidden force put into action by an invisible source—and suggests a public fearful about the way commercial forces exert power. Fredric Jameson defines conspiracy theory as a "degraded attempt to think the impossible totality of the contemporary world system." If the world feels fractured and illogical, if we don't even understand our own desires and compunctions, a conspiracy theory gets all the pieces to fall neatly into place. Advertising is about efficacy and the transmission of message, applying communicative force to achieve some measurable end: higher sales, more votes, more fans. Conspiracy theory explains its sinister success. It suggests a communication so pure and surgical it bypasses interpretation. As visual communicators, our only argument against conspiracy theory is to announce with all sincerity our own haplessness: *Don't worry, we're not really that powerful.* And of course nothing confirms the truth of a conspiracy more effectively than its passionate denial.

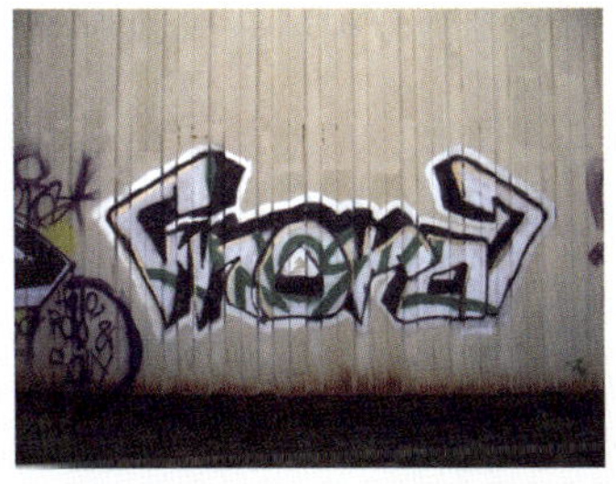

But if you look at the half-century between Vicary and today, conspiracy theory may be the most prevalent theory of design. Consider official Soviet Politburo photographs wherein figures mysteriously appear and disappear, depending on political standing, a condition exacerbated by the ease with which the emergence of Photoshop® has rendered such photographic manipulations possible. Or the subversive effect the retouched bodies of fashion models is understood to have on the psyches of adolescent women. Or the "reading" of architecture as literal messages encoded in buildings. Or product placement in popular movies and television shows, wherein advertising is naturalized in the narrative. Or the analysis of language itself to find inherent biases embedded therein: the emergence of the title Ms. in the seventies was, after all, an attempt to unravel the patriarchal conspiracy of language. Or the railing of the right against the coercive operations of everything from "feminazis" and "ecofascists" to a perceived "radical homosexual agenda." Or the now commonly accepted practice of allowing vast software networks to sift silently through personal computer databases and emails and surreptitiously modify the on-line environment to more efficiently separate us from our cash. All of these have at their core the assumption that there is a sub rosa process at work to skew perception and bend the will of the reader by way of some hidden strategy enacted by some absent power.

"All political behavior requires strategy," Hofstader tells us, "many strategic acts depend for their effect upon a period of secrecy, and anything that is secret can be described, often with but little exaggeration, as conspiratorial. The distinguishing thing about the paranoid style is not that its exponents see conspiracies and plots here and there in history, but that they regard a 'vast' or 'gigantic' conspiracy as the motive force in historical events." And in that it involves the manipulation of content for effect, what is design if not political or strategic?

Which brings us back to typography. Writing for a *New York Times* blog, photography theorist and filmmaker Errol Morris enacts a simple experiment. He asks readers to read a short text, then respond about the perceived veracity of the passage. Unbeknownst to the subject, the texts are presented in six different typefaces. Analyzing the results, Morris finds a clear correlation between typography and the perception of truth of the texts. Apparently we have been involved in a five-hundred-year-old typographic conspiracy without ever realizing it.

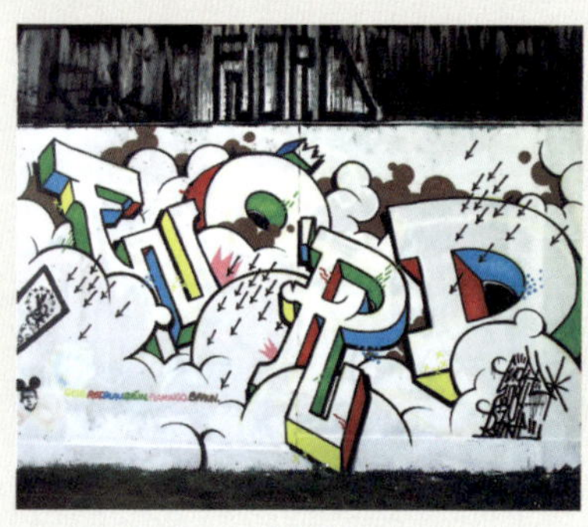

Conspiracy suggests there is, somewhere, an adequate rationale for the sensation of dislocation and suppression of contemporary life on one hand, and the elusive meaning of modernist abstraction on the other, a power that can be felt but not framed. To this day you can find "Fnord" or "I can see the Fnords" tagged on walls, bridges and road signs. Luckily a group called Software Solutions For The Betterment Of Mankind, Ltd. now offers a "Fnord Finder" that promises to "reverse decades of Illuminati mind control [and] to expose the fnords buried in *New York Times* articles." This handy tool is built into the Google Chrome browser—one of the most pernicious information-gathering tools ever devised—and is simple to operate: "When reading a story on nytimes.com, just click the 'F' icon in the upper right of your address bar to find and expose the fnords." In case you were worried, SSFTBOM is "Not affiliated with the *New York Times* or the Illuminated Seers of Bavaria."

If the fnord is the typography of that hidden power, to see the fnords is to fight back. Vision is an act of resistance. The ability to re-visualize the invisible character is to break outside the network of control that links us all. To claim sight is to be inured to the power of suggestion. To be free we must learn to see again.

WIRED DICTIONARY: LEXICONOGRAPHY

WITH IRWIN CHEN

> The composition of vast books is a laborious and impoverishing extravagance. To go on for five hundred pages developing an idea whose perfect oral exposition is possible in a few minutes!
> —Jorge Luis Borges,
> Prologue to *The Garden of Forking Paths*

Typographers manipulate words and letters all day long. Text is a crude slurry poured into page templates and then, through a series of winnowing operations, shaped into compositions. Typography is a plastic art.

We expect authors to write the words we will form into pages, and we expect those words to be chosen and arranged to create a specific effect. The author is saying something (or trying to); the typographer enhances or intensifies that effort (or doesn't). But words themselves have a way of revealing or belying the author's intention. Suppose the process was run in reverse? Could the unraveling of printed pages uncover hidden desires?

The premise of *The Wired Dictionary*, a 300+ page lexicon of every word used in the first ten years of *Wired* Magazine, is that an underlying, subconscious textual intent may be revealed through the simple metric of word frequency. If words are the dream-work of the magazine—abundant and interconnected subjects, verbs and nouns strung together—the word-counting algorithm is the psychiatrist who discerns the magazine's true meaning.

A magazine is the product of the collision of many minds and voices, an act of collective will. While the significance and use of particular words may vary among individual writers, the entire corpus of a magazine's output filtered through a

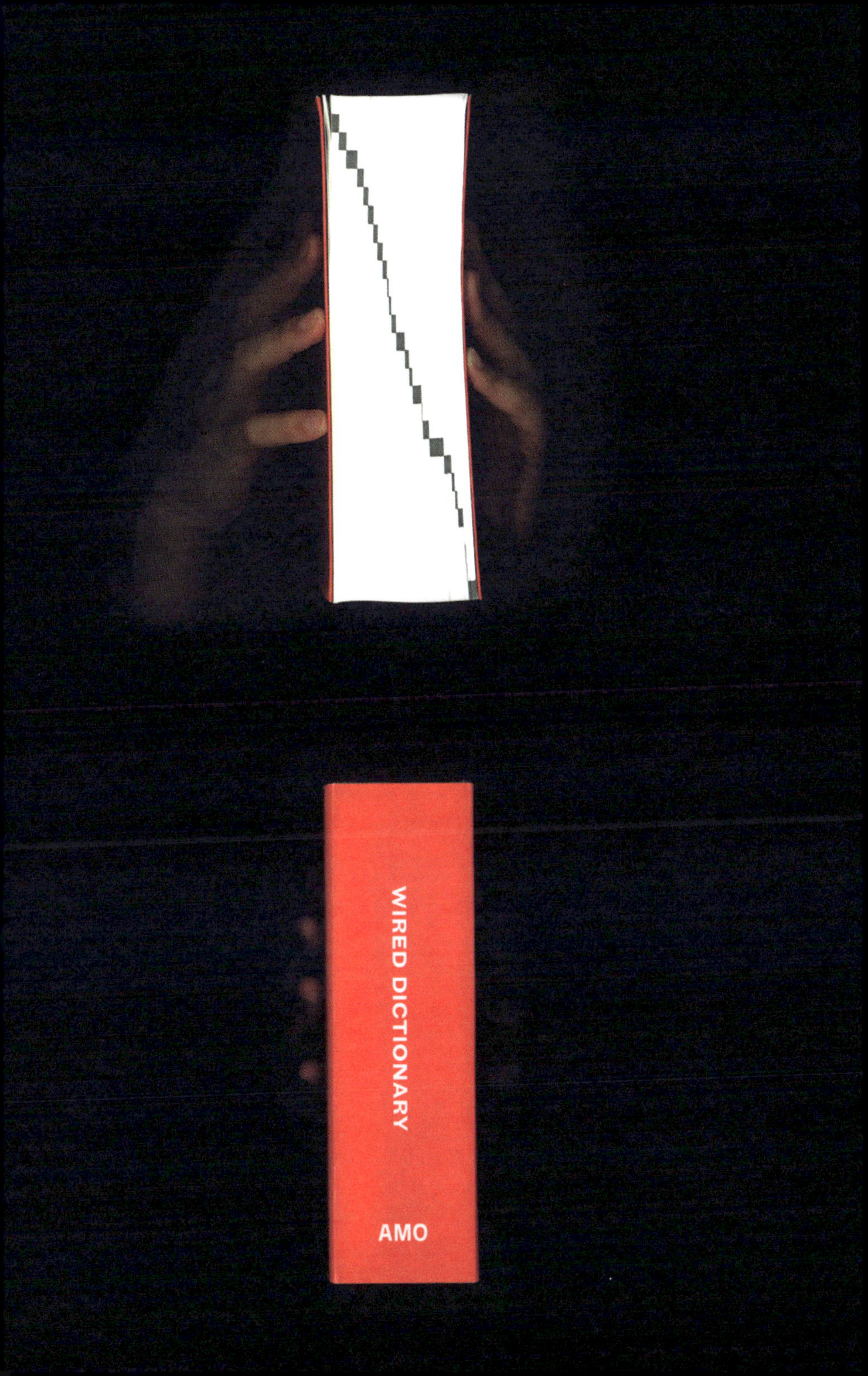

WIRED DICTIONARY

AMO

computer's unblinking eye promises something slightly more deterministic than pop psychology.

The WWII code-breakers at Bletchley Park who keyed their ciphers to language patterns (e.g., the most common word must be "the" and the most common letter, "e") had to do their work by hand. With ubiquitous, massive computational power we can now readily apply this technique to matters far more trivial than national security. In fact, this trope is now so commonplace that Rush Limbaugh counted occurrences of the personal pronoun "I" in President Obama's 2010 State of the Union address as a measure of the president's supposed self-aggrandizement, no doubt inspired by the left's count of his predecessor's use of "9/11" (substitute "fear-mongering" for "cult of personality").

We churned through ten years of *Wired* issues with our algorithm, filtering out the all-too-common articles and prepositions, and discovered that the most published word in *Wired*, up to that point, was not "technology" or "www" or "computer," but "new." What a revelation! *Wired* is not a technology magazine at all, but a magazine devoted to *L'Espirit du Nouveau*!

And there were other revelations. The word ".com" had its own little linguistic bubble that followed the stock market version. "Hacker" started strong and then faded over the years up to the point when the magazine was acquired by Condé Nast, when it abruptly disappeared. Or take the word "revolution." Our algorithm charted how often it appeared from *Wired* issue 1.01 to issue 11.06 and found sharp spikes of exuberance roughly every three months tempered with dips of sobering, perhaps reluctant, restraint. *Wired* was in the predicting business and its message was permanent revolution:

__________ is here. __________ is History.

WORD COUNTING

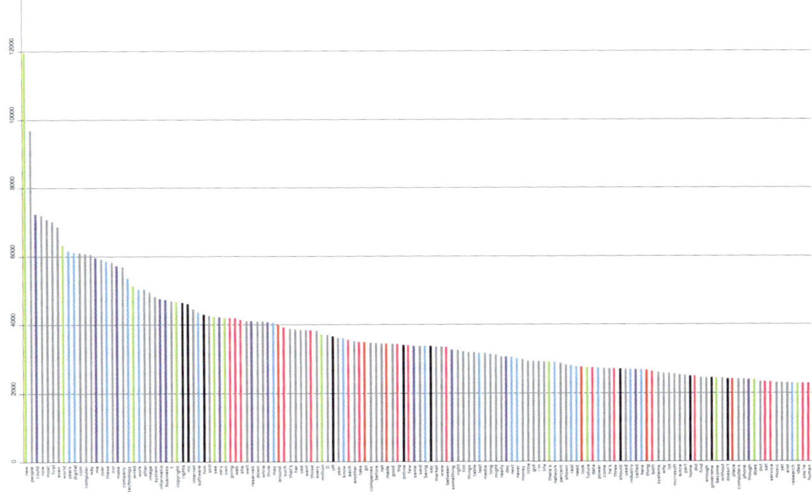

Top 300 Words

The *Wired* dictionary was a joint project with AMO, the research wing of Rem Koolhaas' Office for Metropolitan Architecture. It came about in the course of a larger project for Condé Nast looking at long-term editorial strategies for the techno-futurist magazine. AMO's New York outpost was at that time attached to our studio – it's since moved upstairs – so the collaboration was close and we shared all aspects of the project.

In attempting to analyze what *Wired* had been and in imagining what it could be, we devised a number of research strategies designed to reveal the sometimes hidden aura of the magazine. We were thinking extensively about *Wired*'s very specific brand of language: the magazine had coined a whole vocabulary or at least been instrumental in popularizing a form of techno-geek speak. Someone in the team – primarily Lucia Allais, Katie Andresen, Irwin Chen, Jeffrey Inaba and me working with Rem Koolhaas – suggested we construct a glossary of *Wired*-speak. That idea kept getting ratcheted up and soon we were discussing a *Wired* Dictionary. We wanted to use the form of the dictionary to catalogue the formation of a vernacular.

Irwin Chen set out to figure out how it could be done. First, he collected electronic files of every *Wired* issue published to date. Then he built an algorithm that could search for and count the incidence of every unique word published in *Wired* and the date of its first appearance. Once the data were retrieved, we were able to start to manipulate them. But we also felt it was important to actually make the dictionary itself, with all the words, not just imagine a conceptual project.

So Irwin built an automated program to sort all the words alphabetically and compose pages in QuarkXpress. That way the composition of the entire book, of over 1000 pages, could be accomplished automatically. We were able then to print it digitally and bind it with a simple, commercial binding used for documents. We started to chart the occurrence of certain words: their frequency, trajectories and rhythms. This data became the basis for a number of other diagrams that we employed to reveal the inner desires of the magazine.

The dictionary allowed us to see *Wired* not as a technology magazine but a magazine about Newness, a magazine that perpetually predicted revolutions, a magazine about people and ideas not machines. This led the way for a whole range of other revelations and proposals. All from simply counting words.

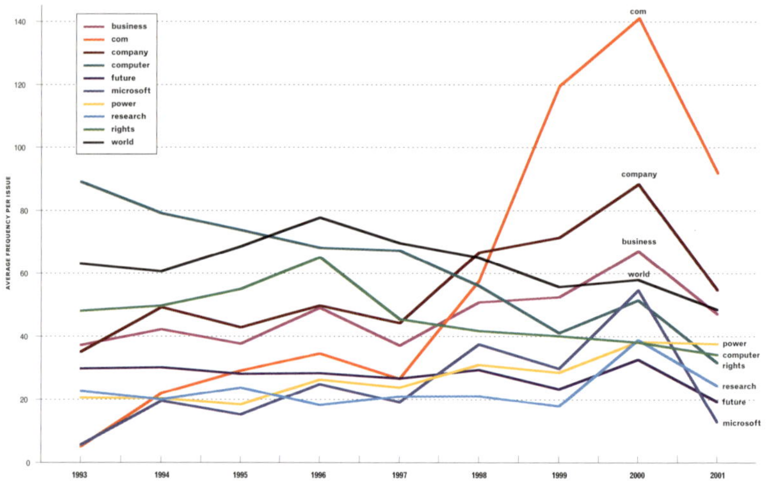

Selected word frequency averaged over time

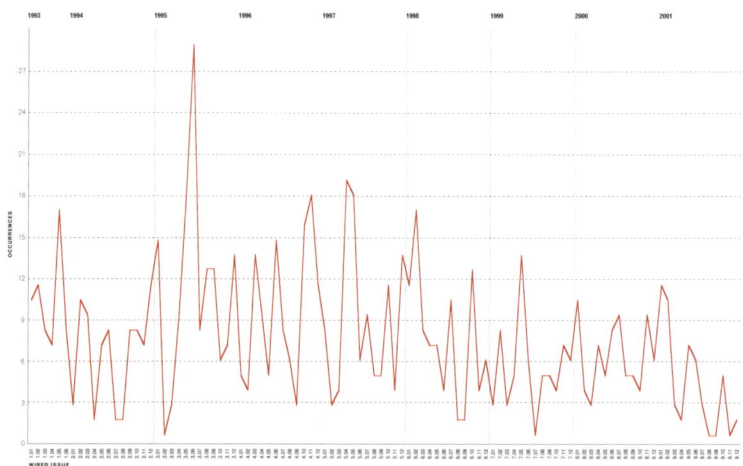

Revolution over time

GENERATION PRAKTIKUM

WITH
ALEXANDER STRUBE

We work in the realm of identity —corporate identity, brand identity, product identity—but rarely do we get to the crux of the definition: the condition of being oneself and not another. But *being onself* isessential, tying the interior and exterior and getting at something, dare I say it, true.

In reality, the territory is hotly contested. The people for whom identity is in active formation—i.e. youth—are also making personal decisions that will have a lifelong effect on their purchasing habits. So marketers are anxious to imprint indelible impressions on the gelatinous mess of the teenage psyche. The perfect site for this pitched battle is the contemporary t-shirt. Literally worn over the heart, the t-shirt links the private and the public, the personal and the promotional. The t-shirt intertwines brand and personal identity in a simple, easy-to-apply package.

At first the form was enough. From its hyper-functional military origins the t-shirt was an act of defiance in itself: think James Dean's plain white "rebel" shirt. Their function as athletic wear introduced the branded concept in the most nonchalant way. Athletic shirts, like their military forebears, served a utilitarian function: the school owned the shirt and the label across the chest proved it. But use-value morphs into exchange-value. The casual college boy with the rumpled YALE CREW shirt made two semiotic points—Ivy League privilege plus athletic prowess—without even trying. The shirt declared status.

By the early 1950s the process had become entirely self-conscious. The t-shirt as marketing tool was established, a development often credited to Floridian Sam Kantor of Tropix Togs, who first licensed Disney characters for his cheap silk-screened shirts. The '60s saw the explosion of the easy-to-print t-shirt as a kind of DIY marketing tool for everything from bands to social movements. Both its cheapness and its rough craft spoke to its anti-establishment credential. Tie-dye as political statement, the shirt eschewed the industrialized system of production. But the DIY shirt evolved into a DIY brand: the sartorial organization of the hippies was almost military in its precision.

As modern marketing continued to develop, the t-shirt developed into a kind of brand-exchange platform: marketers deployed them as grassroots message-distribution networks and consumers adopted them as identity-broadcast devices. To wear a Grateful Dead shirt was to throw your lot in with Deadheads everywhere. It was a public statement of a private state. Their popularity is still deeply rooted in counter-culture history—think Johnny Rotten's shredded "Destroy" shirt or the iconic Che Guevara portrait worn proudly by armchair anarchists since the 1960s. So the t-shirt always has this essential paradox, simultaneously an act of individualism and conformity.

In the past, tribes, cliques and subcultures broadcast their adhesion to the group by means of a certain combination of clothing, behavior, ideals and attitudes. In effect, the movement was the brand. Today, however, the opposite is true. Identity is supported by certain lifestyles, and the lifestyles in turn are associated with specific consumer preferences: brands now offer the owner/user of their respective products a means of differentiation. The consumer speaks through the conspicuous use of the brand.

In 2007 the organizers of the annual design fair in Frankfurt, Germany, invited the studio to organize a special event based on the fair's theme: Private Identity. Our response was to create a t-shirt shop within the confines of the exhibition hall, catering to a small but growing German demographic, the so-called Generation Praktikum: 20-something workers, shut out from the traditional job market, jumping from internship to internship, denied one of the essential aspects of identity, a job. The Generation Praktikum shop offered a helping hand in this frustrated quest for identity: a specially designed collection of shirts, each an edition of one, each a schizophrenic proclamation of identity. The trick was to be both unique and generic at the same time.

The GP t-shirts are easy, timeless, and relatively cheap. They can be produced and printed on demand, work by themselves and as a series, work with the wearer or against her, read in New York but not in Frankfurt or vice versa. The rules were simple: one-color shirt, black type. This assures the communal nature of the project. The messages used the typical devices of marketers: brand associations (logos, slogans, mottos), either/or choices (Nike/Adidas), brand triangulations and psychographics ("Audi, Bulthaup, Cassina"). The focus of the project is choice. As the consumer browses the shop she is in effect mentally trying on possible identities but also buying into the project.

The shop itself was consumed by shopping. Since there was only one shirt in each style, there was no backstock to replace the shirts as they were bought. The GP staffers filled the gaps where those shirts once hung with an image of the consumer and her shirt. The shop transformed into a display or gallery. Products were replaced with people.

GP works by assuming consumers are not completely delusional about capitalism's effect. They are, in fact, fully engaged players in the complex negotiations between brands and individuals. After years of frantic proselytizing about the value of brands, corporations are under increasing pressure to deliver on the brand values they disseminate. Researchers are predicting that the next generation of consumers will assume the power to turn the game to their advantage. (Understanding of course that the golden day when the people finally take over the controls of the machinery has been reliably predicted for decades.)

Audi,
Bulthaup,
Cassina.

- ☐ SLIM / SLENDER
- ☐ ATHLETIC
- ☐ AVERAGE
- ☐ SOME EXTRA BAGGAGE
- ☐ MORE TO LOVE!
- ☐ BODY BUILDER

Kraftwerk
but more
acoustic.

Rammstein,
Michel Houellebecq
und Gerhard Richter.

- ☐ LESS THAN $30K
- ☐ $30K–$45K
- ☐ $45K–$60K
- ☐ $60K–$74K
- ☐ $75K–$100K
- ☐ $100K–$150K
- ☐ $150K–$250K
- ☐ $250K AND HIGHER

hetero-

Airbag, Barkeeper, babysitten, Bluff, Bodyguard, Boom, Camping, Casting, Catering, (etwas) checken, clever, cool, Clown, Coach, Comedian, Container, Controlling, Couch, Countdown, Cover, Dad, Directory, DNA, Dogfight, Drink, Dumping-Preis, fit, Flashback, Flyer, Flop, Friendly Fire, Frisbee, Gentleman, Hand-out, Hearing, (Heck)Spoiler, high, High-End, High-Tech, Hobby, Homepage, Hype, Image, Internet, Jack-pot, Kid(s), Kidnapping, Konvoi, Label, Ladykiller, Layout, Link, live, Look, Looping, Lotion, Mainstream, Making-of, Make-up, Meeting, Mix, Mobbing, Model, Monster, Mom, Motherboard, nonstop, One-Night-Stand, Outdoor, Outfit, Outing/outen, Outplacement, Party, Peak, Pepperoni, Play-off, Power Napping, Public viewing, Recycling, Service, Set, Shop, shop-pen, Sketch, Smalltalk, Sorry, Sound, Soundcheck, Sponsor, Stalker, Standing Ovations, Stuntman, stylen, Tape, Ticket, Team, Tool, Trash, Trend, Trend-setter, Westbank.

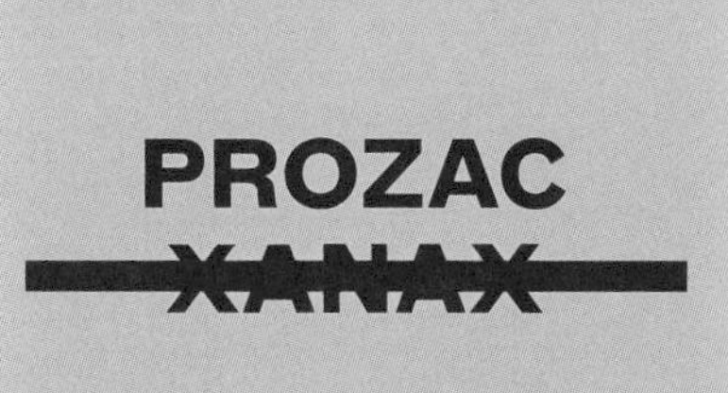

Bentley, Boffi
und Brioni.

Adidas,
Mini Cooper und
Kruder&Dorfmeister.

Nemo
me
impune
lacessit

post- individual
pre- ideology

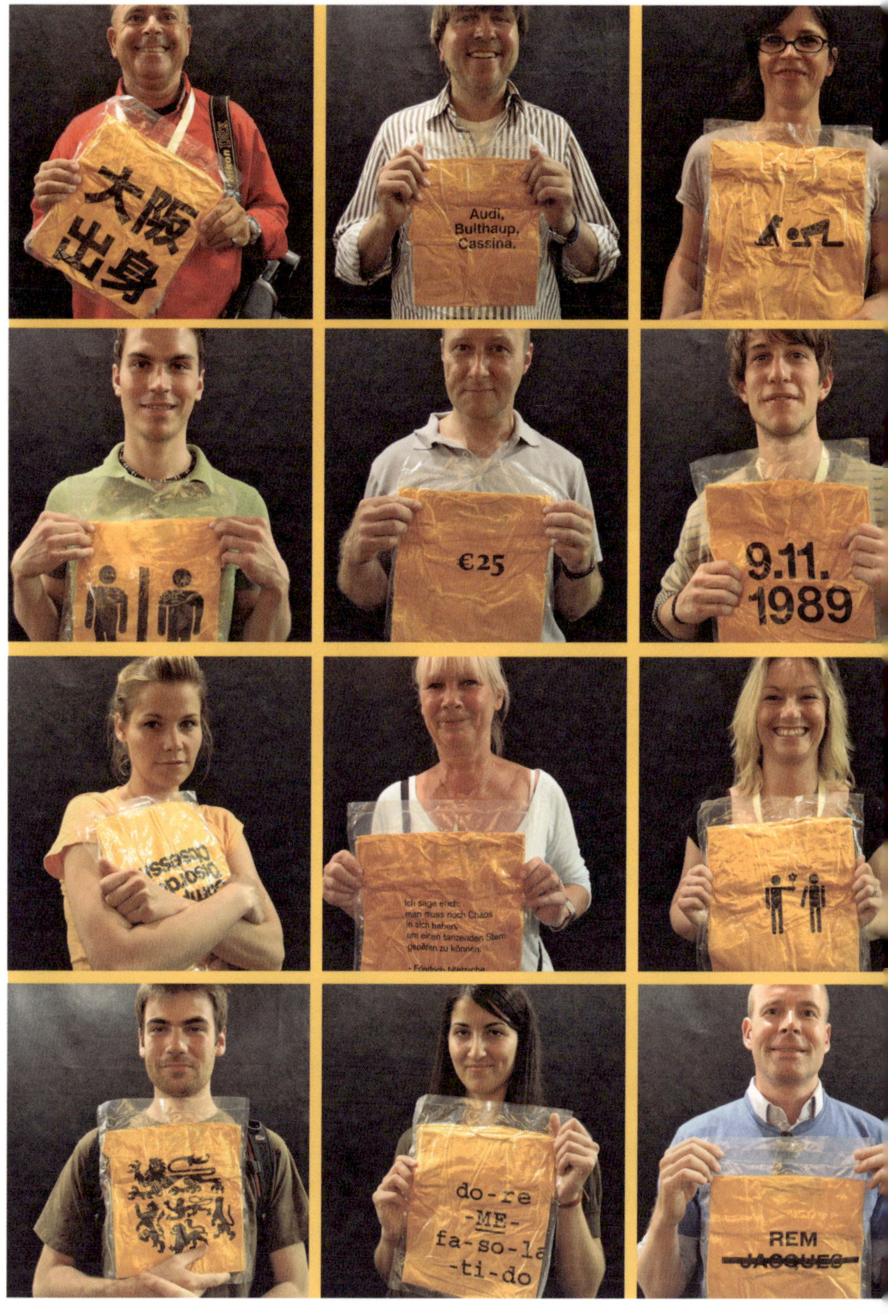
大阪出身
Audi, Bulthaup, Cassina.
€25
9.11. 1989
Ich sage euch:
man muss noch Chaos
in sich haben,
um einen tanzenden Stern
gebären zu können.
do-re
-ME-
fa-so-la
-ti-do
REM
JACQUES

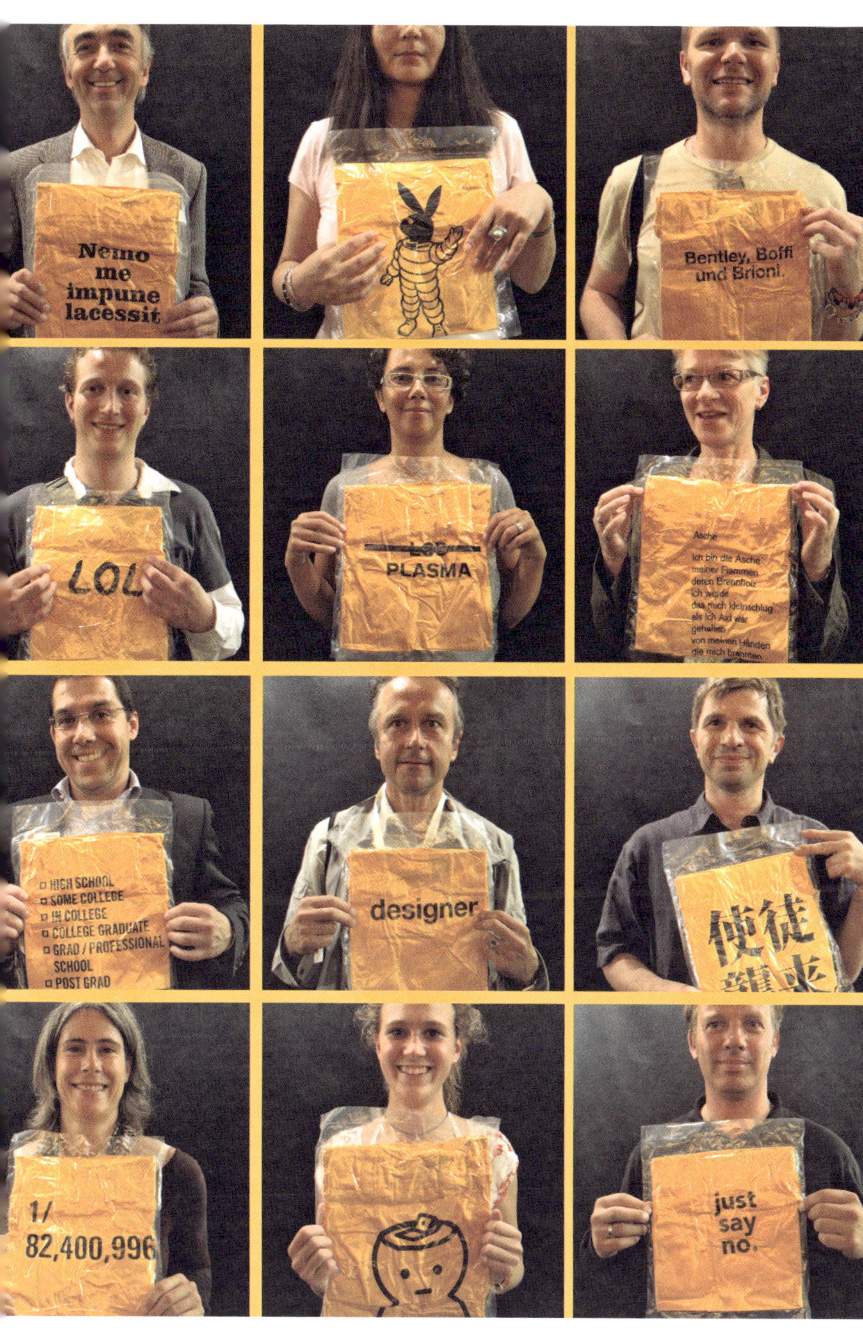
Nemo
me
impune
lacessit
Bentley, Boffi
und Brioni.
LOL
PLASMA
Asche
Ich bin die Asche
meiner Flammen
deren Brennholz
ich wurde
das mich kleinschlug
als ich Axt war
gehalten
von meinen Händen
die mich brannten
HIGH SCHOOL
SOME COLLEGE
IN COLLEGE
COLLEGE GRADUATE
GRAD / PROFESSIONAL
SCHOOL
POST GRAD
designer
使徒
1/
82,400,996
just
say
no.

Will the GenZ consumer be able to make more informed decisions about her consumption with unprecedented access to peer reviews and decentralized information networks? Will she have more agency or less? Will she demand economic, environmental and social responsibility along with sustainability? Have these values arrived, and if so, are they here to stay? Demographically, there will be fewer consumers, with more (inherited) wealth to spend, at least in the developed countries of the western world (after all, no money, no consumption, no heal-the-world). If you accept that even consumption can be counter-culture, revolutionary, game-changing, paradigm-shifting, you might actually end up making a legitimate statement.

TWO TRANSLATIONS

DAN MICHAELSON
TAMARA MALETIC

How to describe the difference between content and form? *What* and *how? Idea* and *voice? Words* and *grammar? Band* and *producer?* Each is too simple. The difference between form and content is unstable, a shiftable thermocline contingent on circumstance. That dynamic differential should itself be an object of design and a predicate to form.

We've been described, sometimes approvingly, as being uninterested in form. But we're actually not that interested in content either, except in the broadest sense. We want users to articulate their own content. More than content, we're interested in tactics, game-play, relationships, duration, and the qualities we can give those moments of exchange.

All economies are focused on relationships. Graphic design is no different, always obsessed with its own duration and use, and with the network effects of its distribution schemes. To borrow a definition from politics, design is concerned with strategizing the art of the possible. The designer creates the rules of the game and tries to plan how the field of play will look and feel in use. One of the greatest and most surprising privileges is to watch the game unfold thereafter, and to react.

The gallerist Julien Levy remembered being taught to play chess by Marcel Duchamp like this: "I was a real amateur at it but I learned what his feeling for chess was .... He said it wasn't a war game, it's an aesthetic game, and you feel the shape of the board as it begins to shift its pattern and you make it become beautiful, even if you lose."

The following two projects suggest the ways in which the role of form in graphic design focuses on such relationships. Both were projects Linked by Air undertook in collaboration with 2x4. At Prada's New York Epicenter, eleven plasma screens hanging among the clothes racks had recently been upgraded with onboard computers. By mounting video cameras above each screen and installing a different computer program in each one, we transformed the displays into eleven kinds of mirrors.

The mirrors had several precedents. 2x4's recent work for Prada and others had focused on surveillance and narcissism, and the ways mosaics may serve to redact. Many artists have experimented with video mirrors; Nam June Paik is a favorite of ours. We weren't trying to invent a new structure. Rather we were curious about what qualities we could create through such a structure: a little punk, a little glam, beautiful, quick, and light. Each mirror ran a different program; visitors experienced them in sequence simply by moving from one screen to the next. The code we used to create each screen was trivial, no more complex than dozens of similar examples that could be found on the Internet at the time. The screens were fun and fast to code, and we rejected as many sketches as we used.

Perhaps in contrast to John Maeda's *Mirror Mirror* from that same year—

part of his Reactive Book series—the Prada digital mirrors weren't so much about algorithm or even interaction, obvious conditions of the modern world, but about creating lived qualities through the disposition of algorithm and interaction. None of the eleven programs contained images; rather, they were algorithmic procedures for processing video streams. The engineering of those procedures, and the way they intersected with the movement of visitors throughout the space, created both form and qualitative experience. So the design object was neither the input (the visitor) nor the output (the constructed image). The object of design was the platform on which the exchange took place.

We later employed the same conceit, with starkly different effects, on a project for a European urban campus comprised of offices, workspaces, labs and public meeting places. Answering a brief for a signing and public-information system, we proposed an invisible wayfinding capability available through mobile-phone text messaging.

Precedents at the time included the new geo-messaging services Socialight and Google SMS; the five-digit SMS micropayment systems common in Europe; telephone interactive voice response (IVR) systems; audio guides, and interactive text adventures like *Zork*. Other inspirations included the voice (or voices) of *The Hitchhiker's Guide to the Galaxy*, and Salvatore from Paul Elliman's *Sirens of Venice.*

We named our voice Johan (56426), relating both to the name of the campus neighborhood (Saint John in English) and suggesting the ethereality of the service. Johan was conceived as a guide. Creating a natural-language conversation system is difficult, but Johan's sphere of expertise was limited.

Users could only ask Johan about the campus, and only particular kinds of questions. Like the Prada mirrors that manipulated input in eleven different ways, Johan supported several specific genres of conversation: greet, locate, describe, direct, inform, identify, and elaborate. While the mirrors translated pixels, Johan processed street names and building numbers, personnel directories, listings, and site-specific markers placed for the project.

Visitors could employ these different conversation modes as needed by texting a question to 56426. A typical query was comprised of a noun (name, building number, marker) and a verb. Punctuation could constitute a verb. "199–88" signified "directions from marker 199 to building 88."

Context was a vital asset that helped minimize difficult user input and maximize the value of Johan's responses.

Johan did not rely on GPS or any other locative technology. Instead, he built on each person's previous query, so the exchange was necessarily dialogic, conversational. He knew, for example, that no markers had the same numbers as buildings. There was

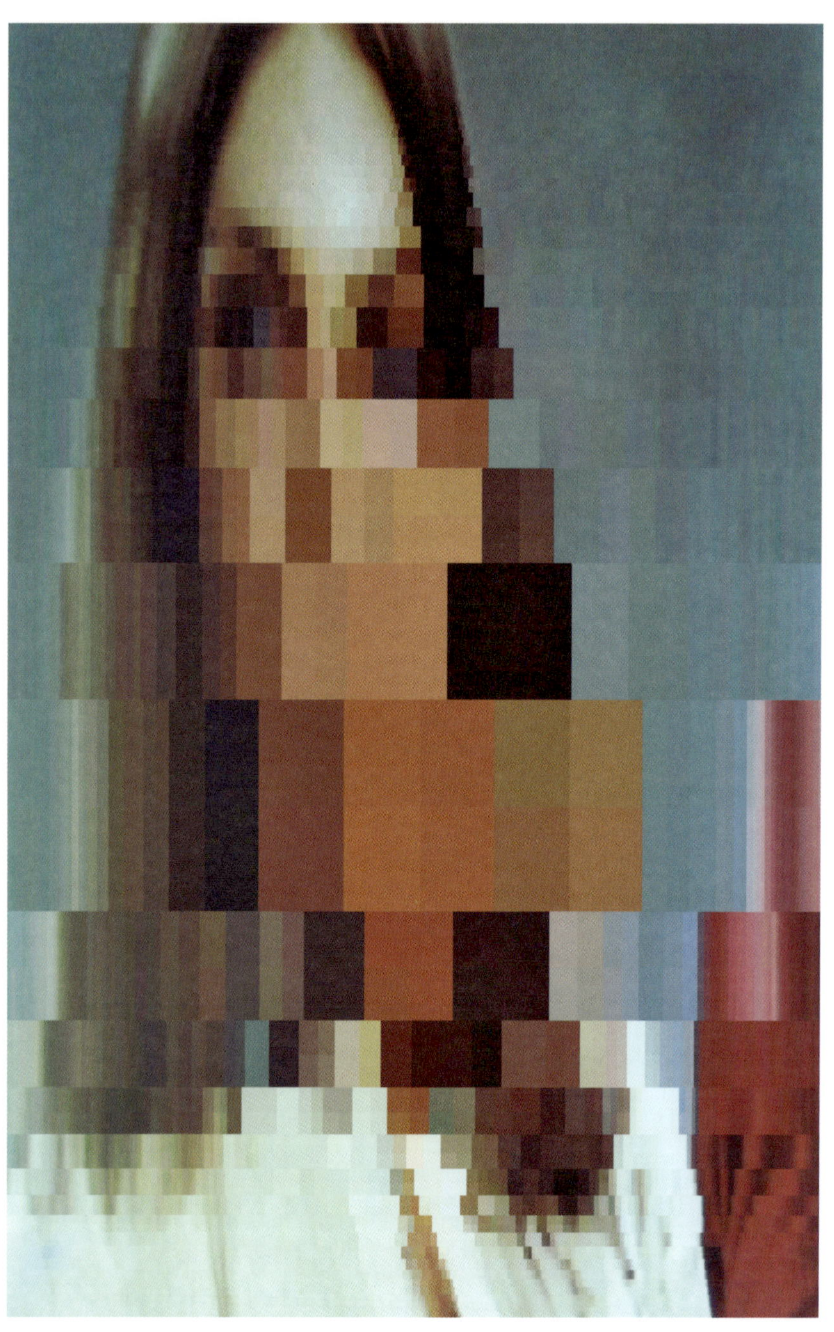

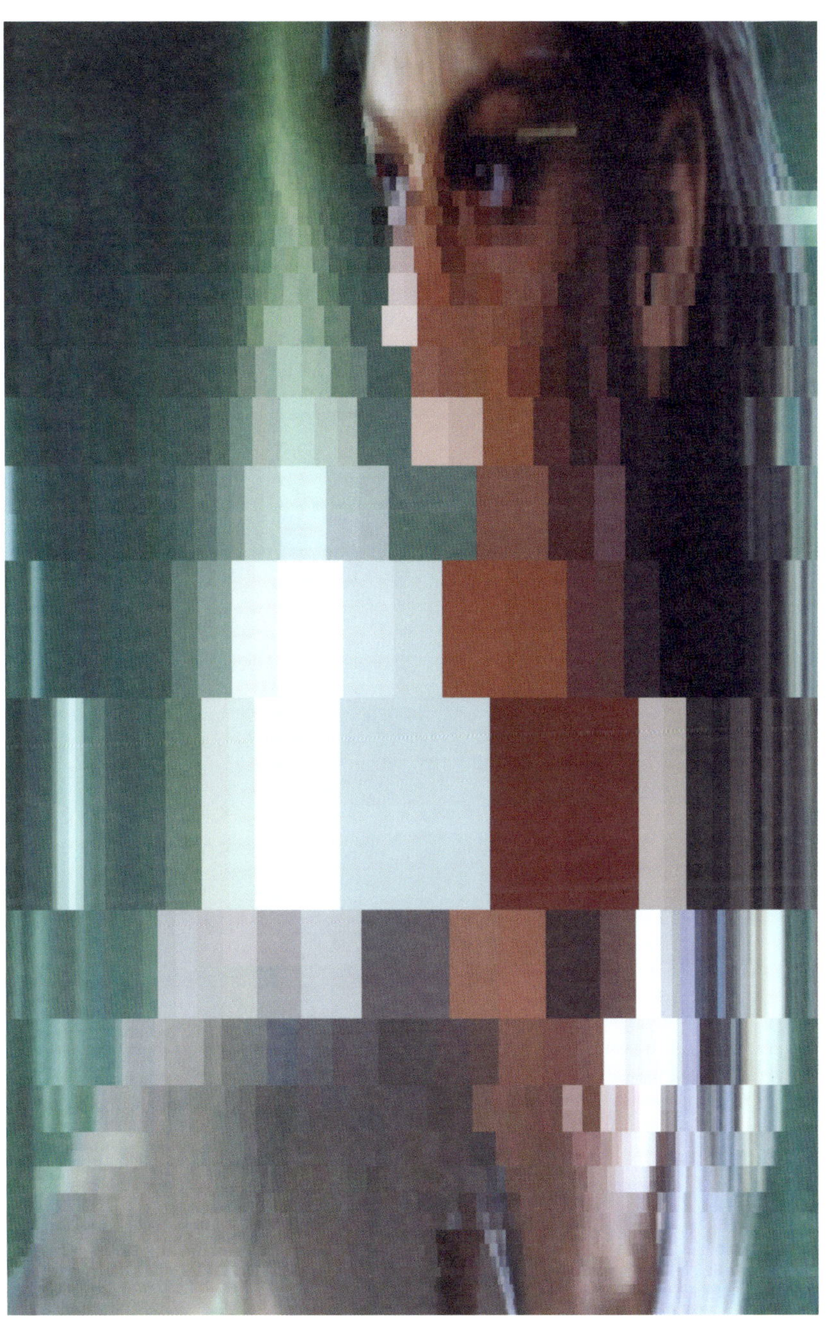

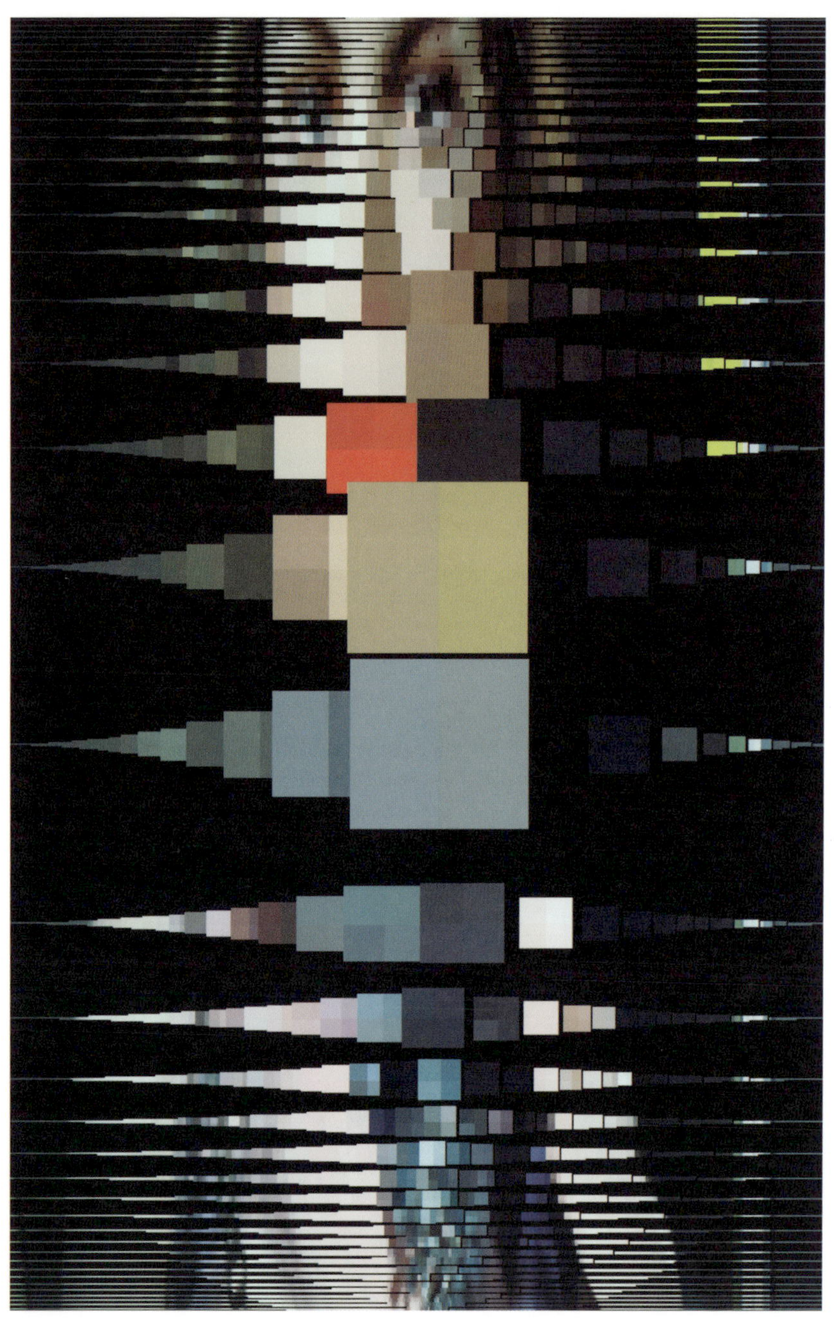

MAGIC MIRRORS
— 2×4 & LINKED BY AIR

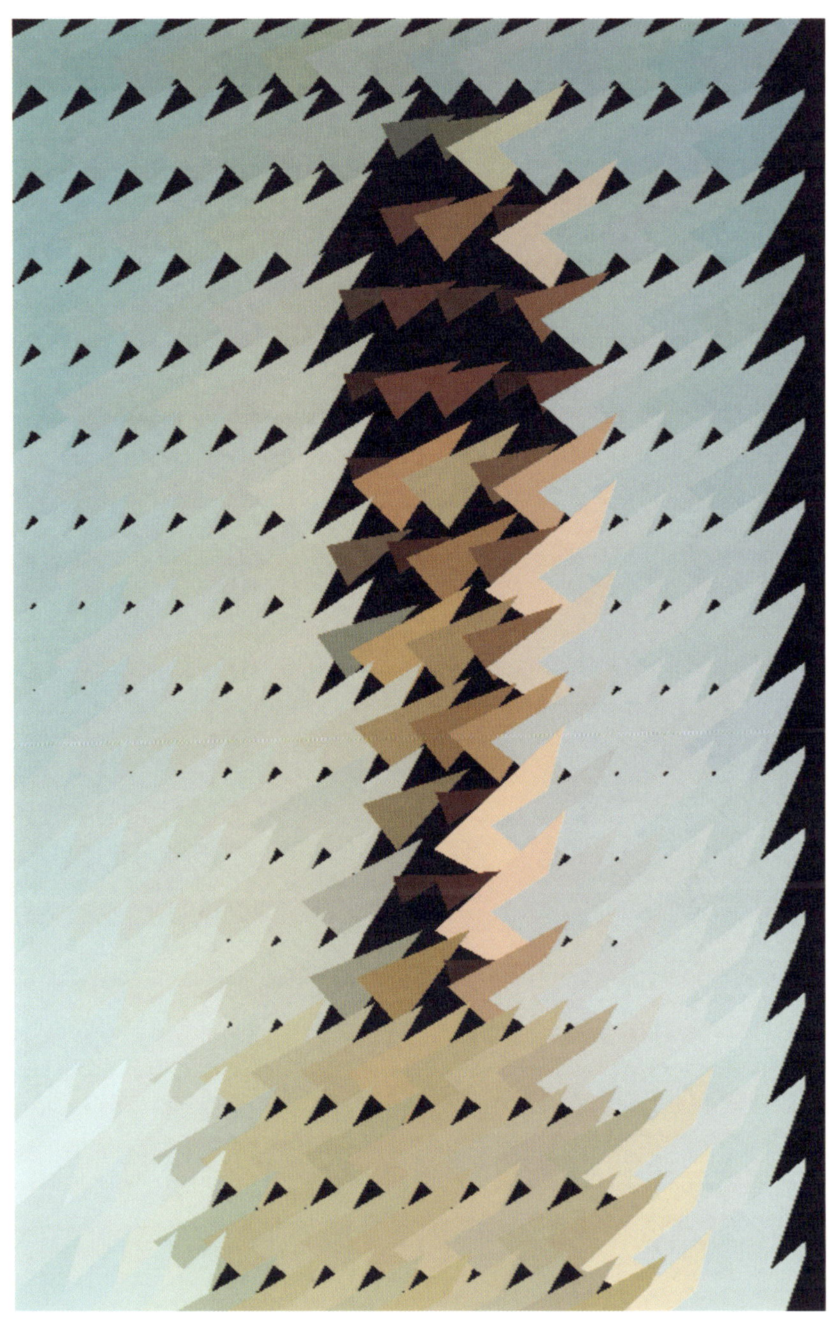

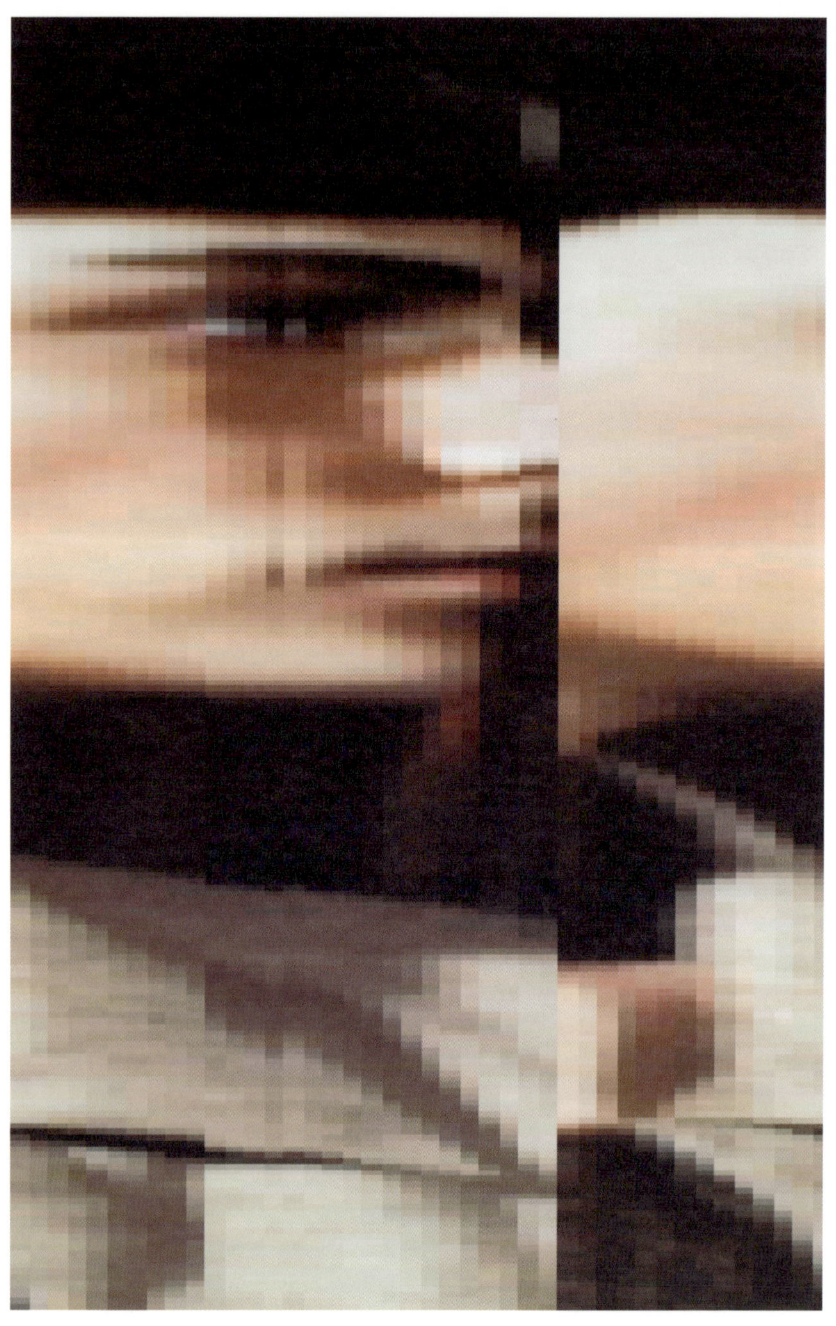

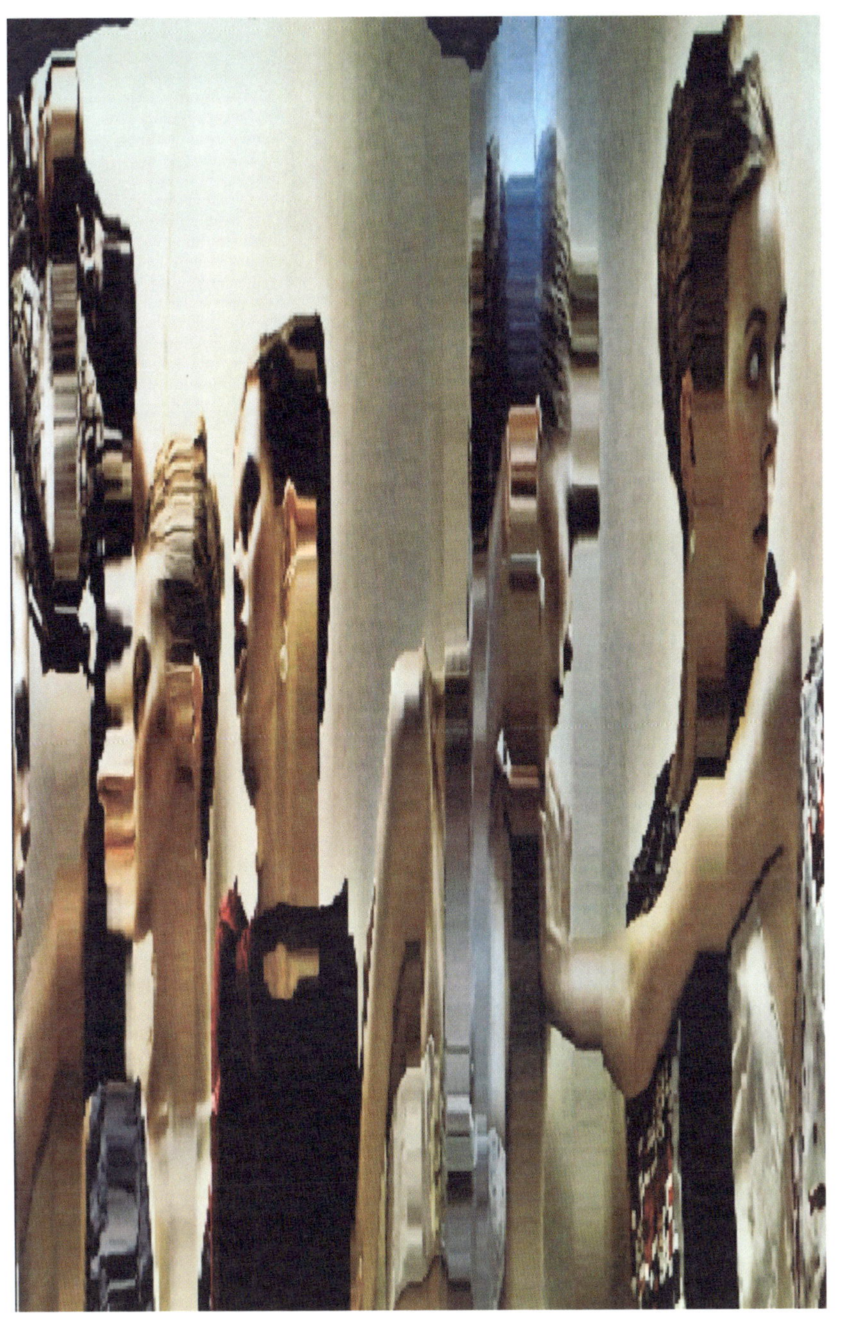

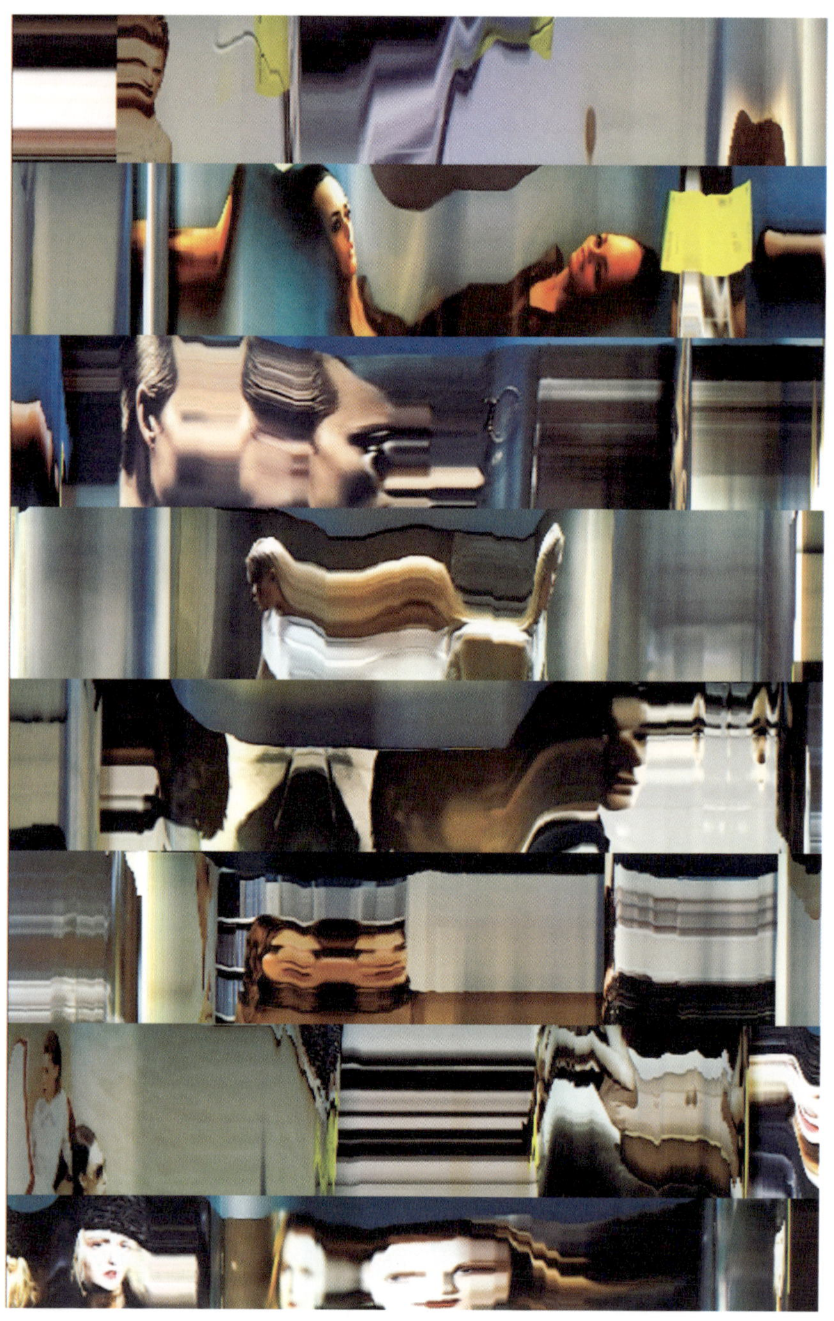

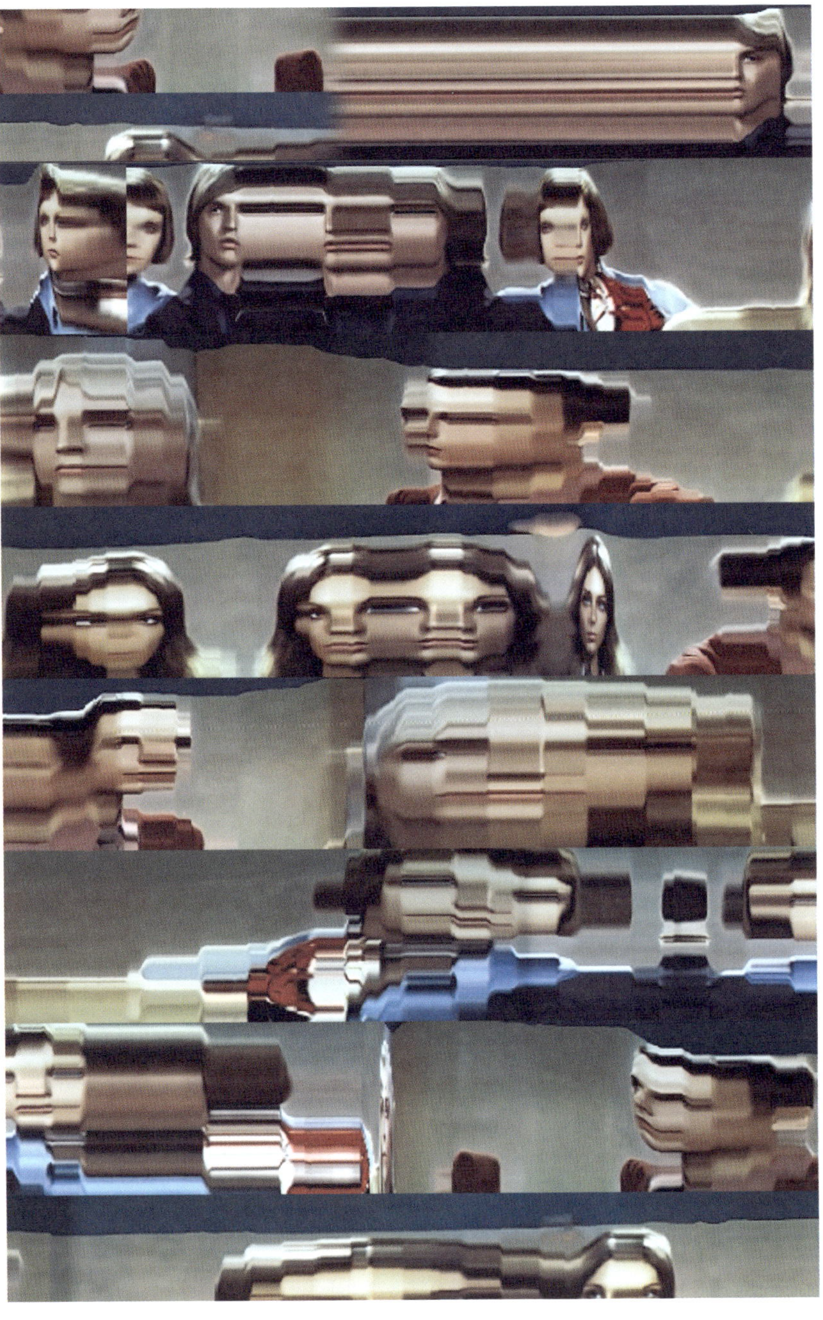

little ambiguity in his database. He wasn't artificially intelligent; he was just a set of filters.

With the nouns and verbs determined, the focus of our work became Johan's typographic language and syntax—his voice. Johan worked through simple SMS messaging, an intimate technology available on every phone. He had to seem comfortable in German, French, and English. We thought about the alternation between male and female voices on the New York City subway, and about the sound effects that are used in some telephone IVR systems announcing a new menu.

We made his voice terse but not brusque, fitting for a concierge, a professional transaction, and an SMS message. At the same time, we used an idiosyncratic punctuation scheme to structure his responses visually within the limitations of SMS, and to give him a certain approachability. As with the mirrors, the establishmentof Johan's database and algorithmic structure was only a predicate for our real interest: the exploration of the constricted typographic structures of the SMS system and their relationship to the movement of the user. Johan was realized as a prototype but never implemented.

One of the most relevant futures of graphic design is the interfaces of people with, and through, the overwhelming transactions and movements of contemporary social and information economies. We have no interest in simplifying, smoothing, or reducing those movements. We are also aware of the pitfalls and potential ethical issues of engaging with design as a set of modern network effects; there are many networks and relationships that we wouldn't touch. In the end, we are not so interested in visualizing or mapping these translations; we want to make them speak.

ON MUSEUMS

WITH
SUSAN SELLERS

Museums hold a unique position in the design profession. Charged with the protection of culturally significant artifacts and masterworks, they lend their gravitas to the objects they contain. Nothing sanctifies a design object more than inclusion in a major museum's permanent collection. (Think how "Included in the collection of the Museum of Modern Art" imbues an object with an undeniable aura.) The museum inoculates design against the infection of fashion and grafts permanence onto the ephemeral. At the same time, design objects are the only museum masterpieces available for sale to the average consumer.

Reading design is dependent on historical, social, economic and environmental contexts. The relevance and significance of an object may be changed (or lost, damaged or enhanced) either because a particular moment has passed or because it has been removed from a the site for which it was intended. The designed product as a visual image or message has no single referent. Instead it is an organic structure, a connection relative to changing consumer positions, values and expectations, constantly shifting and in flux. The traditional design-museum environment, with its dedication to the static and the isolated, is antithetical to the reality of design process. If early concepts of the museum worked on making the private public, what can be done with objects that are, from their inception, inherently public?

While the overriding concern of most design collections has been and is to take "objects out of context in an effort to provoke associations and perceptions that would otherwise not be available—out of the familiar into the unfamiliar," what happens when that process is reversed? What happens when things are viewed *in* context to facilitate looking at familiar objects and environments in an unfamiliar way? What if the city itself were imagined as a designed object of tremendous scale? If the museum were integral to the city—the context for which its exhibits were designed—the recurrent problem about how to recreate context around an artifact would be removed from the start. The museum would be its own context.

A PROPOSAL FOR A MUSEUM OF THE ORDINARY

Against the backdrop of institutionally sponsored "good design," we propose the Museum of the Ordinary, or M.O. This museum is an exhibition space dedicated to the exploration of contemporary design as an urbanist practice. At its heart, M.O. is a *Modus Operandi*, a method of procedure, a way of working, an engine to generate both theory and practice.

We set out to create the structure of the institution purely from the institutional apparatus: the business card, the logo, the mug, the press kit. Signs of legitimacy will conjure legitimacy. (Our motto: The cart drives the horse.) Our primary organizational unit is the name of the Museum itself, which serves as the frame for a range of curatorial activities unified not by an architectural container but by thematic and ideological connections. The name is a perimeter.

Museum of the Ordinary sets out to both reinvigorate and contradict the established precedents of conventional design museums. In M.O., museum and city are one; there is no implied meaning. The semantics of the collection are entirely a function of its curatorial position. The museum is just an urban frame, and the work it contains can only be understood in context.

The city, and our space within it, is a site in which any number of devices have been enacted. As public demands and pressures have changed and shifted, the physical shape of the city has re-formed from a communal pasture to gridded, privately owned parcels. The city bears the impression of the humanity that flows through it.

The map, the primary device of controlling and comprehending change, is an indexical sign. The map reveals the hand of the mapmaker. Through mapping and re-mapping the area, hidden systems from infrastructure to political affiliation are brought to the surface. The gradual effects of history and economic forces are so big, so slow, and so incremental they often occur unnoticed. Thus the Museum gallery plan may include not only current structures, but historic transformations as well.

For our mission, we often returned to Rem Koolhaas' definition of a "new urbanism … not based on the twin fantasies of order and omnipotence; it will be the staging of uncertainty; it will no longer be concerned with the arrangement of more or less permanent objects but with the irrigation of territories with potential … ."

We also found inspiration in conceptual art projects of Richard Long and Hamish Fulton and in the situationist texts of Guy Debord, specifically, in Debord's notion of the intentional drift, the dérive. "In a dérive," Debord wrote in 1957, "one or more persons during a certain period drop their relations, their work and leisure activities, and all their other usual motives for movement and action, and let themselves be drawn by the attractions of the terrain and the encounters they find there." The Museum of the Ordinary is likewise a directed walk, an informed wandering.

The Museum has a perimeter and a permanent collection. The perimeter is inscribed by four coordinates on the grid of Manhattan, determined by one plate of a standard Sanborn real-estate map (Sanborn Map Plate 20/Section 2. Manhattan blocks 472-503). The area is defined by four intersections: Prince Street/Sullivan Street, 6th Avenue/Grand Street, Prince Street/Lafayette Street, Grand Street/Centre Street. These artificial boundaries serve to create some limitations. The Museum, however, reserves the right to expand these boundaries to include other parts of the city, and to open branchesin other cities worldwide.

The area of M.O. is the site of diverse and conflicting communities, the intersection of a traditional Italian-American community that is shrinking and a growing Asian-American community. It is a neighborhood where we live and work, an industrial quarter. The district is highly gentrified—site of galleries and high-priced stores—and also intensely disputed.

The Museum includes all spaces above, on, and below street level. The permanent collection consists of all the designed objects within the perimeter of the Museum. The blocks of buildings form a negative grid of masses ….

The numbered blocks are the basic structural designation:

—The streets, avenues and public spaces are a web of voids and galleries.
—The Museum has multiple points of entry …
… and unlimited passageways …
… and numerous devices of circulation: pedestrian, vehicular, subterranean.

The border between interior and exterior is inscribed by movement. The border patrol continuously circles the perimeter streets, welcoming visitors on the outside, thanking them for their participation on the inside.

Since the collection is so large, it is the responsibility of the curators to subdivide the collection into smaller exhibition spaces. These routinely follow the urban structure (streets, avenues, blocks, individual buildings, individual spaces within individual buildings), but may also inscribe other systems of organization within the cityscape (e.g. all SW corners, building façades, subway tunnels, sewer lines, rooftops).

The name, the logo and the business card call the organization to life, confer titles and positions and establish identity. The logo announces the entrances and defines the Museum's border. The name and the identity are the most important part of the project; by identifying the area, claiming the territory, and lending new value to the objects contained therein, the district of the Museum is reconsidered. The system is made complete with stationery, t-shirts and supporting projects. These ancillary materials build identity and become sites for possible exhibitions: matchbooks become gallery spaces.

All objects within the M.O. perimeter are eligible for exhibition, but our ideological emphasis is on contemporary design in a cultural context, the interface of graphic and industrial design and the urban experience. We are interested in understanding the role contemporary design plays in developing a sense of place and how it shapes the urban character of this area. More important, we are concerned with the city itself, how its physical form is the manifestation of an ongoing, unending process of design.

The devices for exhibition and publicity are typical of any museum, and include the label, frame, vitrine, pedestal, gallery plan, projection, cordon, catalogue, window display, guarded installation, newsletter, museum store, souvenir poster and t-shirt. These devices appear mysteriously in public places throughout the site.

Simple, official M.O. labels are affixed to objects in the city. The labels, marking designed objects as diverse as fire hydrants, Xerox posters and IRT subway stations, parody the seriousness of museum labels. Any manmade object within the perimeter is eligible for labeling.

We mark certain public spaces with official M.O. receipts. They reveal who owns the space, who pays for it, and include an itemized list of the value of visibility and material costs of producing large-scale corporate and public speech.

Museum of the Ordinary frames isolated figures in random advertising posters. The frame contains research and information on the person depicted therein, transforming the image from the general to the specific. The anonymous commercial figure, through meticulous research, is recovered.

Empty spaces call out for M.O. intervention and identification.

Red velvet ropes demark an area of empty wall space with a number of random posters. Museum of the Ordinary placards serve as the "title wall," including the exhibition name and the general curatorial information.

We choose various objects within the Museum as sites for history projects. Social and economic histories are projected onto the objects over a period of time. The stories concentrate on the ownership, property value, hidden events, that shape the form of the object. For a prescribed period of time, items in the collection become ground for their own narratives.

We organize shows using a collection of views of cityscapes. A number of windows in a number of rooms in a number of buildings are identified in a small catalogue. The exhibition consists of the perspectives framed by that particular set of windows. The links—the routes between the objects in the collections (the views)—must be physically traversed and all sites must be visited to complete the experience.

Some exhibitions are the work of private, self-motivated curators. These projects, organized and enacted within the walls of the Museum, may be identified and sponsored by the Museum.

The Museum of the Ordinary website broadcasts live imagery from its streets. In this way, the changing atmosphere of the street corner is framed in real time.

Other efforts reflect individual curators' tastes, fascinations, specialties or fetishes. They may take the form of street events or catalogues. They could be as elaborate as an organized demonstration, or as simple as a temporary security guard imbuing some defended object with a sense of value.

Ultimately, the result of our activity is to continuously catalogue the space. Projects continue to exist as published work and documentation and, in this way, the Museum is a device for inspiring, producing and funding visual projects. Over time, the M.O. publishing initiative will build a visual library of the city site and the curatorial perspectives will be played out in published form.

Finally, the M.O. Store is a virus that infects all commercial ventures within the Museum area, from the Metropolitan Museum store to the specialty boutique to the corner deli. Certain products offered for sale in those establishments—as diverse as canned foods, designer furniture, tabloid newspapers, tea kettles, street jewelry, haute-couture clothing, artworks and subway tokens—may be awarded and endorsed with the Museum of the Ordinary Good Design Seal, a re-creation of the original MoMA tag.

In conclusion, the goal of M.O. is simply to exist. The Museum is a frame and, for the moment at least, it's an empty frame, theory without practice.

If design museums are primarily about control of space and meaning, M.O. is about the release of that control. If traditional museums are about order, M.O. embraces cacophony. Other museums love beauty. We love interest. Design museums extract design as an autonomous proposition; M.O. sees design as a practice without exteriority.

Officially, we identify our goals as follows:

1) Create an institution dedicated to the organization, evaluation and critique of design.
2) Promote exhibition, writing and publishing on the subject of contemporary design in a social context.
3) Contradict the conventional methods of design museology that tend to extract designed objects from culture.
4) Foster an awareness of the social relevance of design in the broadest audience.
5) Encourage a mass audience to discern the effects and presence of contemporary design in daily life.

On a practical level, the Museum is designed as an alternative to our professional studio. As a group we are committed to pursuing a range of projects. The Museum supplies the basic infrastructure to produce work outside of our commissions, also allowing us to collaborate with designers, curators, and writers who could be considered our professional competitors. The project, like the streets, is open to all who choose to wander, or work, within it. Since the Museum is ultimately nothing, that allows us to fill it with everything.

Finally, we'll end with a passage from the Museum Manifesto:
To de-professionalize, to see all acts as interior to the institution, to de-elevate the designer, to foul the water, to make a bed and sleep in it, to bite the hand that feeds us, to burn bridges, to topple the apple cart, to make waves, to bite off our nose to spite our face, to live in glass houses and throw stones, to look gift horses in the mouth, to speak ill of the day before nightfall, to count our chickens before they hatch, and to pull the rug out from under ourselves.

THE MO GRAFFITI MUSEUM

In the years since we proposed the Museum of the Ordinary as a sort of pedagogical challenge at the Design beyond Design conference at the Jan van Eyck Academie in Maastricht, the technological landscape has radically transformed. Many ideas we proposed then are not only possible but more or less in effect, utilizing the enormous potential of distributed information gathering and highly decentralized display options. Collections, carefully organized and arranged, are everywhere. What is Pinterest or Tumblr if not curated display?

The MO Graffiti museum is a project to build a vast permanent collection of graffiti and street art from around the world, submitted by anyone using a smartphone with a camera and the MO app. While the museum is permanent, graffiti is specific to both space and time. One street corner could be the locale for thousands of items in the collection. The geolocation and time-stamp of the telephone network tag each item. The original collector and later visitors can attach commentary. As the collection builds it can be reorganized and filtered in numerous ways. Curators can utilize the collection to create arguments, exhibitions and city tours. Finally, the museum can be pushed back out to the street where each documented surface can be re-explored using the screen as a mediating window that can peel away the accretion and reveal the hidden layers below.

INPUT

4
ADD
COMMENTARY
I ♥
5
INPUT
MULTIPLIED
3
DOCUMENT
LOCATION (x,y)
TIME (z)
M
1
?
2
APP
STORE
Museum
of the
Ordinary

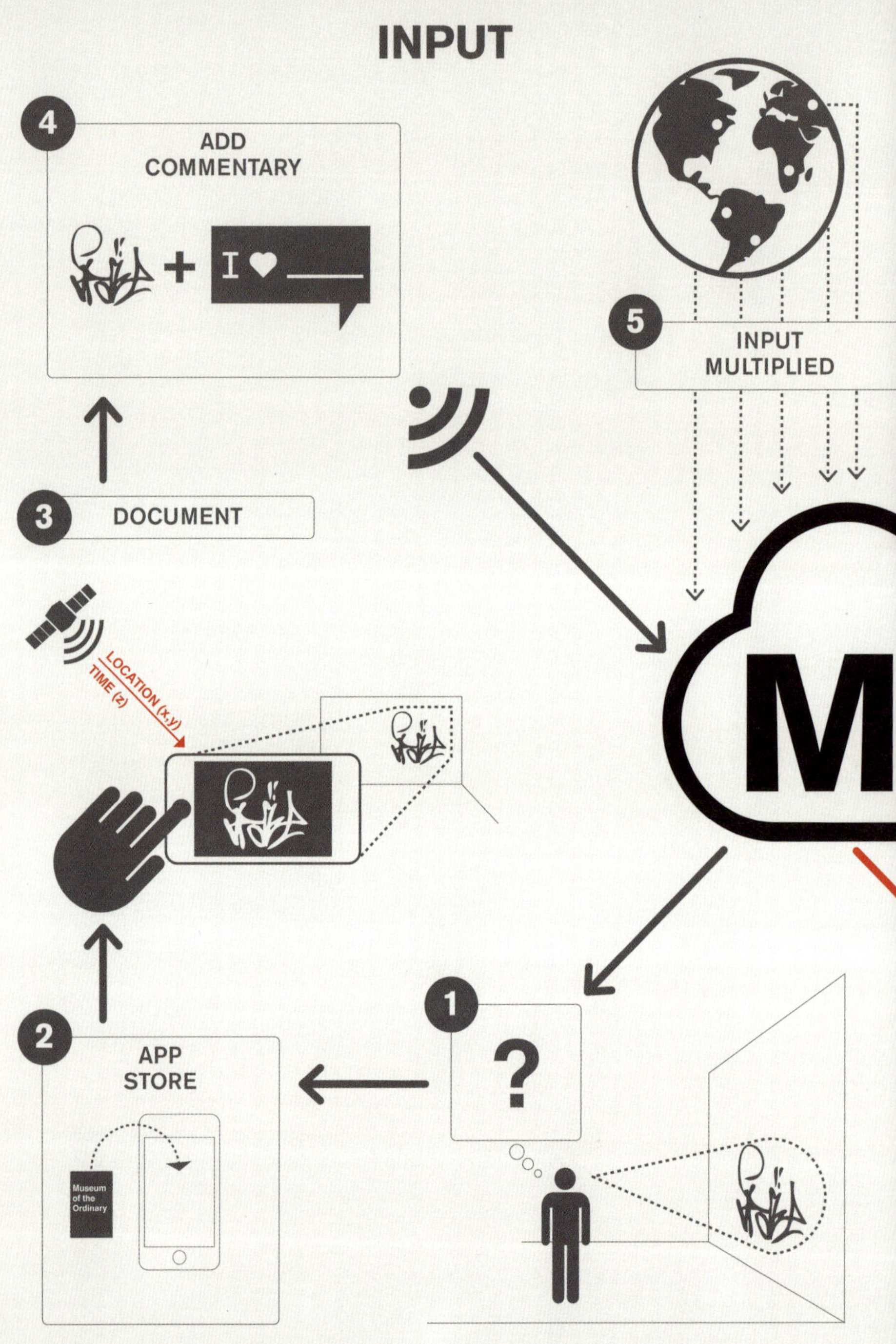

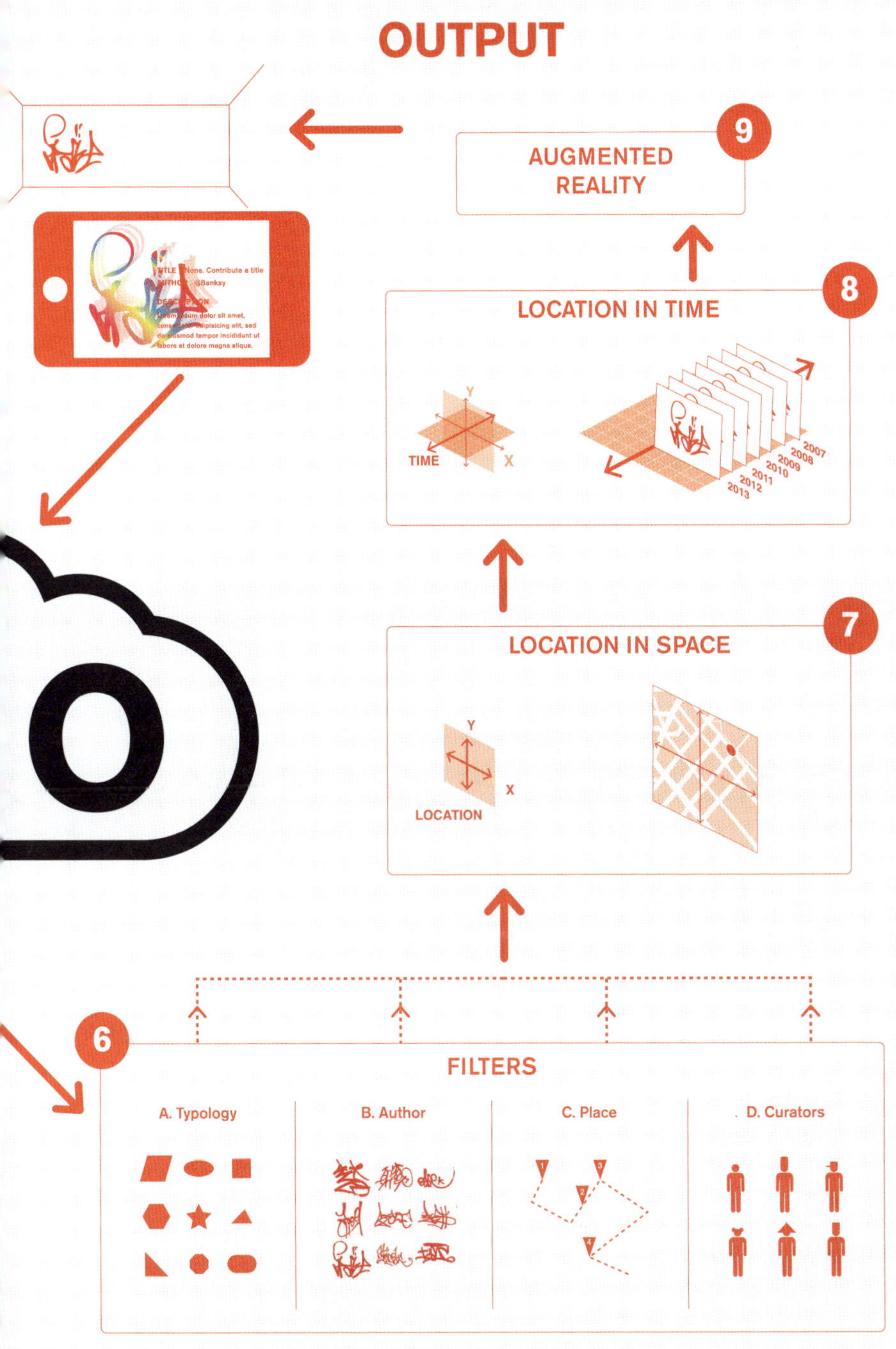
OUTPUT
AUGMENTED REALITY
9
TITLE None. Contribute a title
AUTHOR @Banksy
DESCRIPTION
Lorem ipsum dolor sit amet, consectetur adipisicing elit, sed do eiusmod tempor incididunt ut labore et dolore magna aliqua.
LOCATION IN TIME
8
Y
TIME
X
2007
2008
2009
2010
2011
2012
2013
LOCATION IN SPACE
7
Y
X
LOCATION
6
FILTERS
A. Typology
B. Author
C. Place
D. Curators

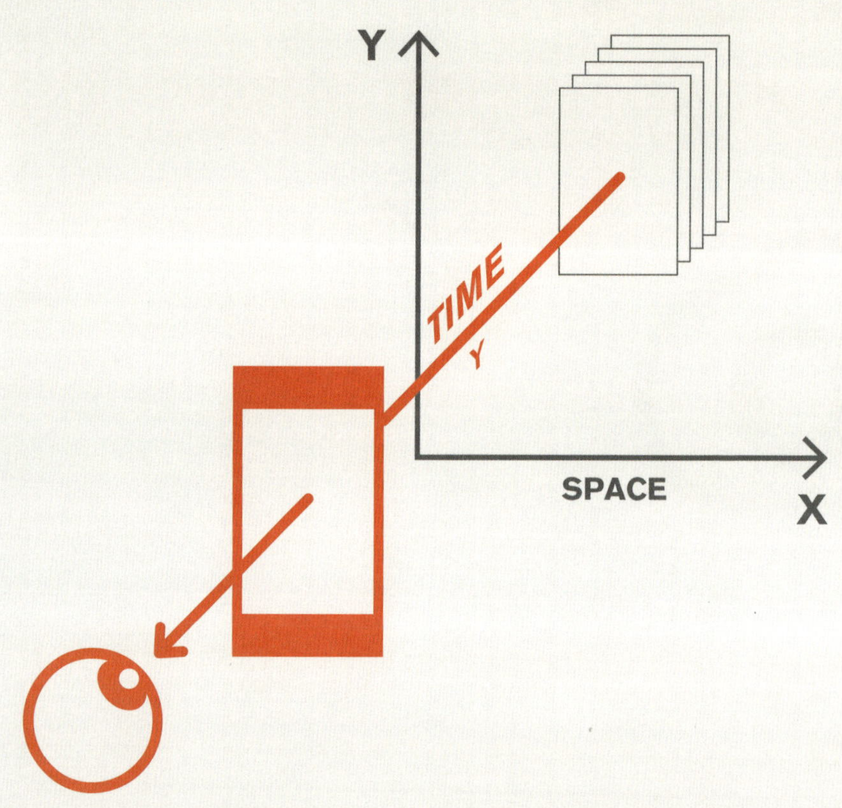
Y
TIME
Y
SPACE
X

DIAGRAM

2×4

The parallax of wayfinding. For most users a building is a series of interconnected, intestinal passages leading to who-knows-where. The spatialization of plan, section, elevation, axonometric perspective is a complex mental trick. And the relationship between exterior and interior is elusive. In a project as complex as OMA's CCTV headquarters in Beijing, the form of the building is reimaged hundreds of times, from multiple perspectives in an attempt to pick through the complexity and make it readable. The user navigates at different scales and comprehensions at different moments in the experience. The whole is always slightly unrenderable.

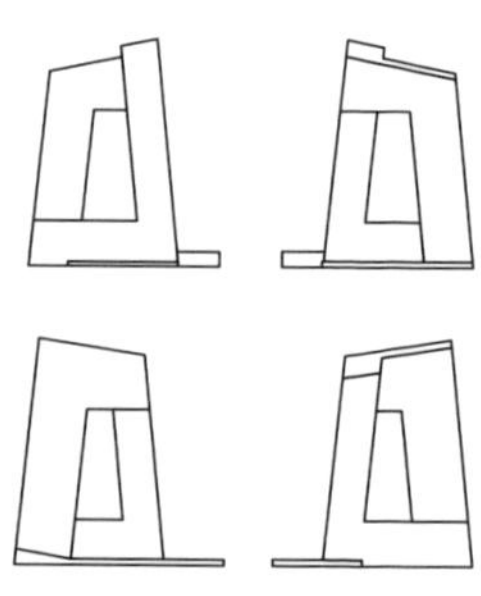

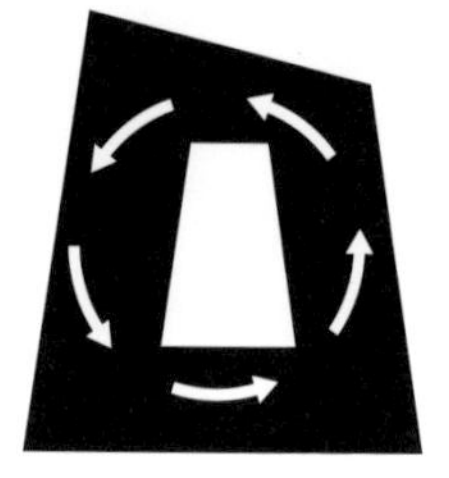

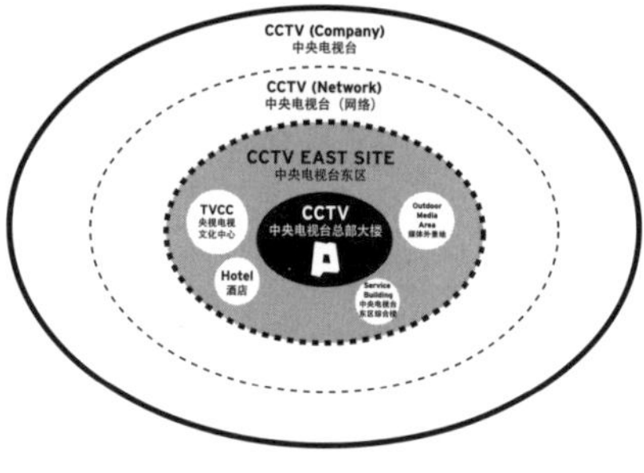

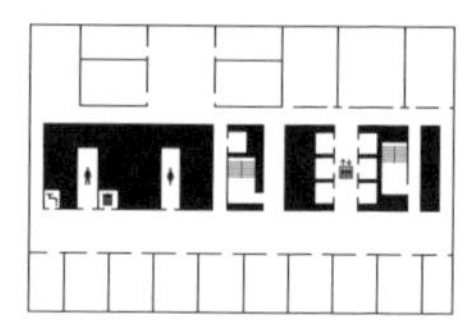

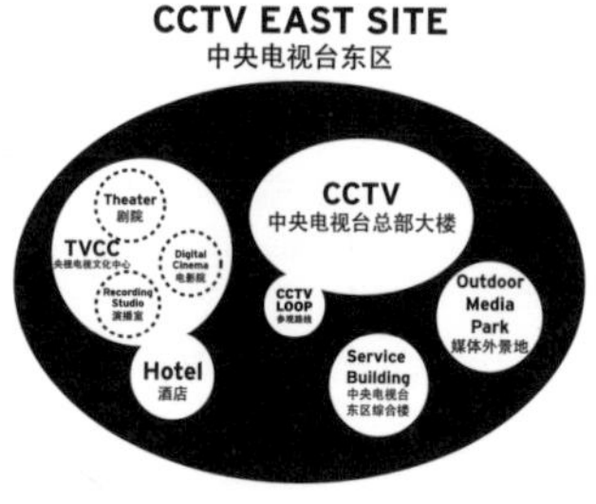

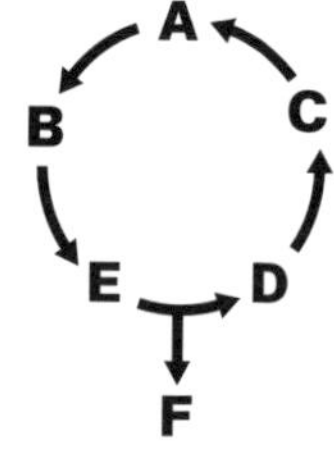

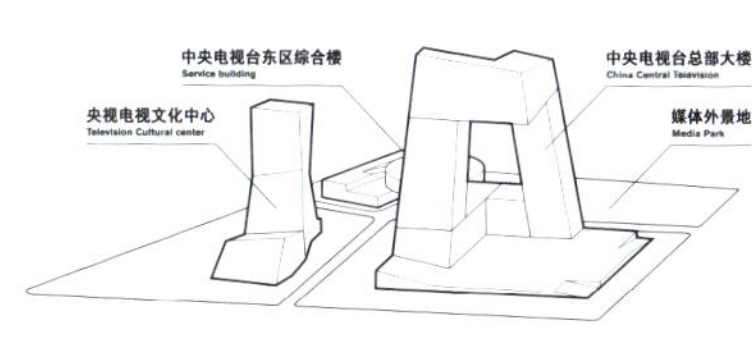

中央电视台东区综合楼
Service building
中央电视台总部大楼
China Central Television
央视电视文化中心
Television Cultural center
媒体外景地
Media Park

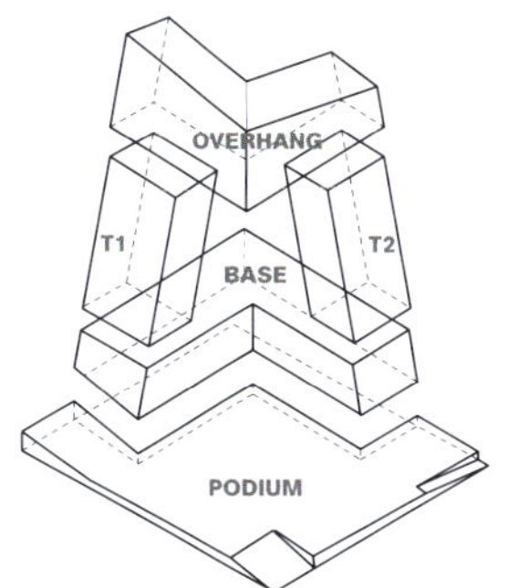

OVERHANG
T1
T2
BASE
PODIUM

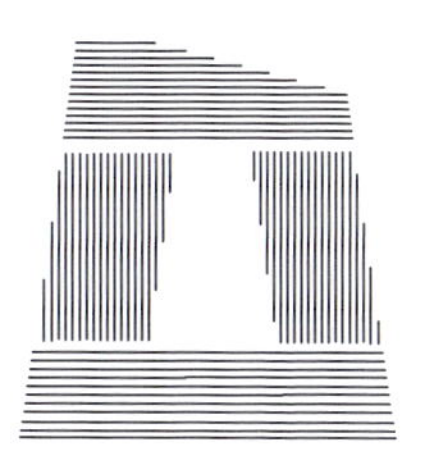

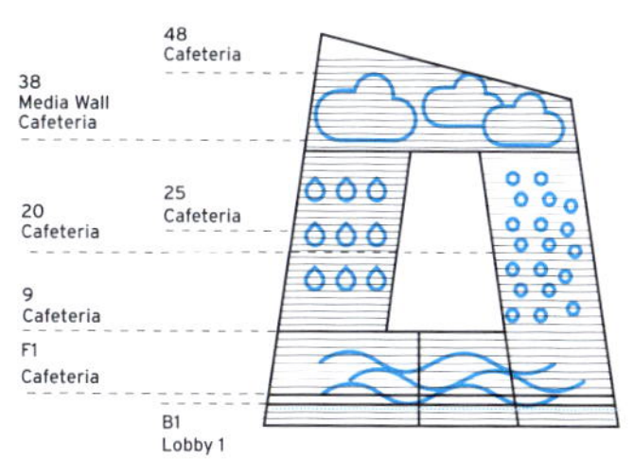

48
Cafeteria
38
Media Wall
Cafeteria
25
Cafeteria
20
Cafeteria
9
Cafeteria
F1
Cafeteria
B1
Lobby 1

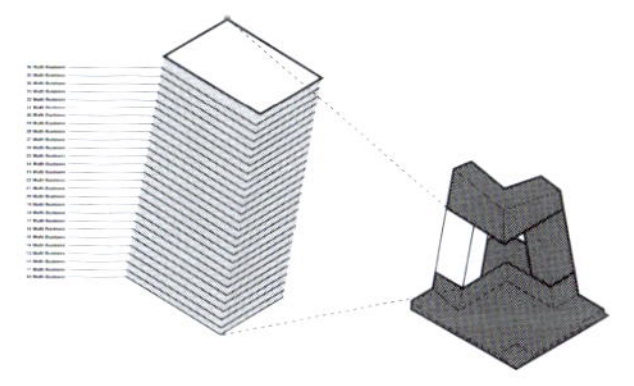

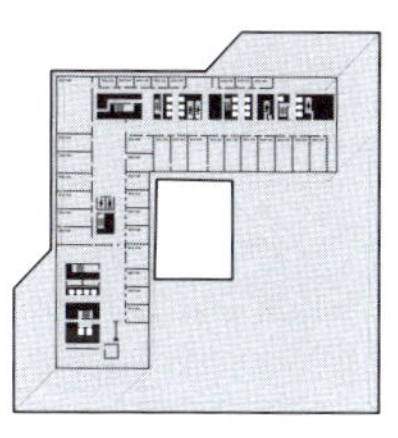

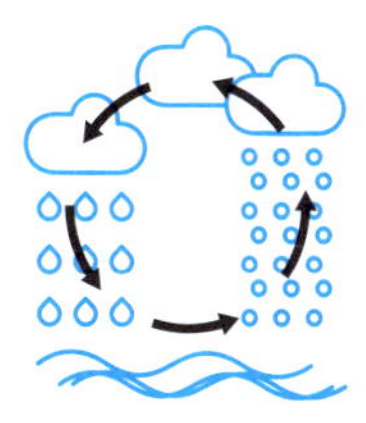

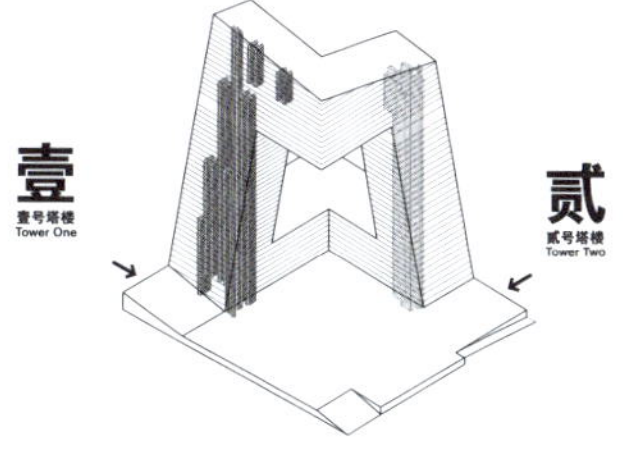

壹
壹号塔楼
Tower One
贰
贰号塔楼
Tower Two

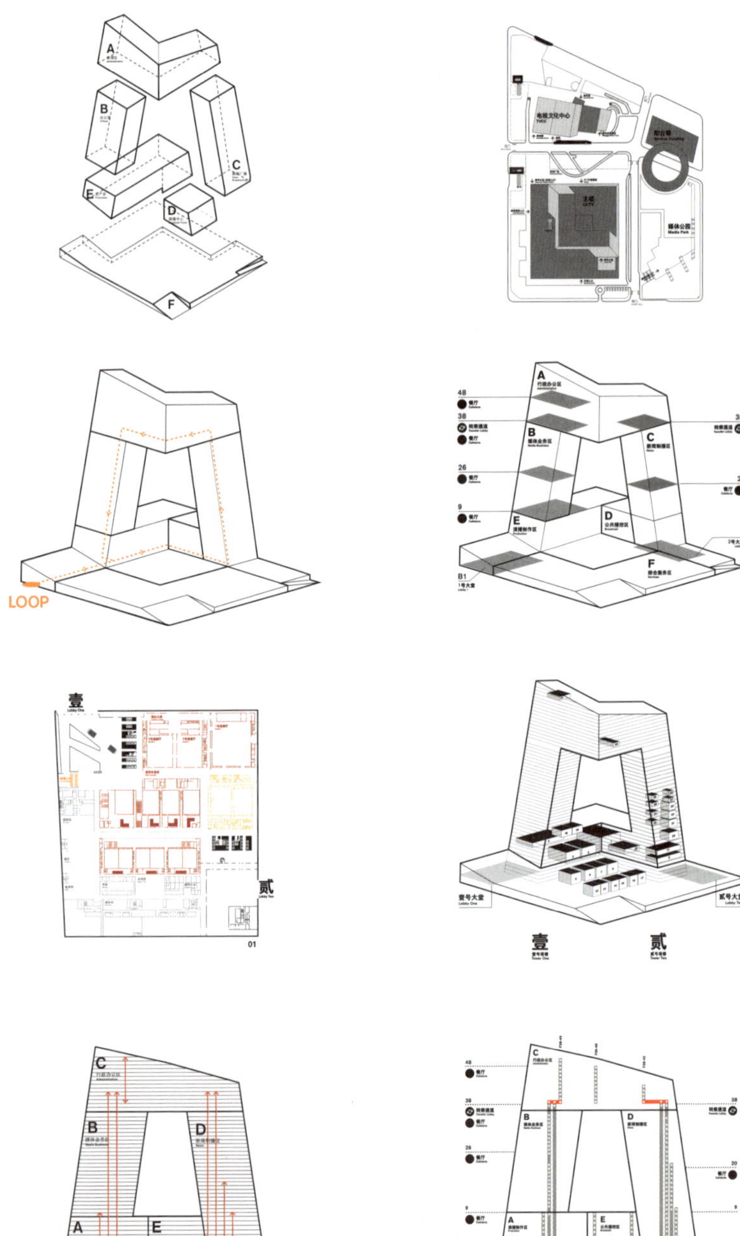

A
B
C
D
E
F
电视文化中心
TVCC
主楼
CCTV
媒体公园
Media Park
LOOP
A
行政办公区
B
媒体业务区
C
新闻制播区
D
公共播控区
E
演播制作区
F
综合服务区
48
38
26
20
9
1
B1
餐厅
转乘通道
1号大堂
2号大堂
壹
Lobby One
贰
Lobby Two
01
壹号大堂
贰号大堂
壹号塔楼
贰号塔楼
C
B
D
A
E

POLE DANCE

FLORIAN IDENBURG
JING LIU

Pole Dance is an exploration of the possibilities and limitations of physical architecture. In response to an increasingly virtualized world, we test architecture's potential to create sensorily charged environments, as opposed to finite forms, and strive to understand how we as designers and users operate both on and in the built world.

We start with this statement:

Freed from the fascination of the finite, and confronted with new ecologies, economies, energies, flows, and fantasies, we can begin to comprehend, and depict, a new image of life on earth: a seemingly elastic cloud. Everything untethered. We bounce about, footloose, on a network of intersections and knots.

If the virtual world uses metaphors of the physical to make it comprehensible—think information architecture—Pole Dance asks what we can extract from the virtual and transplant back in the physical.

Consider the *choreography of situations* rather than object-making. Imagine a participatory environment that reframes the relation between people and structure. Think of an interconnected system constantly affected by human action and environmental factors. Confronted with such an unfamiliar elasticity, *participants*—not visitors or viewers—instinctively engage with the structure: testing its limits, composing games, or joining in its gentle dance.

An open net covering the entire field both controls the maximum pivot of the poles and links the entire grid. A small local action ripples across the larger system. The swaying columns broadcast these ripples over the courtyard walls to the city. The tips of these long stalks generate data that are collected back in the pocket of the participant. Using a custom algorithm, each personal wireless device calculates the data generated by the system and processes it into new forms—both visual and audio—and then rebroadcasts to ever-wider networks.

This loose framework creates a dynamic, deliberately indeterminate, atmosphere. There is no baseline or reboot. With no end and no result, the process becomes an incessant loop—interaction, effect, information, processing, broadcast, interaction—a delicate construct of transforming frames, offering an intensely uplifting experience.

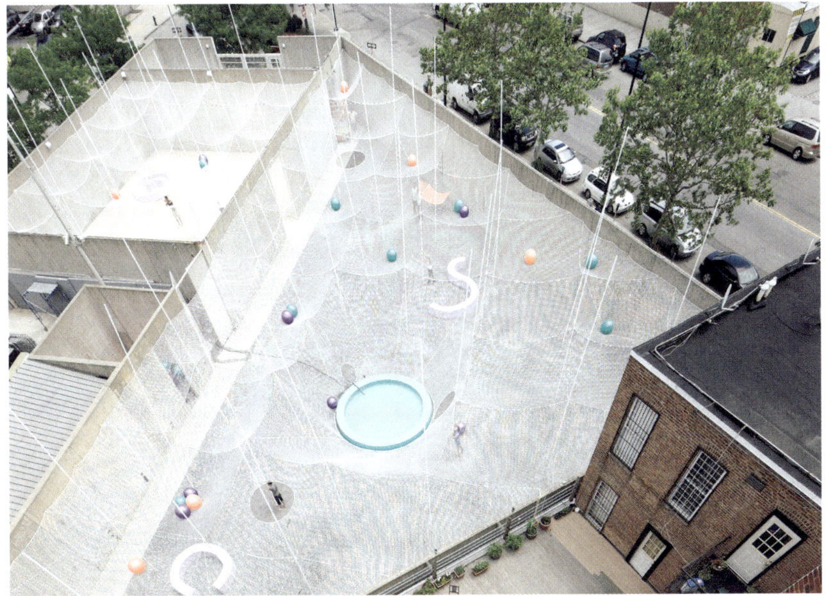

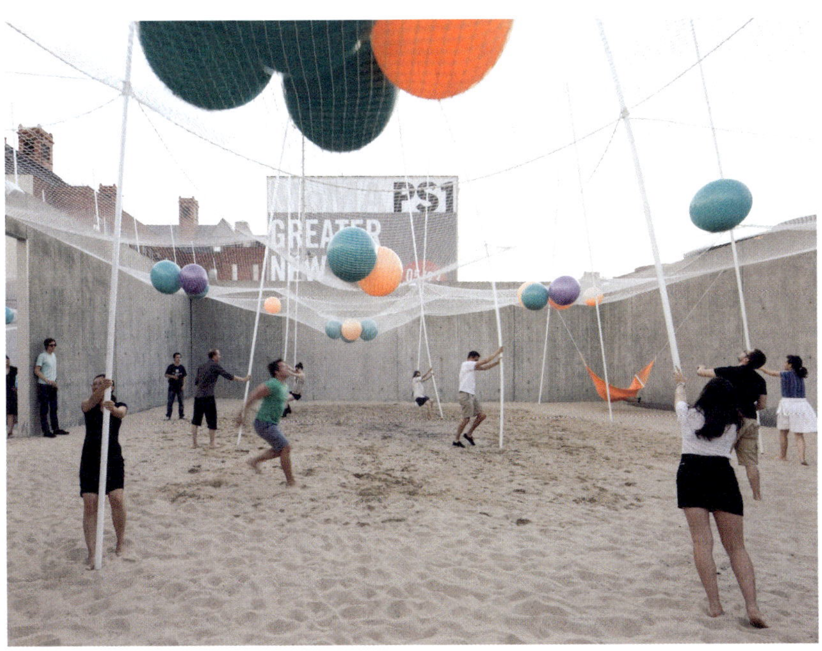

Pole Dance, MoMa PS1 — Photos Iwan Baan

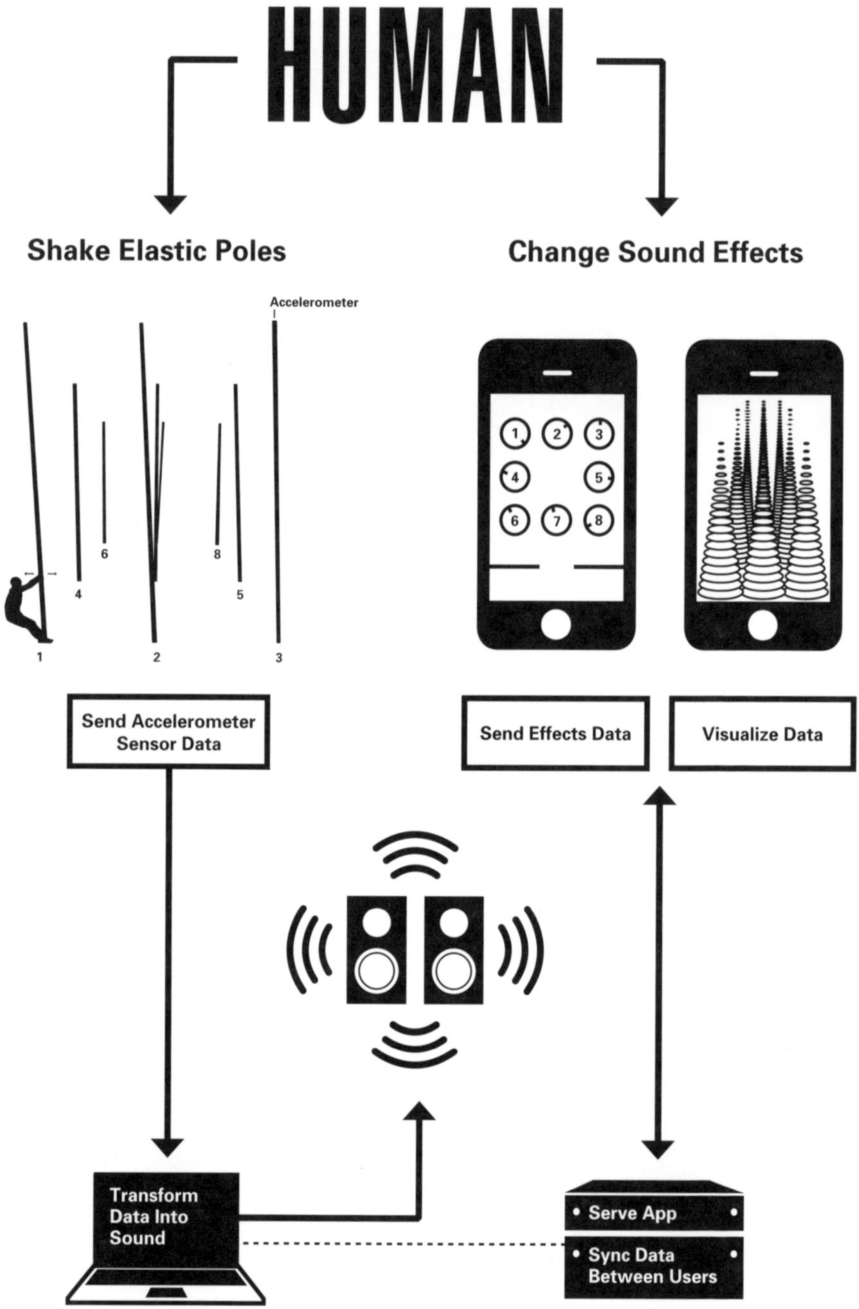

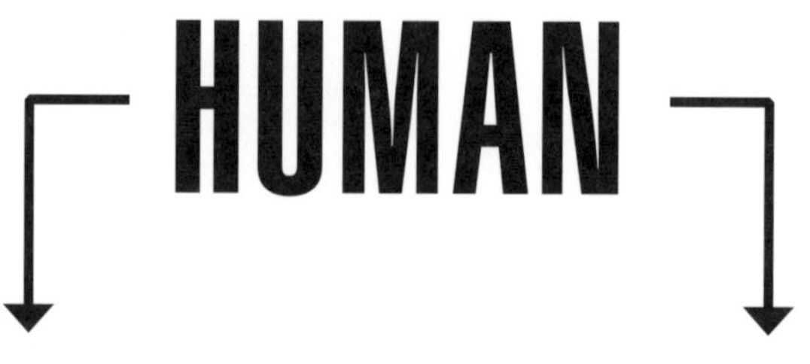

Shake Elastic Poles

Change Sound Effects

Accelerometer

1 2 3 4 5 6 8

1 2 3 4 5 6 7 8

Send Accelerometer Sensor Data

Send Effects Data

Visualize Data

Transform Data Into Sound

- **Serve App**
- **Sync Data Between Users**

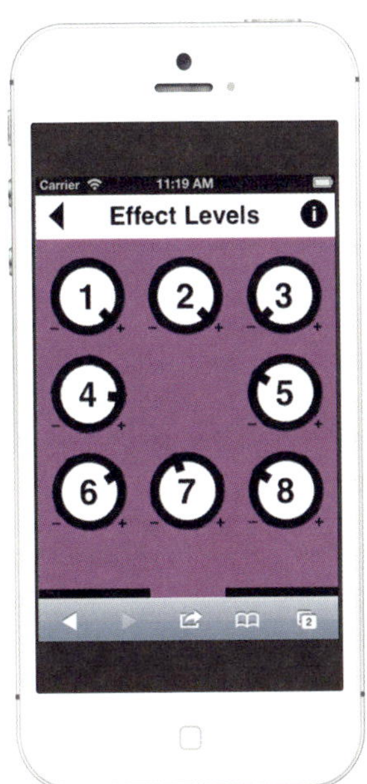
Carrier
11:19 AM
Effect Levels
1
2
3
4
5
6
7
8
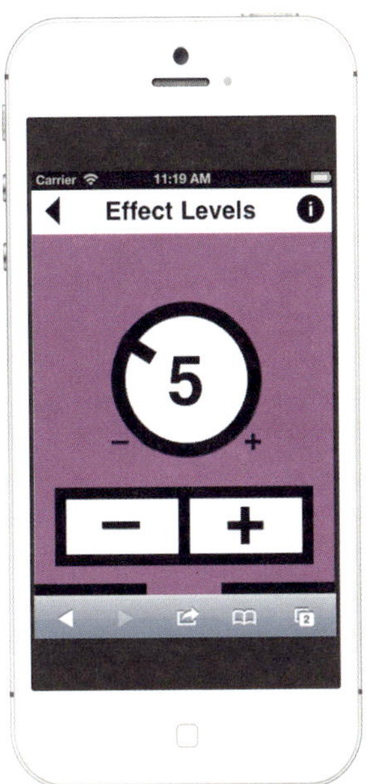
Carrier
11:19 AM
Effect Levels
5
−
+
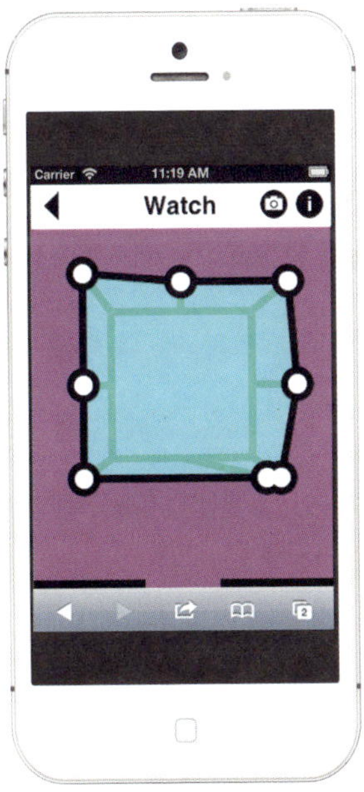
Carrier
11:19 AM
Watch
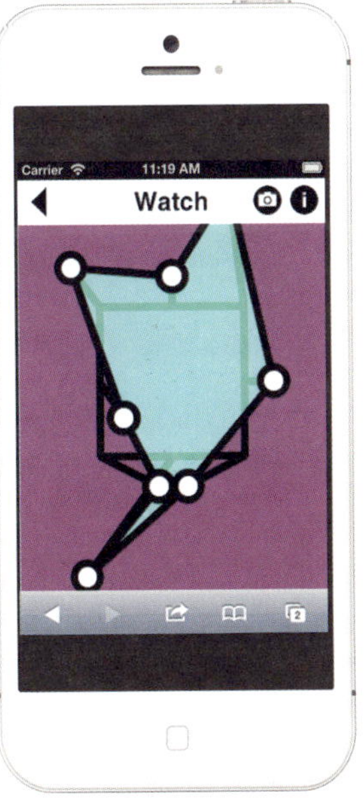
Carrier
11:19 AM
Watch

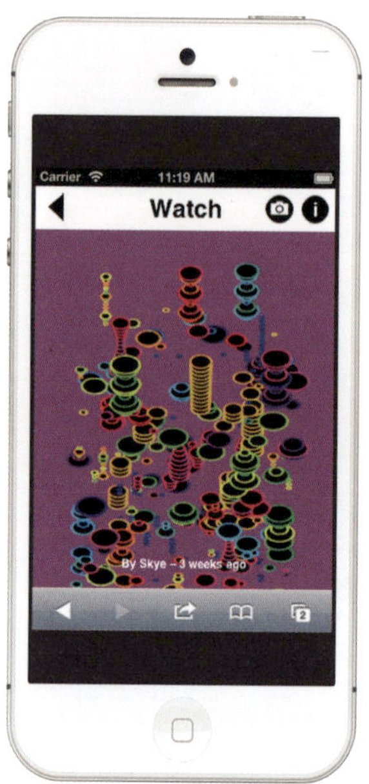
Carrier
11:19 AM
Watch
By Skye – 3 weeks ago

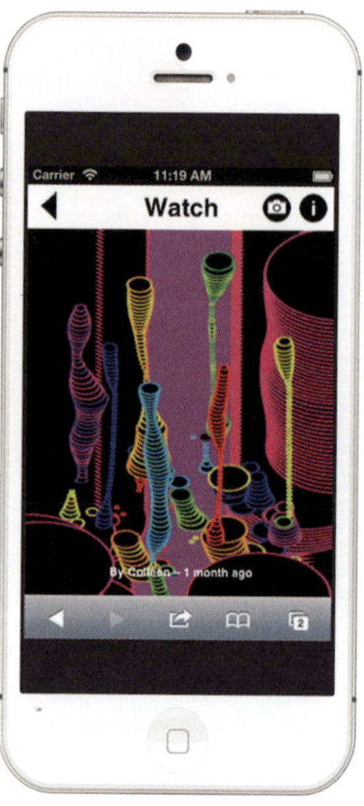
Carrier
11:19 AM
Watch
By Colleen – 1 month ago

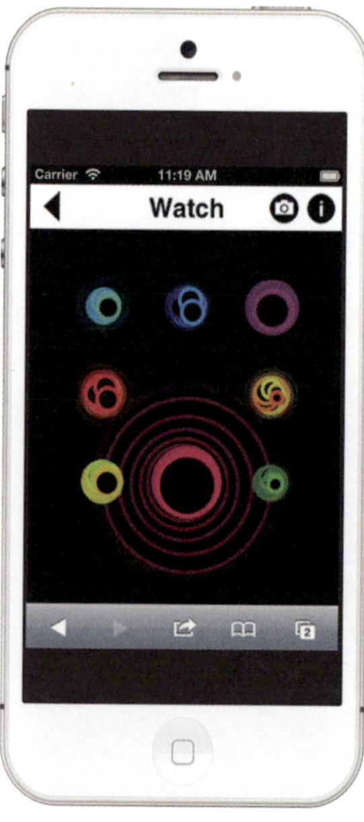
Carrier
11:19 AM
Watch

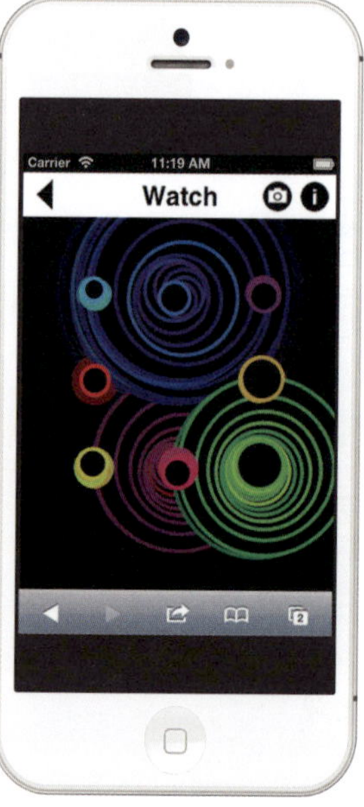
Carrier
11:19 AM
Watch

WAYS OF SEEING

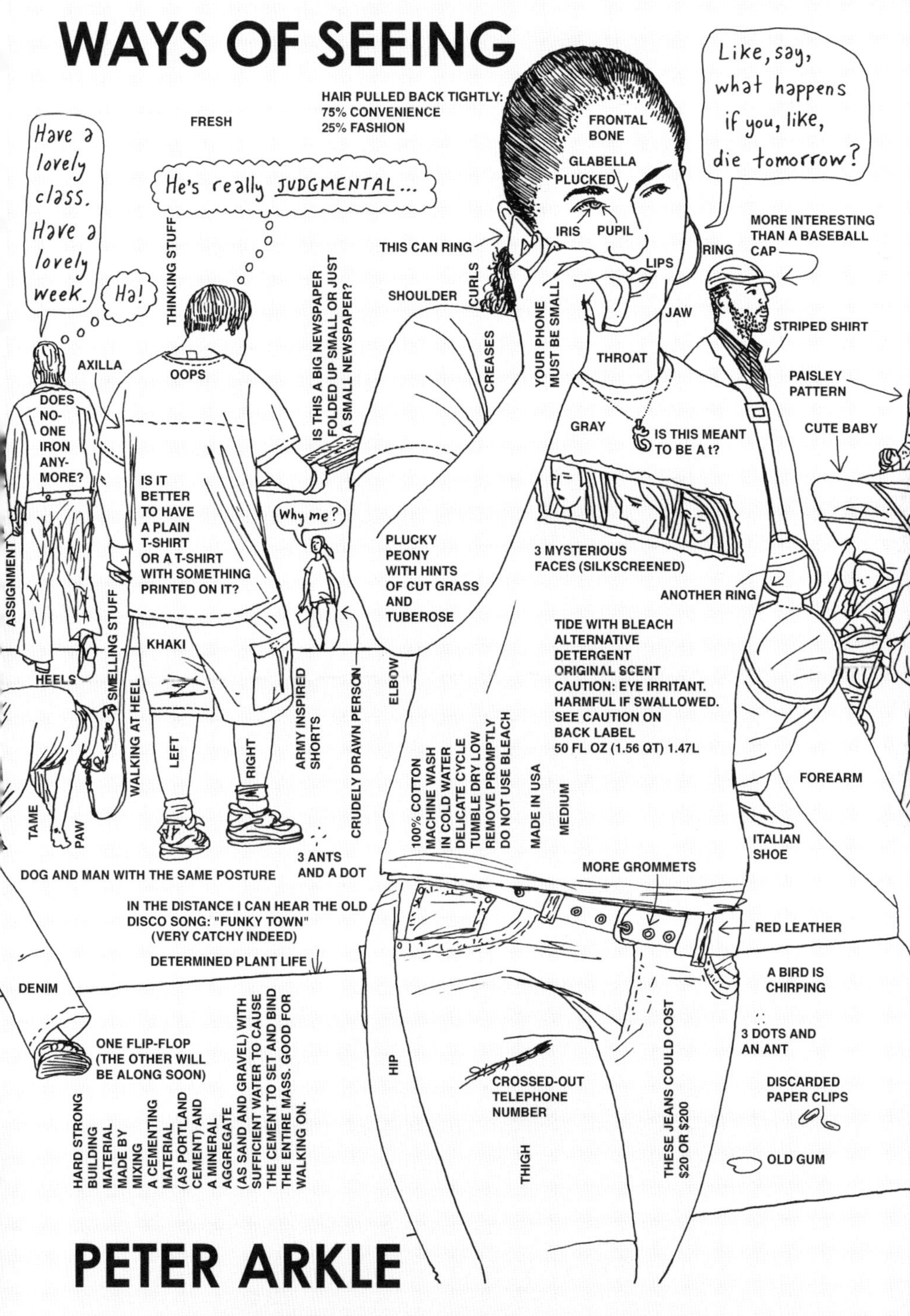

PETER ARKLE

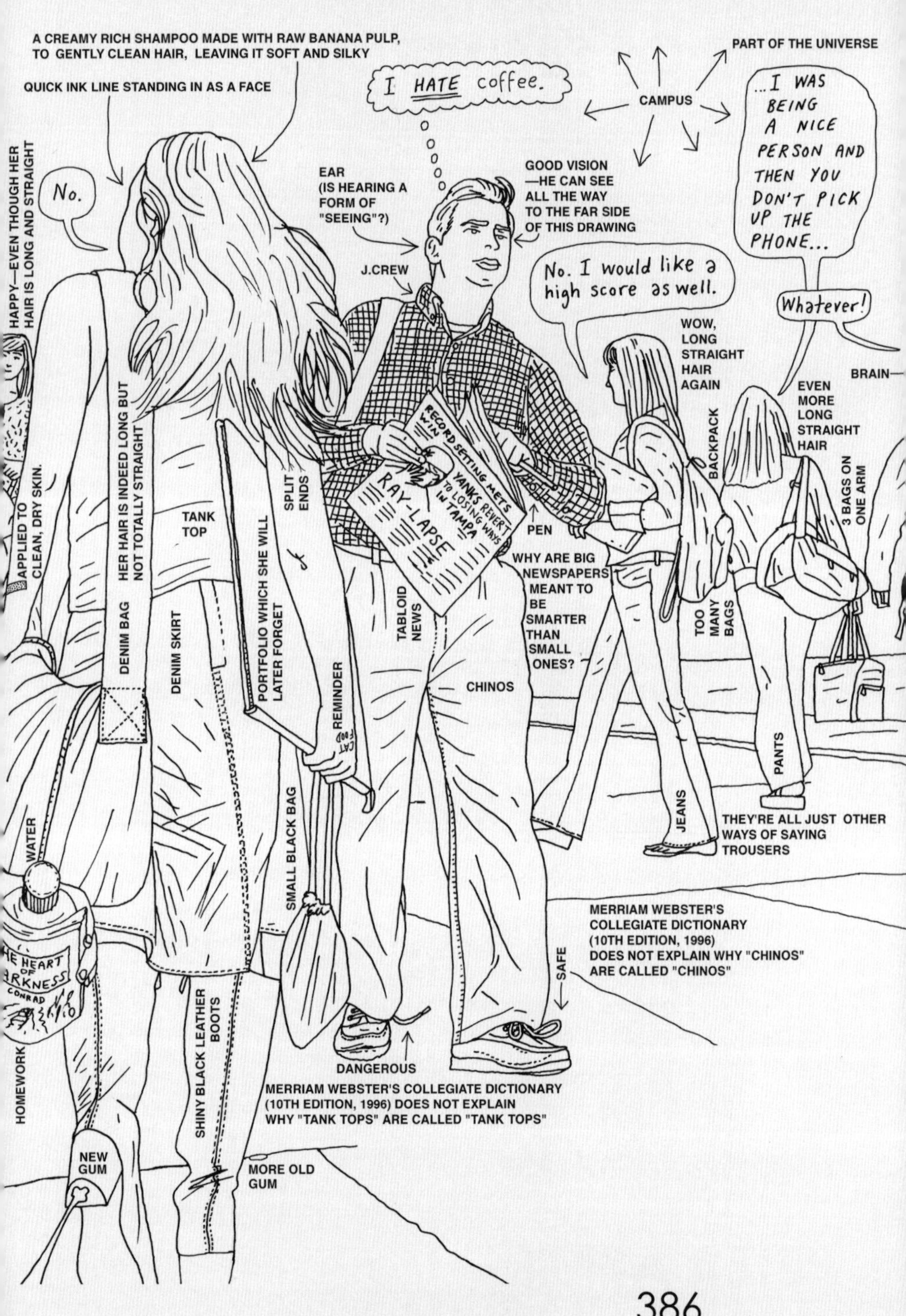

A CREAMY RICH SHAMPOO MADE WITH RAW BANANA PULP, TO GENTLY CLEAN HAIR, LEAVING IT SOFT AND SILKY
QUICK INK LINE STANDING IN AS A FACE
I HATE coffee.
PART OF THE UNIVERSE
CAMPUS
...I WAS BEING A NICE PERSON AND THEN YOU DON'T PICK UP THE PHONE...
HAPPY—EVEN THOUGH HER HAIR IS LONG AND STRAIGHT
No.
EAR (IS HEARING A FORM OF "SEEING"?)
GOOD VISION —HE CAN SEE ALL THE WAY TO THE FAR SIDE OF THIS DRAWING
J.CREW
No. I would like a high score as well.
Whatever!
WOW, LONG STRAIGHT HAIR AGAIN
BRAIN
EVEN MORE LONG STRAIGHT HAIR
BACKPACK
3 BAGS ON ONE ARM
APPLIED TO CLEAN, DRY SKIN.
HER HAIR IS INDEED LONG BUT NOT TOTALLY STRAIGHT
TANK TOP
PORTFOLIO WHICH SHE WILL LATER FORGET
SPLIT ENDS
RECORD SETTING METS WIN
YANKS REVERT TO LOSING WAYS IN TAMPA
RAY-LAPSE
PEN
WHY ARE BIG NEWSPAPERS MEANT TO BE SMARTER THAN SMALL ONES?
TOO MANY BAGS
DENIM BAG
DENIM SKIRT
TABLOID NEWS
REMINDER
CAT FOOD
CHINOS
PANTS
JEANS
THEY'RE ALL JUST OTHER WAYS OF SAYING TROUSERS
WATER
SMALL BLACK BAG
MERRIAM WEBSTER'S COLLEGIATE DICTIONARY (10TH EDITION, 1996) DOES NOT EXPLAIN WHY "CHINOS" ARE CALLED "CHINOS"
SAFE
HEART OF DARKNESS CONRAD
HOMEWORK
SHINY BLACK LEATHER BOOTS
DANGEROUS
MERRIAM WEBSTER'S COLLEGIATE DICTIONARY (10TH EDITION, 1996) DOES NOT EXPLAIN WHY "TANK TOPS" ARE CALLED "TANK TOPS"
NEW GUM
MORE OLD GUM

THE UPPER ATMOSPHERE OR EXPANSE OF SPACE THAT CONSTITUTES AN APPARENT GREAT VAULT OR ARCH OVER THE EARTH

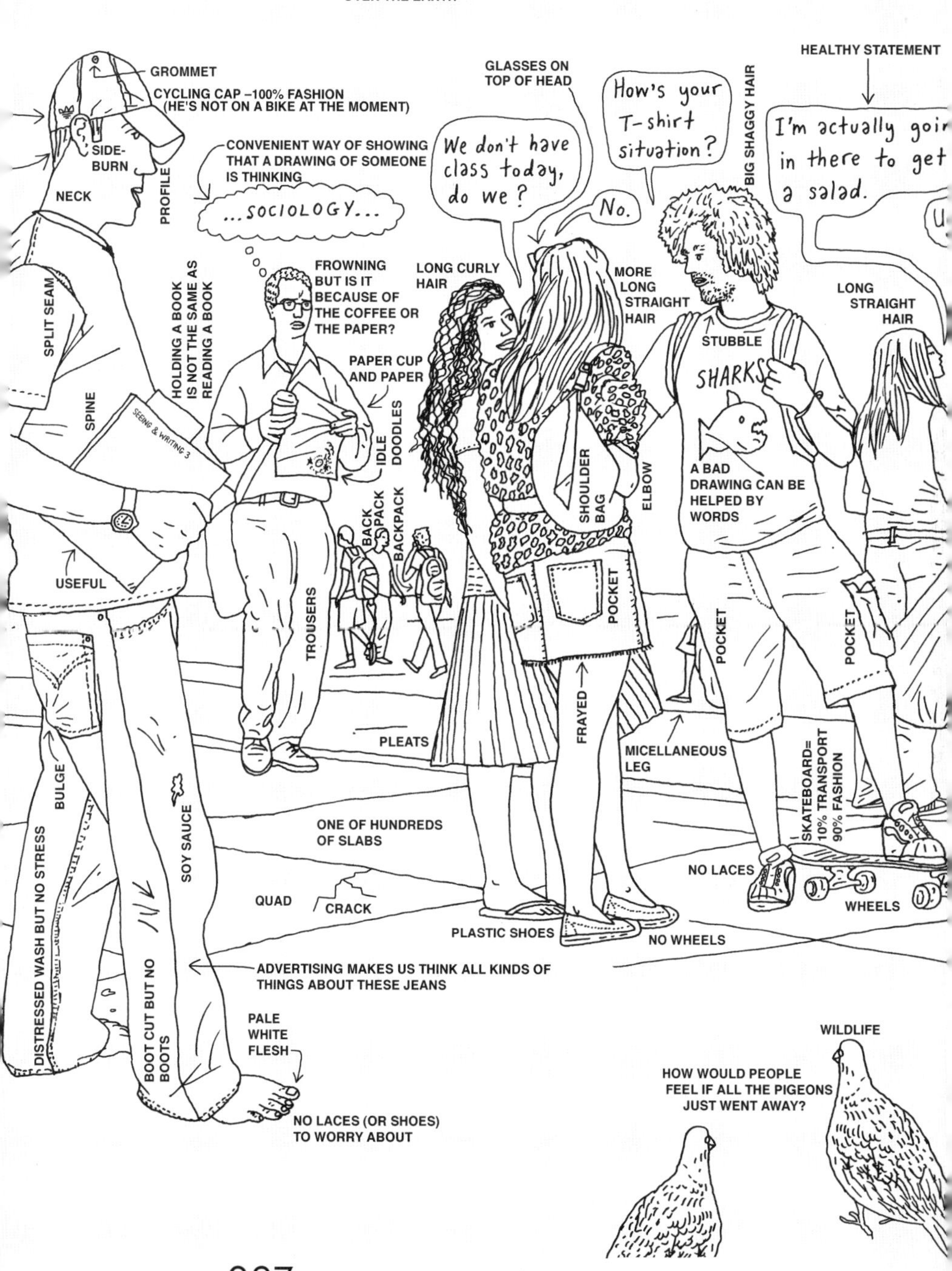

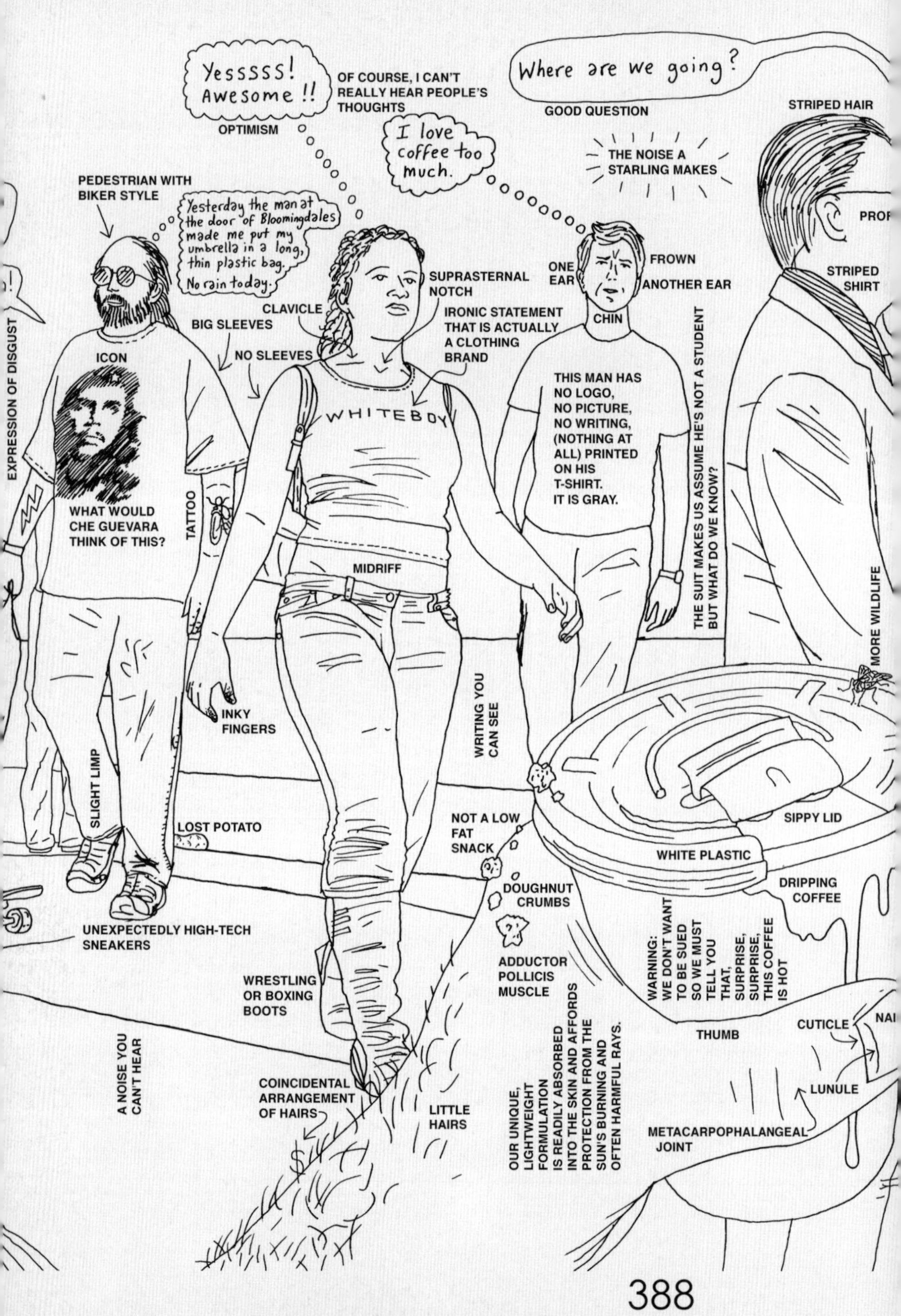
Yesssss! Awesome !!
OPTIMISM
OF COURSE, I CAN'T REALLY HEAR PEOPLE'S THOUGHTS
I love coffee too much.
Where are we going?
GOOD QUESTION
THE NOISE A STARLING MAKES
STRIPED HAIR
PEDESTRIAN WITH BIKER STYLE
Yesterday the man at the door of Bloomingdales made me put my umbrella in a long, thin plastic bag. No rain today.
SUPRASTERNAL NOTCH
ONE EAR
FROWN
ANOTHER EAR
STRIPED SHIRT
CLAVICLE
BIG SLEEVES
IRONIC STATEMENT THAT IS ACTUALLY A CLOTHING BRAND
CHIN
EXPRESSION OF DISGUST
ICON
NO SLEEVES
WHITEBOY
THIS MAN HAS NO LOGO, NO PICTURE, NO WRITING, (NOTHING AT ALL) PRINTED ON HIS T-SHIRT. IT IS GRAY.
THE SUIT MAKES US ASSUME HE'S NOT A STUDENT BUT WHAT DO WE KNOW?
WHAT WOULD CHE GUEVARA THINK OF THIS?
TATTOO
MIDRIFF
MORE WILDLIFE
INKY FINGERS
WRITING YOU CAN SEE
SLIGHT LIMP
LOST POTATO
NOT A LOW FAT SNACK
SIPPY LID
WHITE PLASTIC
DOUGHNUT CRUMBS
DRIPPING COFFEE
UNEXPECTEDLY HIGH-TECH SNEAKERS
ADDUCTOR POLLICIS MUSCLE
WARNING: WE DON'T WANT TO BE SUED SO WE MUST TELL YOU THAT, SURPRISE, SURPRISE, THIS COFFEE IS HOT
WRESTLING OR BOXING BOOTS
CUTICLE
THUMB
A NOISE YOU CAN'T HEAR
OUR UNIQUE, LIGHTWEIGHT FORMULATION IS READILY ABSORBED INTO THE SKIN AND AFFORDS PROTECTION FROM THE SUN'S BURNING AND OFTEN HARMFUL RAYS.
LUNULE
COINCIDENTAL ARRANGEMENT OF HAIRS
LITTLE HAIRS
METACARPOPHALANGEAL JOINT

AFTERWORD

"There are two kinds of sex [design], classical and baroque. Classical sex [design], is romantic, profound, serious, emotional, moral, mysterious, spontaneous, abandoned, focused on a particular person, and stereotypically feminine. Baroque sex [design] is pop, playful, funny, experimental, conscious, deliberate, amoral, anonymous, focused on sensation for sensation's sake, and stereotypically masculine. The classical mentality taken to an extreme is sentimental and finally puritanical; the baroque mentality taken to an extreme is pornographic and finally obscene. Ideally, a sexual [design] relation ought to create a satisfying tension between the two modes (a baroque idea, particularly if the tension is ironic) or else blend them so well that the distinction disappears (a classical aspiration)." —Ellen Willis on sex [Michael Rock on design.]

Faced with such a dichotomy, what's a design-lover to do? Are we classical or baroque? Or maybe more to the point, in the synthesis of the two, are we ironic or earnest? We have, over time, come down on different sides of those questions. One thing is for sure, we are serious about what we do … except when we are not.

But if we have to takes sides I would argue that we most consistently fall in with the baroque: we have a commitment to the political potential of irony. There is a game to be played: author, maker and reader enter into a dynamic wherein the rules are inscribed and elaborate pageants acted out accordingly. The invisible limitations of the system reveal themselves to the participants through the playing. (We can only decry limits if we *see* them!) In our universe those rules are shared understandings: the rules of the mass media, of culture, the fashion system, the shop floor and museum gallery, and the rules of typography, color, composition and line. We expect our readers come to our work well-armed and ready to rumble.

To stay interested in this job you have to take an interest in how that game is played, and what you take away from it, personally. There are projects and there are clients and money and there are big issues to solve and there are big issues we make for ourselves, but are these motivational? I am not sure any of those things are our prime motivation (much as we love to think of ourselves as problem-solvers). At the end of the day we are driven by beauty, that old-fashioned concept we never discuss in public. We like to make things. Beautiful things, ugly things that make you question what is beautiful, secret things that only we think are beautiful, cheap things that when handled correctly become beautiful, luxurious things that try too hard to be beautiful … There is a motivating joy in making something distinct, in being there at the inception. If *beauty* is a combination of things arranged in ways that please the senses, we take an expansive notion of *senses*. We want to touch every nerve. I guess, in the end, we want to be good lovers, in the baroque sense of course, "pop, playful, funny, experimental, conscious, deliberate, amoral, anonymous …."

CONTRIBUTORS

Lucia Allais is an architectural historian and theorist teaching at Princeton University. She is working on a history of international politics and monument preservation in the mid-20th-century, tentatively titled *Designs of Destruction*. Recent publications include "The Real and the Theoretical" in *Perspecta* 42 and "Disaster as Experiment" in *Log* 22.

Peter Arkle is a freelance illustrator of books, magazines, websites, and advertising.

Iwan Baan is a Dutch architectural photographer who has worked with many of the world's most prominent architects. In 2010, he was the recipient of the first annual Julius Shulman Institute Photography Award.

Irwin Chen teaches interaction design at Parsons The New School for Design and is the founder of Redub LLC, an interaction design consultancy based in New York. He is currently serving on the board of AIGA/NY.

Paul Elliman is a London-based artist. Known for his work with a found typography of objects and industrial debris, he also follows the human voice through many of its social and technological guises, often imitating other languages and sounds of the city. In 2012 his work with objects *and* the voice was a central focus of the exhibition "Ecstatic Alphabets/Heaps of Language," at the Museum of Modern Art, New York.

Rob Giampietro is a designer, teacher, writer and a principal at Project Projects in New York. Since 2006, he has been a member of the graphic-design faculty at RISD. His essay on the rise of graphic design MFA programs, "School Days," was published in the Walker Art Center's *Graphic Design: Now in Production* catalogue in 2011.

Florian Idenburg is co-founder of New York–based architectural practice SO – IL and adjunct assistant professor at Harvard University GSD.

Jeannie Kim teaches architectural history and design at the University of Toronto. She is currently working on the centennial history of the Faculty of Architecture at the University of Manitoba in Winnipeg and is the editor of *CC: A Global Report* from Columbia University GSAPP.

Rem Koolhaas is the founder of Office for Metropolitan Architecture, winner of the 2000 Pritzker Prize, and a professor of architecture at Harvard University GSD. He is the author of *Project Japan: Metabolism Talks* (Taschen, 2011), *S,M,L,XL* (Monacelli, 1995) and *Delirious New York* (Oxford University Press, 1978).

Jing Liu is co-founder of New York–based architectural practice SO – IL. A native of China, Liu is currently teaching at Columbia University GSAPP, Syracuse University and Parsons The New School for Design.

Jean-François Lyotard was a key figure in contemporary French philosophy known for his analysis of the impact of postmodernity on the human condition. At the time of his death in 1998, he was university professor emeritus of the University of Paris VIII, and professor at Emory University, Atlanta. He was former founding director, Collège International de Philosophie Paris, and distinguished professor at the University of California, Irvine, as well as visiting professor at Yale University. His books include *The Postmodern Condition* (University of Minnesota Press, 1984); *Just Gaming* (University of Minnesota Press, 1985); *The Differend* (University of Minnesota Press, 1989); *Phenomenology* (State University of New York Press, 1991); and *Libidinal Economy* (Indiana University Press, 1993).

Dan Michaelson and Tamara Maletic are partners in Linked by Air, a design firm focused on the production of public space. Recent projects include the Whitney Museum's website and an all-night urban game in New York, "Midnight Madness," which raised money for a children's charity. Michaelson teaches "Networks & Transactions" and "Mobile Computing" courses in Yale University's graphic-design program. Maletic teaches graphic design at Parsons The New School for Design.

Rick Poynor is visiting professor in critical writing in art and design at the Royal College of Art, London. He was the founding editor of *Eye* and is a co-founder of *Design Observer*, where he blogs regularly. He writes a column for *Print*. His books include *Design without Boundaries* (Booth-Clibborn, 1998), *Obey the Giant* (Princeton Architectural Press, 2001), *Jan van Toorn: Critical Practice* (010 Publishers, 2008) and *No More Rules* (Yale University Press, 2003) which will be reissued by Laurence King in 2013.

Elizabeth Rock is a writer and illustrator living in Providence, Rhode Island, and Washington, D.C. Her editorial illustrations appear in newspapers nationwide.

Susan Sellers is a founding partner and creative director at 2x4 and senior critic at Yale University School of Art.

Michael Speaks is dean of the College of Design and professor of architecture at the University of Kentucky. He was formerly the director of the graduate program at the Southern California Institute of Architecture. Speaks is a founding editor of the cultural journal *Polygraph*, and is former senior editor at *Any* in New York, where he also edited the book series Writing Architecture, published by MIT Press. He is currently a contributing editor for *Architectural Record*.

Georgianna Stout is founding partner and creative director at 2x4. She has been a visiting design critic at RISD and Yale University School of Art.

Jan van Toorn is a graphic designer based in Amsterdam and former director of Jan van Eyck Akademie, Maastricht. His recent works include *Design's Delight* (010 Publishers, 2006) and the print series 10 Still Lives with Borrowed Furniture (2012).

Enrique Walker is an architect and associate professor at Columbia University GSAPP, where he also directs the Master of Science program in advanced architectural design. His publications include *Tschumi on Architecture: Conversations with Enrique Walker* (Monacelli, 2006) and *Lo Ordinario* (Gustavo Gili, 2010).

Mark Wigley is dean of Columbia University GSAPP and the author of *Constant's New Babylon: The Hyper-architecture of Desire* (010 Publishers, 1998); *White Walls, Designer Dresses: The Fashioning of Modern Architecture* (MIT Press, 1995); and *The Architecture of Deconstruction: Derrida's Haunt* (MIT Press, 1993).

INDEX

PERMISSIONS

20–32: Illustrations by Tim Enthoven
101–104: Photographs by Luke Steiner
108–110: *ANY* covers courtesy of ANY Corp
117–120: Photographs by Rob Kulisek
149–154: Images courtesy of Prada
156–163: Photographs by Iwan Baan
171–174: Photographs by Rob Kulisek
179: Guggenheim Las Vegas photograph by Ari Marcopoulos
181: Extrusion photographs by Laurie Sermos
182: Leo's Wall photograph by Sal Mancini; New World Stages photographs by Floto + Warner
183: IIT Founders Wall photographs by Floto + Warner; Prada Parallel Universe photographs by Michael Govan
184: Ali Center photographs courtesy of Beyer Blinder Belle
184: Prada Vomit photographs by CCTV; Canteen photographs by Iwan Baan
185: Novartis wall photograph by Thomas Mayer
186: Prada Hooded Women photographs by Floto + Warner; Smoke and Mirrors photographs by Floto + Warner
187: Prada Chromo photographs by Michael Moran; Prada Notorious Women by Floto + Warner
188: Prada New Masters photographs by Laurie Sermos; Prada HyperWorld photographs by Floto + Warner; Prada Florid photograph by Laurie Sermos
189: Prada Donna Show photographs courtesy of Prada; Guggenheim Las Vegas photographs courtesy of OMA
190: Smoke and Mirrors photographs by Floto + Warner; IIT Clock photograph by Floto + Warner
191: Martin House Visitor Center photograph by Paul Warchol
192: Prada Evil Twin photograph by Laurie Sermos; Vitra Flower photograph courtesy of Vitra
193: NYAS photographs courtesy of H3 Hardy Collaboration Architecture
194: IIT photograph by Richard Barnes

Empire of Screens

312: (top left) Thos. R. Shipp Co. Atwater Kent window, Woodward & Lothrop, between 1918 and 1928, photographer unknown, courtesy of Library of Congress; (bottom left) Edison's greatest marvel—The Vitascope, New York: Metropolitan Print Company, c. 1896, ©Raff & Gammon, courtesy of Library of Congress; (top right) Film still, Wallace McCutcheon and Edwin S. Porter, *Dream of a Rarebit Fiend* (1906); (second right) Proposal for a Cinéorama, Paris Exposition, 1900, origin unknown; (third right) Film still, Georges Méliès, *Long Distance Wireless Photography* (1908); (bottom right) Drawing of Edison's Vitascope in Koster and Bial's Music Hall, 1896, New York City
313: (top left) Eiffel Tower with Citroën ad, 1925, photographer unknown; (bottom left) Textile store window display, Kabul, Afghanistan, 1950s, photographer unknown, courtesy of Mohammad Qayoumi; (top right) Times Square, New York, 1949, photographer unknown; (second right) Film still, Abel Gance, *Napoléon* (1927); (bottom right) Film still, Lois Weber and Phillips Smalley, *Suspense* (1913)
314: (top left) Herbert Bayer Diagram of the Field of Vision, 1930 ©ARS, courtesy of Bauhaus-Archiv Museum, Berlin; (second left) Film still, Charlie Chaplin, *Modern Times* (1936) ©Roy Export S.A.S.; (bottom left) Drive-in movie in Camden, New Jersey, 1933, photographer unknown; (top right) WWII military radar operators, 1947, photographer unknown; (bottom right) Film still, William Cameron Menzies, H.G. Wells' *Things to Come* (1936)
315: (bottom left) Film still, William Cameron Menzies, H.G. Wells' *Things to Come* (1936); (top right) First public postwar showing of moderately priced television set at a New York department store August 24, 1945, photographer Ed Ford, ©AP Photo; (second right) First NBC control room, courtesy of Library of American Broadcasting; (third middle) 1984 Big Brother Poster, 2006, ©Frédéric Guimont; (bottom right) Television control room, photographer Peter Sickles, courtesy of Superstock/Visualphotos
316: (top left) Girl promoting television set, 1950, photographer unknown; (second left) Family watching television, c. 1958, photo by Evert F. Baumgardner, courtesy of the National Archives and Records Administration; (bottom left) Men working in the control room of CBS TV City, 1956, photo by Ralph Crane ©TIME & LIFE Pictures, courtesy of Getty Images; (top right) Alfred Hitchcock, *Rear Window* (1954) poster, courtesy of Universal Studios Licensing LLC; (bottom right) Film still, Alfred Hitchcock, *Rear Window* (1954) courtesy of Universal Studios Licensing LLC
317: (top left) Ray and Charles Eames, *Glimpses of the U.S.A* at the American National Exhibition in Moscow in 1959, ©2012 Eames Office LLC; (second left) First live Transatlantic broadcast from Europe, 1962, ©Bettmann/Corbis/AP Images; (bottom left) J. Svoboda and A. Radok, *Laterna Magika*, Brussels, Expo '58; (bottom middle) 9-camera Circarama rig from Herb A. Lightman, "Circling Italy with Circarama," *American Cinematographer* 43 no. 3 (1962): 162–163; (second right) Ray and Charles Eames, reconstructed stills from *Glimpses of the U.S.A.* made for publication in 1988, ©2012 Eames Office LLC; (third right) Krugovaya Kinopanorama, 1959, photographer unknown; (bottom right) Rod Serling, *Twilight Zone: Black Leather Jackets* (1964), still courtesy of CBS Broadcasting, Inc.
318: (top left) Live broadcast of Mercury launch, New York Grand Central Station, February 20, 1962, photographer unknown, ©Topfoto/The Image Works; (second left) Diagram of New York's World Fair IBM Pavilion, 1964, courtesy of Kevin Roche John Dinkeloo and Associates LLC; (bottom left) New York's World's Fair IBM Pavilion, 1964, courtesy of Kevin Roche John Dinkeloo and Associates, LLC; (top right) Ray and Charles Eames, Number 2

Sequence from the 220-screen presentation of "Think" in the IBM pavilion at the 1964–65 New York World's Fair ©2012 Eames Office LLC; (bottom right) Ray and Charles Eames, V4 sequences from the 22-screen presentation of "Think" in the IBM pavilion at the 1964–65 New York World's Fair ©2012 Eames Office LLC

319: (top left) Drawing of Kenneth Adam's War Room from Stanley Kubrick's *Dr. Strangelove* (1964) ©Sir Kenneth Adam; (third left) Stan VanDerBeek, *Movie-Drome*, 1963–66/2012 "Ghosts in the Machine," installation view courtesy of the Estate of Stan VanDerBeek and New Museum, New York; photograph ©Chang W. Lee/The New York Times/Redux; (bottom left) Elvis Presley's room at Graceland, photograph by Alessandro Gandolfi/Parallelozero; (top right) *Chelsea Girls* poster ©1971 Alan Aldridge; (second right) Film still, Andy Warhol, *Chelsea Girls* (1966) courtesy of the Andy Warhol Museum; (third right) Andy Warhol, "Exploding Plastic Inevitable" with the Velvet Underground, ©1967–2012 Ronald Nameth; (bottom right) Nam June Paik, TV Cello, 1971, ©Nam June Paik Estate

320: (top left) Schematic drawing of the Cinerama's 3-projector screening process from *This is Cinerama* program 1952; (second left) Pacific Cinerama Dome Theatre and Marquee, Welton Becket and Associates, 1963, courtesy of the Office of Historic Resources, City of Los Angeles; (third left) Roman Kroitor, Colin Low, and Hugh O'Connor, *In The Labyrinth*, Expo '67 Montreal, photograph by Jeffrey Stanton; (bottom left) Radúz Çinçera, *Kinoautomat: One Man and his Jury*, Czechoslovak Pavilion at Expo '67 Montreal, photograph by Jeffrey Stanton; (top right) Robert Barclay, *Canada 67*, The Telephone Pavilion at Expo '67 Montreal, photograph by Jeffrey Stanton, (second right), Film still, Roman Kroitor, Colin Low, Hugh O'Connor, *In the Labyrinth*, Expo '67 Montreal; (bottom right) Francis Thompson and Alexander Hammid, *We are Young*, Canadian Pacific Pavilion, Expo '67 Montreal, photograph by Jeffrey Stanton

321: (top left) Plan of Labyrinth Theaters in I. Kalin, *Survey of Building Materials, Systems and Techniques used at the Universal and International Exhibition of 1967* (Ottawa: Queen's Printer, 1969); (second left) Josef Svoboda and Emil Radok, *Prague Musical Spring*, Polyekran, Expo '58 Brussels; (third left) Zbigniew Rybczynski, *Nowa Ksiazka (New Book)*, 1975, film still, courtesy of Zbigniew Rybczynski; (bottom left) Francis Thompson and Alexander Hammid, *We are Young*, Canadian Pacific Pavilion Expo '67, Montreal, photograph by Jeffrey Stanton; (top right) Josef Svoboda and Jiri Sust, *Symphony*, Expo '67 Montreal; (second right) J. Svoboda, E. Radok and M. Pflug, *The Creation of the World*, Polydiaecran, Expo '67, Montreal; (third right) Donald Brittain, *Tiger Child* (1970) Osaka '70 Expo, Fuji Group Pavilion, photograph by Joe Kleiman at the GSCA International Conference and Trade Show, 2006; (fourth right) Fuji Group Pavilion floor plan, Osaka '70, architect Yutaka Murata, courtesy of TensiNet

322: (top left) Mitsubishi's Diamond Vision mega screen at LA Dodger Stadium, 1980, photographer unknown; (second left) Atari Video Computer System, February 1982, photographer unknown, courtesy of AP Photo/HO; (top right) Nam June Paik shows his video sculpture "Fin de Siecle II" at the Whitney Museum of American Art in New York City, 1989, ©AP Photo/Frankie Ziths; (second right) Apple Lisa, screenshot showing stationery pad named "DTC Paper," 1983, courtesy of David T. Craig; (bottom) Christopher Faust, *Suburban Documentation Project,* Metro Traffic Control, Minneapolis, Minnesota, 1993, photo courtesy of the artist

323: (bottom left) Campus Party 2004, photograph by Aythami Melián Perdomo; (top right) IMAX Tycho Brahe Planetarium, Copenhagen, Denmark, 2006, courtesy of Barco; (second right) Michael Bloomberg, New York, NY, 1992, photographer unknown, courtesy of AP Images; (bottom left) NCSA Mosaic Screenshot, courtesy of the Board of Trustees of the University of Illinois

324: (top left) Shibuya, Tokyo, photographer unknown; (top right) Windows sketch by 2x4; (bottom right) CAVE (Cave Automatic Virtual Environment) 2001, courtesy of Dave Pape

325: (top left) Ascendance of the quants, 2007, photographer Chris Goodney, ©Bloomberg, courtesy of Getty Images; (second left) Still from the 2012 presidential campaign, photograph by ©Henny Ray Abrams, AP and Corbis; (third right) Doug Aitken, *Sleepwalkers* (2007) 6-channel video, Museum of Modern Art, New York, photograph by Frederick Charles, Courtesy of Doug Aitken Workshop; (middle bottom) Krugovaya Kinopanorama, 2007, courtesy of Vladimirovich; (bottom right) Kanye West, *Cruel Summer* (2012) photograph by Philippe Ruault, courtesy of OMA

326: (top left) Augmented Reality Traffic, photograph by Christina Zartmann ©ZKM; (bottom left) Augmented reality flash mob at Dam Square, Amsterdam, 2010, by Sander Veenhof; (third right) Google Glass detail, 2012, photograph by Antonio Zugaldia

Fnord images

330: (left) Fnord graffiti on the "Anarchy Bridge" Earlsdon-Coventry (1982) photograph by Walwyn; (right) Fnord graffiti, Portland, Maine, (2008) photograph by Tanya Zivkovic

332: Fnord sticker in Hoxton (2009) photograph by Andrew Bulhak

333: (left) Fnord streetart, Graz, Austria, (2008) photograph by MadC (Flickr); (right) Fnord graffiti in Deering Oaks Park, Portland, Maine, (2006) photograph by Travis H. Curran

334: Fnord graffiti on parking sign (2010) photograph by Fnord_Perfect (Flickr)

335: Fnord graffiti (2006) photograph by puggirl365 (Flickr)

336: Fnord graffiti (2008) photograph by Aaron Smith

337: Fnord graffiti (2010) photograph by peiurban (Flickr)

338: Fnord graffiti in Graz, Austria, (2008) photograph by kami68k (Flickr)

384: Photographs by Iwan Baan courtesy of SO-IL

385–88: Illustration courtesy of Bedford/St. Martin's Press

Multiple Signatures was designed and composed by 2x4—Yoonjai Choi and Michael Rock with Terri Chiao, Sung Joong Kim, Jeffrey Ludlow, Donnie Luu, Liliana Palau and David Yun—in New York City from 2011 to 2012. The majority of the texts are set in three fonts:

Garamond, an old-style serif typeface designed by the 16th-century French punch-cutter and publisher Claude Garamond. Its fluid line and visual consistency have made it one of the most elegant and readable print typefaces. Over the years, numerous iterations of Garamond have been issued. The version used herein is Adobe Garamond Pro, a digital interpretation by Robert Slimbach based on Garamond's original Roman letterforms and Robert Granjon's italics.

Akzidenz-Grotesk, a grotesque sans-serif typeface originally released in 1896 by the Berthold Type Foundry. While thoroughly modern, its proportions are derivative of earlier serif fonts such as Walbaum or Didot. In 1957, Max Miedinger used Akzidenz Grotesk as the basis for his new typeface Neue Haas Grotesk, which was ultimately renamed Helvetica.

Century Gothic, a geometric sans-serif typeface based on Sol Hess's Twentieth Century. The design was influenced by the geometric sans-serif faces of the 1920 and 30s such as Paul Renner's Futura.